16ᵒᵉ

THE AFFAIR

THE

AFFAIR

The Case of Alfred Dreyfus

꙳

Jean-Denis Bredin

Translated from the French
by Jeffrey Mehlman

GEORGE BRAZILLER
NEW YORK

Published in the United States in 1986
by George Braziller, Inc.

Originally published in France in 1983 as *L'Affaire*

Copyright © Julliard, 1983
English translation copyright © George Braziller, Inc.

For information address the publisher:

George Braziller Inc.
One Park Avenue
New York, NY 10016

Library of Congress Cataloging-in-Publication data

Bredin, Jean-Denis.
The Affair: the Case of Alfred Dreyfus.

Translation of L'affaire.
Bibliography: p.
Includes index.
1. Dreyfus, Alfred, 1859–1935. 2. France—Politics
and government—1870—1940. 3. Treason—France—History—
19th century. 4. Antisemitism—France. I. Title
DC354.B6713 1986 944.081'2'0924 85-22374
ISBN 0-8076-1109-3

Book design by Joe Marc Freedman
Printed in the United States of America
First printing, January 1986
Second printing, January 1986

To my daughter Frédérique

Acknowledgments

My thanks to:

Marcel Thomas, Zeev Sternhell, Mavis Gallant, and Erik Arnoult, who have assisted and enlightened me with their advice when I undertook this effort;

My friend Jean-Pierre Ramsay, who encouraged me in this project;

Chief Advocate General Lindon, who facilitated my first encounters;

Jean Favier, the Director General of the French Archives and Madame Favier, who facilitated my research and allowed me both to consult and to reproduce in part the files used by the High Court of Appeal and the numerous documents held in the National Archives;

General Delmas, head of the French Army's Historical Service, who placed at my disposal the "secret file" as well as the administrative files of the officers involved;

Charles Hernu, minister of defense, and Olivier Renard Payen, technical advisor to his staff, who, along with General Delmas, authorized me to take or use photographs of essential documents;

Bar President Bondoux, whose acquaintance with Edgar Demange, helped me greatly, Michel Brichard, Librarian of the Ordre des Avocats, who confided to me the precious documents held by the Ordre at the Paris Bar;

Monseiur Oliver, Justice of the High Court of Appeal, for having opened to me the library of the High Court of Appeal, and the staff of the Court's library for having facilitated my research;

Monsieur Drai, Presiding Justice of the Tribunal de Grande Instance in Paris, and Secretary General Canivet of the Tribunal, for having put at my disposal the Tribunal's archives, and particularly the works and documents left by André Blumel;

Doctor Jean-Louis Dreyfus, Jeanne Dreyfus's son, Charles Dreyfus, Pierre Dreyfus's son, and Francine Beck, Mathieu Dreyfus's granddaughter, for having assisted me with their recollections, their documentation, and their review of my work. Madame Jeanne Lévy, Alfred Dreyfus's daughter, had already done much to enlighten me at the time of her death. Doctor Jean-Louis Lévy was willing to pursue that assistance to me with a measure of patience and intelligence to which I am deeply indebted. My very special thanks to him;

Renaud Fessaguet, who assisted me in my research from the first to the last day. Without his help, I would not have run the full course;

Madame Briquet and Madame Seck, who gave so freely of their time and intelligent devotion;

Madeleine Rebérioux, whose exceptional competence, attentive advice, and friendly lucidity added much to my account. She agreed to read large sections of this work, according me, up to the end, her invaluable support.

My friend Bernard de Fallois, who encouraged and advised me greatly. His opinions helped me to remedy several shortcomings in this work.

I cannot fail to evoke the memory of Pierre Mendès-France. At a time when I hesitated to undertake this project, he encouraged me yet also warned me of its difficulties. Once begun, he sustained me with his friendship. Each of the conversations we had about the Affair opened new perspectives to me. This book, like all that I have tried to do, owes much to the light he shed.

I know all that this work of many years owes to tenderness, as well as what it owes to friendship. To be silent is not to forget.

Goult, June 26, 1983

Contents

II: LONG LIVE ESTERHAZY

III: TWO FRANCES

EPILOGUE
IN THE MIRROR OF THE AFFAIR

THE AFFAIR

PROLOGUE

Judas on Parade[*]

(SATURDAY, JANUARY 5, 1895)

The "execution procession" was scheduled, by government decree, for Saturday, January 5, at 8:45 A.M. in the principal courtyard of the École Militaire on Place Fontenoy. Each regiment of the Paris garrison sent two units, one of soldiers in arms, the other of recruits. Diplomats and journalists were invited to view the spectacle. A section was reserved for the few notables who managed to attend the ceremony, flanked by two regiments.[†] Since the public was not admitted, several thousand of the curious assembled outside the gates, along the trellis, or took to the roofs. The adjacent streets were jammed.

From the Prison of Cherche-Midi, Captain Alfred Dreyfus wrote daily to his wife Lucie:

> My darling, I have learned that the supreme humiliation is for the day after tomorrow. I expected it and was prepared, but the blow was brutal nevertheless. I shall resist, as I promised you. I shall draw the energy that I need from your love, from the affection of you all, from the recollection of my beloved children, and from the supreme hope that the truth will be revealed.[1]
>
> The nights are long . . . it is to you that I turn, from your eyes that I draw all my strength . . . can one imagine a more painful martyrdom?[2]

---

[*] During the Rennes trial, Maurice Barrès assembled and published his recollections of the ceremony of Dreyfus's degradation under the title, "La Parade de Judas" (*Le Journal*, July 4, 1899, July 7, 1899). The text was reprinted in *Scènes et Doctrines du Nationalisme*, Félix Guven, 1902.

[†] Joseph Reinach, *Histoire de l'Affaire Dreyfus*, ed. La Revue Blanche, vol. I, pp. 454 ff. Among the "privileged guests" and journalists present, Reinach mentions: Maurice Barrès, Léon Daudet, Houssaye, and Jules Claretie. The diplomat Maurice Paléologue, assigned by the minister of foreign affairs to follow the Dreyfus Affair for his department, was also present as "guest" of Colonel Jean Sandherr, head of the Intelligence Service. He relates the ceremony in his *Journal de l'Affaire Dreyfus*, Plon, 1955, pp. 37ff.

To his lawyer, Edgar Demange, Dreyfus promised not to give in:

"I shall approach this ordeal, which is worse than death, with my head held high and without embarrassment. To tell you my heart will not be cruelly tormented when the badges of honor I acquired by the sweat of my brow are stripped from me would be to lie. It is certain that I would have preferred death a thousand times over. . . ."[3]

At 7:20 A.M. a squadron of the Garde Républicaine, commanded by Captain Lebrun-Renault, proceeded to the Prison of Cherche-Midi. The convict was taken into custody, meticulously searched, handcuffed, and led to a prison car drawn by four horses. By 7:45, the procession left the military prison; at its head were two horsemen of the Garde Républicaine, followed by a military unit. A second unit followed.

At 7:50, Dreyfus was transferred to a new prison cell, a particularly narrow room of the École Militaire. Captain Lebrun-Renault came to speak to him, after which Dreyfus was obliged to wait more than an hour.* "During those long minutes, I summoned all the energies of my being. . . ."[4] At 8:45 four artillerymen, led by an officer, came in search of the treasonous officer. The morning was glacial: "At times beneath the wintry sky, an acrid and lashing wind whipped snowflakes in our faces."[5] In front of the entrance to the École, on Place Fontenoy, the crowd began to swell, and was contained with great difficulty by the police. Irritation mounted with the delay. The first cries of "Death to the Jew," "Death to Judas," were heard. It was a spectacle, wrote Maurice Barrès, "more exciting than the guillotine."[6]

General Paul Darras was on horseback at the center of the place, with the officers of his staff behind him. He drew his sword. There was a roll of the drums. "Attention . . . present arms!" All held their breath. In the far right corner of the courtyard, Captain Dreyfus appeared, escorted by a brigadier and four gunners, each with a saber in hand and a revolver strapped over the shoulder. He walked resolutely, with his head held high. "Judas walks too well," Barrès would later comment.[7] Midway, nevertheless, he stumbled, then recovered. A few meters from General Darras, he stopped, his heels touching, in military posture. His escort withdrew. A "brief and bloody" ray of sun separated the clouds.[8] Darras glared down at the traitor as the clerk of the Court-Martial read the verdict. Then the general rose in his stirrups and with sword held high pronounced the sacramental words: "Alfred Dreyfus, you are no longer worthy of bearing arms. In the name of the people of France, we dishonor you." Whereupon Dreyfus shouted in a metallic voice that soon cracked: "Soldiers, an inno-

* From that conversation would come the legend of Dreyfus's confession.

cent man is being degraded; soldiers, an innocent man is being dishonored. Long live France! Long live the Army!"[9]

The cries of the crowd, which had been kept at a distance, were heard:
"Death! Death to the Jew!"

Sergeant-Major Bouxin, of the Garde Républicaine, approached the
unmoving convict. Brutally, he ripped the decorations from his cap and
sleeves, the red stripes from his trousers, his epaulets. The badges of rank
were tossed on the ground. The magnificent officer, wrote Barrès, taunted
and flayed the traitor, plunging him into mourning.[10] He confiscated his
saber and sheath, which he broke over his knee. "Next to this helmeted
giant with flowing mane, who dismembered him, Dreyfus seemed very
small indeed."[11] His clothes were in shreds. "He was as submissive as the
stiffest of jumping jacks," observed the journalist Léon Daudet. "I could
see in passing his wan and sly-looking face."*[12] Erect, his held held high,
Dreyfus let out a cry of anguish, a raw howl that ended in sobs. "Long live
France! I am innocent! I swear it on the heads of my wife and my
children!" By this time in rags, "as grotesque as he seemed pitiful,"[13] the
traitor was obliged to march before the troops and to make a tour of the
military assembly. The soldiers maintained an icy silence. Each time he
approached the railing which kept the crowd at bay, the cries of "Death!"
grew louder. Dreyfus persisted in his defense to the point of exhaustion:
"You have no right to insult me. I am innocent."[14] But the clamor drowned
his voice. As he passed before the representatives of the press, he shouted,
"You must tell all of France that I am innocent." Jeers of scorn responded:
"Coward! Judas! Dirty Jew!"[15] Léon Daudet described his progress as
follows:

> Meanwhile, he approached, between his guards, a walking
> corpse, a zombie on parade, frail to all appearances, but magnified
> by the overwhelming shame and hatred that he evoked. Not far
> from us, he managed to find the energy to cry out "Innocent!" in a
> toneless and precipitous voice. And there he was before me, at the
> instant of passing, his eyes dry, his gaze lost in the past, no doubt,
> since the future had died with his honor. He no longer had an age,
> a name, a complexion. His was the color of treason. His face was
> ashen, without relief, base, without appearance of remorse,
> foreign, to be sure, debris of the ghetto. A stubborn audacity
> persisted, which excluded all compassion. This was his last walk

---

* "Let them show us the traitor's obscene face," wrote François Coppée in *Le Journal* of
December 23, 1894, "so we may spit at it, one by one."

among men, yet he seemed to be profiting from it, so great was his
self-control and his defiance of ignominy. It was a terrible sign that
his will had not sunk into the mud, that there had been neither
collapse nor weakness. In circumstances this tragic, tears would not
have seemed cowardly.[16]

Maurice Barrès saw Dreyfus in a similar light:

> As he came toward us with his cap thrust down over his
> forehead, his pince-nez on his ethnic nose, his eyes dry and furious,
> his whole face hard and defiant, he cried out, no, he ordered in his
> unbearable voice: "You must tell all of France that I am innocent."
>
> "Judas! Traitor!" A veritable tempest. Through some fatal
> power he possesses or the force of the ideas associated with his
> name, the wretch evoked in all assembled a measure of antipathy.
> His foreign physiognomy, his impassive stiffness, the very atmos-
> phere he exuded revolted even the most self-controlled of
> spectators.[17]

The diplomat Maurice Paléologue, conversing with his friend Colonel
Jean Sandherr, was astonished by Dreyfus's cold restraint: "It seems to me
that if I were in his skin and I were innocent, I would rebel, I would
struggle—or shout."[18] Sandherr explained: "It is clear that you do not
know the Jews. The race has neither patriotism, nor honor, nor pride. For
centuries, they have done nothing but betray."

The ceremony of degradation was over. When the traitor Dreyfus
arrived at an extremity of the courtyard, two gendarmes seized him, and
hoisted him into a prison car for the trip to jail. Passing by the Pont de
l'Alma, Dreyfus glimpsed through an opening in the vehicle the "windows
of the apartment in which years of such sweetness had just elapsed."[19] In
his shredded uniform, he was taken to prison, searched, photographed,
and measured. Then, toward noon, he was locked in a cell of the Santé
Prison.

The military ceremony was completed without him. The clarions were
sounded; the drums rolled. The band struck up the march, *Sambre et
Meuse.* "The military music spread honor and loyalty over the area and
swept away the stench of treason."[20] The troops began their procession in
lively step. The weather turned a bit less chilly.

"Life resumes," commented Léon Daudet.

> The troops disassemble. Sound the fanfare! Cast over the
> obscene burial site your proud and sonorous mantle. Rifles bristle.

The soldiers march briskly, and the spectacle is forever fixed in their eyes. For the idea of the Homeland is so fundamental and so elevated that it draws energy even from its own antithesis, and assaults against it drive it to excess of inspiration. Above the wreckage of so many beliefs, a single faith remains authentic and sincere: that which safeguards our race, our language, the blood of our blood, and which keeps us all in solidarity. The closed ranks are our own. This wretch is not French. We have all understood as much from his act, his demeanor, his physiognomy. He plotted our disaster, but his crime has exalted us.[21]

Upon returning to the Ministry of Foreign Affairs, Paléologue, who had been rather cold, warmed up with a cup of tea. He recounted the parade to his distinguished colleague, Armand Nisard:

"To have loaned himself so docilely, so passively, to such a humiliation, the man must have no moral sensibility... all of his protests rang false. One felt no warmth of soul; his voice seemed that of an automaton."[22]

While Paléologue recovered, "the batallions bristling with rifles, with their handsome French faces,"[23] finished their procession. The crowd dispersed slowly. A few cries of "Judas," "Traitor," and "Death to the Jew," could still be heard.

What do I have in common with this Dreyfus, Barrès had asked himself. "He is not of my race. He was not born to live in society . . . Be on your guard, patriots! When, then, will Frenchmen learn how to conquer France again? Let us unite to degrade all traitors. May they find in every place, spontaneously organized at their passage, a parade of contempt!"[24]

The same day, January 5, in his prison cell at La Santé, Dreyfus wrote to his wife:[25]

"I will tell you later, when we are happy again, what I suffered today. . . . I wondered what I was doing, why I was there; it seemed to me I was in the throes of a hallucination: but alas, my torn and filthy clothes called me brutally back to reality. . . . "

At 7:00 P.M., he wrote again:

"I have just undergone a terrible lapse, tears mixed with sobs, my whole body shaking with fever. It is a reaction to the horrible tortures of the day. . . . But alas, instead of being able to sob in your arms, instead of being able to lean against you, my sobs resounded in the emptiness of my prison."

He marshaled his remaining forces anew:

"I am concentrating all my energy. Strong with my pure and immaculate conscience, I have an obligation to my name. I do not have the right to desert so long as I retain a single breath of life. I shall struggle in the hope and anticipation of seeing the light emerge. . . . "[26]

· At the same time, his wife Lucie wrote to him:

"You promised me to be courageous, and you kept your word. I thank you for it. I would so much have wanted to be near you, to give you strength. . . . Our darlings are so kind, so gay, so happy. It is a consolation in our immense misfortune to have them so young, so oblivious of life."[27]

The "hideous beast of treason," the "remnant of ghetto debris," did not sleep the night of January 5. He spent the night weeping and writing:

"Innocent, I have braved the most frightening martyrdom that can be inflicted on a soldier. I sensed all around me the contempt of the crowd. I would have been happier in my grave. . . . Make this martyrdom come to an end . . . but do so as quickly as possible, for my own resistance is reaching the point of exhaustion. . . . My heart has bled too much today."[28]

With his degradation over, Dreyfus was to be deported. For a moment he hoped that his wife would be able to follow him:

"We shall reveal in exile the tranquillity of two pure and honest hearts, two hearts all of whose thoughts have always been for our beloved country, for France."[29]

His beloved country? France? How could *he* pretend to talk about it? "The wretch is not French," assured Daudet. And Barrès confirmed:

"Dreyfus does not belong to our Nation, and consequently, how could he betray it? The homeland of the Jews is where their money draws the greatest interest."

Léon Daudet and Maurice Barrès knew how to recognize a Frenchman. The Jew Dreyfus was not one of them.

I

THE TRAITOR
DREYFUS

1

A Child's Pledge

lfred Dreyfus was born in Mulhouse on October 9, 1859, to a family
of Alsatian Jews, established for several centuries. His grandfather
was a poor Jewish merchant from the village of Rixheim in Alsace.[1] From a
rather modest beginning, his father, Raphaël Dreyfus, born in Rixheim in
1818, had set up a small cotton mill, to which was soon added a textile
factory. His business prospered with the manufacture in Mulhouse of
calico, muslin, and broadcloth.[2] In 1869, the comfortable situation of the
family enabled him to leave his small apartment on the rue du Sauvage for
a spacious house, located on the rue de la Sinne and situated in a garden of
splendid trees.

Raphaël Dreyfus had married Jeanne Libmann, a "secular saint,"
according to family tradition. They had thirteen children, seven of
whom—four boys and three girls—survived infancy to grow up in a
family atmosphere that combined severity and warmth. Wealthy, united,
exemplary, the Dreyfus family was widely respected. Apparently, his
mother knew a prolonged period of sickness after Alfred, her last child,
was born, so that his sisters shared in his upbringing. He was, it is said, an
easy child—loving, obedient, at once proud and timid.* Extremely reserved in the presence of strangers, he waxed expansive only within the
family. Dreaming of honor, justice, and generosity, his friends nicknamed
him "Don Quixote." It appeared that every decent sentiment found sustenance in him.

"My childhood," he recalled, "elapsed gently under the beneficent
influence of my mother and sisters, a father deeply devoted to his children,
and under the touching protection of my elder brothers."[4]

The year 1870 would upset that happy and orderly life. First, his elder
sister Henriette married and left Mulhouse. She had been a tender and
attentive presence for Alfred—a second mother. Then, war broke out,
and Alsace was invaded. For several months, the Dreyfus family was forced

* Historians of the Dreyfus Affair have taken little interest in Alfred Dreyfus's childhood.
And the family has remained quite discreet about itself.[3]

to seek refuge in Carpentras. Was it true that the sight of French troops traversing Mulhouse, and the "despair and humiliation" experienced by Alfred when he learned of the occupation of his city of birth, determined, as he was to say, his military destiny?* He was not yet twelve years old.

The Treaty of Frankfurt, which provided in 1871 for the annexation of Alsace to Germany, allowed its inhabitants to opt for French citizenship, but in so doing, they were required to leave Alsatian territory. Raphaël Dreyfus immediately chose French citizenship for himself and for those of his children who were minors. In October 1872, he left Mulhouse to settle temporarily in Basel, Switzerland, thus remaining close enough to supervise the family factories. His eldest son, Jacques, who assumed direction of the mills on the common behalf, was obliged to remain behind. He was the sole member of the family not to assume French citizenship, but he would send his six sons to France and, in 1897, moving a number of the family factories to Belfort, he too would request resumption of his original nationality.

In Basel, Alfred's parents enrolled him in the Real Schule, where he experienced a number of difficulties, as courses were conducted in German. In 1873, Raphaël decided to send his son to Paris for the continuation of his studies. "A sensitive child, accustomed to the comforts of family life," he had a hard time adapting to boarding school.[5] The harsh life of the institution, and the company of his classmates, seemed to him unbearable. He fell sick and returned to his family.

In his autobiography Alfred Dreyfus devotes only one line to the events of his life from 1873 to 1878.[6] He would always remain as shy as he was discreet, harboring an extreme—almost obsessive—sensitivity. His son Pierre summarized these years: "After a suitable period of convalescence, he returned to Paris, attended courses at the Collège Chaptal, passed his baccalaureate, then returned to Sainte-Barbe to prepare for the entrance exams to the École Polytechnique."[7]

It appears that Alfred's destiny was in fact more hesitant; he transferred from boarding school to boarding school and suffered from the instability, withdrawing into himself in an effort at self-protection; he spent several months in Mulhouse serving a business apprenticeship in the family mills, which were in a period of accelerating prosperity; he journeyed to Carpentras, home of his beloved sister Henriette, Mme. Valabrègue, and attempted to develop an interest in the commercial endeavors of his brother-in-law; and he decided to prepare for his baccalaureate on his own and succeeded brilliantly in that exam at the Faculté de Greno-

* Alfred Dreyfus, *Souvenirs et Correspondances*, published by his son, Grasset, 1936, p. 41. Alfred Dreyfus explained his career choice in those terms in a letter to Lucie Dreyfus.

ble.* It was only after that encouraging success that he would choose to attend the Collège Saint-Barbe and prepare for the École Polytechnique.[8]

Why did Alfred Dreyfus decide to become an officer? According to his son Pierre, he never stopped thinking of "Alsace quaking beneath the foreign yoke, of those whose heart had remained French and who so suffered from oppression."[9] The choice of a military career would thus have fulfilled a "childhood pledge." And no doubt his Alsatian origin, an attachment to the land and community of his native region, a hatred of the invader, and a thirst for revenge all played their roles. But there were other, more personal reasons, concerning his character and his ethics. A timid adolescent, as sensitive as he was withdrawn, he no doubt felt the need of a rigorous context, an orderly and protective society. The Army may have seemed to him one vast family, with its crystalline certainties, guaranteeing an organized destiny over a predetermined course. Above all, the values which the Army seemed to embody—homeland, honor, order, and hierarchy—were already his own.

At the same time he could not be unaware that all was not necessarily simple for a Jew in the armed forces. But in 1878, the campaign that would later be launched against Jews in the Army had not yet begun and numerous Jewish officers appeared to be enjoying normal careers. Above all, the wealthy, established, and respected Dreyfus family was quite representative of the assimilated Jewish bourgeoisie.[10] The family observed the principal rituals and several relatives were rabbis, but the Dreyfuses felt only minimal solidarity with the Jewish "community." At age nineteen, Alfred Dreyfus, a Frenchman from Alsace, was passionately devoted to his country and to the Republic.[11] He was proud of his name, of his family, of his social station, all in the manner of a French bourgeois of venerable stock.

After a year of preparation, and without hope of being admitted, Alfred applied to the École Polytechnique. To his surprise, he was successful, and was ranked 182 in an entering class of 236. Of his years at school, he would later say nothing. But his classmates would describe them at length.[12] At his graduation in 1880, he ranked 128 out of 235, and was appointed a sublieutenant in the school of instruction at Fontainebleau. Thus did he emerge an artillery officer, a French officer, a Jewish officer.

* It appears that the young Alfred Dreyfus was being housed by close relatives at the time. In registering for the entrance competition to the École Polytechnique, he gave Bar-le-Duc as his residence.

2

The Army of Revenge

Since the collapse of 1870, the army in which the Sublieutenant Dreyfus began his service was in a state of profound crisis. "An immense disaster, a desperate peace, a series of losses that nothing could compensate, the State without stability, no army other than that just freed from the prisons of the enemy, two provinces confiscated, millions to be paid, the conqueror garrisoned in fully a quarter of the territory, the capital streaming with the blood of a civil war, Europe inclined to irony or indifference. . . ."[1] Thus does Charles de Gaulle describe a defeated France. And how indeed would the Army—humiliated by the surrenders of Sedan and Metz, in disarray from the time of the very first battles, easily defeated—not have been shaken by the national drama?

Barely had the Treaty of Frankfurt been signed and the Parisian uprising crushed than the National Assembly undertook to restore France to her military might. That major legislative effort was accomplished in an atmosphere of unanimous resolve.[2] Laws of 1872, 1873, and 1875 established the principles which were to give the French Army its new foundations: obligatory service demanded of all citizens, a defense maintained by the nation itself, but, simultaneously, the reorganization of an active Army that was to constitute a permanent force and an elaborate school of instruction. In this effort France attempted to imitate the system to which Prussia was thought to owe its success. But by proclaiming service to be obligatory while retaining the prior organization of the Army, the National Assembly instituted an extremely perilous contradiction. "The history of France's military institutions from 1875 to 1914," notes the historian J. Monteilhet, "is at bottom the struggle for existence by the Army in its barracks, bequeathed to the Republic by the Monarchy and the Empire, against a nation in arms, born of obligatory service and daughter of the sovereign nation-state. It was the Army in its barracks that was to end up victorious."[3]

The first twenty years of the Republic undoubtedly constituted a decisive period in the military history of France, characterized by scrupulously patient efforts at retraining and a will perennially alert to innovation and renewal. Antiquated regulations were revised and streamlined to adapt to modern forms of combat. Open field maneuvers were instituted as early as 1874. The École Supérieure de Guerre, founded in 1876, deliberately oriented its teaching toward the critical study of the experiential realities of war and the search for new solutions. It claimed to guarantee intellectual tests as the prime criteria for admission.[4] Under the leadership of General de Miribel, the Superior War Council, then the General Staff of the Army were organized. Reflecting on the lessons of the war just lost, they sought the methods which modern warfare demanded of the military command.[5] "The entire Army," writes de Gaulle, "at present cultivates the field of military intelligence."[6] One ought, nevertheless, to note the limits of this reform, residing in the dogmatism inherent in the various doctrinal schools, the packing of the tightly sealed General Staffs with members of the traditional elites, the reign of a group of mandarins who allowed at the summit of their hierarchy only officers under their protection, and above all the accumulation of prejudices inseparable from the military point of view.[7]

The Army, moreover, was renewing its means of combat. A gigantic plan of mobilization, concentration, requisition, and transportation was gradually elaborated, assigning each man his place and role in the event of war and involving four million men and eight million horses.[8] "There was not a single tool, caisson, or boat," writes de Gaulle, "for which a new model was not adopted between 1875 and 1900."[9] Twelve years after the adoption in 1874 of the Gras model gun—which replaced paper with metal for the encasement of cartridges—the Army adopted the Lebel rifle whose magazine mechanism doubled the firing speed. Shortly thereafter troops on horseback were given cavalry magazine rifles, and cylinder revolvers were put into use. Above all the artillery was the privileged arena of progress, one entailing moreover a bitter competition between France and Germany. Melinite, an explosive powder of great destructive force, was adapted for shells in 1885. The first steel parts, adopted in 1875, were quickly superseded by more advanced models.[10]

The French and Germans studied, in the greatest secrecy, plans for a large-recoil cannon. To the Germans, the difficulties in realizing the project soon seemed insurmountable—as the French Intelligence Service was to learn.[11] More persistent, the French attempted to perfect a cannon of long recoil and oleopneumatic brakes. In 1897 appeared the celebrated 75, whose regularity, speed, and precision of fire would prove incomparable in that era. In 1914, it would save the French Army from being crushed.[12]

Finally, a powerful defensive network was organized on the northern and eastern frontiers, a vast effort of fortification undertaken under the direction of General Sere de Rivières and entailing the installation of a line of fortresses deployed between Épinal and Belfort and the disposition of second-line locations such as Reims and Langres. Paris was now provided with a military belt which would repulse any new invasion.

This renovated army, with its hopes of revenge, gradually became in the following years a powerfully attractive force. "Never in our history," writes Raoul Giradet, "was the prestige of military officers valued so highly as in the twenty-year period following the defeat."[13] Despite the persistent mediocrity of salaries and pensions, "to have a son at Saint-Cyr or to marry one's daughter to an officer, constituted for a family the very consecration of respectability, the avowed goal of the highest ambitions."[14] But the martial renewal and the influence it exerted could not conceal the deep moral and intellectual crisis which was rocking the Army. Military society was profoundly at variance with the nation it had the mission to defend and which it pretended to incarnate.

The Army had been shaken for nearly thirty years by the gusts of history. Where was one's duty? Where one's fidelity? Where legitimacy? With the Republic? The Empire? The Monarchy? "Thus it was," observes François Bedarida, "that legality was no longer necessarily reconcilable with legitimacy."[15] The traditional notions of honor, discipline, and order were called into question by the shifts of a history that seemed to be moving too fast. "From a neutral instrument in the service of the State, the Army became, in the course of the war of national defense and the struggle against the Commune, a politicized body in the service of an ideology. Amid the ruin of principles, every man was to answer according to his own conscience—which meant, most often, according to his temperament, his sympathies, his upbringing, and his social milieu."[16]

And it was precisely this renewed interest in the profession of arms beginning in 1871, the will to participate in the defense of the country, and to prepare for revenge, that attracted to military careers an increasing proportion of young men from the aristocracy and from the conservative and Catholic bourgeoisie. In 1868, the yearbook of Saint-Cyr counted among its graduates 89 names "with the noble particle" out of 284. Ten years later, there were 102 aristocrats out of a class of 365.[17] The proportion of former students of religious institutions grew likewise. In 1847, out of 306 Saint-Cyrians, 2 came from religious schools; in 1886, there were 140 out of a class of 410. Starting in 1873, due to the large-scale economic depression that ravaged rural France, reducing the value of land, the sons of landholders and lords of manors joined the Army as well. Thus an officer corps of aristocrats and bourgeois gradually emerged, far more clerical than their predecessors, and, in a number of cases, profoundly responsive to the influence of the Jesuits. This development is most clear-cut in the cavalry, less evident in the infantry, and even less so in the artillery and the engineering corps.[18] The promotion of officers, moreover, regulated by a law dating from 1832, occurred according to a system smacking of co-option: common sympathies, relations of kinship, and religious and ideological affinities all served to reinforce the proportion and role of conservative and Catholic officers.[19] To this may be added the fact that in many traditional milieus, the Army was experienced as a refuge and a safeguard against the new order of things. It was not, or not yet, an arena of action for the nascent Republic, but, on the contrary, a last haven of the old values, a preserver of the legitimist faith. It was the "holy ark" which the republicans had not yet dared to touch, a precious reserve maintained intact amid the "general subversion."[20]

Bédarida, studying the contents of the republican leader Léon Gambetta's "secret files,"* observes the presence of a large majority of Bonapartist and Legitimist generals in the year 1878. Similarly, most of the colonels at that time felt a profound affinity for the institutions of monarchy. "The higher one rises in the hierarchy, the lower the proportion of officers of popular—or even petit-bourgeois—origin. The system of selection reinforces the conservative character of the career army." In 1890, these tendencies had not been reversed.[22] The Army, or, in any event, the General Staff, appeared to nurture and even embody an attachment to the moral order, a nostalgia for a former France. And quite normally, conservative opinion never stopped depending on the Army, considering it sympathetic, an instrument destined to fulfill conservative ends. The career Army drew to itself and crystallized the aspirations of antirepublican France. It seemed the last force in society which the adversaries of the Republic had the means of controlling and through which they were able to hope for a measure of restitution.[23]

But the crisis of the Army did not consist simply in an increasing divorce between the Republic and military society. It was not the question of the regime alone—republic or monarchy—which divided opinion.[24] A more serious problem faced the officers of France. What was the place of the Army in a democracy based on universal suffrage, a parliamentary system, schooling for all, and obligatory military service? And what was its mission? "Democracy," writes François Bédarida, "means the sovereignty

* These were secret files about the French Army, veritable card catalogues concerning the professional worth and political tendencies of officers, which were discovered in the Ministry of Foreign Affairs among Gambetta's papers. The files shed light on the relations between the Army and the Nation during the ten years following the collapse of 1870.[21]

of the Nation, the law of the majority, broad liberties extended to its citizens, the cultivation of a critical spirit, free debate; what then becomes of the principle of authority, and the law of obedience with which the military spirit is identified?"[25]

At the core of the Dreyfus Affair one encounters repeatedly a major debate over obedience, hierarchy, and authority. Should the tradition of silent discipline be called into question? In 1855, in an anonymous volume, General Gaston Galliffet and the Minister of War Eugène Lamy had defined the military spirit as "the annihilation of all those rebellions which occur in man against the imperatives of suffering and sacrifice . . . the voluntary death of will, in which survives obedience alone."[26] For having championed in 1872 "a free, active, and intelligent competition" between officers and ranks, Colonel Denfert-Rochereau had been challenged to a duel by General Changarnier, for whom "obedience was the living law for the soldier; without it there was no Army."

The Army was, of necessity, guardian of the ancient virtues of obedience and discipline. But it did not fulfill that role for its own sake. Could it retain values that the Nation itself would abandon? Was it not the natural auxiliary of a social order that shared its morality? Were not the principles of authority, established hierarchies, and obedience to one's superiors precisely the rules of a society that the Army embodied and was obliged to protect? "For whoever would reflect the slightest bit," General du Barail wrote brutally, "the republican and military points of view are two contradictory and incompatible states. . . . The Republic represents the sovereignty of public opinion, the absolute equality of all, the crushing of the elite by the majority. It is a pyramid stood on its head. By its motto alone, the Republic is the negation of the Army, for liberty, equality, and fraternity are tantamount to indiscipline, the oblivion of obedience, and the negation of hierarchical principles."[27]

All French officers would not live the confrontation in those terms. Many, out of traditional deference to the law of the State, conviction, or the ruses of ambition, would find compromises. But most would ultimately feel poorly integrated in the republican Nation. Convinced it belonged to an elite, "protected by uniform from the contagious defects of civilian society," the military community would be tempted to exacerbate its contemptuous, proud, and often wounded isolation. The majority of officers withdrew into an extremely restricted circle of relations, removed from the lower classes but also from the governing elites, who opened their doors to only a handful of high-ranking officers.[28] Fundamentally, they were "an Army if not cut off from the Nation, at least living in its margins."[29] An Army intent on preserving the "male sentiments" and "virile habits" of devotion, daring, and bravery, which constituted the military spirit.* An Army which protected the "pride of the French name," the cult of the flag, the "religion of France." An Army which nourished warrior virtues, French virtues, eternal virtues, the very ones later exalted by the writer Charles Péguy, and which would prepare the Nation for the holy war, the war of revenge, from which would come the resurrection of a proud and courageous people. The Army, at the end of the nineteenth century and even at the beginning of the twentieth, would never cease to react to the favorable or nefarious effects of the perceived exaltation of its role. Since it expressed the nation's fervor, since it bore the hopes of revenge and glory, was it not identical with France herself? And was it not, in the accomplishment of its mission, above the rules of justice, even above the laws?

3

Intelligent, Zealous, Conscientious, Quite Active

Alfred Dreyfus was twenty-one years old when he entered the school of instruction at Fontainebleau. He remained there two years, earned good grades, and on October 1, 1882, was named lieutenant of the Thirty-first Artillery Regiment, garrisoned at Le Mans. At the end of 1883, he was transferred to the horse battery of the first division of the cavalry in Paris. His evaluations described him as "intelligent . . . zealous . . . conscientious . . . quite active." In 1887, they noted that he was an "excellent lieutenant of horse battery" and that "he gave orders well." In 1888, they said that "with the advantage of an excellent memory and an

---

* Paul Déroulède, *De l'éducation militaire*. Déroulède proposed a method of teaching the military virtues to all young Frenchmen. "It is a matter of nothing less than transforming the youth of our schools into a legion of warriors."

extremely lively intelligence," he was "the best lieutenant of the batteries group." It was then that he decided to prepare for the entrance examinations to the École de Guerre. In September 1889 he was named captain of the Twenty-first Artillery and was transferred as an observation officer to the École Centrale de Pyrotechnie Militaire in Bourges. There he worked diligently to be admitted to the École de Guerre—not without occasional diversions. To be sure, he frequented women of easy virtue.[1] Shy, lonely, a bit haughty, at times curt, he was not at all comfortable among his fellow officers, which was markedly apparent. Bourges bored him. In Paris, he made the acquaintance of Lucie Hadamard, daughter of a diamond merchant and granddaughter of a graduate of the École Polytechnique. Lucie was tall and shapely, rich and Jewish. She found the young officer with the promising future charming. They were engaged in the course of the winter of 1889, but continued to live apart—he in Bourges, she in Paris. The wedding took place on April 21, 1890. On April 20, Alfred Dreyfus had the pleasure of being admitted to the École de Guerre.

He was enrolled at the beginning of the fall, and for two and a half years worked like a man possessed. His evaluations reveal his zeal and the satisfaction of his superiors. "Rather good health; myopic; easy character; good upbringing; very good posture; general education very extensive; training in military theory very good; knows German very well; mounts a horse quite well; very good officer; keen mind, grasping questions very well; quick to work and accustomed to study. Quite suitable for service with the General Staff." In November 1892, he graduated ninth in a class of eighty-one with the citation "very good" and certification from the General Staff. His excellent ranking resulted in his being called to serve a probationary term with the General Staff of the Army, which he began January 1, 1893. A son—Pierre—was born in 1891, a daughter—Jeanne—in February 1893. "A brilliant and easy career was open to me; my future seemed most auspicious. After a day's work, I returned to the tranquillity and charm of family life . . . our happiness was complete. . . . I had no financial worries; the same deep affection bound me to the members of my family and to those of my wife's family. Everything in life seemed to smile at me."[2]

Thus would Alfred Dreyfus describe the years in which, as a young husband, a young father (he was not yet thirty-four), a brilliant officer of the General Staff, he seemed destined to lead a life of happiness. Of that happiness he would always give the same impression: a peaceful "interior," a united family cultivating in mutual affection the virtues of honor, order, and harmony. In fact had all been as "easy" for Dreyfus as he claimed? At the École de Guerre and at the General Staff, he did not quite resemble the others. He was Alsatian and spoke German: What made him sympathetic to some inspired at times distrust in others. He was a child of the industrial bourgeoisie, a class that did little to conceal its recently accumulated wealth. Whether they belonged to the aristocracy, the traditional bourgeoisie, or the middle classes, most of his comrades enjoyed only limited resources locked into houses and landed estates. Most often they lived on their salaries, which restricted them to a mediocre station.[3] Alfred Dreyfus's fortune may have displeased some because it was so apparent, and because it signified the rise of a new bourgeoisie.

Above all, he was Jewish. Since 1892, Edouard Drumont's newspaper, *La Libre Parole,* had been conducting a furious campaign against the presence of Jewish officers in the Army. They were accused of blocking paths of advancement, populating the École Polytechnique, taking the place of Catholic officers, and preparing the terrain for treason. In the name of the 300 Jewish officers then in the French Army, Captain Ernest Crémieu-Foa challenged Drumont to a duel.* In so doing, he intended to prove that he was an officer like any other, an officer able to defend himself.

Several other duels in 1892 pitted Jewish officers against French anti-Semites.[4] In the course of one of these, the Marquis de Morès, an anti-Semitic agitator, killed Captain Armand Mayer, a young Jewish officer, who was a graduate of the Polytechnique and the nephew of a highly respected rabbi in Paris. Mayer's funeral resulted in a spectacular demonstration: between 20,000 and 100,000 people attended, according to *Le Matin.* Military honors were bestowed. High-ranking officers, a detachment of students from the École Polytechnique, and a company of the infantry followed the coffin. To cries of "Long live the army!" and the roll of drums, the burial took on the appearance of a patriotic parade. The Jewish community was deeply affected. A Jew, an Alsatian, and an officer, Mayer seemed to be the symbol of Jewish devotion to the Nation.†

As a young officer on loan to the General Staff, Alfred Dreyfus could not have remained entirely indifferent to the deluge of insults directed at Jewish officers, branding them potential traitors, on the occasion of Mayer's death. Yet he never mentioned them. Dreyfus's silence on his relationship to the Jewish tradition was absolute: He would speak of it

---

* Both were slightly wounded. Captain Crémieu-Foa's witness was Captain Ferdinand Walsin Esterhazy. See *infra* p. 123.

† The French Chief Rabbi's speech at Mayer's funeral bears witness to this: "His sacrifice of his life will not have been without use to the causes that were dear to him if it has as an effect to dispel unseemly misunderstandings and to reveal in its splendor, through the mourner's veil that covers it today, the flag of France, that glorious and immortal symbol of justice, concord, and fraternity." See Michael Marrus, *The Politics of Assimilation: The French Jewish Community at the Time of the Dreyfus Affair*[5] and the abundant bibliography quoted by Marrus on the subject of Mayer's death.

neither in his memoirs nor in the long correspondence from Devil's Island that he pursued with his wife. That silence, which might be explained by an almost neurotic modesty, an obstinate discretion concerning his intimate feelings and affinities, reveals in 1892 Dreyfus's indifference to the issue. That he was a Jew by name or tradition did in fact impose certain obligations, reinforcing the imperatives of rigor and patriotic fervor. But that singularity, like his character, simply served to isolate him further.

Within the Army, Dreyfus had neither a protector nor a powerful supporter. He was neither friend nor protégé of any of the chiefs of the Army, nor for that matter, of any political personality.[6] It is probable that his name and his Jewishness, which he neither invoked nor concealed, somewhat impeded his professional advancement. At the École de Guerre, General Pierre Bonnefond, who objected to the presence of Jews on the General Staff, gave him a very low grade. When he dropped several ranks,[7] Dreyfus demanded an explanation.* Later, when the General Staff would close ranks to attack him, there would be many officers who would openly express their animosity toward him. General Lebelin de Dionne, under whose orders he had served at the École de Guerre, and who had evaluated him quite positively at the time, would describe him as "intelligent, diligent, and gifted with an extraordinary memory." But he would add:

> His contemptuous and brusque demeanor, his reckless remarks (saying in particular before his classmates that the Alsatians were happier under German domination than under French domination) earned him the antipathy of his teachers and classmates. His personal behavior was improper. Recently married, he did not hesitate to be seen with prostitutes. I was obliged to criticize him on that subject. . . . I have seen many Israelite officers at the École de Guerre. I can affirm that none of them had been the object of the animosity of his superiors and colleagues. If this was not the case for Dreyfus, it was due to his detestable character, his immodesty of language, and his undignified private life, not at all to his religion."[8]

Once he had been accused as a traitor, numerous affairs with foreign women—many of whom were said to speak German—were attributed to him. It would be said that he traveled frequently to Mulhouse, in German

---

* Dreyfus claimed to have protested "in the name of the Israelite officers" to General Lebelin de Dionne. That pointed intervention constitutes one of the very few cases in which Dreyfus affirmed his affiliation with the Jewish community. It would be used against him in the indictment of 1894, when it would be seen as one of the signs of his indiscretion.

Alsace. It would be revealed that he continually asked his classmates questions, collected secret information, and inquired about armaments; that he arrogantly flaunted his wealth; that he gambled frequently and cheated; that he was vain, dissembling, and enigmatic—in a word, suspect.* Even his physique, his myopia, and, of course, his physiognomy, ended up bearing witness against him: Dreyfus seemed flat, commonplace, livid, cunning, colorless, awkward, and prodigiously antipathetic.[9] But the women of easy virtue whom he frequented—"until my marriage," he would specify with evident respect for bourgeois morality[10]— the officers, many of whom were his friends, and who would later be obsessed with destroying him, the life of material comfort which would subsequently be termed ostentatious and unjustly acquired wealth, all seemed part of an altogether tranquil life. His loving family, brilliant career, and the service of "dear France,"† as he would never cease to call it, established for him a peaceful and seemingly natural harmony. Alfred Dreyfus was indeed a happy man.

4

A Jew

What the young officer did not see, or did not want to see, was the increasing strength of the anti-Semitic current which had been agitating French public opinion for several years.

Since the Revolution of 1789, the Jews of France had been living in a tranquillity that was but rarely interrupted. Having become full citizens in

* Captain Junck, Dreyfus's classmate at the École de Guerre, would testify on May 16, 1898: "Very haughty, he enjoyed showing off his wealth. He boasted of having led quite a life when he was a lieutenant in Le Mans and then in Paris. He liked telling of his adventures." Archives of the Ministry of War. Secret File. File No. 1, item no. 13. Captain de Pouydraguin, commenting (on November 8, 1897, and May 13, 1898) on Dreyfus's curiosity during the trips of the École de Guerre, would declare: "What I believed to be the zeal of a diligent and ambitious officer could well have had other causes . . ." These are merely a few examples.
† See in particular, in *Lettres d'un innocent,* the letter of December 7, 1894, to Lucie Dreyfus: "Oh! dear France, you whom I love with all my soul, with all my heart, you to whom I have devoted all my energy, all my intelligence . . ." The theme, and even the words, are constantly repeated throughout the correspondence.

1791, entitled to exercise any craft, with full access to French culture, they had ceased to constitute a community isolated from the rest of society.[1] "Citizenship was the sign of emancipation, the guarantee for the Jew that he was free."[2] Emancipation had as its natural effect assimilation. The Jews were now free to maintain their religion, but without that circumstance affecting their relationship with the French Nation. "'Let there be neither Jews nor Christians except at the hour of prayer for those who pray!' Thus did France proclaim on August 26, 1789, through the Declaration of the Rights of Man. From that day on, France recognized only citizens."[3]

Such were the words of an "assimilated" Jew in 1892. And no doubt, the Jews of France felt "a particular aptitude for imitation," for assimilation:[4] The acquisition of equality and "social fusion" which they welcomed enthusiastically might serve as an example for the rest of Europe. On the hundredth anniversary of the Revolution, special commemorative services were held in all synagogues. The French motto of "liberty, equality, fraternity" was exalted.[5] The Revolution, wrote Grand Rabbi Zadoc Kahn of Nîmes, "is our exodus from Egypt . . . our modern Passover."[6] It appeared that the French Jews had contracted a "historical debt" toward France, that in offering them emancipation, the Nation had acquired "a huge sum of credit redeemable in their loyalty and in the normal activities of their daily life." Among others, the rabbi of Avignon expressed this in addressing his congregation: "May we always attempt to arrive first among honest and loyal workers in all careers that have been opened to us. . . . May we offer an example of civic and social virtue. May we never cease to be irreproachable citizens. Let us be, in brief, worthy children of France."[7]

"When the Dreyfus Affair erupted," writes Michael Marrus, "the theoretical association of Judaism with modern France, the intellectual dimension of assimilation, had become the official doctrine of the Jewish community."[8]

This did not, however, mean that anti-Judaic prejudices, which had been nurtured by Christianity since its origin, had been dispelled. For numerous Catholics and for a large part of the clergy, the Jews remained the people of "deicide." The Talmud was but an "anticatechism" from which the Jews "derived, like serpents, all their vices."[9] Periodically, the old myth of ritual crime was revived.[10] As early as 1806, Louis Gabriel Ambroise de Bonald, one of the best representatives of conservative Catholicism, was writing in *Le Publiciste:* "The Jews, all of whose ideas are perverted and who either scorn or detest us, would find in their history, should they become our masters, terrible lessons to apply to us."[11] In 1858, Louis Veuillot, one of the leaders of the Church of France, revealed in three issues of *L'Univers* such great contempt for the Jews that the Consistoire

Central Israélite felt obliged to issue a solemn protest. Anti-Jewish publications were already numerous during the first half of the nineteenth century, but they appear to have had only a limited audience.[12] A number of Jewish personalities—including the lawyer, Adolphe Crémieux—founded in 1860 the Alliance Israélite Universelle, intended to combat "the injustice, prejudice, and discrimination" embodied in a number of violently anti-Jewish publications as well as in the scandal of a series of "forced conversions" of Jewish children.[13] But that virtually clandestine group appears only to have provoked the distrust of the Jewish community.

It was toward the year 1880 in France that traditional anti-Judaism began to evolve into an anti-Semitism whose tide would continue to rise throughout the remainder of the century.* "The hostility against the Jews," wrote Bernard Lazare, publishing in 1894 his *Anti-Semitism, Its History and Its Causes,* "which was formerly rooted in sentiment, now became philosophical. . . . The new anti-Jews wanted to be able to explain their hatred—i.e., to adorn it. Anti-Judaism had become anti-Semitism."[14] What had up until then been mere prejudice, an irrational hostility, was to become in a few years a veritable doctrine, an explanation of society, the foundation of a politics, even a morality.

The fantastic explosion of intolerance which was to occur during the Dreyfus Affair has received numerous and rather confused explanations. Beginning in 1880, the rise of anti-Semitism could be observed throughout Europe. In Russia it manifested itself in a series of vicious pogroms. And even as France was consolidating its alliance with Russia, the Russian Jews were fleeing westward from the massacres ordered by the czar,[15] many seeking refuge in France. A few years later a wave of brutality was to spread over the whole of eastern Europe. In Germany, an outbreak of anti-Semitic propaganda occurred. But French public opinion did not seem to be particularly responsive. There was no French delegation to the international anti-Semitic congress which assembled 300 German, Austrian, and Russian delegates in Dresden in 1882.† During the 1882 trial of Jews accused of committing ritual crime in Tisza-Eszlas in Hungary, most of the French press denounced an "ignoble," "monstrous" trial, "worthy of the Middle Ages." "It is not a judicial debate," wrote *Le Journal des Débats* of July 16, 1883, "but a racial war." On the other hand, a segment of the Catholic press—and notably, *L'Univers,* whose readership was, to be sure,

---

* The term is generally attributed to Wilhelm Marr, who published a violently anti-Jewish tract in Berne in 1873, which at first went unobserved in France and was subsequently commented on in 1879 in *Le Temps* and *Le Journal des Débats.*

† "The Anti-Semitic Congress in Dresden has just demonstrated that human stupidity is gaining ground" (*Le Figaro,* September 20, 1882).

quite limited—affirmed its certainty of the "Jewish crime," and protested against an acquittal that could only be due to "Jewish gold."[16]

Ought a partial explanation for this growing intolerance in France after 1882 to be sought in what has been called the "Jewish invasion"—the settling in France, and particularly in Paris, of an increasing number of Jews in flight from persecution?[17] In 1840, there were but 70,000 Jews in France, two thirds of whom lived in Alsace and Lorraine. That small community gradually swelled with the arrival of German, Polish, and Russian Jews—quite often to Paris. Jews without resources, they were confronted by a distrustful, vaguely hostile population, itself burdened with religious prejudices, of the myth of the "youpin" or "kike."[18] Between 1870 and 1880, Paris received at least 50,000 Jews from Alsace-Lorraine, who were quickly assumed to be Germans, whereas their very choice of expatriation manifested their loyalty to France. The Jewish community of Algeria—44,000 in 1890—was similarly swollen by the flow of immigrants from Alsace-Lorraine.* In *La France Juive,* published in 1886, Edouard Drumont claimed that France, which had been colonized by the Jews, had a Jewish population of 500,000. In fact, it was less than 100,000.† It is nevertheless the case that the "Jewish invasion," or the myth which it constituted, may have helped feed a latent anti-Semitism.

But the real reasons for the anti-Semitic fever are no doubt to be sought in a large-scale confusion of opinion. In the last quarter of the nineteenth century, the new economic and political forms assumed by French society provoked among those attached to the old order, or who suffered from the changes, anxiety, fear, and frequently anger: the general disarray was an incitement to identify those who were responsible. A number of muddled and incommensurate rebellions all converged in a common desperation and resentment. There were rebellions against the new ways of life that came with technological progress and industrial society, against the rural exodus and the exploitation of workers, but also against the difficulties the development of capitalism was causing industrialists and tradesmen, against the iron law of the banks, and against the abject poverty of some, the ruin of others, by an arrogant and inhuman economic system. There were revolts as well against democracy, understood as government by all, against the principle of equality, against the parliamentary system, and against the government of babbling and impotent lawyers. There were revolts against the denial of God, the secular principle, the destruction of

* In October 1871, by order of Adolphe Crémieux, then minister of justice, the Jews of Algeria were declared to be French citizens.
† According to the census of 1890 (which may have been incomplete), there were 67,780 Jews in mainland France and 43,556 in Algeria.

the Christian virtues, and the dislocation of Catholic influence. And revolts against the liberal values characterizing the Enlightenment, against the Utopianism which had nurtured European thought leading to the Revolution, against the sovereignty of science and reason, and against faith in the inevitable progress of societies.

Those revolts, undoubtedly issuing from different social classes, had little coherence. Some came from conservative forces, nostalgic for the values and hierarchies defended by the Church and the Monarchy. Others betrayed little more than a fear of the upheavals imposed by industrial society and by urban concentration. Still others exploited the misery of the victims of the capitalist system. But they were all united by a common series of refusals: a refusal of the rationalist individualism of liberal society, a refusal of capitalism and its modes of exploitation, a refusal of the parliamentary system, and a refusal of the dissolution of social ties in bourgeois society.[19]

Those refusals, which perhaps reveal less an attachment to the old order than an anxiety at the approach of a new society, found expression in the resurgence of irrational values: the cult of instinct, the affirmation of the self (be it individual ego or national ego), the discovery of the unconscious, and the cult of energy. Thus would emerge a vague ideology, concerning which Zeev Sternhell has observed correctly, that was promulgated at the end of the nineteenth century by men emerging from quite different horizons and from rather distant disciplines in France, Germany, Italy, Austria, and Russia.[20] The uprooted intellectual, the vagabond without country, the wandering Jew, and the international capitalist became equally detestable. They embodied a decadent, mediocre, materialistic, and thoroughly corrupt society. There were condemnations of vast cities "in which heroism was lost" and workers enslaved, of capitalism, which depopulated the countryside and organized a reign of money which knew no homeland. It was common to demand a reform of institutions bringing them closer to an authoritarianism that would rid them of impotence and parliamentary inertia. There were calls for a leader incarnating the virtues of the race. To the pretentions of reason were opposed the virtues of instinct, even animality. Critical intelligence was distrusted, virility exalted. Throughout Europe, that ideology, in its confusion and vigor, would bring substance and strength to anti-Semitism.

For only a vast conspiracy it was believed, could explain the decadence of the times.[21] The Jews—and to a lesser degree the Protestants and the Freemasons—were its organizers and inspirers. A wanderer, the Jew was by nature without a homeland. A merchant, he was removed from the soil. By destiny or by curse, he was "international." He loved money, not war.

He was nurtured on intelligence, not instinct. He appealed to tolerance, not strength. He flourished in an impotent and venal parliamentary democracy. This land was not his, these ancestors were not his. And since what was called for was a culprit, who profited from everything that was hateful, who scorned everything worthy of love, Judas seemed born to the role. "That Dreyfus is capable of treason I deduce from his race," Maurice Barrès, who conferred on anti-Semitism the dimension of political doctrine, was to write.[22] The journalist Charles Maurras would later make of it the necessary basis of any system. "Everything seems impossible, or frightfully difficult, without the providential arrival of anti-Semitism, through which all things fall into place and are simplified."[23]

The brutal rise of anti-Semitism in the penultimate decade of the last century has been frequently described.[24] In 1882, the collapse of the Union Générale, a Catholic bank very close to the Church, which brought a number of small depositors to ruin, was attributed, particularly by the Catholic press, to the machinations of the large Jewish banks, and to a plan fomented by the Rothschilds. About thirty anti-Semitic publications between 1883 and 1892 granted that bankruptcy special attention, denounced "Jewish methods," and placed the French on their guard.[25] Anti-Semites of the right and of the extreme left joined on that occasion to denounce Jewish financiers, Jewish capitalists, and Jewish Rothschilds. Between 1882 and 1886, twenty anti-Semitic works by priests are to be found. They have in common their explanation of all the misfortunes of France by the "persistence of the deicidal people."[26]

In 1886, Edouard Drumont published *La France Juive*, which was to know a violent success.* In two months, approximately 100,000 copies were sold. That extravagantly mediocre work,[27] fueled by gossip and fantasy, was nevertheless sufficiently adept "to elevate the Jewish myth to the level of an ideology and a political method."[28] Above all, it was intent on addressing the working class and the petite bourgeoisie, the victims of international capitalism and large industry. To the first group, Drumont denounced the Jew, symbolized by Rothschild, as the agent of the workers' misery; to the second, he explained that Karl Marx and "all the heads of the cosmopolitan revolution are Jews." Thus was he able to reconcile in anti-Semitism counter-Revolutionary thought, the Catholic tradition, and a populist anticapitalism of socialistic tendency. Thanks to anti-Semitism, class conflicts were dissolved. "There remained," observes Michel Winock, "but a minority of Jewish profiteers crushing the immense majority of

---

* Edouard Drumont, *La France juive: Essai d'histoire contemporaine,* Paris, Marpon & Flammarion, 1886. In 1888, the book's immense success was to justify a popular edition published by Palme. The work would be reprinted in more than two hundred editions.

their Aryan and Catholic victims."[29] Encouraged by his success, Drumont undertook an involvement in political action. In 1889, he founded the Ligue Nationale Anti-Semite, which was to founder,* and in 1892, the newspaper *La Libre Parole,* which, thanks to the Panama scandal of the 1890's, would quickly achieve great success.† Beginning in May 1892, *La Libre Parole* began its violent campaign against the presence of a great number of Jewish officers in the Army, denouncing them as potential traitors, and proclaiming, not without a measure of reason, that "in an enormous majority of French soldiers there existed a sentiment of repulsion toward the sons of Israel."[30] The newspaper of the Assumptionists, *La Croix,*‡ joined vigorously in that campaign. It was to dub itself in 1890 "the most anti-Jewish newspaper in France, the one that bears Christ, the sign of horror for all Jews."[31]

It was in this climate that anti-Semitism was unleashed. It did not yet manifest itself in noisy demonstrations or acts of violence, but was already highly visible in numerous publications and meetings, whose collective audience cannot have been negligible.

An anti-Semitic literature as abundant as it was varied can be divided according to three "angles of attack":[32] a traditional, religious anti-Judaism, which accused the deicidal people, denounced the Talmud as "a body of colossal absurdities and unspeakable turpitude,"[33] and took up the accusation of ritual murders; an "economic" anti-Judaism,[34] which condemned the haughty, indolent, avid, and cowardly Jew who brought wherever he went the spirit of corruption, speculation, and theft, a passion for lucre, and the "banking spirit"; and finally, a racist anti-Semitism, which radically opposed the Jew, sought grounding in the opposition between Aryan (or Indo-European) and Semitic races, and postulated the definitive inferiority of the Jew.[35]

Edouard Drumont attempted to effect their synthesis. He was untrou-

* On the other hand, the Ligue Antisémitique Française (LAF), created in 1892 and revived in 1897 by Jules Guérin, and the Jeunesse Antisémitique de France (JAF), founded in 1894, would enjoy an appreciable success. In 1898, the LAF would count no fewer than 5,000 followers. The figure is far from negligible if one considers that no political organization of the period counted more than 100,000 members (Stephen Wilson, "Jewish Attitudes to Anti-Semitism During the Dreyfus Affair" in *European Studies Review,* VI, no. 2, 1976, pp. 225ff).

† It was discovered that investors were being defrauded by inefficiencies and delays in the building of a canal through Panama. Several Jews, including Baron de Reinach, Arton, and Cornelius Hertz, were involved, and new fuel was added to the distrust of Jews and capitalists combined.

‡ Pierre Sorlin's *La Croix et les Juifs,* Grasset 1967, is the fundamental work on the anti-Jewish campaign—whose violence was frequently hysterical—waged by the Assumptionist newspaper.

bled by the diverse forms of anti-Semitism, but insisted on a global rejection of the Jew, while seeking vague historical support. Ignoble and
nefarious in every aspect, the Jew was the explanation of all the ills
plaguing France and the French. As of 1890, if it is indeed possible to date
an unleashing of hatred, "the anti-Semite attacks the Jew in his totality."[36]
The Jew was "evil" itself. He might have talents; his intelligence might be
respected; his works might even be admired; but he was an "other—an
other whose qualities as well as whose faults separated him from the rest of
the Nation." At times, he was a revolutionary, in which case he threatened
traditional values and the unity of the Nation. At times, he was a capitalist,
in which case he bankrupted peasants, exploited workers, and strangled
small tradesmen. Frequently, he was German by origin or sentiment, or
Alsatian (which amounted to the same), an enemy by nature or a traitor by
calling. Running through this body of literature, the essential elements of
which were supplied by *La France Juive,* was the physical and moral profile
of the abstract Jew, the "ideal" Jew, an enemy of France and a born
traitor.[37] He could be detected at once by his appearance: "The principal
signs," wrote Drumont, "by which a Jew may be recognized are thus: the
famous hooked nose, frequently blinking eyes, teeth tightly together, ears
sticking out, fingernails that are square rather than almond-shape, a torso
too long, flat feet, rounded knees, extraordinarily protruding ankles, the
limp and melting hand of a hypocrite and traitor. They frequently have
one arm longer than the other."[38]

The Jew "smelled bad"; he had "hooked fingers"; he bore on his face
"the signs of infamy"; his face was bloodless, his complexion pale. His
speech was inhuman; he whined, bit, licked, barked, and scratched.[39]
"From both the moral and physical point of view," wrote Léon Bloy, "the
contemporary kike is the confluence of every kind of hideousness in the
world."* In moral terms, what dominated was his rapacity; the Jew was a
miser, a usurer, and a speculator.[40] He was hypocritical, obsequious,
servile, crawling, spineless, and cunning. He dreamed of universal domination. He hated Christians and sought only to expropriate them. He
loved sacrifices and was ritually attracted to blood. He was cowardly, afraid
of brute force, and refused to serve as a soldier. He had no homeland, was
a wanderer and foreigner in every country he inhabited, and a betrayer of
them all. Jewish women were sensual, perverted, and debauched.[41] They
supplied "to every capital city the largest contingent of prostitutes." They
assisted Jews in corrupting and ruining Christians. There was no end to an

---

* Léon Bloy, *Le Salut par les Juifs,* Paris, 1892, p. 14. But Léon Bloy's complicated and
occasionally nuanced book contrasts the Jews with their religion—from which so much else
proceeded.

enumeration of the traits which converged to designate the Jew. But needless to say, the Jew was without personal identity. He was no more than the representative of his race, pale, inconsistent, and anonymous. Thus would Maurice Barrès later describe Dreyfus at the Rennes trial:

> A voice without quality... the voice never corresponds to the words ... the most jellylike of all the Dreyfusards.... Is it not childish to experience a malaise and to speak of mystery just because a foreigner does not react to events in the same manner as one of us? We are requiring of this child of Sem the fine traits of the Indo-European race. He is not permeable to all the stimuli with which our land, our ancestors, our flag and the word "honor" affect us. There are cases of optical aphasia in which one sees written signs in vain; they remain incomprehensible. Here the aphasia is congenital; it stems from the race.[42]

Most often, anti-Semites merely vented their hatred, attributed the national decadence to the Jews, and protested against their role in French society. But a number of them proposed remedies.[43] Some suggested economic measures, including a total or partial confiscation of Jewish wealth.[44] The Reverend Father de Pascal proposed a law forbidding all foreigners from possessing territory in the French countryside, and included Jews among that group.[45] In November 1891, Francis Laur submitted to Parliament a proposal that would expel all Jews from France, and found thirty-two deputies to support him. The abbé Henri Desportes requested "the relegation of the Jews outside the confines of Christian society," for "these people can no longer live the same life as us. They seek to plunge back into the depth of the ghetto, from which they should never have emerged and to which we will soon dispatch them again."[46] Georges Meynie was more vigorous still: "What the Jews need is the gallows in order to allow them to expiate the harm they have done us."[47] As for Drumont, he sought an avenger: "All of France will follow a leader who brings retribution, and who, instead of striking the ill-starred workers of France, will strike the Jews with their pockets lined in gold." On January 18, 1893, addressing the youth of France in *La Libre Parole,* he prophesied, "I feel that it is you who will avenge us when you are older and something tells me that the punishment will be frightening."

To be sure, in 1892 and 1893, this literature had only a limited readership, more numerous in Paris than in the provinces. In the elections of 1893, anti-Semitic agitation played only a secondary role. But the Army, the Church, Catholics, the traditional bourgeoisie, small businessmen, and craftsmen, all victims of economic development, as well as the urban proletariat, were the natural constituency for this ideology. What was missing was a pretext, a spark.

Alfred Dreyfus was concerned with other matters. He was a young husband, a young father, a brilliant officer. Life indeed seemed to reserve for him only smiles.

5

The Republic of Opportunists

At year's end in 1893, the Republic had reason to be satisfied. The attempt by General Georges Boulanger to seize the reins of government had ended in ridicule.

No doubt fortune had played its role in the Republic's success. For a time, it had seemed as though the rise of General Boulanger was irresistible. His strength—and his fragility—were linked to the fact that he seemed to unite all of France's malcontents and to be the vehicle of all of their projects. Royalists concluded that he could be used to further the cause of monarchy. Numerous Catholics saw in him a providential man sent by God to save France and her heritage of Christian virtues. The prestige of the Army—as guardian of the social order and instrument of a future revenge—worked to his advantage. All those who detested the parliamentary system, its impotence, and its apparent corruption, were inclined to favor him. A segment of the popular classes also looked up to the apparently pure and austere leader, who was capable of overtaking Parliament and expelling bourgeois liberalism, capitalist exploitation, and the assorted ills of the era. The fact that Boulanger's own ideas were a bit truncated contributed in a manner to his popularity. His program, "Dissolve, Revise, Reconstitute," contained nothing offensive to anyone. Triumphally elected in March 1887 in Dordogne and in the Nord, then, in August, in Charente-Inferieure, the Somme, and the Nord, Boulanger, it seemed to many, would be the winner of a general plebiscite. "The Republic," lamented Jules Ferry, "has been struck to the quick."[1] In January 1889, Boulanger had the audacity to offer his candidacy in Paris. A stunning success assured him that power was henceforth within his grasp. "To the Elysée! To the Elysée!" his troops chanted . . . and no doubt, given the panic of the government and the complicity of a good part of the police and the military, mastery of France would have been his.

But Boulanger waited, perhaps out of the scruple of a disciplined soldier, a hesitant temperament, or true confusion, leaving the Republic time to react. Constans, minister of the interior, convinced the government to bring the principal leaders of Boulanger's support to trial and to initiate discussion of a proposed law establishing procedures for the High Court of Justice. Boulanger was gently warned that his arrest was imminent— and fled to Brussels. He was tried in his absence. Ruined, desperate, drugged, and increasingly worried about the health of his mistress, Marguerite de Bonnemains, the exiled general "gave himself over to vague reveries of socialism." He dissolved the Comité National Boulangiste in 1890 and after the death of the woman he loved, began to lead an increasingly ghostly existence. On September 30, 1891, at the grave of Marguerite, he shot himself.[2]

Already during the centenary of the Revolution, the Republic of "Opportunists"* had given vent to its satisfaction. The Boulangists appeared to be in disarray. Those nostalgic for the Monarchy or the Empire rarely dared proclaim their loyalty. The elections of 1889 had marked the definitive defeat of the "revisionists" (i.e., the anti-Republicans)† and the victory of the "opportunists," who would thereafter call themselves the "government republicans." The Exposition for the centenary of the Revolution which Sadi Carnot, president of the Republic, had inaugurated on May 6, 1889, a hundred years after the meeting of the Estates-General, displayed the great achievements of French industry as well as works of academic painting, architecture, and sculpture.‡ A luminous fountain represented "France enlightening the world." On September 11, the holiday of the Republic's victory had been celebrated in music with a cantata by the composer, Augusta Holmes. The victorious Republic was given over to celebration.

* Such was the name—with no pejorative connotations—applied at the time to the centrist majority in Parliament.
† Only 38 Boulangist deputies had been elected, including Maurice Barrès, in Nancy, listed as a Revisionist Socialist.
‡ The Exposition had covered the entirety of the Champs-de-Mars, a part of the Esplanade of the Invalides, and the Trocadéro Gardens. The two "sensations" were the "machine gallery," a gigantic hall, 420 meters long with an entirely metallic frame, and the "tower" built by Gustave Eiffel. Electricity allowed the Exposition to be visited both day and night.

And its satisfaction seemed warranted. It had effected a total refutation of those who had predicted its imminent collapse. Discipline had allowed the republicans to win out over the reactionaries. The latter had been largely discredited by their rallying to the Boulangist adventure and would pay the price in the elections of 1893. A new political elite, coming from the middle and petit bourgeoisie—both urban and rural, doctors, lawyers, professors, and modest landholders—rose to power even as the number of former notables—rural aristocrats and extremely wealthy bourgeois—declined.[3] These "new strata," freshly emergent from the masses, gradually took over mayoralties, general councils, and *arrondissement* councils. They acceded to Parliament and consolidated a majority that was often hesitant and amorphous, but sincerely republican and secular.[4]

And the number of accomplishments since the advent of the Republic was impressive. Despite the perpetual increase of military expenses, the state's finances were competently managed. Until 1887, the economic crisis brought with it a small annual deficit. Thereafter deficits were replaced by modest surpluses. The state managed public finances parsimoniously and without imagination, as it would have managed a large private estate. Such a policy meant that the State enjoyed excellent credit both at home and abroad.[5] If the development of French industry—which the Exposition of 1889 revealed to the world—was slower and less spectacular than in England or Germany, its progress was nevertheless constant. "Industry (with the exception of housing) counts for a quarter of total production between 1810 and 1840, for a third in the intermediate period of 1850–1880, and for a half between 1890 and 1910."[6]

At the same time agriculture suffered a relative decline. This was not as a result of what has been exaggeratedly called the exodus from the country or rural depopulation; the statistics, on the contrary, attest to no more than an extremely slow decrease in the active agricultural population.[7] On the other hand, the share of agriculture in the gross national product diminished sharply during the same period, underscoring the disproportion between a segment of the population and its share of the national product.[8] Rigid price and salary structures, a certain tendency toward immobility in the agricultural world, foreign competition, the retirement of certain crops, and the great European agricultural depression extending from 1873 to 1896 furnish partial explanations for a relative impoverishment of the agricultural strata, with its complement of misery, departures from the land, and, in many departments (and notably those affected by the crises in wine production), easily exploitable discontent. It was under the joint pressure of agricultural landowners and textile manufacturers that the Republic gradually gave up on economic liberalism; the progessive return to protectionism, established by the law of January 11, 1892, marked one of the first stages of state intervention. A vast program of public works, inspired by Charles de Freycinet, the minister of war, was another. The role of the state in the economy was thereafter to be debated.

But the two principal domains of republican effort were the Army—identified with the homeland and the vehicle of the national pride—and public schools, which Léon Gambetta had deemed the "seminary of the future."* In point of fact the defense of the homeland and the propagation of knowledge were linked by republican ideology. And it was in its effort to erect a system of secular education that the State was to encounter the aggressive opposition of the Church. In 1893 there remained 15,000 private primary schools as opposed to 68,000 public schools; 84,000 children attended State schools, whereas 52,000 were educated in religious institutions. Unauthorized teaching congregations, which had been dispersed by Jules Ferry, were reconstituted and profited from a large clientele. The Republic's tolerance thus granted a degree of freedom to a system of education which was hostile to it.

The relations between the Catholic Church and the State remained tentative. In his encyclical *Amid Solicitudes,* published in February 1882, Pope Leo XIII may have invited Catholics to accept the Republic and to pursue a revision of the school laws only within the framework of republican legislation. But the majority of bishops were hostile to the institutions of the Republic and a large share of priests faithful to their monarchist convictions. And most country curates, whatever their conviction, were responsive to the authority of local landlords, who dispensed both honors and subsidies.[10] The "poor advice" of the Holy Father was only half needed and the Church had not yet rallied to the secular Republic. Inversely, anticlericalism furnished the republican party with "too solid and too venerable a base," offering "its various factions a common denominator," for traditional republicans not to make vigorous use of it. "The Church wants precisely the opposite of what we want," Georges Clemenceau would repeat.[11] It was a convenient theme. Hostility to the Church would allow one to skirt a number of the great problems posed by modern France and would long serve as a virtuous alibi.

The Army, moreover, for which the Republic asked and consented to so many sacrifices, was hardly more supportive. Strongly influenced by Catholic ideology, distrustful of democratic ideas (contesting the estab-

---

* Secondary education, which was not free, remained (despite a system of scholarships) the privilege of a limited class: 6,616 recipients of the baccalaureate in 1879, 8,000 in 1893.[9]

lished order, questioning hierarchies, and refusing the principle of obedience) which corrupted the national heritage, it remained the "holy ark" of the conservative strata of society.

The escapades of the anarchists were no small worry either. In March 1892, three bombs exploded in Paris, wounding few, but creating a general panic. The attacks proliferated, and were occasionally fatal. Ravachol—arrested, tried, and convicted—delivered a profession of anarchist faith before the Court of Assizes. "Society is rotting. In factories, mines, and fields, there are human beings working without hope of acquiring a thousandth part of the fruit of their labor. They have wives dying of hunger and children whom they can't nourish for lack of bread. Alongside that abject misery, we see overstuffed bourgeois leading lives of pleasure and responding with contemptuous smiles to the tears of the starving." As the attacks increased, to the terror of the bourgeoisie, Ravachol went proudly to the scaffold, singing at the top of his lungs: "To be happy, by God, hang your landlord. . . ."

Less spectacular, but more threatening, was the rise of workers' organizations. It appears that the long depression of 1883–88 had temporarily dulled the will to syndical combat and immobilized the proletariat. But beginning in 1888, a veritable "awakening of labor" may be observed.[12] As early as February 1889, several workers' marches were organized in support of the eight-hour workday. In 1890, for the first time in France, the celebration of international workers' solidarity on the First of May proved a success. A year later, the Army would kill nine of the workers demonstrating at Fourmies. Increasingly numerous and harsh strikes erupted. In 1892, there were 261 strikes involving a total of 50,000 workers. In 1893, 634 strikes would implicate 170,000 workers. Discussion of a general strike was in the air. In August 1892, the strike at Carmaux took on a symbolic aura. Provoked by the dismissal of a socialist militant who had been elected mayor, it soon assumed the dimensions of a political struggle: 3,000 protestors stopped working in order to affirm their right to the free exercise of public functions. Government arbitration—requiring rehiring—was needed to resolve the conflict. Against the Marquis de Solages, an administrator of the Compagnie de Carmaux, a former deputy of the moderate left, Jean Jaurès, would be elected socialist deputy.*

The social crisis was undoubtedly the peril that Parliament was unwilling—and unable—to envisage. The republican majority was blind to workers' conditions and to the revolt of oppressed classes. In passing in

---

* Concerning the development of Jean Jaurès's thought, the works of Madeleine Rebérioux, particularly in the *Bulletin* of the Société d'Etudes jaurassiennes, are fundamental. Among her recent studies, see the preface to the re-edition of *Les Preuves* (Le Signe, 1981) and the preface to the Jaurès *Anthologie* prepared by Louis Lévy (Calmann-Levy, 1983).

1884 a law instituting freedom to organize unions, Parliament believed it was guaranteeing the public peace. Suddenly, it discovered that the syndicats were tools of struggle.* In order to assuage the impatience of the workers, it found itself obliged, on the morrow of the strike at Carmaux, to pass one law establishing optional arbitration to resolve collective differences between workers and management, and another instituting a mandatory weekly day of rest for women and children and limiting their workday to eleven hours. These were, to be sure, but minor concessions. The workday remained cruelly long (twelve to fourteen hours for men). A weekly day off was established only for women and children. The few holidays were unpaid. No system existed to protect the worker in the event of illness, accidents, or old age.[13] Above all, unemployment raged with chronic persistence, attaining a level of 15 percent of the work force in 1893.

But the workers' movement had been launched. The harshly exploited class of employees had awakened to political life. Socialist propaganda was gradually having its effect, and the socialists were gaining in the elections. Jaurès's famous warning to the bourgeois Republic may be recalled. "You have passed laws of education. . . . You have once and for all freed the masses from the tutelage of Church and dogma. . . . You have cut short the old lullaby which rocked human misery to sleep, and human misery has awakened, stood before you, and today demands its proper place."[14]

Boulangism had lured away several of the most dynamic elements of the working class. Anarchism had siphoned off others. But it was henceforth the various schools of socialism that would mobilize this group. The "republicans"—the center—would have to deal both in Parliament and in the country at large with a violent, aggressive left, whose level of organization was ever increasing.

The hostility of the Church, the distrust of the Army, the anarchist agitation, the rise of anti-Semitism, the financial scandals, the instability of the government, and the unpopularity of Parliament were yet insufficient to truly rend the national fabric. On the whole, a "rare stability" in French society could be observed, despite the overthrow of institutions, despite even the economic crises raging through Europe.[15] The buying power of money varied only slightly, but always gaining in value.[16] Whereas income from agricultural property declined slowly, income from labor was constantly on the rise. The French population remained more or less stable: 37,570,000 inhabitants in 1881, and 38,342,000 in 1891.[17] Urban France was developing slowly, without the excesses of England and Germany. From 1886 to 1891, the portion of the population living in agglomerations

* The "syndicalist" movement regained strength after 1890: the number of union members tripled from 1890 to 1895.

of more than 2,000 inhabitants went from 30.5 to 37.4 percent. In 1914, only 13 percent of the French would be living in cities of more than 100,000 inhabitants.[18] The agricultural crisis—resulting in the departure of agricultural workers and small rural landowners from rural to urban centers—did not prevent the rural masses from continuing to participate in the general stability. Most departments still had a majority of rural inhabitants,[19] a situation which did not fail to exert a major influence on the composition of Parliament.[20]

Customs, moreover, had not been deeply modified. The legitimate family remained the cornerstone of all social organization, even if the law of July 24, 1884, inspired by the "Jew" Alfred Naquet, established divorce (under conditions, it may be noted, that were rather difficult to meet).* The practice of birth control increased only gradually, in regions where the influence of the Church was ebbing and in more prosperous milieus. No doubt the aristocracy—ousted from most of the high offices it held, but still strongly represented in the departmental assemblies in Parliament, and in the Army and Navy which had given it refuge—had lost the better part of its influence. But it entertained ever more numerous connections with the upper financial and industrial bourgeoisie, and found in class solidarity— through a tightly knit web of marriages, positions, and shared rituals—a number of new channels.[21] The middle and petite bourgeoisies which were gradually acceding to power, retained for the most part the morality and mentality of the caste they were supplanting. And they did not seriously call into question the mechanisms of domination from which they would henceforth profit.

It was perhaps within the intellectual and ethical sphere that an evolution seems clearest. However limited, the effects of obligatory primary education were being felt. Universal military service functioned as a melting pot. It also furthered education. Above all, the press began to permeate very different milieus. De-Christianization pursued its course slowly, and was especially marked in the case of men. Finally, technical progress, the development of the railroad,† the spread of gas lighting, and the appearance of the telephone and the bicycle all slowly modified the way of life for a segment of the population.

Stability was due less to internal balances than to the obstinate resistance of diverse mentalities to the penetration of industrial life, technological progress, and new ways of life and of thought.[23] A society extremely

---

* The Naquet law would be an intense source of Catholic hostility to the Republic and to Jewry, "destroyers of the Christian family."

† . . . and soon of the automobile. In 1900, there were 3,000 automobiles running in France; in 1905, 22,000; in 1914, 108,000. On the entry into the "automobile era," see Jean Bouvier in Georges Duby, *Histoire de France*.[22]

attached to its traditional values, its prejudices, and its hierarchies . . . A society apt to be quickly rocked by violence, agitated by intolerance, disposed to fanaticism, and easily susceptible to the fascination of a leader or an ideology, but, at bottom, quite conservative and frightened by change. And that society, which claimed to proclaim a democratic message, pursued an existence profoundly withdrawn and distrustful of all that seemed foreign and different.

The elections of 1893 clarified the ambiguities of the Republic of opportunists, and its victory over reactionaries, but also the ordeals it would be obliged to traverse. The right emerged devastated from the elections.[24] Only 76 candidates were elected, whereas in 1889, the conservatives and Boulangists together had won 210 seats.* The "government republicans," that is the center (which replaced the discredited term "opportunists" with that of "progressives") constituted a block of nearly 280 deputies. But the presence on the left of 143 Radicals and 50 Socialists profoundly modified the parliamentary balance.† The "Radical" left had suddenly fortified and expanded its positions, notably in the southwestern and southern portions of the country. Moderately open to social questions, staunchly condemning collectivism, it was no longer an object of fear. Emitting a somewhat vague message of freedom, individualism, and secularism, it spoke to a state of mind increasingly common in France, and was capable of attracting the middle classes. The success of the Socialists in the Chamber—they triumphed in several suburbs of major cities—was the striking effect of the awakening of labor.

As for the collapse of the monarchist right, it seemed to demonstrate that the republican regime was accepted by a large majority of the nation. Above all, one ought to note the troubling lassitude of the voters—out of ten and a half million who were registered, fewer than seven and a half million votes were cast. Do the abstentions indicate that the regime was perceived as a system of impotence and corruption by a segment of the population?[25]

The republican celebrations and electoral victories could not mask the diverse sources of malaise in French society. The popular movement which had supported Boulanger, and the hopes of upheaval which he temporarily embodied, recall that France, after its humiliation of 1871, had never ceased to yearn for revenge; that the parliamentary regime was largely discredited; that the Republic itself was barely tolerated by the traditional elements of society; that the poor and oppressed classes were capable of investing their hope in the virtue of an energetic leader who

* On its fringes was formed a group of 27 who had "rallied" to the Republic and would almost consistently vote for republican cabinets.
† The Socialist vote went from 90,000 in 1889 to 600,000 in 1893.

would master the new forces; that the Army, proud and withdrawn, had barely rallied to the regime; and that the Church was not reconciled to the cult of secularism. "The French malaise is above all moral," observes Jacques Chastenet, examining France in the last decade of the nineteenth century.[26] Boulangism was but one of the symptoms of the crisis provoked in the country by the establishment of the Republic and by the rise of capitalism—a gradual overthrow less of a way of life than of systems of thought. Were a new occasion to present itself. . . .

6

The Ordinary Track

Enthusiastic in its will to command a strong army and to marshal patriotic fervor, the Republic was nevertheless divided as to ways of extending France's power and influence in the world. Colonial conquests had been achieved against the will of Parliament and despite the hostility of numerous republicans—including Georges Clemenceau. They owed a little to chance, and a lot to the obstinacy of a few men—such as Jules Ferry.[1] France intervened in Tunisia in 1881 and occupied Tonkin in 1883. In 1896, Madagascar would become a French colony. But a colonial empire, which would strengthen France's position among the world powers, did not really interest the majority of her statesmen. Public opinion on the subject remained indifferent if not hostile. The public will was oriented to a more traditional endeavor—the search for European allies.

There was in the first place the matter of bringing France out of the isolation into which the defeat of 1870 had brought her. For Léon Gambetta, the republican leader, the first hope had been England. But colonial rivalries and confrontations in Egypt dashed that hope. The German-British colonial treaty of 1890 had profoundly irritated Paris. Nevertheless, Bismarck had been multiplying his overtures and it is possible that Gambetta, and Ferry after him, thought a rapprochement with Germany possible.[2] But the humiliation of 1870 and above all the insoluble problem of Alsace-Lorraine excluded any possibility that public opinion would tolerate such a policy. In May 1891, through a new treaty, Germany extended the Triple Alliance which linked it with Italy and Austria-Hungary, an alliance that seemed overtly hostile to France. In 1892, it renewed a pact signed with Rumania. For France in its isolation, the sole option seemed to be to turn toward Russia.

Such an alliance—between the western democracy and the most autocratic, most reactionary state in the world—was a singular project indeed. To achieve this end, certain errors of German diplomacy, the shrewd will of several political figures such as Charles de Freycinet and Alexandre Ribot, and above all the interest of the Russian Treasury in the vast perspectives opened to it by France's reserves, would all be necessary. Already in 1891, President Sadi Carnot was honored with the Russian Order of Saint-Andrew. A French squadron was heading for Kronstadt. French banks were granting the Russian Treasury credit of five hundred million francs, which had been denied by Germany. Russian crews were received in Toulon amid the delirious enthusiasm of the population. A diplomatic accord, signed in 1891, was strengthened in 1892 by a military agreement. In that unnatural alliance,[3] which seemed to grip Germany within its pincers, the statesmen of the Republic discovered political relief and a measure of naive pride as well. The splendors of Russia impressed them. The Franco-Russian alliance would remain a constant goal for the Republic, to the point of becoming for some—like President Raymond Poincaré—almost an obsession. It would take a war to uncover the illusions it concealed.

France henceforth felt itself stronger, with the support of an immense reserve of men and an alliance with an army that Europe had come to dread. Fear and hatred of Germany were so intimately linked with patriotic sentiment at the time that no effort was made to separate them; the question of Alsace-Lorraine appeared to set between France and Germany a decisive obstacle to rapprochement. For thirty years, the foreign policy espoused by every French government would regularly insist on a modification of the Treaty of Frankfurt and the return to France of the lost provinces. The ephemeral success of General Georges Boulanger, who dreamed of commanding a drive toward the East, was only one sign among many of this situation. No statesman could dare entertain the hypothesis that France might give up Alsace-Lorraine.[4]

And yet the demeanor of Kaiser Wilhelm II toward the French government was remarkably courteous. At times he would dine at the home of the French ambassador. On the occasion of the death of the military leader Patrice de MacMahon, he sent a wreath to the funeral. But all his initiatives were quite coolly received. Since 1890, the representative of Germany in

Paris had been Count Georg Herbert Münster von Derneberg, an old aristocrat as courteous as he was cultivated. He was a determined advocate of a Franco-German alliance, and was prolific in demonstrating his good-will. His relations with the French government were extremely cordial, but did little to change the persistent iciness of the political climate. It was, moreover, not the government that encouraged a mistrust of Germany, but public opinion which seemed to thrive on it. The government sought simply to flatter rather than fight against a popular opinion. At the slightest pretext, national sentiment would awaken, prepared to wage war against the hereditary enemy.

France seemed thus intent on preparing for the conflict which, sooner or later, would pit her against Germany, restoring to her both the con-quered provinces and her national pride. Whence the perpetual military buildup, for which it consented to enormous sacrifices. Whence the Franco-Russian alliance, with its plan to surround Germany. Whence, finally, the organization of a powerful espionage service. If France lost the war, it could not have been because of military inferiority, but because of "betrayals" which paralyzed her forces. The obsession with treason was inseparable from the thirst for revenge. A twofold imperative emerged: unmask the traitors and uncover the military secrets of the enemy.

The war of 1870 had made manifest the superiority of the German Intelligence Services to their barely existent counterparts in France.[5] The Third Republic had become aware of a shortcoming whose gravity it no doubt exaggerated. As early as 1870, at the request of President Adolphe Thiers, police prefects began to set up a crew of informers charged with spying on German diplomats stationed in France; another series of agents would be dispersed throughout Germany.[6] Toward 1872, in the context of a reorganization of the central administration of the Ministry of War, a special service was created, intended to deal exclusively with "statistics": a discreet term for the diverse activities of espionage and counterespio-nage.[7] Located on the rue de Lille, the Section of Statistics was quite near the German embassy.

The section was administratively joined to the second bureau of the General Staff. But because of the importance of its functions and the secrecy they entailed, it appears to have been under the direct control of the chief or deputy-chief of the General Staff of the Army. For several years, apparently, the Section of Statistics had lain dormant under the direction of officers poorly equipped for the function. It came into its own only in 1887 under the leadership of a new head, Commandant Jean Sandherr.

Sandherr, who had already served twice with the Section of Statistics,[8] was well prepared for his new tasks. Born in Mulhouse,[9] a fanatical patriot, fascinated by espionage, he was particularly well informed about security problems in the border regions. Despite the meager resources of the Section of Statistics, Sandherr was able to assure its effectiveness. The service consisted of several officers—five or six members working in a few cramped offices on rue Saint-Dominique—charged with assuming its organization and directing its agents. The section employed a variable number of agents of all sorts, both permanent and part-time. In addition, a whole network of correspondents—in France, Germany, Alsace, and all of Europe—supplied information. Its network of espionage and counterespionage was to assume the most diverse forms: surveillance, shadowing, and the theft of documents. It included as well efforts at mystification, to which Sandherr attributed particular importance: false information and false documents furnished to the "enemy," in general by double agents intent on leading them astray with a variety of false leads.[10] Finally, when it was decided, at the order of General Boulanger, then minister of war, to take a census of foreigners residing in France or living in the border regions, it was this section which was assigned the task of organizing and analyzing the data collected. It was Sandherr who elaborated the plan that would set up two lists of suspects: a Notebook A listing adult aliens living in France, and a Notebook B listing all those, French or alien, suspected of espionage.[11] In utter secrecy, Sandherr drew up the measures to be presented to the president in the event of mobilization: the arrest and detention as "prisoners of war" or expulsion of all persons in Notebook A; the arrest and internment of all persons in Notebook B. A closed session of the Superior Court-Martial on April 1, 1889, in the presence of Generals Jean-Baptiste Billot, Miribel, and Gaston de Galliffet, with Charles Freycinet, then minister of war presiding, was to ratify the measures dreamed up by Sandherr. More than a hundred thousand persons were thus threatened with arrest.[12] As of 1893, Sandherr, together with General Auguste Mercier, who had become minister of war, would draw up instructions addressed to commandants who would thereupon implement his ambitious project, in the event of a general mobilization, through the organization of permanent camps.

Such efforts appear to have created in the Section of Statistics an exasperated climate of overexcitement and intrigue. Sandherr advised his subordinates to have as few human ties as possible, to permanently distrust their colleagues, and to live for their mission alone. The tiny group of officers constituting the Intelligence Service thus lived apart, suspicious of all the other services, and even of the General Staff, proudly convinced that they alone would be able to keep state secrets. The section "considers itself in a sense to be superior to all the other established powers, including the government and its ministers, whose discretion it does not hesitate to scrutinize and whose patriotism and integrity it does not hesitate secretly to sound."[13] As for the indefatigable and impassioned Sandherr, he would continue to refine his mission, seeing spies at every turn and working at his own legend.

In 1894, the Section of Statistics counted five officers under the direction of Sandherr. Commandant Albert Cordier, whose risqué language, severity of temperament, and penchant for alcohol inspired some distrust, was adjunct to the head of the section. Sandherr regarded Cordier cordially, even though the latter, more interested in gossip than information, shared neither his passion for the profession nor his militant anti-Semitism.[14] Below Cordier in the hierarchy came Commandant Hubert Joseph Henry. Born June 2, 1846, in the Marne to a family of farmers, made a sergeant major in 1870, twice taken prisoner and twice escaped, on leaving the ranks he had earned a sublieutenant's and then a lieutenant's stripes. His evaluations for 1872 did not seem to predict more than a modest destiny: "an officer whose sole future will lie in that which seniority by statute confers on him."[15] But General de Miribel, in naming him aide-de-camp in 1875, must have concluded otherwise. In 1877, the general named Henry to the Section of Statistics, even though his ignorance of languages and his crudeness hardly seemed to suit him for the position. Henry left the section in 1886—to take part in expeditions to Tunisia and Tonkin. After that, he went to Oran and then Péronne, returning to the Intelligence Service in 1893. He seems to have been quite successful in a profession he barely distinguished from that of the police. A broad-shouldered giant with an abundant mustache, beneath the brutal trappings of the old trooper, Henry concealed considerable shrewdness, cunning, and even a certain subtlety. He excelled, it appears, in dealings with part-time agents: "procuresses, venal domestics, policemen dismissed from service, traveling salesmen without clientele,"[16] in whom he was able to inspire, as the occasion demanded, sympathy, confidence, or terror. Lieutenant Colonel Georges Picquart, who would later become his superior, would note as much in generally benevolent terms: "Brings a great deal of tact and intelligence to the accomplishment of the delicate tasks assigned to him. An essentially military temperament. Great rectitude and firmness of character, a man of heart, quite vigorous, with much experience as a regimental officer. May end up a colonel."

Commandant Henry, in any event, revealed a blind respect for discipline, great courage, and unreserved admiration for his military superiors. Without respite, he pursued his policelike activity, perpetually in search of new initiatives. With neither education, culture, nor critical spirit, his devotion as an aide to Sandherr was thorough and his zeal indefatigable.[17]

Captain Jules Lauth, ten years Henry's junior, was an entirely different case. "Protestant and desperately so," in Joseph Reinach's phrase, he belonged to a family of an extremely closed segment of the provincial bourgeoisie. Intelligent, proud of his upbringing, and diligent, he possessed a rather unaccommodating character and tolerated opposition poorly. In all spheres—and particularly, in anti-Semitism—he tended toward a fanaticism which his skill and upbringing could not conceal. Strangely enough, he was linked to Henry by a friendship which, with the passage of time, allowed Henry to exercise a considerable influence over his young subordinate. Reinach claimed—though it is difficult to support his hypothesis—that Lauth had become the lover of Henry's beautiful and frivolous wife, a circumstance which would explain their initial tie and subsequent complicity.[18] Fluent in German, Lauth, upon arriving in the Second Bureau in August 1893, was specifically assigned the task of translating German documents, for which his friend Henry was incompetent.

The section also included Captain Pierre Matton, who, after leaving the École de Guerre, was not at all happy in an Intelligence Service, and had few dealings with his colleagues. He was responsible for questions pertaining to Italy. Finally, there was Félix Gribelin, a narrow-minded, carping individual, a servile bureaucrat, gifted with a prodigious memory, who performed the functions of archivist, accountant, and handyman. He recopied and filed secret documents, and one of the two keys to the safe was entrusted to him.

Neither their past nor their training had destined these very different men for intelligence work, but with the single exception of Matton, they all brought to their tasks an incomparable measure of zeal. They were imbued with the importance of their function in the service of France. They employed numerous agents, who received either fixed salaries or fees for items delivered, among whom were a large number of scoundrels, who suspected the presence of spies at all times in all places.

Among the "preferred" agents of the Section of Statistics, two were rendering particularly important services at that time. The first, the Alsatian Martin Brücker, had received the assignment of keeping foreign diplomatic personnel residing in Paris, particularly German diplomats, under surveillance. Among the personnel of the various embassies, he had recruited a sizable number of office boys, valets, and maids, who rifled through drawers, eavesdropped on visits, and stole old papers. But a love affair had compromised his career. An abandoned mistress, named Millescamps née Foret, a merchant of ecclesiastical souvenirs and a marriage broker, had denounced her former lover to the German embassy, where she was not taken seriously. She in turn was denounced by Brücker to the French authorities for having stolen papers from him with the intention of giving them to the Germans. Tried for espiespionage, she was convicted and sentenced by the Paris Correctional Tribunal on January 3, 1894, to five years in prison.* The Section of Statistics, however, was obliged thereafter to consider their man Brücker definitively discredited.

A second invaluable agent was one of Brücker's recruits: Marie Caudron, who became, through her marriage to a former member of the Garde Républicaine, Mme. Bastian. In 1889, Mme. Bastian had been hired by the German embassy to clean offices, scrub stairs, light stoves, and empty wastebaskets. At about that time, she also accepted employment by Brücker—instead of burning discarded papers, she was to collect them. In addition, since she appears to have enjoyed the trust of the embassy, she occasionally replaced the concierge and pilfered various documents from the mail slots.[19] She then turned over her harvest in the course of mysterious meetings (held preferably in churches), initially to Brücker, and subsequently to an agent of the Section of Statistics, who was more often than not Commandant Henry. Torn or crumpled documents were then reconstructed, pasted together, reconstituted, and translated from the German if necessary. From 1889 to 1897, Mme. Bastian was to pursue her tasks without incident. Her remuneration grew with the services she rendered and she earned two hundred fifty francs per month in 1897, a salary to which was added occasional bonuses. Thus it was that Mme. Bastian furnished the French Intelligence Service with a stack of useless scraps of paper, love letters, bills, and receipts, but also, buried in the pile, some essential documents. Working under the pseudonym "Auguste," she constituted what would be called throughout the Dreyfus Affair "the ordinary track."

How the German Embassy failed to perceive Mme. Bastian's illicit dealings remains a mystery. It appears certain, in any event, that before the public revelation, during the Rennes trial, of the uninterrupted functioning of "the ordinary track," over a period of nearly ten years, the Germans did not suspect a thing.[20] And thereafter, for reasons of pride, they would feel compelled to minimize the number and importance of the documents stolen by Mme. Bastian. How was she able to avoid suspicion? Was it her ignorance (since she let it be known that she could not read)? Her apparent stupidity? Maurice Paléologue, whose recollections, to be

---

* At the hearing, Brücker was the only witness. *Le Temps* of January 4 published an account of this "very curious case of espionage." The trial could have alerted the Germans to what was going on at the embassy, but they seem not to have taken any interest in the affair (on this subject see the German documents quoted by Maurice Baumont, *Aux sources de l'Affaire: L'Affaire Dreyfus d'après les archives diplomatiques,* Productions de Paris, 1959, pp 23ff).

sure, are not always reliable, recalls in his *Journal* having described her to a colleague in the Ministry of Foreign Affairs as early as October 12, 1894, presumably on the basis of information from Sandherr, as "a vulgar, stupid, completely illiterate woman about forty years in age."[21] Was it the protection of the German ambassador's daughter, Mlle. von Münster, who appears to have had great sympathy for her? Was her task facilitated by the astonishing frivolity of the German military attaché, Colonel Maximilien von Schwarzkoppen, appointed to Paris in 1892, who elegantly combined his amorous liaisons, functions as a diplomat, and activities as a spy, and threw the torn or merely crumpled refuse of all three endeavors into the wastebasket—rough drafts in gallantry and love letters written or received, along with the most secret documents? Later on, Mme. Bastian, swept up in the torment of the Dreyfus Affair, projected stage-center, would be simultaneously vilified and exalted as a liar, double agent, pathological case or, on the contrary, national heroine.[22] But in the year 1894, Agent "Auguste" was doing her work admirably well. And several times a month, in the shadows of a chapel of the Church of Sainte-Clotilde or the Church of Saint-François-Xavier, the Section of Statistics picked up its delivery from the wastebaskets of the German embassy.

7

Maximilien and Alexandrine

In 1894 the spy war was heating up. More traditionally organized and less craftlike than the French, German espionage was as determined in every respect as its adversary.[1] Numerous German spies were identified; some were convicted. In 1890 the archivist Boutonnet, employed in the office of the technical division of the Artillery, was sentenced to five years for espionage, after admitting to his involvement with the German military attaché von Huehne. Between 1888 and 1890, Sergeant Major Chatelain, Lieutenant Bonnet, Captain Guillot, artificer Thomas in Bourges,

and Joseph Greiner, employed by the Ministry of the Navy, all acknowledged their espionage activities and were sentenced to stiff terms, Joseph
Greiner to twenty years of forced labor. But the Intelligence Service was
not appeased: numerous documents continued to disappear from French
offices. In particular, a number of "master plans"—topographical maps of
French fortifications drawn up by the geographic service of the Army,
generally on a scale of 1/10,000, situating batteries and various defense
installations—were regularly supplied to the Germans. The plans for
Toul, Reims, Nancy, and the eastern fortifications had all been transmitted
to Germany. The elaborate traffic in "master plans" was known to the
Section of Statistics and fueled within its ranks an obsession with spies that
was not without foundation.[2]

During that period, foreign military attachés—especially those from
Germany—were a source of particular concern to France. It was virtually
inevitable that they would become involved in intelligence, but the German officers assigned to Paris seem to have surpassed the accepted limits.[3]
The German military attaché, von Huehne, had been called back by his
government after the scandal caused by his relations with Boutonnet.
Similarly, the American military attaché had been recalled for having
received documents from the spy Greiner, which he then transmitted to
his friend, the German military attaché. Ambassadors promised the
French government to put an end to such abuses, but they were either
unable or unwilling to do so.

In 1892, Lieutenant Colonel Maximilien von Schwarzkoppen had
been named military attaché in Paris. "With this one, you won't have any
problems," the German ambassador, the old Count von Münster is alleged
to have said. He was a diplomat of the old school, who would not tolerate a
military attaché under his authority who engaged in espionage. Born
February 24, 1850, in Potsdam to an old family of officers, Schwarzkoppen, like his father before him, had fought in the war against France.[4] An
impressive and distinguished officer, he was also a likable, cultivated, and
conciliatory man, singularly gifted for the ambiguous profession of military attaché. "A man of royal courts and salons," writes Maurice Baumont,[5] he loved women and men, who, on the whole, reciprocated his
affection. He reconciled—without quite distinguishing them—his role as
a diplomat and his tumultuous personal life. And he spoke French to boot.

When Schwarzkoppen arrived in Paris in 1892, the Franco-Russian
rapprochement was giving Germany understandable cause for alarm.
Schwarzkoppen, taking up the habits of his predecessors, took an immediate interest in Intelligence. But he concealed this irregular activity
from his ambassador, who would certainly disapprove. Like the other

German military attachés, he reported directly—without the ambassador's knowledge—to the German government and perhaps even to Kaiser Wilhelm II, who held Schwarzkoppen in particular esteem.[6] Respectful of hierarchies, courteous, even deferential, Schwarzkoppen was uncomfortable at concealing his activities from Count von Münster, but he obeyed a "higher calling" nonetheless.

Barely had he arrived in Paris than the dashing Colonel von Schwarzkoppen became involved with Major Alessandro Panizzardi, the Italian military attaché. The two soon became quite close, seeing each other almost daily. Until Schwarzkoppen's recall in 1897, they would write each other hundreds of letters, a good number of which, carelessly tossed into the wastebasket, would end up at the French Intelligence Service through "the ordinary track." In their intimate correspondence, Schwarzkoppen occasionally became "Maximilienne" and Alessandro Panizzardi "Alexandrine."[7]

> Dear Maximilien, am I still your Alexandrine? When will you come to bugger me? A thousand salutations from the girl who loves you so. Alexandrine.[8]
>
> My darling . . . all yours and on the mouth . . . Maximilienne.[9]
>
> Here, my dear little girl, is what you request. . . .[10]
>
> Yes little red dog, I shall come for your pleasure. I would be capable of stuffing a meter of swaddling [sic] in you and all the fourteen year old commandants if needed. Oh, the filthy beast. All yours, still coming. Maximilienne."[11]

But the letters were not all so frivolous. Between sighs the two friends would exchange documents and information.[12] They were as mutually bound by espionage as they were by pleasure.

> This morning I saw M. Dubois. . . . We must see each other today.[13]
>
> My little green dog, I'm returning to you (various documents). Farewell, my little Loulou. Your bugger.[14]
>
> I am transmitting to you a copy of the old firing tables for the 80 cannon and the 95 cannon. All yours. Good day, bugger.[15]
>
> My dear little war dog, I am returning to you the notebook of charges with my thanks. We shall have to discuss it together. . . . All yours. Your devoted war bitch. Alexandrine.[16]

Such exchanges were constant throughout 1895, 1896, and into 1897.

> Dear friend, I have something interesting to communicate to you. I shall come to your place this evening. Better yet, be beneath the arcades of the Hotel Continental at 11 P.M. Your Alexandrine.[17]

Schwarzkoppen would dispose of drafts or letters in his wastebasket; some were ripped into little pieces; others simply crumpled and thrown away.* Still others were partially burned.† Madame Bastian would pick up everything that she found: a vast inventory within which the Section of Statistics sorted out love declarations and lewd fantasies from acts of true espionage.

During the same period, Schwarzkoppen wrote and received countless letters from his mistresses, notably from Mme. de Weede, the wife of a Dutch diplomat with whom he pursued a protracted affair.[18] Like the others, those letters were crumpled or ripped, as the spirit moved him, into two, four, six, or even twenty pieces. Gallant, handsome, apparently well loved, as dispersed as he was eclectic, Schwarzkoppen had the drawbacks of his gifts. He was as frivolous as he was attractive.

None of which prevented him from carrying espionage further than his predecessors had. Throughout, he was in contact with an individual whose identity has still not been clarified and who furnished him with "master plans."[19] Occasionally, he and Panizzardi would call the mysterious informer "Jacques Dubois" in their exchanges, after the swindler who had proposed to sell Panizzardi the formula for a new "smokeless powder" in 1893. The traffic in master plans, begun in 1892, would continue through the first half of 1894. The draft of a letter—for Schwarzkoppen wrote and threw away numerous drafts—revealed in January 1894 the fee the military attaché paid his informants: ten francs or more, depending on the fortifications. In April 1894, an intercepted letter, written by Schwarzkoppen to Panizzardi, revealed that an individual designated by the initial D. had transmitted to Schwarzkoppen the plans for Nice, which the military attaché gave over to Panizzardi:

> I truly regret not having seen you before my departure. For the rest, I will be back in 8 days.

---

* An example: Letter no. 263. See also documents 119bis and 121bis of the secret file, Archives of the Ministry of War. It has occasionally—and erroneously—been maintained that Schwarzkoppen was in the habit of tearing into very small pieces the documents he tossed into the wastebasket. He did not always take that precaution.

† Example: Letter no. 280 of the secret file, Archives of the Ministry of War.

Attached are 12 master plans of Nice which that scoundrel D. gave me in the hope of restoring relations. He claims there was a misunderstanding and that he will do all he can to satisfy you. He says he was stubborn and you don't begrudge him that. I responded that he was mad and that I did not believe that you wanted to resume relations. Do as you wish. Good bye. I am quite rushed. Alexandrine. Don't bugger too much!*

The Section of Statistics searched in vain to discover the identity of the German military attaché's informant. A man named Dacher, then a printer named Dubois were first suspected, then cleared.[21] But at the Section of Statistics, and at the General Staff, vigilance was the rule. Treason seemed to permeate the very air one breathed.

8

A Mysterious Visitor

B etween three and four o'clock in the afternoon, on July 20, 1894, a French officer in civilian garb arrived at the German embassy and asked to be received by the military attaché. He wanted, he said, to obtain a passport to go to Alsace. "Of medium height, frail, sickly, he had a sinewy face, dark eyes recessed in their sockets, an abundant head of graying hair, and a salt-and-pepper military mustache." He wore the ribbon of the Legion of Honor.

After being received by Colonel von Schwarzkoppen, he introduced himself as an officer of the French General Staff on active duty, constrained by necessity to engage in a "contemptible" initiative "to which he

---

* The French contains various misspellings by Schwarzkoppen. The letter would constitute the essential document of the secret file transmitted to the Court-Martial judging Dreyfus. See *infra* p. 87. It is dated April 16, 1894. Joseph Reinach, on the basis of statements by officers of the Section of Statistics at the Rennes trial, attempted to demonstrate that the date was false and that the document would have been composed and intercepted in 1893 at the latest (op. cit. p. 32ff and Appendix I). But there is no conclusive argument for doubting the date. Marcel Thomas assumes it to be authentic.[20]

was forced in order to rescue his wife and his children from abject poverty and certain ruin." In order to preserve for his family a small property which he possessed near Châlons, he needed money at whatever price. "There remained to him but a single recourse: to offer his services to the German General Staff." Thus Schwarzkoppen recounts in his *Notebooks*, published in 1930, his first meeting with Commandant Ferdinand Walsin-Esterhazy.*

The officer, who had not yet revealed his identity, spoke of his credentials. During the period 1881–82, he worked in the Bureau of Intelligence, where he was "extremely close" to Colonel Jean Sandherr, chief of the bureau. He was a friend of Deputy Jules Roche, who had promised to name him second in command of his cabinet in the event he became minister of war. At the moment, he was serving with a regiment outside of Paris, and in a few days would attend military maneuvers of great importance at the camp in Châlons.

"I was extremely surprised and indignant at the offer," Schwarzkoppen would write. No doubt intrigued by it as well, Schwarzkoppen claimed that this meeting ended when he showed his mysterious visitor the door. The following day, July 21, the latter left a message. "I am leaving quite soon on the trip of which I spoke." He specified that "thanks to his family relations, he was in a position to furnish important information about Russia."[1]

On July 22, Schwarzkoppen sent a report to the Bureau of Information in Berlin without mentioning it to the ambassador. Four days later, he received instructions to renew contact and to keep Berlin informed.

On the same date, the military attaché tossed into his wastebasket the draft of a letter no doubt addressed to his superiors in which he seemed to speak of the "dangerous" dealings he was about to initiate with a French officer:

> Doubt . . . Proof . . . Letter of service [*brevet* in the German text] . . . a dangerous situation for myself with a French officer. . . . Must not conduct negotiations personally. . . . Bring what he has. . . . Absolute ge . . . [two German words untranslated]. . . . Bureau of Information. . . . No relation. . . . Regiment. . . . An importance only. . . . Leaving the Ministry. . . . Already elsewhere. . . .

* *Les Carnets de Schwarzkoppen: la Vérité sur Dreyfus,* Preface by Lucien Lévy-Bruhl, ed. Rieder, 1930, pp. 6ff. In his innumerable accounts, depositions, publications, and interviews (beginning in 1898), Esterhazy did not deny this version and confirmed the date of the first meeting. Without proof, Joseph Reinach situated the first relations between Esterhazy and Schwarzkoppen in 1893.

Torn into small pieces, this draft appears to have reached the Section of Statistics via the ordinary track.*

On July 27 the decidedly persistent visitor presented himself anew—and without warning—at the embassy. For the first time, he identified himself: "Commandant Count Walsin-Esterhazy, Battalion Chief of the 74th Regiment of the Infantry." Once received by Schwarzkoppen, he specified that his wife was born Nettancourt-Vaubecourt, that he owned the château of Dammartin near Sainte-Menehould in the Marne, that he had ties with the Clermont-Tonnerre. To prove his seriousness, he brought the mobilization papers of his regiment—a document of little interest. He spoke of money; specifically, a fixed salary of two thousand francs per month. Schwarzkoppen refused his demand. His agents were paid only "per item."

But the contact appeared of sufficient interest to Schwarzkoppen for him to travel to Germany on August 3 and 4 in order to discuss the matter with Major Mueller, chief of the German Intelligence Service and the two decided it was worthwhile to pursue contact. Upon returning to Paris on August 6, Schwarzkoppen found at the embassy a letter from Esterhazy specifying his future addresses. "Until 10:VIII: officer staff of the third artillery brigade, camped at Châlons; from the 10th to the 12th: in the country at the château of Dammartin near Saint-Menehould (Marne); thereafter at my habitual residence, which you will find in the registry."

On August 13 Esterhazy, who had left the encampment at Châlons four days earlier, again went to the embassy, at 10 P.M.[3] He claimed that he was able to bring information of exceptional value and promised in particular the mobilization plans of the Artillery, which had just been revised.[4] In addition, he spoke of the "120 short" cannon in which the German General Staff had great interest.†[5] On August 15 Esterhazy did indeed bring the mobilization plans of the Artillery, and the military attaché appreciated their value. "Esterhazy received 1,000 francs from me, and assured me that he was planning to deliver other interesting information in a few days."[6] "I made that decision," Schwarzkoppen would write, "because I believed that in the interest of my Army, I had an obligation to proceed as I did. But I was also well aware that my position was quite dangerous, and that as a Prussian officer, I could be placed in an

* Marcel Thomas[2] dates this draft, which was intercepted on an uncertain date by the Section of Statistics, July 22. It clearly alludes to the visit paid Schwarzkoppen and the offer of services by a French officer. The document would later be included in the secret file and used against Dreyfus. See *infra* p. 87–88.
† An object of experimentation until 1890, the new gun had been put in use in a certain number of batteries toward the close of 1893. This was notably done at the Châlons camp.

extremely disagreeable situation."[7] No doubt the diplomat, who had violated a promise to his ambassador in order to engage in espionage, was ill at ease. But Schwarzkoppen's life was sufficiently diverting for him to think of other matters. And he had good reason to be satisfied for it appeared that much might be expected from this Commandant Esterhazy. Schwarzkoppen began to set down for his new informer a list of "important questions" about which Germany wished documentation.

9

The Dictation

Early in the morning of Saturday, October 13, Captain Dreyfus received at his residence on the avenue du Trocadéro a call summoning him to appear the following Monday at 9:00 A.M. at the Ministry of War on rue Saint-Dominique. The notice was worded as follows: "Paris, October 13, 1894. Summons. The Division General, Chief of the Army General Staff, will conduct an inspection of the officers on duty with the Staff during the day of Monday, October 15. M. Captain Dreyfus, currently with the 39th Regiment of the Infantry in Paris, is invited to be present on that date at 9 A.M. in the office of the Chief of the Army General. Civilian dress."

Captain Dreyfus was then on required duty with the 39th Regiment of the Infantry. The summons surprised him. The hour was rather early for a "general inspection," which ordinarily was scheduled in the afternoon. That "civilian dress" was required was unusual, but he gave the matter little thought. "That Sunday evening we dined as was our habit, my wife and I, at the home of my in-laws. We all left extremely gay, happy as we always were with those evenings spent with the family."[1]

On Monday morning, he kissed his wife and children. His son Pierre, age three, accompanied him to the door. The morning was brisk and beautiful; the sun began to break through a veil of mist. Dreyfus walked to the Ministry, following the quais of the Seine. Having arrived a bit early, as was his habit, he strolled before the Ministry for a few minutes. Then, right on time, he went up to the office.

He was immediately received by Commandant Georges Picquart of the Army General Staff. Dreyfus was surprised not to see anyone else, since officers were normally summoned for group inspection. Picquart and Dreyfus exchanged commonplaces for a few minutes, after which Picquart led his visitor to the door of the quarters of the chief of the Army General Staff, General Raoul de Boisdeffre.

Dreyfus's astonishment was greater still, for General Boisdeffre was absent. He was received instead by an odd and solemn officer in uniform, who introduced himself as "Commandant du Paty de Clam." In the rear of the room were three men in civilian garb who were unknown to Dreyfus. These were Armand Cochefort, head of Criminal Investigation, his secretary, and Félix Gribelin, archivist of the Section of Statistics. Du Paty invited Dreyfus to fill in the identificatory section of his inspection form, as his aides looked on. Then du Paty, whose right hand was covered by a black silk glove, said to Dreyfus: "I have a letter to write and present to General Boisdeffre for his signature. I've hurt my finger. Can you write it for me?" Dreyfus agreed to the odd request, and sat down at a small table, ready for the dictation.*

It was then that Commandant du Paty, leaning over Dreyfus, dictated to him a meticulously composed text.

Paris, October 15, 1894
   Having the most serious reasons, Sir, for temporarily retaking possession of the documents I had passed on to you before taking off on maneuvers, I beseech you to have them brought immediately to me by the bearer of the present letter, who is an individual to be trusted. . . .

Du Paty continued his dictation with deliberate slowness.

"I recall for your benefit that it is a matter of:

1. A note on the hydraulic brake of the 120 cannon and on the manner in which. . . ."

At that moment du Paty brutally interrupted the dictation. "What is the matter, Captain? You are trembling!"[2] "My fingers are cold," answered Dreyfus, who continued to write.† "My fingers were cold," Dreyfus would

---

* "I understood less and less what was going on," Dreyfus would write from his cell at Cherche-Midi, in his evocation of the incredible scene. Handwritten notes written at Cherche-Midi, 1894 file.

† At no point did his handwriting change. It merely got larger after the words: "I recall to you. . . ."

later write, "for the temperature was quite chilly outside, and I had been in a heated room for only a few minutes."[3]

Why did du Paty suddenly challenge Dreyfus? "To unsettle his self-assurance," he would later claim, attributing to Dreyfus alternately a revealing agitation and the perfect calm of a polished fraud. Dreyfus awaited the rest of the dictation. Du Paty addressed him still more brutally. "Pay attention. This is serious." Dreyfus was offended by the harshness of the bizarre remark, but he continued to write in response to the dictation, attempting to "write better."[4]

"it functioned in maneuvers;

2. A note on covering troops;
3. A note on Madagascar."

"Dreyfus had regained his composure," du Paty would write. "It was useless to pursue the experiment." Whereupon du Paty rose, solemnly placed his hand on Dreyfus's shoulder, and in a thunderous voice, spoke these words: "In the name of the law I arrest you. You are accused of the crime of high treason."

"A bolt of lightning striking at my feet would not have produced in me a more violent sensation; I began speaking incoherently."[5] Dreyfus couldn't understand the insane scenario that was unfolding in the office. He protested, grew indignant. Whereupon du Paty opened up a copy of the Penal Code and read out Article 76. "Whosoever will have engaged in machinations or shared information with foreign powers . . . will be punished by death." As he read he revealed a revolver hidden beneath a folder. Dreyfus, persisting in his protests, caught sight of the weapon. "I am innocent. Kill me if you want." Du Paty answered, "It is not for us, but for you to do so."[6] As Dreyfus protested his innocence, Armand Cochefert and his secretary grabbed him in an attempt to search his person. He did not offer any resistance ("Take my keys. Open everything in my home.") He was told there were devastating charges which had been brought against him. He persisted in maintaining his innocence, explained incoherently that he had a wife and children, that he was rich, that he was Alsatian, that he loved his homeland, his profession, that he was incapable of betrayal. "A rather theatrical pose," du Paty would explain.[7] "I allowed the torrent to die down; it may well have been a set piece prepared in the event of an arrest." The other witnesses would say that Dreyfus seemed to be acting, "that he was calmly observing himself in the mirror."[8] Dreyfus begged to be told of exactly what he was accused, but was shown no document.[9] Du Paty pressed him with questions.

"Have you any enemies capable of having fabricated out of ruse the documents that have been seized and which are the cause of your arrest?"

"I don't know of any enemies I may have."

"Have you been traveling with the General Staff, and if so, during what period?"

"During the second half of June."

"Have you had any dealings with the technical section of the Artillery?"

"Yes, on two occasions."

Dreyfus continued to swear to his innocence.

"I want to live to establish my innocence. . . . I can see that a horrendous plot has been fomented against me. . . ."

The minutes of Dreyfus's interrogation are less than twenty lines in length.

Accompanied by an agent of the Sureté, Commandant Hubert Joseph Henry of the Section of Statistics took Dreyfus away. During the trip, he questioned his prisoner. "What are you accused of?" Henry knew, of course, but was laying a trap. At the Prison of Cherche-Midi, Dreyfus was locked up, his detention kept secret. No communication was made with anyone. No one was allowed to speak to him.[10] It was then that he broke down. A few hours earlier, he had been a happy man, a young and brilliant officer. Now he was no more than a suspect cast into the depths of a prison. Dreyfus believed he was going mad: "I fell into a state of terrible overexcitement. I screamed with pain, paced in my cell, banged my head against the walls."* A horrid attack of rage and despair convulsed him. Why had he not consented to kill himself?

---

* Commandant Ferdinand Forzinetti, who was in charge of military prisons, and received Dreyfus at Cherche-Midi, described Dreyfus, whom he went to see in his cell, as follows: "I had before me a true madman, with eyes shot through with blood. He had overturned everything in his room." (Account by Commandant Forzinetti, published in *Le Figaro*, November 21, 1897.) Forzinetti attempted to calm him.

10

The Bordereau

Since December 3, 1893, General Auguste Mercier had been the minister of war. A graduate of l'École Polytechnique, he had built for himself a rather slow career, but he had acquired a reputation as an intelligent and reflective officer. He was regarded as a republican open to liberal ideas, which was not commonly the case.[1] He was tall, extremely thin, cold, severe, with a face that seemed hacked out with a billhook. He invariably kept his eyes half-closed, and his somewhat forced smile was apt to contract into a grimace. Courteous, tactiturn, quite energetic, he was gifted with an extraordinary memory. His nomination to the ministry of war in Jean Casimir-Périer's government appears to have satisfied the Army.

As a minister, he was entirely devoted to the defense of the Army. In May 1894, Charles Dupuy, upon succeeding Casimir-Périer as prime minister, elected to retain Mercier in his post, a circumstance which gave the general the feeling that he was irremovable. "Haughty, cutting, seemingly infallible and sure of his fate, he issued decisions on all matters with a fatuous will to provoke," wrote Joseph Reinach. "There is no form of ambition worse than one that comes late in life. . . . Everything, including the vulgar indulgences of power, had contributed to his intoxication, to the ripening of a parvenu's insolence. . . ."[2] But Reinach, who regarded him as a major criminal, blackened the portrait. Mercier brought to the advancement of his career undeniable qualities of courage, self-control, and shrewdness.

The right was rather suspicious of General Mercier: he was a general who did not attend mass, a republican. Because he had ordered the anticipated liberation of a section of the contingent on August 1, 1894, the reactionary press lashed out against him. He was accused of protecting a spy named Tripone to please his friend General Gaston de Galliffet. "A scrounger, a sniffer, and an idiot," was the *Intransigeant*'s description.[3] "Explain yourself, Mercier, that we may know just how far human imbecility is capable of going." In *L'Autorité* of June 2, Granier de Cassagnac, a writer of the extreme right, attacked him violently. "Mercier should have been expelled from his seat, and he would have been had the Chamber been filled with patriots." Edouard Drumont, the editor of *La Libre Parole,* pursued his campaign against the presence of Jewish officers in the Army, and took specific aim at Mercier. "The Ministry of War, which should be the sanctuary of patriotism, is a cave, a cesspool. . . . There is always something that stinks there."[4] *La Croix* also insulted the minister of war, suspected of concealing and sheltering Jews and spies. In the autumn of 1894, Mercier had ample reason to fear the return of Parliament. Could one remain a minister of war while being disgraced by the right?

Toward the end of September 1894 Mercier was informed that the Section of Statistics had intercepted a document of great importance, issuing from the German embassy. The document was immediately forwarded to him. It was the celebrated bordereau, the memorandum out of which the Dreyfus Affair would emerge:

Having no indication that you wish to see me, I am nevertheless forwarding to you, Sir, several interesting items of information

1. A note on the hydraulic break of the 120 and the manner in which that part has performed;
2. A note on covering troops (several modifications will be effected by the new plan);
3. A note on a modification of Artillery formations;
4. A note pertaining to Madagascar;
5. The *Sketch for a Firing Manual* for the country artillery (March 14, 1894);

This last document is extremely difficult to procure and I am able to have it at my disposal for only a very few days. The Ministry of War has distributed a fixed number of copies to the regiments, and the regiments are responsible for them. Every officer holding a copy is to return it after maneuvers. If you would then take from it what interests you and keep it at my disposal thereafter, I will take it. Unless you want me to have it copied in extenso and send you the copy.

I am off to maneuvers.

"Mercier's emotion upon reading the text," writes Reinach, "was quite strong, as was his irritation."[5] From its first sentence, the letter indicated the existence of a treasonous transaction. The traitor was apparently an officer, and undoubtedly (since the document alluded to the ministry) an officer of the Ministry of War. The information he disposed of seemed to be important. A French officer, probably of the General Staff, was thus implicated. Mercier immediately grasped the gravity of the situation, and understood that if the culprit were uncovered, arrested, and convicted, the political benefit would accrue to him. He would then be able to muzzle the extreme right and its press. The minister's instructions to General Raoul de Boisdeffre, chief of the Army General Staff, and to General Charles Gonse, deputy-chief, were forceful: "The circle of inquiry is small, limited to the General Staff. Search. Find."[6]

How did the famous bordereau fall into the hands of the Section of Statistics? The "official" version, from which the Ministry of War would never depart, was that the precious document had been found by Mme. Bastian in the wastebasket of Maximilian von Schwarzkoppen, the German military attaché, and passed on to Commandant Henry, no doubt on the evening of September 26.* The bordereau was part of a "rather copious" delivery (half a dozen documents), received via the "ordinary track," which were immediately reconstituted and studied.

There are numerous historians of the Affair who have refused to accept this thesis, which they have dismissed as too simple, if not simple-minded. In his *Histoire de l'Affaire Dreyfus*, Reinach assures us that the bordereau must have been stolen from the stall of the concierge of the German embassy by agent Martin Brücker, of the Section of Statistics, who "took the letter, which had probably come through the mails, from the cubby-hole of Schwarzkoppen, then vacationing in Berlin."[8] Such is the thesis that Alfred Dreyfus himself would eventually seem to accept.[9] "The letter which has since become so notorious under the name of 'bordereau,'" writes Maurice Baumont, "did not arrive at the mysterious Office of Statistics via the ordinary track—through the efforts of Mme. Bastian. Brought to the rue de Lille while the military attaché von Schwarzkoppen was absent from Paris, it had been deposited in the concierge's stall, from which it was to fly off into world history."[10]

"A story of—and for—concierges," as Baumont notes. In fact, though the manner in which the bordereau arrived at the German embassy and the path it subsequently took to the office of the minister of war were not without their effect on the roles of the principal antagonists, and each commentator is tempted to adjust the path of the bordereau to the thesis he is advocating or the legend he is telling. When he published his

---

* Marcel Thomas has established that Commandant Henry, delayed while hunting, did not return to Paris until September 25. On the 26th, he would have seen "Auguste," who would have delivered to him an ample harvest of documents, since they had not seen each other in a month. On the 27th, archivist Félix Gribelin listed in his account book a monthly salary of 100 francs paid to Auguste.[7]

Notebooks, Colonel von Schwarzkoppen sided with those maintaining that the bordereau had not been retrieved from his wastebasket. "That the bordereau," he writes, "was not found in the wastebasket follows directly from the fact that I myself never received it. Mme. Bastian or another secret agent must have found it in my mailbox in the concierge's stall and ripped it into small pieces in order to create the appearance that it came from my basket."[11]

The bordereau "was never in my hands," Schwarzkoppen solemnly affirms. But in the eyes of history, the military attaché is a dubious witness. For it was in his interest to conceal—or to attempt to diminish—his incredible negligence. Could he acknowledge having tossed into the basket—after halfheartedly tearing it up—a document that was to assume such importance in world history? And yet the mass of documents retrieved from Schwarzkoppen's basket over a period of eight years reveals that he threw out pell-mell drafts of intimate letters, the most personal correspondence, and important documents detailing his espionage activities.[12] In 1894, Schwarzkoppen was a remarkably unserious spy, and he would remain so until his departure from France. The efforts of the historian Marcel Thomas have established that in all probability Schwarzkoppen was not telling the truth on this point, and the bordereau did indeed arrive by the ordinary track. Thomas has observed that the ordinary track had brought along with the bordereau the draft of a questionnaire* drawn up by Schwarzkoppen for the use of his agents in order to acquire information about the 120 short cannon on the occasion of the maneuvers at Châlons. The bordereau was in part a response to that questionnaire, a circumstance attesting both to Schwarzkoppen's precise preoccupations and to his phenomenal carelessness. "It is in fact as though before leaving on vacation September 24," writes Thomas, "Schwarzkoppen had hastily dumped into his wastebasket the refuse of files deemed outdated."[14] Thus the bordereau, along with Schwarzkoppen's questionnaire, would have come to the Section of Statistics by way of the ordinary

* The questionnaire was composed as follows:
1. What is the composition of the batteries of the regimental corps at Châlons?
2. How many 120 batteries?
3. What shells does it fire?
4. What is the effective strength in manpower of the batteries?
5. The firing manual of the country artillery?
6. The guide strip?
7. Artillery mobilization?
8. The new cannon?
9. The new rifle?
10. The organization of the armed forces, divisions and reserve brigades?
11. The fort at Manonvilliers?[13]

track and would have been transmitted by Mme. Bastian to Commandant
Henry on September 26 among other documents or scraps of paper at
Sainte-Clotilde or elsewhere.

The bordereau was ripped into six pieces, but so hurriedly* that
Henry had no trouble pasting them together and perceiving their intent.
As early as September 27 he showed his friend Captain Jules Lauth and
Félix Gribelin, of the Section of Statistics, his astonishing discovery. They
discussed the matter briefly, then presented the paper to Commandant
Jean Sandherr, head of the Intelligence Services, who immediately attributed to it great significance. Captain Bertin Matton, who entered the
office by chance, was invited to inspect the document. He voiced the
hypothesis that such a letter had to emanate from someone in the ministry,
and undoubtedly from a member of the Artillery.† On the same day, the
document was taken to the minister (as was customary) by either the chief
or a deputy-chief of the General Staff, along with other documents which
had come through the ordinary track.[15] Since General de Boisdeffre was
absent from Paris, it was one of the deputy-chiefs of the General Staff,
General Jean Renouard, in charge for the interim, who informed the
minister of war of the discovery, whereupon Mercier set out to find the
traitor.

Sandherr and Mercier took for granted (as did Matton) that the traitor
was an officer of the General Staff. One of the notes referred to concerned
"covering troops" and the "new plan," which would seem to indicate that
the author of the letter had access to secret files.‡ Within the cir-
cumscribed group in question, a similar handwriting had to be identified.
Sandherr searched through his archives, but to no avail. Renouard distributed photographic copies of the bordereau to the heads of various
bureaus; but none recognized the script of an officer in his command.
During this period, the Section of Statistics forwarded to General Mercier
other documents which had come through the ordinary track, including a
letter from the Italian military attaché, Alessandro Panizzardi, to his
friend Maximilian von Schwarzkoppen.

"My beautiful bugger. I was in bliss, and am returning to you the three
pieces. Farewell, my beautiful bugger. Your friend."[16] A consensus

* It had not been ripped into small pieces. It has occasionally been argued, on the basis of
this, that the bordereau did not come from Schwarzkoppen's wastebasket. But study of the
Archives of the Ministry of War demonstrates that the ordinary track brought in numerous
documents ripped in two, or simply crumpled by Schwarzkoppen.
† Matton was the only artilleryman in the Section of Statistics.
‡ According to Marcel Thomas, the very word "note" would have suggested to the officers,
who were constantly busy preparing, composing, and receiving "notes," that the text came
from the Ministry.

quickly determined that the author of the bordereau, who spoke of the hydraulic brake of the 120 short and promised to procure the temporary *Firing Manual* of the Artillery, was probably an artilleryman. On October 4, a photographic negative of the bordereau was sent to the heads of the Artillery. The result was not encouraging, and by October all leads had been exhausted. It was at that point that Lieutenant Colonel d'Abboville, who had just succeeded Colonel Roger as deputy-chief of the Fourth Bureau, returned to the Ministry from vacation. On October 6, it was he who tipped the scales of destiny.

On that morning d'Abboville arrived at the Ministry quite proud of his new post. He went to the office of his superior, where the two chatted and were joined shortly thereafter by Lieutenant Colonel Boucher, chief of the Third Bureau. They could not escape talking about the bordereau whose author was being searched for everywhere. D'Abboville took note, then withdrew to his office. Colonel Pierre Fabre called him back and showed him the photo of the bordereau. "If I were in charge of finding the culprit," claimed d'Abboville, happy to display his talents, "I think I would have a rather easy time of it." "What?", asked Fabre. Whereupon d'Abboville brought to his attention the fact that the kinds of information referred to in the bordereau indicated quite clearly that the culprit had been affiliated with the First, Second, Third, and Fourth bureaus of the Ministry. Now it happened that "stagiaires," recently commissioned officers of the General Staff who before receiving their permanent assignments spent several months of apprenticeship in each of the bureaus, were the only individuals who fit the bill. The circle of suspects was tightening. An officer of the General Staff? An Artillery officer temporarily serving with the General Staff? There were four or five who had passed through the Fourth Bureau in the last year whom Fabre knew personally. One of them was Captain Alfred Dreyfus, the very man about whom Fabre had written a negative evaluation for the second semester of 1893: "An incomplete officer, quite intelligent and quite gifted, but pretentious, and not satisfying from the point of view of character, conscience, and manner of service, the conditions necessary for employment with the General Staff of the Army." The notation had been composed by Fabre from information furnished by Lieutenant Colonel Roget and Commandant Bertin Mourot.* The case of this "incomplete officer," a Jewish officer, immediately attracted the attention of Fabre and d'Abboville, delighted to have discovered a new lead. What they now needed was a specimen of his handwriting. They found a form filled out by Dreyfus, compared it with

* Bertin Mourot was of Jewish origin on his mother's side, a circumstance he strained to have forgotten through his overt profession of anti-Semitism.

the handwriting of the bordereau, and were struck by the resemblance.*[17] There remained but a single detail. The author of the bordereau wrote that he was "about to leave on maneuvers." It was established that Dreyfus had not recently gone on maneuvers, nor had any of the officers serving apprenticeships with the General Staff. But the officers were already convinced. They found signs of a General Staff expedition to the East during the month of June in which Dreyfus had participated.† Other specimens of Dreyfus's handwriting were sought, and to their surprise, Fabre and d'Abboville were to find in them "almost all the words of the bordereau." So it was Dreyfus's diction. Indeed, they had their culprit.[19]

The drama took on a certain momentum. Colonel Fabre reported matters to General Charles Gonse, deputy-chief of the General Staff, who alerted General Raoul de Boisdeffre, said to be "very affected." De Boisdeffre issued instructions not to allow any leaks, and undertook to report events to the minister of war. Gonse summoned Sandherr, an impassioned anti-Semite, who slapped his forehead and exclaimed, "I should have realized!"[20] He did not know Dreyfus, but claimed that he had seen him loitering about, and that the Jewish captain had asked him a number of indiscreet questions. From then on, each reinforced the conviction of the other. By nightfall, a dozen high officers were already convinced that Dreyfus was the traitor they were looking for.

Auguste Mercier, the minister of war, would say that upon being informed by the chief of the General Staff, he at first experienced "terrible distress." So the suspected officer "wore the very uniform that he himself had worn." He was "a child of the Alsace in which he too had passed his childhood."[21] But Dreyfus was a Jewish officer, an Alsatian Jew. "At first sight," Mercier would note, his guilt seemed to be beyond doubt.

General Mercier, however, observed to General de Boisdeffre that the officers accusing Dreyfus were not experts. It ws imperative to find someone on whom they could count, who was capable of keeping a secret, and who was competent in handwriting analysis. Who was it that proposed the name of Commandant Mercier du Paty de Clam, an officer with the Third Bureau? He was a bizarre and frequently mad individual: Even today he provokes the most divergent judgments. Marcel Thomas de-

* In comparing the words of the bordereau with the same words written by Dreyfus as dictated by du Paty or recopied by him, one is "struck," at first sight, by the resemblance. But it should also be observed that such careful and slanted handwriting was quite common at the time. The schools had not yet "liberated" handwriting. The superficial resemblance of the two handwritings with those of many other contemporaries may be noted.
† "From that first moment on," wrote Joseph Reinach, "the phenomenon that would dominate the entire Affair was in operation. It was no longer carefully verified facts and scrupulously examined matters which formed opinion; it was a sovereign, pre-established, and irresistible belief which distorted facts and realities."[18]

scribes him as a born officer, "called to a great future, intelligent and cultivated, but with a romantic streak and an excessive confidence in his intuitions."[22] Henri Guillemin[23] relates that he had a rather charged past—an "extremely ugly affair" in 1892— and portrays him in a rather ridiculous light: "a monocle-bearing automaton, with an inflated torso, a chin pointing upward, and the mustache of a cat." In addition, he "dripped with goodwill" and ambition. He was a relative of General de Boisdeffre, who protected him, and the friend of Colonel Maximilian von Schwarzkoppen. His grandfather, president of the Court of Bordeaux, had resigned from his functions in order to rehabilitate three persons unjustly sentenced to death. Justice seemed to be a family tradition. It was known in the ministry that du Paty had a taste for graphology and, in agreement with General Mercier, General de Boisdeffre decided to make use of it. On the evening of October 6, General Gonse called upon Commandant du Paty to compare the two scripts, that of the bordereau and that of Dreyfus, but did not reveal to him the identity of the suspect. With great self-assurance, du Paty immediately concluded that they were identical. General Gonse then explained that "we are dealing with a case of treason, and the inquest undertaken by these offices has cast suspicion on Captain Dreyfus," whereupon du Paty asked that he be allowed to repeat his evaluation. By the evening of October 7, after working all day Sunday, du Paty was able to submit to his superiors a statement concluding that "despite certain disparities," the resemblance is sufficient to justify a legal opinion. The suspicion was henceforth a certainty. De Boisdeffre, Gonse, and Sandherr, like d'Abboville, Fabre, and du Paty, were already convinced.

11

The Conspirators

The eight days separating the discovery of the culprit on October 7 from his arrest on October 15 were extremely agitated. Because the German embassy was implicated, the Affair had become an affair of state. General Auguste Mercier, the minister of war, took precautions. He first consulted with the highest military authority in the country, General Félix

Saussier, military governor of Paris and de facto commander in chief of the French armed forces. Saussier did not like Mercier, and their antagonism—a function of circumstance as well as character—was well known.[1] Saussier was prudent by temperament, a realist perpetually in quest of compromise. A bachelor and *bon vivant,* he maintained as a mistress the wife of a Jewish officer, Maurice Weil, a person of extremely dubious reputation whom *La Libre Parole* periodically accused of being a German spy. There were a number of unpleasant rumors in circulation concerning the relationship between Weil and Saussier, which Saussier attributed to the Section of Statistics and to Mercier in particular.[2] Upon consultation, Saussier advised the minister of war against pursuing the affair. The Army would have nothing to gain from the public denunciation of an officer in Germany's service, and he feared the reactions of the Jewish bank. "You would be better off sending this Dreyfus to get himself killed in Africa." Saussier, moreover, had little trust in the fantasies of the Intelligence Service. But he had no illusions: the minister was consulting him in order to ignore his advice.

On his way out of the Cabinet meeting of October 9, Mercier, who was beginning to take initiatives, asked his obscure colleague Guérin, minister of justice, for the name of a handwriting expert. Guérin suggested Alfred Gobert, an expert with the Bank of France, whom Mercier then summoned personally to the ministry.

On October 10, General Mercier requested an interview with the president of the Republic, Jean Casimir-Périer, in order to inform him. Casimir-Périer would later attest that the minister of war took pains to minimize the affair. "The documents turned over were without great importance.... A few measures taken at the War Ministry" would be sufficient to set matters aright.[3] The minister of war then rushed to inform the prime minister, with whom he agreed to act with utmost discretion. At the Ministry of the Interior, a "petty council" would meet to deliberate on Thursday, October 11. It would be composed of the ministers concerned: the prime minister, the minister of foreign affairs, the minister of justice, and the minister of war.

The petty council met as planned. Mercier presented the matter, explained how the bordereau came into the hands of the Section of Statistics, analyzed the document, and affirmed that through a handwriting analysis it had been possible to discover the culprit. He did not, however, name him, but requested advice on what remained to be done.[4]

The minister of justice and the prime minister "examined the various options without managing to choose any of them."* Only Gabriel

---

* According to Maurice Paléologue's *Journal.* At the time, he was in charge of "restricted affairs"—i.e., intelligence matters—in the Ministry of Foreign Affairs. The director of

Hanotaux, minister of foreign affairs, was courageous enough to take a stand. He saw the risks of a judicial procedure initiated on the sole basis of a document illegally obtained from an embassy and which necessarily would implicate duly accredited diplomatic agents. He went through the difficulties in France's relations with Germany, insisting that the slightest diplomatic incident must be avoided. But the minister of war persevered. He invoked the superior interest of the homeland, the imperatives of national defense. The prime minister sought a vague compromise and extracted from Mercier the promise that he would abandon his pursuit if no other proof than the bordereau were found.[6] It was decided that a search, "which efforts would be made to keep secret," would be conducted in the culprit's home. As for the name of the culprit, which was known to the entire General Staff, neither the president of the Republic, nor the prime minister, nor the minister of foreign affairs were informed. Nor did they protest that gap in the information provided.

Troubled by the course of events, the minister of foreign affairs decided to pay a visit to the home of the minister of war in the hope of making him yield. Hanotaux argued for more than an hour, but to no avail. Mercier invoked the law and the risk of scandal, since the officers involved in the inquest might decide to speak. In reality, he had already resolved to arrest the culprit and was already organizing the execution of that plan.

Mercier was extremely pressed, since he was to leave the following day for maneuvers at Limoges, from which he would not return before October 14. No civilian pressure must be permitted to interrupt or delay the plan he was perfecting. He sent Sandherr, Henry, and du Paty to speak with Police Prefect Louis Lépine to confirm his cooperation. He called Alfred Gobert, the expert summoned urgently to the ministry of war, then dispatched him to General de Boisdeffre and General Gonse. There the expert found himself before an "Aereopagus of officers" busy examining documents and comparing handwritings. They immediately attempted to transmit their ardent and unanimous conviction to the unofficial witness designated by the minister. Gobert, to whom the name of the "culprit"[7] was not revealed, took the documents with him and worked on them all day Friday, October 12. On two occasions Gonse came by to encourage him. Without even waiting for the results of his evaluation, Mercier, sensing Gobert's scruples, requested of the prefect of police the assistance of a second expert. Prefect Lepine recommended Alphonse Bertillon, head of the Prefecture's Service of Judiciary Identity.

On the evening of October 12, General de Boisdeffre called in Commandant du Paty and announced to him that as an officer of the judiciary

political affairs, Armand Nisard, gave him a secret and detailed account of the Council meeting on October 12.[5]

police, he had been chosen to execute the arrest of Captain Dreyfus. "You are going to poison my life," du Paty is alleged to have responded. "I am the head of a family; this is a task for a bachelor. Give it to Picquart."[8] But de Boisdeffre found the words with which to convince him. "You, after all, were not educated by the Jesuits . . . you don't have any Jewish connections . . . then there is a real danger." "There remained no other choice than to submit," du Paty would later claim, "but I already had an intuition of the future." The truth is that du Paty required minimal encouragement and demonstrated exemplary zeal.

At 9 o'clock on the morning of October 13, as Minister of War Mercier was arriving in Limoges, Alphonse Bertillon received an urgent order to compare the bordereau and Dreyfus's handwriting. At the same time, the expert Gobert made known his conclusions. The two handwritings were "of the same graphic type," but "presented numerous and important disparities which had to be taken into account."* The bordereau could come "from a person other than the suspect." But nothing could restrain either the minister of war or the General Staff any longer. When one stopped to reflect, after all, from his very first questions, Gobert had seemed rather curious. As an expert with the Bank of France, he must have had dealings with international finance. Perhaps he even knew Dreyfus and his family. And that very evening, Bertillon produced the happy results of his precipitous labors.[10] "If the hypothesis of a document forged with the utmost care is eliminated, it appears clear to us that it was the same person who wrote the various items submitted and the incriminated document." Bertillon was decidedly a remarkable expert.

There remained the matter of bringing that action to pass. It was du Paty, a fervent reader of adventure novels, who invented the scenario and engineered its approval. The culprit was to be invited to appear under the pretext of a general inspection. He would be instructed to appear in civilian dress—in order to facilitate his stay in prison. Du Paty prepared meticulously the text of the "dictation," which in any event would confound the culprit. Should Dreyfus tremble, he would be confessing his crime. If he did not, he would be revealing the depth of his dissimulation. Commandant Henry would be concealed behind a curtain. A mirror would reflect for the benefit of three witnesses the face of the traitor at the moment of his discomfiture. That the plan was not merely insane but absurd—for if Dreyfus were guilty, the bizarre summons would surely put him on guard—seems to have occurred to no one. A few final details were

---

* In his letter of October 13, Gobert specified: "I am obliged to state that the document under consideration is not traced in a disguised handwriting, but, on the contrary, written quite naturally and normally in a rapid hand; this last detail precludes any possibility of a graphic disguise or study" (National Archives BB 19-101, d2, p. 32).[9]

attended to. Du Paty went to Prefecture of Police Lépine to see Armand Cochefort, head of Criminal Investigations, to make sure of his cooperation. Throughout Sunday, October 14, as Dreyfus was celebrating with his wife and children what were to be his last hours of freedom, there was much agitation. A message was brought to Commandant Ferdinand Forzinetti, director of the Prison of Cherche-Midi, "informing him that on the following day, October 15, a high-ranking officer serving with the General Staff of the Army would transmit to him a communication." That was to be Lieutenant Colonel d'Abboville, who was to accomplish that secret mission on the morning of October 15 in order to prepare the conditions for the incarceration of Dreyfus. D'Abboville was to order Forzinetti not to report events to General Félix Saussier, military governor of Paris. Finally, a last meeting toward 6:00 P.M. was to regroup around Minister of War Mercier the principal participants: General de Boisdeffre, Colonel Sandherr, General Gonse, Armand Cochefert, and, of course, du Paty de Clam, who was to be the protagonist. The scenario was rehearsed in detail. As soon as the dictation was over, du Paty was to proceed to a summary interrogation, after which, Dreyfus would be taken to the Prison of Cherche-Midi by Commandant Henry.

"I said to the minister," du Paty would later claim, "what if he chooses to die? There was a moment of silence, whereupon the minister inclined his head and said—yes."[11] It was agreed that a regulation revolver, loaded with a single bullet, would be placed within Dreyfus's reach "so that he might render justice to himself." Cochefert, the sole civilian present, observed that this seemed to conform to the traditions of honor of the Army.

And that evening, those who organized so minutely the trap into which Dreyfus was led discovered—in spite of themselves—their solidarity. In apportioning the roles, they were henceforth bound by an unconscious pact. Under the authority of General Mercier, they had become—without yet realizing it—conspirators.

12

The Capers of Bertillon

Barely had the play been performed than du Paty, faithful to the scenario, hurried to Dreyfus's home on the Avenue du Trocadéro to conduct a search. He informed Lucie Dreyfus of the sudden arrest of her husband, without giving any motives. As she began to panic—crying, "my husband is dead!"[1]—du Paty proceeded to ply her with enigmatic comments. He forbade her from mentioning to anyone either the arrest or his visit. "It would be the downfall of your husband. . . . A single word would mean war." He searched the entire apartment, confiscated private letters, and took from Lucie the correspondence dating from the time of their engagement, but found nothing of interest. "Your husband is a coward, an abject wretch. . . . If I were his guard, I would spy on him in his sleep." Although he had driven Lucie to despair, he then made a feeble attempt to console her. She spent fifteen days, filled with anxiety, without support, without counsel, obsessed with concealing her misery. It was only on October 31 that du Paty allowed Lucie to inform her family of her husband's plight.* And only once would he transmit to her a note which he had allowed Dreyfus to write. "I assure you of my honor and my affection."

From October 15 to 18, du Paty left Dreyfus in his cell, without interrogation. Those days were atrocious for the prisoner.[3] Dreyfus paced in his cage like a wild beast, spoke out loud, shouted out his innocence, screamed, and sobbed. He hurled himself against the iron furniture, at the risk of injuring himself, then threw himself on to the bed but was unable to sleep. "He took only clear soup and sweet wine, without ever touching any food."[4]

Commandant Ferdinand Forzinetti, director of the Prison of Cherche-Midi, came to see him, and attempted to calm him in vain. On October 18, du Paty arrived in the prison, accompanied by the archivist Félix Gribelin, who acted as his clerk, in order to initiate the interrogation.

* Mathieu Dreyfus would be informed on October 31 by a special dispatch received at the Mulhouse Stock Exchange, where he was "as was his custom on Wednesdays." Lucie implored him to come immediately "for an extremely urgent matter."[2]

He would subsequently come every evening, quite late, frequently remaining for several hours. The first day, du Paty asked Forzinetti to enter unannounced into the cell, bearing a projection lamp—in order to surprise the accused "in a violent flood of light, and to unsettle him." Forzinetti refused. In his prison, there would be no recourse to such procedures.

Du Paty had prepared a new series of ordeals with which to confound Dreyfus. On occasion, he would require him to submit to more than ten consecutive bouts of dictation—while seated, lying down, or standing erect. He was made to perform a battery of absurd and exhausting exercises on the sentence, "I am off to maneuvers." On another count, he contrived with utmost ingenuity, through a series of questions whose significance eluded Dreyfus, to establish that the prisoner might have access to each of the documents referred to in the bordereau. But the bordereau itself was still not shown to him, and Dreyfus continued to protest. On October 24, he is quoted in the minutes: "I swear on the head of my children that I am innocent. If I were shown the incriminating items, I might perhaps understand. For eleven days, I have been kept in secrecy, and I still don't know of what I am accused."[5] In addition to the formal interrogations, du Paty would make "all sorts of veiled allusions" to facts of which Dreyfus understood nothing. He questioned him avidly about his private life. "I was struggling in the void," Dreyfus would write.[6] At times du Paty would threaten; at others, wax devout. "You are lost; only Providence can save you now." After which he would withdraw theatrically, his monocle affixed to his eye, followed by his clerk. Dreyfus would fall, "like a beaten animal, unable to bear any more." He had atrocious nightmares. At night, his guards could hear him screaming or laughing like a lunatic. On the morning of October 27, Dreyfus's mental state appeared to be "close to madness" and sufficiently grave for Forzinetti to report it to the minister and to the governor of Paris.*[7] General Mercier accorded carte blanche to General de Boisdeffre, who authorized Forzinetti to have Dreyfus seen by the house physician "under his responsibility and without mentioning it to anyone." The doctor prescribed sedatives and constant surveillance. Isolated, tormented, and desperate, Dreyfus endured "terrible oscillations of fever and prostration." He frequently thought of dying. Commandant Forzinetti was his lone support. "All the goodness of the human species had sought refuge in that jailer."[8]

It was only on October 30—after Edouard Drumont's newspaper, *La Libre Parole,* had revealed the Dreyfus Affair to the public—that du Paty

* See Forzinetti's letter of October 27, 1894, to the minister of war and to General Saussier: "The officer is in an indescribable mental state . . . There is reason to fear that he may resort to some act of desperation or that madness will ensue." National Archives, BB 19.75.

finally revealed to the accused the photographic negative of the bordereau. At last Dreyfus regained a measure of hope. He finally knew what
he was being accused of, and felt delivered from the "maddening mystery." Henceforth he could confront the accusation directly and demonstrate its patent absurdity. No, he had never been to maneuvers. If he
knew the principle behind the brake of the 120, he had never seen any
document concerning its inner structure, and had never seen it in production or operation. In the Second Bureau, he never had any assignment
concerning troops. He never read or knew a thing about Madagascar. He
was not even aware of the publication of the temporary shooting manual
for the country artillery. His innocence could thus be established.[9]

On October 31, du Paty let Dreyfus know that his inquest was completed. It was too late to look for witnesses, too late to verify arguments.
"The Minister is prepared to receive you if you are willing to begin
considering a confession." Dreyfus reiterated, "I declare to you once again
that I am innocent and have nothing to confess." Du Paty drew up a report
for General Boisdeffre.* The inquest, however, had yielded no results.
Dreyfus refused to confess.

As du Paty interrogated Dreyfus, inquiries intended to reveal the
culprit's true nature were proliferating in every direction. Agent François
Guénée, a former policeman serving with the Section of Statistics, began to
make inquiries in various gambling dens and casinos, working incessantly
to establish that Dreyfus gambled, cheated, and frequented unsavory
types. Guénée's efforts did not yield much—except that Dreyfus had been
seen once or twice in gambling circles.†

Guénée's investigation of Dreyfus's private life proved more fruitful. It
revealed that the young officer had several mistresses, married women,
but also ladies of the *demi-monde*, among them Mmes. Déry, Kron, Bodson,
and Dida, concerning whom great care was taken to ascertain whether
they might be spies. Du Paty quickly concluded that Dreyfus was two-
faced, "a monster." When Alfred's nephew, aged eighteen, came on his
father's behalf to request an interview, du Paty told him: "I cannot under-

---

* This report was lost! At Rennes, du Paty would produce a "record" that he claimed to have
kept of it. That document, he claimed, set out the fragility of the accusations and the risk of
acquittal. "As a result, the judiciary police officer is of the opinion that in the present state of
the investigation there are grounds for dropping the case while nevertheless taking all due
precautions against Captain Dreyfus to prevent him from communicating with foreign
agents until the implementation of the new plan."[10]

But at the Rennes trial, du Paty would have a clear interest in minimizing his role by
producing a document advising that the charges be dropped.

† Another report, prepared by the Prefecture of Police and demonstrating that Dreyfus did
not frequent any gambling circles, would later be concealed from the military tribunal.

stand married men who betray their wives. I myself lost my wife, and until the day of my remarriage, I had no further relations with any other women. Your uncle is a wretch."[11] Upon questioning, Dreyfus attempted to minimize his adventures, claiming they had ended with his marriage. Du Paty concluded, "The adulterous husband is a potential traitor." Later on, Dreyfus's classmates would decribe a pretentious and arrogant officer, proud of his good fortune, perennially prepared to fall into the arms of an adventuress, boasting of being able to "pay" more for women than they could. For the moment, though, no trace of a female spy in Dreyfus's entourage could be found.

The serious effort was enlisted elsewhere. It consisted of establishing beyond any doubt that the bordereau was the work of Dreyfus. Alphonse Bertillon, head of the Prefecture's Service of Judiciary Identity, demonstrated great zeal and a desire for personal recognition. It was known, moreover, that he was a notorious anti-Semite. He offered to intiate a new study. Du Paty summarized his interrogations, and in turn Bertillon assisted du Paty with advice. In his first—and all too rapid—report, Bertillon had mentioned the limiting hypothesis of a document "forged" by an unknown individual in order to bring about the downfall of a personal enemy. He would now refine that hypothesis—by adapting it to the circumstance of Dreyfus's guilt. Did the lightweight paper on which the bordereau was written—an extremely rare onionskin—mean that it might be traced? For the moment, Bertillon dismissed that notion, which would reappear later on.[12] Between October 15, the day on which he applied himself anew to the task, and October 20, Bertillon would concoct a new thesis, which would remain famous: that of a "self-forgery." It was Dreyfus himself who had imitated his own handwriting—through a highly technical procedure—in the bordereau in question. According to circumstances, he could thus either pretend that the document had been fabricated or deny any resemblance with his own handwriting.

For Bertillon and the General Staff, such a theory had the advantage of confounding Dreyfus in any situation. Dreyfus made use of the onionskin paper "in order to give himself the option of arguing the case of a forgery, which had been traced." And if the handwriting of the bordereau were not identical to his own, it was because in imitating his own script, Dreyfus interpolated a number of studied disparities, calculated dissimulations, which could serve to exonerate him. That absurd thesis would thereafter be endlessly reworked, adapted, and transformed by Bertillon to suit the needs of the accusation. Bertillon would describe the fabulous calculations of Dreyfus, who submitted the bordereau to a fixed number of "deviations, shifts, or displacements," who traced and pasted words written seven or eight times over, who borrowed from members of his family* certain forms which were not part of his script, in order to arrive, through prodigious effort, at a forgery of his own handwriting! For the Court-Martial, Bertillon would later prepare a diagram conveying, he thought, Dreyfus's system of defense: at the center of the drawing, "the arsenal of the habitual spy," stocked with formidable arms and opening on to various corridors, one of which led to the "citadel of graphic rebusses," a tortuous, underground path connecting "the various tricks to each other" and allowing the spy, if caught, to "retreat to the citadel of rebusses."[13] In December,[14] Mercier would escort Bertillon to the office of the president of the Republic to assure him of Dreyfus's guilt. Jean Casimir-Périer would receive him on two consecutive days, and observe that the expert was a "compulsively rational madman," truly insane.†

But at the time, Bertillon was serving Dreyfus's accusers, and was taken quite seriously. On October 20, he submitted to Prefect of Police Lépine—for transmission to the minister of war—his second report, a monument of extravagance that the General Staff would later celebrate as a masterpiece of science.[16] "The proof," Bertillon concluded, "is there and is irrefutable. From the very first day, you knew my opinion. It is now absolute, complete, and admitting of no reservation."

But Bertillon was an expert without court affiliation, and his bizarre effort might well fail to be entirely convincing. Three new experts were designated with the recommendation of the minister of justice. All three accepted the assignment and were sworn in on October 21. Eugène Pelletier, an expert known for his integrity, was first to submit his report, on October 25. Refuting all of Bertillon's conclusions, he exonerated Dreyfus, observing that the "incriminating document gives every appearance of having been written without precautions in a normal hand. It represents the usual handwriting of its author." And Pelletier refused to attribute the bordereau to any of the suspects.

Expert Teyssonières—whose name would be struck by the court from the list of experts a few days later—reached conclusions similar to those of Bertillon. "The handwriting of the bordereau presents all the signs of a disguise, but in which the spontaneous tendency nevertheless ends up winning out." He concluded that the accused was guilty. There remained the archivist and paleographer Charavay, an expert of high repute. Was he

---

* A letter written by Mathieu Dreyfus and taken from Alfred Dreyfus's blotter served as material for Bertillon. Subsequently, Bertillon would continue to perfect his system, discovering new "borrowings" by Dreyfus from his family. He would thus have borrowed an extended *s* from his sister-in-law Alice.

† "Not bizarre, but completely insane," Casimir-Périer confided to his friend Maurice Paléologue, "given to an extraordinary and cabalistic madness . . . I thought I had an escapee from La Salpêtrière or Villejuif before me."[15]

influenced by Bertillon, on whom he paid a call? Was he (as Joseph Reinach would claim) the object of an attempt at corruption, which would have succeeded in setting him against Dreyfus? An agent of the Dreyfus family is alleged to have come to see him with an offer of money.[17] Whatever the case, he submitted on October 29 a report concluding that with the single conceivable exception of a "handwriting twin, . . . the incriminating document is of the same hand as the items submitted for comparison." But the contradictory reports of the experts were beginning to affect the morale of du Paty and all those who had joined battle against Dreyfus. And the deteriorating health of the culprit—fainting, crying, laughing, and "feeling his sense draining away"[18]—might pose a serious problem.

Through an odd coincidence,* it was at the very moment that the accusation seemed to collapse that the press latched on to the Affair.[19] Until October 29, no news of the arrest or the inquest had leaked out. But on that day, *La Libre Parole* published a menacing paragraph: "Is it true that an extremely important arrest has taken place by military order? The individual arrested would be accused of espionage. If the item is true, why are the military authorities maintaining absolute silence?" Reinach claims to have had in his possession the photo of a letter† "signed Henry" and sent October 28 to one of Drumont's collaborators at *La Libre Parole*, the journalist Papillaud.

> Dear Friend,
>   As I indeed told you, it is Captain Dreyfus, the one residing at 6 Avenue du Trocadéro, who was arrested on the 15th for espionage and who is in prison at the Cherche-Midi.
>   It is claimed that he is on a trip, but that is a lie because they want to stifle the affair. All of Israel has been mobilized.
> Yours,
> Henry.
>   Have my little investigation completed as soon as possible.

Reinach accused Commandant Henry of having authored the letter.‡ He was said to have undertaken the initiative in order to prevent the minister of war from backing out. The article in *La Libre Parole* mobilized the entirety of the press. By the evening of October 31, *L'Eclair*, drawing

---

* There is no coincidence for those who, like Joseph Reinach, believe that the General Staff used the press to "relaunch" the Affair.
† It would be published by Joseph Reinach in *Le Siècle* on April 2, 1899.
‡ But Marcel Thomas[20] notes that the handwriting is not at all like Henry's. And why would Henry have signed his own name to such an indiscretion?

on a different source, confirmed the arrest of an officer, "not, however, a high-ranking officer." On the same day, *La Patrie* spoke of an "Israelite officer serving with the Ministry of War." And it was *Le Soir* of October 31, which revealed to the public that "the officer in question was named Dreyfus, that he was 35 years old, that he was an artillery captain attached to the Ministry of War." At 10:00 P.M. of the same day, the Havas Agency confirmed the arrest of an "officer" without revealing his name. Thus, by November 1, when *La Libre Parole* announced in a first-page headline: "High Treason. Arrest of the Jewish Officer A. Dreyfus," the news was already known.

La Libre Parole had launched the campaign, which would continue to mount and had immediately identified the issue which would remain at its center—anti-Semitism. Under the byline "Commandant Z.," which concealed a habitual collaborator of Drumont,* *La Libre Parole* sketched the portrait and conducted the trial of the Jewish traitor: "We have, nevertheless, a consolation: it was not a true Frenchman who committed the crime."

As though lightning had struck, every newspaper ran the item and Dreyfus's name was heard in all quarters. A number of ministers, including Finance Minister Raymond Poincaré, thus learned of Dreyfus's arrest first through the newspaper. An emergency cabinet meeting was called. Gabriel Hanotaux, minister of foreign affairs, restated his objections, but Minister of War Mercier arrived with a copy of the bordereau. He summarized the reports of the experts, related the arrest, the dictation, the trembling of the hand and the handwriting. He had little difficulty in convincing the ministers, who preferred to be rid of the affair at once and the decision to begin judicial action was unanimous. Thus did *La Libre Parole* opportunely sustain Mercier in his determination. Henceforth the entire government would be committed to the pursuit and Mercier could no longer back out.

On the morning of November 1, Mathieu Dreyfus, urgently summoned by his sister-in-law, arrived in Paris. Tall, blond, with the blue eyes typical of the family, Mathieu seemed to be a man of consummate charm. He was happy, funny, sensitive, at times sentimental, and gifted with unlimited energy and indefatigable intelligence. He was two years older than Alfred, who was more than a brother to him, "the friend of his heart, the chosen friend." Mathieu Dreyfus had also dreamed of a military career but had failed at the École Polytechnique and resigned himself to entering the family business, which he directed with his brothers Jacques and Léon.[21] His refractory patriotism was ardent and uncompromising. When he arrived in Paris, the newspaper vendors were crying the news in the street: the Jewish officer Dreyfus had been arrested. Mathieu did not

* Papillaud or Biot.

for a moment imagine that his brother could be guilty. Lucie recounted to him, between sobs, the little she knew. On a visiting card given to her, du Paty had written these obliging words: "There is still hope. The Council of Ministers is meeting this morning. I will pass by in the course of the day." Mathieu dispatched his nephew to request an interview of Commandant du Paty—in the simple hope of understanding what had transpired. But du Paty arrived in the afternoon, followed by the archivist Félix Gribelin. Mathieu introduced himself. Du Paty explained: "The charges are devastating. There is not one thousandth of a chance that your brother is innocent. Moreover, he has already half-confessed to me." Du Paty pursued: "Your brother was leading a double life . . . he was seeing women. Your brother is a monster, a two-faced monster . . . he had a hole right here." And du Paty, with his finger, touched the middle of his forehead. Mathieu asked to see his brother to console him, interrogate him, confound him if he was a traitor! "Never, never!" exclaimed du Paty. "One word, a single word could mean a European war." Mathieu Dreyfus was convinced he was dealing with a madman. "I was afraid at the thought that my brother was in the hands of that man."[22]

There was no course left but to find a lawyer. The Dreyfus family knew by reputation René Waldeck-Rousseau, a great business lawyer, and in addition a politician of influence with the "centrist majority" then governing. Waldeck-Rousseau received Mathieu Dreyfus, who was introduced to him by Lucien Lévy-Bruhl, a philosophy teacher at the Lycée Louis-le-Grand and Mathieu's cousin. The lawyer seemed hesitant and asked for time to reflect. A few days later, he let it be known that to his great regret he could not accept the case. He no longer pleaded penal cases.[23] Above all, his political situation and his ambition put him in an embarrassing position. He would soon be a candidate for the Senate, and the affair could only prove to be a source of trouble. But he promised his advice and support, and warmly recommended his old friend Edgar Demange.* An expert on penal law, Demange had never been involved in politics. Respectful of the hierarchies (and, in particular, of the Army), a convinced Christian, he was considered to be on the right of the Parisian bar. "He belonged," Reinach assures us, "to that already aged generation of the Palais which espoused liberty and justice."[25] Demange would consent to defend Dreyfus only on the condition that he might first study the case. "If my conscience forbids me from defending your brother," he told Mathieu, "my refusal will be known and discussed; I will be your brother's first judge." But because the judicial inquiry had been secret and did not admit

* "Demange is a nasty, a very nasty individual," Colonel Jean Sandherr would confide to his friend Maurice Paléologue.[24] "He is in the hands of the Jews. At the Intelligence Service we have a file on him that could take him quite far."

the presence of a lawyer, Demange was temporarily unable to proceed. He would be able to visit Dreyfus and see the dossier of the case only on December 5 on the eve of a closed court hearing. It was then that the lawyer would study the meager dossier. A Catholic, conservative, and borne by numerous prejudices to the side of Dreyfus's accusers, he would see only the violations of the law, the fragility of the accusation, and the risk of a monstrous judicial error. He would become the lawyer for the Jewish officer, and remain so through all the ordeals, until the completion of his task.

13

This Jew Protected by Germany

While Mathieu Dreyfus was seeking ways to defend his brother from an unknown accusation, the press was unleashed. Throughout the month of November, and up until the trial, its pitch would continue to rise. The themes would not change: hatred of the Jew, hatred of Germany, love of the homeland and the Army which embodied it, and fear of treason. By November 5, *La Libre Parole, L'Autorité, Le Journal,* and *Le Temps* were assuring all that Dreyfus had simultaneously sold his services to both Germany and to Italy. The journalist Henri Rochefort and Edouard Drumont claimed to have obtained information about documents that had been sold. The "three million readers" of *Le Petit Journal* learned on November 2 that "Dreyfus's rank, his position, the matters of capital importance of which he was in charge . . . gave him the means of providing useful service to the enemy and inflicting irreparable harm on France."[1] In the following days, the accusations varied. Dreyfus was a frenetic gambler; he had a passion for women and gambling; he betrayed for the sake of an Italian spy, a woman of admirable beauty and noble family. Thanks to Dreyfus, *La Libre Parole* and *La Croix* were able to justify their campaign against the presence of Jewish officers in the Army: "He came into the Army with the intention of betrayal." "As a Jew and a German, he detests the French. . . . A German by taste and upbringing, a Jew by race, he did the job of a Jew and a German—and nothing else."[2] "In every nasty affair, there are always Jews. Nothing could be easier than to organize a good clean-up."[3] "One day, a Jew steals secret documents; the next day the same Jew grimaces as he sells papers to a German. The homeland is to be found wherever the money is good." *La Croix* knew no bounds: "Jewry . . . has rotted out everthing . . . it is a horrid cancer. . . . The Jews are vampires . . . leading France into slavery; . . . whether the order be to rob, corrupt, or betray our country, the Jew always leads the charge. . . ."[4] "The frightful Jews, vomited up into France by the ghettos of Germany, can barely jabber our language." Like *La Libre Parole*, *La Croix* demanded again that the Jews be banished, as did *Le Pèlerin*. *La Croix* drew up lists of Jewish officers, manifested particular interest in those who had changed their name, presented an inventory of Jewish journalists, and identified Jews in education and administration.[5] As for the wretch Dreyfus, it was rumored that he was protected by Joseph Reinach, a Jewish politician, a relative of the Rothschilds, and an agent of the banks—that higher international Jewry which had decided on the ruin of the French and the seizure of the land of France. "A ferocious joy," Reinach observed,[6] "is breaking out in the anti-Semitic newspapers." "This crime," affirmed *Le Pèlerin*, "is one of the most considerable events of recent times." In *La Croix*, Ernest Judet pretended to invoke extenuating circumstances on Dreyfus's behalf: "his hereditary stain, the curse weighing on his race." *Le Petit Journal* (whose principal administrator incidentally was a Jew) ran a major article on November 3: "He is not a Frenchman," which began with the words, "The people renounce Dreyfus as a compatriot. . . ."[7] Drumont vituperated in *La Libre Parole* of November 6: "The man does business in the manner of the sons of Sem. Were you to shoot him by accident, after slapping his face with his own epaulets, you still would not succeed in implanting in his brain ideas which he does not possess about honor, duty, and the homeland, which are legacies transmitted through innumerable generations. They cannot be improvised."

With Dreyfus's arrest, anti-Semitism was thus to undergo a brutal reinvigoration. Dreyfus justified everything that had been said, however poorly understood. The betrayal of the Jewish captain demonstrated the treachery of all Jews.* "Such is the fate of the type," observed *La Libre Parole*.[9] "Every Jew betrays his employer," claimed *Le Soleil du Midi*.[10] What

---

* The anti-Semitic press discovered—to its sorrow—that treason was a political crime and that Dreyfus would undoubtedly not face a death penalty—which was abolished in political cases by the Constitution of 1848. The newspapers and their readers (in letters to the editor) competed in imagining tortures appropriate for the "savage beast."[8]

could Mathieu Dreyfus conceivably do to stem a tide that seemed irresistible? He undertook a series of abortive initiatives: "My name sufficed to close many a door."[11] The single journalist who consented to receive him was Emile Bergerat of *Le Journal*, who demanded for a Jew "the right to be innocent." Mathieu, through friends, contacted the newspapers not caught up in the anti-Jewish hysteria: *Le Temps, Les Débats,* and *Le Figaro.* But in vain.

The campaign of the right-wing press was not directed solely against Jews. It sought to taint the minister of war and, beyond him, the government.* General Auguste Mercier was accused of having kept the investigation secret in the hope of stifling the Affair. Drumont and Rochefort let loose a flood of insults against Mercier. "The Minister of War is a cesspool who cannot rightfully be compared to the Augean stables, because no Hercules has as yet attempted to clean it out."[12] "There are almost 40,000 officers in the Army," Drumont commented, "and General Mercier chooses to confide the secret of our national defense to a born cosmopolite. Is this man Mercier not positively vile?"[13] "Are the Jews then sacred even when they betray?"[14] In *L'Intransigeant*, Rochefort denounced Mercier's "carelessness, his stupidity, his bad faith."[15] Mercier was resolved "to save the traitor, his quasi-accomplice." † The minister of war (and undoubtedly the prime minister) were worried. The government was fragile, and there was nothing to gain in appearing weak or hesitant. For Mercier there was even a great advantage in proving his determination. On November 17, breaking his silence, Mercier declared to *Le Journal* that the investigation against Dreyfus would be completed in ten days. *La Libre Parole* was all the more troubled in that Mercier, in his interview in *Le Journal*, seemed to be downplaying the Affair "in order to reassure public opinion."[16] Drumont's newspaper exploded:

> The Dreyfus Affair is taking a very nasty turn for the government. In the course of the evening, we questioned several high-ranking officers, all of whom answered with the following dilemma:
>
> • either General Mercier had Dreyfus arrested without proof, and in that case his lack of seriousness is a crime;
>
> • or he allowed the items establishing the treason to be stolen from

---

* In September 1894, in one of his numerous reports to his minister, Schwarzkoppen predicted the impending downfall of General Mercier. "He has lost the confidence of the government as well as of the Army," claimed Schwarzkoppen, who insinuated that Jules Roche, who was charged with defending the Ministry of War's budget, would probably be his successor.

† *La Libre Parole, La Croix,* and *L'Intransigeant* denounced Mercier's and General Félix Saussier's Jewish "friends." Saussier's ties to Maurice Weil were again used against him.

him, and in that case his lack of foresight verges on stupidity. In either case, General Mercier is unworthy of the position he is occupying. In his situation, one is as guilty for being stupid as for being criminal.[17]

Le Figaro, which disliked Mercier, hinted at the possibility of further incidents. The guilty officer would have communicated confidential items to several members of Parliament. It was at that point that General Mercier, already resolutely committed, but incited by the violence of the campaign and resolved to put it to his own use, accorded an interview on November 28 to Charles Leser in *Le Figaro*: "It is said that Captain Dreyfus had offered secret documents to the Italian government. This is an error. I cannot say more on the subject since the investigation is not over. The only thing that I can say on the record is that his guilt is absolute, certain." To the great joy of the right, the minister of war thus proclaimed Dreyfus's guilt.[18] Desperate, Mathieu Dreyfus rushed to see the lawyer René Waldeck-Rousseau, so that he might attempt to obtain from Mercier a denial. Mercier's intervention created the risk that the Court-Martial would be obliged to choose between the minister of war and Captain Dreyfus,[19] and the choice would necessarily be unequal. Shocked by the minister's public stand, Waldeck-Rousseau agreed to intervene with the prime minister. On November 29, an ambiguous note from the Havas Agency contradicted the interview in *Le Figaro*, but *Le Figaro* protested the denial. For General Mercier, Dreyfus's guilt had become a personal affair. Their destinies were now irrevocably joined.

The campaign against the minister of war that November 1894 was not the sole worry of the French government, which was clearly overwhelmed by "the Dreyfus Affair." On November 9, *La Patrie* announced that the Intelligence Service had seized letters addressed by Dreyfus to Colonel Maximilian von Schwarzkoppen, the German military attaché. The German ambassador was quite properly indignant. He was convinced that Schwarzkoppen, bound by his word, could have no dealings with any spy. In agreement with Schwarzkoppen—whose conscience was clear since he did not know Dreyfus—Count von Münster, the German diplomat, drew up a note which was published in *Le Figaro* of November 10: "Lieutenant Colonel von Schwarzkoppen has never received any letters from Dreyfus. He has never had any direct or indirect relations with him. If that officer is guilty of the crime of which he is accused, the German embassy is not involved in the affair."[20]

The Italian and Austrian governments similarly affirmed that their services had had no dealings with Dreyfus. Quite obviously, those declarations by "enemy" nations had no effect on public opinion. It was natural, observed the French press, that Germany "cover" its agents. When the minister of war claimed in the *Figaro* interview of November 28 that he possessed "certain proof" of Dreyfus's guilt, Schwarzkoppen deemed it prudent to send the Wilhelmstrasse a long report on the Dreyfus Affair, which would be transmitted by the ambassador: "Everything is hypothetical. Naturally, in the public at large there persists the idea that military attachés must be mixed up in stories of espionage, a circumstance which has given a sector of the French press the opportunity to recommend once again the elimination of the institution of military attachés. . . ."[21] Schwarzkoppen's message was both true and false. While it was true that he did not know Dreyfus, he was at the time "utilizing" other French officers. . . .

Count von Münster, who, for his part, did not know anything of what had transpired, continued to vent his indignation at the campaign launched against Germany. The Dreyfus Affair, he wrote to Berlin, is bringing "to a paroxysm among the French the malady which consists of seeing spies everywhere."[22] On November 28, he protested to the minister of foreign affairs, Gabriel Hanotaux: "I declared precisely to M. Hanotaux that I was asking him to protect me from such assaults, both myself and my embassy."[23] Hanotaux inquired of Maurice Paléologue, who oversaw relations with the Intelligence Service at the Ministry of Foreign Affairs.[24] And Paléologue, linked by friendship with Colonel Sandherr, head of the Intelligence Service, and who was in frequent contact with Commandant Henry and Captain Lauth at the Section of Statistics, confirmed to his minister that the letter attributed to Dreyfus had indeed been discovered in the German embassy. "All three of them told me that the letter had been found in pieces in Schwarzkoppen's waste basket." Was the old diplomat lying? Hanotaux—who detested the proliferating complications—reassured the German ambassador somewhat feebly, "Yes, the French government is revolted by the campaign, which has been exceeding all limits and cannot be tolerated."[25] And on November 29 and 30, two notes from the Havas Agency—the first having seemed too "weak" to the German government—strained, in vague terms, to safeguard the German embassy from jeopardy: "Certain newspapers persist in calling into question in various articles published on the subject of military espionage the embassies and foreign delegations of Paris. We are authorized to declare that the allegations concerning them are without foundation."[26]

The denial was so insipid that Count von Münster protested again. He would obtain a third variant on December 13, written as follows: "Several newspapers persist in publishing completely false information about the Dreyfus Affair. It is totally inaccurate that M. von Münster spoke to M.

Hanotaux on the subject for any other reason than to protest formally the allegations linking the German embassy to the affair. We are also in a position to deny the report that the minister of foreign affairs transmitted to Count von Münster any document or item of any sort related either to the Dreyfus Affair or to activities of espionage."*

In point of fact, the French government would have liked to calm matters and to reassure the understandably rattled German ambassador. But what could it do? Was not the press outside of the government's control? The French government sought to navigate between the imperatives of its foreign policy and those of its domestic policy. What could it do against those screaming treason? And what could Germany do to exonerate Dreyfus? Henceforth, every time the Germans would maintain that they had no relations with Dreyfus, they would only succeed in demonstrating their complicity. Nothing, after all, could be more natural than that Germany protect the Jew it was using. . . .

14

I Am Approaching the End of My Suffering

However unfavorably disposed he was to a trial based on the "elucubrations" of the Section of Statistics, General Félix Saussier, military governor of Paris, had no other choice on December 3 than to issue an order to open an investigation. Commandant Bexon d'Ormescheville, judge advocate of the first Court Martial, began hearings. In the course of the twelve sessions he would conduct from December 14 to 29, the inves-

---

* The negotiations between Hanotaux and Münster issuing in this new communique were difficult and even strained. Toward 10 P.M., Prime Minister Charles Dupuy and General Mercier went to the Elysée. At 11:30 P.M., the Havas Agency published the denial to which Ambassador von Münster had finally given his accord. But those several hours would become in General Mercier's imagination the "historic night" during which, he claimed, Germany was on the verge of declaring war and General de Boisdeffre was on alert, preparing to issue mobilization orders at any moment.[27] (See *infra*, pp. 107–10.)

tigating magistrate would repeat—frequently word for word—the questions that had been asked by Commandant du Paty de Clam.* Three interrogation sessions would be devoted to women Dreyfus had known—and particularly to one, Mme. Dida, whom Dreyfus appears to have loved and who was murdered by a young Russian.† Dreyfus was obliged to clarify the declarations of his colleagues at the École de Guerre and at the General Staff, which elaborated on his curiosity, his strange questions, his habits of rummaging about in search of documents, and lingering in offices. D'Ormescheville heard several officers describe Dreyfus as an intelligent man, endowed with a fabulous memory, but garrulous, obsequious, self-contented, indiscreet, and inclined to discussions of espionage. "Wherever he passed," d'Ormescheville would later conclude, "documents disappeared." But aside from the elucubrations of Alphonse Bertillon, the head of the Prefecture's Service of Judiciary Identity, there was nothing new or—above all—conclusive.‡ On December 3, d'Ormescheville submitted a report written in collaboration with du Paty. It was, in fact, an indictment which exploited, line by line, the few elements assembled and above all strained to eliminate anything that might contradict the accusation.§ The report submitted by Alfred Gobert, the handwriting expert—which exonerated Dreyfus—was "tainted," if not by worthlessness, by suspicion. Colonels Fabre and d'Abboville were promoted to the rank of "authorities in graphology." The dictation scene was evoked as follows: "As soon as Dreyfus perceived the object of the letter, his handwriting—which had been regular and normal until then—grew

* D'Ormescheville did not see the police investigation establishing that "Captain Dreyfus was unknown in Parisian gambling circles." Joseph Reinach maintained that the police prefect's "note," which was transmitted to Commandant Henry, had been confiscated by him. D'Ormescheville, in any event, was acquainted only with the two reports of Félix Guénée, the investigator with the Section of Statistics, dated November 4, and November 19. The second referred as follows to the prefect's conclusion: "for Police Headquarters to have responded negatively to the inquiry concerning Captain Dreyfus, it must have been satisfied with answers as negative as they were biased." Guénée explained at length that Police Headquarters was very poorly informed.

† During the Rennes trial, Dreyfus recopied d'Ormescheville's report, annotating it in the margins, paragraph by paragraph, refuting every accusation. Dr. Jean-Louis Lévy, Dreyfus's grandson, was kind enough to transmit to me a photocopy of Dreyfus's moving and significant manuscript.

‡ In particular there was a meticulous study of the record of Dreyfus's revenue and expenses and the accounts of the family factory in Mulhouse. Nothing out of the ordinary was discovered.[1]

§ The following sentence from the report, revealing as it does the prosecution's efforts, may be cited as an example: "The search of his residence yielded more or less the results that he claimed it would. But it is legitimate to suspect that if no letter, even from family members (except for those addressed to Mme. Dreyfus during their engagement) and no bill, even from tradesmen, was found in the search, it was because anything that might have been in any way compromising had been hidden or already destroyed."

irregular; he became agitated in a manner that was clear to those present."
Dreyfus's amorous associations were depicted in particularly somber col-
ors. He knew "a woman named Dida, older than himself, married, quite
wealthy, who was reputed to pay her lovers and who was murdered by
Wladimiroff," and also the "Austrian Dery, a kept woman despite her
advanced age and who has appeared for several years on the list of persons
suspected of espionage."* Dreyfus's indiscretion, his curiosity, "a sinister
attitude analogous to that of persons engaged in espionage," were judged
to be "a serious liability." Did he remain bitter at not being awarded the
rank he had coveted upon leaving the École de Guerre? "Since indiscretion
is at the core of his character, one need not be suprised that he knew the
secret grade given him by the general examiner." It was not established
that he had knowledge of the documents enumerated in the bordereau,
but he could have known them. The investigating magistrate concluded
his report as follows:

> Along with his extensive knowledge, Captain Dreyfus possesses a
> remarkable memory; he speaks several languages, including Ger-
> man, which he knows thoroughly, and Italian, of which he claims to
> have only a vague notion. He is moreover, of a rather supple—even
> obsequious—character, quite suited for relations of espionage with
> foreign agents. He was thus the perfect choice for the miserable
> and shameful mission that he either inspired or accepted and to
> which—quite luckily for France, perhaps—the discovery of his
> intrigues has put an end.

On December 4, on the basis of this "devastating report," Dreyfus was
sent before the first Court-Martial. The secrecy of the preliminary investigation was over, and the lawyer, Edgar Demange, was able to visit Dreyfus
and become acquainted with the case as of December 5. That same day, for
the first time, the prisoner was permitted to write to his wife:

> I cannot tell you all that I have suffered. . . . Do you remember
> when I told you how happy we were? Everything in life was smiling
> at us. . . . The truth will out in the end. My conscience is calm and at
> rest; it has nothing to reproach me. . . . I was devastated, struck to
> the floor of my somber prison, face to face with by conscience. I

---

* The police investigation also was extended to Mme. Kron, Countess de Montelijos, Mme.
de Moncy, who ran on Rue Saint-Lazare "one of the most assiduously frequented houses of
ill-repute in Paris," and Mme. Bodson, known "for her promiscuous tendencies." These
various "leads" appear to have been useless.[2] In the aforementioned manuscript, Dreyfus
refuted the suspicions concerning his personal life. He denied most of the liaisons with which
he was reproached, and claimed that the others were over by 1888.

knew moments of madness, even raving, but my sense remained
alert. It told me: Head high, and look the world in the eye.
Strengthened by your conscience, arise and walk tall. . . . I kiss you
a thousand times over—as I love you, as I adore you. A thousand
kisses to the children. I don't dare tell you any more about them;
tears come to my eye at the thought of them.[3]

Henceforth, he would write daily to Lucie:

> To have worked all my life with the sole aim of wreaking revenge
> against the infamous ravisher who abducted our beloved Alsace,
> and to see oneself accused of betraying this country, no, my dar-
> ling, my mind refuses to comprehend. . . .
> Oh beloved France, you whom I have loved with all my soul, all
> my heart. You to whom I have devoted all my energy, all my
> intelligence, how could they accuse me of so frightful a crime?[4]

Dreyfus recognized his personal shortcomings, the trouble they may
have caused him:

> My somewhat haughty reserve, my freedom of speech and judg-
> ment, my lack of indulgence are at present causing me the greatest
> harm. I am neither spineless, nor cunning, nor a flatterer. . . .
> What I can affirm is that I have always tread the path of duty and
> honor. . . . Money is nothing, honor is all. . . . Tell Mathieu that I
> depend on him in this task; it is not beyond his capacities. If he has
> to move heaven and earth, the wretch must be found.[5]

Throughout his correspondence, Dreyfus would use the same words
over and over again. He was innocent. He valued above all else his beloved
country and the sentiment of his honor. He adored his wife and his
children, loved his family. The truth must be discovered, and honor, the
pride of his name, the respect of all, and happiness be restored to him.
The values in which he believed would never be questioned, not even in
the deepest despair. In his entire correspondence, there is not a single
mention of the Jews, nor is the drama in which he was caught up ever
attributed to the fact that he was Jewish.* He was French, Alsatian, the
head of a family.

* See however the account of Commandant Forzinetti, the Keeper of the prison.[6] Upon being
brought back to his cell after the Court Martial's verdict, he was alleged to have shouted: "My
only crime is being born a Jew."

It was on December 19 that the first Court-Martial was to meet to judge the case of Captain Dreyfus. Neither du Paty's inquest nor d'Ormeschevil-le's investigation had contributed any substantial elements to support the accusation. The central items were still the bordereau and the comparison of handwritings. But those comparisons were by no means conclusive. Even if one attempted to discredit the expert Alfred Gobert, two out of the five remaining experts refused to attribute the bordereau to Dreyfus. Demange was a formidable lawyer. Ought they then to fear an acquittal? The anxiety was mounting at the Section of Statistics and at the General Staff among all those deeply implicated in the affair. General Mercier, minister of war, himself had reasons to worry. In an article in *L'Autorité* of December 13, Granier de Cassagnac, a writer of the extreme right (and a close friend of Demange at the time), put the dilemma as follows: "The Dreyfus Affair is stuck to General Mercier's back like the centaur's tunic to the shoulders of Hercules. . . . If Dreyfus is acquitted, the Minister goes under; that is beyond doubt, since he would be crushed beneath the frightening responsibility for having initiated so frivolously so grave a matter. But if Dreyfus is convicted . . . Mercier takes on greatness and, profiting from the trial, passes for the savior of the country."[7] *Le Figaro* of December 19 says as much in other terms: "If through some extraordinary circumstances he had been deceived, the poor general would become forthwith a wretch, a traitor, a man of infamy deserving of prison." The thought of Dreyfus's acquittal raised frightening prospects.

The Section of Statistics did not lose any time. By order of Colonel Sandherr, Commandant Henry went over all the documents which had arrived at the service in recent years. He studied them carefully with the aim of discovering those that could be used against Dreyfus to "illuminate" the affair of the bordereau.* The note written by the German military attaché, Colonel Maximilian von Schwarzkoppen, to Alessandro Paniz-zardi, the Italian military attaché, which appears to have been intercepted the previous spring through the ordinary track, was quickly retained:† "I would be back in 8 days. Enclosed are the master plans of Nice which that scoundrel D . . . gave me for you. . . ." The text's meaning was not clear. But the initial D. could be applied to Dreyfus.‡ Schwarzkoppen's

---

* Sandherr periodically inquired of his friend Maurice Paléologue, in charge of "restricted affairs" at the Ministry of Foreign Affairs, whether there was not anything he might use from secret intelligence information. He sent Commandant Henry to see Paléologue. "I spread my files before Commandant Henry," Paléologue relates. "He could no more glean anything of use from them than I could."[8]

† See the complete text of this note, whoch would later be referred to under the rubric "Scoundrel D," *supra* pp. 50–51.

‡ The document in fact referred to "Dubois," the name given by Schwarzkoppen and

"memorandum,"* which seemed to be connected to the bordereau, was also retained. To these was added another letter from Panizzardi to Schwarzkoppen, intercepted before February 1894, which would subsequently be called "the Davignon letter " or the "letter of calls."†

> My dear Bugger,
> I am forwarding to you you know what. As soon as you left, I studied the question of those called and saw that certain questions of address, etc., are all subordinated to a major one whose direction is this.
> For a partial call-up, limited, that is, to several regions, are the manifests published only in the affected regions or throughout the State?
> I spoke again to Colonel Davignon, and that is why I am asking you, should you have the opportunity to broach this question with your friend, to do so in particular, so that Davignon not be apprised of it—at any rate, he would not respond—for it must never be known that one attaché has dealings with another. Farewell, my little dog. Everything.

After an initial search of all the files, that is all that was retained.[10] A mere pittance; one would have to do better. Now it happened that François Guénée, the former police agent serving with the Section of Statistics, had protracted dealings with the Marquis de Val-Carlos, a Spanish nobleman and deputy military attaché of the Spanish embassy in Paris.‡ Val-Carlos had supplied abundant information to the Section of Statistics on the subject of military attachés, their lives and loves, and, of course, Schwarzkoppen and Panizzardi. Guénée had extracted ample material for two reports, dated March 28 and 30, 1894, which were communicated to the minister of war, as was the custom, in the form of an "information bulletin."[11] One wonders whence sprang the idea of falsifying Guénée's two reports, of interpolating material with the aim of implicating Dreyfus. Into his old reports of the spring of 1894, Guénée, in any event, inserted

---

Panizzardi to the agent delivering "master plans." The Section of Statistics knew that the document was connected to the longstanding traffic in "master plans" of which Dreyfus could not be seriously suspected. But the initial D was too valuable for the document not to be exploited.

* *Supra* pp. 52–53.

† Du Paty would prepare a commentary on the letter for the Court-Martial, maintaining that "your friend" was none other than Dreyfus. See *infra* p. 96. The letter, which had been transmitted to the minister of war in February 1894, had aroused no particular emotion at the time.[9]

‡ Several members of the Marquis de Val-Carlos's family were French and he made no secret

new sentences intended to incriminate "an officer of the General Staff" who could be none other, of course, than Captain Dreyfus.

The following sentences, attributed to Val-Carlos, were thus added to the original texts, which were reedited, moreover, to give the new document a measure of coherence:

> Tell Commandant Henry on my behalf (who may repeat it to the Colonel [Sandherr]) that there is reason to double the surveillance of the Ministry of War, for it emerges from my last conversation with Captain von Susskind that the German attachés have in the offices of the General Staff an officer who is informing them admirably well. Find out, Guénée, if I knew the name, I'd tell you. . . .*

> Someone in the Ministry of War, almost certainly an attaché, has tipped off the German military attachés. . . . That is further proof that you have one or several wolves in your sheep-pen. . . . Find out, I can't tell you often enough, because I am certain of it. . . .†

The German military attachés, it therefore appeared, had "an officer who [was] informing them admirably well" in the offices of the General Staff. A convenient confirmation indeed of the accusation, even if Dreyfus were not expressly named. There remained only to change the dates of the two reports and to substitute them for the originals.‡

As Marcel Thomas has observed,[12] Guénée could not have acted alone in initiating and assuming responsibility for such forgeries. It is almost certain that Henry and Sandherr organized the cosmetic effort, which was executed by the Service. It is uncertain if the Ministry of War was consulted or informed, but we may venture that it probably was.[13] On that day in November 1894 on which the "Guénée forgeries" were fabricated, the Section of Statistics embarked on a criminal path. A complicity—which later events would only reinforce—was established among Sandherr, Henry, Guénée, no doubt Gribelin and Lauth, and perhaps also General Mercier. They had threatening information on each other, and would henceforth be constrained to solidarity.

While the Section of Statistics was secretly fabricating a dossier against Dreyfus, Mathieu and Lucie were attempting to organize his defense. It

---

of his Francophilic sentiments. Dreyfus's partisans would subsequently refer to him as the *rastaquouère* [i.e., the South American "sharpster"].
* Sentence added in a revision of the report of March 28.
† Sentence added in a revision of the report of March 30.
‡ They would be dated March 28 and April 28.

was known that the Ministry of War favored a debate in closed session, which the defense had every reason to fear. Edgar Demange approached his friend, the lawyer René Waldeck-Rousseau, who promised to broach the subject with the president of the Republic, and did. Joseph Reinach would attempt to do the same, but both to no avail. For the Dreyfus Affair was beginning to poison the life of President Jean Casimir-Périer. Spoiled by fortune, tolerating adversity rather poorly, he had long hesitated to announce his candidacy for the highest office of the state. "He had agreed to become president of the Republic despite his tears," yielding to the pressures of his mother and his friend Burdeau.[14] Now he felt himself surrounded by enemies. He was the butt of fierce attacks in the left-wing press: "usurer, robber, mountebank, exploiter of the workers."[15] He sensed both the mounting disfavor and the hatred of the people, which he did not believe he deserved. He was looking for an exit, as he confided to his friend Reinach on October 12. The Dreyfus Affair proved to him that power was being exercised behind his back. There remained for him only to resign. "Casimir-Périer," observed Reinach, "is letting himself go. . . ."[16] He left matters to Charles Dupuy, the prime minister, who in turn left them to the minister of war, General Mercier. And Mercier gave free rein to Sandherr and du Paty.

As for Mathieu Dreyfus, he knocked at every door in the hope of helping his brother. He sought out character witnesses. General de Dionne, former commandant of the École Supérieure de Guerre, received him courteously but was not willing to testify: the "excellent" evaluations in his record would have to suffice.* General Niox, Dreyfus's former teacher, refused. Commandant Givre, under whose orders Dreyfus had served, responded with an insulting letter. Commandant Clément resisted, then consented to appear. Only Commandant de Barberin responded without hesitation: "It is my duty; I will come." At the clerk's office of the Court-Martial, Mathieu Dreyfus convinced the clerk, Vallecalle, to grant him a glimpse of the bordereau.† "I was shocked," Mathieu recalled. "The handwriting of the document bore only a vague resemblance to my brother's."[18] Finally, Mathieu and his brother Léon, no longer knowing at which door to knock, armed with several letters of recommendation, decided to see Colonel Jean Sandherr, head of the Intelligence Service. Sandherr agreed to receive them in his home on rue Léonce-Raynaud. He was quite cordial, and expressed sympathy for the

---

* Mathieu Dreyfus, *L'Affaire telle que je l'ai vécue*.[17] General de Dionne confirmed to Mathieu Dreyfus the incident of the "low grade" given to Alfred Dreyfus on his final exam by General Bonnefond because he was a Jew. See *supra*, p. 22.

† Only Edgar Demange had access to the file, and he was unable to have any of it photographed.

family, but refused to discuss the case. "Whether my brother be convicted or acquitted," Mathieu assured him, "I will devote my whole life, our whole fortune, to discovering the truth." It was an imprudent comment, to say the least; Colonel Sandherr would one day sue for attempted bribery. The two brothers, he would claim, had offered him money. "And yet," wrote Mathieu Dreyfus, "we were confident! Seven loyal and honest officers will not convict a colleague on the basis of a scrap of paper of suspicious origin, whose attribution is contested since two experts out of five affirm that it is not the hand of Captain Dreyfus."[19]

From his prison cell, Dreyfus too was regaining hope. On December 15 he wrote to his wife: "My confidence is absolute. . . . I will be dealing with soldiers who will hear me and understand me. The certainty of my innocence will enter into their hearts. . . ."[20] On the eve of the opening of the proceedings, he wrote her:

> I am approaching the end of my suffering, of my martyrdom. Tomorrow I shall appear before my judges, my head high and my soul at ease. The ordeal I have just undergone, a terrible ordeal if ever there was one, has exhausted my soul. I will return to you better than I was. . . . Dedicated to my country, to which I have devoted all my energy, all my intelligence, I have nothing to fear. . . . Sleep sweetly, my darling, and don't be at all worried. Think only of the joy we will experience in finding ourselves soon in each other's arms. . . .[21]

"I am approaching the end of my suffering. . . ." "Sleep sweetly, my darling. . . ." But the minister of war was preparing for the hearing and the Section of Statistics was working night and day.

15

This Man Is the Traitor

The proceedings opened at noon on December 19, 1894. The Court-Martial was presided over by Colonel E. Maurel and did not include a single Artillery officer. Six judges were from the Infantry, and the seventh from the Cavalry.* Not without difficulty did Mathieu Dreyfus and one of his brothers manage to find a place in the small room of the Prison of Cherche-Midi, amid a crowd that remained standing. "Bring in the accused," ordered Colonel Maurel. Alfred Dreyfus came forward, apparently quite calm, severe, "his back a bit stooped over, his complexion dull, the fixed, near-sighted stare from behind the perennial pince-nez, the close-cropped blond hair already graying."[1] He stopped and saluted the Court-Martial. The presiding judge asked him about his civil status. "Your age?" "Thirty-five." "Your place of birth?" "Mulhouse, Alsace, Colonel." At the judge's invitation, he was seated.

Barely had the court clerk Vallecalle finished calling the witnesses than Commandant André Brisset, the prosecutor, demanded a closed session. Dreyfus's lawyer was prepared for as much. For several days, the debate over a closed session had been taken up in the press. *La Patrie*, *L'Intransigeant*, *L'Eclair*, and above all *Le Petit Journal* were relentless. "A closed session is our impregnable refuge against Germany. . . . A closed session will shield us from all the madmen who dream of troubling the peace of Europe."[2] *Le Siècle*, *Le Figaro*, and *L'Echo de Paris* took the opposite position. "A closed session would only serve to prolong the scandal," wrote *Le Figaro* of December 11. Edgar Demange had no illusions. He had prepared his conclusions—which were clearly intended to influence the press—whose sole aim was to say publicly that Dreyfus was being tried on the basis of a single piece of evidence, which had been denied by him, and

---

* Commandants Florentin and Patron, Lieutenant Colonel Echemann, and Captains Jules Roche and Martin Freystaetter belonged to the Infantry; Commandant Gallet to the Cavalry. Freysataetter was born in the annexed province of Lorraine. Of the three deputy judges, one was from the Artillery: Colonel Altmayer. The two others, Commandant Curé and Captair Thibaudin, belonged to the Infantry.

whose authenticity was contested.[3] He attempted to read his conclusions, but was immediately interrupted by Colonel Maurel. "You are arguing the case, Maître." "Whether I am or not," responded Demange, "do you accept my conclusions?" "File them without reading them," cried the prosecutor. And since Demange continued, the judge commanded, "I order you to stop; the request for a closed session is becoming a joke." The lawyer protested. "For seven months the honor of an officer of the French Army has been exposed without defense to the most outrageous polemics." The presiding judge rose. "By virtue of my discretionary powers, I order the Court to withdraw." Demange's voice was lost as the judges donned their caps. They were to return in a quarter of an hour. Unanimously, they decided that the proceedings would continue in closed session.

The public slowly emptied out of the chamber. Mathieu Dreyfus departed as well. There remained only the judges, the prosecutor Brisset, the defense lawyer Demange, and the defendant. In addition, there remained two witnesses whose presence was not altogether normal: police Prefect Louis Lépine and Commandant Georges Picquart, commissioned by the minister of war and the chief of the General Staff to report on the trial to them. Picquart observed Dreyfus. The defendant was answering the questions of the presiding judge in a monotonous voice that the police prefect would describe as "colorless, vacant, indolent,"[4] a voice that suppressed intonations, masked emotions, and occasionally cracked when raised. Colonel Maurel "interrogated him, without benevolence, without brutality—as he should have."[5] It appears that the defendant's responses, in their clarity and precision, were making an impression on the Council.[6] The feebleness of the indictment would soon be evident.

Witnesses were heard on December 19, 20, and 21. "The proceedings," observed Lépine, "are languishing in the dull, gray register of a vulgar affair."[7] General Gonse, Colonel Fabre, and Lieutenant Colonel d'Abboville began to discomfit Dreyfus. Du Paty, who was alternately as agitated as a clown and as stiff as a Prussian officer, explained his initiatives and recounted the scene of the dictation. He revealed to the astonished tribunal how, during the interrogations at the Prison of Cherche-Midi, he measured the "emotion betraying Dreyfus's guilt" from "the almost imperceptible movement of the extremity of his foot" as he sat with his legs crossed! Commandant Hubert Joseph Henry, delegated by the minister of war to enter a deposition on behalf of the Section of Statistics, applied himself to demonstrating Dreyfus's guilt. The archivist Félix Gribelin, drawing on the tales collected by the investigator, François Guénée, described in myriad detail the sinister habits of the defendant. His curiosity, indiscretion, and all too frequent and poorly explained absences from service were also submitted as evidence.* Whereupon there ensued a procession of Dreyfus's former colleagues at the École de Guerre and the General Staff. Most of them sketched an unpleasant portrait, but a few, bound by their oath, evoked his virtues. Mercier-Milon testified that he was always "a faithful and scrupulous soldier." Tocanne, his classmate at the École de Guerre, affirmed that he "believed him incapable of a felony." Dreyfus intervened frequently, contributing precise details. Lépine believed an acquittal probable,[9] and Commandant Georges Picquart informed the minister that "the affair was proceeding rather poorly."

Something had to be done. Commandant Henry secretly asked one of the judges, Commandant Gallet, his personal friend, that he be called back to the stand and interrogated by the presiding magistrate about the presence of a treasonous officer in the Second Bureau. The judge complied with the maneuver. Henry returned to the stand, and speaking in a loud voice, proclaimed that this time he was obliged to tell everything. As early as March, an "honorable person" alerted his service to the fact that an officer in the Ministry was committing treason. In June, the same person repeating his warning: the traitor was an officer in the Second Bureau. Whereupon Commandant Henry turned toward Dreyfus, pointed at him theatrically, and said, "This man is the traitor."[10] Dreyfus stood up. Livid with anger, he protested, demanding the name of the informer. But Henry had made a great impression. Edgar Demange interceded, evoked the full horror of an anonymous denunciation, and insisted that Henry tell the whole truth. "With the frank and rude gesture of a trooper," Henry then slapped his peaked cap. "There are some secrets in an officer's head that his cap does well to ignore."[11] Dreyfus, still standing, continued to protest. Colonel Maurel addressed the witness with solemnity, "Do you affirm on your honor that the treasonous officer was Captain Dreyfus?" Henry lifted his hand toward the painting of Christ hanging on the wall, and cried out in a resounding voice, "I swear to it." That deposition was "the stroke of the bludgeon that brought Dreyfus down."[12] "It was the apparition of retribution incarnate," Lépine would say. Only Commandant Picquart—but he already knew, no doubt, that Henry's intervention had been prepared—found him "extremely theatrical." A man of the people, risen through the ranks, to all appearances loyal and unmannered, an extremely courageous soldier (as the Legion of Honor on his chest attested), Henry communicated to the military judges a conviction of total sincerity.[13]

On the following day, the experts were heard. In novel jargon, "bris-

* A statement on "Captain Dreyfus's absences during his time at the École du Guerre" had been prepared on November 20, 1894.[8]

tling with barbarous words," the head of the Prefecture's Service of Judiciary Identity, Alphonse Bertillon, presented the thesis of a "self-forgery."* He referred to Dreyfus as the "culprit," and commented on his fabulous diagram to the bewilderment of the judges. He testified that Dreyfus had made use of at least three specimens of handwriting: his own, his brother's, and his wife's. "I attached no importance to his deposition," Alfred Dreyfus would write, "for it seemed to me to be the work of a madman."[14] But the defendant committed the error of permitting himself—uncharacteristically—a joke. "Let the witness swear that he in fact saw me write the bordereau." The irony produced a negative impression. The other experts merely repeated their conclusions. The handwriting expert, Alfred Gobert—who stuck firmly to his conclusions, which were favorable to Dreyfus—manifestly irritated the prosecution.

Next came the character witnesses for the defense. Alsatians attesting to the honorability of the family and the patriotism of the captain; officers† who agreed, not without courage, to say that Dreyfus had always been a good and loyal soldier; finally, Rabbi Dreyfuss‡ of Paris, the philosopher Lucien Lévy-Bruhl, the physician Vaucaire, and the industrialist Arthur Amson all expressed their esteem for the officer, the man, and the father.

At the session on October 21, Commandant Brisset read the indictment, a tiresome rehash of d'Ormescheville's report. At that juncture, Alfred Dreyfus was confident of an acquittal, but Edgar Demange was less assured. He told Mathieu, "If an order has not been issued to convict him, he will be acquitted this evening." What preoccupied the old lawyer was less the session than the agitation surrounding it, the comings and goings of du Paty, Sandherr, and Picquart, the long conversations he could see or imagine, and the barely concealed exchanges among the prosecution witnesses, the accusers, and the judges. Demange was indeed afraid. On the afternoon of December 22, he argued for three hours. First, he applied himself to demonstrating that the bordereau could not possibly be written by Dreyfus. Then, disputing all the gossip that had been heard, he proved that Dreyfus had no motive and could not have committed treason. "An attorney for jury trials," observed Joseph Reinach, "too inclined to

---

* See *supra* p. 73.

† Colonel Clément, Commandants de Barbarin, Ruffey, and Leblond, Captains Meyer and Devaux. Du Paty intervened again in the proceedings when the witnesses insisted on the absurdity of a crime without motive. He explained that one of the family factories had recently burned down and that the family had received a large insurance indemnity . . . which might well have been disguised payment for treason. Dreyfus grew indignant at such insane slander.[15]

‡ Sandherr related to Maurice Paléologue Rabbi Dreyfus's testimony, mocking his Yiddish accent: "I am the Chief Rabbi of Paris. I don't know anything about this matter, but I have known the family of the accused for a long time and I consider it to be an honest family."[16]

pleading on behalf of criminals, he abided by the precept of Lachaud, who had been his master: Provoke a doubt in the minds of the jurors and let the doubt develop. But the military jurors proved more simpleminded than their civilian counterparts; doubt alone did not convince them."* "Acquittal seemed certain to me," Dreyfus would write.[18] At the invitation of the presiding magistrate, the defendant pronounced a few words: "a son of Alsace the French. . . ," he could not have committed the most hideous of crimes. And the judges withdrew to their chambers.

At seven o'clock in the evening, in Mathieu Dreyfus's apartment on rue Châteaudun where family and friends had gathered, the anxiety was mounting. The deliberations appeared to be lasting longer than expected. The silent vigil continued. As for what was going on. . . . Commandant du Paty de Clam delivered to the president of the Court-Martial a sealed envelope on behalf of the minister of war with "the most compelling moral imperative possible" to transfer its contents to the judges during their deliberation. The minister of war did not mention this secret communication to anyone: not to the president of the Republic, not to the prime minister, not to any other member of the government. Obeying the "moral" imperative he had received, Colonel Maurel broke the seal and opened the envelope. Inside he found the several pieces of evidence collected by the Section of Statistics to sustain the accusation against Dreyfus, as well as a commentary prepared—at the behest of the minister of war—by du Paty de Clam in collaboration with Colonel Sandherr to facilitate a comprehension of the documents and their attribution to Dreyfus.[19] Colonel Maurel read certain of the items, and had Lieutenant Colonel Echemann read others; they were passed from hand to hand. Not a single judge appears to have suspected that such a communication, concealed from the defense, was in violation of the law, the Military Code, or common equity. But did they really need it to sustain their opinion?† The reading of the documents, and the commentaries and discussions they elicited, all took time. And indeed, the deliberations were lasting longer than expected.

At 7:30 P.M. the telephone rang in Mathieu Dreyfus's home. It announced the dreadful news. The Court-Martial had unanimously found

---

* Joseph Reinach, *Histoire de l'Affaire Dreyfus.*[17] Against Labori's advice, Demange would resort to that dangerous strategy again at Rennes (See *infra* p. 424ff). Moreover, he committed the error of not responding to the military prosecutor's line (brandishing the bordereau): "If I have no other proof than this letter, it still remains and it is devastating for the accused."

† "I read only one document," Colonel Maurel would say at Rennes, "and I did not listen to the others, because my mind was made up." "The secret documents had only a minor influence," Captain Freystaetter would tell the High Court of Appeal. But the "scoundrel D" document appears to have remained—with the passing of time—in the judges' memories.[20]

Dreyfus guilty. It sentenced him to perpetual deportation in a fortified enclosure and to military degradation.*

It was Edgar Demange who brought the news to the convict. Demange was sobbing; Dreyfus restrained his tears. He was brought into the vestibule of the courtroom. He was erect, his arms against his body in military posture. Night fell. The clerk read the verdict to him by candlelight. Captain Dreyfus did not move, but remained stiff—as though dead.

He was taken to the infirmary, and there his despair burst forth. He hurled himself against the walls, tried to fracture his skull and his limbs. Guards were obliged to restrain him physically. His officer's cowl was forced over his head like a straitjacket, and he was taken through the already empty streets back to prison.

Mathieu Dreyfus went immediately to see Demange. The lawyer seemed undone, ravaged by the disaster. "I implored your brother not to kill himself; I told Forzinetti, who promised to watch over him." Mathieu asked, begged: "What happened? How were they able to convict him, to convict him unanimously?" Demange explained: "When I began my plea, Colonel Maurel let everyone see himself opening a book . . . the others seemed indifferent . . . then I regained hope. . . . What happened in the deliberation room? I don't know. No, I don't understand; it's horrible." And without conviction, the lawyer added, "He must sign his request for an appeal."

But Commandant Georges Picquart was already bringing the good news to the minister of war, General Mercier. The minister awaited it in full dress, for he was expected at an official dinner at the Elysée Palace. Mercier received the news without uttering a single word. "The poor man!" muttered Mme. Mercier. For the minister of war, it was a great victory. He would dine with the heartiest of appetites.

---

* Once judgment was passed, Presiding Judge Maurel returned the envelope containing the secret documents to Commandant du Paty, who immediately returned them to the Section of Statistics.

16

The Affair Is Over

The day after sentencing, the entire press, from the right to the left, expressed its satisfaction.* Maurice Paléologue took note of the "approbation, relief, and joy, a triumphant, vindictive, and ferocious joy."[1] The traitor, the German, was found guilty, by unanimous verdict.† From the right to the left, not a person could be found to defend Dreyfus. The verdict is a veritable source of relief for all concerned, wrote *Le Matin* the day after. And Georges Clemenceau, in *La Justice* of December 25, seemed to be expressing the common point of view. "He has no relative, no wife, no child, no love of anything, no human—or even animal—ties, nothing but an obscene soul and an abject heart." On December 25, General Mercier, minister of war, proposed to the Chamber of Deputies a law reinstituting the death penalty for treason, and Deputy Jean Jaurès intervened in the debate, maintaining forcefully that Dreyfus could have and should have been sentenced to death. "Captain Dreyfus, convicted of treason in a unanimous verdict, did not receive the death sentence. As opposed to those results, the country sees that simply soldiers are shot without pardon or pity for a momentary lapse or act of violence. . . . We have the duty to ask ourselves whether the nation's justice should remain unarmed in the event that abominable acts analogous to that committed by Captain Dreyfus were to recur."[3] *La Libre Parole* had assured its readers that "all of Jewry was consolidating behind the traitor."[4] But the Jews of France—in their stupefaction—remained silent. The large majority of Jews, the writer Charles Péguy would later note with sadness, kept silent about Dreyfus because they feared trouble—or "simply inconvenience."[5] "They were afraid of the blows. They had received so many. They would rather one didn't talk to them about him." But toward the end of 1894, it was not fear that predominated, but the strength of the evidence. How

---

* Not only the extremist press, *La Libre Parole* and *La Croix*, but *Le Temps, Les Débats, La Paix,* and *Le Figaro.*
† On December 24, the German Chancery issued a further statement recalling again that "the German embassy has never had the slightest direct or indirect relation with Dreyfus."[2]

would one declare one's solidarity with a traitor? At the conclusion of a trial without irregularity, Dreyfus had been unanimously found guilty by seven French officers. What room was there for doubt? How would a Frenchman, a Jewish Frenchman, make common cause with a spy who had sold to Germany intelligence of the greatest importance? Dreyfus had betrayed everything—including the Jews themselves.

Alfred Dreyfus's despair knew no limits. "I turned over in my mind the most extravagant plans."[6] The night after sentencing he was close to suicide. The next day he wrote Lucie: "For you alone, my poor darling, do I manage to struggle. It is the thought of you which stops my arm."[7] In the succeeding days, he sent her several letters a day. He evoked their past happiness: "How happy we were, my darling. Everything in life seemed to smile at us: fortune, love, adorable children, a united family, everything . . . am I then branded with some fatal seal?"[8] He evoked those outside who hurled insults at him. "Those people are right: they have been told that I am a traitor. Ah! how the horrid word 'traitor' tears my heart out!"[9] "Cry out my innocence, cry it out with all the strength of your lungs, cry it out on the rooftops so that the walls shake."

Without any illusions, he signed a petition for an appeal—which could be granted only because of procedural irregularities, Maître Boivin-Champeaux, who composed the written statement, refused to vouch for it orally. Commandant Romain, the prosecutor, was steadfast. "Were there a hundred procedural irregularities, I would still end up rejecting the petition. No appeal. Never."* The petition was rejected December 31. During the night from December 31 to January 1, Alfred wrote a long letter to Lucie. "Midnight is striking at the very moment I light my candle; I can't sleep . . . it seems to me that you are near me as in the wonderful evenings of happy memory." He spent hours crying and was unable to eat.†

On December 31, Commandant du Paty de Clam came to see Dreyfus for the last time—on behalf of the minister of war, he said.[11] That strange initiative would later be justified by General Mercier. "The government still had certain powers concerning the application of the sentence . . . the choice of the place of deportation, for instance. . . . The government was prepared to show some indulgence if he were willing to enter onto the path of repentance, if, in particular, he said which documents had passed into German possession through his agency."

* There was, of course, not the slightest trace in the case file of the communication of secret documents during the deliberations of the judges. Did the Revision Council have no knowledge of it? In any event any chance of an appeal seemed excluded.
† On December 23, 1894, Chief Rabbi Zadoc Kahn had asked General Félix Saussier for authorization "to visit in his capacity as a rabbi the unfortunate Captain Dreyfus and bring him the succor of religion."[10] Authorization was denied.

Du Paty attempted to obtain a confession through some imprudence on Dreyfus's part. But once again, he declared his innocence. "If you are innocent," yelled du Paty, "you are the greatest martyr of all time," and then left.[12] Dreyfus wrote immediately thereafter to the minister of war, recounting the interview, and repeated that he expected no special favor, only the demonstration of his innocence.[13]

> Mister Minister,
>
> I have received, by your order, a visit from Commandant du Paty de Clam, to whom I declared once again that I was innocent, and that I had not even committed the slightest imprudence. I have been convicted, and have no special mercy or pardon to ask of you. But in the name of my honor, which I hope will be restored to me one day, I have the duty to implore you to be willing to continue your search. After I am gone, keep the search alive. That is the sole mercy that I request.

Finally, his wife was permitted to visit him on January 2, 1895. She had not seen him since that Monday, October 15, when he left home, after embracing her, to go to the Ministry of War. The meeting took place in the visiting room of the prison: they were separated by two grated partitions. "Our conversation through the bars did me well. I was trembling on my feet as I came down . . . even now my hand is still not firm. Continue, my dear wife, let us make the world respect us for our demeanor and our courage. . . . I want my honor and I shall have it: no obstacle will stop me."[14]

Lucie Dreyfus wrote to General Saussier, the military governor, and begged to be allowed to meet her husband under conditions less cruel. The governor authorized Ferdinand Forzinetti, the director of the Prison of Cherche-Midi, to let the couple see each other in whatever manner he wished, but under his responsibility.* Thereafter they would meet in the office of the prison director and in his presence. They could speak at length and were allowed to embrace. Lucie made her husband promise that he would not kill himself—"for the sake of herself, of their children, and of honor itself." On January 3, Dreyfus was informed that he would be degraded in the courtyard of the École Militaire on the morning of January 5.

With the conclusion of the atrocious ceremony, he was no longer an officer. He was nothing more than a traitor. For several days, he was imprisoned at La Santé Prison. He and his wife saw each other once again

---

* Commandant Forzinetti wrote on January 3, 1895, to the Military Governor's headquarters, recalling that "relatives of many convicted men had obtained the privilege of using the 'special' visitor's room and that it could be granted to Mme. Dreyfus."[15]

between bars in the visiting room.They exchanged letters of love and desperation. They cried and asked each other forgiveness for their weaknesses. Dreyfus continued not to bear any grudges, to believe himself without enemies. "I can very well excuse the anger," he wrote, "the rage of an entire noble people who are told that there is a traitor. . . ."[16] The rage of an entire noble people? "What have I to do with this Dreyfus?" Maurice Barrès would write. "He was not born to live socially. Alone, in some fallen forest, a tree branch stretches toward him. That he may hang himself from it."[17]

He did not hang himself, but attempted to live. During the night of January 17, he was brutally awakened.[18] He was ordered to dress and clapped into handcuffs, then taken in a prison car to the Gare d'Orléans. A car of narrow cells, intended for transporting convicts, was waiting for him in the station. Each cell had the dimensions of a seated man. With handcuffs on his wrists and irons on his legs, he was taken through the icy night to La Rochelle. He had to beg to be given a little coffee, bread, and cheese. At La Rochelle, he was made to wait for hours in his car, in his cell. The guards, under orders from a representative of the Ministry of the Interior, exchanged orders and signals amid the confusion. The name of Dreyfus was pronounced, and the news spread from mouth to mouth. Soon the crowd outside the car containing the traitor began to swell. He heard the insults, the banging against the walls. When he was taken out of his cell that night, the clamor grew louder. People began to strike him. The guards tried to protect him. He came forward with a certain energy, his hands bound. The blows descended on his head, on his shoulders. More than once, he was knocked to the ground. "Traitor," "Jew," "Death to the Jews." He rose, moved on until he came to the car which drove him away through the crowd. He was cold. His hands were frozen and calloused from the handcuffs. Several of the blows inflicted minor wounds.* He was arriving at the port of La Palice. From there a launch would take him to the Ile de Ré.

He arrived there at night and had to march through the snow to get to the coaling station of Saint-Martin-de-Ré. The director of the prison received him brutally and made him strip. He was meticulously searched† and finally taken to his cell, which was adjacent to a guard station with which it was connected by a large barred opening placed just above his

---

* "Dreyfus now knows," wrote *la Libre Parole* on January 20, "what France thinks both of his crime and of his cynical denials." Séverine, on the other hand, protested in *L'Eclair* against such odious scenes.

† In the inside pocket of one of Dreyfus's vests was found a copy of the bordereau that Dreyfus had used during the trial and which he had kept. The document was sent to Paris and the legend would circulate that the "draft" of the bordereau had been found on Dreyfus—new evidence of his crime.[19]

mattress. Night and day, two guards, replaced every two hours, kept watch. They were under orders not to lose sight of a single one of his gestures.

He was kept for more than a month on the Ile de Ré. Every day he was stripped and searched, after the authorized walk in the courtyard adjoining his cell. As soon as he stepped outside, the guards went on sentry duty. "I have only two happy moments in my day," he wrote to Lucie January 21, 1895, "but they are so short. The first when I am brought this sheet of paper so I may write to you. The second when I am brought your daily letter. I don't dare speak to you of our children."[20]

Having come to Ile de Ré, his wife was permitted to see him for one hour twice a week. Alfred and Lucie would meet in the clerk's office, in a small and elongated room. They were each seated at an extremity of the room with the director of the coaling station seated between them. The guards kept watch over the surroundings. He saw his wife for the last time February 21. On that day he was suddenly instructed to pack his kit bag. Taken to a dock, he was then embarked on a launch and transported aboard the ship *Ville-de-Saint-Nazaire*. No one told him where he was going. Aboard the ship, a cell awaited him which was located beneath the bridge and closed only by a metal grill. The cold was terrible—minus fourteen degrees Centigrade. A hammock was set up so that he might attempt to sleep.

At this juncture, hope was disappearing. "The memory of my wife, whom I had just left, of my children, of all the people I was leaving behind in pain and despair, the uncertainty of the place to which I was being taken, the situation that was now my own, all that put me in an indescribable state."[21] He threw himself to the ground and cried, moaning in the sinister and icy night. The wind and the sound of the sea drowned his laments.

The next day, the *Ville-de-Saint-Nazaire* set sail, bearing the traitor. On that February 22, 1895, the Dreyfus Affair was over.

II

LONG LIVE ESTERHAZY

1

The Legend of a Confession

In the days following the ceremony of degradation, the rumor spread through Paris that Dreyfus had confessed his crime. "The wretch's protests," wrote *Le Figaro*, "and the oath sworn on the heads of his children were so many lies, so much histrionics."[1] During the month of January 1895, the rumor of a confession found a large audience, but then disappeared. It would surface again later when it would become imperative to squeeze out a new verdict against Dreyfus.

On the morning of his degradation, while awaiting the ceremony, Alfred Dreyfus had remained enclosed for an hour in a small office of the École Militaire, guarded by Captain Lebrun-Renault of the Garde Républicaine.[2] In order to break the crushing silence, the two officers had exchanged a few words. "Have you not considered suicide, Monsieur Dreyfus?" Dreyfus spoke of his family and his life. He recounted the visit he had received from Commandant du Paty de Clam by order of the minister of war. "He sent Commandant du Paty to my cell in order to ask me if I had not turned over a document of no significance in the hope of receiving others in exchange." He explained again how he had protested his innocence to du Paty; Lebrun-Renault listened to his story. Four artillerymen appeared to take custody of Dreyfus for the procession. Lebrun-Renault left the room and exchanged a few hurried words with two officers, Colonel Guérin and Lieutenant Philippe. In the report confirming the completion of his mission, Lebrun-Renault wrote the words, "Nothing to report." And Colonel Guérin, whom the military governor of Paris had assigned to attend the ceremony, wrote up the event as follows: "Procession over. Dreyfus protested his innocence and shouted: Vive la France. No other incident."[3]

By nightfall, the rumor had begun to circulate that Dreyfus had confessed to Captain Lebrun-Renault. He had indeed spoken of his innocence, but had specified that "the minister was well aware that if I was turning over documents, they were of no value, and that it was in order to procure others of more importance."

Who was the source of the rumor? The officers with whom Lebrun-Renault had chatted for a few instants just after leaving Dreyfus. Colonel Guérin, Lieutenant Philippe, Commandant de Mitry, and Captain Anthoine remembered what Lebrun-Renault had confided to them at the time. Dreyfus had confessed to him having turned over documents in order to "entice" the Germans and thus obtain more valuable ones. The officers related the story to various journalists, including Ernest Judet and Maurice Barrès. *Le Petit Journal* of January 6 seized on the item. "He would thus have turned over documents, which constitutes a formal confession; but in order to obtain others, which is but one more lie to his credit and nobody will be fooled by it." The press began to accord ample coverage to the confessions of Dreyfus—in various versions. This was the conclusive proof of his guilt.

Commandant Georges Picquart, whom the minister of war had designated to attend the ceremony of degradation as his representative, was astonished. He inquired of Colonel Guérin, who confirmed what Lebrun-Renault had told him. Picquart was disturbed and went to see General Raoul de Boisdeffre, the chief of the General Staff. Together they hurried to the office of the minister of war, General Mercier, who stalled. What ought he to do? At the time, he appeared not to have attached any importance to the stories that had been circulating.

But the rumor was growing. Lebrun-Renault, in search of distraction, went out with a few friends to the public dance at the Moulin-Rouge. Without the slightest forethought, in his pride at the role he had played during the morning, he proceeded to recount his interview with the traitor. The journalist Clisson was present, and he immediately took the story to *Le Figaro*.[4] The press campaign, and the confessions of a traitor in the German camp could only irritate the German embassy and the minister of war was embarrassed. He summoned Lebrun-Renault.

At dawn on January 6, General Gonse sought out Captain Lebrun-Renault, and brought him to the office of the minister of war. "For an officer to be summoned at dawn by the Deputy-Chief of the General Staff and brought at 8 A.M. to see the minister" was no small affair.[5] Lebrun-Renault told the minister what Dreyfus had said to him. He did not actually speak of confessions, but evoked Dreyfus's version of the visit paid him by du Paty de Clam. Now Mercier was intent on keeping that visit secret. The unduly garrulous officer received a reprimand and was ordered to maintain his silence. Under no circumstance was he to mention either du Paty's clandestine mission or the German embassy. All interviews were to be refused.

The matter would undoubtedly have ended at that point had not the president of the Republic, upon opening *Le Figaro*, read the story of

Lebrun-Renault's revelations at the Moulin-Rouge. In order to bring credit to his name, a French officer had thus chosen a public dancehall in order to circulate the confessions of a man convicted of treason! Casimir-Périer knew with what care the German ambassador and the German government read the French press. That very afternoon, he was to receive Count Münster von Derneberg, who had requested a meeting. The article in *Le Figaro* claimed that the bordereau had been taken "from a small chest in the German embassy." What would the ambassador—in a very short while—make of that!

The gossip of Lebrun-Renault had become an affair of state. Casimir-Périer informed the prime minister of the "irritation this new scandal had caused him." Lebrun-Renault was called to the Elysée and was received extremely coldly by the president. No mention was made of any confession by Dreyfus.* But surely, if he had received one, Lebrun-Renault would have spoken about it—if only to clarify the rumors caused by his gossip. The president of the Republic scolded the officer vigorously and ordered him to keep his silence in the future. Shortly thereafter, the Agence Havas published an item specifying that Captain Lebrun-Renault, interrogated by the minister of war, "had certified that he had made no statement to any organ or representative of the press." That evening, Lebrun-Renault, who had so occupied the Republic's attention (for a few hours), returned to the Moulin-Rouge. He was questioned by all present. No, he had said nothing to the newspapers. No, Dreyfus had said nothing to him—except, after the procession, the words, "I am cold, my Captain." And that was the end—for the while—of the legend of a confession.

But it had the effect of further fueling the vigorous campaign the French press was conducting against Germany, the perennial enemy and homeland of traitors. In the days following the verdict against Dreyfus, the press campaign had reached such a pitch that in *Le Figaro* of December 25, the German ambassador had issued a denial of the accusations published concerning the activities of his embassy. "Never has the German embassy had the slightest relation—either direct or indirect—with Captain Dreyfus. No document emanating from him has been stolen from the embassy, and no request has been made for a secret session at his trial."[7]

Germany, it seemed clear, was "covering" her agents. On the day of the degradation, Prime Minister Charles Dupuy, overwhelmed, as he frequently was, by the course of events, had decided to hold a meeting of the Cabinet. Following a proposal by the minister of war, it was decided to ask Parliament to send the traitor to the Iles du Salut—to eliminate any possibility of escape. But among the ministers there was much discussion

* Jean Casimir-Périer would affirm this in his testimony at the Rennes trial.[6]

of Germany's irritation. Several hours after the meeting, the German ambassador transmitted to the head of the government a dispatch emanating from Chlodwig von Hohenlohe, the German chancellor.

His Majesty the Emperor, having full confidence in the loyalty of the President and Government of the Republic, requests Your Excellency to tell M. Casimir-Périer that if it is proven that the German embassy was never involved in the Dreyfus Affair, His Majesty hopes that the Government of the Republic will not hesitate to declare as much.

Without a formal declaration, the legends which the press continues to spread concerning the German embassy would persist and thus compromise the situation of the Emperor's representative.

Signed: von Hohenlohe

Gabriel Hanotaux, the minister of foreign affairs, suffering from an unspecified illness, was convalescing in Cannes. The president of the Republic agreed to receive the German ambassador personally in order to clarify matters. In order to do so, he requested that the Dreyfus dossier be communicated to him.* On January 6, he received the aged Count von Münster, who transmitted to him the solemn protest of the emperor of Germany. Casimir-Périer was intent on reconciling the truth with the courtesy he intended to show the ambassador. He first noted the "unprecedented character" of a communication presented directly to the president of the Republic; by invoking the Constitution, he could have declined the meeting and requested that the ambassador confer with the prime minister. But due to his relations with Count von Münster he was compelled to oblige. He was constrained to tell him that the document written by Dreyfus had been found in the embassy. But the German embassy "was not, of course, responsible for the papers it received," any more than the Imperial government could hold the French responsible for the papers brought to them.[8] The president of the Republic added cordially that

---

* At the Rennes trial, Casimir-Périer would say that he had received the military tribunal's complete file—and specifically the "scoundrel D" document—from the minister of war. It was the case that the minister of war asked the military governor of Paris on January 5, 1895, to have the file of the Dreyfus case delivered to him with due speed, "since the President of the Republic wanted to have it at his disposal immediately" (National Archives BB19 75, d1, p. 73). The "scoundrel D" document was certainly not part of it, since it had been returned with the secret file by Colonel Maurel to du Paty, and by du Paty to Colonel Sandherr. If Casimir-Périer was acquainted with the "scoundrel D" item, it was at a different time and by another channel.

nothing proved that the paper authored by Dreyfus had been solicited by the Germans. The ambassador was both astonished and reassured. What more could he request than a communiqué clarifying the situation. On January 7 and 8, a communiqué of the French government, intended to appease public opinion, was negotiated with Berlin. Every word was debated.* Finally the French and the Germans agreed on the following declaration, which would be published in the evening papers of January 9: "Following the verdict against ex-Captain Dreyfus by the Court-Martial, since certain newspapers persist in calling into question the foreign embassies of Paris, we are authorized, lest public opinion be led astray, to recall the official note issued on the subject November 30, 1894."[9]

The prime minister promised the German diplomat to convene the editors of the principal newspapers, to transmit to them the official note, and to ask them "to become actively engaged in putting an end to . . . the press campaign" which was endangering the "good relations" between France and Germany.[10] But the French communiqué had no more effect—on the overly aroused press—than the declarations from Germany. "Drunk with passion, both real and feigned," wrote Joseph Reinach, "France waxed declamatory."[11] Who cared about hypocritical declarations? Only Dreyfus's punishment mattered. "Dreyfus is no longer a man; he is a number in a chain-gang," wrote *Le Petit Journal* of January 6; *L'Estafette* of January 7 announced, "The convict will pay his debt, for the climate on Devil's Island is less delectable than that of New Caledonia."[12] Not even Dreyfus's attorney was spared the deluge of insults and threats in the press, since he had declared, repeatedly, that he believed in the innocence of his former client. "Whether or not the lawyer lost all sense of dignity amid the frequent indulgences and secondary deceptions of his daily work," wrote Ernest Judet in *Le Petit Journal* of January 13, "is a matter of concern only to the administration of the Bar. . . . Curious as he was to add a monster to his gallery, he may perhaps be excused for accepting to defend a traitor."[13] "Demange's campaign is an outrage to the Army," assured *Le Soleil*.[14] Whatever the displeasure of the "reptiles

* Maurice Baumont, *Aux sources de l'Affaire,* Productions de Paris, 1959, pp. 118–119. At times General Mercier would situate at this date the "historic night" on which the president of the Republic, the prime minister, and the minister of war were awaiting, prepared for war, the result of the telegraphic communications between Wilhelm II and Münster. At times he would evoke two different "nights" on which war threatened: one on December 12, 1894 (see *supra* pp. 82–83), the other on January 8, 1895. At the Rennes trial, Casimir-Périer would maintain that no risk of war was ever raised or feared. This was confirmed by Schwarzkoppen in his *Notebooks.* "Münster's discussions with Hanotaux and Casimir-Périer . . . never took a threatening turn" (*Carnets,* Rider, 1930, pp. 117ff). But the threat of imminent war would be the essential argument developed by General Mercier to justify the illegalities that had been committed.

beyond the Rhine," the French had decided. There was no more to be said! "If Dreyfus himself is not killed, at least let his Affair be dead everafter."[15] In England, Switzerland, and Germany, the press expressed their astonishment at the hysteria in France.

2

The Retirement of Mercier

At eight o'clock in the morning of January 16, 1895, Maurice Paléologue's servant entered his bedroom, "his face profoundly perturbed." "Has Monsieur heard the news? President Casimir-Périer has fled."[1]

He had resigned the previous evening, despite the supplications of his family and friends. "The rising tide of scandals had caused him bitter disgust."[2] Everything around him seemed corrupt. He believed himself surrounded by defiance and hatred. Frequently insulted because of his wealth and his social class, vilified by journalists short on subjects for blackmail, he was tired, particularly of his official function. To make matters worse, he felt that he was not exercising power, but rather playing within the state the role of a "signature machine."[3] The Dreyfus Affair had added to his malaise. His nervous sensibility, native anxiety, and neurotic sensitivity had found nourishment in all circumstances. In utter disgust, he decided to leave.

He had been aided in his intention by a ministerial crisis in which the mediocrity of the government, the ambition of some, the cowardice of others, and the intricacy of the attendant intrigues had all come to light.[4] It was the minister of public works, Jean Louis Barthou, who provided his cue, seizing on the pretext of a decision by the Conseil d'Etat that was mediating to the advantage of the major railroad companies a (minor) conflict in which they were opposed to the state. Raymond Poincaré, minister of finance, who saw in the circumstance a means for advancing his career, announced that he would join his friend in resigning. The decision of the Conseil d'Etat provided them an occasion on which to withdraw in order to stage a more imposing comeback. At which point, the entire government tendered its resignation to the president of the Republic in a maneuver designed to manifest its independence in relation to the large moneyed interests. Casimir-Périer, who was extremely wealthy, thus ran the risk of appearing in solidarity with those interests in the eyes of public opinion. He perceived the maneuver and announced that he would follow the government in resigning. Charles Dupuy, prime minister, was obliged to withdraw his resignation. In the Chambre des Députés, Alexandre Millerand, on behalf of the Socialists, led the attack. He reproached the government with having deferred to the Conseil d'Etat instead of appealing to the sovereignty of Parliament, and he asked for the indictment of former minister of public works Raynal, whom he alleged to have "sacrificed the rights of the State" to the profit of the large companies. It was well known, however, that Raynal was a personal friend of the president of the Republic. On the podium, Barthou, flaunting his resignation, scored a major success. In the wings, Poincaré lobbied his friends to vote against a government of which he was still a member. In the general confusion, a sector of the center split off to join the Socialists and Radicals. On January 5, a majority of twenty-two votes overturned the Dupuy cabinet, whose sole orientation had been to navigate between the various obstacles. That evening, the president of the Republic announced his resignation. On January 16, both Chambers were to hear his final message. "If one ought not to refuse a post at a time of danger, one can nevertheless retain one's dignity only if one has the conviction of serving one's country." Casimir-Périer confessed to being unable to resign himself to "comparing the gravity of his moral responsibilities with the impotence to which he had been condemned."

Public opinion was on the whole quite severe, and the victory of the leftist parties, the result partly of surprise, partly of confusion, could only trouble conservative opinion. The two Chambers convened jointly at Versailles on the very next day, January 17. The Socialists and Radicals supported the candidacy of Eugène Henri Brisson, who was a candidate for the fourth time. The "republicans"—that is, the "progressivist" center—and those deputies of the right who had "rallied" to the Republic were split between two candidates: Félix Faure, a minister in the government that was resigning, and René Waldeck-Rousseau, a lawyer and statesman who "had hesitated throughout the day to yield to the urgings of his friends, and would only reach a decision in the evening when it was already too late." The duc d'Orléans became a partisan of Félix Faure* and carried as well the vote of the monarchist right. As for General Mercier, the minister of war hesitated. The Dreyfus Affair had established his reputation and augmented his prestige. But could a general, even of republican sympathies, be a candidate? Mercier realized that he enjoyed more respect than true affection. He did not dare to announce his own candidacy, but managed to have the idea floated in various circles by his friends. A poster featuring his portrait was distributed in support of the "patriot general": "The Congress should elect the man who delivered the traitor Dreyfus to the Court-Martial." But the Congress paid little attention to him. In the first round of voting, Henri Brisson came in first, followed by Félix Faure. Auguste Mercier received only three votes. In the second round, René Waldeck-Rousseau, in his disappointment, withdrew, thereby assuring the election of the "President of the Rightists."† Once again, the republican Constitution had proven adequate to its task.

The son of a cabinetmaker, a former tanner who had set up in Le Havre a skin-dressing shop, a deputy from Le Havre for the previous twelve years, Félix Faure had never occupied any other than secondary posts in preceding governments. As a minister of the navy in the Dupuy government, he had not attracted any particular notice. He was regarded as intelligent and cautious and had managed to gain the warm sympathy of all sides. In addition, he was of "fine health, fine humor, and fine presence."[5] He was barely fifty-five years old, rather proud of his appearance, much taken with women, and taken to by them. On all matters, he seemed to have only centrist opinions.

The new president of the Republic began by calling on Léon Bourgeois, the head of the Radicals, to form a government, well aware that Bourgeois could not succeed in that task. He then solicited the conservative sage Alexandre Ribot, who in twenty-four hours constituted a "government of republican unity and democratic progress"—that is, a shrewdly proportioned government of the center, which was immediately approved by a crushing majority.‡ Gabriel Hanotaux stayed at Foreign Affairs; Raymond Poincaré was shifted to Public Instruction. The presence of two Radicals gave an impression of an opening to the left.

Alexandre Ribot thought it prudent to delay the difficult assignment of the portfolios of War and Navy. But General Mercier had no illusions. The new prime minister had little affection for him. It was up to him, then, as (departing) minister of war to take certain precautions. As early as

* Who had formerly taken a stand against the expulsion of princes.
† By a vote of 430 to 361. It was during the night following the election of Félix Faure that Dreyfus was transferred from the Santé Prison to La Rochelle.
‡ The vote was 329 to 79.

January 8, he indicated to General Félix Saussier, the military governor of Paris, that "by analogy with what had transpired in trials of similar importance," the files of the trial of ex-Captain Dreyfus would be kept in the Ministry and not in any municipal office.* Mercier called in Colonel Jean Sandherr, head of the Intelligence Service. In his presence, he presented the secret file and handed the documents transmitted to the Court-Martial to Sandherr so that he might distribute them "among the various folders from which they had come."[6] Did he take the time to ask of Boisdeffre, Gonse, Sandherr, du Paty, and Henry their "word of honor" never to reveal anything clandestine or illegal? In his account, Marcel Thomas assumes that he did.[7] In any event, no one would ever reveal such an "oath," which may have been imposed by the architect of Dreyfus's conviction.

Thereafter General Auguste Mercier would be free to take his leave. President Ribot rid himself of the "cumbersome" general to whom the Dreyfus Affair had given such importance. Mercier would take command of the Sixteenth Army Corps. He was replaced by the very distinguished General Emile Zurlinden—an Alsatian and an artilleryman who sported a monocle virtually riveted to his eye. "Dreyfus has been avenged," wrote *La Patrie* of January 29. "The trip to the Iles du Salut should cause him a little less bitterness."

Two days later, the new minister of the colonies, André Lebon, requested the immediate discussion of projected legislation—prepared by Mercier—which would reestablish the Iles du Salut as a deportation site. Without any debate, voting by a show of hands, Parliament passed the law allowing Dreyfus to be imprisoned on Devil's Island.

* The letter from the minister of war to the military governor of Paris, kept in the National Archives (BB19 75, d1, p. 6), bears the written notation: "Don't mention this letter to anyone." Commandant André Brisset, military prosecutor for the Court-Martial, informed the military governor the next day that the "complete file" had already been given to Captain d'Affry de la Mounaye, the minister's aide-de-camp (BB19 75, d1, p. 77), at the request of the minister himself, so that it might be put at the disposal of the president of the Republic.

3

Don't Do That;
It's Not Nice

" A fter the ceremony of degradation," wrote Mathieu Dreyfus, "a vacuum seemed to settle in around us. . . . It appeared that we were no longer like other people, that we had been cut off from the world of the living."[1] A few intimate friends came by, to be sure, to rue de Chateaudun where Mathieu had moved, with words of consolation. But they gave the Dreyfus family the impression that they believed the Affair was now over.[2] Mathieu, like Lucie Dreyfus, and their two families, was convinced of the innocence of his brother. He would not for a moment entertain the slightest doubt. But what could be done?

Mathieu went to thank Commandant Forzinetti, who, throughout Dreyfus's detention in the Cherche-Midi Prison, had demonstrated a measure of generosity and courage which was admirable. Forzinetti gave him a roll of paper. "This is the copy your brother made of d'Ormesche-ville's indictment. He added his own comments; this copy will be very useful to you." Mathieu Dreyfus took the precious document and asked Georges Hadamard, Lucie's brother, to take it to Basel for safekeeping. An odd precaution, but Mathieu knew he was being followed, as was the whole family. Their correspondence was quite plainly being opened. Moreover, the agents charged with keeping track of Mathieu, Lucie, and the Hadamard family did not even bother to conceal their activities. Mathieu decided to hire an agent for himself, who coincidentally answered to the name of "Dubois." Dubois quickly discovered that the concierge of Mathieu's building was on the police payroll, as was the domestic he had recently hired.[3] Traps of all sort were set for Mathieu and Lucie. People came to see them promising documents, suggesting, as a sign of sincerity, to leave in their deposit compromising papers, and, of course, asking for money.[4] Mathieu grew distrustful—and extremely suspicious. As early as January 4, Edgar Demange warned him that he risked being arrested as his brother's accomplice. Commandant du Paty de Clam, whose zeal did not flag, continued to tell anyone who cared to hear it that the Dreyfus family had received and deposited in Alsace the wages of treason in the form of an insurance indemnity. Might Mathieu then be his brother's accomplice? The threat seemed sufficiently serious for him to write on January 5, at Demange's suggestion, to Colonel Sandherr, who was inquiring into the matter. He recalled their interview and protested with indignation, proposing to name two experts to investigate the finances of the family in Mulhouse.* The letter received no answer. Did it serve to avoid—or delay—his arrest? The Dreyfus family lived not only with its anguish but with unrelenting anxiety as to the future.

Mathieu knocked at every door. He called on journalists, including Ernest Judet, whose articles, particularly in *L'Intransigeant*, had been quite hostile to Dreyfus. Judet agreed to hear him out, appeared to be moved, and offered his hand. He solicited politicians. M. Siegfried, formerly minister of commerce, told him outright, "I have five minutes to give you," but promised to intervene to assure that the prisoner was favorably treated. Auguste Scheurer-Kestner, a senator for life, the last representative of French Alsace in the Parliament, vice president of the Senate, received him cordially, asked for time to think things over, and had him come back, then told him that he could not take an interest in his brother. "The information I have received leads me to believe in his guilt."[6] M. Zurcher, a cousin of the new minister of war, General Emile Zurlinden, lived, it seemed, in Mulhouse. Mathieu arranged to meet him and begged him to intervene with the minister, but the latter informed his cousin that there existed in the Ministry of War "copious and clear evidence proving" the guilt of Alfred Dreyfus.[7] What evidence, the minister did not say. No initiative seemed to produce any results. "I was struggling in the void,"

---

* "How can it be, Monsieur, that at the Ministry of War my brothers are accused of complicity in the abominable crime alleged to have been committed by my brother, who, I assure you again today on my honor—which is the equal of that of many a man—is innocent, a circumstance you will realize later when the truth will out. The person who invented that odious accusation is Commandant du Paty.

"I have the right and the duty to ask the man on what grounds that lie is based.

"It is time, Monsieur, that an end be put to these insinuations; you are better equipped than anyone to know who we are.

"In order to clarify matters, if need be, I propose to delegate M. Engel and M. Braun to examine our accounts in Mulhouse for the last thirty years. If those gentlemen, whom we both know, find that any sum whatsoever was paid to us by the German government, or that we ever received any sum whatsoever whose origin we are unable to justify, or that we possess any valuable bought without written record, I will hand myself over to the courts, for I will not leave Paris and will place myself at their disposition. . . ."[5]

Mathieu would write. "The hours and the days seemed endless to us."*

The first glimmer of light came by accident and by a rather curious path. One January morning in 1895, Mathieu Dreyfus was informed by a mutual friend that Dr. Gibert, a physician from Le Havre, believed in Dreyfus's innocence. The good Dr. Gibert had two distinguishing characteristics. As a specialist in incidents of mental suggestion, he had performed some extremely interesting somnambulist experiments with a woman named Léonie,[9] and it was common knowledge that he was an old friend of the president of the Republic, Félix Faure. Dr. Gibert asked Mathieu to come to Le Havre.

Mathieu went at once. He did not want to neglect a single lead, not even the most eccentric. And hypnotism and all of its derivatives—magnetism, spiritism, clairvoyance—were in style. In Paris, many were competing for entry into the salon of Henriette Covedon, "the clairvoyant of the rue de Paradis," whose ecstasies had provoked a number of impassioned polemics. Why not hear out Dr. Gibert's clairvoyant, in Le Havre?

Mathieu described his first encounter with Léonie as follows:

> I beheld a peasant woman seated on a couch, her eyes closed. She appeared about 50 years in age, had regular features, and wore a Norman bonnet on her head.
>
> The doctor told me to sit down facing her.
>
> She took my thumbs, felt them in every direction, scratched them, and then told me slowly, searching for her words, with pauses and, occasionally, protracted stretches of silence: "You are his brother, your wife is with you, you have two children, a little girl and a little boy; they are not with you; he is suffering a great deal." She then abandoned my hands and proceeded to speak as though she were in the presence of my brother. "Why are you wearing glasses? Who gave you those glasses?" But, I said to her, my brother never wears glasses. He always wears a pince-nez. Aren't you confusing glasses and a pince-nez?—"No, no," Léonie shouted in anger, "I know what I am saying; I say glasses, because they are glasses. You will go farther, much farther (and she made a gesture of horror), but you will return. That much is sure. I don't know in how much time; we do not know about time, but it is sure, sure, that you will return."[10]

Mathieu was impressed. On every point—except for Alfred's glasses—Léonie had spoken the truth. But Lucie Dreyfus—returning

* The Bonapartist writer Arthur Lévy, the author of *Bonaparte Intime*, who was convinced of a judicial error, proposed, however, a vigorous written protest that Lucie Dreyfus would sign.

from Ile de Ré*—informed him that the prisoner, in order to spare his pince-nez, which quite frequently fell, had just requested a pair of glasses from the director of the prison. At that point Mathieu became quite concerned. He returned frequently to Le Havre. Dr. Gibert would call for him as soon as he believed Léonie to be "well disposed." At times she would say things that were implausible, even incomprehensible. At other times what she said fascinated Mathieu. She declared that the true culprit was an officer of the Ministry of War, whose name she could not determine, but who was in contact with a German agent named Greber. She said that the document on the basis of which Alfred had been found guilty had been taken from the German embassy. She said that the guilty officer was a friend of Alfred Dreyfus to whom he refused to lend money. At the beginning of February, Mathieu Dreyfus heard her say: "What in hell are those documents they are showing secretly to the judges. Don't do that; it isn't right. If M. Alfred and Maître Demange saw them, they would thwart their purpose." Dreyfus asked Léonie, "What do you mean by those documents?" Léonie responded, "Documents that you do not know about that were shown to the judges; you will see later."[11]

Was it in fact Léonie who was first to speak to Mathieu about "secret documents" that would have been concealed from Demange during the trial of 1894? Mathieu Dreyfus, in any event, was so struck that in agreement with Dr. Gibert he brought Léonie to Paris. He first installed her in an apartment on rue de l'Arcade, in the home of his own sister, Mme. Cahn. Soon she would be living in his own home. Dr. Gibert patiently taught his pupil how to put Léonie in a hypnotic trance. Soon, Mathieu was putting her to sleep for several hours at a time, even for several days. And with Léonie the somnambulist, he would undertake numerous experiments which confirmed her astonishing faculties. Léonie began to occupy more and more space in the life of the Dreyfus family. At times she was lucid; at others, incoherent. Mathieu asked her to follow several officers "psychically." "Often, through nothing more than prolonged contact with my hands, or with one of my hands, and it was her habit to take one of my hands in hers, she perceived my physical or moral state (if I was well or poorly disposed), sometimes my thoughts, which were not always related to the matter under consideration. . . ."[12] Mathieu convinced himself that he was gifted with the power of suggestion; he attempted a few long distance experiments on Léonie, devoting much time to the effort.† He had been reduced to desperate solutions.

Demange advised categorically against the initiative, which was not followed up.[8]
* The scene occurred a few days before Dreyfus's departure for Devil's Island.
† On occasion he would put her to sleep and say to her: "Go to Devil's Island. Give me news of my brother." In 1897, Léonie would one day say to him, while in a hypnotic trance: "Poor

In Le Havre, Dr. Gibert had been the physician of Félix Faure, and remained his friend. The news of the deportation of Alfred Dreyfus to Devil's Island frightened him, for he knew that Dreyfus ran the risk of dying there. On February 20, 1895, Dr. Gibert, in agreement with Mathieu Dreyfus, asked Faure for a hearing, which was granted at the Elysée at seven o'clock on the morning of October 21, while Mathieu awaited his friend in the Hôtel de l'Athénée.[14] Dr. Gibert returned from his meeting overwhelmed. The president of the Republic had told him that Dreyfus had been convicted on the basis of neither the bordereau nor the incidents of the courtroom. "He was convicted on the basis of items communicated to the judges in the deliberation room, items that could be shown to neither the defendant nor his lawyer for reasons of State." Dr. Gibert attempted in vain to interest the president in Dreyfus's cause, but at the end of their interview he asked Faure: "My friend Mathieu Dreyfus is aware of my initiative in seeing you. Will you authorize me to convey to him our conversation?" Yes, replied the president.[15] But he demanded silence toward all others. A strange fate indeed: It was an indiscretion by the president which on February 21, 1895, revealed to the Dreyfus family that a secret file had been transmitted to the judges in the deliberation room. For Mathieu this was a terrible piece of news, but one which bore with it a certain hope. A monstrous illegality had permitted the conviction of his brother.[16] "My brother, then, had not been tried," wrote Mathieu, "he had been murdered." It was impossible to make public the extraordinary admission of the chief of state,* for he would issue an immediate denial. How might one verify and demonstrate the illegality which Félix Faure had revealed? And what were the "secret items"?

In fact, Mathieu had just learned what others were already aware of during those first months of 1895. The vice president of the Senate, Auguste Scheurer-Kestner, had learned from the former minister Charles de Freycinet that the judges had been convinced in their chambers by a letter from Panizzardi to Schwarzkoppen in which Dreyfus had been named.† How did Freycinet know this? Several of the judges—who had convicted Dreyfus—were given to gossip. Lieutenant Colonel Echemann had explained to a journalist from *Le Gaulois*[17] that the transmission of

---

Monsieur Alfred, he can no longer see the ocean. They've built a stockade for him." Mathieu Dreyfus maintained that that was how he learned that a stockade had been built around his brother's hut.[13]

* How had Félix Faure himself learned what had happened? Surely not from General Mercier. Perhaps through Gabriel Hanotaux, minister of foreign affairs in the Dupuy government, who remained in his position during the Ribot regime.

† At the time, that information was not enough to persuade Scheurer-Kestner of Dreyfus's innocence. He would later be convinced and would become one of the most active supporters of the revisionist cause.

items unknown to the defense and even to the government prosecutor during the final hour had determined the verdict. Commandant Martin Freystaetter had mentioned it to one of his friends, a Jewish officer, Captain Picard, who had been Dreyfus's classmate at the École de Guerre, and who, because of poor grades received from an anti-Semitic officer, had not been able to enter the General Staff. Picard had mentioned it to his friend Léon Lévy, an engineer. A second judge, Commandant Florentin, had told the same story to Captain Potier, who had revealed it to a Jewish attorney.[18] "At the Ministry," wrote Joseph Reinach, "twenty officers knew of the secret communication, deemed it an acceptable maneuver, and spoke openly of it with their friends."[19] The blatant illegality appears not to have moved many. All quickly convinced themselves that *raison d'état* had made such a precaution necessary.

The new minister of justice, Ludovic Trarieux,* was a serious and scrupulous man, for whom the Affair and the rise of anti-Semitism were of great concern. As soon as he arrived in the Chancelry, he inquired of his colleague Gabriel Hanotaux, who had remained as minister of foreign affairs. Hanotaux explained to him that personally he was quite opposed to the trial but that General Mercier, the minister of war, had attempted to appease him with a document in which "Dreyfus's initial allowed one to conclude that the Jew had maintained guilty relations with a foreign power."† Thus it was that Edgar Demange learned from his colleague Maître Albert Salle, who himself had received it from one of the judges, that Dreyfus had been convicted on the basis of a secret document, containing the words "that scoundrel D." Shocked and indignant, Demange consulted with Trarieux, who confirmed the existence of such a document. "I have it from my colleague M. Hanotaux, to whom General Mercier gave the item in order to set his conscience at ease." The lawyer insisted, "Was the document shown to the judges?" The minister of justice protested. "Certainly not. That would be monstrous." Mathieu Dreyfus was gathering information from all sides. Who then could this *D.* be, this "scoundrel," if not his brother? A "functionary in Criminal Investigations" informed him that the document had arrived at the Ministry of War during the spring of 1894, that one or two employees whose name began with *D.* had been placed under surveillance, but to no effect. Mathieu did his utmost to track down a suspicious officer, whose family name began with *D.*, but none had been found.

If "devastating" documents had been secretly transmitted to the judges, what was their content? What influence did they exert on the

* Trarieux would found the League of the Rights of Man and would become one of the most ardent fighters in the Dreyfusard cause.
† The "scoundrel D" document.

verdict? Illegality alone was not sufficient to provoke indignation in France in 1894. And the political class of the day seemed as indifferent to the independence of the judiciary as to respect for procedure. The point would later be made by the thoroughly decent Ludovic Trarieux, to Auguste Scheurer-Kestner: "If the man were a traitor and formal procedure were violated in his case, I would not make bold to raise my voice." "In a similar circumstance," Reinach would write, "no Englishman would have pronounced such words."[20] In France, in 1894, in any event, those decisive documents, however secret, complicated rather than simplified the impossible task of Mathieu Dreyfus.

What remained was the essential element: the bordereau. Mathieu Dreyfus had seen it for a brief moment. Demange had not received a photographic copy. In any event, out of professional decorum, he refused to transmit any document to the Dreyfus family. Without a photo of the bordereau, how might one seek out its author? Mathieu speculated that the bordereau had perhaps been fabricated by individuals intent on destroying his brother and who possessed specimens of his handwriting. He inquired in all quarters, without a worthwhile lead. "We were in the pit of an abyss, absolutely unable to emerge from it. On one side, a family and a few friends; on the other, all the powers of society, a whole world it would have been necessary to move."[21] The autumn came, then winter and the anniversary of Dreyfus's arrest. Exhausted by so many useless efforts, Mathieu lapsed into despair.

4

A Fabulous Gambler

The Dreyfus Affair had not clouded the good humor of Colonel Maximilian von Schwarzkoppen. He had never met Captain Dreyfus. The German military attaché, moreover, had simply never engaged in espionage. On December 13, his ambassador, who trusted his word of honor, recalled as much publicly.* "Nobody at the embassy, not even Lieutenant Colonel von Schwarzkoppen, ever knew anything of

---

* See also the official statements of December 25, 1894, and January 9, 1895, supra, p. 108–09.

Captain Dreyfus or had even heard of him." And Schwarzkoppen himself specified in a report to his government on December 14, 1894: "Total obscurity continues to reign concerning the Dreyfus Affair. Up until the present, the contents of the document alleged to have been given by Dreyfus to a military attaché or foreign agent have not been established. The nationalist press continues to maintain that it was the German military attaché, a circumstance linked to attacks against the German embassy in the most imprudent manner."[1] No, the Dreyfus Affair was of no particular concern to Colonel von Schwarzkoppen.

However, this did not prevent Schwarzkoppen from receiving regular visits from Commandant Esterhazy. As early as September 1, 1894,* the commandant had returned bearing "a multitude of interesting communications." He had brought the military attaché "the following items written by himself":[3]

1. a list of the covering troops
2. a description of the 120 short gun
3. a copy of the *Temporary Firing Manual for the Country Artillery*†

Commandant Esterhazy had indicated to von Schwarzkoppen that the Madagascar expedition had been approved. He also specified that he was returning from maneuvers and that he would turn over to him shortly "a report on the observations he had made."

With growing urgency, Esterhazy returned September 5 with a detailed description of the maneuvers in which, he claimed, he had participated. On September 7, he delivered to the embassy a report on the projected expedition to Madagascar. He came yet again October 13 with the "correspondence regulator,"‡ as well as "an extensive work on the state of the French Army." Esterhazy returned thereafter approximately once every two weeks. The value of his information "continued to grow."[4] As did his rewards.

Commandant Esterhazy showed up again November 3. On that day, Schwarzkoppen was worried. Ought not the clamor surrounding Dreyfus's arrest and the implication of the German embassy have imposed a need for greater caution? Was there not a risk that Esterhazy's visits were being observed? But Esterhazy remained confident. He assured von Schwarzkoppen that he had taken "the necessary measures so that even if

* Several days, that is, after the bordereau's arrival at the embassy, which may be dated August 27.[2]
† As compensation, Schwarzkoppen paid him 1,000 francs. Esterhazy in fact had brought an old set of instructions and not the new set expected by Schwarzkoppen. The three items are listed in the bordereau.
‡ A small instrument designed to regulate the firing of 120 guns.

his visits were discovered they would not arouse any suspicions."[5] Schwarzkoppen questioned him about the arrest of Dreyfus. Did he know anything about the matter? Esterhazy knew nothing, but he counseled the military attaché to take increased precautions when transmitting information to Berlin. Persistently, Esterhazy returned again and again. He was seriously in need of money.

During the year 1895, however, the relations between Schwarzkoppen and Esterhazy underwent a gradual deterioration. Esterhazy was transmitting information of extreme inaccuracy[6] and boasting of personal relations which turned out to be false. Schwarzkoppen perceived as much and began to grow distrustful. Esterhazy made a show of zeal, but could manage to furnish the military attaché with nothing but information that was alternately vague and imaginary.[7] On February 20, 1896, he came to see Schwarzkoppen bearing the plans for a nonexistent gun.* The diplomat was wearying of the visits of the increasingly demanding and increasingly inefficient agent. Already on February 20 he threatened to break off relations with him, and he sent to his superiors on the German General Staff a report in which he set out his doubts as to Esterhazy's sincerity and ability. "We have kept our word; he has not. Not a single item of information that can be trusted."[9] The General Staff no doubt authorized Schwarzkoppen at the time to keep his distance from an increasingly useless—if not dangerous—agent.

But Commandant Esterhazy had monetary needs which could never be satisfied, and the money received from Germany was insufficient; his activities, his life, and his resources bore many faces. He was the intimate friend of Maurice Weil, a corrupt but influential Jewish officer, whose attractive wife was the mistress of General Félix Saussier, military governor of Paris. Weil had never ceased interceding on Esterhazy's behalf. Esterhazy had also managed to become the protégé of the former minister Jules Roche, who dreamed of becoming minister of war. The commandant had performed a thousand petty services for him in the hope of one day being his *chef de cabinet*. Above all Esterhazy had become by 1894 one of the secret collaborators of Edouard Drumont's journal, *La Libre Parole*. He was the friend and would soon be the collaborator of Commandant Biot, who under the byline "Commandant Z." wrote the newspaper's military chronicle. By the beginning of 1895, "the pseudonym indicated the dual personality of Biot and Esterhazy."[10] Esterhazy, inhibited by neither cynicism nor prudence, did not hesitate to transmit the same information (if not the same texts) to *La Libre Parole*, to Schwarzkoppen,

---

* In 1908, he would admit to having given Schwarzkoppen diagrams of a rifle "quite incapable of firing a single shot." But it appears that Esterhazy also was being duped by his informers.[8]

and no doubt to his protector Jules Roche. Marcel Thomas has established the (occasionally word-by-word) similarity between the notes transmitted to Schwarzkoppen and certain articles published in *La Libre Parole*.[11] But Esterhazy's links with journalists, "the profession for which he was most gifted,"[12] were not restricted to his secret collaboration with Drumont's newspaper. He contributed several notes to *L'Autorité* as well,[13] and his friend Maurice Weil would open up the columns of the *Journal des Sciences Militaires* to him in 1896. Esterhazy would sign several articles with the pseudonym Z.

Journalism and gallantry were linked in Esterhazy's life. More attracted, it seems, by their wealth than by their beauty, he seduced numerous women. And he stole the mistress—Marguerite Pays, whom he met on a train from Le Havre to Paris—from a journalist at *La Libre Parole*, Ponchon de Saint André (pen name, Boisandré). In the worst of circumstances, moreover, she would remain faithful to him.

There was nothing that Esterhazy would not dare. Within the Jewish community, he had also sought out money. He had been the second of the Jewish Captain Ernest Crémieu-Foa in his duel with Edouard Drumont on June 1, 1892. Did that not mean that the Jews were in his debt?* In July 1894 he succeeded in extorting two thousand francs from Edmond de Rothschild, his former classmate at the Lycée Bonaparte.[15] At the beginning of 1895 he returned. He was indeed intent on tapping his "dear friend," the millionaire baron, for a little cash.[16]

My Dear Friend,
Even though we had lost track of each other for thirty years, you were, when I contacted you, good to me, whereas some who could have, who should have helped me out did nothing; I am deeply grateful and although in the more than precarious situation in which I find myself and which can change only with the death of my uncle it seems impossible for me to do anything to convey to you how grateful I am, I might nevertheless be of some use to you. The extremely cruel necessity which I am forced to confront (without succeeding at it, moreover) has forced me to undertake in secret and outside of my profession certain (extremely honorable) tasks which my uniform nevertheless forbids. Those efforts have allowed me to penetrate into circles in which I have learned things of gravity which, I believe, you would have an interest in knowing. I repeat that I am neither a madman nor a fool.

---

* He had taken the precaution, on the day after the duel, of sending his calling card to Drumont with a few courteous words. And he had initiated a correspondence with the Marquis de Morès, Drumont's witness and a famous anti-Semitic agitator.[14]

Esterhazy was "neither a madman nor a fool," but he had a passion for clandestine activities and an insatiable thirst for money. He liked to manipulate those he met, women and men, like so many marionettes. His life was an incoherent assemblage of ruses and machinations. This prodigious gambler, capable of playing any role, this cheat that no risk could stop, was about to change history.

5

Dreyfus the Deportee

The crossing from the Ile de Ré to the Iles du Salut was long and painful. During the first days, the cold of the open cell was unbearable. Dreyfus was fed the daily ration of deportees, served in old tin cans. On the eighth day the temperature grew warmer, then, little by little turned torrid. "I realized that we were approaching the equator, but did not know where I was being transported."[1] On March 12, 1895, after a crossing of fifteen days, the ship entered the harbor of the Iles du Salut.* Since nothing had been prepared, he was kept in the ship's hold for several hours. The temperature was 104 degrees Fahrenheit. He then disembarked and was taken to the prison of the Ile Royale.† He was kept there

---

* "I will not relate my trip to you," he wrote on March 12, 1895, to his wife. "I was transported in a manner befitting the vile rogue I am taken to be; that is no more than just. It would be out of the question to show any pity to a traitor; he is the lowest of wretches, and in so far as I represent such a wretch I cannot but approve. My situation here cannot but follow from those same principles."

Dreyfus would never doubt that the inhuman treatment he was subjected to would have been justified had he been a traitor. It will be observed that throughout the Dreyfus Affair no voice was heard denouncing the treatment given a deportee, even if he were a traitor.

† An unpublished work, *Dreyfus à l'Ile du Diable*, by A. B. Marbaud, written in 1960,[2] constitutes an exceptional document on Alfred Dreyfus's deportation. It was written, the author states, from drafts and notes written by certain of Dreyfus's guards, which were found in a cell on Devil's Island. Dreyfus's prison file, established at Cayenne, was destroyed in 1906 after Dreyfus was restored to his rights. The precision and coherence of the information and documentation contained in *Dreyfus à l'Ile du Diable* argue in favor of its authenticity. Most often, it confirms documentation already assembled from other sources. The arrival ashore—on the 12th—is described as follows in the report of Chief-Guard Pouly:

"The deportee was disembarked from the Ville-de-Saint-Nazaire at 2 P.M. by the Director of the Penitential Administration and the High Commandant of the Iles du Salut. He was

for a month, and April 14 was transported to the Ile du Diable—Devil's Island.

Volcanic in origin, the Iles du Salut (formerly the "Iles du Diable") constituted an archipelago of three islands, separated from each other by a narrow channel: Ile Royale, Ile Saint-Joseph, and the third and smallest, which retained the sinister name of Devil's Island.[3] Twenty-seven miles from Cayenne, they had more or less the same climate as French Guiana, characterized by continuously high temperatures. Malarial fever raged relentlessly in what had become a preferred site for deportation. The victors of recent wars, including Napoleon, had "deported there those enemies which the hypocrisy of the day prevented from being dispatched to the executioner." Almost all died quite rapidly. The Second Empire revived a tradition which had been interrupted by the Restoration: a few hundred republicans, along with a number of convicts, were sent off to the Iles du Salut.* The National Assembly had then assigned New Caledonia as the destination of those deportees to be kept under high security. At the suggestion of General Mercier, the minister of war, the law had been modified for Dreyfus.

Smaller than its neighbors, as uncultivated as a desert, with vegetation of brush and stunted trees, Devil's Island seemed to be made of rocks.† Fifteen dilapidated huts, the remains of a deserted leper's colony, had been burned down to prepare for Dreyfus's arrival. The place was suited for the traitor. And the high commandant of the Isles, Commandant Bouchet, was prepared to take delivery of a person "whose hideousness was a thousandfold more frightening than that of the wretches who had preceded him."[5]

Dreyfus described his quarters, a small square edifice of brick and stone masonry with a metal roof, agreed upon by the Ministry of War and the Penitential Administration, as follows:

> The cabin assigned to me was made of stone and measured 4 meters by 4 meters. The door was a grated gate armed by simple iron bars. That gate opened on to a booth 2 meters by 3 meters affixed to the front of the cabin and closed by a full wooden door. A guard was stationed inside the booth. The guards were relieved

---

assigned to a guard's room at the entry of the prison-cell area. There were distributed to him: 1 iron bedstead with three planks; 1 troop mattress; 1 troop mosquito net; 1 wash-basin with a porcelain pot; 1 jug; 1 tub; 1 bracket lantern (with brass lamp); 1 table; 1 straw chair. He receives a soldier's rations, without the wine."

* Out of 7,000 individuals shipped to Ile Royale in 1856, 2,500 had died by the end of the year. But the Empire regarded deportation to such a site punishment enough. Deportees were free on the island.

† With a shoreline of less than 3,000 meters, it had a median width of 400 meters.[4]

every two hours and were not to lose sight of me day or night. In order to allow that second function to be exercised, the cabin was illuminated day and night. At night, the door of the booth was closed from both within and without, so that every two hours, at the changing of the guard, there was an infernal clatter of keys and hardware. Five watchmen plus a chief were charged with keeping my guard. During the day, I was free to move about only in the part of the island between the wharf and the little valley in which the former lepers' colony was located, that is, over an area of about 200 meters which was completely unsheltered, and I was absolutely forbidden to exceed that limit under penalty of being locked up in my cabin. As soon as I went out, I was accompanied by the guard on duty who was not to lose sight of a single one of my moves. The guard was armed with a revolver; later on, a gun and an ammunition belt were added. I was formally forbidden from speaking to anyone. . . .[6]

Dreyfus wore a deportee's uniform: cotton shirt, flannel belt, canvas jacket, cloth pants. The few objects he was authorized to have in his possession were returned to him. He would receive a soldier's ration of food, without the wine.

On April 14, 1895, the deportee began "the journal of my sad and frightening life." He was given sheets of paper which were numbered and initialed. He had no news from his wife.* He could not sleep, but listened to the roar of the sea. "I am rediscovering a violent feeling (which I already experienced on the ship) of a deep and almost irresistible attraction for the sea . . . the sea's tyranny over me is violent. . . . Where are the fine dreams of my youth, the aspirations of my mature years? There is no life left in me; my brain goes astray under the pressure of my thought." Dreyfus would keep his journal, almost daily, until September 10, 1896.[8] On that date, "so exhausted, so broken in body and soul," he would decide to abandon it. He had neither a talent nor a taste for writing. He always composed in the same style: "correct, flat, even resigned in its placidity." But modesty and discretion prompted him to restraint as well: his letters were read with great care by his jailers.[9] On occasion, his writing would catch fire, a touch of rhetoric would be introduced, but most often, it was without relief. Dreyfus sought only to describe faithfully and seriously what he experienced. He was frequently exhausted, crushed by the heat or racked by fever. His writing betrayed as much.

* He would receive his first letter from Lucie, dated February 18, on May 2. On June 12, he would be given letters that had arrived in Cayenne at the end of March and had been sent to Paris to be read by the offices of the Ministries of Colonies and of War.[7]

In the journal, as in the letters written to his wife, he spoke endlessly of his honor: "Tell yourself that you have a sacred mission to fulfill, that of having my honor restored to me—the honor of the name borne by our dear children."[10] "It is a matter of our honor, of theirs; we must, then, dear and good Lucie, accept all our sufferings, overcome them until the day on which my innocence will be recognized."[11] "You ought to find among those who are in charge of the affairs of our country men of courage . . . who will understand the frightful martyrdom of a soldier for whom honor is everything."[12] My body is indifferent to everything, for it is moved by an almost superhuman force: a concern for our honor. That is the sacred duty which I must carry out for you, for our children, for my family. . . ."[13] In his journal of May 9, 1895, he wrote: "My body must not give in before honor is restored to us. Without it, I would rather know that both our children were dead."[14]

He also repeatedly referred to his love for France. Above all else there was his country—the country which regarded him as a traitor: "I have just caught a glimpse of the mail arriving from France—how the word sets my soul astir! To think that my country, to whom I have devoted all my energy, all my intelligence, can regard me as a vile scoundrel."[15] On July 14, 1895[16] he wrote: "I have seen the tricolor flag aloft everywhere—the flag that I served with honor and loyalty. . . . My heart, as you know, has not changed. It is a soldier's heart, indifferent to every form of physical suffering, placing honor before everything, above everything; living, and resisting the collapse of everything which makes me a Frenchman, a man; of everything, in brief, which allows one to live.[17] "My life belongs to my country—today as it did yesterday. Let her take it; but if my life is my country's, my country's indefeasible duty is to clarify this horrible drama completely, for my honor does not belong to her; it is the patrimony of our children and of our families."[18]

Always he spoke of his innocence, his loyalty, the justice he awaited. He demanded courage, of himself and of Lucie. "As I have told you, it is neither wearying tears nor useless words that are needed, but acts."[19] At times he would break down: "If you would have me live, my darling, bring my honor back to me as soon as possible, for I will not be able to bear this martyrdom indefinitely. I would rather tell you the truth, the whole truth, than lull you with deceptive illusions."[20] "Such torture ends up surpassing the limits of human energy. It has to end," he wrote in September.[21] "If there were only myself, my disgust with people and things is so deep that I would long for nothing but that great repose—eternal rest."[22] But he sprang back quickly: "Every time that I break down during my long solitary days and nights . . . and would like to close my eyes in order to see, think, and suffer no more, I stiffen in a violent effort of my whole being and shout to myself, 'You are not alone, you are a father, you must defend your honor, and that of your wife and your children. . . .' "[23]

He and his wife served as sources of mutual encouragement; they became rivals in heroism. But they understood their mutual suffering and perceived their brief weaknesses. "Each of them," wrote Joseph Reinach, "emerged equally defeated from their struggle in magnanimity. Both would henceforth try to shut their eyes to their misery, to restrain their hearts. . . ."[24] Between them, throughout a correspondence in which love found expression in every line, through words that they adapted from each other, the ties of tenderness, of a shared ordeal, of the courage to which they inspired each other, and of faith were woven ever thicker. Love nourished their energy. Endlessly, they spoke of their children, their name, their honor, their future: "I think of my wife, of the suffering she must endure. I think of my darling little ones. . . ."[25] "I must gather all my strength and resist still more, still murmuring softly those three names, my talisman: Lucie, Pierre, Jeanne."[26] To his son Pierre, to whom Lucie had explained that his father had gone on a long trip, he wrote, "When papa comes back from his trip, you will come to look for him at the station, with little Jeanne, mama, and everybody."* Not a single letter failed to evoke the children, their gestures, their shouts, "our dear children," "our little ones," "our dear little ones." It was for them, for their honor, their future, that Lucie and he must fight on.†

On Devil's Island, cut off from all sources of information, no letter was to speak to him of his plight. He knew nothing. He speculated and improvised. Lucie must go and throw their children at the feet of the president of the Republic.[28] "Be heroic, it is you whom the duty befalls." He grew impatient: Were not she and Mathieu wasting time? Were they daring enough? He wrote to Commandant du Paty de Clam, to General de Boisdeffre, to the minister of war. On October 5, he wrote the president of the Republic, Félix Faure,

> Accused and then convicted on the basis of my script of the most infamous crime a soldier can commit, I declared and declare again that I did not write the letter attributed to me, that I have never betrayed my honor.

* Letter to Pierre, May 18, 1895. Dreyfus wrote very little to his children. But he was undoubtedly restrained by the painful deception that he and Lucie would keep up until he returned.

† On several occasions, Lucie Dreyfus requested to join her husband on Devil's Island, in conformity with the laws of 1872 and 1873 which recognized "the right of families of deportees to travel to deportation sites." The Council of Ministers would consider the issue twice. No explicitly justified refusal was ever given her, but she was informed that her presence was incompatible with the conditions under which the convict was living.[27]

For a year, alone with my conscience, I have struggled against the most frightful fate by which a man might be beset.

I am not speaking of physical suffering, which is nothing; the pains of the heart are all.

To suffer in this way is already frightening, but to feel all one's family around one suffering is horrible. The agony of an entire family for an abominable crime I did not commit.

I come to solicit neither pardon, nor favors, nor moral convictions. I request, I beg that a full clarification be made of the machination whose unfortunate and frightening victims I and my family have been.

If I have lived, Mister President, if I manage to continue living, it is because the sacred duty that I must fulfill toward my own fills my soul and governs it; otherwise, I would already have succumbed beneath a burden too weighty for human shoulders.

In the name of my honor which has been stripped from me through a frightening error, in the name of my wife, in the name of my children—Oh! Mister President, at that last thought alone, my heart as a father, as a Frenchman, as an honest man roars and howls with pain—I ask you for justice, and that justice which I am soliciting you for with all my soul, with all the strength of my heart, my hands joined in a supreme prayer, is to cast a full light on this tragic story, to stop the frightful martyrdom of a soldier and of a family for whom honor is all.

He would receive a response on January 12, 1896: "Rejected without comment."

He would write again to Faure a year later, on September 10, 1896, sending him the journal which—"broken in body and soul"—he would stop writing that very year:[29]

Mister President,
I take the liberty of requesting of you that this journal, written day by day, be conveyed to my wife.

There will perhaps be found in it, Mister President, cries of anger and fear against the most frightful condemnation which has ever befallen a human being—and a human being who has never sacrificed his honor. I do not feel within me the courage to reread it, to reembark on this horrendous journey.

I recriminate no one; everyone thought himself acting within the fullness of his rights and his conscience. I simply declare once again that I am innocent of this abominable crime, and I continue to make but one request, which remains the same: to search out the true culprit, the author of this heinous crime. . . .

"I recriminate no one": It is true that in the long howl of courage and pain comprised by his journal and correspondence, Alfred Dreyfus never attacked anyone—except, on one or two occasions, Commandant du Paty de Clam and Alphonse Bertillon, the handwriting expert whose testimony condemned him. But he lost confidence in neither the civilian nor the military authorities. It was from the president of the Republic, the government, the Army, its chiefs, the minister of war, and the chief of the General Staff that he expected the demonstration of his innocence. He sought "neither pardon nor special favor." But he maintained his trust. Even in jail Dreyfus was a French officer. He requested an end to "the frightful martyrdom of a soldier and a family for whom honor is all." The Army and France were his reasons for living and believing. It was from them that he awaited justice.

Even in moments of despair, it does not appear that any religious sentiment came to his aide. The ethic which sustained him, composed of the great traditional virtues—Honor, Justice, Courage, Loyalty, Duty— sought no sustenance in God. The word *God* occurs twice in his writings—and quite incidentally.* The word *Jew* does not occur even once. Nor did Lucie ever mention the subject. And yet he must surely have heard the shouts of "Death to the Jews!" and "Death to Judas!" in the courtyard of the École Militaire and in the streets of La Rochelle.

Dreyfus had been sentenced to perpetual deportation, a political punishment. But the minister of colonies had elaborated for his case an original system, not based on any legal text. It was imperative to punish him simultaneously with exemplary severity and to eliminate any risk of escape.

Within his "cage," the deportee could not sleep. He would nod off only intermittently for several brief minutes. Insects ran over his skin. The guards relaying each other appeared to him through the lattice of the entrance like so many ghosts. The heat was crushing: 104 degrees Fahrenheit when he arrived on Devil's Island. At night, he was racked by fevers which would grow only worse in the course of his stay.

In the morning, within the space of a few hundred square meters within which he could walk, always with a guard, he chopped wood. At eight o'clock, he was brought a serving of bread, and occasionally a piece of raw meat. His habitual "diet" consisted as well of lard and dry vegetables with a handful of coarse salt. Only exceptionally did he have green vegeta-

---

* On December 3, 1895, in his journal, he evoked Schopenhauer's line: "If God created the world, I would not like to be God."

bles and pork.[30] For dinner he was given bread and water. The diet in fact was so abject that he wrote to the governor of Guiana to get permission, as the law allowed, to have canned foods transported from Cayenne at his own expense.* "All my time is spent in the struggle for life."[31] He attempted to construct a grill with old scraps of sheet metal. Rusted sheet metal served as his pot. He had no plate. There was a supply of them at the hospital stockroom, but Commandant Bouchet was opposed to allowing Dreyfus to have one.[32] In the course of his walks. he discovered several cultivated areas abandoned by the lepers, a few wild tomatoes which he avidly devoured.

His diet improved somewhat when the high commandant of the islands "had the kindness" to have him sent some cans of concentrated milk,[33] then to bring him tea, four plates, and two pots.[34] As of the end of April, his schedule became rigid: his day began at 5:30 A.M. The preparation of his miserable meals took up a part of his time. From 10:00 A.M. to 3:00 P.M., the heat was unbearable. During that time, he would smoke, try to learn English, and write his journal. As soon as the heat subsided, he would chop wood and wash his laundry. at 6:00 P.M. he dined and was then locked up. There was no lamp in his hut, so he was obliged to go to bed. The oppressive heat, the sudden storms, the wind blowing up a tempest, the animals one had to kill, the nervous tension, and the rising sadness all prevented him from sleeping. "How much better death would be than this slow agony, this martyrdom of every minute."[35]

In May the oppressive humidity was interrupted by the arrival of torrential rains.† He fainted on several occasions and ran high fevers. The doctor came to see him and cared for him as best he could. "A bad day, fever, upset stomach, disgust with everything. What is happening in France all this while?"[37] June brought him great joy: he received from his wife and family letters which, though more than three months late, helped him to survive. The rainy season was drawing to a close. The same sufferings persisted: insect bites, unrelenting surveillance, obsessive concern with the injustice that had befallen him. He could not manage to work more than a few minutes at a time. He did little but wait for the mail and write letters. He spent nights without shutting his eyes. In June, the high commandant paid him a visit. Dreyfus attempted to speak with him.

---

* Mathieu Dreyfus would attempt in vain to find a correspondent in Cayenne. The tradesman whom he chose, M. Dufourg, would be the object of police harassment in Cayenne on several occasions. He would renounce his mission.

† On May 7, there was a meticulous search of his quarters, his clothes, and his books. It appeared that what was being sought (on orders from the Ministry of Colonies) was a "code" that would have allowed Dreyfus to correspond with his family and prepare his escape. The assumption of his duties by Chief-Guard Lebars on May 20 appears to have coincided with a general overhaul of instructions.[36]

Chief-Guard Lebars would note, "He could not proceed . . . his words were cut short by sobs, and he wept copiously for about a quarter of an hour.[38] "The foul weather kept him from going outdoors," observed Lebars on July 9 in his daily report. "After eating, he composed his English composition, then went to bed." In August the heat was horrendous. "If I succumb, and these lines ever reach you, my dear Lucie, know that I shall have done all that is humanly possible to resist so long and painful a martyrdom."* In September he underwent violent palpitations, and fainting spells which grew in frequency. He had received a few books, but found it difficult to read. His head caused him tremendous suffering. During the following months, Dreyfus was to seem crushed by despair and weakness. His headaches became unbearable. "I have had enough," he wrote, "of this life of perpetual suspicion, being treated like a wild beast. . . ."[40] His guards were ordered not to speak to him. With the doctor's authorization, he requested permission to take a swim in the ocean. Permission was denied him. In December the rain fell without surcease. "My blood is burning my skin, the fever devouring me. When will this torture end?"[41]

On December 31, he received a few letters—dated from October and November—and in January 1896 a "considerable shipment" of books.† "But I can no longer read for long periods; everything is out of joint in me."[42] As of February 1896 the journal entries were less frequent and their wording more repetitious. "It's been a long time since I've added anything to my journal," he wrote in July 1896. His nights were long, seemingly interminable bouts of fever and delirium. Throughout the month of July he lay in bed for the most part, prostrated by malarial fever. Along with his medication of quinine, his nourishment consisted of little more than milk. "How much longer will I still be able to resist? . . . I hope this wretched ordeal will end soon, if not I bequeath my children to France, to my country which I have always served with devotion and loyalty, imploring with all my soul and all my strength those who are in charge of the affairs of our country to cast an unsparing light on this frightening drama."[43]

On the evening of September 6, 1896, Dreyfus was "clapped into

---

* Journal entry of August 10, 1895. On August 15, the Director of the Penitential Administration, M. Guégen, visited Dreyfus in the company of the High Commandant of the Islands. He asked Dreyfus whether he had any requests. "M. le Commandant du Paty," answered Dreyfus, "had promised me before my departure from France to continue his inquiries. I did not believe that could last so long . . ."[39] Lebars noted on September 1: "The deportee has been crying since he awoke. He says 'this' can not go on much longer, that his heart will end up bursting. . . . I am keeping a close watch on him."
† He read Montaigne, Spinoza, and the works of Napoleon, for whom he had great admiration.

irons" following the announcement by an English newspaper of his escape.* "Received an iron bed," Lebars was to note in his report, "to which were fitted a bar and two rings. In accordance with orders received, the deportee has been placed this night in double shackles and will remain there until new orders so instruct."[44] Why this treatment was suddenly imposed on a prisoner who was depressed and seriously ill, Dreyfus did not know. "As long as I have been here, I have always followed the strict path that was set for me and obeyed the orders I was given absolutely. . . . My duty is to go on until the exhaustion of my strength," he wrote on September 8. "I will—simply—go on."[45] On September 9, Bravard, the commandant of the islands, who was inflexible but sympathetic to his plight, came to see him and explained with some gentleness that his being clapped into irons was not a punishment. It was merely a security measure ordered by Paris.[46] Thereafter, by order of the minister of the colonies, Dreyfus would be locked up in his cabin night and day—with "double shackles at night."† The perimeter of the walking area around his cabin was to be surrounded by a double stockade, and a sentinel placed within it. The communication of letters and dispatches would be suspended until further notice. "Would that I were in my grave!" Racked with fever, mentally crushed, Dreyfus cut short his journal. He ended it on September 10, 1896, asking the president of the Republic to transmit it to his wife.‡ It seemed likely to him that he would die on Devil's Island. "On the day that the truth will come to light, I request that my beloved wife and children receive the pity inspired by so great a misfortune."

Dreyfus would never receive a response.[48]

---

* See *infra* p. 164.

† In *Cinq années de ma vie*,[47] Dreyfus describes as follows the torture to which he was subjected from September 6 to October 20: "Two U-shaped irons were affixed at their bottom to the sides of the bed. An iron bar was run through those irons, to which were attached two shackles. At one end of the bar, there was a terminal stop, at the other a padlock, so that the bar was affixed to the irons and consequently to the bed. When my feet were thus placed in the two shackles, I was no longer able to move; I was attached to the bed. The torture was horrible, especially during those torrid nights. Soon the very tight shackles on my ankles inflicted wounds." The iron bars, gradually making their way into Alfred Dreyfus's bruised flesh, left a lasting mark. Dreyfus attempted in vain to protect his ankles with rags.

‡ See *supra* p. 129.

6

The First Jew to Rise on Behalf of the Jew

As the months of the dark year 1895 passed, Mathieu Dreyfus grew desperate at his inability to do anything for his brother.[1] His sole consolation was the visits of Ferdinand Forzinetti, the courageous director of the Prison of Cherche-Midi who, at the risk of his career, openly championed Dreyfus's innocence. It was a second "jailer," Patin, who had given the Dreyfus sisters, during the convict's brief stay in his prison, the idea of seeking the help of a writer, a journalist capable of being heard. "It is before public opinion," he told them, "that your brother's cause must be defended." Patin suggested Edouard Drumont or Bernard Lazare. Drumont, editor of *La Libre Parole*, the most fanatical of anti-Semites? The idea seemed absurd. Instead Mathieu contacted Bernard Lazare. They each had relatives in Carpentras, who organized a meeting.

Lazare-Marius Bernard, known as Bernard Lazare, was at the time a very young man, descended from a Jewish family, who in the course of a few years had won for himself an intellectual audience.* He had been noted and feared for the positions he had taken in favor of revolutionary thinkers and anarchists. On their behalf, he had testified in court and done battle in newspapers. In 1894, he published a long essay on *L'antisémitisme, son Histoire et ses Causes*, which had been a *succès d'estime*. Drumont wrote at the time that it was "a remarkable book, nourished with facts and domi-

---

* He was born in Nîmes on June 14, 1865. After studies at the École des Hautes Etudes, he entered swiftly into the world of journalism. A cousin of the poet Ephraïm Mikhaël, he had collaborated with him in writing *La Fiancée de Corinthe*. He had produced a number of literary works, such as *Le Miroir des Légendes, La Porte d'Ivoire,* and *Les Porteurs de Torche.* Along with a few friends, he had founded a journal: *Les Entretiens Politiques et Littéraires,* in which young avant-garde writers published. He also wrote for the *Revue Bleue* and a number of dailies, such as *L'Echo de Paris* and *Le Journal.* "He occupied a worthy place in the literary generation immediately preceding my own," Léon Blum would write.[2]

nated from end to end by a fine effort at impartiality, a discipline imposed on the mind not to yield to influences of race."[3] Scrupulously examining the causes of anti-Semitism, which he explained in large measure by the behavior and character of the Jews,* Lazare affirmed in the book the necessity of a gradual assimilation, whose difficulties he nevertheless noted.[5] At the conclusion of his work, which claimed to be an objective study, Lazare announced the end of anti-Semitism,† concomitant with a disappearance of the religious impulse which he took to be part of the irresistible progress of revolutionary development: "Between the emancipated French Jew and the Talmudic Galician Jew, the gaps grow wider every day . . . the Talmudic spirit is slowly disappearing." The day would come when the Jew would no longer identify himself as a Jew and would no longer be identified as such.

Anti-Semitism was thus but a stage, bound to a prior order of things, of Jewish history. It partook of a declining system of thought—religion, nationalism, and capitalism. Soon that system would be brought to ruin by the forces of social revolution and by the transformation of the structures of society.[7] Lazare had thus adapted for his own use the prevalent theory of the inevitable assimilation of the Jews, which he situated in a perspective of social revolution.

At the very beginning of the Dreyfus Affair, Bernard Lazare had given his answer to the publisher and journalist P.-V. Stock, who had advised him to take a position. "Why? I know neither him nor his people. If he were some poor devil, I would be worried for him. But Dreyfus and his family are very rich, they say; they'll be able to take care of themselves very well without me, especially if he is innocent. . . ."[8] Angered by the anti-Semitic explosion which had surrounded the arrest and trial of Dreyfus, he had, nevertheless, taken a stand. In "Le Nouveau Ghetto," an article published in *La Justice* of November 17, 1894, he had denounced the "atmosphere of hostility and defiance, of latent hatred and prejudice, a

---

* "The Jew," wrote Bernard Lazare, "is certainly more gifted than anyone else when it comes to success. If he has been degraded by mercantile practices, those practices have armed him over the ages with qualities which have become central in the contemporary organization of society. He is cold and calculating, energetic and flexible, persevering and patient, lucid and precise, and all those qualities have been inherited from his ancestors, the traffickers and handlers of ducats. If he applies himself to the activities of commerce and finance, he benefits from centuries-old ancestral training, which has not made him more open, as his vanity would have it, but more suited to certain functions."[4]

† "Thus anti-Semitism unconsciously prepares its own downfall, bearing within itself the seed of its own destruction. And this is ineluctable, since in opening the path to socialism and communism, it works to eliminate not only the economic causes, but also the religious and national causes which engendered it and which will disappear with the present society whose products they are."[6]

ghetto more terrible than any from which one might escape through revolt,"* and in an article entitled "Antisemitisme et Antisemites," published by *L'Echo de Paris* of December 31, 1894, he had violently attacked anti-Semites in all quarters who were profiting from the Dreyfus Affair.

Mathieu Dreyfus showed Lazare the few documents in his possession, in particular the commentary his brother had written on the report prepared by d'Ormescheville, the judge advocate of the first Court-Martial. It appears that he had little difficulty in convincing the young writer of a judicial error. "Thus it was that the famous defender of anarchists and revolutionaries accepted to do everything in his power to aid the wealthy Jewish family." Anti-Dreyfusards would never relinquish their claim that Bernard Lazare had been "bought" by the Dreyfus family.[10]

Lazare set to work immediately. By the spring of 1895, he was writing the first draft of his essay for Dreyfus.† He had extremely few documents at his disposition and committed numerous errors. But his intelligence, precision, and, on occasion, his prescience were astonishing. A simple and rigorous style shorn of all declamation gave force to the argument. Lazare, thoroughly convinced, wanted to publish his text forthwith. Mathieu Dreyfus was hesitant and delayed publication. Dreyfus's lawyer, Edgar Demange, advised him to wait for an auspicious moment; at the time, more direct routes ought to be tried, and public protest avoided.[11] "I lived that year," Lazare would say, "waiting in a state of impatience, feverish to enter into action."[12] The young writer found it hard to understand Mathieu's prudence, but submitted to it.[13]

In Parliament, the Dreyfus Affair was not even mentioned, from the left to the right. Only a few discussions provided an opportunity for anti-Semitism to be voiced. In May 1895 deputy Denis from Landes intervened, asking that the Jews "be rechanneled toward the center of France, where treason is less dangerous." The Socialist, Rouanet, rejected the question of race: "There are neither Jews nor Christians, but capitalists." And Alfred Joseph Naquet, a Jew, mounted the podium to discredit anti-Semitism: "From religion, it borrows the spirit of fanaticism and intolerance. To conservative or capitalist thought, it offers the idea of

* During the same period, the Austrian Jew Theodore Herzl was completing the writing of a play entitled *The Ghetto*, in which he developed ideas close to those expressed by Bernard Lazare in his article of November 1894. Marrus believes that Herzl and Bernard Lazare had already met when the Affair erupted.[9]

† At the same time, on June 9, 1895, the Chambers were passing legislation, under discussion for five years, which in expanding the grounds for revision of penal convictions, authorized thereafter cases of revision for reason of the discovery of "new facts." It was within the perspective thus opened up that Bernard Lazare would work. He would never stop revising his text, bringing it up to date—right up to the date of publication.

envy and fear; it invokes socialism only out of its propensity to disorder; and it retains of patriotism only its suspicion and hatred."[14]

The extreme right protested, drowning the voice of the apostle of divorce, the Jew who was defending himself. President Henri Brisson called Denis back to order, and in a long speech the minister of the interior explained why one could not and should not "rechannel the Jews." After that brief debate the Chamber, bored but appeased, simply approved the motion.

If the debate was aborted in Parliament, it pursued its course in the public mind. In the spring of 1896, Bernard Lazare, desperate to act, entered the polemic. The occasion would be an article published on May 16, 1896, by the writer Emile Zola under the title, "Pour les Juifs." In it, Zola denounced in violent terms the anti-Semitic furor which had been unleashed in the press:

> Let us return then to the depth of the forests, let us begin again the savage war of species against species; let us devour each other because we don't share the same shout and our hair is implanted differently. . . . The Jews have their faults, their vices: they are accused of being a nation in the nation, of being above all frontiers, a kind of international sect without real homeland; above all of carrying in their blood a need for lucre, a love for money, a prodigious intelligence for business which, in less than a century, have accumulated enormous fortunes in their hands. But these separatist Jews, so poorly melted into the nation, overly avid, obsessed with the conquest of gold are in fact the creation of Christians, "the work of our eighteen hundred years of imbecilic persecution." They have been restricted to deplorable neighborhoods, like lepers; why be surprised, then, that in the prison of their ghetto, they have tightened their family bonds![15]

Drumont responded to Zola more violently still, in *La Libre Parole* of May 18, attributing Zola's articles to the vilest of motives: the poor sales of his most recent novels, and the wish to enter the Académie Française. It was at that point that Lazare entered the battle. In a series of articles published in May and June 1896 in *Le Voltaire*, he attacked Drumont and warned the anti-Semites that the Jews would not let themselves be bullied much longer. Lazare observed with regret the general passivity of French Jews. "There are a great number of them who have retained from past persecutions a deplorable habit: that of receiving blows and not protesting, of bending the spine, waiting for the storm to pass, and playing dead lest they attract a bolt of lightning."[16] The Jews are, wrote Lazare, the victims of "an ancient tradition of humility" and an "ancestral pusillanimity."[17] But not all are so timorous.

> I know some who have different conceptions. I know many others who advocate far less meekness. They have had enough of anti-Semitism; they are tired of the insults, the slander, the lies, the dissertations on Cornelius Herz and the prosopopeias on Baron de Reinach. And tomorrow they will be legion, and if they believed as I do, they would group openly, courageously, against you, against your doctrines, and no longer satisfied with defending themselves, they would attack you; and you are not invulnerable, neither you nor your friends.

The controversy, which would continue until the summer, would end, as was customary, with a duel. On June 18, 1896 Drumont and Lazare exchanged shots, to no effect. But Lazare had changed his convictions and his struggle. He was no longer the observer of a gradual and desirable assimilation. He considered himself thereafter the defender of the Jews, "the spokesman of a Jewish resistance too long deferred."[18] "From one day to the next," he would write, "I became a pariah. Since my ancestry had long prepared me for such a state, I did not suffer morally from it."[19]

Mobilized in the service of the martyred Jew, "he was the first of the Dreyfusards," Léon Blum would write, "the one from which would come almost all the others."[20] One of the first, in any event, and as of the fall of 1896, a tireless combatant. He wrote to Alexandre Millerand in the Chambre des Députés; visited the journalist Henri Rochefort; tried to enlist Deputy Jean Jaurès; to persuade Auguste Scheurer-Kestner, the vice president of the Senate, to move the writer François Coppée to action. He met at the time only indifference and skepticism, but nothing could discourage him. And little by little, article by article, year by year, he would become the champion of the Jewish cause. He had come to believe that French anti-Semitism was in no way an aberration, a historical accident, but that it was an integral part of French society, "even as Russian anti-Semitism was part of Russian society." He believed that such anti-Semitism was linked to Christianity, that it was "born on Calvary," and also that it reflected the degeneration of French society, of the societies of Europe in general. Dreyfus was the symbol of the persecuted Jew. The deportee of Devil's Island incarnated "the centuries of suffering of the people of martyrs."[21] In his jail, he was "the tragic image . . . of all those whose despair seeks a refuge in all corners of the world, a refuge in which they will at last find that justice which the best among them so called for on behalf of humanity in its entirety."

The Jews of France were hardly prepared to hear such words. Did Bernard Lazare's passion merely aggravate the problem by giving credence to the idea of Jewish solidarity? Daniel Halévy, a writer and an "assimilated" Jew, described Lazare as "a skillful business agent, an intermediary between the intellectuals and Jewish money. . . ."[22] For most French Jews, this intransigent, overly vehement, revolutionary writer lent support to the legend of a Jewish syndicate of cosmopolites and compromised the Jews dangerously by supporting, because he was Jewish, the cause of a traitor. He would never stop fighting, striking as many blows as he received, until he reached the point of exhaustion. "I wish," he proclaimed, "that it be said that I was the first to speak, that the first one to rise on behalf of the Jewish martyr was a Jew, a Jew who has suffered in his blood and in his flesh the suffering borne by the innocent man, a Jew who knew to what people of pariahs, of the disinherited, of unfortunates he belonged and who derived from that awareness the will to fight for justice and truth."[23] Lazare would die of cancer at the age of thirty-eight on September 2, 1903. A few wealthy Jews took up a collection to assist his widow. In Nîmes, some of his few friends would erect in his memory a modest monument. The indifference was almost universal.

"I will tell of his burial.* Who we were, how few, in the cortege, in the gray and faithful procession descending and passing through Paris. In the middle of vacation. . . . A few, the same madmen, the same fanatics, Jews and Christians, a few—very few—rich Jews, a few—very few—rich Christians, the poor and wretched Jews and Christians, themselves in rather small number. A small troop, in brief, a very small troop."[24] Thus did the writer Charles Péguy exalt the memory of his friend Bernard Lazare. "I never saw a man, I am not saying *believe*, but *know* to that extent. I am not saying merely that a conscience is above jurisdiction but that it is, that it itself exercises a jurisdiction, that it is the supreme jurisdiction, and the only one. . . ." For Péguy, Lazare "had aspects of a saint, of holiness." He lived and died "for the Jews like a martyr." And since he was a prophet, "it was just that he be buried prematurely amid silence and oblivion. In perfect silence and concerted oblivion."[25] The Jews had rejected him. "He was dead before he died. As though they were ashamed of him."[26] "He possessed to the highest degree that morality of the group or band, which is perhaps the only morality."[27]

---

* It took place on September 4, 1903. Few people bothered to attend. Mathieu Dreyfus was present; Alfred Dreyfus was not.

"He was a hero," Péguy would proclaim. And in identifying with the Jew who was "the first to rise," the fighting Jew, the mystical Jew, the detested Jew, Péguy would bear witness for history. "We were heroes. We should say so quite simply, for I do not believe that anyone will say it for us."[28]

7

The "Petit Bleu"

Colonel Jean Sandherr, head of the Intelligence Service, was growing sicker by the day. The first symptoms of a general paralysis were beginning to appear.[1] It became imperative to consider a replacement. His adjunct, Commandant Albert Cordier, who was ill at ease in the Statistics Section, did not want to take his place, and undoubtedly could not have done so. Commandant Henry, who was actually running the office, dreamed of becoming the head of French Intelligence, but he was lacking in stature. In point of fact, General Raoul de Boisdeffre, chief of the General Staff, had already made his decision and persuaded the new minister of war, General Emile Zurlinden to agree. It was Commandant Georges Picquart who appeared best equipped to assume such an imposing responsibility.

Picquart was of Alsacian origin,[2] born in Strasbourg on September 6, 1854. He had studied at Saint-Cyr academy, graduated fifth in his class, served with the General Staff, where he emerged as second in command, then went on to conduct a series of splendid campaigns in Africa and Tonkin. At age thirty-three, he was a battalion chief. As an instructor at the École de Guerre, he had had Alfred Dreyfus as a student. He had given him a mediocre grade in a specialty, topography, in which Dreyfus did not excel. General Gaston de Galliffet had called Picquart to his General Staff; for five years he had directed the Intelligence section. He was an extremely intelligent officer—quite gifted, quite diligent, but whose character was as concealed as it was complex, an officer of rare intellectual distinction.[3] His superiors had appreciated his competence and devotion. It was to him that the chief of the General Staff, in December 1894, had confided the task of "following" and reporting on the Dreyfus trial.* It was he who had represented the minister of war at the ceremony of dismissal.

After a few hesitations (since he had no particular taste for his new specialty), Picquart accepted the post that he had been offered. On July 1, 1895, he was named head of the Section of Statistics and simultaneously scheduled for promotion to the rank of lieutenant colonel.

The ailing Sandherr received Picquart in his home in order to brief him. He was advised that General de Boisdeffre continued to be preoccupied by the "Dreyfus question." "If you need any evidence to convince people, you need but ask Henry for the small file which was transmitted to the judges in their chamber."† That act of confidence could not have surprised Picquart. A few days later, de Boisdeffre confirmed to Picquart that "the Dreyfus Affair is not over. It is only beginning. A new offensive by the Jews is to be feared." He explained to him that it would be necessary to continue feeding the file.

Commandant Henry, who was disappointed at being superseded, had the shrewdness to rally to his new chief, whom he already knew. Picquart was attracted by Henry's ruggedness, his limitless devotion, his experience as a former trooper. For a long time Picquart would continue to have full confidence in him.

Picquart had never questioned the guilt of the Jew Dreyfus, whom he had observed at length throughout his trial. Neither during the debate, nor at the ceremony of degradation could Dreyfus move him. He seemed to him to be merely acting. Respecting the instructions of de Boisdeffre, he would try, like his predecessor, to "fatten" the Dreyfus file,‡ without finding anything against the deportee of Devil's Island worthy of interest. He had, however, numerous concerns besides Dreyfus. The ordinary track continued to bring in numerous documents. And he was obliged to supervise the case of other suspected officers, such as Hecquet d'Orval, of whom Zurlinden had asked him to keep special track.[6] There were numerous spies and counterspies to be supervised, much to be done. . . .

Picquart wanted to assert his authority within the service and to im-

* "He never seemed to have doubted that the accused was guilty," General de Boisdeffre would state at the Rennes trial. Why would he have doubted it? Joseph Reinach observed that like most officers, he was anti-Semitic. He was angered when his name was misspelled "Picard." When charged with assigning the officers serving their apprenticeships to the various offices of the General Staff, he asked Commandant Mercier-Milon to excuse him "for having given him the Jew Dreyfus."[4] It appears that on the last day of the trial, fearing acquittal, he pushed for the communication of the secret documents.
† Sandherr specified that the documents were in Henry's closet, but did not add that General Mercier had ordered them to be dispersed.
‡ Henry persuaded him to contact François Guénée, who made new inquiries at the clubs where Dreyfus would have gambled and with the women he had known.[5]

prove its organization. He decided that henceforth Commandant Henry would receive Madame Bastian's "cones" only in order to assure their delivery. He would immediately convey any papers received to his superior, who would examine them personally. It was thus Picquart who would see them first, and then confide them to Captain Jules Lauth who would reconstitute them.* On another count, Picquart decided to increase surveillance of Lieutenant Colonel Maximilian von Schwarzkoppen and Major Alessandro Panizzardi, the Italian military attaché. But the new chief of the Section of Statistics had scruples unknown to Sandherr. Since he was intent on not violating the law, whenever a problem arose he had the habit of consulting his old friend from Strasbourg, Louis Leblois, a former magistrate who had become a lawyer in Paris. At Picquart's call, Leblois would come with increasing frequency to the Ministry.† Finally Picquart eliminated the access to the service of its "seedy" agents. His subordinates were to meet them outside their offices. It appears that Picquart's seriousness, prudence, and efficiency were well received by his superiors. De Boisdeffre could not stop singing his praises. The three ministers of war who succeeded each other in less than a year, Generals Emile Zurlinden, Godefroy Cavaignac, and Jean-Baptiste Billot, were unsparing in their demonstrations of esteem for him.

In the month of March 1896 the routine of the Section of Statistics was somewhat disturbed. Commandant Henry was to fulfill several missions in Paris and in Toul, and he journeyed to the bedside of his severely ill mother in Pogny in the Somme. In the course of a brief stay in Paris, between either March 1 and 3, or March 4 and 15, he met Madame Bastian in a chapel of Sainte-Clotilde.[9] She handed him voluminous bagfuls, the harvest of more than a month. Henry brought them to the Ministry without taking the time to look at them. Picquart locked them in his closet, then entrusted them on the following day or the day after to Commandant Lauth, who began the long and arduous assignment of reconstituting them. In one of the "cones," he discovered the numerous fragments of a letter-telegram, on blue paper, known in

* Henry, disappointed by the new arrangement, would not always respect his superior's order. He was to take several paper cones home with him and examine their contents before Picquart. He would thus be able to proceed to a first "sorting out" of material.[7]
† Leblois was the son of a pastor who had been one of the leading figures of Alsatian Protestantism. In Strasbourg, he had been Picquart's schoolmate. Throughout the Affair, his personality would be the subject of debate. Some would judge him cunning, meddlesome, hesitant, and awkward. Others would detect in him a number of discreet virtues: scrupulous integrity, kindness, modesty (see P.V. Stock's portrait of him in *Mémorandum d'un éditeur*, op. cit., p. 887). At his death on January 6, 1928, Leblois would leave a manuscript that his widow would publish under the title *L'Affaire Dreyfus: L'Iniquité/La Réparation*.[8]

Paris under the name of *petit bleu*. He gathered thirty or forty pieces, "of which the largest was less than a square centimeter," assembled them as in a puzzle, then glued them together "with transparent paper cut in thin strips more or less following the outline of the tears." Lauth brought to his chief the reconstituted document, which was to become famous as the *petit bleu*.

It read as follows:

Sir,
Above all I await a more detailed explanation than the one you gave me the other day of the question in abeyance. Consequently, I am requesting you to give it to me in writing so I may judge if I can continue my relations with the R. house or not. Signed: C.

On the side reserved for the address the name and address of the addressee were to be found:

Monsieur le Commandant Esterhazy 27, rue de la Bienfaisance— Paris

The *petit bleu* was not stamped. The addressee had thus not received it. The sender had quite meticulously ripped it up without sending it. He had thrown the pieces into the wastebasket.[10]

Lauth was aghast at his discovery. "It's frightening," he told Picquart. "Is there then still another one?" Picquart said nothing, took the fragile document, and began to reflect. The initial *C* was one of the conventional signatures of Schwarzkoppen, and the fragments had been found in the embassy. Clearly, the document designated a traitor. Picquart reflected on the best way in which to begin an inquiry. A few days later, he asked Lauth to photograph the letter-telegram and to delete any trace of its having been ripped up. Lauth was unable to comply. But why such bizarre instructions? "I want to be able to claim that the document was seized in the mails," was Picquart's alleged response to Lauth.[11] It is in fact probable that he was not eager for there to be any new discussions of the "ordinary track" outside his service. There had already been too much said about in 1894.

But on the same day the "ordinary track" had brought a second document of equal importance which has not achieved the notoriety of the *petit bleu*.* It was a letter written in pencil and partially mutilated by a vertical rip that destroyed a considerable number of words. Its text may

* Curiously enough, Joseph Reinach scarcely accords any importance to this document.[12]

nevertheless be reconstituted—in its meaning if not in its exact letter. Marcel Thomas has restored it as follows:[13]

To be delivered by the concierge.

Sir,

I regret not speaking personally (to you) about a matter which (will annoy you considerably). My father has just (refused) the funds necessary to continue (the tour) in the conditions which were stipulated (between us). I will explain to you his reasons, but I begin by telling you already today (that he deems) your conditions too harsh for me and (fears greatly) the results that (might issue from a prolongation) of the trip. He proposes to me (a different) tour concerning which we might (agree. He regards) the relations I have (made) for him up until now out of proportion (with the amount) I have spent on the trips. The point is (I have) to speak to you as soon as possible.

I am returning to you with this the sketches you gave me the other day; they are not the last. C.*

The document was confirmation of treason and also of the dissatisfaction of the German military attaché. Schwarzkoppen wanted to return to Esterhazy the plans the latter had confided to him. He seized on the occasion to tell him that his superiors (my father) deemed Esterhazy's services too costly and too compromising. Their collaboration would have to be worked out on new grounds. Esterhazy, as Marcel Thomas has commented, was to be bought at a discount.[14]

The *petit bleu*, even with the light shed on it by the second document, still contained its enigmas. Above all it allowed for the elaboration of many a legend. Some, against the evidence, have challenged its authenticity.† Its date has been the subject of controversy. During the course of his depositions, Commandant Lauth would date the arrival of the document in the fall of 1895, then in March, then in April. Picquart himself would attempt to "delay" the arrival of the *petit bleu*, situating it in May, then in April, only to acknowledge later on that it had arrived in March. In particular, the author of the *petit bleu*—and of the second document, since they were clearly written by the same hand—still remains unknown. But that Colonel Schwarzkoppen was responsible for its content has never been doubted. The military attaché would acknowledge as much, moreover, in his *Notebooks*:

* The words in parenthesis are hypothetical, but quite plausible.
† Picquart would be accused by the General Staff of having fabricated the *petit bleu*.

I have already said that at the time I had reason to be dissatisfied with Esterhazy's intelligence work. I did not conceal this from him during his visit of February 20 and in fact threatened him with a break in our relations. Since Esterhazy, after that occasion, did not show up for a rather long period of time, toward the beginning of March I sent him a *petit bleu*—a sealed pneumatic letter, with the following contents. . . .[15]

But Lauth, and undoubtedly Picquart as well, had immediately noticed that the handwriting of the reconstituted *petit bleu* was not Schwarzkoppen's. Why had he not himself written his message to Esterhazy? Joseph Reinach adopted the generally accepted point of view when he wrote his *Histoire de l'Affaire Dreyfus* that Schwarzkoppen would have had the *petit bleu* written by one of his mistresses who happened to be with him when he decided to break with Esterhazy. Maurice Paléologue, without any proof, categorically designated the culprit to be the charming Hermance de Weede, wife of an advisor at the Dutch embassy in Paris.[16] But the numerous letters from Madame de Weede seized by the Section of Statistics in the wastebasket of the military attaché between 1895 and 1897 are glaring proof that she did not write the *petit bleu*.[17] There is not the slightest resemblance in penmanship. Are we in fact obliged to conclude, as Joseph Reinach would have it, that the *petit bleu* was written in a woman's hand?* There is at present no possibility of ascertaining with certainty who wrote the two documents which arrived the same day by the ordinary track. Would Schwarzkoppen have had them written by some obscure embassy secretary, as claimed by Marcel Thomas, who, unlike Reinach, judged the handwriting to be "rather masculine"?[18] That is but one hypothesis among others.

The *petit bleu* bore with it a second enigma. Why was the document not sent, but torn up by the military attaché and thrown into the basket where "Auguste" got hold of it? Thomas supposes that the *petit bleu* represented a first—and more brutal—version of a message which Schwarzkoppen decided not to send. He would then have replaced it with a second letter "to be delivered by the concierge." That version would have come to the recipient along with the sketches of guns which were attached. Since it was less uncompromising, it allowed Esterhazy an opportunity to pursue their collaboration. Before sending it off, as was customary, Schwarzkoppen

---

* Von Schwarzkoppen had many other female friends in Paris. And the ordinary track brought in numerous letters (which were occasionally insignificant) from Mme. de Winterfield, wife of a German general, Mme. Fredericks, wife of the Russian military attaché, and Mme. Ghika, wife of a Rumanian diplomat. None of these handwritings recalled that of the *petit bleu*.

would have written a draft which he would then have torn up and placed in the basket.*

Schwarzkoppen, in his *Notebooks*, gives a completely different version.

> I do not know how the letter came into the possesssion of the French Ministry of War; in any event it was not found ripped up in my wastepaper basket, and it did not arrive there by way of the ordinary track. I am certain of having thrown it myself in the post box of the post office of rue (illegible). I do not believe it impossible that I was followed, and that the letter was seized there, in the post office, before being stamped.[20]

Was Schwarzkoppen erring in good faith? Was he not rather attempting to find an explanation favorable to himself in the eyes of history? First the bordereau in 1894, then the *petit bleu* in 1896, both ripped up and thrown into the wastebasket, would together seem to establish a veritable pattern of irresponsibility. Schwarzkoppen plainly wanted to minimize the role of the ordinary track, which was too clear a reminder of his blameworthy negligence.[21]

At the beginning of the month of April, after the burial of his mother, who died on March 28, Commandant Henry returned to his office. His friend Lauth showed him documents that had been discovered. A new case of treason had thus been uncovered. Esterhazy's name was not unknown to Henry. They had worked together between 1877 and 1880 at the Section of Statistics. Perhaps they had seen each other again in the interim. Had Henry in fact known of Commandant Esterhazy's clandestine activities? Did he feign astonishment because he was in fact a friend of the spy, whom he was protecting, as Joseph Reinach claimed?† Did he panic and rush to Esterhazy's home to warn him, "You are compromised"?[22] That Henry was from the start Esterhazy's accomplice and that they never stopped acting in collusion would be a thesis dear to the Dreyfusards. It was never based on anything more than a few—hardly conclusive—clues and the will to link up Esterhazy the spy and Henry the forger, from the

---

* The document "to be delivered by the concierge" would thus be the draft of the one that Esterhazy would in fact have received.[19]

† See Joseph Reinach, vol. II, p. 250. The thesis was taken up by Mathieu Dreyfus (*L'Affaire telle que je l'ai vécue*, op. cit., p. 193) and numerous historians of the Affair. Marcel Thomas, on the other hand, rejects it for lack of conclusive evidence: "When he read it for the first time on the photographs of the *petit bleu*, the name of Esterhazy, his old friend from the Section of Statistics, cannot but have struck Henry, even if (as seems certain), he had lost track of him over ten years' time" (op. cit., p. 231). Marcel Thomas claims that Henry was quick to discover—no doubt before Picquart—that Esterhazy was the author of the bordereau.

very first united by crime.* It is more plausible that Henry was at first dumbfounded that Esterhazy, the old friend of whom he retained such a fond recollection, had become a spy. Henry knew in intimate detail the dossier on which Dreyfus's conviction had been based, and how it had been fabricated. Henry had a police detective's mind—inquisitive and inventive. Was it then that the idea occurred to him to compare the handwriting of the bordereau with Esterhazy's? Did he suspect already that there had never been but a single spy?

To Picquart, who asked Henry whether he knew Esterhazy, Henry answered that they had been together eighteen years earlier in that very office, along with the Jewish officer, Maurice Weil. Picquart asked if there was anything suspicious about him. Henry replied that he did not know, that he had lost sight of him, but that Weil, Esterhazy's friend, was extremely suspect. Picquart consulted Henry on the choice of the agent to be assigned to keep the spy under surveillance.

Picquart would undertake his inquest concerning Esterhazy without mentioning it to either General de Boisdeffre, General Gonse, or the minister of war. A curious silence indeed! Picquart discovered that a French officer, a "second Dreyfus," was betraying, and he kept the secret for the Section of Statistics. "He luxuriated in solitude," explained Reinach. But was such a predisposition capable of causing him to deviate from his duty? Ought we to see in it, as does Marcel Thomas, the sign of a perilous pride, "an illusion of power"? Did the youngest lieutenant colonel in the French Army, the brilliant head of the Section of Statistics intend to keep first the secret, then the profit of his discovery? Was it not also true that he had but limited respect, even scorn and distrust, for his hierarchical superior, General Gonse, the second in command of the General Staff? But Picquart spoke to neither General de Boisdeffre nor the minister, with whom he had relations of complete confidence.

The ordinary track allowed Colonel Picquart to discover a second incident. A treasonous officer was at large. Against all reason, and despite his own duty, Picquart mentioned nothing of it to his superiors. That silence, that failing were soon to furnish a formidable weapon against him.

---

* *Infra* pp. 506–07. The thesis of large-scale complicity between Esterhazy and the Section of Statistics—Henry, but also Lauth, and, for some, Sandherr—gives support to the notion of criminal premeditation on the part of the General Staff.

8

I Was Terrified

Lieutenant Colonel Picquart immediately began his inquest. The military register informed him that Commandant Walsin-Esterhazy was serving with the Seventy-fourth Regiment of the line, then stationed in Paris. It happened that Picquart was well acquainted with a high-ranking officer of precisely that regiment, Commandant Curé, an old friend from Saint-Cyr academy, and they met frequently at the home of their mutual friend, Mlle. de Comminges. He invited Curé to the Ministry. "In your regiment there is an officer named Esterhazy. Strictly between us, what do you think of him?" Curé did not know much about him, but had no respect for an individual who was leading a dissolute life, seemed perpetually short of money, and was obsessed with financial considerations. "Does he not tend to seek out confidential information?" Curé recalled that Esterhazy was particularly interested in artillery and guns, that he had himself twice chosen for firing school, that he went there a third time without salary at his own expense, that he perpetually had soldiers—and in particular one Ecalle whose name he recalled—copying all sorts of documents—in brief, that he was nosy, inquisitive, and indiscreet. Picquart asked Curé to procure for him a specimen of Esterhazy's handwriting—which was a routine request. Curé did not have a sample at his disposal, but refused to procure one. "Ask the Colonel."[1]

Picquart, moreover, having consulted with Commandant Henry,[2] entrusted to one of the two police officials serving with the Ministry of War, Desvernine, the task of initiating a discreet inquest concerning Commandant Esterhazy. He met the police agent, who had been summoned by a letter-telegram signed "Robert," in front of the Louvre on April 9 or 10. As of April 17, a first police report on the "benefactor"* was ready. The benefactor had serious financial problems. He was keeping a mistress, Marguerite Pays, whom he visited every evening before returning to his conjugal home at night. He was renting an apartment for her at 49, rue de Douai, and gave her a monthly allowance. He had numerous creditors and

---

* A pseudonym assigned Esterhazy, who resided at 27, rue de la Bienfaisance.[3]

could not pay his bills on time. He was an intimate of the Jewish officer, Maurice Weil, who procured funds for him. He was in contact with Edouard Drumont, editor of *La Libre Parole*. He was negotiating his entry into the board of directors of a British firm in London. But "nothing suspect from the national point of view" had been observed. It was simply noted that "his mood has grown somber recently."* Other reports, dated April 22 and 25, were barely more interesting. But at the end of the month, Picquart, who had met his agent again at the Gare Saint-Lazare, learned that Esterhazy had been seen on two occasions entering the German embassy. Upon investigation, it was ascertained that he had a legitimate motive: Colonel Abria had asked him to obtain a passport on his behalf for travel in the annexed province of Alsace.† During May and June, the surveillance produced no results. During the month of May, Commandant Curé met Picquart leaving the Ministry. "What's new with Esterhazy?" Picquart asked. Curé had not seen him again. He inquired of Picquart, "Do you still suspect him?" "I don't suspect him," answered Picquart. "I am certain." "Be careful," Curé advised. "In cases like this, many proofs are needed and you are dealing with someone stronger than yourself. . . ." By 1896, procedures were significantly more cautious than in 1894. And what did Commandant Curé know of Esterhazy's "strength"?[5]

During this period, there arrived some new information through the channels of a double agent located in Brussels, Edmond Lajoux, who occasionally used the services of a German agent, Richard Cuers. Cuers had provided several good leads and made possible in 1894—shortly after Dreyfus's arrest—the arrest of two German lieutenants suspected of espionage. Short of money, Cuers, in June 1896, had "spontaneously" offered his services to the French military attaché in Germany, Lieutenant Colonel de Foucault, who was doing in Berlin what Schwarzkoppen was doing in Paris. He claimed that he had interesting information about a "decorated" person who was frequenting the German embassy in broad daylight and who was supplying Schwarzkoppen with a host of intelligence.‡ Picquart, once apprised of this, met with Colonel de Foucault, who confirmed the information. He then staged a mysterious meeting in Basel—neutral territory. Cuers met there with Captain Lauth, who spoke German, Commandant Henry, and police agent Tombs. The contact took place August 7. Cuers did not have much to tell—or at least chose not to. Henry grew angry and Lauth argued, but to no avail. There was an

---

* This is one of the arguments used by Joseph Reinach to deduce that Esterhazy had been "warned" in the interim by Henry.[4]
† Esterhazy had thus arranged to have a plausible motive for his trips to the embassy.
‡ It appears that Cuers spoke to Edmond Lajoux, as early as the end of 1894, about this "decorated" individual who was frequenting the German embassy in Paris.

attempt to intoxicate the spy, which was equally unsuccessful. The report written by Lauth for Picquart upon his return nevertheless included an interesting bit of information: the "decorated" individual who was inform- ing Schwartzkoppen was a "battalion chief," like Esterhazy? Picquart was nonetheless disappointed. He concluded that Lauth and Henry had not been sufficiently adept in getting Cuers to talk. But as soon as he returned to Germany, Cuers immediately went to the French embassy to register a complaint. He claimed to have been mistreated. One of the Intelligence Service's envoys, "a corpulent and ruddy individual, who claimed to be a police agent, but whom [he] had recognized as an officer, constantly bullied him to prevent him from speaking." Later on,* Cuers would claim that he had "told a lot to Lauth and Henry": that Dreyfus had never been working for Germany; that Schwarzkoppen had never had any other informer than a commandant, of an Austrian family, who had begun his strategy of betrayal as early as 1893; that the "corpulent individual," namely Henry, had insulted and threatened him in order to prevent him from speaking! Henry, to be sure, would maintain that the opposite was the case. Whom was one to believe? They were all, after all, professional liars.[6]

All of Picquart's inquiries thus seemed to be in vain. It was at that juncture that he decided to finally report to his superiors the grave suspi- cions of which Esterhazy was the object.†

At the end of July, he wrote to General de Boisdeffre, the chief of the General Staff, who was in therapy at Vichy, requesting an urgent meeting. De Boisdeffre, who was to arrive at the Gare de Lyon on the evening of August 5, asked Picquart to meet him there. Sitting in the car reserved for the chief of the General Staff, Picquart broke the news to him: "I believe that we have just discovered a new traitor. . . ." Picquart named Comman- dant Walsin-Esterhazy. The name meant nothing to the chief of the General Staff. De Boisdeffre encouraged Picquart to pursue his investiga- tion. He did not at the time reproach him for not having first informed General Gonse, second in command of the General Staff and Picquart's hierarchical superior. He even authorized Picquart to discuss the matter with the minister. General de Boisdeffre was quite calm, almost noncha- lant, in marked contrast to his reaction at the discovery of the bordereau.

On the following day, Colonel Picquart saw General Jean-Baptiste Billot, minister of war. Billot held Picquart in high esteem. He listened to him attentively, approved of his prudence, and recommended that he

---

* Letter of July 15, 1899, to an editor of *Le Figaro*.
† It appears that Picquart had been affected by the death of his mother in June. In any event, his friend Louis Leblois saw in the period of mourning one of the explanations for Picquart's delay in informing his superiors.[7]

continue his investigation. But he could not bring himself to authorize Picquart to request of Colonal Abria a specimen of Esterhazy's handwriting, which seemed inappropriate. On several occasions during the month of August, amid the apparently fruitless investigations and surveillance, Boisdeffre and Picquart were to meet. They dined and went horseback riding together. Picquart was of the opinion that the time had come to begin legal proceedings. But the chief of the General Staff betrayed a remarkable propensity to prudence. "I do not want a new Dreyfus Affair. . . ."[8] Neither the minister of war nor the chief of the General Staff seemed particularly excited by this Esterhazy Affair.

During this time, Commandant Esterhazy, after having unsuccessfully attempted to become an administrator of a British firm then being organized,[9] undertook numerous initiatives to have himself appointed . . . to the Ministry of War. He wished to enter either the technical division or the Intelligence Service, "where his perfect knowledge of German and of the German Army would allow him to be of real service." Deputy Jules Roche, vice president of the Army Commission, wrote to the minister of war, his "friend" Billot, recommending to him "this officer of the most signal merit, a true man of war, a soldier of a cast of which there are not many. I would like you to see him for just ten minutes." Maurice Weil also undertook to help out his old friend, intervening with the minister's Cabinet. Throughout the month of August, Weil and Esterhazy augmented their efforts and wrote to each other. Picquart, to be sure, who was intercepting letters received by Esterhazy, and particulary those sent by Weil, remained informed. General Boisdeffre was also informed, as was the minister of war. He even ordered his Cabinet to transmit all letters received from, or on the subject of, Esterhazy to the Section of Statistics. And Esterhazy, in his urgency to enter this section, wrote incessantly to all quarters.*

At the end of August, Calmon-Maison, chief of the civilian Cabinet of the minister of war, obeying instructions from the minister, communicated to Picquart two letters sent by Esterhazy on August 25: one to Commandant Theveney, Weil's friend who was serving with Billot's Cabinet, the other to Calmon-Maison himself. They were two letters of ardent solicitation. Picquart read them and grew deeply perturbed. That regular handwriting, with its slant and its precision seemed familiar to him. The bordereau which had served to convict Dreyfus flashed in his memory. In his offices, he had facsimiles of it. He opened a drawer and took out a photo of the bordereau. He placed the bordereau and the letters

---

* Would he have done so—with such imprudent ardor—had he known of the suspicions weighing on him and the investigations being conducted? In his letters to Jules Roche, Esterhazy protested against the bad faith of the minister, who was stalling in taking him into his staff. "He is putting me off as one would not put off the lowest of lackeys."[10]

written by Esterhazy which he had just received, side by side. "I was terrified," he would later say.[11] The handwritings were not similar. They were identical. The evidence struck him like lightning: the bordereau had not been written by Dreyfus. It was the work of Esterhazy.

9

An Idealist?

The Esterhazy family claimed that they descended from Attila.[1] The Esterhazys were already well known in the thirteenth century; they were said to come from the village of Zerhas, on one of the islands of the Danube. Theirs was a long dynasty of soldiers and diplomats which, from the thirteenth to the eighteenth centuries, never ceased their quest "to conquer great properties and great responsibilities." In the eighteenth century, Paul Esterhazy, "the Palatine," helped to save the Austrian Empire. He crushed the Hungarian rebels, and was regally compensated with the title Prince of the Holy Empire. The Esterhazys were the largest property holders in Europe: 29 manors, 21 châteaux, 60 towns with markets, and 414 villages.

Under Louis XIV, one of Prince Paul's nephews, Count Antoine I, "turbulent and driven to pleasure," placed himself in the service of the rebel Rakoczy. Sentenced in his absence, he was obliged to seek refuge in France. Born in France, his son Valentin settled there, became recognized for his bravery, and in 1734 received a commission to form a new regiment in Strasbourg: the Royal Esterhazy. Out of a passing romance there was born to him in 1740 a son, Ladislas-Valentin. A lieutenant colonel at the age of twenty, the steward of the Royal Esterhazy, and soon to become field marshall, Ladislas-Valentin accumulated a variety of honors and, thanks to his "brutal beauty," became the favorite of Marie-Antoinette. "A Frenchman by second choice," Joseph Reinach maintained,[2] he remained an Austrian at heart. The Revolution forced him to leave for Koblentz a few days before the flight to Varennes. He would settle in Grodek and die there in 1805.

Ladislas-Valentin had a young sister, Marie-Anne, born like himself of the passing loves of Valentin. She had never married and had received from the King the consoling title of "Dame." With a minor nobleman, Marquis Jean-César de Ginestous, a magistrate and governor of Vigan, she had a child. Jean-Marie-Auguste had been "declared" on May 7, 1767, born of "unknown father and mother." Marie-Anne—who raised him with great diligence—gave him the nickname of Walsin. Settling in Nîmes, she died in 1823 at the age of eighty-one.

Jean-Marie-Auguste, known as Walsin, the natural descendant of the Esterhazys, married a demoiselle Cartier, the daughter of a comfortable merchant, in Nîmes during the Year V of the Revolution. He himself had a go at business. But a soldier's blood undoubtedly beat in his veins: he had three sons, two of whom entered the Army. Both Walsins became generals during the Second Empire. The younger of the two distinguished himself during the Crimean War. From his marriage with Mlle. Dequeux de Beauval he had a daughter and a son. Thus it was that the natural heir of a glorious familial line, Marie Charles Ferdinand Walsin Esterhazy, who engineered the Dreyfus Affair, was born in Paris, on rue de Clichy, December 26, 1847.

He did his studies at the Lycée Bonaparte.* His schoolmates retained a recollection of a slender boy, of dullish complexion, poorly dressed, and always keeping to himself. His father died when he was ten. His mother died when he was seventeen. Life was not easy for him. He abandoned the lycée after the fifth form and would never receive the baccalaureate. "He was attracted to Parisian society and intent on striking a figure in it."[4] For several years we have no trace of him. Reinach maintains that he spent some time in Germany and learned the language. Marie-Charles resurfaces in 1869, serving with the Pontifical Legion. He spent a year in Rome, then resigned, and thanks to his uncle General Walsin managed to be appointed by Imperial decree on June 24, 1870 as sublieutenant of the Foreign Legion. He was soon to do combat with the Army of the Loire. While the French troops were being routed, he was named sublieutenant with the First Regiment of Zouaves and soon to be promoted captain. But in 1871, the Commission for the Revision of Rank demoted him, making him a sublieutenant again. It was a circumstance that left him profoundly bitter.

In 1875, he was garrisoned at Beauvais, but managed to become involved with the editing of a bulletin in Paris published by a collective of

* Where he would learn German. There have been misguided attempts to locate "Germanisms" and "exotic" turns of phrase in his letters. As Marcel Thomas has observed, he had only one sixteenth Hungarian blood and did not speak the language of his glorious family. In 1898, the head of the Esterhazy clan would file suit to force him to give up the title of Count and take on the added name Walsin, a reminder of his illegitimacy.[3]

officers as he had an adequate speaking knowledge of English and Italian. He wrote articles for the bulletin on all sorts of military subjects. In 1877 he succeeded in getting himself transferred to the Information Service, which was still quite lacking in organization, and in which he rejoined his old friend Captain Maurice Weil, the Jewish officer. He spent three years there as a translator from German. It was there that he got to know Captain Hubert Joseph Henry, who entered the service through the patronage of General de Miribel in December 1877, and may have become close to him.* In 1880, he received his third stripe, was transferred to Cholet, then left to participate in the Tunisian campaign. In Tunisia he was sufficiently shrewd to manage to have an entirely imaginary honor included in his record of service. Soon he would be stationed at Sfax with the Tunisian intelligence services. He wrote to his beautiful cousin, Madame de Boulancy, who was one of his numerous mistresses, requesting a loan.† Everywhere he passed he accumulated debts. His generous cousin never stopped sending him—increasingly large sums of—money: 36,500 francs in two years.[5] Esterhazy was extremely bitter that France did not recognize his merits more amply. He wrote a series of vigorous diatribes and sent them off to his creditor: "General Saussier [military governor of Paris] is a clown ... the Germans will put all of them in their proper place. ... All of those grotesque generals still bear the imprint of the Prussian boot a bit lower than their back. ..."[6] A series of obscure but suspicious deals forced the resident general, Paul Cambon, to have him sent back to France. In February 1884, he was to take the boat for Marseille, transferred to the Seventh Batallion of Light Infantry. He was furious, almost desperate. He wrote his cousin a furious phillipic against France. Madame de Boulancy shortly thereafter revealed enough spirit to ask for her money back, whereupon Esterhazy broke with her.

What was left if not a lucky marriage? Esterhazy wrote to specialized agencies,[7] to no effect. Through a priest from the Madeleine, he would claim, he came to know a family of venerable nobility from Lorraine, the Nettancourt-Vaubécourts. The marquis was financially ruined and suffered from neurasthenia, but his wife, whose origins were bourgeois, possessed a certain fortune. Their second daughter, Anne, seemed difficult to marry off. A dowry of two hundred thousand francs was promised. On February 6, 1886 Count Esterhazy married Anne de Nettancourt-Vaubécourt. Despite numerous vexations, the countess would remain faithful to her husband, devoted until the very end of his tumultuous life.

---

* This is one of the residual mysteries of the Affair that will, no doubt, never be elucidated.
† His correspondence with Mme. de Boulancy was to be published in part in Le Figaro, starting on November 28, 1897, at the instigation of Mathieu Dreyfus.

After his death, she would even try to defend his memory. Esterhazy, on the other hand, found his wife disappointing, foolish, and basely sensual:

> Marriage is either an association of financial interests or the satisfaction of a very crude physical passion or the fusion of two individuals who have come to think and feel alike in all matters.
>
> Concerning financial interests, my wife never for a moment realized, never even tried to understand, that when people as poor as we marry and when they have been mad enough to begin with a host of foolish expenses, then they have to be thrifty and not buy themselves dresses, coats, and hats at the slightest whim, not travel first class, not pay their maids 60 francs a month.
>
> As for the fusion of our thoughts and feelings, I can say that I did everything that I could, but that my wife, who had inherited from her mother an immeasurable reserve of passive stubbornness, never made a single effort to be close to me, in that regard. "I'm bored," was her sole refrain. It was uttered on the first day and I heard it up until the end.
>
> What remained was physical passion. I believe that my wife loved me intensely through her senses. But of all the forms of love, that is the most base, the least lasting, and it was not to that sole end that I had gotten married. . . . Of all the women with whom I have dealt in the course of my life and who have had a greater or lesser quantity of tenderness for me, the only one not to have any true affection for me was my wife! I have had no luck! For I do not call love that physical passion, so fleeting when it alone exists, which attracts a woman to a man—especially to the first man—and it was that and that alone which Mlle. de Nettancourt felt for me. My mistresses loved me with their heart, my legitimate spouse had for me nothing but a sensual attraction. It is remarkably ironic![8]

But this "idealist" was drowning in debts. In 1888, when the couple set up house in Courbevoie, he was already bankrupt. In order to save any cash at all, the Countess was obliged to request a separation of their properties. This did not, however, prevent Esterhazy from purchasing a château in the Marne, at Dommartin-la-Planchette—for his old age. His married life became increasingly difficult. Husband and wife bickered incessantly, to the despair of the Count who dreamed of a life of serenity. "The scene we are playing," he wrote, "is the death of the marital hearth." He gambled and went into debt. He deceived his wife as much as possible. Everywhere, he was on the lookout for money and adventure. He requested help from wealthy Jews and simultaneously linked up with militant anti-Semites. In 1892, when he was to be named a commandant and wanted to be transferred to the Seventy-fourth Regiment of the Infantry, he solicited the help of his "Jewish friends": Maurice Weil, of course, who intervened with General Saussier, and several others, including Joseph Reinach, who appears not to have intervened. But on several occasions, he obtained satisfaction.

But he also had to make a living. And the year 1894 began rather ominously for Commandant Walsin-Esterhazy. His accounts at the Crédit Lyonnais were empty and the Crédit Foncier threatened him in June with legal action if he failed to pay back almost five thousand francs, for the equivalent of a year and a half overdue payments on a mortgage loan that he could not manage to reimburse. He attempted to live through his influential relations and to enter into a ministerial Cabinet. But the minister of war, General Auguste Mercier, detested his protector, Jules Roche, who was scheming to become his replacement.

In all quarters, Esterhazy would invoke his influential connections: his friend General Félix Saussier and his friend Jules Roche. He mingled with members of Parliament and with journalists, and by dint of claiming that he was a personality of note, he became one. But his monetary situation was growing progressively worse. His château at Dommartin was extremely costly; his creditors were pressing him daily. He accused his wife of being a spendthrift. She was incapable of living, he would sigh, with the thousand francs per month he claimed he was giving her. At the stock market he attempted a few purchases on margin which ended up badly, for he was speculating on the decline of stocks whose value continued to rise.[9] From whom could he extract money? His in-laws no longer wanted to do anything for him. Ever since he served as a second for Captain Ernest Crémieu-Foa, they reproached him with his Jewish connections. He composed a letter which he fraudulently attributed to his maternal uncle, the diplomat de Beauval: "You defended the Jews, and now you are going under because of money. It is the hand of God." Maurice Weil circulated the letter, which was capable of moving a few wealthy Jews. On July 5, Baron Edmond de Rothschild had two thousand francs sent to him.* Grand Rabbi Zadoc Kahn also attempted to find some funds for the unfortunate, who appeared to be suffering for having defended the Jews.[10] But such support could not be sufficient. "I will even resort to crime," he affirmed, "before seeing my family die of hunger." What could he do? Collaborate with a few select newspapers that would exploit his knowledge and his talent, which he would do in 1895, becoming the

---

* Esterhazy would renew such efforts in 1895 (see *supra* p. 123).

anonymous editor of *La Libre Parole*. Become an ex-patriot, as he was often inclined to imagine? Commit suicide? Sell himself to Germany since France was incapable of compensating him for his worth?

He was "sick," wrote Joseph Reinach.[11] And physically, he was. Esterhazy had tuberculosis. He slept only rarely. He was overexcited, dangerous, irritable, oscillating between extremes of anger and depression. Always he believed himself persecuted—his wife, his mistresses, his friends, the General Staff, France, the whole world was united against him.* And he hated them for it. He did not distinguish truth from lies, and believed everything he said. He would betray whenever it became necessary, and always remained convinced that he was innocent. Everything about him seemed the fruit of some usurpation: his name, his nobility, his relations, the duels he claimed to have fought, the missions he said he had fulfilled, the moments of glory that he flaunted. In love with appearances, avid for luxury and even ostentation, perpetually in search of new pleasure, he squandered the money he had and the money he didn't have, the funds of all the women and men on whom he could lean. He lived out of cleverness, schemes, gimmicks, and blackmail, but also out of dreams. A liar, a robber of banknotes, titles, and jewels, nasty with all those who devoted themselves to him, envious of all, cruel with women, he was, in the last analysis, quite unhappy. A prodigious adventurer whose inventiveness and daring were immeasurable. But in the middle of the year 1894, a fallen, exhausted adventurer who was gasping for breath amid the thousand intrigues he had woven around himself.

Such was the man who came knocking at the door of the German military attaché on July 20, 1894. He was dry, bony, and stooped, his body too thin for his massive head. His high-cheekboned face was crossed by a thick black mustache and almost without a chin. "An aquiline nose, small, black, impenetrable deep-set eyes which were always in movement, abruptness of speech, his voice trembling between extremes of violence and gentleness"[12] rendered him an odd and even "exotic" character. But Count Esterhazy was also an "ingratiating and seductive" officer. Those who knew him admired the sharp sallies of his curious, supple, and perpetually mobile wit.[13] His febrile imagination, ardent speech, and marvelous intensity of life seduced and often fascinated. He seemed to have accumulated enormous talents and enormous vices in an incoherent mosaic. Seated in front of Colonel Maximilian von Schwarzkoppen's desk, he spoke of his wife and his sick children, the poverty which overwhelmed him. He threatened to lodge a bullet in his head. A born actor, he had entered into his new role.

* One moving strain of fidelity in his life of treason: an impassioned love for his two daughters.

10

The Serenity of France

Even as the Chief of the Intelligence Service was secretly investigating Commandant Esterhazy, during that autumn of 1896, France had almost forgotten the Dreyfus Affair. "Dreyfus? I vaguely remember the name, but I can no longer remember anything of the story." Thus spoke one of the guests at a gathering of friends that also included Léon Blum, the Socialist. An officer who was present, Lieutenant Colonel Gaudérique Roget, had to recount the Affair.[1] France had other worries: its finances, the congregations, the "troubling" rise of workers' demands. Because it advocated the passage of a fiscal law, called the law of subscription, which taxed the religious congregations, the government of Alexandre Ribot had provoked an unleashing of hostility on the right and even among the Catholics who had "rallied" to the regime, without managing to reassure the left. It fell on October 28, 1895, because of an insignificant scandal, but one which once again demonstrated the collusion between business and politics. The Radical chieftain, Léon Bourgeois followed Ribot with the formation of a homogeneously Radical government. Without a majority, it could survive solely thanks to the "tolerance" of the government republicans; that is, the center.[2] But it quickly lost that tolerance. In announcing a law governing associations, prior to a general reordering of the relations between the Church and the State, Bourgeois provoked the hostility of the entire Catholic right and of a sector of the center as well. He increased parliamentary dissatisfaction by advocating the principle of a tax on revenue, which had long been a plank of the Radical platform. Bourgeois claimed to be defending it as the axis of a policy intended to correct the inequalities of society and to establish national solidarity, but a tax on revenue opened up the path to the inquisition, to collectivism. The opposition swelled from all sides. With great difficulty the government convinced the Chamber to approve the principle of a progressive tax.[3] But starting with the spring of 1896, fifty-five departmental assemblies declared themselves opposed to the project. Those deputies who were hesitant abandoned the government. Without a majority in the Chamber, Léon

Bourgeois was obliged by the Senate to resign, after three months of impassioned conflict.[4]

He was followed by Jules Méline, Jules Ferry's former minister, and the apostle of protectionism. He formed a homogeneously moderate cabinet. Gabriel Hanotaux returned to Foreign Affairs, Jean Louis Barthou to Interior. Steering his course with great shrewdness, Méline would manage to maintain a government for twenty-six months.[5] He split sharply with the Radicals, and sought his majority in an alliance of the "government republicans"—that is, of the center and the right. He was thus obliged to renounce anticlericalism, which he attacked as "a tactic of the Radicals to feed the voters a deceptive solution" and to appease the forces of religion. That is why the government closed its eyes to the return of the con-greganists, the development of ecclesiastical property, and of religious instruction.[6] Méline, who had reserved for himself the position of minister of agriculture,[7] claimed to "take his base of support in the countryside": the protectionist policies he would promote with such vigor were intended to reassure the peasants, particularly the grape-growers, who were threatened by foreign competition. But the government would concede at least a few welfare laws[8], such as the 1898 law protecting workers who were injured at work. Nevertheless, for the Socialists, who conquered fifteen large cities, including Lille and Marseille, in the municipal elections of 1896, and for the Radicals, who were gaining a broader hearing in rural France and who insisted on a return to a secular and militant Republic, the Méline government thereafter would appear as the embodiment of reactionary power.

It was during this period that the "colonial party" was organized.[9] In the Chamber, the "colonial group" had become powerful and active. The Ministry of Colonies was created in 1894. Apparently, the public no longer viewed the idea of colonization with the same indifference or hostility that it had ten years earlier. France continued to expand its possessions in Africa. Madagascar, following the costly campaign of 1895, was annexed the following year. Tradesmen, soldiers, and functionaries were organizing their departures, often fleeing a difficult or mediocre life in metropolitan France. The Empire seemed to be recognized, indeed consecrated. And if it is doubtful that it functioned as a source of economic profit, at least it served to distract "a whole sector of the nationalist movement."[10]

But it was still the endless reinforcement of the Franco-Russian alliance which united and assuaged public opinion. The French and the Russians multiplied their displays of courtesy and speeches of friendship. In October 1896, young Czar Nicholas II agreed to pay an official visit to France in the company of the Czarina Alexandra. The Republic greeted them with its full range of pomp. In Cherbourg, amid the frenetic cries of the crowd, President Félix Faure greeted the sovereigns of the immense empire. A special train took them to Paris; a station was built at the edge of the Bois de Boulogne to receive the crowned heads. In the capital, the welcome was delirious. Nearly a million inhabitants of the provinces swept into Paris. Celebrations and spectacles for the sovereigns proliferated. A sumptuous dinner awaited them at the Elysée. There were embraces and toasts to the friendship, the union between the two populations. "In a Europe which is almost entirely monarchical, the Republic has demonstrated that it can indeed strike a fine figure."[11] At the Bourse, Russian properties were perpetually increasing in value; the enthusiasm of the French knew no reservations.[12]

During the year 1896, the government of the center succeeded in reassuring and strengthening the right. The Church and the congregations were the object of numerous acts of deference. The tax on revenue was shelved. The Army was at the height of its power and prestige. Farmers were jealously protected. Through its military strength and its powerful alliances, France showed a proud face to the rest of Europe. To be sure there were dark spots: the strikes which were proliferating and growing increasingly severe; the rise of the Socialists, who were winning votes and seats with each new election. On May 30, 1896, the Socialist lawyer Alexandre Millerand delivered in Saint-Mandé a programmatic address. "Society's property must gradually come to replace capitalist property." Certain industries, such as sugar production, were "already ready to be appropriated." But socialism, Millerand proclaimed, "in no way threatens small property owners. Socialists were internationalists, but they did not have "the impious and insane idea" of destroying their country. Yes, they were patriots. And if they wanted to transform society, it was "through the conquest of public offices through universal suffrage." The next day, October 31, 1896, the "Saint-Mandé program" was adopted as the platform of the Socialist group in the Chamber. The Socialist Jules Guesde appended only a few reservations concerning style. He expressed his satisfaction at seeing "the essential elements of socialism . . . increasingly shared by our neighbors in struggle." First the government must be won. Thus did the French Socialists become disciplined.[13]

Technical progress was tranquilly pursuing its course as the century ended. There were already taxi-automobiles riding through the streets of Paris. Louis Lumière brought off the first public projections of motion pictures. The bicycle was perfected. At the end of 1896, the Parisian public was enthralled by the first exhibition of bicycles and automobiles. Did anyone really care that the traitor Dreyfus was agonizing on Devil's Island? But then, who even remembered?

11

Keep the Two Affairs Separate

T wenty months had more or less effaced all memory of Alfred Dreyfus. Yet within four months, Lieutenant Colonel Georges Picquart and Mathieu Dreyfus, one through stubborn rectitude, the other through awkward devotion, would unknowingly resuscitate the Affair.

When Colonel Picquart discovered, upon comparing the bordereau with Esterhazy's two letters, that Esterhazy was to all appearances the author of the bordereau, he took several precautions before informing his superiors. First he asked Captain Lauth to photograph Esterhazy's two letters while blocking out those parts of the documents which betrayed the identity of the sender and the recipients. In one of the letters, he substituted the words "dear sir" for "my dear friend": this device was to permit him to reveal the photos of the documents without revealing to whom they had been sent.* At the end of August, Picquart called in Commandant du Paty de Clam. He showed him the photos he had "prepared" and the photo of the bordereau. "Do you see an analogy?" Picquart would testify at the Rennes trial that du Paty responded, "But that is Mathieu Dreyfus's handwriting." An odd response, and one that did little to enlighten Picquart.† A few days later, the chief of the Section of Statistics summoned Alphonse Bertillon and showed him the photos of Esterhazy's letters. "That is the handwriting of the bordereau," Bertillon exclaimed without hesitating. "But what if it were written quite recently?" Picquart objected. Bertillon replied, "Then it is because the Jews have trained someone in the

---

* Lauth would subsequently exploit this tactic in order to claim that Picquart, proceeding as a forger, had wanted to denature Esterhazy's letters.
† Was du Paty invoking Bertillon's system, maintaining that the bordereau written by Dreyfus had been forged in part in imitation of Mathieu's handwriting? Marcel Thomas has discovered an unpublished note by du Paty, dated December 1, 1896, in which the officer wrote: "Not only is there an analogy, but, at sight, an absolute identity."[1]

course of a year to imitate his handwriting." That thesis would later be adopted in various versions by Esterhazy's friends.

Thereafter Picquart was convinced: the bordereau was Esterhazy's work. He knew of the secret file which had been communicated to the judges of the military tribunal during their deliberations. Colonel Jean Sandherr, head of the Intelligence Services at the time, upon turning over his responsibilities to Picquart, had specified, "You need only ask Commandant Henry for the file communicated to the judges in their council chamber. When you open it, you will see some convincing items of evidence." Picquart had probably known of the existence of the enigmatic file already during the 1894 trial. But he did not know precisely what its contents were. He had not been sufficiently curious to consult it since his arrival at the Section of Statistics. On August 30 or 31,* he asked Félix Gribelin, in Henry's absence, "Give me the small file which was communicated to Dreyfus's judges and is in Commandant Henry's safe." Gribelin complied. Picquart took the dusty file, which had been resting in a closet for a year and a half. He expected to find "serious things," crushing evidence. He found "nothing." The "scoundrel D" document might not refer to Dreyfus at all. The "Davignon letter" revealed nothing conclusive. Picquart knew François Guénée, the agent working for the Section, too well not to realize the limited importance of his reports. Picquart examined the insignificant papers at length. Because of them, Dreyfus was even then enduring torture on Devil's Island. Picquart thought back to the days of the trial. He saw himself seated behind the tribunal, observing . . . a traitor? An innocent man? He passed long nights pondering. He was certain of a judicial error. His conscience, the elevated idea of the Army he held, and reason as well—for inevitably the truth would eventually out— dictated his duty. He would thereafter never waver from it.

On September 1, 1896, he completed for General de Boisdeffre, the chief of the General Staff, the signed report in which were assembled the essential elements of a matter requiring, in his judgment, "immediate decisions." In it he demonstrated Esterhazy's guilt. He evoked the bordereau, revealed the similarity of handwriting, recalling in a brief footnote that the bordereau had been "the occasion of other legal action." That was intended to be sufficiently clear for Picquart to be understood. He attached to his report the relevant documents. He resorted, however, to the ruse, which would eventually be used against him, of saying that he had received the *petit bleu* through the ordinary track "at the end of the month of April 1896." Apparently, he was embarrassed at having been so late in informing his superiors of the *petit bleu*, and he wanted to "rejuvenate" its

---

* According to Joseph Reinach[2]; between August 28 and 31 according to Picquart; on August 28 according to Gribelin.[3]

date.* His adversaries would seize on that circumstance as grounds for arguing that he had tampered with the document accusing Esterhazy, or even that he had forged it.

Picquart sought out de Boisdeffre to convey to him his conclusion. The General listened to him impassively, barely surprised. When the colonel referred to the secret file, de Boisdeffre seemed startled. "Why was it not burned as had been agreed?" That was the sole point on which he became moved. Picquart expected a reaction, orders, congratulations, the indignation of the chief of the General Staff upon discovering that an innocent man had been convicted. But de Boisdeffre said nothing. When Picquart returned the following day, de Boisdeffre simply said to him, "Do you think I have slept after what you showed me yesterday?" And he ordered Picquart to present the matter to the deputy-chief of the General Staff, General Charles Gonse. "I was intent," de Boisdeffre would explain at Rennes, "on following a hierarchical path and on knowing the opinion of General Gonse, an opinion that was quite valuable to me."

In a state of astonishment, since de Boisdeffre had never demanded such scrupulous respect for the hierarchy, Picquart went to see General Gonse, who was then on sick leave at Cormeilles-en-Parisis. He presented the matter during a long two-hour meeting with Gonse, who also listened without responding, with the exception of the comment, "So we must have been wrong?"[5] Gonse gave Picquart a single recommendation. "Keep the two affairs separate." Picquart wondered how he could keep them separate. "I did not see how, in focusing on Esterhazy, we could not focus on the bordereau . . . and the bordereau, in a word, was the Dreyfus Affair."[6] De Boisdeffre, however, confirmed Gonse's instructions. "Keep them separate."[7] Plainly Picquart and his superiors did not see their duty in the same light.

Mathieu Dreyfus—who, to be sure, knew nothing of what was going on in the General Staff—was growing desperate as the end of 1896 approached. The news of his brother was alarming. What could he do to attract attention to the martyrdom of an innocent?† In London, Mathieu sought out the services of an "agency," whose director, Mr. Cook, promised to obtain through a mysterious Mr. X, the support of several English newspapers. Mr. X rolled into vigorous action and was copiously paid. One August day, he let Mathieu know that it was time to start a rumor through

---

* Picquart would frequently vary in his statements concerning the date of arrival of the *petit bleu*. In the Zola trial, he would situate it during the month of May.[4]

† "Judging by the methods used," writes Hannah Arendt (*Sur l'antisémitisme*, Calmann-Lévy, coll. Diaspora, 1973), "one might have thought that the Dreyfusses were trying to shield a guilty man from justice rather than to save an innocent one. They were extremely fearful of publicity, and trusted only under-the-table maneuvers."[8] This severe judgment makes short shrift of the difficulties encountered by the Dreyfusard cause at the time.

the newspapers that Alfred Dreyfus had escaped: to prevent the silence from growing thicker still, and to avoid public opinion from considering the Affair closed.[9] Mathieu Dreyfus thought the idea a good one. No sooner would the escape be announced than it would have to be denied, but public opinion would be reawakened in the process. On September 3, *The Daily Chronicle* announced "the escape of Captain Dreyfus." The news was said to have been brought to London by Captain Hunter of the good ship *Non Pareil*: neither the captain nor his ship existed. Immediately retransmitted by the press agencies, the false news arrived in Paris on the same day. It was taken up by the evening dailies. On the evening of September 3, the minister of the colonies, André Leblon, cabled to Guiana and was reassured. Dreyfus was still there.

On September 4, the government issued a denial. But the same day, the minister of colonies—who panicked nevertheless—took precautions. Until further orders, the traitor would be kept in his cabin under "double shackles at night."[10] At the time, Mathieu's maneuver had only aggravated the plight of the prisoner of Devil's Island.

Fortunately, it did have other effects. On September 8, Gaston Calmette published in the *Figaro* an article in which, with the help of information confided to him by a government functionary recently back from Guiana, he described the tragic existence of the convict, "ageless, his body stooped over, his hair white, his face sallow and hollowed, his beard gray, weary and slow of pace." *La Libre Parole* of September 11, 1896, reacted violently. "Dreyfus is living like a brute. He could read, but prefers to eat. He guzzles, he eats, and he drinks. . . ." Camille Chautemps, who had preceded Lebon as minister of colonies, declared himself slandered by Calmette, because the latter had dared to write that the minister had temporarily considered allowing Mme. Dreyfus to rejoin her husband. "Infamous slander," the former minister stormed, terrorized that one day the voters would reproach him for such an inclination to benevolence. He demanded a retraction, but was confounded when *Le Figaro* published Chautemps's coded telegram to the governor of Guiana asking whether Mme. Dreyfus might eventually be authorized to rejoin her husband. Feelings were growing heated. Henri Rochefort fulminated in *L'Intransigeant* and Edouard Drumont in *La Libre Parole*. The syndicate of Dreyfus's friends was accused of propagating erroneous information and of bribing Dreyfus's guards. The Jews, claimed *La Libre Parole* of September 22, would already have assembled four million francs to execute the traitor's escape.[11] Granier de Cassagnac, a violent anti-Semite but Edgar Demange's friend, published on September 14 in *L'Autorité* an article entitled "Le Doute," which recalled examples of judicial error. The entire press was waxing polemical on the subject of the deportee of Devil's Island.

Above all, *L'Eclair* of September 10 published a long article that was violently hostile to Dreyfus and denounced the traitor's "civilian accomplices," "his family, the soul of all this agitation." The article contained a mysterious sentence.

> If this doubt in favor of the traitor should continue to grow, it is believed, even within the military, that it would be appropriate to dot all the i's and to very frankly reveal on what irrefutable grounds the Court-Martial based its decision to brand as a traitor to the country the man who seems to be benefiting excessively from an inexplicable sense of pity and a feeling of doubt which seems more generous than perspicacious.

It was a strange text, which seemed to reveal, in ambiguous terms, the existence of the secret file. Some would say Commandant Henry was behind it. Others would claim it was the Dreyfus family. Picquart too would be accused. Whatever the case, the article caused a sensation. On September 11, André Castelin, deputy from the Aisne, made public a letter to the prime minister: the deputy warned Premier Jules Méline that he would be called to account when the Parliament reconvened for "the government's indulgence toward Dreyfus and his friends." Now the political situation was in turmoil. And on September 14 *L'Eclair* struck again, specifying still further:[12]

> In September 1894, the military attachés of the German embassy addressed a letter in code to their colleagues in the Italian embassy. That letter successfully left the hands of its authors and arrived in those to whom it was addressed, but between the point of departure and the point of arrival, it was skillfully and prudently photographed.
>
> It was a letter coded in the manner of the German embassy. That code was in our possession, and it may be imagined that it was of too great a usefulness for the public diffusion of such a secret to be possible. Later on, it will be seen that such was the reason for which the letter in question was not included in the official dossier and that it was only in secret, in the deliberation room, out of the presence even of the accused, that it was transmitted to the judges of the Court-Martial.
>
> About September 20, Colonel Sandherr, head of the Section of Statistics, communicated to General Mercier the letter, which had

been deciphered. It concerned the espionage service in Paris and contained the sentence: "Decidedly, that animal Dreyfus is becoming too demanding."

Of which Dreyfus were the German and Italian military attachés in fact talking?

The long article in *L'Eclair* was plainly well informed. It summarized more or less correctly the text of the bordereau without however reproducing it. It contained a detailed and faithful account of the arrest and the scene of the dictation. It named the principal actors in the Affair: du Paty, Henry, Gonse, Gribelin. And if it was in error on an essential point—the words "scoundrel D." were replaced by "that animal Dreyfus"—it revealed, this time without any ambiguity, the existence of the secret file and part of its contents.

Finally, the communication of a secret file to Dreyfus's judges was known to all. One of its documents, although misquoted, was summarized. Mathieu Dreyfus regained hope. He thought he detected in the articles in *L'Eclair* "a response by the General Staff" to the articles by Calmette and Cassagnac. That hypothesis was quite fragile, for if *L'Eclair* contributed new elements supporting the conviction of Dreyfus, it revealed to public opinion the abuse of 1894. And that revelation was not without its risks for Mercier, du Paty, Sandherr, Henry, those who had been the original architects and agents of the breach of procedure.

Commandant Picquart, in any event, was to benefit from the revelation. What he had feared was beginning to occur.* On September 14, he wrote to General Gonse, sending him as well the article in *L'Eclair* that Gonse had already read.

> My General,
>
> On September 8, I had the honor of bringing to your attention the scandal that certain individuals were threatening to provoke quite soon and I took the liberty of telling you that in my opinion we were going to have a major problem on our hands if we did not take the initiative.
>
> The article in *L'Eclair* which you will find appended unfortunately confirms me in my opinion. I am going to search out carefully the persons who have so carefully planted the bomb. But I feel

---

* Picquart—no doubt informed of Mathieu's initiatives in every direction—feared that the family might sponsor a press campaign in favor of Dreyfus. Events were to prove him right. Picquart appears to have been convinced—as was the General Staff—that Dreyfus's friends were at the origin of the article in *L'Eclair*.

obliged to affirm once again that in my opinion it is imperative to act without delay.

If we wait any longer, we will be overwhelmed, locked into an inextricable position, and we will no longer have the means of either defending ourselves or ascertaining the real truth.

Accept, my General, the expression of my respect and devotion.

P.S. The papers I showed you in Cormeilles are in my briefcase, which is sealed.

Should you need it, Lauth would give you the briefcase. Neither he nor anyone else, by the way, knows anything about the matter.

But General Gonse seemed not to hear him. For days, he had been attempting to bring Picquart back to a more prudent course, restricting him to his narrowly defined mission: the head of the Section of Statistics was to supervise surveillance of Esterhazy's suspect activities without concern for the bordereau. "It seems useful to me to proceed in this entire matter with great prudence, distrusting one's first impressions." Gonse, whom Picquart had seen so agitated, so panicky at the time of the discovery of the bordereau in 1894 was now so calm that nothing could perturb him. Still Picquart warned him. The time was coming when people who believed that an error had been made would attempt and indeed provoke a major scandal. . . . It would be an ugly and useless crisis that could be avoided if justice were restored soon enough.* But Gonse appeased him. "We must avoid all erroneous maneuvers and above all initiatives which might be irreversible," repeated Gonse, whom Picquart's zeal was beginning to worry. Picquart sought recourse in General Billot, the minister of war.† With de Boisdeffre's authorization, Picquart saw the minister on September 9 or 10. He explained to him everything that he knew: the identical handwriting, the existence and contents of the secret file. He listened to Picquart attentively. General Billot did not like General Mercier and this judicial error might prove interesting.[15] He would think about it.

When Picquart returned to see the minister, he found him "completely changed." De Boisdeffre had taken the precaution of speaking to him in the interim. "Military solidarity" was being invoked to the hilt. Billot remained

* Picquart had heard it said by François Guénée that Deputy André Castelin was in fact working for the Dreyfus family.[13]

† Joseph Reinach describes the minister of war as follows: "Billot regarded himself as a great military and political figure. He was a wily old trooper, sly, quick-witted, but without character, not evil, but without any goodness, too intelligent not to admit in his inner mind that Picquart was right, but not enough to make his own, at whatever cost, the cause that was offered to him."[14]

silent about all that he had just learned. Dreyfus's probable innocence and the discovery of a treasonous officer became "military secrets." He spoke of them neither to the prime minister nor to any of his colleagues. Picquart despaired of convincing anyone. He had the impression that his insistence was becoming annoying.

On September 15 Picquart had a discussion with Gonse that ended poorly. It seems that Picquart wanted to precipitate matters by either arresting Esterhazy or laying a trap for him.[16] For the first time the deputy-chief of the General Staff lost his calm. "What does it matter to you that that Jew is on Devil's Island?" Picquart was astonished. "But since he's innocent. . . ." he replied indignantly. Gonse shrugged his shoulders. It was possible that Dreyfus was innocent. "It doesn't matter. Those are not matters which ought to enter into consideration." And Gonse insinuated, "If you don't say anything, no one will know." Picquart exploded. "What you are saying is abominable. I do not know what I will do. But in any event, I will not take this secret to the grave with me." Picquart left the room without waiting for an answer.*

The conflict was now out in the open. Picquart knew there was nothing more he could expect from Gonse. The next day, the two men, upon seeing each other, acted as though they had forgotten the scene. "What are you going to do?" asked Gonse. Picquart again suggested that they set a trap for Esterhazy: a forged telegram appearing to emanate from Schwarzkoppen, the German military attaché, would be sent to Esterhazy according to the code which they already knew. "An important and urgent matter concerning the R. house. Come immediately to Paris. You will be awaited at the station. C." Gonse was hesitant, and consulted Boisdeffre who hesitated as well. Picquart was sent back to the Ministry. "No, Colonel Picquart, we must not do such things. You don't have the right to. I, Chief of the Army, do not have the right to subject a high officer to such a thing." Thus would Billot describe his edifying action at the Rennes trial.[18] And Gonse would claim for himself no less virtue. "That unworthy maneuver, needless to say, did not receive the approval of the minister, to whom, moreover, I had submitted it with a negative recommendation." Picquart's proposal was as absurd as it was inappropriate.† That was simply not the way one dealt with a French officer!

On September 18, Lucie Dreyfus sent the president of the Chamber of Deputies a petition composed by Edgar Demange. The prudent attorney had finally allowed the family to take public initiatives.

* Such, at least, was Picquart's account.[17] Gonse denied the terms, if not the spirit, of the conversation.

† General Gonse, along with General de Boisdeffre, had previously approved the trap set for Dreyfus.[19]

Deputies,

The newspaper *L'Eclair* in its edition of September 15, appearing Monday morning, published, in defiance of all contradiction, that there was irrefutable, material proof of my husband's guilt, that that proof was in the hands of the Ministry of War, which had communicated it confidentially during their deliberations to the judges of the Court-Martial, whose conclusion it helped to form, without the defendant or his lawyer knowing it.

I refused to believe that such could be the case, and I expected the denial that the semi-official Agence Havas supplies in the case of all erroneous news, even of lesser importance than the present case.

The denial did not come. It is thus true that after debates enshrouded in the most utter mystery, because of a closed session, a French officer has been convicted by a Court-Martial on the basis of an accusation that the prosecution has produced without his being informed and with neither he nor his counsel being able to discuss it.

This is a denial of all justice.

Subjected for almost two years now to the most cruel martyrdom, as is he in whose innocence my faith remains absolute, I have restricted myself to silence despite all the odious and absurd slander propagated amid the public and in the press.

Today it is my duty to break that silence, and without commentary, without recrimination, I address myself to you, Gentlemen, the only power to whom I can resort, and I demand justice.

Lucie Dreyfus.

The newspapers, including *Le Figaro*, reproduced the petition.[20] Now the Dreyfus Affair had truly begun.

12

The Patriotic Forgery

I n October, however, the agitation seemed to subside, lost amid the *fêtes russes*. The Republic was welcoming the czar and the empress. France appeared to have given her heart to Russia, gratified to feel herself loved.[1] In an effort to be worthy of their imperial guests, the republican men of state commissioned new official uniforms and deliberated at length on the subject of meals and celebrations. On such sumptuous occasions, patriotism, the pleasure of ostentation, and vanity were fused.

Lieutenant Colonel Georges Picquart meanwhile was secretly doing his duty. He pursued his investigation and expanded it to the author of the articles in *L'Eclair*, whom he attempted to locate. "There is reason to believe, my dear Colonel," Félix Gribelin, at the Section of Statistics, hinted perfidiously to him, "that since Commandant Henry has been away since the end of August, the article was written by you or me." "Don't worry, I'll shield you," answered Picquart.[2] But could he himself remain calm? The systematic interception of Esterhazy's correspondence had proved fruitless, as had the verification of Esterhazy's past activities.* The investigation of the leaks exploited by *L'Eclair* had led nowhere. Picquart sensed that these failures were being imputed to him. Might he not be protecting the culprits? A thousand clues, none of which was conclusive, led him to foresee his imminent disgrace. Commandant Henry returned from leave. Captain Jules Lauth, Félix Gribelin, and François Guénée would join him in a "bureaucratic conspiracy"† against their solitary and pretentious superior. Generals Gonse and de Boisdeffre of the General Staff kept Minister Billot regularly informed. The unfortunate Picquart was neglecting his service. He was concerned only with his obsessions: the Esterhazy Affair and the Dreyfus Affair. Toward the middle of October,

---

* Agent Desvernine had searched Esterhazy's apartment on the rue de la Bienfaisance (in his absence) to no avail. All that was found were some burnt papers and two of Edouard Drumont's visiting cards.[3]
† As of October, Commandant Henry was plainly assigned with keeping his superior under surveillance.[4]

de Boisdeffre stopped concealing from Picquart the extent of his displeasure. The head of the Intelligence Service was lacking in "balance" in his investigation of Esterhazy. He was wrong to have mentioned it to Alphonse Bertillon, who was speaking about it to all and sundry. And had one not begun to see rather often, all too often, Maître Louis Leblois at the Ministry? Why was Picquart so interested in the alleged innocence of Dreyfus? Commandant Henry reported to General Gonse, who discussed the case with General de Boisdeffre. The head of the Intelligence Service seemed to suffer from an obsession. De Boisdeffre recommended to the minister that he reassign Picquart elsewhere in the interest of the Service. It would be important to isolate him from the unfortunate influences that might be exerted on him. Picquart had previously distinguished himself in Tonkin. Might he not be transferred there—even in his own interest? The minister of war was embarrassed. He was searching for a compromise. He claimed to want to avoid a renewal of polemics in the press. It would be best, no doubt, to invent the pretext of a mission. Picquart would be asked to reorganize the Intelligence Service affiliated with the various armed corps stationed on the eastern and southeastern borders. He would thus not be permanently replaced. Gonse would be temporarily in charge of the Intelligence Service and Henry would be responsible for its daily workings.

On October 27, the minister signed the order mandating Picquart's mission. "I immediately understood," Picquart would state, "that it was a matter of keeping me at a distance, but I didn't convey that feeling to anyone."[5] He began to understand that his zeal, his curiosity to discover the "real truth," were upsetting the General Staff and his own subordinates as well. He saw clearly that Dreyfus's innocence was of concern to no one. Had the case been closed? Was the Army's prestige or the reputation of France at stake? Or was it simply the embarrassment caused by the illegality of the secret file?* The mission which had been invented for him was in no sense urgent. It was November 14 that the minister had him informed that his fate was sealed: he was to leave within forty-eight hours. On November 15 and 16, Colonel Picquart handed all of his files over to General Gonse, including the investigation of Esterhazy. He gave the original of the *petit bleu* to Commandant Henry. General Gonse saw him

---

* Schwarzkoppen described the situation as follows in his *Notebooks*: Gonse, de Boisdeffre and the minister of war did not want to allow for any relaunching of the Dreyfus Affair. They regarded Picquart's discovery and the great energy with which he seemed to want to pursue it as extremely embarrassing and fraught with difficulties. Like their acolytes, du Paty and Henry, they must have feared that if Picquart succeeded in proving Dreyfus's innocence and Esterhazy's guilt, it would be all over for them, for the Army's prestige, and for France's reputation. They had thus to render the pursuit of Picquart's investigation impossible and to establish Dreyfus's guilt once again."[6]

off with an "affectionate farewell." "You will come back to us in December," Gonse promised with growing amiability. When Picquart entered the train that was to take him to Châlons, he could sense the relief
caused by his replacement.

But between the signature authorizing the mission that would remove
Picquart from Paris and his departure, there occurred a rush of events that
appear to have justified his disquiet. The return of the two Chambers,
scheduled for October 27, brought with it the impending threat of the
official questioning by Deputy André Castelin, to all appearances violently
opposed to Dreyfus, but alleged by François Guénée to be in the "pay" of
the Dreyfus family. General Billot was increasingly concerned. A confidential note from Guénée to Gonse, dated October 30, introduced a new
dilemma: it revealed that Picquart, in his study of the secret file, had
pressed his investigation further than had been thought, that he had
worked on Commandant du Paty de Clam's commentary, and—with
perilous curiosity—on Guénée's two reports.* He had summoned Guénée
and questioned him on the odd remarks by the Marquis Val-Carlos, the
deputy military attaché of the Spanish embassy, which he had reported. A
perilous curiosity indeed. . . . Had Picquart "uncovered the weak point" in
the reports by Guénée that were transmitted to the Court-Martial?[7] Had
he perceived or suspected the forgeries that had been committed? And
what was—or might be—known of the matter outside the Ministry?

At the end of October, Gonse had brutally reclaimed possession of the
secret file from Picquart. A note by Guénée, revealing that Picquart may
have had suspicions about the events of 1894, recalled the file's fragility.†
What was lacking, in the face of the new danger, was a document that
would be truly devastating for Dreyfus. A decisive piece of evidence was
needed. Did Gonse, who saw Henry on October 3, suggest to him or order
him to "invent" the document that would provide definitive proof of
Dreyfus's guilt? Or was it Henry who had the idea—to please his
superiors, to render them a service, to help Esterhazy, out of military zeal
or friendly complicity?[9]

On Sunday, November 1, All Saints Day, Commandant Henry worked
calmly in his home. He had taken with him two or three documents that
had arrived through the ordinary track, selected from the archives of the
Section of Statistics. One was a letter from Alessandro Panizzardi, the
Italian military attaché, to Colonel Maximilien de Schwarzkoppen, the

---

* Concerning which it will be recalled that they were padded in order to strengthen the secret
file. See *supra* p. 88–89.
† Guénée ended his note of October 30 by specifying that Picquart had told him of conveying
his "doubts" to a third party. Henry and Guénée would claim that Picquart had mentioned
them to his friend, the lawyer Louis Leblois.[8]

German military attaché, a brief letter written in blue pencil during the second half of June 1896 and found, as was the custom, by Mme. Bastian in Schwarzkoppen's wastebasket.

> My dear friend,
>   Here is the manual. I paid for you (180) as agreed. Wednesday, eight in the evening, at Laurent's place is fine. I have invited three from my embassy, including one Jew. Don't miss it. Alexandrine.[10]

There was in addition a second document, an envelope which had also come by way of the ordinary track. The front bore Schwarzkoppen's address, written by Panizzardi's hand. On the back was the Italian's initialed seal. For his labors, Henry had acquired a blank half-sheet of graph paper, the very paper habitually used by Panizzardi.

Perhaps on his own, conceivably with the assistance of a forgery expert,[11] in any event aided by his wife, who enveloped him with her advice, Henry, after numerous trials, proceeded to execute his task. With a blue pencil, he traced on his sheet—which had been previously ripped so that it might appear to have come through the ordinary track—a text of his invention which was devastating for Dreyfus.

> I have read that a Deputy is to pursue questioning about Dreyfus. If Rome is asked for new explanations, I will say that I never had any relations with the Jew. If they ask you, say the same, for no one must ever know what happened with him.

He imitated, as best he could, Panizzardi's handwriting. He took the precaution of including two or three words appearing in his model. With the help of transparent adhesive tape, he aligned and attached the heading of the model letter "My dear friend" and the signature "Alexandrine." He then glued to the original model, whose heading and signature had been amputated, the heading and signature of an insignificant document—an invitation to dinner[12]—which he subsequently destroyed. The forgery was crude. Henry, who was no polished professional, failed to perceive that the lines of the graph on the paper used for the forgery were bluish in tint, whereas the heading and signature were traced on paper whose squares were mauve. Inversely, the second document, written on a graph of mauve, was provided with a heading and signature written on bluish-gray paper. The size of the squares, moreover, was not exactly the same.

Those lapses would eventually prove incriminating to Commandant Henry, but at the time, he was quite proud of his effort. On November 2, he brought his document to General Gonse. Gonse and de Boisdeffre rushed to see the minister, informing him of the "discovery" that Henry had just made. They could all rest easy again. The ordinary track had thus brought them proof that would definitively confound Dreyfus's partisans. Why not show the document to Colonel Picquart, who still had a few days left as head of the service? "Because," de Boisdeffre would say, "the minister thought it better not to, and so did I. Colonel Picquart's departure was a decision that had already been made, and the minister had decided that it was preferable to no longer speak to him about anything."[13] Was that in fact the minister's decision? The minister had been shown only a photograph of the document. "I will say that I never had any relations with the Jew." Unfortunately, the photo was not clear. The original was "replaced" in the secret file by a copy of the forgery written entirely in Gribelin's hand and preceded by a description of the envelope and the seal. The precaution was admirable: the copy had been "authenticated" in hierarchical order by Gonse, Henry, Lauth, and Gribelin, with mention of the rank and function of each. All four attested to the authenticity of the copy, which had been substituted for the original.[14]

A strange procedure. . . . For Marcel Thomas, it signifies clearly the complicity of the General Staff and the Section of Statistics. Thereafter, "each of the associates had a hold on the others." If de Boisdeffre kept his distance, his deputy Gonse gave his endorsement to the forgery, presumably by order or counsel of the General Staff. When Henry would tell his wife, upon leaving for Mont-Valérien, "I am doomed; they're letting me go,"* he would be telling the truth. His accomplices would be abandoning him.

But even as the General Staff was eliminating Picquart, as Henry was fabricating the forgery intended to confound Dreyfus's supporters, as the General Staff and the Section of Statistics were consolidating their criminal complicity, Mathieu Dreyfus was initiating a vigorous attack. On November 7 and 8, all members of Parliament, all the principal journalists of Paris, and numerous personalities of note, received a pamphlet, signed by Bernard Lazare, *Une Erreur Judiciaire: La Vérité sur l'Affaire Dreyfus*.† It was, as Marcel Thomas has observed, a "veritable declaration of war" by the partisans of Dreyfus. The contents of the bordereau were reproduced in their entirety. Lazare affirmed that "the secret document did not contain the name Dreyfus, but only the initial D." The text, which the

* *Infra* p. 330.
† The brochure was secretly printed in Brussels and sent in sealed envelopes. It will be recalled that Bernard Lazare had written his first text in favor of Dreyfus in June 1895. Demange and Dreyfus had constrained him to wait patiently for almost a year and a half. Bernard Lazare had constantly revised and improved his work in the interim. The brochure was printed in an edition of 3,000 copies.

young writer had been revising up until the last day, particularly in order to refute the articles of *L'Eclair*, was given a rather reserved reception.[15] But at the General Staff its impact was more marked. Lazare appeared to be extremely well informed. Did he have in his hands the complete text of the "scoundrel D." document? Did he know the other items in the secret file, even if he did not refer to them? Before departing, Picquart had the time to make a hasty investigation. He discovered that Lazare's brochure had cost the Dreyfus family twenty-five thousand francs. But concerning the source of the leaks that had informed Lazare, he found nothing. In any event, he said nothing. Thereafter, for the General Staff, Picquart would be the suspect.

On November 10 lightning struck: *Le Matin* published a facsimile of the bordereau.* This time no effort was made to conceal the suspicions aimed at Picquart. Gonse asked him curtly if he had in his files a copy of the bordereau. He answered in the negative—incorrectly, as it happened. "After verification," he was obliged to acknowledge his error.[16] In addition, the minister of war learned that Picquart was having the postal service intercept letters exchanged between the Jewish officer, Maurice Weil, and Esterhazy. The letters obtained were not without interest. They revealed Esterhazy's personality, his relations with Edouard Drumont and *La Libre Parole*. A pattern of humble requests and threats of blackmail could already be observed.[17] But Billot was infuriated by "procedures" that he deemed unloyal and that might soon implicate his friend General Félix Saussier. The minister, whom matters were driving to a state of panic, learned on November 12 of an anonymous letter written to Maurice Weil. "You are aware that Castelin is going to denounce you as an accomplice in the Dreyfus Affair, you and Esterhazy. Commandant Pierre." Weil surely must have warned Esterhazy, and undoubtedly Saussier as well.† The future seemed rife with insurmountable problems. Gonse threatened to resign if Picquart was not removed immediately from his post. On November 14, the minister received Picquart along with Boisdeffre and Gonse. He berated him severely. "Your investigation of Esterhazy has been leaked to the public. . . . You will leave your office tomorrow." Gonse and de Boisdeffre remained silent.

But the publication of the bordereau had done more than precipitate Picquart's exile. Esterhazy was terrified. He read in the newspapers that

---

* The facsimile had been sold, it appears, to the newspaper—under the title "La Preuve: fac-similé du bordereau écrit par Dreyfus"—by Teysonnière, the handwriting expert, who had kept it and was intent on profiting from the press campaign.
† It is certain that Maurice Weil showed the letter to Esterhazy, whom the publication of the bordereau had already thrown into a panic. Weil transmitted the anonymous letter to Deputy Adrien de Montbello (from the Marne), a member of the Armed Services Commission, who conveyed it to the minister of war.[18]

the bordereau was written in his own hand. He knew that there were many who could recognize his handwriting. At the General Staff, the disquiet was mounting. Where did the facsimile come from? Where would the leaks stop? As for Mathieu Dreyfus, he finally had the long awaited means to assure an authentic investigation. He had the facsimile, framed on each side by letters of his brother, reproduced as a poster. In revealing the disparities in handwriting, the poster would at last open people's eyes. "Our circle of action was growing, expanding from day to day," wrote Mathieu.[19] There remained but to find the author of the bordereau. . . .

The publication of the bordereau revealed to Colonel von Schwarzkoppen the frightening truth. "I immediately recognized Esterhazy's handwriting," he would write. He understood that "Dreyfus had been condemned in Esterhazy's place."[20] I told this, he added, "to my friend Panizzardi, to whom I revealed for the first time the name and position of my correspondent." Schwarzkoppen maintained that his situation at the time became "extremely painful." Ought he to proclaim the truth and confound Esterhazy? His "duty" as an officer—or as a spy—forbade him from doing that. After a struggle with his conscience which he presented with great care in his *Notebooks*,[21] he opted to remain silent. On November 22, he nevertheless sent his superiors a long report in which he attempted to reconcile his secret with his scruples.[22]

> As far as the Dreyfus Affair is concerned, it remains as mysterious as ever. . . . Here we can but repeat still again and forever that Dreyfus was and is absolutely unknown to our embassy, that we have never had any relations—be they direct or through an intermediary—with him, and that consequently, there has never existed in the embassy the alleged document written by him and stolen from the embassy, which is said to have led to his conviction. If Dreyfus's conviction did indeed result from an alleged document emanating from him and stolen from the German embassy, that conviction is an error, and after the declaration by the German ambassador to the minister of foreign affairs that the embassy never had the slightest dealings with Dreyfus, the French government should alone assume the weighty responsibility for this act of judicial murder.[23]

As of November 10, Schwarzkoppen had in his hands the proof of Dreyfus's innocence, and the proof of Esterhazy's treason. He held their fates in the balance. But he was the German military attaché and an intelligence agent. The truth and the affairs of France were of secondary importance.

Once again, Count Münster von Derneberg, who knew nothing of espionage activity, waxed indignant at the thought that the German embassy was being called into question. "The minister of foreign affairs has the duty to protect resolutely the Imperial Embassy from deceitful and absurd attacks."[24] In November, he would send the German emperor, Wilhelm II, a report summarizing Lazare's theses concerning Dreyfus's innocence, which Wilhelm II would annotate with the words, "This was and still is my idea."[25]

The questioning by Deputy André Castelin took place on November 18. The great and much feared encounter would last less than two hours. General Billot was in good spirits. He now knew that there existed in the Ministry a decisive document, the very one whose photo he had been shown by de Boisdeffre and Gonse. He kept a copy of it in his file. He would make use of it only if Castelin truly provoked him. But the investigation seemed to work against Dreyfus rather than for him. The minister, upon ascending the podium, hid behind the authority of the previous verdict and his respect for the closed session. He refused to broach the central issue. Castelin had gathered all the gossip to be culled from articles he had read. He denounced the "civilian accomplices" aiding Dreyfus, the attempts at bribery aimed at judges and experts. He asked for legal action against Bernard Lazare, against all those apologists for the traitor. He did not mention the names of either Esterhazy or Weil. Billot was relieved.[26] Against so weak an assault there would be no need to reveal the weapon he had in reserve. A few Socialists (Edouard Vaillant and Marcel Sembat) and several anti-Semitic deputies proposed motions inviting the government to take effective measures "in order to suppress treason." The premier, Jules Méline, protested that the government was executing its duties in full and had no need of reeducation from anyone. He finally accepted the formulation of a unanimously voted motion (with the exception of five adversaries and several abstentions—including Joseph Reinach) according to which the Chamber "declared itself united in patriotic sentiment and confident that the government would seek out, wherever and whenever needed, any whose responsibility has come to light during and since the conviction of the traitor Dreyfus, and would continue to suppress them."[27] "That matter was brought to trial," Billot proclaimed, "and no one has the right to question the results." De Boisdeffre and Gonse were reassured; the government had maneuvered adroitly. The Assembly had unanimously denounced the partisans of "the traitor Dreyfus." Picquart had gone off on his lengthy mission. . . . Commandant Henry, who had labored so well for the Army, would take his place. However poorly it had begun, the trimester was ending rather well.

But there were now glimmers of hope in the evening gatherings of the

Dreyfus family. The infraction of the law which had allowed Dreyfus to be judged guilty was now known to all. It even began to disturb many who believed in Dreyfus's guilt—rigorous students of the law, men of uncompromising conscience. The photo of the bordereau was widely circulated and one could easily see that it was not written by Alfred Dreyfus. Indeed, there were grounds for hope. But on Devil's Island, the deportee was chained to his hut, held in double shackles, while the double stockade was built around him. The copies of his letters—the administration kept all the originals[28]—which reached Lucie with three or four weeks' delay contained extremely bad news. He was exhausted, at the brink of despair. Time itself was a mortal enemy.

13

Speranza

The conspirators had not waited for Lieutenant Colonel Picquart's departure to begin their "investigation": Commandant Henry was in charge of the operation. On November 18 he ordered Police Inspector Tombs to investigate the leaks that *Le Matin* had been exploiting. The inspector soon discovered that the culprit had been the handwriting expert Teysonnière, who had sold his copy of the bordereau to the journal. Disappointing news indeed: it was plainly not Picquart. Henry then commissioned the very devoted agent Félix Gribelin to pursue the inquest. Using the pseudonym Lescure, Gribelin questioned a journalist from *Le Matin*. He said—or Gribelin had him say—what was expected of him. "It was an official who had custody of the bordereau" who was responsible for informing the newspaper. "An official? Picquart." And François Guénée—who could always be counted on for his zeal—drew up the report of the confidences that his superior, Picquart, had made to him before leaving his post. "You see, M. Guénée, when I find myself confronted with a delicate matter, I have the habit of going to consult an old friend of mine who lives nearby."[1] The "old friend" was the lawyer Louis Leblois, a Protestant and an Alsatian, whom Guénée portrayed in the most odious terms: "embittered . . . weasel-faced . . . detested by his classmates from the time he entered school." So Picquart, it seemed, had already been seeking the advice of Leblois in November 1896. Before long it would be said that Picquart had been seen showing his friend Leblois the documents of the secret file that were spread out on his desk. That indiscretion would be denounced as a "serious professional breach," with which both Picquart and Leblois would be reproached.

That was not enough. Commandant Henry's zeal knew no limits. All correspondence addressed to Picquart—who was still nominally the head of the Intelligence Service—was unsealed, carefully read, then reexpedited to its addressee, or occasionally retained. It would take some time for Picquart to perceive this. But then Colonel Picquart was preoccupied in his new location. General Gonse sent him affectionate letters.[2] Picquart's mission was prolonged, bringing him ever closer to the Mediterranean. "General Billot orders you to continue your tour with the 7th Corps without returning to Paris. . . . The Ministry wants you to go forthwith to inspect the 14th and 15th regions. . . ." The Section of Statistics informed the minister that the doings of the Italian consuls in Tunisia were in need of investigation. And Picquart was surely the man needed for such an inquest.

On November 27, through a felicitous coincidence Commandant Henry intercepted a letter, written in Spanish and addressed to Colonel Picquart by a former soldier named Germain Ducasse, who was quite devoted to Picquart, who had periodically served as an agent of the Section of Statistics, and who had become, no doubt thanks to his protector, the private secretary of the Countess de Comminges, an aging spinster who maintained a salon frequented by Picquart and other officers. Under the name of Durand, on November 24 and 26, Ducasse forwarded to Picquart two rather enigmatically phrased reports that were intercepted by Henry. Even more noteworthy, on November 27, he sent a mysterious note, composed in Spanish.

> Most honorable sir:
> Never would I have believed it had I not seen it myself. The masterpiece is complete as of today: we are to call Cagliostro Robert Houdin.
> The Countess speaks incessantly of you and tells me each day that the demi-god is asking when it will be possible to see you.
> Your devoted servant who kisses you on the hand. "J."[3]

A coded message—surely suspicious. The first paragraph referred to a professional matter that Picquart had entrusted to agent Desvernine (here named Cagliostro). The second concerned worldly relations in the

Countess's salon. A Captain Lallemand was the "demi-god" whereas, for the devoted Ducasse, Picquart was the "good Lord." But that mattered little: the document was sufficiently bizarre to be useful. Henry consulted Gonse. They took pains not to consult the note's author, whom they knew quite well. What was called for was a demonstration that the missive revealed Picquart's relationship with Dreyfus's supporters. Thus might they extract from the minister the definitive removal of the cumbersome colonel.

The indefatigable Henry returned to work. On December 14, in the course of a few hours, he produced a new forgery based on the intercepted document. It was a letter that would arrive by mail at the Ministry on December 15, would be "opened by error," and carefully retained.

> Paris, Midnight 35—I am leaving the house, our friends are in a state of consternation; your unfortunate departure has upset everything. Hasten your return here; come quickly, quickly! The holiday season being quite auspicious for the cause, we count on you for the 20th. She is ready, but cannot and will not act until she has spoken to you. Once the demi-god speaks, we will act. Speranza.[4]

The forgery said what was necessary: the Jewish syndicate, Dreyfus's friends, were awaiting the return of Picquart. Around Christmas they would act in concert. The minister of war was shown the new document. This time he was convinced. On December 24 he made the decision to send Picquart to Tunisia. It was Gonse who sent the news to Picquart. "The Minister has just told me that he is expanding the range of your mission and charging you with the organization of the Intelligence Service in Algeria and in Tunisia. . . . You are to leave on the boat departing from Marseille on Tuesday, December 29, for Philippeville."[5] With Colonel Picquart in Africa, they would be rid of him at last.

Front side of the famous "bordereau" out of which the Dreyfus Affair emerged. Intercepted toward the end of September 1894 by the French Intelligence Service, by October 6 it was attributed to Captain Dreyfus, who was serving an apprenticeship with the General Staff.

Reverse side of the same "bordereau."

The "bordereau" as recopied by Dreyfus in the Cherche-Midi Prison. The various resemblances and disparities on the basis of which expert Bertillon based his thesis—that Dreyfus had imitated his own handwriting—may be noted.

The "Dictation": a text dictated to Captain Dreyfus by Commandant du Paty de Clam on October 13, 1894, in order to confound him. The handwriting gets a bit larger with the words: "Je vous rappelle…" "What is the matter, Captain, you are trembling…" was du Paty's response.

A letter by Commandant Esterhazy, written early September 1894, to the German military attaché Maximilien von Schwarzkoppen. When compared to the bordereau, one can see the similarities in handwriting discovered by Colonel Picquart.

"Le petit bleu." A rough copy of a "telegram" addressed by the German military attaché to Commandant Esterhazy and intercepted in March 1896 by the French Intelligence Service. This document enabled Colonel Picquart to identify Esterhazy as the author of the bordereau.

The "scoundrel D." letter, signed Alexandrine and addressed by Schwarzkoppen to his colleague, the Italian military attaché Panizzardi. Schwarzkoppen passed on "12 master plans of Nice" confided to him by a secret agent designated by the letter D. The document, "stolen" from the diplomat's waste basket, was the principal item in the "secret file" given on orders from the minister of war to Dreyfus's judges during their deliberations.

"The Henry Forgery." The document was forged by Commandant Henry during the night of October 31, 1896, to augment the file assembled against Dreyfus with a devastating document. The cross-rulings of the paper, which allowed Captain Cuigent to detect the forgery, are still visible in the pieces at the top and bottom.

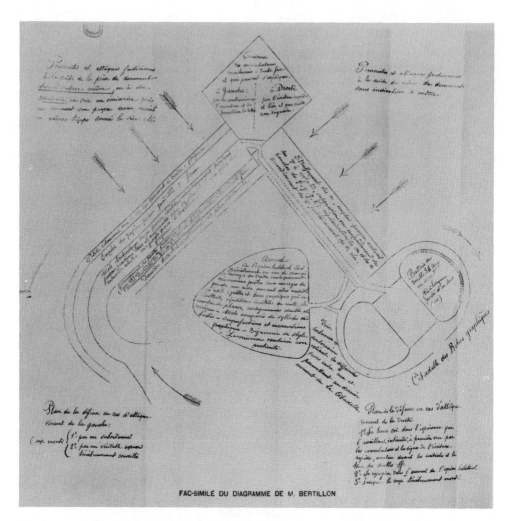

FAC-SIMILÉ DU DIAGRAMME DE M. BERTILLON

The famous "redan" drawn up by expert Bertillon to demonstrate to the military judges the "self-forgery" attributed to Dreyfus in writing the bordereau. At the center: "the arsenal of the habitual spy," stocked with formidable weapons. To the right: the corridor leading to the "citadel of graphic rebuses." Toward the top: the job dubbed "Works of double-sided spoilt sheets," flanked by a corridor fortified on its left and right with five trenches, one of which was underground. The diagram specifies the "lines of defense" envisioned by Dreyfus.

Alfred Dreyfus at age 19 in 1879, a student at the École Polytechnique. He was a shy and idealistic adolescent.

Alfred Dreyfus (on the first step, at the extreme right) in his class picture at the École de Guerre, August 1891.

Son effort de prédilection s'est porté sur les lois d'éducation nationale, le budget des Ecoles a été doublé, et l'instruction de tous assurée.

Pour la première fois le respect absolu de la liberté de Conscience dans l'Ecole a été constitué par les lois, qu'il s'agisse du Prêtre, du Pasteur ou du Rabbin.

Avec un soin jaloux, la République a réformé tout notre outillage militaire. La France aujourd'hui peut être tranquille.

Elle n'attaquera jamais personne, mais elle ne craint plus qu'on l'attaque.

La situation de Retraite de tous les officiers et soldats a été améliorée: l'Armée sait que la République a pour elle une constante sollicitude.

Campaign illustrations for the legislative elections of 1881, celebrating compulsory education, freedom of religion, the renovation of "military equipment," and the situation of officers and soldiers in the Nation.

Beneath portraits of eminent statesmen, the Army proclaims its fidelity to the Republic.

General Raoul de Boisdeffre, Army Chief of Staff

Commandant du Paty de Clam

Commandant Henry

General Auguste Mercier, minister of war in 1894

A consummate man of the world, a secret agent, beloved by both men and women, combining pleasures with espionage, Maximilien von Schwarzkoppen (above), the German military attaché, tossed into his waste basket both love letters and priceless documents. On behalf of the French Intelligence Service, Madame Bastian, a cleaning lady at the embassy, would undertake her collections.

The man who altered history: Commandant Count Walsin-Esterhazy (right). His Legion of Honor decoration on his unbuttoned uniform, his cap pulled low, his moustache drooping, his eye aflame, perpetually shifting, thus Esterhazy appeared, a prodigious gambler and a cheater whom no risk could impede.

January 5, 1895. In the principal courtyard of the École Militaire, before the regiments of the Paris garrison and numerous guests, Captain Dreyfus submits to his degradation. Sergeant-Major Bouxin of the Garde Républicaine had just stripped the galloons from his cap, which lie with his epaulets on the ground.

14

From Colonel to Lawyer,
Lawyer to Senator

General Gonse and Commandant Henry, who were the principal actors at the time, also wanted to appease Colonel Picquart, for they knew that it was not in his character to submit without resistance. Henry assured Picquart of his loyalty in a letter of December 4: "I feel as you do the malaise you refer to, but I must tell you quite frankly and man to man that if you had been willing to listen to me on the day that you told me I was speaking so wisely, that malaise would have disappeared a long time ago. . . ." For the new year, General Gonse sent Picquart his best wishes. "Good health on your splendid trip"; his signature was preceded by the words, "affectionately yours." Picquart was assured that all his expenses would be reimbursed. He was promised all the "leaves" he would need. They would take care of his horse, the "old friend" he had left behind in Paris. Picquart pretended to be their dupe, and undoubtedly in part he was. He remained deferential to Gonse, warm with Henry. But since it was clear that the urgency of his mission was fabricated, on January 16, he requested bluntly to return to the ranks.[1] The minister refused. To have acceded would have been an acknowledgment that Picquart was in disgrace.

In Paris, at least, that was the rumor. His friends were worried. "He is on a mission," Gonse affirmed flatly.[2] In March 1897 Picquart was allowed to spend a few days in Paris. Was it then, as he would later maintain, that he had the "revelation" of the duplicity of Commandant Henry, whom he had until then regarded as his faithful aide?[3] Did his friends, who were better informed than he, warn him that his situation was more perilous than he imagined? Whatever the case, upon returning to Sousse, he added a codicil to his will. In it he explained the coincidence that had put him on Commandant Esterhazy's track. He spoke of the influence commanded by Esterhazy, his relations with Weil, who was "perhaps his accomplice," and the possible influence of General Saussier. He explained how he had discovered that Dreyfus had been convicted for the crime of another on the basis of secret evidence, how General de Boisdeffre had manipulated the minister of war, and how he himself had been sent to Africa "with the evident intention of removing him far away from the Intelligence Service." He enclosed his account in a sealed envelope on which he wrote the words: "In the event of the death of the undersigned, deliver this envelope to the president of the Republic who alone is to know of it. G. Picquart, Lieutenant Colonel in the 4th Sharpshooters."[4]

On May 18, in returning to Henry an agent's letter, Picquart appended a rather nasty note:

Commandant Henry,
    Let it be publicly admitted once and for all that I have been relieved of my functions, or that I am no longer fulfilling my functions.
    I have no reason to be embarrassed by that circumstance; what embarrasses me are all the lies and mysteries that my actual situation has inspired in the course of the last six months.

Henry responded on May 31 with an extremely insolent letter, which he undoubtedly composed with Captain Lauth and Félix Gribelin and probably submitted to Gonse for his approval. In it, for the first time, he leveled serious charges against his former superior:

My Colonel,
    I have the honor of informing you that as the result of an investigation conducted here after the receipt of your note of May 18, the word "mystery" may be applied to the facts related below, which occurred at the S.S. in the course of the year 1896:
    1. The opening of letters unrelated to the Service for reasons that no one here has ever understood.
    2. Propositions made to two members of the staff of the S.S. and which consisted of testifying if need be that "a classified document of the Service had been seized in the mails and emanated from a known individual."
    3. The opening of a "secret file" and the examination of its contents, concerning which certain indiscretions then transpired to ends unrelated to the Service.
    The material proof of these facts exists here. As for the word "lies," which is also contained in the aforementioned note, our inquiry has not yet been able to determine where, how, and to

whom the word should be applied. Rest assured of my respectful sentiments. Henry.*

The letter reached Picquart on June 7 at Gabès. This time Picquart was without illusions. It was a declaration of war.[5] "Overwhelmed, he reflected for three days."[6] On June 10, he responded curtly: "Received letter of May 31. I protest in the most formal manner the insinuations it contains and the manner in which the facts are presented." Henceforth he was aware that he would be obliged to defend himself and was intent on taking precautionary measures.

He asked for permission to go to Paris and arrived there on June 20. The following day, he went to see his old friend Maître Louis Leblois, the only lawyer whom he knew. He presented matters to him in detail, showed him the documents in his possession, including the letters from Gonse. He told him that he was now convinced of Dreyfus's innocence and of Esterhazy's guilt. But he did not yet specifically mention to him the *petit bleu*, since he judged that item subject to professional secrecy. Leblois immediately perceived the drama of conscience in which his unhappy friend had been plunged and he sympathized with his scruples. He anticipated the danger of the intrigues that were closing in on him. Had not Picquart fallen into a trap? They spent every evening from June 21 to June 29 together. Leblois was in Reinach's words, "more insistent as the hours passed, more curious for details, more impassioned by the great cause it was his ambition to make his own; Picquart, perplexed, racked by doubt, utterly disoriented."[7]

Before leaving for Sousse, Picquart gave his valued friend "complete power of attorney." "If he felt it necessary," Leblois was authorized to inform the government of what he knew. But he forbade the lawyer from communicating with Dreyfus's brother or lawyer. Any indiscretion would be "an abuse of confidence." Leblois pledged his silence and the two friends separated.

Bound by his pledge, Leblois did not know what to do with the information confided to him. He felt a dual responsibility—toward his friend Picquart and toward the innocent Dreyfus. But he was the captive of his promise. To be sure, he could not speak to his colleague Edgar Demange. One day in July, he dined at Ville-d'Avray with members of the Alsace-Lorraine Committee. Among those present was Auguste Scheurer-Kestner, the former deputy from Alsace and the vice president of the Senate. Scheurer-Kestner, who was by then himself preoccupied with the Affair, expressed his doubts as to the guilt of the deportee on

* In barely guarded terms, the letter accused Picquart of having "altered" the *petit bleu* and of having communicated the secret file to his friend, the lawyer Leblois.

Devil's Island. Leblois listened without uttering a word. A few days later, Leblois met Scheurer-Kestner's nephew, Charles Risles, mayor of the Seventh Arrondissement. Risles spoke to him of his uncle's preoccupations with the Dreyfus question. Brutally, Leblois made his decision: "Take me to see your uncle." On July 13, he paid a visit to the vice president of the Senate in his home, and on that day occurred one of the decisive events of the Dreyfus Affair.

The lawyer told all he knew. He showed Scheurer-Kestner the letters Picquart had left with him. He made the vice president swear that he would not make use of these confidences without his prior agreement. In the memorandum he would draw up that day, Scheurer-Kestner, overwhelmed, "dumbstruck" as he would say, affirmed his beliefs: "Here is the truth about the Dreyfus Affair."

At the time of his conviction, everyone, military judges and functionaries of the Ministry of War, was convinced of his guilt.

Today, the opposite is the case. Some doubt; others, and the minister of war is among them, recognize the situation as it is: Dreyfus is innocent.

But the Affair is being stifled and in order to be free of it, the story of an accomplice is being invented.

Not only is it known in the Ministry of War that Dreyfus is innocent, but the identity of the culprit, the criminal, is known.

The culprit is named Walzin [sic] Esterhazy; he is an Austrian [crossed out] Hungarian who has been naturalized French, a commandant in the French army, recently retired from service, allegedly because of temporary infirmities, and residing at 27, rue de la Bienfaisance. He was commandant with the 74th Line only three months ago. They began by retiring him from active duty—temporarily, since at the Ministry of War they proceed on a day by day basis. He is a man riddled with debts, a gambler and a rake. I am about to procure a specimen of his handwriting by purchasing one of his letters of credit. His handwriting, which I have not yet seen, is exactly the same as the handwriting of the document which served to convict Dreyfus, according to the person who made this staggering confidence to me, which I am alone in sharing with him. Walzin had been caught in another espionage affair after the Dreyfus Affair and it was then that the similarity in handwriting with the Dreyfus document became patent.

Commandant Walzin was Mayer's second in his duel with Morès and he has flaunted it ever since in order to ask all of Jewry for money.

This Walzin has an accomplice; his name is Maurice Weil and he lives at 97, Faubourg Saint-Honoré. Let's turn to Weil. Weil is a commandant of the territorial army; he is a stockbroker, it is thought, a former horse trader. He has entered into the confidence of General Saussier, who at present still knows nothing of all this; in June 1896, Saussier, who is, it is said, on excellent terms with Mme. Weil, dined at the Weil home with Walzin. . . .

Difficulties of the situation:

1. M. Picquard [sic] must remain out of it.
2. The Ministry defended Dreyfus's conviction in November 1896, while knowing he was innocent.
3. Weil's relations with Saussier.
4. Any mention would expose Picquard, since General Gonse would guess at the source of the indiscretion.

. . . Commandant Henry knows everything.[8]

The memorandum contains several errors. It offers hypotheses—such as Weil's complicity with Esterhazy—but on the whole, Scheurer-Kestner was correct in his assumptions. There were now three men of integrity who knew the truth. But Picquart was in Africa and bound by professional secrecy. As for Leblois and Scheurer-Kestner, they were each captives of the oath they had taken. A few days later, on August 11, Scheurer-Kestner would appeal to Picquart. Picquart had to speak out. "Your friend is plainly an honest man; he has already proven it; but his honesty must not stop honest man; he has already proven it; but his honesty must not stop midway." Leblois, without even contacting Picquart, countered with a categorical refusal. He called Scheurer-Kestner back to a measure of prudence. "All these people will defend themselves, and we know that they have no scruples. If one cannot make an omelette without breaking a few eggs, for this omelette, the quantity broken would be appalling." The vice president of the Senate could obtain no promises from Leblois. He would have to act on his own. He authorized his friend Joseph Reinach, whose influence in political circles of the "center" was considerable, and several other friends—including the politician Arthur Ranc—to say "that he had come to the firm conviction that Dreyfus was innocent." To be sure, he could not utter a single word as to his reasons. He authorized Reinach to inform Mme. Dreyfus of his assistance, "the first ray of sunlight to warm that poor heart in three years."[9] The support of the vice president of the Senate, whose moral authority far exceeded his functions, who had numerous and powerful friends, was not insignificant. Finally, a politician, who was influential and would be heard, appeared to support Dreyfus's cause.

But Scheurer-Kestner wanted to complete his file and to verify the charges against Esterhazy. He lacked a specimen of the traitor's handwriting. He charged a retired police agent, Jaume, to hunt for some evidence. Imprudently, Esterhazy wrote copiously and specimens of his handwriting were to be found everywhere.[10] Jaume brought one to him on July 27. Reinach sent Scheurer-Kestner a photo of the bordereau. The resemblances were striking!* Bound by his pledge, Scheurer-Kestner, of course, mentioned Esterhazy to no one. On the other hand, he proclaimed his support for Dreyfus everywhere, and in political circles it gradually became known that the vice president of the Senate was convinced of the innocence of the deportee of Devil's Island, that he had the "proof" in his hands. Dining at the Elysée on July 19 with his friend Félix Faure, the vice president of the Senate took aside the daughter of the president of the Republic "whom he knew to be intelligent and good."[12] "My heart is heavy, my conscience racked. It's an atrocious business; Captain Dreyfus is innocent. Don't mention it to your father, for I cannot yet tell him very much; I am not free to; but have sympathy for me."[13]

Needless to say, Lucie Faure mentioned it forthwith to her father. Two days later she wrote to Scheurer-Kestner. He must speak quickly to the president. And Joseph Reinach transmitted to Scheurer-Kestner the pleas of the Dreyfus family, who were by then holding on to the promise of his support for dear life. Scheurer-Kestner would have to speak.

But bound by his pledge, as Leblois was by his, what could he say? Picquart was silent. Leblois could say nothing, nor could Scheurer-Kestner. Mathieu and Lucie Dreyfus knew nothing of what the others knew and refused to divulge. At the General Staff and at the Section of Statistics, the declarations of the vice president of the Senate were examined with the utmost care. Here was a new danger. What exactly did the new enemy know? And how might he be paralyzed?

---

* It does not appear that Scheurer-Kestner at that point experienced the certainty of "absolute identity" which had struck Picquart. But his conviction was established.[11]

15

I Have a Closetful

At what moment and in what circumstances did Commandant Esterhazy learn that he was the focus of serious suspicion? Was he
informed by Commandant Henry at the very start of the investigation? Or
by Maurice Weil during the course of 1897? Or was it later, when the
General Staff, in a state of panic, initiated contact with him? Whatever the
case, at the beginning of the year 1897, he had lost neither his composure
nor his cynicism. He was furious only that Minister of War Jean-Baptiste
Billot and his friend General Félix Saussier had abandoned him, furious at
not having been appointed to the ministerial cabinet in spite of all his
maneuvers. During the month of March, he succeeded in unleashing
through *La Libre Parole* a violent press campaign against the minister of
war. "I asked Drumont to have him attacked from every angle—without
respite. He has been just perfect. Paul de Cassagnac was very good as well,
and thanks to Drumont, who is the force behind not only his own sheet,
but others—including *L'Intransigeant*—the bastard doesn't have a moment's rest. . . ." And to be sure, he threatened as well. "If I am not
reassigned, if I leave, I have reserved for them a story that will create a
scandal throughout the world."[1] There was no doubt what he was referring to.

His disappointments did not prevent him from seeking everywhere,
and by all means, the money of which he was in ever greater need. Under
the alias of Rohan-Chabot, he became partner with the proprietress of a
brothel at 43, rue du Rocher. He invested only 2,000 francs, but supplied
the addresses of more than 1,500 potential "clients," most of them officers.
That deal appears to have furnished him with some resources during the
difficult year of 1897.[2] Above all, the death in October 1896 of his first
cousin, Paul Esterhazy, provided him the opportunity for a new swindle.
His cousin had left behind a widow, several daughters, and a twenty-year-
old son, Christian, who dreamed of a life of leisure and who spent a certain
amount of money. Esterhazy persuaded Christian and his mother that he
alone was capable of investing their holdings wisely, since he had so many

Jewish friends. In a series of payments, he received from his gullible
nephew nearly 40,000 francs that he claimed to invest with the
Rothschilds. He took what he needed, gambled with the rest at the Bourse,
and lost. At the end of 1897, he was incapable of returning any of it to
Christian, sought to arrange a wealthy marriage for him as compensation.
He failed at that, but nevertheless managed to have him declared unfit for
military service.[3] Thus did a French officer, suspected by the minister of
war, by the General Staff, and by the Intelligence Service of being an agent
in Germany employ, shifting from deception to deception, pursue his
tranquil existence.

During the month of October 1897, Scheurer-Kestner's maneuvers in
the political sphere, Mathieu Dreyfus's campaign in the press and—
through the distribution of his posters—through public opinion in general, were beginning to be a source of serious concern for Generals de
Boisdeffre and Gonse. They were convinced that Colonel Picquart, at
however great a distance, was informing Scheurer-Kestner. They had
proof that Scheurer-Kestner and Leblois were meeting,* and that they
were in contact with Dreyfus's friends and family. The Jewish "syndicate"
and its partisans were threatening. The General Staff would have to react.
Starting in October 1897, their initiatives would increase, diversify, and
two months later, give way to a veritable frenzy.

It was General Gonse, amiable, "saccharine . . . with an ingrained
affinity for deception,"[4] who appears to have taken the initiative. In a
lengthy secret note of October 15, he "restored" the morale of his minister,
who was quite susceptible to being affected by Scheurer-Kestner's campaign. Gonse assembled all the elements marshaled against Dreyfus:
notably the document furnished by Henry on Gribelin's interrogation,
Dreyfus's confessions, which resurfaced for the occasion, and the "Weiler"
letter, which indicated "a clandestine correspondence and the beginnings
of a scheme to substitute a different person for the convict."† The minister
had to be in a position to respond to Scheurer-Kestner.

But that precautionary measure could not suffice. Would it not be
necessary as well to "warn" Esterhazy? If one wanted to maintain the

---

* Specifically on November 10, at Fribourg.
† This was a "letter" addressed to the prisoner on Devil's Island on August 31, 1896, which
had been intercepted at the time by the Ministry of Colonies. Written in invisible ink, and
signed "Weiss" or "Weiler," it seemed to emanate from a relative of Dreyfus. The deciphered
text was extremely compromising: "Impossible to decipher your last communication; return
to the former procedure in your answer. Indicate precisely where the interesting documents
are and the arrangements made for the closet. Actor ready to begin immediately."
   The Weiler letter was an obvious forgery which was subsequently attributed alternately to
Commandant Henry and to Alphonse Bertillon. At the time of the discovery of the Weiler
letter, it had been attributed, notably by Bertillon, to the Dreyfus family. It appears that
Picquart immediately sensed a forgery.[5]

dogma of Dreyfus's guilt, would one not also have to protect the person the syndicate wanted to accuse? Above all, it would be imperative to prevent Esterhazy from committing any blunders. On October 16, General Gonse, after consulting with General de Boisdeffre, decided to call on their man for all seasons, the architect of Dreyfus's arrest, Commandant du Paty de Clam, who was capable of anything as long as his military conscience was appeased. Du Paty, an enlightened servant, rushed to speak to Gonse. Henry, du Paty, and Gonse deliberated. Du Paty proposed calling in Esterhazy to "order him to remain calm and not to do anything foolish." The move was dangerous and would immediately cause suspicion. By an odd coincidence, the minister of war received on that very day, October 16, an anonymous letter claiming that the Dreyfus family had been looking for treasonous officers who might be guilty of the actions attributed to Dreyfus, and had found two suspects.* That letter provided some inspiration. Du Paty would fabricate an anonymous letter, intended to warn Esterhazy, which would more or less repeat word for word the letter sent to the minister.† But the minister of war, when consulted by General Gonse, opposed sending an anonymous letter.

The situation was extremely awkward. How could Esterhazy be warned? Henry pressed du Paty: "Du Paty, this is our predicament. Do you understand? This is our predicament."[8] Du Paty understood that it was up to him to take the initiative. "I am ready," replied du Paty. On the following day there was sent to Esterhazy's address in Dommartin-la-Planchette a letter signed "Espérance," which was to inform him of the situation:

> Your name is about to become the focus of a major scandal. The Dreffus [sic] family is going to accuse you publicly of being the author of the text on which the Dreffus trial was based. The family possesses numerous specimens of your handwriting to serve as items for examination. It is a colonel who was with the Ministry last year, M. Picard, who transmitted the papers to the Dreffus family. That gentleman is now in Tonkin, I believe. The Dreffus family intends to provoke you to panic by publishing your handwriting in various newspapers, and for you to flee to your relatives in Hungary. That would indicate that you are guilty; and they would then ask for a new trial to proclaim Dreffus's innocence. It is M. Picard who gave the information to the family. This M. Picard purchased your handwriting from noncommissioned officers in Rouen last

---

* Joseph Reinach attributes this anonymous letter to Commandant Henry,[6] a circumstance Marcel Thomas regards as highly unlikely.[7]

† The draft of du Paty's forgery would be kept by Henry, who would add the initials P.D.C. (Paty de Clam), in order to compromise (as additional insurance!) his devoted accomplice.

year. I learned all this from a sergeant in your regiment who was given money in exchange for your handwriting. You are hereby forewarned of what these scoundrels plan to do in order to ruin you. It is now up to you to defend your name and the honor of your children. Act quickly, for the family is about to act to assure your doom. Your devoted friend, Espérance. Never show this letter to anyone. It is for you alone and in order to save you from the grave dangers with which you are threatened.*

Thus began what has been called the "collusion."[9] In point of fact, the deception was merely continuing, but it is true that on that day it took the indisputable form of treason. In order to further their plan, the deputy-chief of the General Staff and the actual head of the Intelligence Service, assisted by a superior officer, secretly warned a German spy that he risked being arrested.

On October 19, when he received the "Espérance" letter, Esterhazy panicked. He took a train, got off in Paris, and went to the home of his devoted mistress, Marguerite Pays. For three days, he remained prostrate, slumped in a chair, annihilated. "I am dishonored. I will have to flee; I will have to kill myself." He must have thought of it, since he took the precaution on October 20 of writing to the landlord of his building to ask that the lease of his apartment be transferred to the name of Mme. Pays. He was truly desperate, yet did nothing more constructive than compose an anonymous letter, filled with insults, that he had sent to Dreyfus's father-in-law in Lyon, M. Hadamard. He felt abandoned by all, and ignominiously persecuted.

He was not, however, alone. On October 22, toward 7:00 P.M., a stranger in blue-tinted glasses knocked at the door on rue de Douai. Esterhazy was out. The visitor, who left a message to arrange a meeting with him, was none other than Félix Gribelin, the archivist from the Intelligence Service. He had, it is true, at first resisted accepting a mission so out of keeping with his profession. Henry had advised him to "wear glasses and a fake beard," which did little to preserve the dignity of an officer.

The mysterious meeting was arranged for that very evening, across from the Parc Montsouris, at the corner of the Vanne reservoir. If Esterhazy was disturbed[10] the message that had been left sought to reassure him: he was told that he had "powerful protectors who wanted to rescue

---

* The work of a presumably "feminine" hand, it appears to have been written by Mme. Henry, for Mmes. du Paty de Clam and Henry were by then collaborating with their husbands. In 1896, Commandant Henry had signed "Speranza" the forgery urging Picquart to return to resume the task that his departure had jeopardized.

him and to whom it was in his interest to listen."[11] Before going to the meeting, Esterhazy rushed to the office of Colonel von Schwarzkoppen. He did not know that he was being followed.* It had been almost a year since the German military attaché had broken off relations with him, nevertheless, Schwarzkoppen agreed to receive him. Esterhazy told him the object of his visit: their relationship had been discovered. Esterhazy was threatened with "replacing" Dreyfus on Devil's Island. Schwarzkoppen would be dragged into the scandal. There was only one solution. The military attaché would have to see Mme. Dreyfus and assure her that her husband was guilty and that all efforts would be in vain. "You are insane, monsieur le Commandant," replied Schwarzkoppen. Esterhazy collapsed onto a couch, shouting and sobbing, drew his pistol, and threatened to shoot the military attaché. At last he calmed down. "I would have shielded you," Schwarzkoppen told him, "were it not that the other one is over there."[13] And he politely saw Esterhazy to the door. Esterhazy regained his coach, and stopped on rue de Medicis to see a senator who was also a friend of Mme. Pays. Finally, he went to the Parc Montsouris and waited.

After a time, two individuals emerged from a carriage. One—Félix Gribelin—was disguised as he had been in the morning. The other, "tall, erect, rigid, like a Prussian officer, bearing a fake black beard," was none other than Commandant du Paty de Clam.[14] The "Prussian officer" approached Esterhazy brusquely. "Commandant, you know why we are here." "Messieurs, I do not know who you are, but I declare to you that I am the victim of a frightful plot." "If we were not convinced of it, we would not be here." While the conversation continued, Commandant Henry waited in the carriage. Du Paty began to explain to the spy the "plots" that were woven around him. He showed him the facsimile of the bordereau. "It is incredible," exclaimed Esterhazy, "how certain words resemble my handwriting." His answers appeared firm and his "accent sincere."† Esterhazy must understand that henceforth he had defenders who were resolute and indefatigable. But he would have to obey the instructions that he would be given and do nothing without consulting his defenders. Esterhazy was reassured. They separated, with the promise of maintaining daily contact. Esterhazy returned to the German embassy to take leave of Schwarzkoppen, whom he would not see again. He was quite cheerful,

---

* He continued to be under police surveillance, a circumstance that complicated the task of his "protectors." It is known from the police report of his "tail" that he went first to the Crédit Lyonnais, then to the newspaper offices of *La Patrie,* before arriving toward three o'clock at the German embassy.[12]

† It appears that Esterhazy at that point attempted to explain to his two interlocutors that he was employed by Colonel Jean Sandherr and that Gribelin curtly contradicted him.[15] After Commandant Henry's death, Esterhazy would reaffirm that thesis, according to which he was a double agent.

even wearing a rose in his lapel. He told of his meeting, which had been extremely reassuring, with "two representatives of the Ministry of War," who assured him of the "government's assistance." Schwarzkoppen was delighted that things had worked out so well.* But he did not share Esterhazy's confidence. Ought he to tell all, to confess his error to Count Münster von Derneberg? Whatever happened, Schwarzkoppen could not but know that he would soon be leaving his post. Count von Münster could not retain a military attaché who was suspected by everyone. On a hundred occasions, the ambassador had vouched for his virtue. Would he still be so certain? On November 2, 1897, the imprudent Schwarzkoppen would be called back to Germany and appointed to command the Second Regiment of Grenadiers of the Guard in Berlin, a flattering promotion indeed.[18] On November 11, he would present his farewell to the president of the Republic. In order to assuage his troubled conscience, he would reaffirm to Félix Faure, "I have never known Dreyfus." As for the German ambassador, at the time he appeared to have harbored no ill feelings toward his military attaché, to whom he would write on November 20:

> My Dear Colonel,
>
> I sincerely regret that you are no longer here. The fact that the newspapers have been connecting your departure with Dreyfus astonishes me, but hardly worries me. We both well know that poor Dreyfus, as far as we were concerned, was absolutely innocent. That is why the cries of the newspapers leave me cold and should leave you equally cold. Esterhazy is defending himself quite poorly and appears to be a man of rather dubious honor.
>
> All of Paris thinks of nothing but Dreyfus. . . . You must have much to do in getting acquainted with the regiment, finding and setting up an apartment. We miss you here a great deal.
> Very amicably yours,
> Munster.

It was only later that the ambassador would discover to what extent Schwarzkoppen had deceived him.

Thereafter the conspirators of the Parc Montsouris, du Paty, Henry, and Esterhazy, would see each other often. Undoubtedly, Esterhazy and Henry were also meeting without the knowledge of their confederate. Esterhazy was sufficiently self-assured to ask for a meeting with General Ferdinand Millet, head of the Infantry, on October 23. By October 25 the meeting was arranged. Esterhazy explained to the general, who did not

---

* This second visit was not recounted by Schwarzkoppen in his *Notebooks*.[16] But Schwarzkoppen described it to his friend Panizzardi.[17]

understand much of what he was told, the plot whose victim he had become. He admitted that his handwriting resembled that of the bordereau, but stressed that a commandant in the Infantry would know nothing about artillery. Nor could he suggest what this Colonel Picquart could have against him. He wept and had difficulty speaking. "Everything is confused in my head." He claimed that he had sent to the Ministry in 1893—more precisely to Captain Bro of the General Staff*—a short text he had written on the Battle of Eupatoria in which his father had distinguished himself. "My daughter was gravely ill at the time and I was looking after her," he claimed. It was du Paty who prompted him to invent some insignificant story of a manuscript he would have sent to the Ministry on some past occasion.[19] In the difficult times that were about to beset him, he would thus be able to claim that Dreyfus had known—through Captain Bro—his handwriting and succeeded in imitating it.

On the same day, the indefatigable Esterhazy sent a lengthy report to the Ministry of War in which he repeated all that he had just told the head of the Infantry. And since he was henceforth subject to his protectors, he faithfully recopied a text prepared by du Paty, taking the precaution of retaining the original.† The treasonous officer had indeed become a docile aide. But it was learned—through the police—that he had gone on October 23 to the German embassy and spent more than an hour there. A glaring imprudence. He must not commit similar blunders in the future. So it was that du Paty and Henry, increasingly compromised with every passing day, lectured a German agent because he risked being observed during a visit to the German embassy.

The entire matter was reported to General de Boisdeffre. There was no indignation on the part of the chief of the General Staff, but he found his subordinates rather careless. A "discreet" intermediary would have to be found to speak with the difficult commandant. M. de Nettancourt, Esterhazy's brother-in-law, was suggested, but as Esterhazy was estranged from him, Marguerite Pays, and later Christian Esterhazy, would serve as contacts when they would be needed. Esterhazy had understood that it was in his greatest interest to "stick" to his generous protectors, and, of course, to compromise them as well. Thereafter he manipulated du Paty far more than the latter, overwhelmed by his turbulent protégé, managed to control him. Esterhazy also saw Commandant Henry with increasing frequency. Together they pondered a thousand ways of dishonoring Picquart, ridicul-

* This was in fact a lie, which Captain Bro would deny. But du Paty recalled that when he had first confronted Dreyfus with the bordereau, the latter, who subsequently withdrew the remark, had the momentary impression of recognizing Captain Bro's handwriting.
† The original has disappeared, but there are several uncontested photographs of it extant.[20] In his letter to General Billot, Esterhazy acknowledged having had the *Firing Manual* in his hands in 1894. It had been loaned to him by a Jewish officer, Lieutenant Bernheim.

ing Scheurer-Kestner, forcing the syndicate to retreat. If they had not been accomplices before, during the month of October 1897 the two banded together.

But Commandant Henry and his very devoted Gribelin were pursuing another task in their offices as well. With daily application, they were building up the dossier that was to devastate Captain Dreyfus. Quite opportunely, they remembered Dreyfus's confessions. It would be wise to secure an official version that was signed. Once located, Captain Lebrun-Renault of the Garde Républicaine did not seem difficult to convince. On October 20, in the presence of Gonse and Henry, he attested to having received Dreyfus's confession in the course of the ceremony of degradation.*

A slew of letters collected from the German embassy through the ordinary track after Dreyfus was sentenced were also added to the secret file. The "Henry document"—his forgery—was also included, to be sure, and would bear the numeral 3 in the list of documents concurrently prepared by Henry. There was also added a brief—and, in fact, quite insignificant—letter sent by Alessandro Panizzardi, to Schwarzkoppen in March of 1894, which read:

> My Very Dear Friend,
>   Last night I ended up calling the doctor, who has forbidden me to go out. Since I am unable to visit you tomorrow, I am asking you to come to my home in the morning, since P . . . has brought me many things of great interest and since we have only ten days to us, we shall have to divide the work.
>   Try, then, to tell the the ambassador that you can't go up.
> All yours,
> Alexandrine.

But in order to give the letter a measure of interest Henry took the useful measure of scratching out the letter *P* and replacing it with a *D*. Finally, he predated a document from after Dreyfus's deportation, a note sent by Panizzardi to Schwarzkoppen on March 28, 1895.†

---

* In order to augment the authenticity of his declaration, Gonse and Henry attested a few days later in an appended note which was predated October 20, that Lebrun-Renault's statement had been made in their presence.[21]
† This was the so-called "railroad" document. Henry cut out the words "28 March, 3 o'clock," which allowed it to be dated, and wrote in his own hand, in red ink at the bottom of the letter "April 1894." The forgery was beyond dispute. It would serve in implementing the second revision.

. . . You must be good enough to send to me immediately what you have copied, for I have to finish up because I'm sending things off to Rome on the 31st and before then you still have to copy the part copied by me.

I can tell you that I will have the organization of the railroad. . . .

The interest there lay in compromising Dreyfus, who had worked in the office in charge of military transport by railroad in March 1894. During this period, Gribelin as well was busy composing "secret notes" that were devastating for Dreyfus and above all falsifying the accounting books of the Section of Statistics in order to conceal Guénée's fraudulent reports, which, it was feared, Picquart had begun to suspect. It was an impressive dossier indeed which they thus filled out and transmitted to General Gonse, who would now be able to allow the minister of war to resist the pressures of his "friend" Scheurer-Kestner, and France to fight off the maneuvers of the Jewish syndicate.

Commandant Henry was quite proud of his work. He would soon be promoted to lieutenant colonel. On November 3, 1897, he met Maurice Paléologue from the Ministry of Foreign Affairs, on the Quai d'Orsay. Like a number of others, the diplomat was becoming concerned. Might the judges in 1894 by any chance have erred? "Don't worry," replied a jovial Henry. "Dreyfus was convicted quite justly. While he has been fishing for sharks on his island, we have discovered the most devastating evidence against him. I have a closetful."[22] And since Paléologue seemed skeptical, Henry reassured him still further. "We have a top secret document . . . we have a letter from the Emperor of Germany . . . a letter addressed to Count von Münster . . . in it the Emperor speaks of their relations with Dreyfus."* This time Paléologue was shocked: Would an emperor be writing to his ambassador about espionage? "It must have been a letter from Münster or Schwarzkoppen to the Emperor in which Dreyfus was discussed." But Henry in his boldness did not have the slightest doubt. "It is a letter which is absolutely conclusive . . . you won't get another word out of me." Whereupon he hurried off, with his lumbering pace, in the direction of the Invalides. . . .[23] Commandant Henry had served the Army and his country very well. He had by then a "closetful" of devastating evidence.

---

* If Paléologue's recollections are correct, this was the first allusion to the famous bordereau "annotated" by Wilhelm II. The bordereau that had been discovered was alleged to have been merely traced from the annotated version. The legend would later make the rounds.

16

My Dear Friend, Just Listen to Me

Mathieu Dreyfus continued to exhaust himself in maneuvers and inquiries. Throughout the long year 1897, in France and abroad, he had commissioned more than ten expert analyses of the handwriting of the bordereau.[1] The experts solicited all concluded that the handwriting was not that of Alfred Dreyfus. There was disagreement only on a single point: was the bordereau written in a normal fluent hand or was it the result of a disguised handwriting? With the help of the indefatigable Bernard Lazare and Joseph Reinach, who were convinced early on of Dreyfus's innocence, he began a vast public information campaign, particularly among academics, writers, and jurists, all those who might be moved (if not convinced) by the illegality that had been committed and by the fragility of a conviction resting merely on a resemblance in handwriting. In his *Souvenirs sur l'Affaire Dreyfus*, Léon Blum tells of how all the "canvassers" of goodwill began to split up their task.[2] And indeed the small band originally drawn to the family by chance or generosity—Commandant Ferdinand Forzinetti, the director of the Prison of Cherche-Midi; Dr. Gilbert, the specialist in mental suggestion; Bernard Lazare, later Joseph Reinach, the lawyer Louis Leblois, and, with his special authority, Auguste Scheurer-Kestner—was now growing with every passing month. A number of their initiatives had proven in vain. Bernard Lazare, assisted by Commandant Forzinetti, paid a visit to Henri Rochefort. Ought not the former ally of General Boulanger, who had once been convicted by the High Court and who had recently returned from exile, be sensitive to the injustice of an irregular trial? He had had his own "Devil's Island." And then he liked to defy authority, to take exception to tradition.[3] Above all, through his articles in *L'Intransigeant*, he exercised a veritable tyranny over the "most frivolous, mercurial, and consequently impassioned sector of public opinion." Rochefort listened to Lazare, appeared interested, promised a benevolent neutrality, and the next day published in *L'Intransigeant* an account of the visit,* an extremely violent article entitled "Vain Attempt to Rehabilitate a Traitor."

For his part, the writer Léon Blum went to see Maurice Barrès. "For me he was not only the master but the guide; we formed a school around him, almost a court." Blum was virtually certain that he would succeed in moving him. "I would almost have been willing to sign for him myself."[4] Blum found Barrès in his small painter's studio, in the middle of the dueling lesson which the writer had made part of his morning routine. "I can still see the proud and charming grace of his welcome. . . . I am certain that he had true friendship for me, almost the solicitude of an elder brother. . . ." Barrès received him warmly, saying, "Three years ago I attended Dreyfus's dismissal. . . . I wrote an article in *Le Journal*. . . . You recall? Well, I wonder whether I was not wrong. Was Dreyfus a scoundrel, or was he a stoic, a martyr? I no longer have any idea." Barrès did not consent or disagree. "I will write to you . . ." was his only response. The implication, notes Blum, was "that those five words contained a refusal." Barrès would write to him a few days later. He could see no demonstrable truth on either side. But in cases of doubt, "it was the national instinct that he would choose as his rallying point." "That letter descended on me like a veil of mourning. Something was shattered, over; one of the paths of my youth had reached its end. . . ."[5] Barrès would soon throw all of his talent and verve into the battle against an appeal of the Dreyfus trial.

But there were not only refusals. Emile Zola had already committed himself vigorously to the cause. In his articles, he landed violent blows against all those blinded by anti-Semitism and against the General Staff. Anatole France let his sympathy for the deportee of Devil's Island be known. Neither his skepticism, nor the distance he seemed to prefer, nor his status as an honored and well-known writer were enough to prevent him from taking sides.† The University and the École Normale were contributing supporters whose number and authority began to reassure the Dreyfus family. Little by little, Gabriel Monod, Charles Andler, Paul Dupuy, and Gustave Bloch began coming in the evening to the home of Lucien Herr on rue du Val-de-Grace, where the librarian of the École Normale exercised a decisive intellectual and moral influence on generations of Normalians. A few friends, academics, and students who were preoccupied with the Dreyfus verdict, together sought to make the truth

---

* One of the consequences was that Forzinetti was relieved of his functions as head of the military prison of Cherche-Midi.

† "No one would have dared hope for Anatole France," according to Léon Blum. Analyzing the reasons for the involvement of a writer for whom everything it seemed would be an obstacle for their cause, Léon Blum wrote: "France was a Dreyfusard because the methodical and scientific efforts of human intelligence were in his eyes the only reality that was certain."

known.[6] They shared a common hatred for traditional authority, social hierarchy, and institutions such as the Church and the Army, which claimed to be founded on rigid ideas. "There is an absolute opposition," wrote Lucien Herr, "between the imperialistic, militaristic principle and the radical principle. The duty to obey or the duty to question." They exalted the secular spirit of freedom in its opposition to all prejudice. A critical attitude toward all judgments, anticlericalism, and a rejection of anti-Semitism were the bases of a doubt that would gradually become a firm belief. As yet they were sources of sympathy rather than support, and without great influence, but they would draw Dreyfus's supporters out of the solitude and cold in which they had been isolated.

In the struggle that seemed forthcoming, however, the rallying of several politicians seemed still more important. Georges Clemenceau, who after 1871 had been the representative of a jingoistic and chauvinistic nationalism and who had been seriously tainted by the Panama scandal, seemed to be revising his initial position against Dreyfus. Perhaps having been temporarily excluded from political life, he was seeking a way back in. He was also undoubtedly sensitive to injustice, to the hatred and slander of which he had had his fill; perhaps he was "touched by the striking similarity that the Dreyfus story seemed to bear to his own misfortunes."* He could become an extremely useful ally, since as political editor of the newspaper *L'Aurore*, he had at his sway a rather considerable sector of the public. On November 2 and 10, he was already publishing articles in which—without dismissing the idea that Dreyfus might be guilty—he wrote that the nation nonetheless had the right to see things in "broad daylight." If there were "specific presumptions of error, then the trial should be revised." The Socialist Jean Jaurès, initially hostile toward the wealthy Jew protected by money, began to question the commonly held views, as much through the influence of Lucien Herr as out of "chivalric generosity," a kind of "quixotic calling."[8] Detesting all injustice, inclined, in addition, to seek in every injustice "a symbolic explanation of collective iniquities," he was troubled by the Affair.[9] Yes, Mathieu Dreyfus was no longer alone.

It was, nevertheless, through the authority of the vice president of the Senate, Auguste Scheurer-Kestner, that some immediate influence was to be hoped for. Mathieu Dreyfus remained convinced that remedial action must begin through the government: "It is the government that French law endows with the exclusive power of initiating a judicial appeal . . . nothing, then, is possible without the government." Such was the opinion of Joseph Reinach and Scheurer-Kestner. Like Jules Méline, the prime

---

* In the Panama Affair, Clemenceau had been the victim of falsified documents.[7]

minister, and Minister of War Billot, Reinach and Scheurer-Kestner had been friends of the former republican leader Léon Gambetta. Their past and common loyalties had created ties that joined them. Even more than Reinach, Scheurer-Kestner hoped to move a government he believed to be composed of men of scruples. He stubbornly confided in them.[10] He was intent on legality and intransigent regarding the respect for formalities. It was thus that the vice president of the Senate sought a meeting with the president of the Republic to tell him what little the lawyer Louis Leblois authorized him to say. In the corridors of the Chamber and the Senate, Scheurer-Kestner's intervention was eagerly awaited. The meeting was arranged for October 29. The General Staff was concerned once again. A few hours before the scheduled meeting, Commandant Esterhazy had delivered to the president of the Republic, "the supreme chief of my country," a letter, which was undoubtedly prepared by du Paty and in which he asked Félix Faure to put an end to the "machination" whose victim he had become, threatening, should he not obtain satisfaction, to appeal to the emperor of Germany, "suzerain" of his family:[11]

Mister President,

I have the honor of forwarding to you the text of an anonymous letter that was sent to me on October 20, 1897.

It is I who am referred to in that letter as the intended victim.

I do not want to wait for my name to be delivered over to the newspapers in order to find out what the attitude of my superiors will be.

I have addressed myself to my superior and natural protector, the minister of war, to find out whether he would shield me at the time my name would be pronounced.

The minister has not responded. Now my House is sufficiently illustrious in the glories of the history of France and the histories of the great European courts for the government of my country to be concerned lest that name be dragged through the mud.

I am thus addressing myself to the Supreme Chief of the Army, to the President of the Republic, and I ask him to put an end to the scandal, as he can and should do.

I am asking for justice against the infamous instigator of this plot, who has delivered over to the fomentors of the machination the secrets of his Service in order to substitute me for a miserable wretch.

If I were to know the pain of not being heard by the supreme head of my country, I have taken measures so that my appeal will reach the patron of my coat of arms, the suzerain of the family

Esterhazy, the Emperor of Germany. He is a soldier and will know how to place the honor of a soldier—even an enemy soldier—above the petty and sinister intrigues of politics. He will dare to speak loud and clear to defend the honor of ten generations of soldiers.

It is yours, Mister President, to decide if you ought to force me to shift the question on to such terrain.

An Esterhazy fears no one except God. Nothing and no one will prevent me from acting as I say should I be sacrificed to I know not what miserable political arrangement.

I am with the deepest respect, Monsieur le Président de la République, your very obedient and very respectful servant.

Signed: Esterhazy

Scheurer-Kestner would find Félix Faure, his long-time friend, both irritated and cutting. Scheurer-Kestner wondered whether power had not changed him. Faure, "in former years so friendly and gay, a fine companion," had been transformed, wrote Joseph Reinach, as though "in the limitless pride that had befallen him from his prestigious wealth and the frequentation of emperors and kings, he had acquired the habit of confusing his own person with France."[12] Faure had become "calmly and serenely ridiculous." Above all, it is probable that the president of the Republic, in receiving the vice president of the Senate, was aware of the problems that initiative, indeed the entire matter, might cause him. Invoking his constitutional role, he refused to receive the confidences of his friend. Scheurer-Kestner insisted, "At the very least, grant me your benevolent neutrality." Faure gave his promise, relieved of a staggering burden.[13]

Scheurer-Kestner, much vexed, went the following day to see the Minister of War, his old friend General Jean-Baptiste Billot. The two interlocutors, who knew each other extremely well, proceeded cautiously.* "I have proof," assured Billot. "My information was given me by a man of valor, General Gonse." "Demonstrate to me that Dreyfus is guilty and I'll go away with peace of mind." Billot then spoke of Dreyfus's confessions. He quoted from memory the "Henry forgery" in order to confound his friend. Scheurer-Kestner persisted in refuting the minister's every argument. "I did not believe you were that naive." But Billot diverted the conversation elsewhere. "I find myself in a den of Jesuits here. Ever

---

* On the previous day, the minister had received a note from du Paty concerning Dreyfus's "confession" and a note from Gonse demonstrating that Picquart, passing through Paris in June, had undoubtedly met with Scheurer-Kestner and Mathieu Dreyfus.[14]

since Miribel passed through, the Ministry has been invaded by pupils of the Jesuits. The only one who is not a Jesuit," and he slapped his chest, "is Jean-Baptiste Billot."[15] They came back to Dreyfus. Billot finally agreed to investigate the matter personally. In exchange, he asked Scheurer-Kestner to promise not to do anything for fifteen days. The two friends separated quite displeased with each other. An hour later, Esterhazy received a note from either du Paty de Clam or Commandant Henry, which read as follows: "The minister has just left Scheurer-Kestner with whom he lunched; a lengthy confidential discussion. Everything is going quite well. The enemy has been restrained.[16]

On the following day, October 31, the newspapers announced that Scheurer-Kestner had gone to see Billot to speak to him about Dreyfus. *Le Matin* published a detailed account of their conversation. Where were the leaks coming from? From Henry, who was kept up-to-date by General Gonse, whom the minister had informed immediately? An indignant Scheurer-Kestner protested to the minister on November 1:

> Who committed the indiscretion? You are quite poorly served, or rather you have received a disservice. . . . I have not told you everything that I know . . . just seek . . . seek . . . and you shall find. . . . In what way would the Army be hurt if the Generals themselves acknowledge that there may have been a judicial error? They would emerge with greater stature, General Mercier and the others. My dear old friend, just listen to me.

The dear old friend did not listen. But the press was unleashed. *Le Matin, La Patrie, La Libre Parole*, and *L'Intransigeant* doused Scheurer-Kestner with insults: "the grey eminence of treason," "lipomatose gorilla," "slime that had to be washed into the sewer." "A vague clanging of large coins could be heard." He was a "Kraut," a "Prussian," the "valet of the Germans." "If he is not a scoundrel, he is a madman, and an asylum is called for."[17] Scheurer-Kestner, the old voice of protest from French Alsace, a man whose very reason for living was patriotism, was deeply affected. He nevertheless pursued his initiatives without flinching. On November 2, he paid a visit to Prime Minister Méline, in order to convince him, brought various handwriting specimens—from the bordereau, from Dreyfus, and from Esterhazy. In his presence, he compared them. Méline was plainly uncomfortable with this unprecedented tactic. "I am not an expert," he objected with evident ill humor. It seemed to him that Dreyfus's handwriting resembled that of the bordereau more than the other one. . . . The next day, Scheurer-Kestner returned to the prime minister with the lawyer Leblois, whom he was able—not without difficulty—to persuade to join him. While Leblois waited in the antechamber, Scheurer-Kestner attempted to convince the premier that he must receive the lawyer. For the first time, Scheurer-Kestner named Picquart. The laywer, who was waiting outside, could show the prime minister General Gonse's letters to Picquart . . . he had them in his pocket. . . . Méline grew impatient. He replied that the whole matter was the concern of the minister of war. He refused to receive Leblois. The visit was a failure.

The two men decided to themselves see Minister of War Billot. But Leblois had second thoughts upon entering the building. "No, this is really too stupid. We are going to throw ourselves into the lion's mouth."[18] This time it was Scheurer-Kestner who was furious. He had compromised himself in a series of vain initiatives. Leblois's hesitations were beginning to make him look ridiculous. On November 5 he went to see Jean-Baptiste Darlan, the minister of justice, who was anxious not to receive any confidences. If a request for an appeal were one day registered, it would have to pass through him. Thus it was that everyone, turning a deaf ear, invoked the duties of his office. That same day, Scheurer-Kestner made a declaration to *Le Figaro*: he had already transmitted to the government, he said, "the elements of his conviction" and he was leaving it to them to take "the necessary measures." The declaration was rather clumsy; he appeared to be placing his trust thereafter in the government. Scheurer-Kestner pleaded with Leblois, begging him to "give over Picquart" without reservations, to go tell "everything" to the minister of war. It was the only way to bring the truth to light. The lawyer, divided between his oath and his duty, finally gave in. He agreed to see Billot, news which Scheurer-Kestner, now reassured, brought to the prime minister. "It is too late," replied Méline, "you have brought the whole matter to the governmental level. . . ." And the meeting of ministers of November 6 ratified Méline's position a few minutes later. It would be expressed in a semiofficial note published in *Le Temps* that very evening. The Dreyfus family had no other recourse than to register an official appeals investigation, "which would be examined and which would follow its natural course. . . ."

After so many "unsuccessful maneuvers," the results of Scheurer-Kestner's efforts were rather tentative. By promising revelations which never surfaced, Scheurer-Kestner, according to Marcel Thomas, had "discredited the cause of an appeal in the public's eyes."[19] By using Lieutenant Colonel Picquart's name without exploiting what Picquart knew, they had put him in a perilous position and weakened his case. Did not Picquart now appear to be the secret fomentor of all the initiatives that had been taken?

Méline and Billot had had little difficulty in maneuvering their "old friend," who was too inhibited by his principles, too rigorous in the choice of his means, too scrupulous to be a real threat. The Scheurer-Kestner "alert" was now over, as the General Staff well knew. The dangerous man had been Picquart.

17

Help Me, My Prince, to My Rescue!

It was Lieutenant Colonel Picquart whom they would have to get rid of. Commandants Esterhazy, Henry, and du Paty de Clam would devote the month of November to this task.

On October 31, Commandant Esterhazy, whose correspondence was inexhaustible, addressed a new letter to the president of the Republic. In it he observed that "neither the Chief of the State nor the Chief of the Army had answered him with a word of support or consolation." So that was how "the services rendered to France by his ancestors for one hundred sixty years" were to be rewarded. He would thus be reduced to resorting to all the means at his disposal. Now it happened that the generous woman who was protecting him had given him a precious document, "the photograph of a document stolen from a foreign legation by Colonel Picquart." If he did not obtain justice, he would publish it.

> ... The generous lady who warned me of the horrible plot fomented against me by Dreyfus's friends with the assistance of Colonel Picquart has succeeded since then in procuring for me, among other documents, the photograph of an item she was able to extract from that officer. This document stolen by Colonel Picquart in a foreign legation is highly compromising for certain diplomatic personalities. If I receive neither support nor justice, or

if my name comes to be mentioned, this photograph, which is
presently in safekeeping abroad, will be immediately published. . . .*

Esterhazy was prudent enough not to reveal the contents of this secret
and presumably "liberating" document. In Commandant Henry's
mind—and it is probable that he prepared the letter with Esterhazy—the
liberating document was most likely a photo of the "scoundrel D." letter.[2]
As for the mysterious woman who had confided it to him, Esterhazy would
later say that she had come to a meeting she had arranged with him
"tightly veiled." Who then was this providentially veiled woman who
transmitted to her protégé the photograph of a document stolen by
Picquart? She was "an extremely elegant, quite refined lady of the world,"
the Countess of Comminges, a great friend of Picquart, he would first
maintain. The meeting had taken place on the Pont Alexandre one Good
Friday evening.† Later he would identify her as the Marquise du Paty,
whom her husband would have sent to the Pont Alexandre. In the interim
he would tell du Paty that the veiled lady was "merely a lower-class woman,
perfumed like a woman of dubious reputation."[4] Esterhazy would produce numerous versions of the mysterious encounter, which would eventually fuel a number of the legends of the Dreyfus Affair. Thus it was that
the president of the Republic would gain knowledge of a letter of
blackmail written by a French officer seriously suspected of espionage and
claiming to be the bearer of a stolen document. Félix Faure did little more
than discuss the correspondence with the minister of war. And the sole
result was that November 1 a coded telegram was sent from the Ministry of
War to General Jérôme Leclerc, Picquart's hierarchical superior, asking
him to interrogate the officer about the stolen document.

> The government has received letters saying that Lieutenant Col-
> onel Picquart of the 4th Sharpshooters would have allowed himself
> to be robbed by a woman of a photograph of a document coming
> from a foreign legation that would be highly compromising for
> certain diplomatic personalities.
>
> I am asking you to question said superior officer in the utmost
> secrecy and to ask him for explanations whose summary you will
> send to me with all urgency via coded telegram. You will then send

---

* On the same day, *La Libre Parole*, pitching in, reported "that a high functionary of the
Ministery of War had surrendered documents to Scheurer-Kestner."[1]
† Du Paty appears to have panicked at this explanation, which was proposed by Commandant Henry. For in 1892 he was involved in blackmailing the Comminges family, and traces of
the case remained at the Prefecture—as Commandant Henry was well aware.[3]

to me urgently your detailed report. Lieutenant Colonel Picquart is to remain at your disposition for any additional information that might be asked of him.

It was a fine victory for Henry and Gonse: The president of the Republic and the minister of war were yielding to the demands of Esterhazy. And Picquart found himself in the position of the defendant.

As soon as he received the dispatch from the Ministry, General Leclerc called Picquart in for questioning. The interview took place in a cordial atmosphere since Leclerc had great respect for his subordinate. No, no document had left Picquart's office and no woman had gained entry to it. On the other hand, Leclerc was to confirm to the Ministry that Picquart had been "on leave or on holiday" from June 15 to July 7. The General Staff was thus assured that Picquart, having come to Paris, could quite possibly have been Scheurer-Kestner's informer. That was enough to justify their suspicions. He was indeed the essential agent of the "Dreyfusard syndicate." On November 5, Esterhazy, encouraged by his success, wrote the president of the Republic a third letter that was still more threatening:

> This is the last time I shall be addressing myself to the public powers. The lady who informed me of the horrible plot woven against me has transmitted to me, among others, a document which is a protection for me *because it proves the baseness of Dreyfus* and a danger for my country because *its publication with the handwriting facsimile* will force France to either *humiliate herself or go to war*.
>
> I shout out the ancient French cry: Help me, my Prince, to my rescue. I shout it to you, Monsieur le Président, who before being chief of state are an honest man and who must in the depth of your soul be profoundly disgusted by the cowardice you perceive.
>
> Defend me and I will transmit the document to the minister of war without a single person casting his eyes on it. But defend me quickly for I can no longer wait and I will recoil from nothing to defend or avenge my unworthily sacrificed honor. . . .

The sentence about the "baseness of Dreyfus" plainly refers to the "scoundrel D." document. Was it that allusion and the imminent threat the letter contained which finally provoked a reaction? On November 6 the minister of war wrote to General Saussier informing him of Esterhazy's letters. Such a correspondence should have immediately led to an arrest and to the initiation of legal proceedings. But Esterhazy seemed invulnerable. Saussier, who knew Maurice Weil's friend well, was satisfied with calling in Esterhazy and "cleaning out his mind." Esterhazy excused himself for being overexcited. Matters seem to have gone no further than that. That very day, Esterhazy, overflowing with self-assurance and cynicism, sent Picquart an insulting letter and dispatched a copy to General de Boisdeffre.

> My Colonel,
> I have received these last days a letter in which you are formally accused of having fomented against me the most abominable machination to substitute me for Dreyfus. In that letter it is said, among other things, that you have bribed non-commissioned officers in order to have specimens of my handwriting, a fact which is true, since I have verified it. It is also said that you have diverted from the Ministry of War documents entrusted to your honor in order to compose a clandestine file that you have delivered to the friends of the traitor. The matter of the clandestine file is precise, since I have in my possession today items that were taken from that file.
> In the face of such a monstrous accusation and in spite of the proof that has been given me, I hestitate to believe that a superior officer of the French Army could have been trading in the secrets of his Service in order to attempt to substitute one of his comrades for the wretch the proof of whose crime he had evidence of. It is unthinkable that you evade a clear and frank explanation.[5]

Reassured by his protectors, constantly manipulated by Henry, assisted by du Paty, Esterhazy could not let up on his assault. He was at once shrewd and imprudent. He would improvise rather dangerously and began to irritate his friends. On November 9, the minister of war enjoined Saussier to have Esterhazy return the "liberating document." Saussier called him in again and attempted to make him understand that he had to give the minister the famous document. "Whether he will do it or not I do not know," wrote Saussier in his report. Quite clearly annoyed, the military governor of Paris did not wish to assume any responsibility in the matter, leaving it to the government to intervene:

> In brief, the government alone can determine the importance to be attributed to the letters written by Commandant Walsin-Esterhazy to the president of the Republic and to yourself, as well as the measures to be taken against him.
> Judging from the strictly military point of view, there would be

no reason to submit his case to a Court-Martial or at least to an inquest, corresponding to the formal breach of discipline constituted by his acts.

Esterhazy seemed increasingly nervous. On November 10 he sent General Saussier an insolent letter with a threat between its lines:

> This morning I committed myself personally to you, but in the course of the day I found those close to me quite agitated after the appearance of an article in this morning's *L'Intransigeant* in which they believed they saw an allusion to my person and I do not believe I will be able to prevent them from acting and seizing the initiative. . . . Everything seems to prove that it is indeed I whom Colonel Picquart decided to substitute for Dreyfus through use of forged documents and others removed from my service. The secret file would be in the hands of one Lebois [sic] and the government would already be decided, it is said, on the subject. . . . Dare I ask you, Monsieur le Gouverneur, to exercise your exalted influence with members of the government in order to obtain from them some act—be it official or not—that will extricate the person of a man whom they know to be perfectly innocent? . . . As of today I have been looking for a way to return the document I promised you quickly; if I haven't found it in 48 hours, I will ask one of my associates to go personally to London. . . .[6]

Saussier forwarded the letter without comment. Henceforth he would await instructions from the government. But the minister of war and the chief of the General Staff seemed to be in complete harmony. Against the officer who was a traitor to his country and who was blackmailing the highest-placed persons in the State, it was not yet time to act.

On the other hand, Henry and Esterhazy, who were by then inseparable, pursued their project of establishing that Picquart was nothing more than an agent of the "syndicate." He would thus be definitively discredited and his accusations without effect. On November 10, 1897, an unknown individual delivered to the office on rue La Fayette a telegram addressed to "Colonel Picquart, Tunis."

Colonel Picquart, Tunis
> Stop the demi-god. Everything is discovered. Very serious matter.
>
> Speranza.

The telegram thus appeared to continue the correspondence fabricated by Henry a year before in December 1896.* And the signature "Speranza" evoked the benevolent "Espérance" who had warned Esterhazy of the dangers awaiting him. That lack of imagination, indeed that rank imprudence, impeded neither the forger that Henry had become, nor Esterhazy, the fabricator of the deceptions.†

That same day, a second telegram, sent from the office of the Bourse, was dispatched to Picquart at his correct address:

Colonel Picquart, Sousse
   We have proof that the *bleu* was fabricated by Georges.
                                                          Blanche

That text was intended to be transparent. Blanche was Mlle. de Comminges, Picquart's friend. The *bleu* was to all appearances the *petit bleu*. Thus Picquart's friends were seeking to warn him that his crime had been discovered: he had fabricated the *petit bleu*. Henry, of course, issued an order to intercept the two false telegrams. The "Blanche" telegram was to reach Picquart on November 11, the "Speranza" telegram, forwarded from Tunis to Sousse, on November 12. And finally an anonymous letter—reading: "To be feared. Our whole labor discovered; withdraw quietly; write nothing"—came to Picquart on November 17.

The incriminating telegrams, photographed at Henry's request, were forwarded with copies, needless to say, to General Gonse, who transmitted them to the minister. All pretended to be scandalized. So the "syndicate" was tipping off Picquart! But who knew of the existence of the *petit bleu* at the time? Billot, de Boisdeffre, Gonse, Henry, Gribelin, and Lauth.‡ For Picquart, who was receiving dispatches, the mysterious correspondent was necessarily one—or several—of them, and most probably Gonse and Henry. But for the Criminal Investigation Division whom the minister asked to begin an inquest, everything was clear. The demigod was plainly Scheurer-Kestner. Georges was Picquart. Blanche was, of course, Mlle. de Comminges, the colonel's dear friend. This business of telegrams was taken quite seriously, to the point that the minister of the interior chose to inform his colleagues, during an official session of the Ministerial Council, of this grave turn of events. Picquart was at the heart of a clandestine plot. The minister of the PTT had all telegrams addressed to Picquart transmit-

---

* *Supra* p. 179.
† In 1898, Marguerite Pays would admit to Examining Judge Paul Bertulus that she had in all probability composed the message—without even disguising her handwriting—at the request of her lover, Commandant Esterhazy.
‡ It was not yet known by Leblois, to whom Picquart chose not to mention it.

ted to him. Only two were found—and they were authentic. Addressed to Picquart on November 6 and 7, they read: "Have written only today. Henceforth address to Avenue de la Grande-Armée" and "Have received letter. Alice must return immediately Berthe's packet of letters. Am writing today."[7] It all seemed very suspect indeed. In fact, these were two dispatches sent to Picquart by his mistress Mme. Mounier, the wife of a functionary in Foreign Affairs, who was taking precautionary measures to conceal their secret affair. But at the time, all these telegrams, both the authentic and the invented, were fed into the dossier of suspect Picquart. And on December 12, General Billot, predating his order by a day in order to justify the initiatives taken by the minister of the PTT, delegated Gonse "to initiate a secret judicial inquiry in Paris against Lieutenant-Colonel Picquart." This time the conspirators were fully satisfied. Their audacity had borne fruit. It was not against Commandant Esterhazy that a judicial inquiry was being opened, but against Colonel Picquart.

But at this point chance entered into the affair and brusquely began mucking up their splendid victory. On November 7, while strolling on the boulevards, a stockbroker named de Castro, who happened to buy one of the facsimiles of the bordereau and of Alfred Dreyfus's handwriting that Mathieu had had distributed widely, had a "shock." He recognized the handwriting of one of his clients, Commandant Esterhazy. Through the mediation of a mutual acquaintance, Castro called on Mathieu Dreyfus. He showed him Esterhazy's letters. Mathieu studied them, at length. There was no doubt. "They were identical. This was the handwriting of the culprit." Mathieu asked for an urgent meeting with Scheurer-Kestner. "I shouted at him: I am going to tell you the name of the traitor. It is Esterhazy." And Scheurer-Kestner, with relief, since it was not he who had mentioned the name, could at last reply, "Yes, he's the one."* There had been a ghastly time lag which had been of great service to Esterhazy's "friends." On November 11, 1897, Mathieu learned by chance what the minister of war, the General Staff, and the Section of Statistics had known since the month of August 1896.

For Mathieu Dreyfus, this was a decisive step forward in the Affair. What he had been looking for for nearly three years he now knew. The author of the bordereau was a French officer, Commandant Esterhazy. But how could one inform the public? On November 12, a meeting was arranged between Scheurer-Kestner; Leblois; Mathieu; the lawyer, Edgar

---

* For Dreyfus's enemies, it would be apparent that the Castro "fable," invented by Mathieu, served to conceal leaks from Scheurer-Kestner. It was Scheurer-Kestner who—betraying his pledge—would have told Mathieu that the author of the bordereau was Esterhazy. But the versions given by Scheurer-Kestner (in his *Memoirs*), by Mathieu Dreyfus, and by Castro coincided precisely.[8]

Demange; and Emmanuel Arène, a deputy from Corsica and editor of *Le Figaro*, who declared that he was ready to publish articles in order to "prepare public opinion." Arène was to conduct a campaign of gradual revelations. But proceeding somewhat rashly, under the byline "Vidi," he published on November 14 an article in which he revealed the essential facts. Esterhazy was not named, but the article referred to the author of the bordereau as an "officer who is quite well known and frequently seen about Paris . . . who has a title, is married, quite well related. . . ." The article was too clear for those who knew, too obscure for the readers of *Le Figaro*.[9] In addition, it contained an allusion to a "new document" that the minister of war was alleged to have mentioned to Scheurer-Kestner, an item that mentioned Dreyfus. Upon reading the article, Commandant Henry suddenly had the feeling "that an abyss was opening up beneath him."[10] The only document bearing Dreyfus's name was his forgery. Would the minister, then, have been imprudent enough to have mentioned it to his adversaries? Henry rushed off to see du Paty. In a state of great excitation, the two paid a call on Esterhazy. The three accomplices deliberated amid great agitation and finally decided that Esterhazy would deliver to Edouard Drumont a text in response, a kind of brochure which they had already prepared and which they hastily set about revising. The article appeared the next day, November 15, in *La Libre Parole*, under the title "Dixi." It presented in summary the thesis that would thereafter— with a few variants—be that of the General Staff. The officer denounced in *Le Figaro* was innocent. He was the victim of an infamous machination fomented by Picquart and Dreyfus's supporters[11] that intended to substitute an innocent man for the true culprit, the Jewish officer. As a precaution, that very evening Henry brought to the Ministry of War the "liberating document," which was thus "spontaneously" given by Esterhazy to his minister.*

The polemic in the press forced Mathieu Dreyfus to action. On the evening of December 15, he made public the letter, composed with Edgar Demange, in which he denounced to the minister of war the true author of the bordereau, Commandant Esterhazy:

> Mister Minister,
>   The sole basis of the accusation brought in 1894 against my unfortunate brother is an unsigned, undated letter establishing that confidential military documents were delivered to an agent of a foreign military power.

* Marcel Thomas has established that Esterhazy had never had the liberating document, the "scoundrel D." letter, in his hands, and that he did not even know of it. It was Henry who imagined and executed the pseudo-restitution.[12]

I have the honor of informing you that the author of that document is M. le Comte Walsin-Esterhazy, an Infantry Commandant, withdrawn from active duty last spring for reason of temporary infirmities.

Commandant Esterhazy's handwriting is identical to that of the document in question. It will be quite easy for you to procure a specimen of the handwriting of the officer.

I am prepared, moreover, to indicate to you where you may find letters of his, whose authenticity cannot be contested and which date from before my brother's arrest.

I cannot doubt, Mister Minister, that knowing the author of the treason for which my brother was convicted, you will act swiftly that justice be done.

On the same day, November 15, Picquart filed a complaint with his minister against Commandant Esterhazy, "who having been informed, I know not by whom, of the investigation I conducted concerning him in the exercise of my functions, has brought slanderous accusations against me, first in the form of a private letter, then in the form of telegrams." The accused Picquart was thus also joining the offensive.

The secret war that had been waged for two months to eliminate Picquart and to save Esterhazy was now brought before public opinion. For the minister of war, the first imperative was simply saving face. On December 16, he announced to the Chamber that faced with Mathieu Dreyfus's denunciation, the government's duty was now clearly defined:

> It owes it to justice, to the honor of the accused, to insist that the author of the denunciation produce his justification. Matters will then be resolved in strict conformity with the law. The Ministry of War, the guardian of the Army's honor and the entity charged with keeping vigil over the nation's defense and the country's security, will not be found amiss in the execution of its duty.

General Billot ordered General Saussier to open an investigation. On November 17, General Georges de Pellieux, military commandant of the Department of the Seine, under whose authority Esterhazy fell, was designated to "investigate," but not to open legal proceedings—since no such order had as yet been issued.

As Marcel Thomas has observed, the "collusion" intent on eliminating Picquart appeared to have failed. The conspirators "had not been able to prevent the initiation of an official investigation, which was bound—for better or for worse—to open up an initial breach in the wall of silence and mystery which alone could protect Esterhazy."[13] In order to protect Esterhazy, Henry and du Paty had taken so many imprudent initiatives, produced so many forgeries, that the announced investigation—indeed any investigation—could not but be dangerous. Generals de Boisdeffre and Gonse, who had encouraged or sanctioned them, Gonse day by day, de Boisdeffre while keeping his distance, were worried. Numerous precautionary measures would have to be taken. Had one of de Boisdeffre's aides-de-camp, Commandant Pauffin de Saint-Morel, gone to see the writer Henri Rochefort and supplied him with information? De Boisdeffre placed him under close arrest. Had Esterhazy and du Paty been seen together in the Passage Landrieu? They must no longer see each other, or if they did, only with the greatest prudence. The time was now over when the conspirators could do anything they wished under the cloak of secrecy. In the government, in the General Staff, and in the Section of Statistics, panic was widespread. An investigation had been ordered; public opinion was aroused.

Only Esterhazy retained his cool daring. He gave numerous interviews to *La Libre Parole*, *Le Matin*, *L'Echo de Paris*, *Le Figaro*, and *Le Temps*. Did the handwriting of the bordereau bear a "frightening" resemblance to his own? Of course it did. Dreyfus had traced it. Esterhazy did not defend himself for knowing Colonel von Schwarzkoppen: his relatives in Austria had ties with the military attaché's family. A veiled woman had warned him of the plot against him. As had his friend Edouard Drumont. He had done well to himself inform Félix Faure and to shake up a bit the indolent president of the Republic. As for his slanderers, he "shat" on them. In editions of hundreds of thousands of copies, the declarations of a "true soldier" unjustly harassed were sold. All Paris was fascinated with the episode of the veiled woman. Was she the wife of a diplomat? An adventuress? A beautiful Jewess seeking vengeance against Picquart? In all quarters, Esterhazy proclaimed his innocence, swore that he would reveal it to the world, even if it meant setting Paris aflame. "Dreyfus," observed Joseph Reinach, "never had used such language." As opposed to the Alsatian Jew, "no sooner was the Hungarian gentleman accused than he was innocent."[14]

How could Commandant Esterhazy *not* be vainglorious and insolent! For two months, he had held all of France beneath his boot. He threatened the president of the Republic, defied the minister of war, reprimanded the military governor of Paris. A spy, a traitor, a blackmailer, and a thief, he had manipulated the highest civilian and military authorities. Why indeed should the generous woman who had never stopped protecting him, mysterious Espérance, fail him now?

18

I Speak to You
as from the Grave

Every night from September 6, to October 20, 1896, deportee Dreyfus was placed in shackles. Although he tried to attenuate the abrasion of the iron by wrapping rags around his ankles, there was soon little left of them but wounds. These had to be dressed every morning. All day long until November 12, during the time the double stockade was being erected, Dreyfus remained locked in his hut without a minute's freedom to walk outside. On October 29, the director of the Penal Administration wrote to the high commandant of the Iles du Salut to specify the measures to be taken in the event of the deportee's decease. The corpse was to be sent to France, but before being placed in a coffin and as soon as possible after confirmation of death, a cast of the face was to be taken. During this period, Dreyfus sent only brief letters to his wife. "The very emptiness of his correspondence was an index of his martyrdom."[1] "I have suffered so; I have endured so many things that life is profoundly indifferent to me, and I speak to you as from the grave, from the eternal silence which places you above all else."[2]

On November 12,[3] when his guards opened the door of his hut for him, Dreyfus could no longer see the sea. His prison was henceforth surrounded by a double stockade 2.5 meters in height. One wall, at about 1.5 meters from his hut, deprived him of air and light; the other surrounded a walking space 16 meters wide and 40 meters long. No trees. Not a corner of shade. During the day, the deportee could move about the enclosure, always trailed by a guard. From then on he would see nothing but the wood of the stockades and the tropical sky above his head. The months that followed were a true inferno. "The deportee had a major crisis," noted Chief of Surveillance Kerbat on November 27. In December he complained of lightheadedness. The high commandant and the physician came to visit him.*

Lucie's letters reached the deportee after a delay of two months.[4] As of March 1897, they came to him recopied "by a common hand."[†] Orders forbade Dreyfus from being kept abreast of his Affair, and the letters he received could only describe the days and nights, speak of the health of dear ones, express feelings, suffering, despair. Of the efforts taken to reveal his innocence, the progress in the struggle Mathieu and Lucie were waging in Paris, Dreyfus knew nothing.

During the month of August 1897, his physical and mental health had become so alarming that, based on the physician's concerned report, it was decided to build him a new cabin. It would be divided in two by an iron grid, with the deportee on one side and a guard on the other, so that his every move, day and night, might be observed. The new cabin was, however, higher and more spacious. A view of the island and of the sea was still blocked by a stockade—2.8 meters tall—but which was at a greater distance from the cabin. Alfred Dreyfus would have been a bit better off if the humidity were not so great. The construction did not allow for any ventilation, and water tended to stagnate inside. Above all, the harassments inflicted out of fear of an escape were more numerous. The slightest incident, "the slightest wisp of smoke breaking at the horizon the monotony of the sky,"[6] became a pretext for more rigorous measures and new precautions. In September a schooner showed up about three miles from the coast. "We were for a moment at the point of shooting at it," noted Kerbat, "and sounding the alarm." New "rules" were posted in the hut and often reinforced.[‡] The deportee was in so weakened a state that

---

* On Devil's Island, the year 1897 would be largely devoted to reinforcing security arrangements on the island, which was gradually becoming a veritable fortified bastion. The prospect of Dreyfus's escape had become the terror of the Ministry of Colonies. But with the passage of time, Daniel showed "less passion in his activities as a jailer, less febrile zeal." Was it the misgivings inspired by Dreyfus's wretched state? Perhaps also the effect on the local administration of the evolution of the Dreyfus Affair.

† He received two from his children, dated October 10. "Dearest Papa . . . I would like you to come back soon. You must ask the Good Lord. As for me, I ask him every day . . . Many kisses. Your little Jeanne." And "Pierrot" wrote him the same day: "Dearest Papa, I cried this morning because you are not coming back, and it causes me too much pain. . . ."[5] Dreyfus, Kerbrat noted, wrote numerous letters which he then burned. Most often, he composed drafts of his letters, which the administration confiscated and burned.

‡ 1. The deportee was required to ensure the cleanliness of his "hut" and of the walking area allotted him.

2. He had to prepare his own meals.

3. He was authorized to improve his ration with other foodstuffs and to receive liquids "in a reasonable quantity of which the administration alone was judge."

4. Any objects sent to him would be carefully inspected and given to him only to satisfy his daily needs.

5. Any letter or other text written by the deportee was to be submitted to the head of the

he did not know whether he would survive. "I have long hidden from you," he wrote to Lucie on October 2, 1897, "my horrible distress in the face of such torture in order to prevent you from growing weak in turn . . . if I have not hidden anything from you in the last few months, it is because I believe that you have to be prepared for anything."

He admitted his physical and cerebral collapses. "Exhausted as I often am, I collapse beneath the blows of a bludgeon. At such times, I am no more than a poor human being of agony and suffering."[7]

"I have terrible moments in which my brain goes mad," he wrote on December 25, 1897. Far from improving, the deportee's state grew still worse at the beginning of 1898. On the other hand, the surveillance appeared to have slackened off. He was allowed to see the ocean, to take a few walks by the cliff.* Several of his wife's letters—it would later be learned that they spoke discreetly of Scheurer-Kestner's initiatives—reached him with two months' delay and only "partially recopied"; that is, quite obviously censored. Lucie's courageous and consoling letters betrayed her fatigue and sadness. "It was decided that we would not even have the consolation of suffering together, that we would drink the cup of bitterness to the last drop. . . ."[9] In February 1898, Dreyfus sent the presidents of the two houses, both deputies and senators, a fervent and dignified letter which would never be dispatched. He requested "full and glaring light on the matter . . . justice for those close to me, the life of my children, an end to this frightful martyrdom."[10]

For he never lost confidence in the civilian and military authorities, in the government, his hierarchical superiors, and the Army in which he was a soldier. He wrote Lucie on January 7, 1898:

> I have placed our fate, the fate of our children, the fate of innocent people who have been struggling for three years in the most implausible circumstances, in the hands of the president of the Republic, in the hands of the minister of war, in order to request an end, at last, to our frightful martyrdom.[11]

---

camp. This was also the case for requests and claims.

6. The doors of the "hut" were to remain open until nightfall. During that time, the deportee would be free to walk about within the stockaded area.

7. All communication with the outside world was forbidden. In the event of presences other than those habitually necessitated by the service, the deportee was to be locked up until the departure of the fatigue party.

8. During the night, the premises assigned the deportee were to be illuminated "within" and (as during daylight hours) occupied by a guard.

* Dreyfus's treatment improved during the first months of 1898 as the revisionist campaign developed. It appears that Dreyfus was kept informed of the principal events in his affair not through letters but by guards commenting in his presence on the news from France.[8]

On January 25 he repeated:

> I have asked the president of the Republic, the minister of war, and
> General de Boisdeffre for my rehabilitation and for a revision of
> the trial. I have placed the fate of so many innocent victims, the fate
> of our children in their hands; I have confided the future of our
> children to General de Boisdeffre. With feverish impatience, with
> all the strength I have left, I await their response.[12]

The following day he reiterated to Lucie the faith he had in his
superior.

> This is the situation as I believe I understand it and that I take to be
> not far from the truth. I believe that General de Boisdeffre has
> never refused to accord us justice. Profoundly aggrieved, we ask
> him to show us the light. It has not been in his power to let it shine
> any more than in ours. It will emerge in some future that no one
> can predict.[13]

The deportee Dreyfus no longer even knew how he managed to
survive, "so immense is my cerebral and nervous exhaustion." As he was
afraid of dying there in his hut, he prescribed to his wife her duty:

> I am asigning you as an absolute duty to go find General de
> Boisdeffre in person, and after the letters I have written, the feeling
> which, I am sure, is at the bottom of his heart to grant us rehabilita-
> tion, once you have understood that revealing the light is a long-
> term labor, that it is impossible to predict when it will emerge, I
> nevertheless have no doubt that he will grant you immediately a
> revision of the trial, that he will put an end to a situation that is so
> atrocious for you and for the children; my hopes spring not only
> from the loyalty of my past, but from the absolute loyalty of my
> behavior for three years, amid all kinds of tortures, I have never
> forgotten what I was: a loyal soldier devoted to his country. I have
> accepted everything, submitted to everything, with sealed lips. I
> am not bragging of this, however, I have done only my duty,
> nothing but my duty.

For Dreyfus, the president of the Republic, the minister of war, and
General de Boisdeffre embodied his country. "I have never forgotten that
transcending men, their passions and their confusions, there is the country."[14] He had confided his innocence, his children, and his increasingly
fragile life to his superiors; that is, to France.

19

Let Us Not Allow Ourselves to Be Devoured

On November 17, 1897, General Georges de Pellieux, temporarily in charge of military operations in Paris, began his administrative investigation. He immediately called in Mathieu Dreyfus, who brought him the facsimile of the bordereau and the letters from Commandant Esterhazy that he had procured. Mathieu explained to the general how Esterhazy was in a position to identify each of the items referred to in the bordereau. When Mathieu Dreyfus evoked Esterhazy's personality, Pellieux cut him short: "We know the dubious morals of the officer in question. It is useless to insist."* The investigating general promised to have an expert handwriting analysis performed. Mathieu emerged quite satisfied from this first meeting. On the same day, Pellieux spoke with Scheurer-Kestner. "See Leblois," the vice president of the Senate replied to most of the questions addressed to him. He also recommended that Pellieux receive testimony from Colonel Picquart, without which there could not be a serious investigation.

Esterhazy was called in on the morning of November 18. He recounted in detail everything that the article entitled "Dixi" had already revealed. He asked to be confronted with Gribelin and with "the officer who conducted the investigation of Dreyfus." He did not name du Paty de Clam, of course, since it was assumed that he did not know his identity. He was already preparing—through a series of allusions—the thesis that he would adopt and flesh out later on: Dreyfus had composed the bordereau by tracing Esterhazy's handwriting, a specimen of which he had obtained from Captain Bro. On November 19 Pellieux heard Louis Leblois. The lawyer did not conceal that he had occasionally worked at the Ministry of

---

* "The information in the bordereau is of no value whatsoever; it is known to everyone," General de Pellieux was also alleged to have told Mathieu Dreyfus.[1]

War with Picquart, who had consulted him on questions relating to his service. Leblois vehemently demanded the immediate arrest of Esterhazy and his appearance before a Court-Martial.

It was then that Pellieux paid a visit to the chief of the General Staff. It appears that General de Boisdeffre was quite adept in keeping the investigator in rein. He explained to him the "underpinnings" of the Picquart Affair. He showed him the "telegrams" received by Picquart.* General Gonse also opened up his files for him.[3] By November 20, Pellieux had signed the report concluding his first investigation. Esterhazy appeared to be cleared of all suspicion. But Picquart had every appearance of being guilty.

> In my soul and conscience, I hereby declare:
> Esterhazy seems to me cleared of all suspicion. However unappealing a case he may be, because of the grave deviations of his private life, he cannot, in my opinion, be accused of treason.
> Picquart seems guilty. I believe that unfortunately the documents to be found at the General Staff (intercepted letters and dispatches) do not allow for any doubt on the subject. Should the investigation be continued and expanded?
> If Picquart is questioned in Tunis, it will be said that we were afraid to bring him here.
> If he is questioned here as a witness, it will be difficult to isolate him from his advisers.
> It seems to me that Lieutenant-Colonel Picquart's situation is such that he should be brought before an investigatory board and questioned under conditions of the utmost secrecy. . . .

On the following day there took place an official ministerial meeting at which the Pellieux report was discussed.† The matter was assumed to be over and done with. . . . But the council of ministers declared itself unsatisfied—a strange scruple on the part of the civilian government that would prove rife with consequences. A few hours later, General Saussier was informed that in the government's estimation "the investigation should be completed and be granted the extra-judicial status invoked in Articles 84, 85, and 86 of the Code of Military Justice." They were conceiv-

---

* He specified—as General de Pellieux would note in an appendix to his report—that Lieutenant Colonel Picquart had never "either transmitted or showed to him a single document of the investigation he had conducted concerning Commandant Esterhazy."[2]
† Minister of War Billot had received a letter from Picquart, dated November 15, 1897, denouncing Esterhazy as the author of the false telegrams and filing a complaint against him. Billot, according to Marcel Thomas, "was now concerned with preserving an appearance of fairness even if he was profoundly hostile to revision."[4]

ably interested in initiating proceedings against Picquart as an order was simultaneously given to bring him back to France. But the General Staff had no illusions. General Billot had maneuvered quite clumsily at the council of ministers. Esterhazy, who was furious, dashed off an anonymous letter to Prime Minister Jules Méline: "Thanks to the colossal stupidity of your Minister Billot, the Picquart affair is about to explode with all of its consequences. It is impossible to imagine ineptitude of such dimensions." And General de Boisdeffre, who perceived the danger, noted: "We will have to march. Everyone will have to join in. Let us make use of all of our weapons, and let us not allow ourselves to be devoured."[5] On November 2 1, Pellieux began his new investigation. It would last until December 3.

Esterhazy, out of prudence, enjoined the services of Tézenas, a young trial lawyer—"supple, likable, a skeptic since childhood, with a gift for facile oratory"[6]—whom Esterhazy's personality seems to have won over. Esterhazy would speak with Tézenas for hours on end about the most varied subjects. The lawyer discovered "a living encyclopedia who knew everything and could speak of anything with great charm and novelty."[7] But for the most part, Esterhazy was alone in defending himself. And as a first measure, he took the precaution of remaining quite close to his "protectors." He would see Commandant Henry secretly with great regularity. For Commandant du Paty de Clam, with whom he was no longer to meet, he found an intermediary, his dear cousin Christian, who still believed his money to be invested with the Rothschilds, and who agreed to perform this delicate service for his uncle now that he was in difficult straits. Du Paty and Christian Esterhazy would meet almost every evening in out-of-the-way locations—on the banks of the Seine, in public squares, and in churches. In public urinals, du Paty would read Esterhazy's notes. He kept up his morale. Was not Godefroy Cavaignac, du Paty's cousin, prepared to rise to Esterhazy's defense on the podium of the Chamber? Had not Félix Faure confided to an intimate: "As long as I am President, the revision of the trial will not take place"? Christian was unceasing in his efforts on behalf of his uncle, who was affectionately managing his fortune, but who could not, for the moment, return his money to him because of the problems the Jews were causing him. The good Christian was the most zealous of messengers. Every morning he carried a new note to Pellieux. With such support, Esterhazy moved quickly to seize the initiative. He knew that the real peril came from Picquart, whose return to France had been announced. On November 2 2, Esterhazy asked Pellieux for a house-search of the "maid's room" Picquart had rented on the sixth floor of the building in which he had an apartment, 3, rue Yvon-Villarceaux. He claimed that the papers held by Picquart could be found there.[8] And he added, "It is my opinion, my general, that you are the best guardian of my honor." Pellieux—who appeared more docile every day—authorized the search. Nothing was found except a few packets of letters of little interest which were returned to Picquart.

On November 22, Pellieux committed the indiscretion of requesting the "original" of the bordereau. The General Staff was immediately worried. Would the investigator be imprudent enough to request an expert analysis? Pellieux was promptly obliged to reassure de Boisdeffre and Gonse:

> In asking for the communication of the original bordereau of the Dreyfus trial, it could not have entered my mind to make it the object of a new expert analysis with Esterhazy's handwriting, since I indicated myself in my report that such was Mathieu Dreyfus's aim and that the revision of the trial would have thereby begun, something which could not happen through such channels.
>
> I will add that such an analysis does not even appear useful to me, since Commandant Esterhazy himself recognizes that certain words of the bordereau are identical to his handwriting. . . .
>
> The expert analysis that I might perhaps be inclined to order would be the following one, which has no relation to the original trial.
>
> Given Esterhazy's handwriting before the trial and the publication of the bordereau, after that publication and recently, has he modified his handwriting and has he returned quite recently to his original handwriting as the accusation claims?
>
> What I want to be sure of is that the facsimiles one can find on the street are precise, that the bordereau is actually on tracing paper, in order to arrive, if possible, at some knowledge of the path through which it came to the press and of the person who transmitted it, all of which may have an importance for the legal proceedings currently underway.

No, there was no need to panic. General de Pellieux, who was the subject of daily attentions from General Gonse and Commandant Henry, could not be entertaining ill intentions. He was by then convinced of Esterhazy's innocence. Upon being called in anew, Mathieu Dreyfus found the general completely changed.[9] He asked his questions curtly, and jotted down the answers, without uttering a single word outside the formal interrogation.

Having arrived in Marseille on November 25, Colonel Picquart was questioned on November 26 and 27. He spoke precisely of the entire investigation that he had conducted in 1896, his conflicts with Gonse and de Boisdeffre, Esterhazy's maneuvers, including the bogus telegrams, and finally his relations with Leblois.[10] Pellieux spoke to him "with an affected and malevolent formality."[11] The investigator confronted the witness with the *petit bleu*. "I believe that I recognize it; but it seems to me that the handwriting was more uniform. . . ." Picquart was unaware that Commandant Henry had crudely "scratched out" part of the *petit bleu* in order to give the impression that his superior officer had attempted to doctor it. When the witness sought to talk about the bordereau, Pellieux prevented him: "I cannot allow you to broach the discussion of the possibility that the bordereau was materially the work of Esterhazy, since the bordereau at the conclusion of a trial was attributed to Dreyfus and the question has the authority of legal verdict." On the other hand, Pellieux questioned Picquart at length concerning "Speranza," Mlle. de Comminges, the women surrounding him, the Jews he frequented.* When Picquart bridled, the investigator reassured him, "You are a witness; you are not a defendant." But he also spoke to him of the "grave errors" he had committed. "Pellieux," in Joseph Reinach's summary, "conducted his interrogations with increasing brutality and harshness. Paternalistic and familiar with Esterhazy, obsequious with Scheurer-Kestner, he treated Picquart as though he were guilty. It would have been more honest to have him questioned by Esterhazy and Henry."[13]

But the General Staff was not counting on General de Pellieux alone. The press also contributed its support. It was flooded with articles denouncing the acts of the Jewish syndicate and exalting Esterhazy, the magnificent French soldier whom the Jews wanted to implicate in the crimes commited by the deportee of Devil's Island. Traps were set for Mathieu Dreyfus and for Joseph Reinach. There were attempts to persuade them to buy forged documents which they would subsequently use; they could thus be confounded publicly.[14] On all sides, Dreyfus's family and friends had to be on their guard.

At the end of the month of November, it was clear that Pellieux was going to dismiss the charge. The press had already said as much. But at this point there emerged Mme. de Boulancy, Esterhazy's former mistress, from whom he had borrowed and swindled a large amount of money and who decided to seek revenge. She transmitted to her lawyer, Maître Julliemer, the old letters of her cousin, lover, and debtor, in which he gave vent, in rather delirious terms, to his hatred for France and his scorn for the French Army. The lawyer met Scheurer-Kestner through the aid of a mutual friend and showed him the letters. He entrusted to him the most

---

* Inquiries would subsequently be made concerning the "Jewish origins" which some attributed to Picquart. They would yield no results.[12]

violent of the diatribes, in which Esterhazy wrote—thirteen years earlier—to Mme. de Boulancy:

> If someone were to come tell me this evening that I would be killed tomorrow as a Uhlan captain running through Frenchmen with my saber, I would certainly be perfectly happy. . . .
>
> You are totally mistaken about my nature and character; from a general point of view I am certainly worth infinitely less than the least of your friends, but I am a being of a species completely different from theirs; it is about that, moreover, that people err most often in my regard; but right now, exasperated, embittered, furious, in an absolutely atrocious situation, I am capable of great things given the opportunity, or of crimes if they could avenge me.
>
> I would not hurt a puppy, but I would have a hundred thousand Frenchmen killed with pleasure. Which is why all the petty gossip of a hairdresser on a spree drives me into a foul rage; and if I could, which is far more difficult than is thought, I would be with the mahdi in fifteen days.
>
> Ah! The cases of "people say," with their cowardly and anonymous "people," and the obscene men who go from one woman to another vending their whorehouse gossip, to which everyone listens, what a depressing sight it would all make in a Paris taken by storm and given over to the pillage of 100,000 drunken soldiers!
>
> That is a celebration that I dream of!
>
> So be it.

That very day Scheurer-Kestner undertook to present the letter to Pellieux. He was somewhat embarrassed by the task.* He requested that all of Esterhazy's letters be seized in Mme. de Boulancy's residence. Pellieux resisted. The situation was souring. He was suddenly taken with juridical scruples. He asked Commandant Henry for the name of a magistrate he might consult concerning the legal problems raised by the matter. Henry recommended an intelligent and shrewd young examining magistrate to whom matters of espionage had been confided in recent years, Judge Paul Bertulus. Henry had frequently discussed with Bertulus the dossiers assembled against Dreyfus and against Picquart. He believed him to be sufficiently forewarned. On questions of penal procedure, Pellieux thus decided to take the advice of Bertulus, who himself, out of surprise at

---

* The anti-Dreyfusard press would view the exploitation of Mme. de Boulancy (first by Scheurer-Kestner, then by Mathieu Dreyfus) as one of the "ignominies" of the Jewish syndicate.

the confidence he enjoyed, took the precaution of seeking authorization from the Ministry of Justice. A house-search was decided upon. On November 27, a police investigator appeared at the door of Mme. de Boulancy, who "spontaneously" surrendered the letters. Thus did she consummate her revenge. And on the morning of November 28, *Le Figaro*, receiving its documentation from Mathieu Dreyfus and Joseph Reinach, published the famous "Uhlan letter," which informed French and foreign public opinion of the sentiments of Commandant Esterhazy toward France and her Army.

This time Esterhazy panicked. It appears that upon learning of what was in store, he thought of fleeing France.* His only recourse was to claim a forgery. A large sector of the press immediately rushed to his support, assuring that the bordereau had been traced from his handwriting. And so it was that the "Jewish syndicate," for 17,000 francs according to *L'Echo de Paris*, for 20,000 francs specified *Le Matin* of the same day, had purchased from a spiteful woman old letters sent in full confidence almost fifteen years earlier by an officer to his mistress, whereupon an "expert laboratory job" had succeeded in distorting them. "General de Pellieux is going to demonstrate that the letters are forgeries," proclaimed *L'Echo de Paris*.[16] "The letters are fake," assured Henri Rochefort in *L'Intransigeant*. "We do not wish to become guilty of forgery ourselves by reproducing them."[17] The culprit was the Jew Reinach, "the dispenser of the syndicate's millions and Scheurer-Kestner's inspiration."[18] Reinach was a professional forger, but he would soon be in the hands of justice. At that point no punishment could be too severe, prophesied *La Libre Parole*.[19] From London, the Duke of Orleans joined in the debate. "For my part, should it please God to restore the crown to me, I dare say that I will know how to find within the awareness of my duty and my right, and within the powers of the institutions of the monarchy, the strength necessary to protect, as needed, the honor of the soldiers of France."[20]

Confronted by Mme. de Boulancy, who was now in hot pursuit of him, Esterhazy was soon obliged to concede that most of the letters turned over were indeed from him: with the exception of the Uhlan letter which he persisted in calling "dressed up." It was then conceived that attenuating circumstances might be invoked to defend the honor of this French officer. His letters were the talk of an embittered or exalted man, but not of a traitor.[21] Denys Cochin, a deputy from Paris, asked Joseph Reinach: "Who has never had such fits of anger?" In *La Revue des Deux Mondes*,[22] Francis Charmes, in the name of morality, blamed Mathieu Dreyfus, who

---

* Barthou, the minister of the interior, appears to have believed it: on November 26 at 2:00 A.M., all border stations were alerted to arrest Commandant Esterhazy should he attempt to cross the border.[15]

must have been behind the publication: "There are limits which a certain moral delicacy simply does not allow one to trespass." And in any event, what did all the details add up to? Was there really any relationship between these letters and the bordereau? "Dreyfus continues to be the traitor," affirmed Alphonse Humbert, editor of the Radical newspaper, *L'Eclair*, and the press rallied to the fairness of his statement.[23]

But Esterhazy's denials concerning the Uhlan letter presented an obvious advantage for the Dreyfus family. They would force Pellieux to order an expert handwriting analysis. But could he limit the analysis to the letters addressed to Mme. de Boulancy, as he had begun to do, by compelling the expert Belhomme, to concentrate solely on that question?* How could he not broaden the expert's assignment to an examination of the bordereau? Under the byline of Emmanuel Arène, *Le Figaro* denounced the scandalous denial of justice that was in the offing. In *L'Aurore* of November 30, and December 2, 1897, Georges Clemenceau took a firm stand. With scathing and pitiless talent, he raised the real questions:

> Who is protecting Commandant Esterhazy? The law stops short, impotent before this aspiring Prussian disguised as a French officer. Why? Who is it that is trembling before Esterhazy? What secret power, what unstatable reasons are countering the action of justice? Who is obstructing its path? If need be, we will say!

And while the Senate forced Jean-Baptiste Darlan, the minister of justice, to resign on the basis of a nebulous administrative question,† the minister of war invited Pellieux to "take possession" of the bordereau from the Ministry. Pellieux had already received the original of the *petit bleu* and the dossier of fake telegrams. Was there not a risk that he would expand his inquiry and insist on having the complete file? It would be a catastrophe if the document previously forged by Henry, which de Boisdeffre and Gonse well knew to be no more than a crude forgery, were seized in order to satisfy the needs of the moment.

To complicate matters further, the Italian ambassador, Count Tornielli, had the ill-starred idea of writing to Minister of Foreign Affairs Gabriel Hanotaux on November 28 to announce that Alessandro Panizzardi, the Italian military attaché, would be constrained to declare publicly

---

* An official note of November 29, 1897, announced: "Although the letters published yesterday do not have an immediate relation with the Dreyfus Affair, General de Pellieux has decided to submit them to expert analysis."[24]

† Joseph Reinach concluded that the Senate wanted—on this pretext—to call the government and particularly the minister of war back to a respect for the law. But Darlan was undoubtedly the sole member of the government favorable to revision.[25]

"that the sentences alleged to be written by him and that would have designated Dreyfus either by name or initial were inauthentic." Clearly, the reference was to the document fabricated by Henry. In addition, the ambassador requested that Panizzardi be heard as a witness. This time, the General Staff panicked. Would they be required to produce the dangerous document, discuss it publicly, perhaps submit it to an expert analysis? de Boisdeffre would have to parry that threat without delay. He dashed off a note, quite vigorous in tenor, intended for the council of ministers convening on November 30. At whatever cost, Panizzardi must not be allowed to make a deposition. And throwing the full weight of his authority into the discussion, the chief of the General Staff wrote:

> The General Staff of the Army judges that the request by Count Tornielli cannot be granted for the following reasons:
> 1. Since Colonel Panizzardi is a party with direct interests in the question, his testimony would not be acceptable. He is necessarily suspect and the affirmations of such a witness could not be of value.
> 2. The General Staff of the Army has in its possession three letters from Colonel Panizzardi to Colonel von Schwarzkoppen in which Dreyfus is referred to.
> The first two letters speak only of D. . . .
> The third spells the name of Dreyfus out letter by letter.
> These three letters are appended herewith: the last is even accompanied by its envelope, which bears a wax seal initialed A.P. That seal is habitually used by Colonel Panizzardi.*

This crucial document casts light on de Boisdeffre's behavior and on his tranquil audacity. In it he vouched personally for the authenticity of two documents he knew to be forgeries,[27] in order to prevent them from being included in the investigation conducted by Pellieux. And he used his authority to prevent the testimony of a witness who might well have been decisive. Extremely impressed by the peremptory opinion of the chief of the General Staff, the council of ministers was hard put to act. Panizzardi would thus not be heard. The crucial document, the "Henry forgery" would return to the Ministry. It would only reemerge much later, provoking a host of other episodes.

The investigation was coming to a close. Pellieux had been quick to eliminate any possibility of a general analysis on the pretext that no

---

* Attached to the note were the documents known as "scoundrel D.," "for D brought me," and the "Henry forgery," plus various other items come by way of the ordinary track for purposes of comparison.[26]

experts could be found who were not already involved in the Dreyfus Affair. It was enough for him to question Esterhazy about "the identity of the original and the photos of the bordereau"—which Esterhazy, of course, recognized.[28] Before concluding his investigation, Pellieux was to hear Henry, Captain Lauth of the Second Bureau, and Félix Gribelin. Henry was shown the *petit bleu*. Henry, who harvested the "cones" coming in on the ordinary track, was categorical. He had no recollection of the document. It could not have arrived by way of the ordinary track. What he was certain of, on the other hand, was having seen Colonel Picquart and Maître Leblois in October 1896 together examining a photo of the "scoundrel D." document laid out on the colonel's desk. He did not want to attack his former chief who was, he said, "no more than a skeptic, a neurotic." "I consider him to be an unwitting agent of agents who are propelling him."[29] Lauth and Gribelin confirmed his statements. They too had witnessed discussions held between Picquart and Leblois at the Ministry on the most confidential subjects. Might du Paty de Clam also be heard? In order to be sure of not contradicting Esterhazy, du Paty sent him a note—which would subsequently be known as the "note with two handwritings"—in which he set forth what he planned to say to Pellieux and what Esterhazy should say.

> So long as you have not received an official letter, you are not supposed to know me;
>
> Remain silent as to the nature of the relations we have had by retreating behind commitments to third parties;
>
> Maintain that those relations have been simply encouragements, calls to moderation, and appeals to your good feelings so as to return the document and that they have nothing to do with the matter of the veiled lady; I have never divulged anything confidential to you and it was not I who denounced Picquart to you. That is the terrain on which I shall stay: absorb well everything I have marked in red and then destroy this. You will perceive how important it is for us to be in agreement, both for you and for me. . . .[30]

Pellieux would not call in du Paty. Esterhazy, however, prudently retained the note. It might be useful someday. It was.

While Pellieux prepared his report, which was inclined to dismiss charges against Esterhazy, General Billot was preparing to answer questions before the Chamber prepared by the celebrated right-wing deputy and monarchist, Count Albert de Mun, who had promised revelations. The General Staff wanted to assist the minister of war and simultaneously to find a way to put the whole question behind them once and for all. Generals Billot, de Boisdeffre, and Gonse deliberated together. The dismissal of charges toward which Pellieux was inclined would provoke a great clamor. There was a risk that they would have to bring Mathieu Dreyfus, Esterhazy's slanderer, before a criminal court. The Dreyfus trial would be reconducted before a jury. Might it not be better to exploit their advantage? Let Esterhazy spontaneously ask to be sent before a Court-Martial. . . . He would be acquitted. He would redeem his compromised reputation. Above all, through Esterhazy's acquittal, Dreyfus's guilt would be established a second time. Such was the opinion of Esterhazy's lawyer, Tézenas. Such would soon be Pellieux's opinion as well. But Esterhazy was recalcitrant . . . and what if there were a risk? General de Boisdeffre, upon being consulted, stood firm. There was no doubt of an acquittal. All then joined in staging their clever project, which was to put a juridical end to the Esterhazy Affair and to the Dreyfus Affair. Between Esterhazy and Pellieux, who met outside the office of the general investigator, Tézenas negotiated the terms of the "spontaneous" letter Esterhazy was to send to Pellieux. The letter—whose draft had been corrected by Pellieux—reached its addressee on December 2:

My General,

As an innocent man, the torture I have been enduring for fifteen days is superhuman.

I believe that you have in your hands all the evidence of the infamous plot that was fomented in order to ruin me. But that evidence must be produced in the course of as broad a judicial debate as possible so that the light may emerge.

Neither a refusal to prosecute nor a dismissal of charges are at present enough to assure me the reparation due me. As an officer accused of high treason, I have a right to a court martial, which is the highest form of military justice. Only a decision reached therein will be able to blight—by acquitting me before public opinion, which they dared to address—the most cowardly of slanderers.

From your high equity, I await to be called before the Court Martial of Paris.

An admirable attitude, whose merits were much praised in the press the next day. Courageous Esterhazy! Imprudent Esterhazy! Was he not running the risk, asked a worried Rochefort, of falling into the trap of the Jews? On December 3, General de Pellieux transmitted to General Saus-

sier a report which was a lengthy plea in favor of Commandant Esterhazy.*
As had been predicted, the report concluded, despite Esterhazy's request,
with a refusal to prosecute. Pellieux described the *petit bleu* as "a document
without authenticity or plausibility which he was willing to believe was not
fabricated for the needs of the cause." As for Colonel Picquart, Pellieux
saw in him the "unwitting agent" of a person who had caused him to come
very close to dishonor. And Pellieux, who had not received a mandate to
prosecute Picquart, nevertheless concluded by submitting his case to an
investigating board called on to reach a decision concerning this discharge
for infringements against honor or grave errors committed while in
service.

Their mission was now accomplished. The commandants of the Army
corps assembled in Paris for the commissioning of officers, intervened that
very day with a plea to President Félix Faure. The Army was indignant
that its officers were criticized and subject to suspicion.[32] According to the
joint plan, on December 4, General Saussier, in agreement with Generals
Billot and de Boisdeffre, refused to ratify Pellieux's conclusions. Acceding
to Esterhazy's request, Faure signed the order that would initiate legal
proceedings.

Everything was thus set for the interrogation by Count de Mun. The
event took place on December 4. Prior to any debate, the indefatigable
André Castelin, the deputy from the Aisne, asked to be allowed to pose a
question to the prime minister. He requested that Méline reassure "the
Army, public opinion, and the Chamber." Méline responded immediately.
"I will say right away what will be the last word in this debate: There is no
Dreyfus Affair. There is none at present and there will be no Dreyfus
Affair." Whereupon Count de Mun mounted the tribunal. Declaring
himself to be the defender of the country and the Army, he denounced the
Jewish syndicate, "which had been working for German wages." In a
strong and solemn voice, he united and comforted the Chamber, which
was unanimous in its patriotic fervor. "It is to the minister of war that my
question is addressed, for it is he, the head of the War department, whom I
want to ask to come here, in a solemn address, to avenge the chiefs of the
Army and, in particular, the chief of the General Staff."

Applause broke out on the right and in the center and soon spread to
the left. Soon "almost the entire Chamber had arisen to acclaim such
magnificent words."[33]

> We must know whether it is true that there is in this country a
> mysterious and hidden power strong enough to be able to cast

---

* It appears that General Mercier spontaneously went out of his way to attest to Dreyfus's
guilt before the investigator. See *L'Echo de Paris,* December 4, 1897.[31]

suspicion at will on those who command our Army, those who, on the day when great duties will befall it, will have the mission of taking our Army to the enemy and conducting a war.

We must know whether such a hidden power is strong enough to overwhelm the entire country, as it has been for more than fifteen days, introducing thoughts of doubt and suspicion of officers . . .

Emotions had reached a peak. Joseph Reinach, whom the speech designated, remained silent. "I could feel over my head the hatred of three hundred hypnotized individuals. . . . I crossed my arms. A single word, a gesture, would have transformed their madness into a furor."[34]

De Mun continued:

Ah! you asked that there not be any political questions raised here! No, there aren't any. There are assembled here neither friends, nor adversaries, nor ministries, nor enemies of the cabinet; there are representatives of the country; there are Frenchmen concerned to conserve intact what is most precious, what remains, in the midst of our partisan discord and struggles, the common domain of our invincible hopes: the honor of the Army.

De Mun called on the prime minister to request that the minister of war speak. An effort was made to locate Billot. When the session resumed, the minister of war mounted the tribunal as in an assault. "The Dreyfus Affair was adjudicated justly and without irregularity. For my part, in my soul and conscience, as Chief of the Army, I consider the verdict to have been fairly rendered and Dreyfus to be guilty."

The Chamber acclaimed him. The Socialist Alexandre Millerand mounted the tribunal. "Harsh, acerbic, hammering out his words, he crushed the government beneath the astonishing accusation of being a friend and accomplice of the promoters of a revision."[35] He denounced the cowardice of the government, its blunders, and also Joseph Reinach, "who is conducting his own campaign right here, whereas instead of attempting to rehabilitate a new Calas, he should perhaps find in his own family other rehabilitations to pursue."

That allusion to Baron de Reinach, who had been compromised in the Panama scandal, provoked the applause of the Socialists and of the right.[36] By a huge majority, the Chamber voted, paragraph by paragraph, for a motion in which it declared itself "respectful of the verdict" and "associated itself with the homage rendered by the minister of war to the Army." It was scathing toward "the leaders of the odious campaign undertaken to trouble the public conscience." Almost all of the Radicals and a majority of the Socialists voted along with the right for the motion that buried the Dreyfus Affair.

A few days later, on December 7, Scheurer-Kestner had his turn to question the government in the Senate. Romain Rolland, who attended the session, described the spectacle as follows:[37]

> Old Scheurer, tall, erect and pale, his beard white with yellow locks and the austere air of a Huguenot of the sixteenth century, climbed the steps of the Tribune with a jerky stride as if he were climbing to the scaffold. . . . He read his honest appeal to reason and justice in a strong, slow, heavy, glacial voice before a hostile, blind, and ferocious crowd which punctuated his speech with hoots and insulting laughter. When he stepped down from the Tribune, it was as though he were stepping into his grave; a cruel silence enshrouded him.

In point of fact, it appears that the Senate listened politely to its vice president as was its custom. But Scheurer-Kestner was embarrassed, trapped between his beliefs, "the reserve that had been imposed on him . . . the respect, the impassioned devotion he had for the Army," and finally the confidence that he insisted on having in the government. Billot exploited quite shrewdly the awkwardness of his friend. Once again he declared "in his soul and conscience, as a soldier and as chief of the Army," that Dreyfus was guilty. Like Count de Mun in the Chamber, with simpler words, he unified the Senate by demanding their respect. "The Army springs from the entrails of the country. It is submissive, patient, patriotic; all of our children are under her flags. Think of France!"

Was there anything left to say? Bravely, Ludovic Trarieux, the former minister of justice, came to Scheurer-Kestner's support. He evoked the serious errors that had been committed in the exercise of his functions. It was a crime, he maintained, not to do everything to rectify them. But the prime minister interrupted him, proclaiming "There is no Dreyfus Affair." The Senate passed unanimously a motion approving the government's declarations.

For Dreyfus's supporters, this was the hour of defeat. Military justice, the government, and the Parliament had all proclaimed Dreyfus's guilt and lashed out against those who dared to defend his innocence publicly. Edouard Drumont, Ernest Judet, the Assumptionists of *La Croix*, Henri Rochefort, and Granier de Cassagnac (who had joined up with the most impassioned of Dreyfus's enemies) were overflowing with satisfaction, pouring a daily wave of insults over the treasonous Jewish syndicate. Was there no longer a Dreyfus Affair as the prime mininster had assured? For the General Staff, there remained one final scene to play. There remained to have Esterhazy acquitted, to make sure that the matter had been "doubly adjudicated." It would not prove the most difficult of their tasks.

20

They Would Not Have Done as Much for a Poor Man

Commandant Esterhazy's acquittal may have appeared extremely probable, but it was still essential to keep an eye on every detail. On December 4 General Saussier entrusted the judicial inquiry to Commandant Ravary, a recorder with the First Council of Paris. An aged and retired commandant who—according to Joseph Reinach—"could understand nothing but following orders,"[1] Ravary began anew General de Pellieux's investigation. Every evening, to make sure that he had not blundered, he would report his doings to General Gonse. Gonse kept Commandant Henry up-to-date. And Commandant Henry and du Paty de Clam would concert with Esterhazy. "You will be questioned tomorrow," du Paty wrote him on December 14, 1897, "concerning your relations with Schwarzkoppen. Restrict yourself to the terrain agreed upon, and don't elaborate on any details."[2] In such manner, slipups might be avoided. The inquiry entailed but a single risk: the handwriting analysis that Ravary was obliged to order and confide to three experts—Varinard, a former architect; Couard, a paleographer and former student at the École des Chartes; and Belhomme, an old secondary-school inspector. Ravary asked them to compare the handwriting of the bordereau with Esterhazy's. They were not, however, asked to evaluate in any way Dreyfus's handwriting,

since such action would taint an established verdict. Under the leadership
of Belhomme (whom Esterhazy called "the idiot," and Reinach "the senile
one"),[3] the experts, sequestered at the Prison of Cherche-Midi with Commandant Ravary, went to work. On December 26, they concluded unanimously that the bordereau was not Esterhazy's work. "At first glance," it
appears to be a rather "dubious" document. No doubt, it contains "many
letters identical to those of Esterhazy's normal handwriting." But "had
Esterhazy written the document, he would have disguised his handwriting." Thus both the resemblances and the disparities worked to Esterhazy's favor. The bordereau was a fake, with "sections that had been
traced" in order to compromise Esterhazy. But the forger, of whom it was
said merely that he "was not a professional," was not named. Dreyfus, no
doubt. The report enchanted the General Staff. Only Esterhazy, who was
more demanding than his protectors, declared it absurd, and "insufficient." More subtle in their evaluation of the Uhlan letter, the experts
concluded that it "seemed rather" an improvised imitation of Esterhazy's
script than an original document. This was more than had ever been asked
for. On December 31, 1897, the investigating magistrate was able to sign a
report concluding: "Although the accusations against Commandant Esterhazy have been brought with a precise theatrical sense of how best to
stir and trouble public opinion, in reality, there is no convincing evidence
of his guilt." He offered the opinion that under the circumstances, it would
be appropriate to dismiss the charge.[4] Following the prearranged plan,
Esterhazy then persisted in requesting to appear before a Court-Martial,
"which alone could bring to light my innocence and reduce to nought all
the accusations of my slanderers."[5] On January 1, 1898, General Saussier,
rejecting the conclusions of the investigating magistrate, ordered Esterhazy to appear before the First Court-Martial.*

   In the meanwhile a few final precautions were taken. By order of
General de Boisdeffre, General Mercier managed to have Gonse transmit
to him the famous commentary prepared by du Paty, to accompany the
secret file and which Colonel Sandherr, head of the Intelligence Service,
had retained. In Gonse's presence, Mercier proceeded to burn the document which was tormenting him, since it was written proof of the illegal
communication during the Court-Martial which convicted Dreyfus. "The
only tangible trace of Mercier's abuse of authority" thus disappeared.[7]

---

* The indictment contained the words "acts committed in 1894," thus localizing in time the
crime imputed to Esterhazy. The date was subsequently scratched out. The decision acquitting Esterhazy was thus to cleanse him juridically of all treasonous acts, without reference to
the year 1894. Concerning this matter, which reveals the fraudulent procedure used to
protect Esterhazy with a prior verdict, General Luxer, who presided over the Court-Martial,
would be questioned during the revision procedure. He would say that he had not noticed
what had been so conveniently scratched out on Esterhazy's behalf.[6]

Juridically, everything was proceeding as planned. But difficulties were emerging elsewhere, which the conspirators had to face, frequently after careful consideration, occasionally by improvisation. On December 12, the newspaper *L'Intransigeant* had accused the emperor of Germany and Ambassador Münster von Derneberg of having direct relations with Dreyfus. "One of the famous secret documents," wrote *L'Intransigeant*, "is a letter by the Emperor of Germany. . . . In that letter to M. von Münster, the name of Captain Dreyfus could be found written from one end to the other." Several newspapers had taken up that legend, adding on myriad details,* and the German ambassador had protested still again to Hanotaux and to Méline. The prime minister offered his apologies, deplored what had happened, and promised to do whatever he could. What he needed, he said, was a good censorship law. Annotating by hand his ambassador's reports, Emperor Wilhelm II expressed his dissatisfaction. "The French government is doing nothing. The provocations have not stopped." The old ambassador attempted in vain to explain to his emperor the "Parisian" mentality.† "In all matters political and especially concerning Germany, the Parisian is completely lacking in discernment. His frivolity and impassioned character do not allow him the time to reflect. As a result, the press here exercises a most pernicious influence. . . ."

The Italian government was growing irritated as well. The Italian ambassador issued numerous protests against articles in the press which presented Dreyfus as an agent of the Italian military attaché. The ambassador reiterated that Panizzardi had never seen or known Dreyfus. Panizzardi had volunteered his testimony, which had been declined by the government. "In our legal system, we do not recognize spontaneous testimony, but only testimony requested in the course of juridical proceedings."[9] Heartfelt excuses were tendered to the Italian representatives, but there was no possibility of acceding to their request. Schwarzkoppen—by then returned to Germany—and Panizzardi—still in Paris—continued their correspondence. Their relationship had changed somewhat and their letters now contained only words of reproach. Panizzardi wrote anxiously on December 21. "The Affair will surface again more vigorously than ever," wrote Panizzardi on December 21, "a few days from now when the Court-Martial will convene. It has been decided to produce at whatever cost Esterhazy's innocence, and that is good for you. It will be said that the bordereau was not his."[10]

Writing to his friend, he specified on December 31: "Everybody believes that the famous affair will end during the first week of 1898 with an

---

* This was the legend of the annotated bordereau which would play an important role during the second phase of the Affair.
† Report of December 16, 1897, to Wilhelm II.[8]

acquittal of Esterhazy for espionage. The government has interests which are too great for it not to arrange things thus."[11]

Panizzardi attempted to calm his friend, whom he found "agitated" by the Affair. "Reserve for me always your precious friendship." The tone was friendly, but a bit distant, and preoccupied. The days of Maximilien and Alexandrine had passed.

But little attention was paid these diplomats, whom the French government could always reassure with a few cajoling words. Nor to Empress Eugenia and Emperor Wilhelm II, who claimed that they were convinced of Dreyfus's innocence. It was to be expected that they would sympathize with a traitor, and France had no lesson to learn from foreigners. The real problems were in France, where the syndicate, on the eve of the Esterhazy trial, was attempting to stir up public opinion. Emile Zola, "seeing no newspaper that would accept his articles," pursued his campaign with the publication on December 13 of a *Lettre à la Jeunesse*, a veritable call to the students of the Latin Quarter, then on January 4 with a *Lettre à la France* which was not without reverberations.[12] The newspaper *Le Temps* maintained a neutrality which would slowly become favorable to Dreyfus's cause. On December 9 several women, including Marguerite Durand, Madame Séverine, and Hélène Sée founded a newspaper, *La Fronde*, in which could be heard the voice first of pity, then of sympathy. In *Le Siècle*, Yves Guyot took sides and published, at Joseph Reinach's request, the act of indictment of the 1894 trial in order to demonstrate its vacuity. Georges Clemenceau, in *L'Aurore*, was evermore active and waxing increasingly scathing. On the other hand, reacting to a campaign of subscription cancellations, *Le Figaro*, which had long been loyal, deserted the cause. On December 13, Fernand de Rodays, the director of *Le Figaro*, offered his explanation in an embarrassed article: "Reasons of State made it his duty." The newspaper would remain neutral—for the while. Francis de Pressensé, Joseph Cornély, Emile Duclaux, the director of the Institut Pasteur,* Ferdinand Buisson, a professor at the Sorbonne, Louis Havet, a member of the Institute, Anatole France, and Octave Mirbeau all revealed a sympathy that would little by little become an active force. After Gabriel Monod and Salomon Reinach, Appell, the dean of the Paris Faculté des Sciences, joined the Dreyfus camp. Lucien Herr gave of himself immeasurably, drawing in former students at the École Normale such as Léon Blum and Victor Béraud and other young men such as Charles Péguy, Paul Langevin, and Jean Perrin, who in turn would recruit others.

It was in the political sphere that it was hardest to find adherents.

* He was persuaded, it appears, by the incoherence of d'Ormescheville's report, which was published by *Le Siècle*.

Ludovic Trarieux, the former minister of justice, went from a distaste for the illegal procedures to a belief in Dreyfus's innocence. He had become an extremely active source of support for Dreyfus's cause. But such a commitment was the exception. The legislative elections of 1898 were approaching, and it seemed dangerous and useless to the few members of Parliament intent on a revision to get involved in an Affair in which one could only be hurt. On the right and in the center Dreyfus's treason was an article of national faith. On the left, sentiment remained hostile or at best hesitant. The majority of the radicals, Léon Blum noted, were and would long remain opposed to any revision. Godefroy Cavaignac, Paul Doumer, and Berteaux subscribed to the theses of the General Staff. Only Léon Bourgeois and Henri Brisson, who were scrupulously republican, were attracted to Dreyfus's cause. But as yet they did not dare say so. It was common knowledge that the Radical newspaper *L'Eclair*, edited by Alphonse Humbert, was at the beck and call of the General Staff, for which it served as a forum. The mass of the Radical party was "jingoistic": from its point of view, the honor of the Army was indistinguishable from the service of the country.[13] Among the Socialists, distrust of the syndicate was fueled by left-wing anti-Semitism and a hatred for that commercial bourgeoisie that the Dreyfuses and especially the Reinachs seemed to represent. "They would not have done as much for a poor man," wrote René Viviani, giving vent to a sentiment that was quite widespread among the Socialists. Jean Jaurès himself revealed the dominant sentiment among the Socialists when he wrote in *La Petite République* of December 11: "If the terrible sentence had befallen a man without relations, without money . . . converging on the trial there are two fractions of the privileged class which are clashing; Protestant and Jewish opportunist groupings, on the one side, and clerical and military groupings on the other are pitted against each other."[14]

Why should the Socialists enter into a conflict that was dividing the middle class and in which so many capitalist interests were at stake and in opposition? The gradual rallying to the cause of men like Jaurès, borne by his generosity, his conception of a humane socialist ideal, would exercise considerable influence on the course of the Affair. But for a long time he would remain isolated. Was not Jaurès—"entirely preoccupied and, as it were, mystically exalted by the task he had undertaken"[15]—deviating from the true mission of socialism? The Socialists would follow Jaurès only gradually, some in spite of themselves, and most of them constrained to overcome prejudices in the process. Up until the end, men like Alexandre Millerand and René Viviani would keep their distances from the debates surrounding the Affair. Was it the professional deformation of lawyers

overly sensitive to the authority of an established verdict?* Or the prudence of men of ambition? The shrewdest of politicians, such as Louis
Barthou, Raymond Poincaré, or Eugène Caillaux, those who would dominate the political scene a few years later, strained as long as possible not to
take a stand and became committed only when they were assured of
deriving some advantage from it. It was nevertheless the case that in
December and January 1898, the small band of "Dreyfusards" (as they
began to be called), was growing and becoming organized. The days were
over when they counted not even ten. This was the period—December
1897—when Mathieu Dreyfus met Joseph Reinach for the first time.[17]
And Mathieu still had not met Clemenceau, Zola, or Jaurès. Bernard
Lazare, Scheurer-Kestner, and by then Joseph Reinach, Ludovic
Trarieux, and Lucien Herr expended themselves incalculably. Meetings
proliferated in the homes of one or another of them. Newcomers to the
cause of Dreyfus were introduced. Some wrote and others commissioned
articles. Tasks were shared. When money was needed, and it frequently
was, Mathieu contributed or managed to find it. The "Syndicate," as
Drumont, Rochefort, and the General Staff called it, the Jewish syndicate,
the syndicate of traitors, was growing perpetually stronger.

It was the syndicate's patron, Mathieu Dreyfus, who had denounced
Esterhazy, whom Esterhazy's friends sought to discredit. Efforts were
made to plant suspicious papers on him. Mathieu warned his colleagues
not to accept anything. He was offered meetings that would discredit
him; traps were set for him, as they were for Joseph Reinach.[18] Mathieu
grew extremely distrustful, perhaps excessively so. On all sides he saw
traps that he would have to thwart.[19] But he had reason to be prudent.
On December 29, a legal action was initiated against him and his brother
Léon for attempted bribery. The two brothers were accused of having
offered money to Colonel Sandherr when they had gone to see him on
December 14, 1894, a few days before Alfred Dreyfus's trial three years
ago. Upon being summoned by Judge Bertulus, Léon and Mathieu
learned that there were three witnesses for the prosecution: General
Gonse, Commandant Lauth, and the archivist Gribelin. All three testified under oath that Colonel Sandherr, who died in 1897, had told
them at the time of the attempt to bribe him. What were they defending,
these officers who would not recoil before any ploy? Commandant Esterhazy? The reputation of General Mercier, whose illegality they continued to cover up? The honor of the Army, whose trustees they claimed
to be? Were they bound by an oath they had taken, locked into discipline,

---

* Millerand would write in *La Lanterne* of January 9, 1898, after admiring Cavaignac's
speech, which had "relieved the public conscience": "Enough is enough: now the Affair is
over, over for us."[16]

captives of a complicity consolidated every day by the actions they perpe-
trated together? Was it a hatred of Jews, a fear of the syndicate, the
power of the hierarchy, a love of their class, or simply the instinct of
self-preservation which moved them? At every step, they were obliged to
commit a new abuse in order to shore up the preceding one. The next
stop was Esterhazy's acquittal.

21

Long Live Esterhazy

E vents transpired as planned.
Two sessions—on January 10 and 11—had been scheduled for the
proceedings of the First Court-Martial, a sign that military justice was
expected to operate with remarkable swiftness. "As in 1894, the victory of
deception was faced with one final obstacle, the publicity accorded to the
proceedings."[1] The partisans of revision took the offensive by attempting
to avoid any closed session that—by stifling Lieutenant Colonel Picquart's
testimony—would facilitate the acquittal. Joseph Reinach sent an open
letter to the minister of war, protesting the anticipated closed session. In
Le Temps of January 6, 1898, Ludovic Trarieux published a letter denouncing "the simulacrum of justice which is in the offing." General Billot
faltered, then found a clever compromise: Commandant Esterhazy and
the civilian witnesses—with the exception of Louis Leblois—would be
heard in a public session. The military witnesses and the experts would be
heard secretly. The General Staff thus achieved what was essential to its
designs. The press would not hear Picquart's deposition.

Could Mathieu Dreyfus, whose complaint was at the origin of the
proceedings, file a civil suit? The question was unclear from a legal point
of view. The lawyer, Edgar Demange, and Ludovic Trarieux, the former
minister of justice, judged it crucial to be present during the deliberations,
even if the military tribunal should (as was probable) declare the civil suit
inadmissible. At least they would be heard. Demange would represent
Mathieu Dreyfus, just as he had represented his brother in 1894. A lawyer
would have to be found for Lucie Dreyfus, who would also attempt to file a

civil suit. Various names were mentioned, but it was Leblois's suggestion which was retained: Fernand Labori would be approached.

At the time, Labori was not yet thirty-five years old.[2] He had already argued several cases which had provoked a stir. His plea for the anarchist Edouard Vaillant had made him famous in the Palais. He had also intervened in the course of the Panama trial, thus confirming his courage and his talent. He was a powerful attorney, with a sonorous voice and broad, deliberately theatrical gestures, who was capable, when carried away, of superb moments of eloquence. Admirable in his improvisations, he was also extremely diligent and methodical. He knew every document of his cases and wrote the essential sections of his arguments with great care. His passion and boldness actually concealed a mastery that rarely faltered, a perpetually alert mind, and even, at times, a prudence inclined to calculation. Quite ambitious, regarding the courtroom as too narrow an arena for his career, he had unsuccessfully attempted in 1893, with the support of the moderate republicans, to be elected as the deputy from the Marne. He thought of offering his candidacy in Rheims against Léon Bourgeois, one of the leaders of the Radical Party.

When Leblois asked him to represent Dreyfus's wife, Labori hesitated. He was not certain that Dreyfus was innocent. He would later say that his certainty became complete only after the proceedings of the Esterhazy trial.[3] Studying the case, he discovered an indictment which was in itself "a complete defense."[4] An excellent jurist, he perceived the illegalities surrounding the Affair and the results that a lawyer might derive from them. No doubt he also saw the risks that the case entailed for his practice, which was thriving, and for the political career to which he aspired. He was courageous enough to accept the case, but he took certain precautions. He wanted to be officially appointed to the case by the president of the bar. He told Mathieu, "It must be known that if I am representing your sister-in-law, it is because my conscience impels me, and that the question of fees has had no influence on my decision."[5] The older Demange, who looked on the arrival of his young and tumultuous colleague with a not altogether favorable eye, protested. What would *he* look like, he who had always accepted honoraria? "The difference can only diminish me and make me look like a man eager for money." The two attorneys discussed the matter in private, while Mathieu, in an adjoining room, awaited their response: a first conflict to be followed by numerous others. Finally Labori yielded, nearly overcome: "I defer to the categorical wish expressed by Demange; but this is the greatest sacrifice that could be asked of me."[6] He would receive a fee, and would soon adapt quite satisfactorily to the sacrifice.[7]

On January 10, just before 9 o'clock, Lucie and Mathieu Dreyfus arrived at the Prison of Cherche-Midi in the company of their lawyers.

General de Luxer, presiding over the Court-Martial, had reserved seats for them facing the platform on which the table of military judges was situated. The defendant's bench was located a scarce two meters away.

The public and the witnesses entered gradually. The benches filled up with officers. Mathieu noticed a lieutenant colonel who seemed isolated, alone. The "sky blue" jacket of his uniform—characteristic of the Algerian sharpshooters—clashed with the "black jackets of the others."[8] He was Colonel Picquart, whom Mathieu was seeing for the first time. The court usher announced, "Court Martial. . . . Present arms." Officers flooded in, following the seven judges. General de Pellieux was seated behind the judge presiding over the military tribunal.

"Have the defendant enter." For the first time, Mathieu saw the man who had written the bordereau, who had sent his brother to jail, the traitor whom the French Army seemed to be protecting. "He grazed me as he passed by, so narrow was the space."[9]

Mathieu looked at him. The profile was that of some great bird of prey. The deep dark eyes, set well back in their orbit, were in constant movement. It was impossible to hold their gaze. Mathieu thought of his brother. Where was he at that precise moment? In what state? Was he still alive? Why had all the forces in society coalesced to convict his brother, even as they were uniting that very day to find this officer innocent? And then the witnesses were called. They all withdrew into two small rooms. Mathieu Dreyfus introduced himself to Colonel Picquart, who was seated beside Auguste Scheurer-Kestner. Colonel Henry came in—"his vulgar, ruddy face, blotchy in complexion, planted on his heavy, massive body." He spoke noisily with another officer. His shoes touched Mathieu's, who pretended not to notice.[10] Commandant du Paty de Clam paced incessantly, his body erect, head high and thrown back, monocle in place, eyes devoid of expression. Commandant Lauth was there, "his thin, supple body and a face that seemed carved by a knife—dry, harsh, and prodigiously ugly." Meanwhile with elbows lazily propped on a table, his eyes half-closed, with a "pained and benevolent expression," General Gonse seemed to be only nominally present. They were all there, the men who had jointly sent his brother to Devil's Island—and then kept him there. They were surrounded by officers who spoke loudly and gesticulated, apparently quite comfortable in this setting. They were all there, except for Generals de Boisdeffre and Mercier.

The Court-Martial ordered as planned a "delayed" closed session. "The proceedings will be public until the stage when their publication might appear to endanger national defense." After hearing the explanations of Labori and Demange, who invoked on behalf of Lucie and Mathieu, "above the law of silence, the immutable principles of justice," the court rejected unanimously the filing of civil suits. The decision retained as its essential basis the fact that "ex-Captain Dreyfus was justly and lawfully convicted."

The interrogation of Esterhazy, who had been registered as a prisoner the day before by General Luxer was dispatched expeditiously. The defendant responded in a calm and curt voice. He was perfectly at ease, and played quite well the role which he had taken on, that of a slandered warrior.[11] The audience, a large majority of whom were officers, manifested its sympathy for him.

Mathieu Dreyfus's deposition, on the other hand, was interrupted by bursts of laughter and occasionally by howls, on cue at times from Esterhazy's lawyers, at other times from the officers grouped around General de Pellieux and seated behind the judges. When Mathieu responded to the cross-examination of Maurice Tézenas, stating, "I defend my brother in every respect," he was flooded with hoots from a large segment of the audience. The moving and precise testimony offered thereafter by Scheurer-Kestner in the form of a public confession, fell upon more receptive ears. But when the vice president of the Senate expressed his certainty that the bordereau was not written by Dreyfus, several officers sneered loudly. Scheurer-Kestner challenged them. "You find that funny?" His immense respect for the Army was tested quite harshly by such sarcasm, which seemed to be mocking both himself and the truth. There followed a procession of additional witnesses, including Marguerite Pays, who "lived from her investments," and who was visibly in a state of panic, and Maurice Weil, the Jewish officer, who had nothing to say. After which the secret session was decreed.

It was thus in secret that Colonel Picquart furnished his explanations late that afternoon and the following day. Serene, precise, and without apparent emotion, he related everything that he knew. As soon as he pronounced the names of Billot, de Boisdeffre, and Mercier, General de Pellieux, who had remained silent throughout the public session, intervened in the discussion. He forbade Picquart to implicate such glorious names in such an affair. With utter contempt for the law, the presiding magistrate allowed the investigating officer to speak.* Inversely, de Luxer treated Picquart so poorly and interrupted him so often that one of the magistrates, Commandant Rivals, believed it his duty to intervene: "I see,"

* "If I participated in the task of acquittal," General de Pellieux would declare at the Zola trial, "I am proud of it."[12] Upon being questioned during the revision procedure concerning the role he had allowed General de Pellieux to play throughout the trial, in defiance of normal procedure, General de Luxer would acknowledge that General de Pellieux had intervened on several occasions "in a manner favorable to the accused" or hostile to Picquart. General de Luxer would claim to have threatened Pellieux, at the suggestion of one of the judges, with expulsion.[13]

he said, "that Colonel Picquart is the true defendant. I request that he be permitted to present all the explanations necessary to his defense." De Luxer allowed Picquart to complete his demonstration. When the latter returned to the witnesses' chamber, Mathieu conveyed to him his gratitude. Picquart replied, "You have no reason to thank me. I was obeying my conscience."

Next, Gonse, Lauth, and Henry all accused Picquart with concerted violence. Henry recalled that he had seen his superior leafing through the secret file with Leblois. Picquart was called back. "When did you see us?" asked Picquart. Henry got lost amid the dates and became confused. Pellieux intervened once again, rising to Henry's aid. "At a year's distance, it is quite difficult to give a date." Gribelin, from the Section of Statistics, also swore that he had seen the two friends reading the secret file together. Under such circumstances, what effect could Leblois's testimony have? He was listened to indifferently. There followed the final witnesses. Only one of the three expert analysts was called. "Esterhazy listened distractedly, as might a spectator bored by a mediocre play in the theatre."[14]

All went extremely well. The government prosecutor relinquished the indictment. Although suffering from a severe sciatic condition, the lawyer Maurice Tézenas argued for five hours out of respect for traditional formalities. "His meticulous plea gave the judges the illusion that they were going to reach their decision with complete freedom of conscience."[15] At 8:05 P.M., the judges withdrew to their chamber. The guards led away Esterhazy, who, upon passing in front of Picquart, sprang to attention. The deliberations took about three minutes.* At 8:10 the doors of the courtroom were reopened to the public and General de Luxer, in a firm voice, proceeded to read the verdict. Commandant Esterhazy was acquitted unanimously.

Applause broke out in the room, along with shouts of "Long live the Army!" "Long live France!" "Death to the Jews!" and "Death to the syndicate!" Colonel Picquart and Mathieu Dreyfus walked out slowly and with difficulty, insulted by some, threatened by others. Esterhazy found it hard to make his way through the crowd in order to return to prison for his official release. The officers wanted to carry him aloft in triumph. Between 1,000 and 1,500 people were besieging the approaches of the Prison of Cherche-Midi: hands stretched out toward the glorious officer. At the threshold of the prison, a loud voice proclaimed, "Hats off to the martyr of the Jews."

Thus did Esterhazy leave prison, free, smiling, surrounded by officers and friends who formed his escort. During the night, the cry was launched

* "I did not have time to collect my papers," one of Tézenas's collaborators would write in *Le Temps* of January 13, 1898, "and already the judges were filing back in."[16]

from street to street. "Long live Esterhazy; long live the Army!" He had finally become the hero he dreamed of being.

The next day, Colonel Picquart would be arrested, confined to a fortress, and taken to Mont-Valérien. That same day in the Senate Scheurer-Kestner would be stripped of his vice presidency.

Evidently the syndicate was unable to open up a path to revision. By then, the Dreyfus Affair had been doubly adjudicated and the deportee of Devil's Island doubly convicted.

III

TWO FRANCES

1

J'Accuse

It thus seemed that Auguste Scheurer-Kestner's republican virtue, waiting for the government to seek out the truth, Joseph Reinach's diplomacy, hoping for the revision to spring from a growing awareness amid political circles, and Mathieu Dreyfus's daily effort knocking at all doors, were in vain. "We were quite discouraged," Léon Blum confessed.[1] "Everything was over; all was lost." Dreyfus had been convicted a second time. . . . His friends had been uneasy throughout the preliminary investigation and throughout Esterhazy's trial. But "not for an instant," Blum assures, "did the idea even occur to us that Esterhazy's acquittal was possible."[2] No doubt they suspected that the General Staff had organized everything in advance. But in spite of this, they expected the truth to emerge. Esterhazy's acquittal by a unanimous vote without discussion descended on them "like a sledgehammer."[3] A revision seemed entirely impossible. It would henceforth be in conflict with a "complete and self-sufficient system of resistance."

More lucid than most of Dreyfus's friends, Emile Zola had not for a moment doubted that Esterhazy would be acquitted. Even before the verdict, he had begun writing the famous text that was to "shatter the windows of that bolted chamber in which the cause of revision was being asphyxiated to death."[4] Zola's genius lay in understanding that at the time there was nothing more that could be expected from legal options, that the only recourse was public opinion. In order to mobilize it, it would be necessary to stop presenting the Dreyfus Affair in small fragments, in details that were often incomprehensible. With total scorn for considerations of prudence, without any ethical or juridical precautions, what was needed was to deliver to the public a striking text which would summarize the Affair at the risk of simplification and bring to light the crimes of the General Staff. With a single, energetic blow, the order of things might be changed.

At the beginning of 1898, Zola was an author of world renown and considerable wealth. He knew that in involving himself in the Affair, he

ran the risk of upsetting his life and alienating the larger part of his
readers, who came from the generally anti-Dreyfusard middle class.* He
realized as well that he would have to relinquish the ambition, which he
had long coveted, of entering the Académie Française. But disturbed for
several years by the ongoing nationalist and anti-Semitic campaigns, and
convinced early on of Dreyfus's innocence, he plunged into the
struggle—passionately and without looking back.[5] In his first pamphlet,
Lettre à la Jeunesse, published on December 13, 1897, he addressed the
French students shouting Scheurer-Kestner's name in the streets:

> Where are you off to, young men, running in groups through the
> streets, demonstrating in the name of your anger and enthusiasm?
> We are off to hoot at . . . an old man . . . who imagined that
> without risk of punishment, he could lend his support to a gener-
> ous cause, hoping that clarity emerge . . . for the very honor of the
> French nation.[6]

Then, in his *Lettre à la France*, published by Eugène Fasquelle on
January 7, 1898, he called on that "good-hearted and commonsensical
people" not to allow themselves to be abused to the point of reaching "the
ferocity of fear, the shadows of intolerance" by the lies of the press, the
base insults, and the moral perversions to which the country seemed to
him to be given. In an article published by *Le Figaro* on December 5, 1897,
he vigorously analyzed the role of the "so-called serious and honest press."

> We have seen the gutter press in heat, making its money out of
> pathological curiosity, perverting the masses in order to sell its
> blackened paper. . . . We have seen higher up on the scale the
> popular newspapers, selling for a sou, addressed to the majority
> and forging the opinions of the crowd; we have seen them inspire
> atrocious passions, and furiously conduct a sectarian cam-
> paign. . . . Finally, we have seen the higher so-called serious and
> honest press witness all this with an impassiveness—I was going to
> say a serenity—that I declare stupefying. These honest newspap-
> ers have contented themselves with recording all with scrupulous
> care, whether it be true or false. . . .

* This would not prevent Zola from being accused of seeking glory and wealth in the Dreyfus
Affair. "After himself," Sarraut would write in *La Dépêche* of January 23, 1898, "Zola
worships only one thing: money. Zola saw in the Dreyfus Affair an immense and colossal
advertisement. He in fact could not care less for Dreyfus; what interests him is himself,
Zola. . . ." Zola, in fact, would emerge from the Affair virtually ruined.

Zola was thus composing his text on Esterhazy's acquittal in full awareness of the role achieved by the press. Since it was the press which—in
weighing on the government even more than on public opinion—was
stifling any chance of a revision, it was through the press that Zola decided
to accomplish the act that the Socialist Jules Guesde would call "the greatest revolutionary act of the century." Zola knew the risks he was taking.
He saw the crimes and misdemeanors he was committing in writing his
text and also the hatred and resentment it would unleash. Nor did he fail
to realize that he was one of the only writers—perhaps the only one—
commanding a readerhip that might give his initiative a vast diffusion. He
knew that he was not only a "popular novelist" who dominated his time,
but a writer of worldwide reputation. He realized that he could strike
hard—and far.

Without awaiting Esterhazy's acquittal, he set to writing amid fever and
anger. He spent two nights composing the sheets of his letter to the
president of the Republic.* He brought his finished labor to Ernest
Vaughan, director of *L'Aurore*, since *Le Figaro*, where he customarily
wrote, had just left the Dreyfusard camp. Even more than Vaughan,
Georges Clemenceau was immediately enthusiastic. The writer François
Coppée, on the other hand, to whom Zola showed a few pages, implored
him not to publish anything.† On the evening of Esterhazy's acquittal, Zola
gave a reading of his finished text to the staff of *L'Aurore*. They applauded.
It was Clemenceau who came up with the spectacular title: *J'Accuse*.
Clemenceau and Vaughan organized the posting of placards and the
publicity. *L'Aurore* would be brought out in an edition of 300,000 copies,
and the letter would be spread throughout the streets thanks to the
exceptional employment of several hundred news criers. And so it was that
on the morning of January 13, 1898, Paris received like a lightning bolt,
the special edition of *L'Aurore*, in which could be read "aflame in large
letters"[7] "J'Accuse, Letter to the President of the Republic by Emile Zola."
In a few hours, more than 200,000 copies were sold. It was "the greatest
day of the Affair,"[8] the one, in any event, which restored strength and
confidence at a desperate time to Dreyfus's partisans. It was also the one
that has remained in popular memory.

* The text had originally been prepared for publication as a brochure, like his previous
efforts. It was at the last moment that Zola had the idea of publishing his letter in a newspaper
to reach a wider public.
† Coppée had been on the verge of joining the Dreyfusard camp at the end of 1897 in the
wake, it appears, of a visit from Lucie Dreyfus. He had even written an extremely partisan
article for *Le Journal*, which that newspaper rejected. Coppée was subsequently to become a
relentless and militant anti-Dreyfusard.

Zola's long letter to Félix Faure ends with the conclusion that inspired its title:[9]

I accuse Lieutenant-Colonel du Paty de Clam of having been the diabolical artisan of the judicial error, without knowing it, I am willing to believe, and then of having defended his nefarious work for three years through the most grotesque and culpable machinations.

I accuse General Mercier of having become an accomplice, out of mental weakness at the least, in one of the greatest iniquities of the century.

I accuse General Billot of having had in his hands the definitive evidence of Dreyfus's innocence and of having stifled it, of being guilty of an outrage against humanity and outrage against justice for a political end and in order to save the compromised General Staff.

I accuse General de Boisdeffre and General Gonse of being guilty of the same crime, one, no doubt, out of clerical passion, the other, perhaps, out of that *esprit de corps* which makes of the offices of War an impregnable holy ark.

I accuse General de Pellieux and Commandant Ravary of having conducted an inquest which is vile, by which I mean an inquest of the most monstrous partiality, of which we have, in the latter's report, an imperishable monument of naive audacity.

I accuse the three handwriting experts, Mssrs. Belhomme, Varinard, and Couard, of having composed deceitful and fraudulent reports, unless a medical examination declares them to be stricken with an impairment of vision or judgment.

I accuse the offices of War of having conducted in the press, particularly in *L'Eclair* and in *L'Echo de Paris*, an abominable campaign designed to mislead public opinion and to conceal their wrongdoing.

Finally, I accuse the first Court Martial of having violated the law in convicting a defendant on the basis of a document kept secret, and I accuse the second Court Martial of having covered up that illegality on command by committing in turn the juridical crime of knowingly acquitting a guilty man.

In bringing these accusations, I am not without realizing that I expose myself in the process to Articles 30 and 31 of the press law of July 29, 1881, which punishes offenses of slander. And it is quite willingly that I so expose myself.

As for those whom I accuse, I do not know them, I have never seen them, I have neither rancor nor hatred for them. They are for me no more than entities, spirits of social malfeasance. And the act that I hereby accomplish is but a revolutionary means of hastening the explosion of truth and justice.

I have but one passion, one for seeing the light, in the name of humanitywhich has so suffered and which is entitled to happiness. My fiery protest is but the cry of my soul. Let me be brought then before a criminal court and let the investigation be conducted in the light of day!

I am waiting.

Rest assured, Mister President, of my deepest respect.

The errors contained in the celebrated *J'Accuse* were of little import. Zola was working hastily, with few documents, and did not claim to be doing the work of an historian. No doubt he exaggerated the importance of Commandant du Paty de Clam, whom he erroneously situated in the first rank. He neglected to name Commandant Henry, the principal criminal agent. He minimized the role of General Gonse. He did not see the essential responsibility of General Mercier. Joseph Reinach observed that he rendered all the actors "too mediocre, too null," as though they were all led on by du Paty. He was mistaken about the hierarchy of their roles.[10] Reinach—whose admiration for Zola was marked by a certain mistrust—even criticizes the writer's style.

> The further he advances in his discourse, the less he tells; he exclaims and vituperates. Now once he has repeated the word crime ten times in twenty lines, one can no longer see the crimes he is denouncing, only the orator in a state of fury. His anger provokes mistrust. A naked crime is a hundred times more horrible than a crime clothed in adjectives.[11]

"It was quite knowingly," observed Marcel Thomas, "that Zola enlarged, exaggerated, and schematized—in order to impress public opinion."[12] He ran the risk of error and excess. He appealed to his "intuition" rather than to "evidence which remained out of his reach." But what is astonishing is the luminous force of that intuition, what Reinach called "the terrible penetration" with which Zola discerned and denounced what was essential: *esprit de corps* in the "holy ark," hierarchical exasperation, clerical passion, *raison d'état*, the conspiracy of deceived masses and panicking officials, criminal stubbornness, crimes committed and covered up in order to "save the compromised General Staff." Beyond any errors of detail, Zola, who had neither time nor documentation, discovered the very substance of the Dreyfus Affair.

Is *J'Accuse* a "masterpiece," as Léon Blum has written,[13] a polemical text of "imperishable beauty"?[14] It is, in any event, a great document, one which marks an essential date in the history of journalism. In the article, published two days after Esterhazy's triumphant acquittal, the violence of expression, the daring metaphors, the vehement adjectives, the deliberate repetition of certain words in order to endow the letter with an incantatory air ("the word *crime* is repeated ten times in the course of twenty lines"), the inflamed style, and finally the breathless progression, as if inspired by anger, up until the final words of defiance, make of it a text which was admirably conceived and written to shake up public opinion.

Was it a "revolutionary means of hastening the explosion of truth and justice" as Zola affirmed at the end of his letter? Zola was not without knowing that virtually every paragraph was subject to legal action, that he could and indeed would provoke a number of lawsuits. "My fiery protest is but the cry of my soul. Let me then be brought before a criminal court and let the inquest take place in broad daylight." Zola assumed the risk of standing up against the civilian and military authorities. He appealed to public opinion as a higher power. It was from that power that he awaited the movement that would shake up the legal authorities and draw them out of their state of compromise or fear. Had it been adequately sensed, wrote Léon Blum, that "Zola's act was that of a hero"?[15] It is true that by 1898 Zola had acquired a fortune, worldwide fame, and was enjoying his success with bourgeois satisfaction. Zola was not, like Bernard Lazare, a young man borne aloft by his anger, a fighter of daring wit, eager to cross swords. Convinced of Dreyfus's innocence, Zola could easily have joined the struggle with more limited arms and been useful to Dreyfus's cause without harming his own. But there he was suddenly risking "the fruits of forty years' labor," exposing himself to every form of hatred, every outrage, plunging, against the powers that be, into the most perilous of battles. Out of a taste for publicity, as would be claimed already the day after the publication of *J'Accuse* by the newspapers which would thereafter be storming against him? Out of a passion for money and in order to help sell his "obscene" books? Because he had been copiously remunerated by the syndicate? Because he was a half-crazed pervert, a foreigner? "Who exactly is this Monsieur Zola?" Maurice Barrès, reflecting on his act, would later write. "The man is not French." Barrès would not call into question his Dreyfusard sincerity, but claimed, "there is a frontier between us. Which frontier? The Alps. . . . Emile Zola thinks quite naturally with the thoughts of an uprooted Venetian."[16] Zola's adversaries were not mistaken. The celebrated writer was not simply defending Dreyfus's innocence. The entire text of *J'Accuse* is an indictment of the forces and virtues of traditional France, its religious passion, military spirit, and hierarchies, which required Dreyfus's conviction and then Esterhazy's acquittal. And Zola claimed to be acting in the name of the moral principles which constituted in his eyes the foundation of the Republic.[17]

> We are told of the honor of the Army and asked to love and respect it. Well, yes. To be sure, the Army which would rise at the first threat, which would defend French soil, is the whole of the people, and we have nothing but tenderness and respect for it. But they are not talking about that Army, whose dignity, in our insistence on justice, is precisely what we want. They are talking about the saber, the master they may well impose on us tomorrow. And as for devoutly kissing the saber's tip, by God, no!

Beyond the Affair, Zola lashed out at all the traditional forces intent on impeding "the work of truth and justice."

> It is also a crime to seek support from the gutter press, to allow oneself to be defended by all of the scoundrels of Paris, in such manner that it is now the scoundrels who insolently parade their victory in the defeat of law and simple decency. It is a crime to have accused of troubling France those who wish her to be generous, at the head of free and just nations, when one has oneself fomented the impudent plot of imposing deception before the eyes of the world at large. It is a crime to have misled public opinion, to have used for a labor of death that opinion which has been perverted to the point of insanity. It is a crime to poison the meek and the humble, to exasperate the passions of reaction and intolerance while seeking shelter behind an odious anti-Semitism from which the great liberal France of the rights of man will die if it is not cured. It is a crime to exploit patriotism for works of hatred and it is, finally, a crime to make of the saber the god of modern times, when all of human science is laboring toward the future work of truth and justice.

That was perhaps the heart of it. Zola was the first—since Bernard Lazare was not in a position to endow his involvement with this dimension—to make of the struggle for the revision of the Dreyfus trial a moral cause and a republican duty.

In the process, he gave the action of the partisans of Dreyfus a new coherence which transcended the cause of the deportee of Devil's Island. "The party of justice had been born," claimed Joseph Reinach. And in like manner, Zola, through his excommunications, would help Dreyfus's enemies to recognize each other and regroup. The reasons motivating each—on the one side, the democratic ethic, the respect for law, the ideal of justice and truth; on the other, the traditional virtues whose refuge and guardian the Army took itself to be, the exaltation of national sentiment—were clearly, perhaps even crudely separated and opposed. Thus in a single day, Zola had greatly influenced the Dreyfus Affair. He had established the boundaries of the two camps, and he had situated himself within the divide.

In Paris, the effect was immense. "Dreyfusism," wrote Léon Blum, "was reinvigorated . . . we could feel the confidence well up and rise within us."[18] Rare were those who, like Scheurer-Kestner, perceived above all the risks to which Zola might expose Dreyfus's cause. "Here we are," wrote Scheurer-Kestner in his *Mémoires*,

> in full military crisis. What had to be avoided is precisely what is happening. Instead of giving the country time to reflect, . . . the solution will be assigned to a dubious tribunal, for juries are always dubious. It was imperative to allow the country, which we had exhausted for three months, time to breathe. . . . Zola has entered onto revolutionary terrain in an affair that requires public opinion. What an error! The era of stupidity is about to begin. . . .[19]

But old Scheurer-Kestner had remained attached to a strategy of patience and prudence whose failure, in January 1898, was patent. "Giving the country time to reflect" meant undoubtedly giving up any hope for a revision.

On the morning of January 13, the government, which was horrified by the impact the publication of *J'Accuse* was having in Paris, had a clear awareness of the plan Zola was pursuing. The writer wanted to continue to agitate public opinion with a major criminal trial that would begin anew both the Esterhazy case and the Dreyfus Affair. Clearly it would be best not to bring legal action against Zola. Just a few more days and the effect of *J'Accuse* would fade. Such was the opinion of Méline and General Billot. It was also Esterhazy's hope once the panic caused by this new torment had subsided. "In a few days no one will give it any thought,"[20] he confided to Marguerite Pays and his nephew Christian. But how could one avoid filing suit? The Parliament had been in a state of turmoil ever since the morning of January 13. Count de Mun let it be known that he would begin questioning in the afternoon in order to defend the honor of the Army, a task which could no longer wait. And the Radicals meanwhile perceived an opportunity to overthrow the Méline government.

Henri Brisson—who had been reelected president of the Chamber two days earlier—opened the session with a vague and solemn speech evoking "the perils of dictatorship" and the "endless circle of revolutions and regressions." The prime minister tried to appease the right by venting the government's displeasure in the face of Zola's "abominable attacks" and requested that the Chamber decline any discussion of the matter. Count de Mun replied vigorously that Zola's article was "a bloody outrage to the leaders of the Army" and demanded reparation. The minister of war mounted the tribune, extolled the Army, and in the face of the Assembly's applause, committed the error of promising legal action.[21] The radical, Godefroy Cavaignac, a former minister of war, intervened in turn, judging no doubt that the time was ripe "to overthrow the government by a simple push."[22] He affirmed that he "did not want to let it be said that the defense of the Army came from the right." He assured the Assembly that Dreyfus had issued a confession, coroborated by "testimony contemporaneous" with the Dreyfus trial.* He claimed to be exasperated that the government was stifling such testimony out of he knew not what compromises "with hidden powers."[24] On that day only Jean Jaurès dared to raise a discordant voice. "What, once again the Ministry's intervention, instead of being spontaneous, occurs in response to a summons from the right. . . . I tell you that you are in the process of delivering over the Republic to the generals."

General Billot protested, "Never have the great military chiefs been more respectful of the law, more subject to discipline." Méline surrendered without resistance to the pressures of the right, supported by a majority of the Radicals. He recalled that the Dreyfus Affair had already been adjudged, that the Chamber should not and could not do anything that would open up the path to revision. He too promised legal action against Zola.[25]

Thereafter, the government could no longer retreat. On January 18, the Council of Ministers deliberated on the complaint to be deposed by the minister of war. Quite shrewdly, it was decided to retain for the suit but a single sentence, that in which Zola accused the Court-Martial of having acquitted Esterhazy "on command" and of having "committed the juridi-

---

* Charles Dupuy, prime minister at the time of the Dreyfus trial, attended the session. He was well aware that Dreyfus had issued no confession, that there was no testimony. He said nothing. Nor did Barthou, Poincaré, and Hanotaux.[23]

cal crime of knowingly acquitting a guilty man." Now it was plainly impossible for Zola to bring to court proof that the Court-Martial had acquitted a guilty man on command. Such an order, which was in fact not needed, no doubt never existed. With that stroke, the charges against Zola were narrowed to an extreme, the accusations concerning the Dreyfus Affair were kept at a distance, and above all the conviction of the writer was made certain. Esterhazy, who was informed even before the complaint was filed, had the wise intuition that such precautions would not be sufficient, that the Zola trial would necessarily exceed the bounds that were thus being fixed. "This Zola trial is a serious error," he wrote on January 28 to his nephew Christian. . . . "The insulter should simply have been the object of contempt."[26] He went off expressing his unhappiness in nightclubs, newspaper offices, and in the home of his new friends M. and Mme. de Pellieux, who had become his protectors and taken him into their intimacy. But he was not alone in fearing the trial. General Billot was quite aware of the difficulties which had been piling up for two months. "We are swimming in shit," he told one of his colleagues,[27] "but it is not my ass that did it." General de Boisdeffre also seemed to have submitted to legal action from which there was little to expect and much to fear.

A few precautions were hastily taken. General Gonse had already composed a letter, addressed to General de Boisdeffre, telling how in March 1895 he had accompanied Captain Lebrun-Renault to the office of General Mercier, then to that of the president of the Republic in order to tell them of Dreyfus's confession, "half-admissions or incipient admissions" that boiled down to this, "The minister of war knows that if I have handed over documents, they are documents of no significance, and it was in order to obtain more significant ones from the Germans." In order to give the letter more credibility, Gonse thought it wise to predate it . . . to January 6, 1895, as though he had reported to his chief the convicted traitor's "confession" the very day after the event.* Gonse, moreover, collected carefully the testimony of several officers: Captain Bernard, who had heard a few words of Dreyfus's confession; and Captain Anthoine, who had received the confidence of his friend Captain d'Attel, now deceased, who had also heard Dreyfus tell Lebrun-Renault, "As far as what I handed over, it wasn't worth the effort." Thus it was that in 1898 memories returned with surprising clarity. They gave reality to Dreyfus's confessions, which were taking on increasing importance even as the bordereau was losing its own.

Justice was swift. On February 7 before the Court of Assizes was to

* This was no doubt the letter that Cavaignac had "seen" and that he would refer to in his interpellation of January 13.

begin the trial of Emile Zola and Perrenx, the managing editor of *L'Aurore*, on the basis of a complaint deposed by the minister of war less than three weeks earlier. Colonel Picquart would clearly be the principal witness for the defense. It would be a good idea then, before the hearing, to slap him with a disciplinary measure, which was quickly arranged. On February 1 Picquart appeared before an investigatory board composed of officers of the General Staff. "The board will be happy," declared the defendant, "if Lieutenant Colonel Picquart is expelled from the Army while Commandant Esterhazy still struts around today with his cross and his rank." Neither Picquart's defense, repeating that he never communicated to his friend Leblois any secret file, nor General de Galliffet's favorable deposition accomplished anything. By four voices to one, the board declared Colonel Picquart "in the situation of being retired for reason of grave misdeeds while in service." The decision, which was no more than a recommendation to the minister, was immediately made public. That would suffice to discredit Picquart's testimony a few days later in criminal court. General Billot received the recommendation and prudently delayed any decision.

But by then the Chamber had grown excited at the approach of the trial. On January 22 the Radical Cavaignac, for whom the Dreyfus Affair was serving as an effective vehicle, once again summoned the government to produce the decisive documents establishing Dreyfus's confession. Méline was aware that Cavaignac's goal was to overthrow him. He confirmed to the Chamber Dreyfus's confession without producing a single item of evidence. "Captain Lebrun-Renault's declaration, received the very day of the execution of Dreyfus's verdict. . . . I recognize, and everyone knows, that that declaration exists." The Chamber did not ask for further evidence, but in order to be rid of Cavaignac, Méline continued his assault. He insulted Zola. "No one has the right to pour contempt on the chiefs of the Army. It is through such measures that new editions of *La Débâcle* are prepared. . . . Why not take him to court for the whole article? Because the honor of our generals is in no need of being submitted to the appreciation of a jury, because it is above all suspicion." And then he went after Cavaignac himself. He would gladly yield his place if only Cavaignac were capable of taking it. And the prime minister excited the enthusiasm of the Chamber. "What we are defending are the permanent interests of the country: our military power and the renown of France abroad . . . like soldiers, we will remain at our posts." The Assembly accorded him a standing ovation. At this point, Jaurès intervened. For the first time, he took a clear stand, vehemently, as though he had suppressed the cry of his conscience for too long. "The ones who are preparing future debacles are not those who warn us in time of our errors, but those who commit them, yesterday court generals protected by the Empire, today Jesuit-spawned generals protected by the Republic."

And lashing out at Méline, he issued, amid a growing tumult, a devastating indictment of the government's policies. "Do you know what we are suffering from? What we are all dying from? I say so assuming full responsibility: ever since this affair began, we have all been dying from half-measures, reticences, equivocations, lies, and cowardice! Yes, equivocations, lies, and cowardice!"[28]

"He was no longer merely speaking," wrote Reinach, "he was thundering, his face gone purple, his arm stretched out toward the ministers who were protesting and the right all aroar."[29] The more the clamor waxed furious, the more Jaurès raised his voice "like the cry of some great bird of the sea in a storm." Soon insults were voiced in an attempt to prevent him from continuing. Count de Bernis, a deputy from Gard, shouted, "You are the syndicate's lawyer." "Monsieur de Bernis," Jaurès shot back, "you are a wretch and a coward." There was a tumult. Socialists and right-wing Deputies hurled invective at each other and soon came to blows. Bernis managed to strike Jaurès. President Brisson shook his bell in vain. Soldiers had to be called in to evacuate the premises.

Two days later, on January 24, Jaurès was able to proceed with his intervention. Concerning the very basis of the Dreyfus Affair, he said that as yet he was not certain. "I affirm on my honor that if I were, I would say my thoughts out loud." But he pressed Méline with questions on the illegalities which had been following each other for three years. "Yes or no: have we respected or violated the legal guarantees which are the common patrimony that all citizens must defend, even if it profits the Jews?" Méline responded from his seat with a few sentences of disdain. He did not want to say anything that would serve the cause of revision. He had too much respect for the duly delivered verdict. By a vote of 360 to 126, a vote of confidence in the government was passed. Most of the Radicals voted with the center and the right. In the corridors, a number of republican deputies who voted their confidence in Méline surrounded Jaurès. He had been excellent, and quite courageous. He had asked the right questions. But what was at stake was France, her Army, and her reputation. And above all, there were elections only a few months away. . . .

Maurice Paléologue recounts in his journal the furor caused by these new developments.[30] There was widespread talk of the Zola trial soon to take place. Mme. Aubernon, who had established an influential *salon*, had gathered "revisionists" such as the novelist Paul Hervieu and Gabriel Séailles, a professor of philosophy at the Sorbonne, and adversaries of revision such as the novelist René Bazin and the critic Ferdinand

Brunetière. The discussion grew heated. Brunetière, between courses, began a monologue:

> But what is Zola getting mixed up in? The *J'Accuse* letter is a monument of stupidity, presumptuousness, and incongruity. And that petition that they are having circulated among intellectuals. . . .
>
> Intellectual aptitudes, which, to be sure, I do not scorn, have only a relative value. For me, within the social order, I place a far higher value on stamp of will, strength of character, sureness of judgment, and practical experience. And so I would not hesitate to place some farmer or businessman whom I know far above some scholar, biologist, or mathematician whom I would rather not name. . . .

At dessert Brunetière caught fire. "Without tribunals, there is no society, gentlemen! So have some respect for the *res judicata*! Don't destroy the very powers that you yourselves have instituted." Paul Hervieu replied that justice was founded on law, and that the honor of a man was no less precious than the honor of an Army. As for *raison d'état*?, it was no more than a convenient cloak for covering up the ignorance, stupidity, or skullduggery of an oligarchy. "Yes, it is the intellectuals, and not the generals, not the bawlers of *La Libre Parole* who embody the true traditions of the French conscience and the French mind. . . ." Paléologue thus passed a fine, even a fascinating evening. Despite all the scandals and baseness, France was decidedly a great country, for the drama in which it was convulsed was not lacking in greatness. "It pits against each other two sacred sentiments: the love of justice and the religion of patriotism."[31]

The love of justice . . . the religion of patriotism. . . . Paléologue would sleep well, lulled by such sentiments. From his prison, Alfred Dreyfus, "almost dying," wrote to his wife. He counted the hours, almost the minutes with whatever strength he had left. His "cerebral and nervous exhaustion was immense." He was afraid of dying.[32] He placed his trust in General de Boisdeffre. "It has been no more in General de Boisdeffre's power than in yours to bring things into the light. . . ."[33] "I want to wish that I will still have a minute of happiness on this earth; but what I have no right to doubt is that justice will be done; that justice be rendered to you and to our children. I will say to you, then: courage and trust."[34] Justice and patriotism were two realms Dreyfus was unable to separate. How could his country want to stifle justice? How could the Army, the government, and the Parliament stand for an innocent man to die in jail?

2

The Question Will Not Be Raised

Zola was preparing for his trial.[1] Barboux, president of the bar, an old republican convinced of Dreyfus's innocence, had declined the honor of representing him. Zola's revolutionary—or romantic—act frightened him. Bar President Henri du Buit had let it be known that he would accept the case "only on condition of entering a plea of insanity."[2] It was Louis Leblois, once again, who advised Zola to speak to Fernand Labori, who accepted enthusiastically.[3] Albert Clemenceau, Georges's younger brother, was to represent Perrenx, the managing editor of *L'Aurore*. Georges Clemenceau, who was not a lawyer, obtained from the presiding magistrate authorization to speak along with his brother, but not to ask questions.

A defense committee was organized, which grouped around Zola and his attorneys Ludovic Trarieux, Louis Leblois, Joseph Reinach, and Mathieu Dreyfus, who remained somewhat at a distance, not to give the appearance of overinvolvement in a trial other than his own.[4] Léon Blum, an extremely fine jurist, placed himself at Labori's disposition. He prepared the delicate questions of penal law and was to write up a large number of the conclusions presented by Labori throughout the trial.[5] It was decided to call nearly two hundred witnesses: Ministers of War Mercier and Billot; all the chiefs of the General Staff and their collaborators; the seven judges who had acquitted Esterhazy;[6] Esterhazy himself; General de Pellieux; Commandant Ravary; Picquart; Leblois; Captain Lebrun-Renault; Major Ferdinand Forzinetti, commandant of the Cherche-Midi prison; Edgar Demange; President of the Bar Salles; the handwriting experts called in for the two previous trials; the former president Casimir-Périer; the Cabinet ministers of 1894; a large number of politicians, including Auguste Scheurer-Kestner, Arthur Ranc, Jean Jaurès, and Ludovic Trarieux; intellectuals (as they were beginning to be called), including Anatole France, Emile Duclaux, and Edouard Grimaux; archivists; professors at the École des Chartes and the Collège de France to perform scientific analyses of the bordereau; journalists; foreign diplomats; and military attachés, including Panizzardi and Schwarzkoppen. Up until February 7, it would be necessary to spend day and night preparing the questions to be put to each witness. The aim was evident. It was a matter of seizing the opportunity provided by the Zola trial to demonstrate Dreyfus's innocence and Esterhazy's guilt. Beyond that, for some in Zola's entourage, it would be an occasion to bring the Army to trial. In the Palais a trial of such dimensions had never been seen. It was scheduled to take up fifteen sessions, from February 7 to 23. Presiding Judge Delegorgue, a "big and rotund man who was neither mean nor lacking in sense or wit,"[7] was manifestly divided between the haughty pleasure of presiding over such a huge affair and his concern not to cause the government displeasure. The prosecuting magistrate's role was taken by Advocate General Edmond Van Cassel, who was "surly and brutal." He would be quickly overwhelmed by events.

On the defendants' bench would sit Zola, receiving hundreds of messages, and Perrenx, timid in his "Sunday suit." Behind them were Labori and his collaborators, the lawyers Hild and Monira, and the Clemenceau brothers, "two editions of the same man, Vendeans with energetic features, vivid and penetrating eyes that promised a battle."[8] Never before had so large a crowd, agitated by so many passions, invaded the Court of Assizes. Lawyers piled in alongside officers, elegant women, journalists, and actors. Parisian high society, accustomed to theatrical premiers, did all it could to snatch up the few passes available.

The jurors consisted of two wholesale merchants, a stockholder, a linen-draper, a wine merchant, an agricultural contractor, a brass setter, an employee, a wire-maker, a tawer, a corn-chandler, and a market-gardener. "Little people," observed Joseph Reinach, who characterized them solely by their profession.[9] As soon as the trial began, Van Cassel, whose distrust was aroused by the number of witnesses listed, asked that the debate be restricted by court order to the single grievance retained in the minister of war's complaint, the offense against Esterhazy's judges. "We do not have the right to call indirectly into question a case that has been duly adjudged. What they want is a revolutionary revision." Labori, then Albert Clemenceau, argued the inseparability of the charges against Zola. The Court issued a first order limiting discussion in conformity with the conclusions of the public prosecutor. The defense did not appeal, "agreeing to do battle in that narrow pass,"[10] and the trial began.

It was, throughout, "a prodigious struggle,"[11] wrote Mathieu Dreyfus who abstained from coming to the Palais in order not to provoke disturbances. It was also a "grandiose and dramatic spectacle"[12] pitting the combatants face-to-face, deepening day by day the ditch separating "the men of the revision and the men of the resistance."

Lucie Dreyfus, "the widow of the living corpse," came to the first session. Dressed in black, extremely pale, trembling before the large audience, she could not utter a word. As soon as Labori had asked his first question—"What do you think of Emile Zola's good faith?"—the presiding judge interrupted the lawyer with a formula that would be repeated thereafter hundreds of times. "The question will not be raised." Lucie Dreyfus remained silent at the witness stand as the procedural battle began. The Court issued a new judgment: "The judge has rightly refused to pose to Madame Dreyfus the questions solicited by the defense." Whereupon there began a procession of all the actors of the Affair. Leblois testified shrewdly, and related the matter of the bogus telegrams. Scheurer-Kestner described at length the genesis of his convictions. But the judge refused him the right to read the letters exchanged between General Gonse and Picquart.* Then came Casimir-Périer, who provoked an ovation from the revisionists by beginning with the words, "I am a simple citizen at the order of my country's justice." But a new order from the Court forbade him from answering the questions of the defense.

During the evening of the first session there was fighting in the galleries of the Palais. Zola, who was awaited by an enormous, threatening crowd, could leave only under the personal protection of the police prefect. In the street, the anti-Semitic agitator Jules Guérin was leading his groups. The Dreyfusards were taunted and assailed. There were shouts of "Death to the Jews," "Death to the traitors," "Kikes to the water." The windows of Jewish-owned shops were smashed, workshops invaded, machines broken. Such demonstrations would continue throughout the trial.† "This is the people's noble fury," observed *La Libre Parole* of February 12.[14] "If there's one thing that must smell bloody awful, it's grilled kike." *Le Siècle* and *L'Aurore*, on the other hand, supported Zola and Dreyfus's cause quite resolutely.

On the following days, generals and officers of the Intelligence Service came to the stand. The first was General de Boisdeffre, in uniform, wearing the badge of the Legion of Honor, "distinguished, calm, without stiffness." He affirmed that "Dreyfus's guilt has always been a certainty." Pressed by Labori with questions, he continued invoking the prior verdict

---

* Joseph Reinach would have them published the next day in *Le Siècle* and *L'Aurore*.
† "Every day," wrote Labori, "Zola came to pick me up on Rue de Bourgogne. We would go to the Palais together. We would arrive amid a huge crowd of adversaries and friends, simultaneously hooted and acclaimed."[13]

or state secrets in order not to respond. After him, General Gonse repeated his chief's deposition. Then came General Mercier: "haughty,
imperturbable, precise, disdainfully entrenched in the awareness of his
own infallibility."[15] He denied that "he had boasted of having communicated secret documents to the Court Martial." But he refused to respond
as to the very existence of the secret documents. Like de Boisdeffre, he
swore that Dreyfus was guilty. "I have no reason to return to the Dreyfus
trial. But if I did, since my word as a soldier has been requested, it would be
in order to say that Dreyfus was a traitor who has been justly and lawfully
convicted." Commandant du Paty de Clam then made a deposition which
was much noted. Buttoned tight at the waist in his finest uniform, a
monocle riveted to his eye, he crossed the courtroom with the cadenced
step of a Prussian military parade, stopped like a robot two feet from the
stand, heels together, knees braced, back arched, saluted the Court and
the jury in military fashion and waited, stiffly, as would a soldier before his
superior officers. Once the oath had been taken, he refused to answer
most of the questions. He then saluted the Court and the jury, pivoted, and
left the room, pursuing his earlier formality amid laughter and sarcasm.[16]
After that singular spectacle, came Colonel Henry's deposition. To all
appearances, he had but a single preoccupation, which was to finish his
testimony as soon as possible. Ruddier than ever, he claimed to be sick,
congested with fever. He came armed with a medical certificate. Clutching
the stand, according to Reinach, "with his terrible butcher's hands" to
support himself, he claimed not to understand the questions, said he was
"in a stupor as a result of a night of insomnia and medication. . . ." He
remained more or less mute, moving, and pitiful until he withdrew at the
express request of General Gonse. "Colonel Henry is extremely ill; he has
made a great effort to be here; I ask the Court to authorize him to
withdraw."[17]

Next, Alphonse Bertillon, the handwriting expert, took the stand. He
provided the court with a few hours of amusement. He explained why the
bordereau was surely Dreyfus's work:

In order to guide his handwriting, the writer of the bordereau
made use of a kind of transparent template inserted at every line
beneath the tracing paper of the bordereau. The template consists
of a double chain: the first chain is composed by the word "*intérêt*"
raced end to end indefinitely and meshing with each other; that is
written in such manner that the initial *i* merges with the final *t*
preceding it; the second chain is identical to the first, but displaced
1.25 mm. to the left.

The transparent template is traced from the word *intérêt* which concludes a letter found in Dreyfus's blotter. The word itself is not written naturally, but constructed geometrically.[18]

And in front of the blackboard, he defended his famous diagram, expressed surprise that the facsimile of the bordereau had not reproduced the "point of the blotter," but declared himself incapable of answering Labori's question of whether the point should be placed "in the arsenal or in the trenches." Furious at provoking the hilarity of all present, Bertillon protested that after his death, he would be judged "from the point of view of history." He accused the lawyers of tormenting him. Then, on the verge of collapse, he decided to seek "shelter in the future behind the court order forbidding discussion of the Dreyfus Affair." The judge, who was for once irritated by testimony hostile to Zola, but which managed to provoke the laughter of the generals themselves, concluded: "Let us say that the witness does not want to speak." And the unhappy Bertillon withdrew amid hoots of laughter as Labori observed: "Here is the accusation of 1894. There is a single charge: the bordereau. And there is the principal expert."[19]

Esterhazy testified only at the end of the trial. He had begun looking increasingly sinister and agitated as the hearings went on, prophesying at times that "the streets of Paris would be strewn with 100,000 corpses before the end of this miserable affair," at times that if Dreyfus were to set foot in France again, "there would be 5,000 Jewish corpses in the streets of Paris," and warning that he had the intention "of not merely speaking but of taking action in the courtroom." Finally, he agreed to submit to the prudent silence imposed on him by General de Pellieux, who had become his protector. Esterhazy came to the stand, and with his arms crossed, silent, his eyes in constant motion, he listened—without answering—to the questions posed by Labori and then to the sixty questions prepared by Albert Clemenceau on the subject of his life, his letters to Mme. de Boulancy, his swindles, and his forgeries. For more than thirty minutes,[20] while the lawyer hammered out his precise and devastating questions, waiting in vain for an answer, then returning with renewed emphasis on his every word, Esterhazy kept his silence, looking pale, desperate, and tragic. For one of Clemenceau's questions, the judge had to come to the witness's aid: "Does Commandant Esterhazy acknowledge . . . having had relations with Colonel von Schwarzkoppen?" "Let us not speak, Maître Clemenceau, of officers belonging to foreign countries." "Why not, Mister President?" "Because there is something which is above everything else, and that is the honor and the security of the country." "From which I conclude, Mister President, that the honor of the country allows an officer to perform these acts but not to speak of them." After which, Esterhazy, almost fainting, returned to his seat in the audience amid a crowd of officers in uniform who gave him an ovation.

Was there a risk that the Affair would turn out poorly for the General Staff? Despite the insistence of the presiding magistrate on confining the trial within narrow limits, despite the determination of officers punctuating the proceedings with their words of honor, Labori and Clemenceau had scored a number of points throughout the hearings. There were too many awkward silences, embarrassments, and abrupt retreats behind the "prior verdict," *res judicata*. Too many appeals to *raison d'état*. On several occasions, the defense had achieved a clear advantage.

The first major breakthrough was during the testimony of the most eagerly anticipated of witnesses, Colonel Picquart. He stepped up to the stand "quite rapidly, quite erect in his blue uniform braided with gold, tall, thin, supple, looking young at age 43, his eyes narrow and his gaze distant, his face closed, his expression a bit fatigued." He seemed a man of meditation, as much an artist as a soldier.* With tranquil courage and frequent intervals of silence, his voice at times choking, he related for more than an hour, amid general fascination, how he had discovered Esterhazy's treason and all that had followed. He spoke with moderation of the maneuvers and then of the hatreds whose victim he had been, without voicing any complaint, but expressing, nevertheless, his sadness at having been expelled from the Army. Maurice Paléologue found him to be inhibited, "hesitating to take a stand between the duties of professional discipline and the risks of open rebellion, much as would a priest who—having strayed into a theological controversy—might feel hovering above him the lightning of anathema and excommunication."[21] Others perceived in his moderation, on the contrary, a certain cleverness, "the sign of a cunning and two-faced mind." He was "of the race of the great felines."[22] In point of fact, that manner was his very style. To all matters, Picquart applied the same seriousness, the same sense of exactitude, always disciplining his passion. "More warmth would not hurt," noted Reinach. "A little emotion would be appreciated."[23] The same criticism would later be made of Alfred Dreyfus at Rennes. What is certain is that in concluding his deposition, he left a great impression. The revisionists, including a number of lawyers in judicial robes, gave him an ovation. An odious demonstration: the military witnesses considered themselves insulted. A lawyer was even heard to shout, "Long live Picquart!" At the court's recess, General de Pellieux, leading the other officers, issued a protest. "Long live

* In *Jean Santeuil*, Marcel Proust describes "the oblique bearing of his head . . . the extremely fine timbre of his voice. . . . His long deposition was continually marked by a swaying of his body from right to left. . . ." (*Jean Santeuil*, 1952, vol. II, pp. 134ff).

Picquart," claimed the general, meant "Down with the Army." In the name
of the *Ordre des avocats*, its presiding officer Ployer, with ceremonial cap in
hand, led a procession of his colleagues to beg the generals' pardon, and in
order to reassure them, they cried out twice in the corridors of the Palais:
"Long live the Army!"

After the intermission, Picquart was confronted with a number of
officers—his former subordinates—who, of course, bore down on him
quite harshly. Henry, who was more or less recovered but still fragile,
returned to the stand. Picquart had little trouble putting him in a difficult
situation. Henry admitted that if he had said that he had seen Leblois
going through the secret file with Picquart, it was in a "figurative sense."
And then, suddenly apoplectic, banging on the stand with his hand, he
thundered, "And I, I stand by everything that I said and I will add that
Colonel Picquart has lied." Picquart, livid, his teeth clenched, restrained
his temper* and then suddenly, forgetting all prudence, revealing his
passionate soul, he "burned his bridges," and said everything that he had
been holding back for months.

> You will understand it when you learn that these same men, Henry,
> Gribelin, aided by du Paty and directed by Gonse, were the princi-
> ple artisans of the other affair!. . . At the time, I am prepared to
> believe they were heeding their conscience, believing that they
> were proceeding in truth. They then received from Colonel Sand-
> herr, who already at the time of the affair was stricken with a
> serious illness from which he has since died, instructions, as a kind
> of last will, to defend against attack the verdict which was the honor
> of the Bureau!
>
> As for myself, I thought otherwise when I was at the head of the
> Service, and since I had my doubts, I wanted to be enlightened and
> believed there was a better way to defend a cause than locking
> oneself into blind faith.
>
> Gentlemen of the jury, it has now been I don't know how much
> time, months that I have been heaped with insults by newspapers
> that are paid to spread such slander and untruth. . . . For months, I
> remained in the situation most horrible for an officer, since my
> honor was attacked and I was unable to defend myself! Tomorrow,
> perhaps, I will be expelled from the Army that I love and to which I
> have given twenty-five years of my life! That did not stop me, when
> I thought it my duty to pursue truth and justice. I did so, and in so
> doing I believed I was rendering a greater service to my country

---

* They would fight a duel on March 5. In the course of an impassioned encounter, Henry
would be wounded in the arm.

and to the Army. It was thus that I believed it incumbent upon me to perform my duty as an honest man.

Then he returned to the reserve from which he had emerged for a moment of superlative anger, as Albert Clemenceau proceeded to press Henry, increasingly embarrassed and—once again—ill, with questions.

The defense achieved a further advantage during the hearing of its expert witnesses, archivists, and scholars, including Professors Paul Meyer and Auguste Molinier, from the École des Chartes and Louis Havet, from the Collège de France; most devastating was the testimony of Giry, a professor at the École des Chartes and the École des Hautes Etudes, who came not merely to say that Bertillon's theses were insane, something that the Court and the jury already suspected, but that the handwriting of the bordereau was "fluent," without hesitation, and that it was identical to Esterhazy's. "The bordereau and Esterhazy's letters are written by the same hand in the same script," affirmed Auguste Molinier.[24] On that day, the General Staff could sense the faint premonition of defeat.

It was then that General de Pellieux, elevated to the role of leading actor, plunged into the conflict. On February 16, he opened fire, quite candidly, with a veritable plea on behalf of Esterhazy, with whom he could be seen endlessly conferring. These so-called scholars were merely "amateurs," who had only been able to work from photographs. Moreover, the whole matter of handwriting was secondary. Pellieux applied himself to demonstrating that Esterhazy did not know any of the documents referred to in the bordereau, whereas Dreyfus knew them all. And quite quickly he turned to the jury, allowing his soldier's indignation to overflow:

> What do you want this Army to become on the day of danger, which may be closer than you believe? What do you want the poor soldiers, who will be led into fire by leaders that have been discredited in their eyes, to do? It is to the slaughterhouse that your sons would be led, gentlemen of the jury! But Zola would have won a new battle; he would write a new *Dèbâcle*; he would carry the French language throughout the universe, in a Europe from which France would have been expunged on that very day.

The jurors listened to him in a state of great emotion. In the courtroom, officers were standing to better witness this appeal. And with consummate craft, Pellieux began his peroration:

> I will not be contradicted by my comrades: the revision is of little

concern to us; it is even a matter of indifference. We would have been happy had the Court-Martial of 1894 acquitted Dreyfus; it would have proven that there was not a traitor in the Army, and we are still in mourning over that fact. But what the Court-Martial of 1898 would not admit, the abyss it would not negotiate, is this: it did not want an innocent man to be put in the place of Dreyfus, be he guilty or not. I have finished.

"A superb swordsman," in Paléologue's words, "deploying in the service of his conviction the ardor, eloquence, and fearlessness of a believer attesting to his faith,"[25] Pellieux was applauded at length. But once again Picquart took the stand. He demonstrated that Esterhazy had quite easily obtained all the information listed in the bordereau. Confronted with Gonse and Pellieux, he was still imposing. And then, after recess on February 17, Pellieux suddenly asked to return to the stand. He found a pretext in the fact that the lawyers had given a public reading of a passage in d'Ormescheville's report for the first Court-Martial. That was, he observed, a document relating to the Dreyfus Affair. The "pact of silence," he said, which the officers, for their part, had scrupulously observed, had been broken and he was thus free to tell all. For the first time, he was going to speak to the Court of the "devastating" document which could be found in the Ministry.*

I will repeat the quite characteristic words of Colonel Henry. You want the truth? Well, here we are!

At the time of the Castelin interpellation, there occurred an event that I would like to bring to your attention. We had at the Ministry of War—and note that I am not speaking of the Dreyfus Affair—absolute proof of Dreyfus's guilt! And that proof I saw. At the time of the interpellation, there came to the Ministry of War a paper whose origin cannot be contested and which says—I will tell you what it contains: "There is going to be an interpellation concerning the Dreyfus Affair. Never disclose the relations we had with the Jew."

And gentlemen, the note is signed, not with a name that is known, but accompanied by a personal card, and on the back of that card there is an insignificant meeting noted and signed with a made-up name which is the same as that of the document. And the personal card bears the name of the person. . . .

This is what I have been anxious to say!

* That is: the "Henry forgery."

Had Pellieux received an assignment from the General Staff to strike that blow because, as Mathieu Dreyfus wrote, "the generals in their panic decided at that point to make one supreme and decisive effort to crush Dreyfus once and for all?"[26] The hypothesis is dubious. De Boisdeffre and Gonse knew or suspected that the document furnished by Henry was not authentic. And their entire effort until then had consisted in making use of it in testimony without ever producing it. Pellieux's outburst seemed a grave error.* He ran the risk of being obliged to produce the forgery, which the defense would then discredit. No doubt Pellieux was acting alone, carried away by his convictions, by the pull of the role that he was taking in the debate, and irritated as well (since he was not aware that the document was a forgery) that the General Staff hesitated to exhibit—"to be over with it once and for all"—the conclusive proof of Dreyfus's treason.

At the time, Pellieux scored a triumph. The trial seemed to be over. Labori pretended to be dumbfounded. In point of fact, he knew from Scheurer-Kestner (who had it from Billot) of the existence of the document, and it is probable that he was also aware of the doubts entertained as to its authenticity.[28] He immediately grasped the jeopardy in which Pellieux's intervention risked placing the General Staff. He requested that the document be included as part of the proceedings.

> After something like this, it can no longer be a matter of restraining or restricting the scope of courtroom debate. May General de Pellieux allow me to very respectfully bring to his attention that there is no item, whatever it be, which has any value at all and which scientifically constitutes a proof before it has been submitted to adversarial debate. . . . Whatever respect I may have for General de Pellieux's word as a soldier, I cannot accord the slightest importance to this document. So long as we do not recognize it, so long as we have not discussed it, so long as it will not have been made publicly known, it will not count. . . .

General Gonse saw the disaster in the offing and attempted to parry the blow. "The Army does not at all fear the light. It does not at all fear saying where the truth is in order to save its honor. But prudence is needed; and I do not at all see how one can publicly bring here evidence of that nature, which exists, which is real, which is absolute." Once again, the appeal was to *raison d'état*. Pellieux understood his error. But borne on by his success, he called to his aide-de-camp Commandant Delcassé, to find

* Marcel Thomas refers to Pellieux's declaration as an "enormous blunder," which in the long run would "deliver up the key to Henry's machinations."[27]

General de Boisdeffre immediately. Pellieux was by then master of the courtroom. The judge would not dare to interrupt him. The general berated the public. "I will ask not to be interrupted by sneers. . . . I have had about enough." And he went still further: "And there are other documents, which General de Boisdeffre will describe."*

De Boisdeffre was heard on the following day.† Calm, buttoned tight into his large uniform, in a slow and energetic voice he spoke a text which had plainly been learned by heart. "I will be brief. I confirm on all points General de Pellieux's deposition as being exact and authentic. I have not a single word more to say; I don't have the right to; I say again, gentlemen, I don't have the right to."

He bore down on the words "I don't have the right to," indicating that relations with Germany were at stake, and that there was a threat of war. And he went on, more gravely still, raising his voice a bit. "And now, gentlemen, allow me, in conclusion, to say one thing: You are the jury, you are the Nation. If the Nation does not have confidence in the leaders of its Army, in those who bear the responsibility for the national defense, they are ready to relinquish that onerous task to others. You have but to speak. I will not say a single word more."

And he withdrew, to an accompaniment of applause. Labori protested that he had questions to ask, but Judge Delegorgue refused him the floor. "The incident is closed." Amid hoots and outcries, Labori developed his conclusions, requesting the communication of a document which "offered no semblance of value or authenticity." "That is the ultimate indecency," the judge cut him short. And the Court rejected Labori's conclusions. At that point Zola's lawyers considered leaving the courtroom, then decided against it.

In order to avoid producing a document he knew to be false, the chief of the General Staff had thrown the generals' sword into the balance. "The Third Republic no longer exists, . . ." an English newspaper, the *Westminster Gazette,* would comment. "General de Boisdeffre's *coup d'état* differs from Napoleon's only in the degree of brutality of the attendant circumstances." Clemenceau would be indignant: "A threat of imminent war, the slaughter announced, the resignation of the General Staff ready to be tendered . . . no more is needed to bring twelve trembling citizens to the point of making the law bow before the saber."[30]

---

* As a precaution, on the morning of Boisdeffre's testimony, Pellieux had Lauth give him the principal items "devastating" Dreyfus.[29]

† Proust describes him thus in *Jean Santeuil:* "He seemed quite calm, quite slow, although clearly rather preoccupied. . . . As he passed, hats were removed and he saluted with great politeness . . . blinking at times, stretching out his stiff leg, stopping, drawing out his mustache, passing his hand over his reddened cheek like an old warhorse that he himself would have tired out. . . ." (*op. cit.,* vol. II, p. 124).

"What Pellieux has done is idiotic," Henry commented to his friend Paléologue, quite aware of the consequences.[31] As were Gonse and de Boisdeffre. But for the moment, de Boisdeffre's moving and threatening intervention had reestablished a measure of order. And the chief of the General Staff had posited the principle which would dominate the entire debate for the Army: to doubt the authenticity of a document held by the General Staff, to doubt the word of its generals, was to declare oneself in opposition to the Army, to declare its leaders incapable, and to threaten the country's defense. De Boisdeffre had cast into the debate not only the honor of the Army, but the defense of the imperiled nation.

For the moment, de Boisdeffre had won the battle. Nothing further could reverse the course of the trial. It was in vain that Picquart returned the next day, affirming that the document of which General de Pellieux had spoken could not but be a forgery.* In vain as well was Jean Jaurès's superb deposition, addressing the jurors, and beyond them the people, describing the terrible role played by General Mercier, provoking applause even among his adversaries. In vain did Emile Duclaux and Anatole France step up to bolster Zola with the testimony of their admiration and solidarity. On the morning of February 21, the prosecution began the dull, dismal, and long drawn-out summary of its case. It managed to arouse consternation even among the "patriots," who were keyed up to hear an impassioned accusation. The courtroom, filled with officers and other supporters who had come en masse,† was disappointed by the prosecutor's speech, which resembled, in the words of *La Libre Parole*, "falling rain, a winter's rain, monotonous and cold, without lightning," or "a drizzle from a grey sky," as the pseudonymous Séverine was to put it in *La Fronde* of February 22. Zola answered the advocate general, reading a text that he had prepared, in order to reach the jurors' hearts:

> You are the heart and the reason of Paris, of my great Paris, where I was born, and of whom I have been singing for almost forty years. . . . I can see you with your families in the evening by a lamp. . . . In striking me, you will only make me greater. . . . Whoever suffers for truth and justice becomes august and sacred. . . . Dreyfus is innocent, I swear it . . . by my forty years of work, I swear that Dreyfus is innocent.

* It will be recalled that the document had been concealed from Picquart at the time of its "discovery." Pellieux took the floor again to denounce "the attitude of a gentleman who is still wearing the uniform of the French Army and who has come here to the bar of justice to accuse three generals of having fabricated a forgery or of having made use of one."[32]
†.Placed by the royalist lawyer Jules Auffray, who had accepted the assignment from the General Staff of "doing the courtroom."

"He spoke," according to Reinach, "like the characters in Victor Hugo when they make a political speech."[33] His voice was so drowned out by jeers, so interrupted by insults that he could barely be heard. Labori then argued for three sessions. Zola asked him to plead for Dreyfus more than for himself. Sidestepping the violence that had marred numerous incidents in the trial, arguing with care, Labori, mastering his emotion, pursued the implacable demonstration of Dreyfus's innocence. He concluded with a few ringing lines about the Army's honor. "May your verdict mean several things: first of all, 'Long live the Army!'—I too want to shout: 'Long live the Army! . . .' But also 'Long live the Republic!' and 'Long live France!' that is: 'Long live justice!' 'Long live the eternal ideal!'"

Applause broke out, combined with an uproar. The officers banged the floor with their scabbards. In the middle of the courtroom, Paul Déroulède, the leader of the Ligue des Patriotes, shouted his indignation.

It was then George Clemenceau's turn to argue for Perrenx. Amid the unrelenting uproar, he explained that "there were the greatest presumptions that Dreyfus was innocent." He offered a critique of *raison d'état* and *res judicata,* the authority of a prior verdict. He provoked laughter when he pointed to the Christ hanging over the courtroom and cried out: "There you have your *res judicata!*" With Déroulède at their head, the patriots did not let up in their efforts to prevent him from speaking. He concluded emotionally: "It is up to you to decide less concerning us than concerning yourselves. We appear here before you. You appear here before history."

The advocate general replied, "Take as your guide the country's soul." Labori responded, reminding the jury that it was about to render a historic judgment.

But nothing could override the impression made by General de Boisdeffre. The deliberations lasted thirty-five minutes. By majority vote, Zola and Perrenx were deemed guilty. Attenuating circumstances were not acknowledged. Zola was sentenced to a year in prison, the maximum penalty, Perrenx to four months, and each to fines of three thousand francs. There were shouts of joy and acclamation greeting the verdict. Officers embraced each other. Slogans shouted a hundred times over during the trial were heard again. "Long Live the Army!" "Death to Zola!" "Death to the Jews!" The sinister uproar rose outside the Palais. Insulted and threatened, Zola walked out sadly, protected by his friends, still leaning on his cane. "They are cannibals," he said simply. Clemenceau would later comment, "Had Zola been acquitted, not one of us would have come out alive."[34]

Thus a jury of the people had convicted Dreyfus, as had the Army, this time "after a great public debate, in the open."[35] The trial, intended to serve Dreyfus's cause, ended with a third conviction. And the "heroic" act of *J'Accuse* would now have to be paid for by Zola. A year in prison. There were outbursts of joy all over France. "I will not attempt to describe," wrote Maurice Barrès in *Le Figaro* the next day, "the excitement, the fraternity, the joy of the day's end." All through the night and the following day, demonstrations erupted spontaneously or were organized. People ran through the streets jeering at Jews and acclaiming the Army. The bars of Lyon, Grenoble, Tours, and Le Mans voted motions of congratulations to the Army. Military circles hoisted the flag. Newspapers trampled on Zola, the foreigner, Dreyfus's employee; on Labori, "that lawyer of Germanic origin, married to an English Jewess"; on Picquart, "a divorcee whose children are being raised in Germany."[36] Zola's acquittal would have meant war, the journalist Henri Rochefort assured. But now, the order of the day was an end to the plots of Jews, foreigners, and traitors. It was the victory of France!

The next day, February 24, the prime minister drew the happy conclusions to be derived from the verdict before the Chamber: "There is at the present time neither a Zola trial nor a Dreyfus trial; there is no trial at all . . . all this has to stop. . . . As of tomorrow, all those who would continue the struggle would no longer be arguing in good faith. . . . We will apply to them the full severity of the laws, and if the arms at our disposal are insufficient, we will ask you for others."

On February 26, the minister of war had the president of the Republic sign the decree officially discharging Colonel Picquart for reasons of "grave misdeeds while in service" and liquidating his pension. For having testified in the trial, Professor Grimaux was deprived of his chair at the École Polytechnique. Leblois was relieved by Louis Barthou, the minister of the interior, of his functions as deputy mayor of the Seventh Arrondissement. Summoned to appear before the Paris Bar on March 22, Leblois was suspended for six months "for having consulted outside his office and betrayed to Scheurer-Kestner the confidence of his client."

And yet there were not many on that day after February 23 who were convinced that the Zola trial had definitively buried the Dreyfus Affair. Méline might repeat that "there is no more trial"; the Parliament might vote to post a speech which once again declared the Affair to be closed; but neither de Boisdeffre nor Mercier had any illusions. They would have to gird up for new battles that every victory seemed to make more difficult. Mathieu Dreyfus, who had been discouraged by Esterhazy's acquittal, regained hope.[37] It mattered little that Zola had been convicted. "We were convinced," assured Léon Blum, "that the Zola trial had been decisive for the Affair." What counted was "the slow advance of the proof, the logical progression of the truth."[38] In *La Revue Blanche,* Léon Blum drew up a balance sheet of the Zola trial.[39] The illegality committed in the 1894 trial had been established.* The absurdity of the attribution of the bordereau to Dreyfus had been demonstrated. The plots of the General Staff against Picquart had been publicly exposed. The suspicions weighing on Esterhazy "had accumulated with great probability, not to say certitude." Once again, in order to win a conviction, it was necessary to have recourse to a secret dossier, a document that was not entered into the proceedings. The Army had to throw its sword into the balance. That Zola had been convicted in no way impeded the truth in its march. . . .

Abroad it appeared that Dreyfus's guilt was less certain.[40] In Brussels, Saint-Petersburg, Warsaw, London, and New York, the press was unanimous the day after the verdict in deploring the French madness. The Affair, the Russian press explained, symbolizes the decadence of people hypnotized by the terror of truth. . . . "Paris is becoming a large village in Asia or Africa . . . in which justice is called the right of the strongest." "Zola's true crime," wrote *The Times* of London, "has been in daring to rise to defend the truth and civil liberty . . . for that courageous defense of the primordial rights of the citizen, he will be honored wherever men have souls that are free. . . ." "France is disappearing from the list of civilized nations," opined *The Daily Mail.* "The French Republic cannot and should not live," wrote an American newspaper, "if a military caste, Jew-devourers, or a mob of students can put it in a hysterical state impelling it to trample underfoot the freedom of its citizens." "Poor France, what a regression," wrote *Le Genevois.* The Belgian essayist, Count Maurice Maeterlinck, referred to the French revolutionary Joseph Sieyès's famous line: "They want to be free; they don't know how to be just," and the poet Emile Verhaeren wrote, "In what has by now become this historic Dreyfus Affair, all of Europe defended the spirit of France against France itself." But who read those newspapers in France, and who listened to those writers? Méline had received the virtually unanimous approval of Parliament. "We are defending the good name of France abroad." He was above all defending the longevity of his government.

Similarly, it mattered little that the German secretary of state, von Bulow, had declared on January 24 to the Budget Commission of the Reichstag, that "there have never been relations or dealings of any sort between ex-Captain Dreyfus, presently in detention on Devil's Island, and any German agent."[41] A large sector of the French press—*Le Gaulois, Le Soleil, Le Petit Journal,* and *La Libre Parole*—replied by mocking the declarations of the German minister, which were obviously intended to dis-

---

* By the testimony of *bâtonnier* Salles, who was prevented from speaking by the presiding judge. By that of Maître Demange, relating the confidences of *bâtonnier* Salles. Above all by the "silences" of General Mercier.

credit France. Similarly, on February 1, when Count Bonin, the Italian undersecretary of foreign affairs, made an identical statement to the Italian Chamber ("We are in a position to affirm as explicitly as possible that neither our military attaché nor any other agent or representative of the Italian government has ever had any relation—be it direct or indirect—with ex-Captain Dreyfus"), the French newspapers reacted with derision and indignation.

The day after Pellieux's "blunder" in evoking a letter between the military attachés of Italy and Germany—from which it would appear that the two officers were committed to concealing their relations with Dreyfus—Italy's ambassador to Paris, Count Tornielli, wrote to Rome to express his indignation to his government. Both in writing and orally, he had already warned the French minister of foreign affairs that such a document did not exist, that it could only be a forgery.[42] Alessandro Panizzardi himself was growing indignant. On February 22, 1898, he wrote to his former friend, Maximilien von Schwarzkoppen, to express his anger.

> Our governments, we, and our ambassadors have given their word that Dreyfus is unknown to us. The chief of the General Staff, de Boisdeffre, has had . . . the nerve, despite all that, to say before a criminal court that they received proof of Dreyfus's guilt two years after his conviction via a letter that came into their hands. He took care, it is true, neither to say our names nor to identify our rank; but everyone knows that it is us. . . . He gave his word and swore to the authenticity of the document as though he himself had seized it in my place or yours, disavowing not only our declarations and those of our governments, but also designating us as dishonest, as liars.
>
> And to you all that probably sounds like nothing! I regret to inform you that on that score not only am I no longer of your opinion, but I am of the belief that something must be done. At this point, it is no longer a matter of saving an honest man in order to convict the true culprit; it is a matter of saving our dignity and simultaneously giving a lesson to this de Boisdeffre, putting him in his place. . . .[43]

But the two friends, by this time, were somewhat estranged. Panizzardi had the feeling that he had been deceived. "I am asking if it would not have been better to admit everything at the beginning of the affair; by this point, you would be tranquil and as for me, although I am not implicated in the Esterhazy affair, neither would I be in the Dreyfus case, which, like the first, does not concern me at all. . . ." But what could Schwarzkoppen—who was bound by discipline and professional reserve—do? Could he publicly admit that Esterhazy had worked for him? He sought a compromise. He made a series of confidential statements to an Italian political columnist, Henri Casella, who had been recommended to him by Panizzardi. They dined together at the Kaiserhof on January 3 and 5. In Casella's presence, he stated categorically that Dreyfus was innocent. Concerning Esterhazy, he was alleged to have said, "I believe him to be capable of anything." But soon thereafter Schwarzkoppen learned that his much appreciated Casella was in fact working for Mathieu Dreyfus.[44] And that completed the estrangement of the two military attachés, each one reproaching the other for his indiscretions.

When Mathieu Dreyfus thought to bring the information furnished by the indiscreet Casella to Zola's defense, it was decided to decline such testimony by a witness who would relate in criminal court the confidential statements of the German miltary attaché. Neither Schwarzkoppen nor Panizzardi could effect any change in French public opinion. Their statements could only make the worst of impressions. . . . The muzzled Casella would seek revenge by publishing in Belgian newspapers in March 1898 the account of his meetings with Panizzardi and Schwarzkoppen. Then, in April and May, he would publish them in France, in *Le Siècle*, thus provoking a turbulent reaction. It was at that point and in that way that the German ambassador, Count Münster von Derneberg, would understand that he had long been deceived by his military attaché, who had been using Esterhazy and secretly engaging in espionage. Münster would send a written reproach to Schwarzkoppen a few months later. "I can demand of you, as your former superior, that you no longer deceive me, as you unhappily have done in this affair."*

But Schwarzkoppen would answer, draped in the folds of his duty, "I have never deceived Your Excellency. I have kept silent at given times about many things, because I thought it incumbent upon me to do so, but I have never knowingly told a lie or acted in a manner contrary to honor."[45]

The attaché had brazenly lied, but he had done so in the name of higher interests. And no doubt he was sincerely pained that his duty had forbidden him from telling the truth to his ambassador. Nor could he do anything to help Dreyfus. How could he acknowledge that Esterhazy had been employed by him as a spy from 1894 to 1897? Espionage allowed little margin for truth.

It is uncertain if, had Schwarzkoppen revealed his dealings with Es-

* Letter of December 19, 1898, from Münster to Schwarzkoppen on the subject of the *petit bleu*. In his answer of December 22, 1898, Schwarzkoppen would acknowledge being the author of the *petit bleu*.

terhazy, anything would have changed. Ever since 1897, the chiefs of the General Staff and most of the members of the French government could no longer fail to know that they were engaged in defending a German spy, that they were keeping an innocent man in detention on Devil's Island. But they were concerned with a different issue now, the honor of the Army and *raison d'état*.

3

Logicians of the Absolute

Z ola's resounding entry into the struggle, the impassioned trial which ensued, the great spectacle which was extended through newspapers, street demonstrations,[1] and public meetings, had at least one of the effects that had been hoped for. The Dreyfus Affair was henceforth to be pursued in the light of public opinion. Ever since the fall of 1897, what had begun to be called the Affair had gained a much larger audience. Mathieu Dreyfus's denunciation of Commandant Esterhazy, the parliamentary debates, and Esterhazy's acquittal had greatly occupied the press. But it was Zola who, in less than a month, had given the Dreyfus Affair its national dimension.

Zola's manifesto had the almost immediate result of encouraging and almost imposing a commitment on the part of all those—writers, teachers, scientists, and artists—who until then had hesitated to plunge into a judicial, military, or political struggle that did not concern them directly. Not that Zola was the first "intellectual" to take a stand. We should forget neither the courageous battle waged by the journalist Bernard Lazare, starting in August 1895, nor the action of those who—like Lucien Herr, Edouard Grimaux, Anatole France, Charles Andler, and Gabriel Monod—had demonstrated before December 1897 their sympathy for the cause of the deportee of Devil's Island. But those commitments were few and isolated, barely coordinated by the moral authority of men such as Herr, and taking place at meetings at individual homes. What was new on the morrow of the publication of *J'Accuse* was not only that involvement in the Affair—for or against Dreyfus—became natural for all those who pretended some influence or authority in the realm of ideas, but also that such involvement became collective. The role in the city of those who would be called intellectuals, assembled as an influence or pressure group by a community of beliefs or ideas, dates from the beginning of the year 1898.[2]

A first "petition for a revision," insisting on "the violation of juridical norms in the 1894 trial and the iniquities surrounding the Esterhazy affair," launched the day after *J'Accuse* by Zola and Emile Duclaux, gathered in a few days several hundred signatures, principally from academics, writers, scientists, artists, and poets. A group of young writers divided the task of collecting signatures: Fernand Gregh, Elie and Daniel Halévy, André Rivoire, Jacques Bizet, and Marcel Proust. A second petition, intended for the Chambre des Députés, requested "the preservation of legal guarantees for ordinary citizens." Every day it received additional signatures. From the Institute came the names of Monod, Duclaux, Grimaux, Frédéric Passy, Louis Havet, Charles Friedel, Arthur Guy, Paul Mages, Charles Richet, and Paul Viollet. From the Sorbonne, those of Gabriel Séailles, Charles Seignobos, Fernand Brunot, and Jean Psichari. "Older" academics, such as Lucien Herr, Charles Andler, Victor Berard, and Léon Blum, and younger scholars such as Charles Péguy, Jean Perrin, and Paul Langevin signed and had others sign. To be sure, those already enrolled in the battle—Joseph Reinach, Louis Leblois, Ludovic Trarieux, Auguste Scheurer-Kestner, Yves Guyot, Arthur Ranc, and Anatole France—signed readily. Artists (Gallé, Claude Monet, Clairin, Alfred Roll, and Eugène Carrière) and poets (Ratisbonne, Bouchos, Barbier) also adhered. To which may be added teachers, students, and sympathizers, whose names were gathered from the whole of France. Since the first signers of the petitions were men of letters and men of science, they were qualified by their adversaries as "intellectuals," a term already used by de Maupassant in 1879, then by Maurice Barrès in 1888, and which gained currency thereafter in small, hermetic, and elitist literary journals. The word, in its pejorative sense, would deprecate the vanity of men of thought who gave their opinion on public issues. It was proudly taken up by those it was intended to ridicule, and Georges Clemenceau, in *L'Aurore* of January 14, 1898, published the petition and its signatures under the title: "Manifesto of the Intellectuals." "In calling us intellectuals," observed Anatole France, "they were hurling an insult at intelligence, neither more nor less than that. They were making sport of people capable of understanding. These were slandered and outraged. It was said that they were getting mixed up in things that did not concern them. . . ."

The intellectuals—demi-intellectuals, as Barrès was to write in *Le Journal* of February 1—quickly became frequent targets of ridicule and insult.* "The mere fact," the critic Ferdinand Brunetière claimed, "that the word 'intellectuals' has been forged recently to designate as something in the order of a noble caste people living in laboratories and libraries is a condemnation of one of the most ridiculous foibles of our era—the pretention of raising writers, scientists, professors, and philosophers to the rank of supermen." Barrès denounced in still more vigorous terms

> this who's who of the elite, . . . who would not want to be part of it? Holders of a *licence* joined in and marched in closed ranks behind their teachers. A demiculture destroys instinct without replacing it with conscience. All these aristocrats of thought insist on flaunting the fact that they do not think like the vile multitude. That fact is all too clear. . . . These intellectuals are an inevitable waste product of society's effort to create an elite: in every operation, there are in this manner a certain percentage which must be sacrificed.[3]

What depressed Barrès was the presence of Anatole France among such simpletons. He looked for ways to excuse him. "Anatole France is less convinced of Dreyfus's innocence than of the general guilt. He acquits the traitor of Devil's Island only in order to condemn society."[4] But Barrès lashed out at all the others, theoreticians without roots, *métèques* like Zola or Jean Psichari, philosophers crushed by German influence, the ambitious, the perverts, at best young men athirst for illusions, men of abstraction for whom "the country is an idea," the one they find "most useful." "For example, the idea that all men are brothers, that nationality is a prejudice to be destoyed, that military honor reeks of blood. . . ."[5]

The flocking of intellectuals to Dreyfus's defense appears to have surprised the anti-Dreyfusards as a new and incongruous phenomenon. All the "logicians of the absolute" could not but have—in particular through the press—an influence and a public. It was not enough to oppose them, as did Brunetière, to appeal to the masses. The anti-Dreyfusard intellectuals themselves must organize. They would do so late, and as though in spite of themselves, since they found such collective action repugnant. The "Ligue de la Patrie Française," intended to unite them, would not be founded until the end of 1898. Directed by the writers François Coppée, Jules Lemaître, Ferdinand Brunetière, and Maurice Barrès, it took as its mission to defend, amid "the crisis of France" that

---

* In May 1898, Ferdinand Brunetière would publish under the title *Après le procès* a "Response to several 'intellectuals' ": "The intervention of a novelist—even a famous one—in a matter of military justice seems to me as out of place as the intervention, in a question concerning the origins of Romanticism, of a colonel in the police force" (Librairie Académique Perrin. p. 1).

began with the new year, respect for the nation and loyalty toward the Army, uniting all those in search of a "social discipline." It would very quickly enjoy a huge success.

In his analysis of the division in the literary world effected by the Dreyfus Affair in the course of the year 1898,[6] Christophe Charle has observed a massive commitment to the intellectuals' position—that is, to the revision of Dreyfus's trial—on the part of what he calls the "dominated pole," essentially represented by a literary or artistic "vanguard" of marginal individuals, as yet unrecognized poets, daring artists, writers such as Marcel Proust, Fernand Gregh, and Halévy of the *Banquet* group; André Gide of the *Conque* group; and above all the collaborators of *La Revue Blanche*, Stéphane Mallarmé, Charles Péguy, Léon Blum, Jean Psichari, Jules Renard, and Julien Benda. The Symbolists, Count Maurice Maeterlinck, Saint-Pol Roux, Paul Fort, and Verhaeren were a natural part of this camp. From this perspective, Dreyfusism appears to have been lived not as a passive position, but as a militant function, and for certain of its advocates, Péguy for example, as a "mystique." It was conceived of as a prolongation of individual autonomy, a refusal to compromise with institutions, the established order, and specifically the Army, the Church, and the realm of *res judicata*. The intellectuals were issuing a moral protest: "They were defending," writes Christophe Charle, "justice and law, which had been flouted, even as they defended pure literary values against the pressures of the marketplace and mercantilism."[7]

Inversely, anti-Dreyfusism would gradually attract the intellectuals of the "dominant pole," those, that is, who had received substantial social and institutional recognition. "Caught up in worldly pursuits, gratified by multiple honors, laden with decorations," they were essentially members of the Académie Française and the Institut and officially recognized poets, such as the Parnassians. Thus it was that *La Patrie Française* would group among its first partisans twenty-two members of the Académie Française. In joining the anti-Dreyfusist cause, Charles Bourget, Vincent Brunetière, Jules Lemaître, Pierre Loti, François Coppée, José Hérédia, and André Theuriet were defending a social order which had showered its blessings on them, established values with which they felt solidarity, the "sizable cultural and social capital" which they managed to have at their disposal. Within the University, Christophe Charle observes, the split occurred according to analogous criteria. The newer disciplines (like sociology, whose legitimacy was contested) or those that were evolving (like history) furnished the Dreyfusards with Emile Durkheim and Lucien Lévy-Bruhl, sociologists; Henri Hauser, an economic historian; and Gustave Lanson, the student of literary history.[8] On the other hand, historians of the Académie, such as Paul Thureau-Dangin, and professors of literature at the Sorbonne, such as Louis Petit de Julleville or Emile Faguet, were generally anti-Dreyfusard. Within the University, the polemic would thus oppose disciplines as much as men.[9] When Brunetière, in *La Revue des Deux Mondes* of March 15, 1898, denied intellectuals the right to call into question the Army and the courts in the name of a fallacious concept of individualism, it was Durkheim who responded:[10]

> If, then, in recent times, a certain number of artists, but especially of scientists, have deemed it their duty to refuse assent to a verdict whose legality appeared to them suspect, it is not because, as chemists or philologists, philosophers or historians, they have assumed for themselves I know not what special privileges and a right to veto duly delivered verdicts. It is rather because, being men, they intend to exercise their full rights as men and retain as their own a matter that falls within the jurisdiction of reason alone. It is true that they have shown themselves to be more jealous of this right than the rest of society; but that is simply because, as a result of their professional habits, it is closer to their hearts. Accustomed by the exercise of scientific method to reserve judgment as long as they are not informed, it is normal that they would yield less easily to the movements of the masses and the prestige of authority.

Thus Zola, in radically unsettling the world of ideas, forced intellectuals to be pitted against each other. Zola, as Charle observes, belonged to neither one nor the other of the two camps. He was located in an "intermediate" group, that of writers of "large-scale production," which included novelists and playwrights. Such writers, who were well known yet not part of the academic establishment, went toward one or the other camp, according to their age, temperament, conviction, or simply chance. Zola and Octave Mirbeau were Dreyfusard. Huysmans and Alphonse Daudet were anti-Dreyfusard. Jules Claretie, Ludovic Halévy, Victorien Sardou, Courteline, de Flers, Abel Hermant, Edmond Rostand, and Georges de Porto-Riche were Dreyfusard, and Lavedan and Edouard Pailleron anti-Dreyfusard.

Zola undoubtedly had all the qualities needed in order to polarize the realm of letters. He was capable of carrying along a large segment of lesser known writers. "For us," Léon Blum was to note, "he was an unexpected and inestimable ally." But for Dreyfus's enemies, he was a vulnerable writer: foreign, perverted, half-crazed, a man of wealth, a venal agent of the syndicate. He was not sacred, like Anatole France, for example, whose situation within the dominant pole would shield him from the harshest attacks.

Charle's analysis accounts nicely for the split among men of letters and also for the division within literary studies in the universities. It makes of the Dreyfus Affair an index for a kind of class struggle within the intellectual class, or rather for a struggle between rival movements within the dominant social class.[11] Writers thereafter would arrogate to themselves the role of leader, projecting onto the social sphere the crises and rivalries they experienced within the republic of letters. But Charle is forced to admit the existence of some important exceptions, which blur his linear split of the literary domain. Anatole France and Sully Prudhomme were Dreyfusard, but their official situation should have inclined them otherwise. Inversely, Paul Valéry, Léautaud, and Pierre Louÿs would long remain anti-Dreyfusard, even though they were only marginally established. Yet such exceptions do not invalidate an analysis which, in essential terms, gives a good account of the emerging division and of its causes.

It appears, however, that intellectuals of scientific training or discipline frequently elude Charle's criteria, which are more applicable to the realm of letters. In their case there came into play a rigorous concern for facts, the requirements of demonstration and logical proof, the very method which such intellectuals had acquired and were inclined to extrapolate to other areas of consideration. This explains, for example, the involvement of Edouard Grimaux, professor at the École Polytechnique, who characterized himself as "one of those chauvinistic patriots who start running when the troops begin to parade," but who testified as follows at the Zola trial:

> I must bring to your attention this rather odd movement of so many men of science, so many men of letters, of artists, of these men who do not follow the fluctuations of daily political reality and many of whom do not even know the names of the ministers! These men have left their laboratories, their studies, and their studios in order to make their voices heard because they have understood that what is at stake today is Liberty and the honor of the Nation.*

* A letter from Gaston Paris, Administrator of the Collège de France, sent on January 23, 1898, to Gabriel Hanotaux, minister of foreign affairs, expressed similar preoccupations. "The facts, moreover, are so clear that in order not to perceive them one has either to be blind or to close one's eyes. I am very unhappy, believe me, and there are many others in that situation with me. If I write as much to you, it is not in order to ask for an answer that no doubt you are unable to give me: it is to let you know what is being thought in the milieu to which you belong and that we were happy to see represented by you in the ranks of power, the world of sincere and disinterested men who search for truth and are accustomed to criticism, the world of the École des Hautes Études and the Collège de France." And from the Collège de France, Gabriel Monod would write to similar effect on February 20 to his friend Hanotaux: "The French have such a need for a creed and for masters that now that they no longer believe in God, they believe in the infallibility of the Army."[12]

A scrupulous investment in the truth, the spirit of research and free inquiry, in fashioning if not a mentality at least a method, thus played a role in the involvement of numerous intellectuals.* An additional factor to be taken into account is the imperatives of a secular morality, which influenced a majority of teachers at the time, and, beyond them, many intellectuals. Based on a respect for the individual, a tolerance for the opinion of others, an irreducible devotion to critical thought, "the superior form of the doubting mind," confused with the secular spirit itself, that morality may have been at the source of support, however timid, discreet, or, on the contrary, impassioned it may have been.

The "demi-intellectuals," the "logicians of the absolute," as yet had only a limited public. The few newspapers in which they could write, *L'Aurore* and *Le Siècle*, counted for little in comparison with the enormous influence of the anti-Dreyfusard press: what were the 200,000 subscribers to *L'Aurore* compared with the 500,000 readers of *La Libre Parole* the 1,500,000 readers of Judet's *Petit Journal*, which was hysterically anti-Dreyfusard, the 170,000 readers of *La Croix*, to which should be added all the provincial editions of *La Croix*, which numbered almost a hundred.[14] In 1898 the Dreyfusard press was less than 10 percent of the press, restricted essentially to Paris. The intellectuals, nevertheless, held a few bastions from which their influence might spread.

The first of these was the École Normale Supérieure, whose large majority was Dreyfusard.[15] Not only because of the personal influence of Lucien Herr, and also of Charles Andler, Gustave Bloch, Paul Dupuy, and Gabriel Monod, but above all, because the very spirit of the École was resolutely hostile to authority, permanent institutions, and, to be sure, the Army. The critical attitude was natural to its students. It had nothing in common with the "almost feudal" spirit that seemed to be embodied by the Army: hierarchy, obedience, and submission of the individual to the group. In addition, the École was on the whole anticlerical. The Church was distrusted because it was a hierarchical organization, and above all because it was a force for obscurantism and regression. Finally, the École disapproved of anti-Semitism in general. Many students and the most respected masters were Jewish.

Another center of action for Dreyfusard intellectuals was the Librairie Bellais, located at the corner of rues Cujas and Victor-Cousin, which opened its doors during the summer of 1898, thanks to the dowry of Charles Péguy's wife. The bookstore quickly became the meeting place not only of those who, like Péguy, were interested in socialist literature, but

---

* Madeleine Rebérioux has observed that the twofold method of the scholar—reasoning and verifying—characterized the work of many of those—archivist, researchers, historians—who became Dreyfusards. Rebérioux linked Jaurès' *Les Preuves* to that method.[13]

also of Dreyfusard intellectuals. Péguy recruited a handful of young
Normalians, socialist students enlisted to protect the Dreyfusard professors of the Sorbonne such as Louis Buisson, François Aulard, and Charles
Seignobos, who had been threatened by anti-Semitic gangs. When Péguy,
followed by his troops, stepped out of the Librairie Bellais, it was, he would
say proudly, the little army of Justice and Truth that ascended the rue
Saint-Jacques: "In those days, I was, so to speak, the military leader of the
former École Normale. Or rather there were two leaders. I was the military
leader on the days when there was fighting. Herr was the military leader on
the days when there was none."[16] Léon Blum relates that during the
Affair, he spent almost every morning in the bookstore. The Tharaud
brothers, Jérôme and Jean, frequently came to visit. As well as Albert
Thomas, and the physicists Paul Langevin and Jean Perrin. The writer
Romain Rolland came as well, until his quarrel with Lucien Herr.[17] "You
were wrong to tease me on the subject of our difference of opinions," he
wrote on February 1, 1898 to Herr.

> If I have no sympathy for either Picquart or Zola, it does not follow
> that Quesnay and Esterhazy do not make my stomach turn . . .
> that does not prevent the fact that the day on which you will
> be defeated, pursued, exiled, and perhaps shot (and I don't be-
> lieve that day is far off), I will be on your side, because in
> this conflict, victory—which ever it be—is what is most odious to
> me.

The Librairie Bellais—where friendship and enthusiasm were of the
essence—was, as Herr had predicted, on the brink of bankruptcy at the
end of its first year. It would have to be reconstituted in August 1899 by a
group of about twenty stockholders, almost all of them former students of
the École Normale, most of them Socialists, and all of them committed to
the fight for revision. More than the École Normale, which was republican,
anticlerical, antimilitarist, and antiracist, but Radical rather than Socialist,
the Librairie Bellais was a locus for young Socialist intellectuals attracted
to Dreyfus's cause.[18]

Although limited to a small circle, *La Revue Blanche* also played a role
that was not insignificant.[19] Under the influence of the Natanson brothers,
who had assumed editorship in 1891, it had evolved as of 1897 toward
Dreyfusism. Léon Blum, who had succeeded Lucien Muhlfeld on February 1, 1896, was then the resident literary critic. He would remain until
replaced by André Gide on February 1, 1900.* Starting in February 1898,

* André Gide, who was traveling with his wife in Italy at the time of the Esterhazy trial, was at
first extremely enthusiastic about Zola's *J'Accuse* and sent his signature for the *Aurore* petition

La Revue Blanche became involved in the case, protesting openly against the power of the military, "a concealed power capable of organizing unanimous verdicts when it wishes." For the first time, Lucien Herr dared to denounce Maurice Barrès, whom *La Revue Blanche* had always saluted as "the master writer of the age." On March 1, *La Revue Blanche* published a "homage to Zola," to whom it extended "ardent congratulations." Thereafter, the premises of *La Revue Blanche* were to become, along with those of the Librairie Bellais, one of the centers of militant Dreyfusism. It was there that were held the veritable war councils that would run on into the night. "The Dreyfus Affair is our passion," exclaimed Jules Renard. "For it, we would compromise women, children, and fortunes." From November 1898 to November 1899, Charles Péguy would contribute sixteen articles. Octave Mirbeau plunged into the battle unsparingly. Almost every evening, he would come to *La Revue Blanche*, opening the door with a crash, filling the waiting room with his resonant voice and his bursts of laughter. Jean Psichari was frequently there. Julien Benda would soon join them.[21] Mallarmé would stop in with an article. They would villify Jules Lemaître, who was emerging as the intellectual leader of the anti-Dreyfusards. If *La Revue Blanche* was not the fortress of an aristocracy of the spirit, whose mission, according to Julien Benda, would be "the slow formation of superior beings" under the influence of Blum, then of Benda, it was in any event the meeting place of a group committed to the cause of revision.

Yes, Zola had accomplished a miracle. It became increasingly rare to find writers, academics, or artists, who refused to take a stand. The calls to unity launched by *Le Temps* in the beginning of 1899 to gather the mass of those who did not wish to be "revolutionary or internationalist along with certain defenders of Dreyfus or anti-Semitic and nationalist with certain adversaries of Dreyfus," would attract only a few signatures, those of Sully Prudhomme; Victorien Sardou; Ludovic Halévy; the historian, Ernest Lavisse; and the writer, Abel Hermant. That effort at pacification would have no future. Even the world of salons was divided throughout 1898 between Dreyfusard salons, such as those of Mme. Strauss and Mme. de Caillavet, where Anatole France held sway, and anti-Dreyfusard salons, such as that of Mme. de Loynes, whose oracle was Jules Lemaître, and that of Mme. Adam, where Paul Bourget could be heard. And it was undoubtedly the intellectuals, whatever the limits of their public, who in their divisions and passions made of the Dreyfus Affair a national debate.

Another effect of their division was that, at the beginning of 1898, the

---

from Rome. It appears that later he was more hesitant and proved sensitive to the arguments of Paul Valéry, who was anti-Dreyfusard.[20]

Dreyfus Affair had ceased to be merely a fight on behalf of an innocent convict. Its scope had been limited as long as Mathieu Dreyfus, at first by himself and then with the aid of a few, had been organizing all efforts in favor of a revision. Henceforth, Dreyfus had become for many a symbol, and for some an instrument. The struggle was now against institutions, against hierarchy, against military authority, and against the Church as much as it was for Alfred Dreyfus, dying on Devil's Island. No doubt at the time those struggles were inseparable. But the battle in which hundreds of intellectuals had become involved far transcended an individual fate. For some it had become a political battle, for others a mystique. At stake was a moral cause, a society in which justice and equality would reign. "We would have died for Dreyfus," Péguy would proclaim.[22] "We did indeed plan," Léon Blum would write, "to transform the revisionist coalition into a permanent army in the service of human rights and justice."[23] That moral, mystical, and political coalition around the deportee of Devil's Island was serving his cause in 1898. Yet it harbored the potential for discord which would erupt when Dreyfus would later cease to be the hero of his own cause. In the same way, the anti-Dreyfusards had now nearly forgotten Dreyfus. Rather, they subsumed the "Jewish traitor," as a symbol, into their hatred of all the social and intellectual types that seemed to them cut off from the organic unity of their country: Jews, socialists, Protestants, liberal priests, emancipated women, striking workers, all those who threatened the stability and continuity of the true France.[24] "What was our aim?" Léon Blum asked. "To obtain the revision of an unjust sentence?"[25] It would remain so for some, but for many, in the course of the year 1898, the perspective was more vast and yet more vague as well. Eventually the deportee on Devil's Island might seem not at all to conform to his symbolic role, indeed to be a positive hindrance, in the immense confrontation that was fomenting. The "Affair Without Dreyfus" would soon begin.

But what was most remarkable was that the activism in the world of letters was not without its influence on the world of politics. In 1897, even in 1898, Méline was no doubt correct in saying that from a political point of view, there was no Dreyfus Affair. The near totality of the political world was anti-Dreyfusard—by instinct, prudence, or ignorance. And it was only individuals like Scheurer-Kestner, Trarieux, soon thereafter Clemenceau and Jaurès who one by one rejected the common belief that Dreyfus was guilty. Throughout the year 1898, the professionals of politics would begin—rather slowly, since the May 1898 elections inspired a certain distrust—to align themselves. The centrists, who rejected the Dreyfus Affair, would not resist. It is not the influence of the intellectuals alone which explains the breakup of the centrists, but it would help give shape to the split and fuel the political conflict with ideology. The division of interests and ideas which would take place at the end of 1898, and even more in 1899, separating, in sum, a Dreyfusard left from an anti-Dreyfusard right, would to a large extent follow the lines traced by the intellectuals. "It was the logic of the world of letters," observes Christophe Charle,[26] "which created this new division, redrawing the contours of the right and the left, giving militant ideologies to the parties in power, which had run out of ideas: nationalism on one side, anticlericalism and defense of the Republic on the other." Thus, Emile Zola had not merely staked out for the first time in France the role of intellectuals in the polity, he also revealed the capacity of intellectuals in French society to delineate political divisions, to open the way to new realignments. This trend would become increasingly familiar in the twentieth century.

4

The Fury of France

If the anti-Dreyfusard intellectuals, as though surprised by Zola's revolutionary stance and the concerted action following in its wake, were late in responding, anti-Semitic agitation, on the contrary, found in the publication of *J'Accuse* fuel for a brutal renewal.[1] The first wave of incidents broke out the day after Zola launched his "bomb." On January 17 in Nantes, 3,000 youths paraded through the streets shouting cries of death. Windows of Jewish storefronts were shattered, and an attempt was made to force open the synagogue door. That evening in Nancy, Jewish-owned shops were invaded and the synagogue besieged. At Rennes, a mixed crowd of 2,000 peasants and city dwellers attacked the homes of the Jewish professor Victor Basch, and of Professor Andrade, who had sent a letter, which had been published, to General Mercier. In Bordeaux, violent demonstrations erupted to cries of "Death to the Jews!" "Death to Zola!" and "Death to Dreyfus!" The police were barely able to prevent the pillage of Jewish shops. There were similar scenes in Moulins, Montpellier, An-

goulême, Tours, Poitiers, and Toulouse. On January 19 it became necessary to keep Jewish shops closed, and the dragoons were called in to
reestablish order. On January 21 at Angers and at Rouen, the cavalry had
to charge to prevent pillaging. On January 22, it was the Gendarmerie that
had to defend Jewish stores in Châlons. In Saint-Malo, Dreyfus was
burned in effigy in a public square. In Marseille, several thousand people,
led by a few young men, applauded the officers on the balcony of the
military club, broke the gates of the temple, and shouted death threats to
the rabbi, who had to be protected. During the last week in January the
riots shifted eastward. All of Lorraine was affected. In Epinal, Nancy, and
Bar-le-Duc, there were street processions and broken windows to repeated
cries of "Down with Zola! Down with the Jews!" Demonstrations attracted
4,000 people in Marseille and Bordeaux, 3,000 in Nantes, 2,000 in Rouen.
They lasted six days in Rouen, five days in Marseille and Bordeaux, four
days in Nantes, Dijon, and Châlons. Each time, the police had to intervene
to protect synagogues and Jewish commercial establishments. In Paris, the
anti-Semitic agitator Jules Guérin exercised his troops in the Latin Quarter, on the boulevards, and around the Palais de Justice during the Zola
trial. Huge placards were carried throughout the streets of Paris, bearing
the words: "Zola to the gallows. Death to the Jews." In *Le Figaro* of January
19, Guérin proclaimed that the people of Paris would henceforth hold two
hostages: Bernard Lazare and Joseph Reinach. Almost every evening
public meetings were organized, in which the Jews, Dreyfus, Zola, and the
syndicate were condemned to death. Religious services were celebrated
during which the officiant invited the faithful to continue the sacred battle
against the deicidal people.[2]

But it was in Algeria that a veritable crisis of anti-Jewish hysteria
occurred. Anti-Semitism had increased a good deal there in recent years.
The Crémieux decree of October 14, 1871, which had naturalized *en bloc*
all the Jews of Algeria, integrating them into the Republic, had been
rather poorly accepted by the majority of non-Jews. They saw in it a
scandalous act of favoritism on the part of the nascent Republic. More than
320,000 citizens of French origin had maintained the 50,000 Jews settled
in Algeria as an isolated community, living from commerce if not usury,
scorned by the Arabs, detested by the nonnaturalized foreigners
(Spaniards, Maltese, and Italians), antipathetic to all and, as a result,
withdrawn, self-absorbed, and unable to maintain a normal existence. As
of May 1897 cases of violence, stemming from Mostaganem, had erupted.[3]
Jewish stores had been pillaged, notably on May 20 in Oran, and
synagogues ransacked. Between January 18 and 24, 1898, bloody riots
broke out in almost all the cities of Algeria. Jewish shops were sacked and
the police, who frequently intervened ineffectively and late, counted a

number of casualties of its own. The fighting that began in Algiers on January 18 lasted for several days. Most of the Jewish bazaars were devastated. Christian shopkeepers were obliged to display placards reading "Catholic House" or "No Jew in the House." Every day Zola was burned in effigy. The mayor of Algiers attempted to flatter the population in order to reestablish order: "You are indignant at the doings of those who are trying to taint that sacred thing, the honor of the French Army. . . . But do not let that explosion of splendid sentiments degenerate into chaos." And further still: "You have given a superb demonstration of your French fury. Show now that you have calm and strength."[4] On the evening of January 22, the principal leaders, Pradelle, Lebailly, and a young student named Max Régis Milano, an agitator of rather proud aspect, of Italian stock, harangued a crowd of 6,000. Max Régis, who had had numerous duels with Jews, proposed to "water the liberty tree with Jewish blood." Langlois, a lawyer, proclaimed: "The Jews have dared to raise their heads. We must crush them." Attacked on January 22 and 23, the Jews defended themselves and their shops with sticks and rocks. A rioter was killed and numerous policemen wounded. Governor Lépine, who came to inspect the situation, was himself struck by a projectile, "amid the screams of a crowd gone delirious." No Jewish shop escaped the damage. On January 23, during the funeral procession of a rioter who was killed, several Jews were stoned, and one massacred with a bludgeon. More than 600 persons were arrested, more than 100 seriously injured. This was but the first wave of riots which would extend over several years. There was barely a day that passed in 1898 without an anti-Jewish demonstration erupting in Algeria. Régis gradually became the idol of a population that saw in him the most courageous of anti-Jewish militants. Tall, handsome, strong, and energetic, he was the object of a veritable cult: "our Jesus-Régis," as his loyalists called him. He would soon found a newspaper, *L'Antijuif*, which would immediately achieve a colossal success. Régis's bands could be found strutting through the streets everywhere, marking the rhythm of their anti-Semitic songs, including the "Marche Antisémite."

> A mort les Juifs! A mort les Juifs!
> Il faut les pendre
> Sans plus attendre
> A mort les Juifs! A mort les Juifs!
> Il faut les pendre
> Par le pif!
>
> (Death to the Jews! Death to the Jews!
> We must hang them

Without further delay
Death to the Jews! Death to the Jews!
We must hang them
By the nose!)

And the "Marseillaise Antijuive."

Il y a trop longtemps qu'nous sommes dans la misère,
Chassons l'étranger,
Ca f'ra travailler;
Ce qu'il nous faut, c'est un meilleur salaire,
Chassons de notre pays,
Toute cette sale bande de youdis!

(We have lived in misery for too long,
Let's chase out the foreigner,
That'll give us work;
What we need is a better salary,
Let's chase out of our country,
The whole filthy band of Kikes!)

In February 1898, Régis would offer Edouard Drumont, the editor of
La Libre Parole, the honor of being a candidate in the legislative elections
from Algiers's second ward. To the accompaniment of oft-repeated shouts
of "Long live the Army!" and "Down with the Jews," the author of *La
France Juive*, with Régis's backing, would conduct a victorious campaign
and would be elected in the first round on May 8 with a margin of 13,000
votes over his rival Samary. Four out of six Algerian deputies in May 1898
would be members of the "anti-Semitic caucus" in the Chamber. In
November, Régis himself would be elected mayor of Algiers. At that point,
Algerian anti-Semitism, a veritable mass movement, illustrated not merely
by the violence of its riots but by its electoral successes, would take on the
appearance of a challenge to the public powers.[5] If the agitation was tamer
in metropolitan France, where there was better control of the demonstrations, where anti-Semitism did not seem to receive (as was the case in
Algeria) true popular support, it was nevertheless the case that throughout
1898 and 1899, French society seemed in the process of isolating its Jewish
community.

During those two years Catholic anti-Semitism was to develop explo-
sively. A large number of Christian families nourished their children with
daily hatred for the Jews. François Mauriac relates that as a young boy it
was no surprise to him that his chamber pot was called "Zola," and that

beside him in the study hall at Catholic school "a little boy played at the degradation of Dreyfus, removing the wing of a fly, then a leg, then another wing."[6] In the private schools of the southwest, use was made of a reading book published in Toulouse, and recommended by several bishops,[7] in which could be read: "The Jews have been an accursed race since they sold Our Lord and failed to perceive His goodness. They tend to enslave all the nations on which they sweep down like so many vultures on a choice prey. They are dangerous and insatiable parasites who are to be found wherever there are crimes."* Numerous priests wrote and published anti-Jewish songs denouncing "the Jews and Masons . . . who want to devour a priest every day . . . and chase away the divine master, . . ." lumping together Judas, Rothschild, Dreyfus, and other scandalous Jews. The brothers of the Christian schools considered Dreyfus's guilt to be an untouchable dogma, of the same order as the infallibility of the Pope, and they distributed violently anti-Jewish texts and brochures.[8]

But the most dramatic action was that pursued by the Augustinian Fathers of the Assumption, thanks to the Maison de la Bonne Presse, a formidable arsenal at the service of Catholic thought and which, as of 1897, devoted an essential portion of its publication to the struggle against the Jews. In 1897, *Le Pèlerin* was appearing in editions of 40,000 copies, while *La Croix* printed more than 170,000.† *La Croix*, which called itself the "most anti-Jewish newspaper in France," as well as the numerous publications surrounding it, derived from the "renewal of the Affair" as of December 1897 a new source of fury. At that point the anti-Semitism of the Bonne Presse was to know no bounds. In February 1898, Abbé Loutil, a normally moderate columnist, entitled an editorial devoted to Zola, "Disembowel Him!" and Abbé Debauge did not hesitate to write, "All this will finish badly for the Jews . . . if the police and the government continue to be impotent, the citizens in their disgust will be obliged to render justice themselves." In July, *La Croix* would take a full page to reproduce a poster: "Judas Dreyfus has sold France. . . . The Jews have snatched, sullied, and destroyed everything. . . . Let us unite to smash Jewish omnipotence and boot the Jews out of France." But beyond the guilt of Dreyfus, a Jew and a traitor, *La Croix* denounced in the Jew the symbol of evil, the historical vehicle of sin. The baptized, become God's soldiers, owed it to themselves to vanquish the Jews, and the Assumptionists regarded themselves as veritable Crusaders, off to war, as in former times, against pagans and men of evil. They were defending Christ, the Church, and France. For the Catholics *were* France: "True patriotism is that of the baptized," wrote

* The book would be legally banned on September 5, 1898.
† To those newspapers may be added the provincial *Croix,* nearly a hundred publications adapted for regional audiences and spreading the Assumptionist ideology.

Father Bailly. "To be Catholic and to be French are one and the same thing."[9] To defend France was also to defend a traditional civilization. The Assumptionists detested factories and capital, over which the Jew and Lucifer held sway. They extolled the earth, since the Lord was the master of the fields.[10] The village represented the good, and the city embodied evil. The transition from an economy of the land to an industrial economy was a disaster for which the Jews were responsible and from which they derived profit. *La Croix* and *Le Pèlerin* were thus certain they were defending the people—peasants against capitalism, small businessmen against the bazaars and department stores from which the Jews extorted their profit. "One finds perfectly undistinguished Lévys settling into a country, and through techniques possessed by the Jew alone, soon obliging local business to go under before their competition. . . ."[11] No doubt the Assumptionists were seeking to gain a large readership with this propaganda, especially in the North, where their press was quite well ingrained. But they had a sincere horror of industrialization: "the machine and the workshop devouring the individual. . . . King Capital with his entourage of speculators, brokers, and industrialists of every stripe. . . . Modern France is abandoning God, and lives only for money, under the culpable influence of the Jews." La Bonne Presse thus reflected nostalgia for a feudal past. "All was not perfect in the France of former times, and yet the people seemed gay, faces were open . . . people sang and danced on any pretext."[12] Dreyfus was but the representative, the symbol, of the forces of evil destroying France.

To be sure, *La Croix* was not the authorized organ of the Church in France. But, as Pierre Sorlin has observed, "its title, its editorial staff, its vaunted fidelity to the Pope's directives,"[13] had the result that it seemed to many to be the "official newspaper" of the religious world. And the Church would do little to call *La Croix*—and especially the various local editions,[14] some of whose issues were veritable calls to murder—back to a different conception of Christian charity.[15] When Leo XIII invited the faithful to exercise a measure of prudence, it was essentially their hostility to the Republic—and not toward the Jews—that he deplored. So that the Catholics of France were to find in the Assumptionist press daily nourishment for the old reserve of anti-Semitism latent within the traditions of French Catholicism.[16]

But it was not the Assumptionist press alone that performed this task. The activity of the "integrist" clergy,[17] whose most vehement representatives were Abbé Barbier and Monsignor Delassus, the director of *La Semaine Religieuse*, should not be neglected. "If the Church had been heeded," opined Delassus, "never would the Jews have been admitted to form part of the French nationality. . . . Dreyfus was rich; he did not betray for money but out of instinct, if not obedience." And Delassus never ceased to elaborate, in his writings and his preachings, on the "misdeeds of the Jews." The social Catholics themselves frequently participated in anti-Jewish hostility, which was common to almost all Catholics. In the journal *La Sociologie Catholique*, Paul Lapeyre, discussing the Jewish question in March 1898, denounced usury as a manifestation of the pride and egotism of the Jew. La Tour du Pin—who would exercise a significant influence on Action Française[18]—proposed liberating France from the Jewish evil, which would entail "treating the Jews like foreigners, and dangerous foreigners at that," and reconstituting within the economic and political order the organs of our life which "rendered us, before the Jewish invasion, independent of the Jews and masters in our homes"—that is, parishes and corporations. The Christian Democrats themselves, Abbé Sir and Abbé Lemire, included in their program the struggle against Jews and Freemasons "who have marked their hatred of the poor even as they have marked their hatred of Christ."[19] At the Christian Democrats' national congress of November 1896, held in Lyon, it was Edouard Drumont, "the pope of anti-Semitism," who presided over the closing banquet. The Jews were characterized there as "robbing the children of the people"; it was proposed to find Jewish proletarians to pull the rope from which Rothschild would be hanged.[20] Abbé Henri Desportes—who was part of the Christian Democrats' general staff—the founder in 1890 of a monthly journal of "social and religious defense" entitled *L'Alliance Antijuive*, then of another, *La Terre de France*, was to become for years the sounding board for all anti-Semitic accusations, specifically those concerning the ritual murder of Christian children.[21]

What could the protests of a few Catholic Dreyfusards accomplish against this broad movement, that seemed to sweep up all of Catholic thought?[22] The publication in 1899 by one Ginevra, of a brochure entitled *Catholique Dreyfusard*, dedicated by a Christian, "a simple observer of the evangelical law," to M. and Mme. Alfred Dreyfus, "persecuted Israelites"? The writings and sermons of Abbé Fremont, who did not hestitate, in homilies that were regarded as scandalous, to stigmatize anti-Semitism and to speak of "our brothers the Jews"?[23] To what effect the formation in February 1899—through the inspiration of the great Christian disciple of the École des Chartes, Paul Marie Viollet—of the Comité Catholique pour la Défense du Droit, which rejected the spirit of intolerance and denounced the profound harm caused to the country by anti-Semitism?[24] And yet the Comité counted in 1899 more than a hundred members, including about fifteen priests. Similarly Abbé Pichot, publishing consecutively in 1898 and 1899 *La Conscience Chrétienne et L'Affaire Dreyfus* and *La Conscience Chrétienne et la Question Juive*, dared to condemn anti-

Semitism as a violation of the Gospels. Anatole Leroy-Beaulieu also stigmatized that simplistic doctrine,[25] "derived from haughty Germany and amorphous, enormous Russia," and applied himself to refuting all the arguments against the Jews: "I have often wondered what would have been different had there not been any Jews in France. There would have been nothing or almost nothing changed. We would have lost a few men of great distinction . . ." Starting in 1896 and throughout the Dreyfus Affair, Leroy-Beaulieu had the courage to organize an increasing number of lectures, which were quickly interrupted and which gained for him the outraged indignation of *La Libre Parole*. Over and over again, it excommunicated this monstrous "philo-Semite."[26]

It was perhaps the writer Charles Péguy, suggests Pierre Pierrard, who was if not "the only Christian of note to see his Jewish brothers with an unobscured vision, illuminated from within and loving them for what they were,"[27] at least the only Catholic writer of the period to answer the anti-Semites with an "evangelical" passion capable of challenging their own!* No doubt Péguy would accord his love to a Jew of his own conception, an "ideal" Jew, impoverished, deprived, eager for justice, the authentic heir of the prophetic race, a Jew "streaming with the word of God," to whom he would give the voice, features, and courage, "the heart devoured by fire," of his friend Bernard Lazare. He would construct a mystical image of the Jew which would merge with that of Christ. But beyond the exasperations of his cult of the prophets, the lyrical furors that would occasionally cause him to be unjust (particularly toward Jean Jaurès and Dreyfus himself, accused of "acquitting himself lamentably" of his appointed role as victim and hero[29]), beyond even certain traces of anti-Semitism (as when he spoke of capitalism), Péguy was perhaps the only one to have attacked—with luminous ardor—the very foundations of the aged hostility of the Catholics: "It is not the Jews who crucified Jesus Christ, but the sins of us all. . . . Bourgeois anti-Semites only know bourgeois Jews. We who are poor, it happens, know poor Jews and even Jews living in misery. . . . Anti-Semites speak about Jews. I warn you that I am going to say something outrageous: anti-Semites don't know the Jews; they talk about them, but they don't know them." But in 1898, Charles Péguy was still a young socialist Normalian, who, along with a few comrades, was using his fists to defend Dreyfusard professors. Catholic thought found its embodiment and expression in *La Croix*.

Anti-Semitism at the century's end found nourishment as much in

---

* But Péguy's militant involvement in the Affair in 1898, was a socialist—and not a Christian—commitment. There would gradually develop in Péguy the notion of the Affair's twofold roots in French revolutionary tradition and in Christian morality and faith. That version of the Affair would blossom in *Notre jeunesse*, which appeared in 1910.[28]

Rothschild as in Judas. Drumont himself proclaimed in 1898, on the occasion of the reconstitution of the former Ligue Antisémite, "Anti-Semitism has never been a religious issue; it has always been an economic and social issue."[30] The principal themes of such anti-Semitism, whose function was to integrate and mobilize the population, had been developed by Toussenel, a disciple of Fourier.* The decadence of France, parliamentary corruption, and the weakness of government had permitted the Jews to become the masters of banks, transportation, and trade, and to seize control of the nation's economy. In that context, the Protestant was gladly coupled with the Jew.[31] Toussenel's work was about the only anti-Semitic book known to the pioneers of French socialism. In like manner, Proudhon had expressed in violent terms his hostility to the Jews: "The Jew is the enemy of the human species. The race should be sent back to Asia or exterminated. A hatred of the Jews and of the English should be an article of our political faith."[32] For Louis Auguste Blanqui too, anti-Jewish socialism had been elevated to the dignity of an article of faith. The Jews embodied the reign of money, lust, and rapaciousness. The struggle against the combined figure of capitalism and the Jews dictated his denunciation of the universal suffrage on which the parliamentary Republic had been founded: "Universal suffrage," wrote Blanqui, "is the definitive enthronement of Rothschild, the arrival of the Jews. . . ."[33] Albert Regnard, who took up the intellectual legacy of *Blanquisme* in *La Revue Socialiste*, could salute the publication of Drumont's *La France juive* as a work of public welfare. Did not Drumont claim, as had Blanqui, that capitalism was "the immediate product of Semitism"?† There was thus a strong French tradition of popular anti-Semitism which linked the hatred of Jews and of capitalism.[35] In 1898, Maurice Barrès, a candidate in the legislative elections in Nancy, would take up and give precision to that theme in his platform. The Jew was responsible for economic insecurity. Resistant to manual labor, unsuited for work in the field, he would never be other than "a merchant of men or goods, and if need be, a usurer. . . . For twenty years now, the opportunist set-up has favored the Jew, the foreigner, and the cosmopolite." Criminal policies had delivered France over to the Reinach family and Alfred Dreyfus.[36] Frenchmen must be protected, proclaimed Maurice Barrès, from foreign products, foreign workers, naturalized citizens, and above all from international finance, that is, from Jewry.[37] Jules Guérin would say more or less the same thing in

* In his book *Les Juifs, rois de l'époque*, from which Drumont derived much of his inspiration.
† August Chirac's *Les Rois de la République*, published in 1883, but which was far from having known the success of *La France juive*, also developed the themes of popular anti-Semitism: "'Jewishness' is a conception of the world, a way of life; it is the domination of money, the exploitation of the people by capital."[35]

articles published throughout the year 1899 in the journal *L'Antijuif*: "The further one is from the Jews, the closer one is to the people." A Republic founded through the collusion of the Jews, the Freemasons, and the Protestants had given the French workers over to the powerful banks and to Jewish finance. Along with the socialist and revolutionary workers, the anti-Semites were the most recent Frenchmen to invoke the cause of the people.

No doubt the Socialists sitting in Parliament at the time Zola published *J'Accuse* were not openly anti-Semitic. There is no overt anti-Semitism to be found in any of the four dominant rival socialist organizations. Neither Jaurès, to be sure, nor Jules Guesde, nor Edouard Vaillant took up the anti-Semitic themes circulating in the traditions of French socialism. Socialist intellectuals, such as Lucien Herr, vigorously condemned all anti-Semitism. Adherence to Marxist principles did not lead to anti-Semitism as a doctrine. It remained, nevertheless, that *The Jewish Question* was ambiguous on the subject, and that in the work best known at the time to French militants, *Class Struggles in France*,[38] Marx had on several occasions conflated Judaism and capitalism, lashing out at Jewish financiers and the "Jews of the Bourse." Zeev Sternhell has concluded that Marx, however discreetly, had also helped fuel the idea that socialism implied anti-Semitism.[39]

And Léon Blum was undoubtedly too enthusiastic when he claimed not to perceive among the Socialists during the Affair "the slightest indulgence toward the anti-Semitic trend."[40] In 1898, the tradition of plebeian anti-Semitism was not extinct among French socialists. In numerous Guesdist federations, the Dreyfus Affair provoked overtly anti-Semitic reactions.[41] On February 20, 1898, when riots had already broken out in several French cities and Jews in various places were victims of violence, the Socialist group in Parliament, which included Jean Jaurès, René Viviani, Jules Guesde, and Alexandre Millerand, made public a "Manifesto on the Dreyfus Affair." It made no reference to those acts of violence, but denounced the Affair "as a struggle between two rival factions of the bourgeoisie" which must not distract Socialists from the real fight against the capitalist system.* It was implied that Dreyfus's campaign was being financed by Jewish capitalists attempting, through the rehabilitation of Dreyfus, to gain the country's support for their own misdoings and to "wash clean . . . all the blemishes of Israel."† It would take resolute action by Juarès beginning in January 1898, and during the

---

* In 1898, *La Petite République* published a "letter from Jewish workers" to French Socialists, assuring them that its signers had nothing to do with Rothschild.
† "Le Manifeste," *La Lanterne,* January 20, 1898.

subsequent months, to argue that the danger was "not only for the bourgeois republic but the social republic." The publication at the end of September 1898 of Jaurès's volume, *Les Preuves* (distributed at cost by the Socialist daily *La Petite République*)* gradually convinced the Socialists to adhere to the thesis "that if the bourgeois Republic, in opposing the military conspiracy, needed Socialist energy, it was, on the contrary, for a daring party eager for conquests an opportunity sent by destiny, an historic opening." But for this end, months of agitation, riots, and even the threat of a *coup d'etat* would be necessary. And even then, Jaurès's involvement, because it risked turning socialism away from its essential task, would provoke some protracted reticence. After the fact, Léon Blum would note that Jaurès endowed socialism with a new moral greatness, but that he had not "provoked the avalanche of agreement and conviction" that he had hoped for.[42] And later on, when Georges Clemenceau, one of the most symbolic patrons of the Dreyfus struggle, would implement a policy of antilabor repression, the extreme left would denounce the mystification, from the proletarian perspective, constituted by involvement in the Dreyfus Affair, the "triumph of the Jewish party" in the war between two factions of the bourgeoisie whose battleground the Affair had been, and finally the installation, at the workers' expense, of a "domesticated, middle-class socialism," born of the support given to bourgeois ideology.[43]

Catholic anti-Semitism and popular anti-Semitism might seem to diverge; nationalism, however, gave them coherence. By way of nationalism, anti-Semitism ceased being a confused combination of prejudices, fears, animosities, and refusals. It was undoubtedly Barrès who, through the articles he published during the Affair and in his electoral "programs," gave national anti-Semitism its most forceful expression. Nationalism, affirmed Barrès, "is a discipline and a method." He argued further, "We are the men of France's continuity."[44] In that progression could be found pell-mell the refutation of industrial society; of machine technology, which made man the slave of his work; of bourgeois civilization, responsible for the spread of mediocrity; and of the corrupt and corruptive parliamentary system. "Nationalism consists in resolving every question in terms of its relation to France."[45] It entailed defending workers from

---

* Assembling the articles he had published in *La Petite République* on the Dreyfus Affair, Jaurès demonstrated Dreyfus's innocence luminously in *Les Preuves*, clarifying and denouncing the crimes committed in the name of the honor of the Army and reasons of State. He concluded: "Let's have justice in broad daylight! In broad daylight: the revision—to save an innocent and to punish the guilty, to instruct the people, and to honor the nation!" In his preface, Jaurès explained that the proletariat could no longer be satisfied with "general formulas," that it now wanted to know "in depth and even in the recesses of its operation the mechanism of these great events."

foreigners and work itself from capitalist exploitation. It made protectionism imperative, a patriotic duty: "In France the Frenchman must march in the first rank, the foreigner in the second." The nation was the sole reality. "For lack of Greek blood in my veins," wrote Barrès, "I understand neither Socrates nor Plato." Neither the foreigner nor the Jew could think or live as a Frenchman.

"I don't need to be told," Barrès would claim, "why Dreyfus committed treason . . ."[46] Dreyfus was not a member of the true Nation. "Dreyfus is nothing but an uprooted plant who feels ill at ease in our French garden."[47] It remained that "the Dreyfus Affair was but a tragic sign of a general state." The French nation was divided, weakened in all respects. Its moral unity had to be restored. A definition and shared idea of France was needed. "A nation is the common possession of an ancient cemetery and the will to preserve that heritage undivided." One had to protect that legacy. "We have wanted to maintain the house of our fathers in which foreigners are trespassing."[48] The intellectuals supporting Dreyfus's cause were dividing France and in judging "everything abstractly," understood nothing of the true nation: "I am not an intellectual," proclaimed Barrès, "and I desire above all that people speak in French."[49] The uprooted fueled the disquiet of the nation. Certain foreigners, in order to destroy the Army, "have picked up this little Jew like a weapon, like a knife from the dust."[50]

Whether Dreyfus were guilty or innocent did not really seem to matter. The Dreyfusard plot was dividing and disarming France. "Even if their client were innocent, they would remain criminals." What was sure, claimed Barrès, borrowing a formula from the writer Paul Déroulède, was that "France was innocent." Barrès would go further still: "Dreyfus is the representative of a different species. . . . The problem of race has been raised." And were it not a necessity to judge him "according to French morality and our justice," the case of Dreyfus would be fit matter for a "chair of comparative ethnology."[51]

Anti-Semitism thus seemed to flow from nationalism as from a source. "The Jewish question is inseparable from the national question."[52] How might it be resolved? Barrès and most of the nationalists proposed in 1898 a program of measures in which federalism played an important role.[53] In vague terms, Barrès called for defending Frenchmen from insecurity, fighting off the barons of finance, protecting the nation's workers, prohibiting the hiring of foreigners in the shipyards, and protecting French products. Barrès did not specify what anti-Jewish measures he expected, but what was clear was that the Jewish invasion must be halted and the economic conquest of France by the Jews prohibited. France would have to be "reconquered," the "traitors dismissed,"[54] and the "blemishes of rot on our admirable race" eliminated.[55] Barrès left to others the task of specifying the means.

Faced with the unfurling of anti-Semitism over France during the years 1898–99, which was no longer restricted to the publication of such opinions alone but included violence and exactions, the Jewish community was in turmoil, but its reactions were few and timid. "The French Jews," wrote Léon Blum, "abandoned the cause. They no longer spoke of the Affair among themselves. A great misfortune had befallen Israel. They submitted to it without saying a word, waiting for time and silence to efface its effects."[56] Even after the publication of *J'Accuse*, when the Affair was brought before public opinion, the Jews of France remained for the most part silent. There was, said Blum, a kind of "timorous and egotistical prudence." They also did not want to be accused of defending Dreyfus merely because he was Jewish—that is, a will not to bring new fuel to the passions of anti-Semitism.[57] Deep-rooted in the hearts of most Jews, there was also an impassioned attachment to France, which entailed a stubborn trust: "We are convinced," wrote Louis Lévy in *L'Univers Israélite* of 1898,[58] "that France will soon come back to her senses, will be ashamed of the madness into which she has let herself slip, and will shake off her error."*

If—after Bernard Lazare and Joseph Reinach—there were Jews fighting to defend the deportee of Devil's Island, it was not out of any concerted solidarity. It was rather to perform a duty dictated by love of country and passion for justice.† For "the Dreyfus Affair was in no way Jewish, but entirely humanitarian."[59] There would be not a single Jewish movement of active resistance to anti-Semitism constituted throughout the Affair—with the exception of a small Committee Against Anti-Semitism whose activity and membership would be kept secret; its existence would be officially acknowledged only in 1902, "once the storm had passed."[60]

The Jews of France, or rather, the French citizens of Jewish belief maintained their only recourse was to "seek refuge in the France of 1789,

* Formulating his wishes for the new year 1899, Chief Rabbi Zadoc Kahn reaffirmed the historic faith of French Jews in the French Republic. "With all my heart, I wish for our beloved France to remain faithful to her admirable natural genius, composed of reason, common sense, loyalty, and generosity; not to abandon anything of the glorious traditions which in the past have earned her the gratitude and the love of the oppressed; to seek always to be in the first rank among nations in the defence of the principles of justice, humanity, and social solidarity, so that she may be strong and respected abroad, and united and prosperous at home."
† Many joined the League of the Rights of Man as soon as it was founded by Ludovic Trarieux in February 1898. Out of thirty-four members in the League's office, only three were Jews, as was observed "with satisfaction" by *Archives Israélites* on the morrow of the foundation of the League.

in a promise of emancipation that had never been completely kept."[61] What was left them as an option if not to be still more scrupulous in their love of France and their passion for justice? Nothing, neither the anti-Semitism nor the shouts of hatred, nor the acts of violence against random persons and properties could shake the strength of the assimilationist tradition. "For the majority of Jews," concludes the historian Michael Marrus, "it was vain to appeal to a Jewish specificity in the face of the powerful attraction exercised by France. In adversity French Jews have always been inclined to seek the protection accorded them by the ideals of the French Revolution and the charms of patriotism."[62]

But what could be the meaning of a Jewish "national consciousness" for Frenchmen of "Israelite" persuasion or tradition who did not recognize in themselves either community or solidarity? Bernard Lazare might claim to speak "as a Jew," affirm that "Dreyfus belongs to a class of pariahs," make of the deportee of Devil's Island the symbol of the persecuted Jew throughout the world,[63] and finally demand that the Affair reinforce the "feeling of Jewish nationality" and awaken in French Jews a "Jewish national conscience."[64] What meaning did he attribute to those words? And how might they be understood? Bernard Lazare appeared to be an extremist, at best a romantic, who ran the risk of compromising the Jews, if not discrediting them. If Theodore Herzl's ideas of a Jewish state* knew great success with the Jews of Eastern Europe, notably in Russia and wherever there existed an isolated and mistreated Jewish proletariat, he was barely heard by the assimilated Jews of Western Europe. In 1896, Herzl presented his ideas to Baron Edmond de Rothschild, who took him to be a dreamer. Rothschild was convinced that the twentieth century would quite naturally resolve the Jewish problem, were it still to exist, through the gradual assimilation of all minorities. At the first Zionist Congress, held in Basel in 1897, there were twelve delegates from France and eighty from Russia.[66] Starting in 1897, Lazare, who had become editor in chief of the journal *Zion*, succeeded in winning over a few Jewish students—rare Jewish intellectuals—to Herzl's ideas. In 1899, the Zionist newspaper *Le Flambeau*, founded by one of the French delegates to the Basel congress, Jacques Bahas, and supported by Lazare, would also attempt—in expressing its contempt for assimilated French Jews such as Chief Rabbi Zadoc Kahn and the wealthy Joseph Reinach—to attract

* Theodore Herzl, who attended the ceremony of Dreyfus's degradation as a correspondent of the Austrian newspaper, *Neue Freie Press*, grew aware of the illusions of assimilation. In 1896, he published his book *The Jewish State: An Attempt to Solve the Jewish Question*, which presented for the first time a coherently developed thesis of the creation of a Jewish State as the sole solution to the Jewish question: "We are a united people. And because the Jews form a Nation that does not want to, can not, and should not disappear, that Nation must engender a State."[65]

French Jews toward a Jewish nationalism. But the efforts of Bernard Lazare and Jacques Bahas would bear only limited fruit amid a few Jews detached from French society—anarchists, revolutionaries, foreigners unhappy with life in France. In their immense majority the French Jews would remain united in their response to persecution, even in their own country. They would have to be more French than other Frenchmen.[67]

5

Thou Shalt Not Follow the Multitude

General Billot, the minister of war, was not reassured by either Commandant Esterhazy's acquittal or Zola's conviction. The vast current of popular opinion which had come to support the cause of revision was plainly a sign of future developments in the Affair. The approach of legislative elections made it necessary to take precautions. Were General Billot to be replaced, it was imperative that he leave his successor orderly files. Throughout the Esterhazy trial, and later the Zola trial, the documents of the Dreyfus dossier had been in constant circulation among the Ministry, the General Staff, the Section of Statistics, and the military tribunal. It would be imperative to put things in order and, if he were able, to further complete the dossier indicting Dreyfus.

Billot entrusted his son-in-law, Wattine, a young magistrate, with the task of compiling a complete inventory of the Dreyfus file, under the direction of General Gonse and with Commandant Henry's aid. In his archival work, Wattine would soon be assisted by Captain Louis Cuignet. A dossier of 365 documents was constituted, in which were to be found in chronological order the old items of the secret file. Undated papers were assigned dates. Gonse numbered and initialed each document personally. He did not hesitate to change the dates of certain documents in order to shore up the accusation.[1] To the principal file were appended several adjoining files intended to show that wherever Dreyfus passed, documents had been leaked. The entry on confessions was completed by an account of Captain Lebrun-Renault's declarations addressed by General Gonse to General de Boisdeffre. Guénée's doctored reports, however, which had been part of the secret file in 1894, were—for reasons of prudence—withdrawn from the dossier. On June 1, 1898 Gonse finished the report intended to accompany the collection of documents thus assembled and classified. He concluded:

> To what mental aberration must passion be capable of bringing people that they have maintained, in order to rescue a guilty man, that French officers have committed forgery or made use of counterfeit documents! The documents appended herewith and the ten cartons of the Intelligence Service respond. One does not fabricate 1,500 documents!
>
> Designated by Panizzardi's letters, convicted by the bordereau, devastated by the sequence of proofs as well as by the subsequent correspondence in which his name is spelled out, Dreyfus did certainly betray his country and one can affirm in one's soul and conscience along with the judges of the Court Martial of 1894: "Yes, Dreyfus is guilty."

General de Boisdeffre authenticated the work and the report by adding his signature, preceded by the words: "Read and approved."

While the Ministry of War was busying itself with putting the Dreyfus dossier "in order," the Zola trial took a new turn. Maître Mornard, a lawyer with the High Court of Appeal who was to become one of the best artisans of the revision, had retained in Zola's favor seven grounds for appeal, one of which was that the minister of war had no right to lodge a complaint with the Court Martial that Zola had made the accusation that Esterhazy was acquitted "on command." Designated as judge advocate, Appeals Judge Chambereaud of the Criminal Chamber had decided on that last score to reverse the judgment convicting Zola. And on April 2 at a session of the Criminal Chamber, Attorney General Manau,* almost eighty years old, his eyes still ablaze beneath bushy white eyebrows, took the floor. He had attended most of the sessions of the Zola trial. He refused to limit his motion to the juridical debate submitted to the High Court of Appeal. In an ardent voice, at times cracking with emotion, he affirmed that the promoters of a revision were "neither traitors nor sell-outs, but the honor

---

* He was, Reinach relates, "one of the last survivers of that generation of 1848 which had borne in their lifetime boundless illusions of justice."[2] He had become a magistrate after the fall of the Empire after thirty years as a lawyer.

of the country." He spoke of his disgust at the anti-Semitic furor, and concluded by recalling to the Criminal Chamber the biblical precept, "Thou shalt not follow the multitude to do evil and when thou shalt speak at a trial, thou shalt not proceed so as to pervert the law." Astonished, and undoubtedly divided, the High Court of Appeal listened to its public prosecutor, a hoary combatant for law and justice, take so vigorous a stand. It postponed its deliberations for two days. And on April 2 it overturned the verdict convicting Zola.

There was great joy among the revisionists[3] and an explosion of furor in the other camp. Granier de Cassagnac, Edouard Drumont, and Henri Rochefort outdid each other in invective. The High Court of Appeal had put itself in the service of Jewry. The presiding magistrate of the Criminal Chamber—the Alsatian Protestant Loew—was, like Dreyfus, a German Jew. The "obscene" Manau was himself a concealed German. His name would be pronounced thereafter "Manaüh." Within the government the decision was received dumbly. Neither the "Dreyfusist" address of the public prosecutor nor a judgment complicating the task of the political powers had been expected. The prime minister, much vexed, allowed himself, from the tribune of the Chamber, to be carried away, a few hours after reading the decision, to the point of criticizing the juridical theory of the High Court of Appeal. He found it opportune to cast blame on "the unfortunate words of the public prosecutor." He gave his promise—to a few deputies who declared Manau's speech "shameful"—that the government would examine "with complete impartiality," the "incriminated language." This was a new stage in the evolution of the Affair. The judiciary had entered into conflict with the will of the executive. It had "besmirched the Army." On April 8, the judges of the Court Martial who had been defamed by Zola met to draw the consequences from the decision of the High Court of Appeal. They deliberated for more than eight hours. Should they lodge a complaint? Ought they to run the risk of a second Zola trial? Méline, whom the proximity of elections had rendered quite prudent, inclined toward abstaining from further action. But the honor of the Army demanded . . . by a vote of five to two, that the military judges file suit, restricting themselves to a single sentence of Zola's letter. "A Court Martial has just dared to acquit Esterhazy on command, a supreme offense to all truth and all justice. . . ." And they expressed simultaneously the wish that Zola be stricken from the lists of the Legion of Honor. In its embarrassment, the government could do no better than attempt to limit the damage: it would try to prevent another Zola trial. On the pretext that public order might be disturbed, it was decided that the second trial would take place not in Paris, but Versailles. In Versailles, the

Army's presence was everywhere, and the courtroom rather small. There would be few people and many officers. Hearings were set for May 23. By that date, the legislative elections would be over.

On April 7, *Le Siècle* published the text of the deposition Henri Casella would have made had he been heard in court. The Italian journalist told of his conversations with Panizzardi and Schwarzkoppen,* their declarations of Dreyfus's innocence and Esterhazy's guilt. He recounted in detail Esterhazy's last visit to Schwarzkoppen, which he claimed to have heard from Schwarzkoppen's own mouth. Lies, cried Drumont and Rochefort. But neither Panizzardi nor Schwarzkoppen issued a denial. . . . Whereupon the press invented new theses in order to exculpate Esterhazy. Esterhazy was indeed dealing with Schwarzkoppen, but in so doing he was following orders. He was deceiving Schwarzkoppen by giving him spurious or insignificant material. It was the German who had been deceived and betrayed.[4] But the decision of the High Court of Appeal, Casella's revelations, and the forthcoming elections were a great source of worry for Esterhazy, who was more lucid than many of his supporters. He grew agitated and began feeding he newspapers contradictory confidential information. He complained to General de Pellieux. All this was going to finish badly. France was governed by imbeciles. . . .[5]

6

A Republican Majority

The Dreyfus Affair was more or less absent from the election campaign of May 1898. For the candidates of the right and the center, Dreyfus's guilt was a dogma that upheld the honor of the Army and the defense of the nation. The great majority of Radicals remained convinced of Dreyfus's guilt. Henri Brisson, who entertained a few doubts, barely mentioned them. The Radical leader Léon Bourgeois was infinitely prudent. The verdict had been reached. Camille Pelletan was certain that Auguste Scheurer-Kestner, vice president of the Senate, had been misled. For the rest, Pierre Miquel observed, "There are not four deputies in the

---

* See *supra* p. 274.

Chamber who doubt the verdict of 1894."[1] The small number of those who hesitated were in any event convinced that the French were not interested in the rehabilitation of the Jew on Devil's Island. "We are with the crowd, and not at all with the intellectuals," affirmed *La Dépêche de Toulouse*, which claimed to express the thinking of the Radicals. As for the Socialists, for the most part, they wished to commit themselves to "neither of the clans of the bourgeois civil war." "They are afraid," claimed the Socialist Jean Jaurès, whose Dreyfusard ardor was strenuously opposed by his friends: "They are tearing off flaps of my clothes in order to prevent me from mounting the rostrum."[2] Jaurès himself, seeking reelection from the Tarn, did not mention a word of the Dreyfus Affair in his election manifestos.* Historians are in agreement that the Dreyfus Affair was hardly discussed—if at all—during the election campaign. From this, however, it has perhaps been too quickly concluded that the Affair had not yet aroused a great interest in France, with the conceivable exception of the major cities. Silence concerning the Affair was a matter of political precaution. In speaking of it, one faced great risks. In order not to alienate anyone, the most prudent course was to remain silent. Thus the most astute politicians, who could sense the direction of the wind, said nothing on the subject.

For both rounds of the legislative elections, on May 8 and 22, the results verified, in any event, that there might be drawbacks in being a Dreyfusard. Joseph Reinach, a deputy from Basses-Alpes for eight years, could not collect a thousand votes. In 1893 he had had more than seven thousand.† Jean Jaurès was defeated in Carmaux. Paul Déroulède and Granier de Cassagnac, anti-Dreyfusard combatants, were elected. Similarly, Edouard Drumont was elected triumphantly in Algiers on a platform drawn from *La France Juive*. But these were exceptions. On the whole, the Chamber of 1898 revealed a stunning continuity in its electoral divisions; 270 centrists replaced 270 centrists. The conservatives, royalists rallying to the Republic, and nationalists gained a few seats at the expense of the Radicals and Socialists. The minister of the interior, Louis Barthou, could flaunt his satisfaction. The Méline majority remained stable. In its first session, the new Chamber carried the very moderate Paul Deschanel to its presidency. Supported by the conservatives and the progressives (i.e., the center) he won by a few votes over the Radical Henri Brisson.

And yet the immobility was only apparent. New divisions seemed to be

---

* It is true that the Tarn region was then agitated by pitiless class warfare. The owner of the mines at Carmaux would take Jaurès' seat from him after a campaign that reached a rare level of violence.
† Joseph Reinach had courageously affirmed his commitment in his professions of faith: "It is possible that I will lose my seat in this battle. It is certain that I will retain the satisfacton of having done my duty."

emerging. On the right, there was a resurgence of the "nationalists," who—taking up in many respects what was left of Boulangism—claimed to defend against all modes of abandon and betrayal, the country, the Army, and the traditional values whose principal gravediggers were the Jews. Drumont, Déroulède, Rochefort, and Barrès—who was defeated in Nancy—all declared themselves "nationalists." That new current, in alliance with the conservatives and the *ralliés* had won nearly a hundred seats. It had apparently bitten off a share of the radical electorate. Throughout the campaign, the Fathers of the Assumption, and particularly the most active, Fathers Adéodat, Bailly, Picard, and Jaujoux ("men of the people, rough in appearance, crude of speech")[3] had become ardently involved in supporting the nationalists through the publications of La Bonne Presse (which had taken a stand in a majority of districts against Socialist and Radical "miscreants") and also through meetings and committees of propagandists who had given of themselves immeasurably. Four hundred monks, a thousand friars and novices, and a few thousand knights of *La Croix*, lay members enlisted beneath the banner of the Catholic newspaper, had moved through villages and crowded neighborhoods in order to mobilize the patriotic electorate against all the agents of treason.[4] "Justice, Equality" committees, founded under the aegis of the Assumptionists throughout France (starting in 1896),[5] had constituted extremely active organizations for selling La Bonne Presse and election propaganda. With such backing from the Assumptionists (and more discreetly from the other religious congregations)* and numerous priests, a "hardcore" right made its entry into Parliament. Anti-Semitism was, of course, one of its preferred themes. And that new force was not without influence on the other parties. Among those elected from the center, many had observed with disquiet the rise of a violent, clerical right, that recalled to them the worst days of Boulangism. The election campaign convinced many deputies that the "republican spirit" was threatened by those newly elected—or by the forces supporting them. Thus it was that members of Parliament elected from the center, who until then had been satisfied with a conservative right and who were sincerely republican, would be gradually driven toward the Radicals. Such was the case in particular for Louis Barthou, Raymond Poincaré, Georges Leygues, Eugène Caillaux, and many others, who would henceforth look toward a moderate left. On the right the power of the Church made them uneasy, and they could see arising beneath the mantle of nationalism, an appetite for revenge against the Republic. Cracks were forming in the

* Joseph Reinach raised the issue—without conclusive evidence—of the clandestine activity of the Jesuits.[6] He lashed out in particular against Father du Lac, "astir in every intrigue." Father du Lac was the confessor of a number of generals, including General de Boisdeffre.

party of order. In the heat of the summer of 1898, they would lead to a veritable disintegration of the "progressive" center, which would burst and split into a right and a left.[7]

The first sign of this occurred on June 14. Méline imagined that he could continue to govern through the support of the right against the Radicals. But Henri Brisson, removed from the presidency, was lying in wait. He had two Radicals propose a motion pledging to approve in the future "solely policies based on a strictly republican majority,"[8] and which would condemn any alliance with the nationalists. By a vote of 295 to 246, the motion—against Méline's strenuous opposition—was passed. Drumont and his friends had undoubtedly voted with the left because, in Drumont's words, "the worlds of high finance and Jewry had imposed on Méline and on Félix Faure an ambiguous posture in the Dreyfus Affair." But Méline's defeat was achieved because a large number of progressivists had sided with the left in the vote. "The Chamber had made its choice," wrote Pierre Miquel. "Between the Socialist and collectivist peril, on the one hand, and the reactionary clerical peril on the other, the Radicals and the progressivists had given priority to the more threatening of the two, that coming from the right. The politics of *ralliement* were condemned and along with it all those filling the ranks of opportunism."[9] The condemnation was not yet that clear, and in point of fact, the Chamber was barely aware in 1898 of a socialist "peril." But it was the case that the centrist bog was swerving away from a right that had become too dangerous. Even if no one, with the exception of Drumont, had specifically named Dreyfus in Parliament, the recent developments of the Affair, the brutality of the nationalist right, and the violence of the anti-Semites had worked toward a decisive reclassification of political forces.

Beginning on June 15 with Méline's resignation, the political crisis was to last twelve days. After failing with Alexandre Ribot, then Jean Sarrien, Félix Faure called on the Radical Henri Brisson, in the hope, it appears, of seeing him fail in turn.* But Brisson succeeded in constituting a Cabinet, whose deft ambiguity would not be long in appearing. While the prime minister reserved the Ministry of the Interior for himself, and entrusted the essential portfolios to his Radical friends, he offered the Ministry of War to Godefroy Cavaignac, a Radical no doubt, but of nationalist stripe, who had distinguished himself in recent months by his anti-Dreyfusard energy. Thus the government's composition meant that the lay Republic would be defended against clerical intrigue, but also that the cause of Dreyfus would be of little import to the new government. François Goguel has observed that the Radicals were as yet "far removed from linking their

* In order to clear the way for Cavaignac, according to Joseph Reinach.[10]

cause to that of revisionism."[11] Nearly all wanted the Affair to be over once and for all, and for the agitation underway since the beginning of 1898 to come to an end. The nationalists did not fail to perceive this. Against all logic, they decided to vote for the Radical government "because," proclaimed Déroulède from the tribune, "Cavaignac was minister of war and that was a guarantee that the Army's honor would be safeguarded." "The prime minister," exulted *La Libre Parole* on May 29 "is no more than a dummy on whom Cavaignac will be seated."

Virtually alone in this regard amid his military associates, Commandant Esterhazy despaired at the arrival at the Ministry of War of the "narrow-minded Polytechnicien, . . . an ignoramus of austere countenance, who takes his stubbornness for energy, a cardboard sectarian . . ."[12] And while the anti-Dreyfusards congratulated each other, Esterhazy warned Drumont that this "imbecile Robespierre" would make them long for his predecessor, General Billot. Before yielding his office to Cavaignac, Billot found the time to submit to the president of the Republic for signature a decree rescinding Joseph Reinach's rank in the reserve army "for having, outside of his period of service, published against his superiors an injurious article." Billot, upon resigning, countersigned the decree. "He would not have wanted," claimed Reinach, "to leave the honor to Cavaignac."[13]

7

All This Is Going to End Badly

I f Henri Brisson was the head of the government, it was Godefroy Cavaignac who was its preponderant personality. A grandson of the Revolutionary *conventionnel* Jean-Baptiste Cavaignac, a son of General Eugène Cavaignac, Godefroy Cavaignac, a deputy from Sarthe since 1882, illustrated a new conception of Radicalism, in which were fused an impassioned nationalism, projected reforms, and a call for true republican virtue hostile to all forms of corruption. His influence and popularity were gaining. In the debate over the Panama scandal, he had distinguished himself by his rigor and severity. He had supplied the Radicals with the theme on which they had based their campaign in 1898: the fight against fiscal inequality.[1] Because he shared their patriotic intransigence, he had gained a large following among the nationalists. The image he had achieved—as a man of honor, inflexible on questions of money, a loyal but uncompromising dispenser of justice—gave him authority far beyond the Radical party. He was borne aloft by an exalted awareness of his own merits and by his great ambition. He did not conceal the fact that the presidency of the Republic was his goal.

For several months already, he appeared to have linked his political fate to the antirevisionist cause.[2] Passionately convinced of Dreyfus's guilt, he had become the symbol—and perhaps the recourse—of all the forces opposed to revision. But his temperament, reputation, and pride prevented him from adopting the strategy used by Méline and General Billot, seeking refuge behind the principle of *res judicata,* navigating between the most immediate obstacles. Shortly after arriving at the Ministry, Cavaignac announced his plan, more courageous and more effective than that of his predecessors.* It was he who would decisively clarify Dreyfus's guilt and the sordid machinations of the partisans of revision. He would reduce the syndicate to impotence and ridicule. For that, there would be no need of Commandant Esterhazy, a lost soldier of whom he would "unburden" the party of patriots: "When I have broken Esterhazy, I will have all the more authority to catch the whole band." As for Lieutenant Colonel Picquart, the "cornerstone" of the project, what Cavaignac had in store for him was the ordeal of a court-martial.

On June 28, Cavaignac requested the secret file. He wanted it examined by Colonel Gaudérique Roget, chief of the Fourth Bureau, who had become the head of his military staff, and by Captain Louis Cuignet, who was already involved in the task, and in whom he had complete confidence. He was hoping to find the elements that would definitively confound Dreyfus's supporters. General de Boisdeffre immediately perceived the disaster to which the new strategy might lead. This new zealot did not know that Esterhazy and the General Staff had long since joined causes, that the dossier was filled with fabricated documents. De Boisdeffre would try to circumscribe the problem. For a time, he hoped that Cavaignac would be discouraged by the sheer bulk of the dossier, but that was not at all the case. Cavaignac asked de Boisdeffre if he had indeed

---

* He had insisted that the Ministry of Justice be given over to Jean Sarrien, a pale figure of anti-Dreyfusard persuasion, whom he hoped to turn into his docile instrument.

verified the authenticity of all the items. The chief of the General Staff had to admit that he had not. "The authenticity of the whole and the unlimited trust he had in Lieutenant Colonel Henry had seemed to him a sufficient guarantee."[3] The minister expressed astonishment. De Boisdeffre, increasingly worried, began feeding Cavaignac copious advice for the definitive stance that the latter already had in mind. It would be better not to talk of secret documents, either to acknowledge or to deny their existence. Better not to mention the names of the military attachés. Nor to refer to Germany or Italy. While Cavaignac appeared to take note, he would do exactly as he wished. Esterhazy began to panic, since he was informed from all sides that Cavaignac was preparing to execute him. On July 3 he rushed to see his friend General de Pellieux, told him that his life was "no longer bearable," that he was about to kill himself, and that he would bring down those who had abandoned him in the process. De Boisdeffre and General Gonse attempted—with due caution—to mollify Cavaignac, who only grew more obstinate.

On July 7 there was scheduled in the Chamber debate on a new challenge by the indefatigable André Castelin concerning the shameful maneuvers of Dreyfus's friends. This was the occasion chosen by Cavaignac to deliver the "major address" that would dispel once and for all the legend of Dreyfus's innocence. Along with Roger, his cabinet head, and Captain Louis Cuignet, he went to work assiduously.[4] He did not consult Lieutenant Colonel Henry nor General de Boisdeffre. Cavaignac was already thinking of naming him ambassador to Saint-Petersburg, in order to be rid of him, fulfilling in the process an old dream of de Boisdeffre's, who had been one of the architects of the Franco-Russian alliance. He would thus be able to place one of his own men at the head of the General Staff. The minister persisted in pursuing his plan, certain he was right and determined to prove it to all. Until the very last moment, Gonse busied himself with the accusation. On July 4, Captain Lebrun-Renault brought the minister a sheet from his notebook of 1895 in which, he claimed, he had taken Dreyfus's confession. Cavaignac took the sheet, read it, recopied it, and returned it to Lebrun-Renault, who, strangely enough, would later claim to have destroyed it, having deemed it "no longer of any utility." For the while, the minister was confirmed in his conviction that Dreyfus had confessed.

On July 5, Cavaignac received at the Ministry of War, Prime Minister Henri Brisson, Minister of Justice Jean Sarrien, and several ministers. On a large table in the middle of the minister's office were displayed the decisive documents—about sixty in number—of the secret file. Captain Cuignet commented on each, and General Gonse waited in an adjacent room in the event that clarification was needed. The prime minister and

Sarrien were particularly interested in the document in which Dreyfus's name was actually spelled out.* It was "very interesting," observed the prime minister, to whom Cavaignac explained that he could examine the dossier in its entirety, which Gonse would keep at his disposal. Cavaignac was rather proud of his evidence. He was going to "pulverize" the syndicate. Brisson allowed him to proceed. Was he actually convinced? Or did he see an opportunity to allow "an overly imposing princeling" to discredit himself?[5]

On that same day, July 5, Lucie Dreyfus sent Sarrien an official request to annul the 1894 verdict on the grounds that it had been based on the secret communication of a document to the judges. She asked that he bring before the High Court of Appeal the violations of law that had allowed for her husband's conviction. That request, which was made public, reinvigorated the minister of war in his project. He was fully prepared to execute Dreyfus.

As was customary, Deputy Castelin mounted the tribune on July 7 to demand "not new and superfluous evidence of the Jew's crime," but exceptional legislation intended to punish the traitor's "champions." He accused Mathieu Dreyfus, Georges Picquart, Joseph Reinach, and the lawyer Edgar Demange, of conspiring to "appeal simultaneously to foreign powers and to the forces of revolution."

Breaking a long silence, Cavaignac then stepped up onto the tribune. In the dry and harsh tone which the Assembly came to recognize as that of a Grand Inquisitor, he delivered his response. He began by "liquidating" Esterhazy: "There has been an effort to substitute for Dreyfus an officer who will be stricken tomorrow with the punishment he deserves." The right was stunned, and the left broke out in applause. Then the minister approached the subject of Dreyfus himself. He spoke, beyond the confines of the Assembly, to the defenders of Dreyfus, whom he saluted as men of good faith. "A misunderstanding threatens to arise between them and that Army whose sacred mission it is to defend the patrimony of France, not only her material patrimony, but her intellectual and moral patrimony." It was for the sake of Dreyfus's defenders above all that he was going to speak; for them that he would bring forward the "proof of the truth." He pledged his absolute certainty as to Dreyfus's guilt: "Never could any consideration of public welfare, whatever it be, impel me to keep an innocent man in jail. . . ." Then he brought forth his proof. He had selected three items "out of a thousand." There was Alessandro Panizzardi's letter to Maximilien von Schwarzkoppen of September 1896.† There

* That is: the "Henry forgery."
† Which Henry had dated March 1894, adding the initial D., which he had substituted for P. after scratching the original out. *Supra* p. 195.

was the "scoundrel D." letter, which had served in the secret file of 1894,* and above all, since it clarified the other two, there was the letter which spelled out Dreyfus's name.† Exclamations resounded on all sides. The Chamber seemed braced in a state of thunderous unanimity. No one present seemed to remember that Auguste Scheurer-Kestner, Georges Picquart, and twenty journalists had already denouced that last document as a fraud, after Pellieux had imprudently referred to it in the Zola trial. No, the proof appeared conclusive to the Assembly: "The abject misery of ignorance and fear," Jean Jaurès would comment. "They did not know because they did not dare to know."⁶ Cavaignac then threw his own authority into the balance: "I have assessed the material authenticity and the moral authenticity of this document," and with considerable talent he undertook to demonstrate them both. Then, "continuing his lecture like a professor at the blackboard,"‡ he turned to Dreyfus's confession. He attested that Captain Lebrun-Renault had heard this testimony. He had proof of it in his hands. Once his demonstration was over, he concluded with a ringing tribute to the Army. "May all Frenchmen be able to come together tomorrow to proclaim that the Army which is their pride and their hope is not only mighty with its own strength . . . is not only strong with the nation's trust, but strong as well in the justice of the acts that it has accomplished."⁷

As he descended from the rostrum, the entire Chamber rose in acclamation. The prime minister insisted on noting that Cavaignac had spoken "in the name of the government." He was intent on not allowing the glory of such a speech to accrue solely to Cavaignac's profit. By unanimous vote, it was decided to post the speech in all the communes of France. Only fifteen Socialists abstained . . . along with former Prime Minister Méline.

"We had had our hopes for Cavaignac," the Socialist, Léon Blum, would write. "We knew him to be upright, hardworking, and methodical." And there he was declaring Dreyfus guilty. He had vouched personally for the authenticity of the documents he had read—even for the accuracy of the confession to Lebrun-Renault! "What was frightening, horrendous was that he could believe all that in good faith. And the entire Chamber had acclaimed him."⁸ "We were floored," continued Blum. "The atmosphere had changed and was once again hostile to us."⁹ On the following day the press vented its near unanimous satisfaction. The "Dreyfus question," wrote Cassagnac in *L'Autorité*, remains open "only for those who have a racial or private interest in proclaiming his innocence." The Socialist Alexandre Millerand, wrote in *La Lanterne* of July 9 that Cavaig-

* *Supra* pp. 50–51.
† The Henry forgery.
‡ Drumont, *La Libre Parole* of July 8, 1898.

nac had "relieved the public conscience." *Le Figaro* and *L'Echo de Paris* expressed moderate satisfaction: common sense had triumphed. There was no need to speak further of the Dreyfus Affair. . . . "We were there with our heads in our hands," explained Léon Blum, "Mathieu Dreyfus, Lucien Herr, and myself. We were silent, immobile. Were we crying? Did the oppression constrain our tears? I search in vain for words to convey that burden of despondency, consternation, and mourning. . . ."[10]

Whereupon Jean Jaurès appeared. In his warm voice, he both consoled and berated his friends. "There was vehemence and anger in his voice, but also something triumphant and radiant. . . ." He rekindled their zeal and soon persuaded them that the documents whose authenticity Cavaignac had guaranteed were forgeries. They reeked of falsity. The forgers have come out of their hold. "We've got them by the throat." "Stop looking as though you were at a funeral; be like me; rejoice! . . ." To be sure his triumph was tinged with regret. "The silence, the acquiescence, the unanimous vote, all that was sad. . . . It was sad that there was not a single person. . . ." But who cared about the complacency of the Assembly? Cavaignac's speech should not have been a source of consternation for Dreyfus's friends but of comfort. Cavaignac had stepped out of the fortress in which Méline could not be touched. Out of clumsiness, passion, or stubborn blindness, Cavaignac had conceded everything except Dreyfus's innocence. "He had conceded," wrote Joseph Reinach, drawing up an inventory of Cavaignac's errors,

> that the intellectual elite that had denounced the judicial error was in good faith; that *raison d'Etat* could not prevail against justice; that the poisonous argument based on foreign repercussions was the most contemptible of pretexts; that France had a right to resolve the matter one way or another without having to fear a war; that the alleged necessity of a closed session was a lie and a position of cowardice; that the entire question is judicial and not political; that *res judicata* is no more than a legal formalism; that anyone had the right, following the minister's example, to proceed to examine the documents and facts of the case and to review them in detail; that again following the minister's example, it was permissible to base an argument—without lacking in patriotism—on German and Italian documents; that secret documents had been communicated to the judges in 1894, since the minister had not dared to adopt as his own Billot's sacrosanct formula; that the bordereau, the sole legal basis of the accusation, of which Cavaignac had said not a word, was insufficient to prove Dreyfus's guilt; that someone other than himself might indeed have been its author; and that

Esterhazy, since Cavaignac was about to expel him from the Army, was at least a scoundrel and perhaps a bandit.

After that, what was left, after the abandonment of all the most solid outposts engaged in the citadel's defense? A legend and a forgery.[11]

Like Joseph Reinach, Mathieu Dreyfus, in his memoirs, claims that Cavaignac in his speech of July 7 "was also responsible for the revision."[12] But it was only with the passage of time that the actual effects of Cavaignac's intervention would be seen. At the time, the minister of war seemed to have routed Dreyfus's partisans. His speech was posted, and the "Henry forgery" with it, in the thirty-six thousand communes of France.

All the political parties appeared to have buried the Affair. From the bed which he could no longer leave, the aged Scheurer-Kestner continued to proclaim his conviction: "It would be unworthy of an old republican like myself, in the presence of a task imposed by his conscience, to recoil because a temporarily disoriented sector of public opinion has risen against him. . . ."[13] But Scheurer-Kestner was afraid, by then, of dying before Dreyfus was freed from prison. . . .

It was no doubt within the General Staff that the risks entailed by Cavaignac's strategy were best gauged. By regrouping behind the authority of a prior verdict, Méline and Billot avoided acting, allowing the General Staff to move in their place. Now the civilian authorities, in confiscating that initiative without foreseeing its consequences, were courting disaster. Esterhazy, in a state of panic, was capable of the very worst. Pellieux's "blunder" at the Zola trial, that Boisdeffre had skillfully set aright, had now been aggravated by Cavaignac. They were several—including Boisdeffre, Gonse, and Henry—who knew that two of the documents whose text was now posted on every city hall in France were forgeries and rather crude forgeries at that. A handful of politicians knew it as well.* And why, if not for that reason, had the very prudent Méline abstained from the vote on posting Cavaignac's speech?

In General Gonse's office, a few officers gathered on the evening of Cavaignac's "triumph." "The minister would have done well not to have read the letters," murmured Commandant Henry.[14] "All this is going to end badly," commented General Gonse.

---

* At the least, Hanotaux and Billot, who had been ministers in the Méline government.

8

We Need a Lightning Bolt

The day after the "triumphant speech," Jean Jaurès published in *La Petite République* an open letter to the minister of war in which he took up quite vigorously the thesis he had developed in the presence of Léon Blum and Lucien Herr. Godefroy Cavaignac had, in spite of himself, rendered the greatest service to the cause of revision.*

> Yesterday in the Chamber you performed both a useful labor and a criminal labor. You performed a useful labor in presenting to the country a part of the dossier.
>
> Henceforth it will no longer be permitted to talk of the necessity of a closed session; through you the problem has become the business of the Nation itself. Through you the debate has begun. And first of all, a major fact, a decisive fact will strike all minds once the rapid torrent of parliamentary approbation will have passed.
>
> You did not say, you did not dare to say that secret documents had not been communicated to the judges without being given to the defendant. Better still, by quoting the documents which, in your opinion, ought to be the basis of one's belief and which do not figure in the bill of indictment, you admit, you proclaim the monstrous iniquity of the military proceedings and you furnish your colleague Sarrien with the elements needed for a revision. But permit me to tell you this: at bottom, your arguments don't carry; they have no merit. Far from shaking my deep conviction, they have, on the contrary, confirmed it and more than ever I am convinced that a monstrous judicial error has been committed.

* In *L'Aurore* of July 8, Clemenceau observed that the secret communication to the judges in 1894 was now an established fact, and that the revision was consequently inevitable. Guyot wrote the same in *Le Siècle* of the same day.

More than ever I am convinced that it is Esterhazy and Esterhazy alone who is the traitor.

When the Socialist groups of Paris are willing, when they are willing to leave behind equivocation, ignorance, and deception in order to grasp in its workings the monstrous functioning of the military machine, I will be prepared to demonstrate for them the proof of what I am saying.

What then have you come up with? You have posited in opposition Dreyfus's alleged admissions to Captain Lebrun-Renault. But if the General Staff accorded any merit to that story, why did it not require the latter to set it down in writing in a formal report and sign it? Why above all was the transcription of such a confession not submitted to the accused, as law requires? Why is the only trace of it to be found in a jotting in Lebrun-Renault's notebook or in a letter to General Gonse?

But there is more still, and if one is willing to read carefully that letter from General Gonse, one will have the whole key to the Affair.

In the Zola trial, Labori read an authentic extract from du Paty's interrogation of Dreyfus. There it may be observed that du Paty attempted in vain to extract a confession from the accused. He promised to arrange a meeting with the minister of war for him if only he would embark on the path of confession, if he confessed at least to an imprudence. And the accused, despite that trap, affirmed his innocence.

And here is how General Gonse, following Lebrun-Renault, relates Dreyfus's alleged confession:

"The minister is aware that I am innocent; he had me say as much by Commandant du Paty de Clam in prison three or four days ago and he knows that if I turned over any documents, they were documents of no significance, and that it was in order to obtain others, which were important."

Yes, I thank you for communicating those texts to us, for they allow us to see fully through what transformation the conversation recorded in the minutes of the interrogation and repeated by Dreyfus in his defense has been denatured—no doubt, unconsciously—by Captain Lebrun-Renault. We can also observe how dangerous it is to base a judgment on the alleged remarks of a defendant when such remarks are not submitted to the defendant himself so he may acknowledge and sign them.

Otherwise, there is no limit to arbitrariness, fantasy, uncertainty, and error.

But, Mister Minister, there is a man who should have risen before the Chamber to shout out that you were in error. I refer to Charles Dupuy. I affirm once again, I swear once again that he told me that Captain Lebrun-Renault, when he called on him, affirmed to him that he had not received a confession from Dreyfus. What! Charles Dupuy knows that and keeps his silence! He sees that you are basing your belief and that of the country on those alleged admissions. He knows they are false, and out of prudence and calculation, he remains silent. What name can one give to such a crime? And with what brand will history stigmatize this man when it will know the truth?

In any event, in order to establish that D. . . . applies to Dreyfus, you are obliged to quote a document seized in 1896 and in which the name of Dreyfus is spelled out.

That document had already been quoted by General de Pellieux, and it was already clear that it was the crudest and most glaring of forgeries, produced just in time to save Esterhazy.

After what you have cited, this is still more certain. You attribute the 1896 document to the persons who wrote those of 1894 and it is enough for you to observe that they were written by the same blue pencil. But just compare the language in them. The 1894 documents are in perfect French.

The 1896 document contains the crudest errors. The forger, wanting to imitate a foreigner's style, took delight in fabricating the most pitiful French.

But have you even thought about these things? Have you taken the time to study and compare? No, for what you needed was an immediate success, a success on the tribune and with public opinion. You are fascinated by the Elysée and thought that chauvinistic passion would bring you there. Be careful, though: law, justice, and truth cannot always be violated with impunity.

The acclamations will pass: the truth will remain.

And intrepid consciences will continue their implacable struggle against all the lies, all the baseness. You have unleashed anew the passions of our misguided country. It matters little. The truth is patient and her friends will not flinch.

Thus did the Dreyfusards, with Jean Jaurès at their head, mount their assault. The same day, the attorney Edgar Demange met with the lawyer Fernand Labori, Lieutenant Colonel Georges Picquart, Ludovic Trarieux, and Joseph Reinach.[1] Demange decided to send Sarrien a letter, intended to support the request for an annulment of the 1894 verdict which Lucie

Dreyfus had brought before Sarrien.* He affirmed that "the documents dated March and April 1894 and read from the tribune of the Chamber of Deputies by the minister of war were known to neither Dreyfus nor to his defense." He observed that the only document legally known to the Court Martial—the bordereau—had not even been mentioned by Cavaignac in his address. Finally, in order to demolish the legend of a confession, he sent the minister of justice a copy of the note written by Alfred Dreyfus immediately after Commandant du Paty's visit of December 31, 1894, a note reporting that du Paty had come to ask him "on behalf of the Minister" if he had not simply wanted to "entice" the Germans, and specifying, "I answered him that I had never had relations with any German agent or military attaché, that I had not engaged in any act of enticement or baiting, that I was innocent." Why would Dreyfus have said otherwise to Captain Lebrun-Renault?

But the crucial letter was no doubt that sent on July 9 by the dismissed Colonel Picquart to Henri Brisson, the prime minister:

Mister Prime Minister:

Until now I have not been able to express myself freely on the subject of the secret documents on which it has been claimed to base Dreyfus's guilt.

Since the minister of war has quoted from the tribune of the Chamber of Deputies three of those documents, I consider it a duty to inform you that I am in a position to establish before any competent jurisdiction that the two documents dated 1894 cannot be applied to Dreyfus and that the one dated 1896 has every appearance of being a forgery. It will then appear that the good faith of the minister of war has been caught unawares and that such is as well the case for all those who have believed in the value of the first two documents and the authenticity of the last.

Kindly accept, Mister Prime Minister, etc.

G. Picquart

Picquart did not have any illusions. He knew that the letter would provoke the minister of war's fury, against which he was without defense. He calmly performed what he took to be his duty. And in fact Cavaignac took the letter—addressed to the prime minister by an "agent of the syndicate"—as a personal offense. He urged the prime minister to announce the filing of a complaint against Picquart and Leblois. Brisson fell sick. The minister of war dragged Sarrien to the bedside of the prime

* The letter was published in *Le Siècle* of July 9.

minister: he wanted, he demanded legal action. But Cavaignac, who only the day before had routed the syndicate, had other worries that day. The most serious came from a totally unexpected source.

Examining Magistrate Bertulus had been investigating for several months the forgery charge brought by Colonel Picquart because of the two telegrams—one signed "Speranza," the other "Blanche"—that had been sent to him in Tunisia on November 10, 1897 with the intention of making him appear to be an agent of the syndicate. That investigation had made little progress, although Bertulus was conducting it with care. Then in May, the lawyer Herbin brought to his colleague, Fernand Labori, a new witness of crucial importance: Christian Esterhazy. Well-intentioned Christian, tired of asking his uncle for the return of the money he had loaned, made some inquiries on his own and discovered that the funds given to his uncle had never been invested with the Rothschilds. His uncle, in brief, had swindled, humiliated, and, in addition, manipulated him by using him as an intermediary. Furious to avenge himself, Christian Esterhazy went to tell all to the lawyer representing both Zola and Lucie Dreyfus. With documents in hand, he revealed the role he had played between du Paty de Clam and his uncle, and the meetings arranged in churches and on riverbanks. He told everything that he knew about the "liberating document" and about the false telegrams. He revealed the continuous communications between Commandant Esterhazy, General de Pellieux, and the General Staff. That much had never been hoped for. Since Christian thought he recalled that at least one of the counterfeit telegrams sent to Picquart was in Mlle. Marguerite Pays's handwriting, Mathieu Dreyfus had the idea to send flowers, through a confederate, to Esterhazy's mistress, who, extremely moved, answered with a note of thanks.* It was thus verified that the handwriting of the Speranza dispatch was that of Esterhazy's mistress.

It appears that the revisionists waited a certain amount of time before exploiting such precious revelations. On July 4, Picquart had written to the magistrate asking that Christian Esterhazy be heard. And on July 9, two days after Cavaignac's speech, Christian became a witness. Seized with remorse, he first denied, then confessed his exploits.† But he had en-

---

* The procedure was not beyond reproach, and Mathieu, implicated in the maneuver, did not stop there.[2] The anti-Dreyfusards would maintain that Christian was "bought" by the syndicate, and that all the rest was no more than a carefully staged deception.[3] "Christian," wrote Reinach, "did not request a *sou,* and did not receive any."[4]

† Esterhazy, informed in a manner that has not been ascertained, wrote to his nephew on July 8: "It is said that in April you went to turn me in, to betray me, to sell me, to tell abominable and monstrous stories about me to my worst enemies. . . . You, after Boulancy! No, it's enough to make one want to renounce God!"[5]

trusted the "documents" proving the collusion of Esterhazy, du Paty de Clam, and the General Staff to Labori.

The lawyer and the examining magistrate then organized a complicated scenario. Accompanied by his clerk, the magistrate would appear on July 11 at Labori's home. Labori would protest against the visit as "an attack on lawyers' rights." Refusing to transfer the documents to the magistrate, Labori would consent to hand them over to Christian, who would have come with the magistrate in order to take back his dossier. And Christian himself would transfer them to the judge. The scenario was played out and the judge received the precious documents. Bertulus immediately informed the public prosecutor that he intended to have Esterhazy and his mistress arrested, on twin charges of swindling and forgery. Feuilloley, the prosecutor, was dumbstruck. He informed Minister of Justice Sarrien who, in turn, warned Cavaignac. They attempted to dissuade Judge Bertulus, but by then matters had turned into a race between various legal proceedings. On July 11 the minister of war signed an order bringing Esterhazy before an investigatory board. But the magistrate seized the initiative away from Cavaignac. At 6:00 P.M. on July 12 there was a house-search in the home of Marguerite Pays, where a considerable number of papers of little significance were discovered. Esterhazy, who was expecting the search, had hidden the essential documents. At 8 o'clock, when Esterhazy arrived to take his mistress to dinner, he was arrested, and broke down. Then, he issued a threat, "I will speak, and I will reveal what I have concealed until now." The public prosecutor's representative, who was present, tried to turn Bertulus away from his insane determination, but nothing would stop the magistrate. Toward midnight Commandant Esterhazy was taken to La Santé Prison and Marguerite Pays to the Prison of Saint-Lazare.

That evening a military party was being held at the Elysée where Cavaignac was being honored. It was there that he learned the news and became furious. This petty magistrate was upsetting all his projects. At the General Staff the atmosphere was one of impending disaster. General de Boisdeffre chose to fall sick and take a leave of absence. General Gonse remained at his post, but would also become ill during the following days. As for Commandant Henry, who could "feel the ground quaking," he sank into despair.[6]

By July 12, Minister of War Cavaignac had regained the initiative and had extracted from the prime minister authorization to file suit against Picquart, who was accused of divulging secret materials. The plan was to have him arrested swiftly.* The charge was based on the accusations of

---

* Brisson, who was ill, resisted for three days. And then, as he yielded to pressure from Cavaignac and Sarrien, he realized that to allow a complaint to be lodged was also to authorize Picquart's arrest.

Félix Gribelin, Captain Lauth, and Commandant Henry. Picquart was alleged to have shown three dossiers—including one on "carrier pigeons" and the famous "secret file"—to his friend, the lawyer Louis Leblois. A particularly "efficient" examining magistrate was found in Albert Fabre, a personal friend of Henri Brisson. On the same day, the magistrate ordered a search of Picquart's home in his absence. Arrest was imminent. In order to bend the government's resolution, former Minister of Justice Ludovic Trarieux wrote to Sarrien, "If the arrest of Lieutenant Colonel Picquart must take place, I insist—in order to spare him useless harassment—that it be under my roof that he is seized. That should tell you my feelings." Sarrien did not reply. The next day, Judge Fabre, after apparently having resisted for several hours, surrendered to the will of the Ministry. He would place Picquart in detention. Picquart, summoned to the Palais de Justice, scarcely had time to affirm his innocence. He was arrested, then brought to La Santé Prison . . . where Esterhazy had already been in detention for the previous two days.

Through Cavaignac's furious determination* and Brisson's weakness, the Affair had reached a point of total incoherence. The government was unable to master different but related legal proceedings that were as complicated as they were unpredictable in their developments. Since Christian Esterhazy, in Bertulus's presence, had "charged" Colonel du Paty de Clam, Picquart, from the depths of the prison, was now filing a suit for forgery against du Paty. He was under the impression that du Paty had been the author of the telegram signed "Blanche." Cavaignac, who was energetically pursuing his own investigation, received Gribelin, who placed all responsibility on du Paty and Gonse. General Gonse, now trying to extricate himself, claimed that the Montsouris meeting between Esterhazy and du Paty had been organized without the knowledge of the General Staff. He too accused du Paty, who within a few days had become a scapegoat. Cavaignac thus called in du Paty, to whom he was distantly related, and heard his arguments at length. Du Paty seemed sincere, but it was clear that he had been imprudent.

During this period the examining magistrates were quite relentless, even competitive, in their zeal. Judge Bertulus heard Esterhazy several times; he had by now chosen to deny everything. But the magistrate seemed carried away by his own daring. On July 18 he received a visit from Commandant Henry, who had been chosen as the minister of war's representative at the examination of the papers that had been seized. The

---

* "An *idée fixe*," wrote Reinach, "that most terrible of neuroses, is most terrible when it lodges in the brain of a mathematician who imagines that he has reached it through reason. Such men of science, even when they are healthy, are extremely dangerous when they become involved in politics."[7]

magistrate and the forger had known each other for a long time. The magistrate told Henry everything that he knew about the collusion and the accusations that were mounting against Esterhazy and du Paty. Henry appears to have become frightened. Did Bertulus then attempt to accuse Henry, to "shake him up" in order to learn the truth? Did he attempt to demonstrate that he knew Henry to be, of necessity, Esterhazy's provider, the center of the entire conspiracy? At the Rennes trial, Bertulus would relate that the giant suddenly broke down; that Henry, weeping profusely, embraced him, shouting through his tears, "Save us; save us . . . you must save the Army's honor."[8] Clerk André would testify to having heard, in a voice convulsed with sobs, the desperate words, "You must save the Army's honor." But at Rennes, Henry would not be present to give his version of the strange scene in which an examining magistrate, outside of any formal interrogation, managed to get a guilty man to "crack."

Judge Fabre proceeded, for his part, to conduct a meticulous investigation of Georges Picquart. He would interrogate the accused nine times and hear all the actors of the Affair, who had already testified at the Zola trial, with the exception of de Boisdeffre, who was decidedly ill. Gribelin, Henry, and Lauth maintained their accusations. Fabre also proved quite zealous and decided to indict Leblois as well for divulging secret information. But as one of the defendants was a soldier and the other a civilian, Fabre and the lawyers were plunging ever deeper into the quagmire of the law. Should the two accomplices be separated and each sent before the appropriate jurisdiction or should they both be sent before a court of summary jurisdiction? In the meanwhile Picquart remained in prison.

During this period, various legal procedures were conducted. When the second Zola trial had come before the Court of Assizes of Versailles on May 23, Fernand Labori had succeeded in having it postponed by insisting, prior to all discussion of substance, on a judgment as to the court's jurisdiction,* which was in turn immediately appealed. After the appeal was rejected, Zola was again assigned to appear before the Assize Court on July 18. Once again Labori refused discussion. Perhaps he expected decisive elements to emerge from the Bertulus investigation, or felt that a prolonged discussion was unnecessary with the revision progressing through other channels. Two days before the trial, Zola sent the prime minister a vehement letter, which was published by *L'Aurore* on July 16. "You incarnate republican virtue. You were the high symbol of civic honesty. . . . You fall into the Affair and there you are, stripped of your

---

* Zola lived in Paris and the article on which the trial was based had been published in Paris. Labori consequently maintained that the criminal court of Versailles was incompetent to adjudicate it.

moral sovereignty, you are no more than a fallible and compromised human being."

That letter became part of a strategy. Fernand Labori and Georges Clemenceau, the editor of *L'Aurore,* had persuaded Zola to default, to leave France if the Assize Court did not allow him to prove his accusations, not merely in the three lines retained in the indictment, but in all the "adjoining" statements—that is, in the whole of *J'Accuse.* There was not the slightest chance that the Court would approve. The public prosecutor, Bertrand, had received vigorous instructions: he emotionally denounced Zola's maneuvers to flee "into the procedural jungle-growth." As foreseen, the Court rejected Labori's pleas. The lawyer immediately filed an appeal, but the Court judged that the appeal would not stay the procedures. Zola left the defendant's bench, and slowly traversing the crowd, walked away, amid jeers and shouts. Paul Déroulède, mounted on a platform, shouted: "Leave France! Go to Venice!" Insults were showered on the old writer: "Coward," "Traitor," "Go back to the Jews." All that remained for the Court was to sentence Zola and Perrenx, the managing editor of *L'Aurore,* in their absence, to the maximum penalty—one year in prison. To avoid arrest, Zola left for London at nightfall. The following morning, he had become no more than "M. Pascal," named after a character in one of his novels, living in exile in a small London hotel.*

It appears that it was only with difficulty that Zola embarked on this clandestine departure. There were numerous revisionists, like Joseph Reinach, who disapproved of such an evasion.[9] Was it really necessary for Zola, who was so courageous, to give the appearance of fleeing, the subterfuge of a guilty man? Labori and Clemenceau (who published under Zola's signature an article in *L'Aurore* of July 20 which justified his departure) had convinced the author that his flight was "a tactical necessity for which they assumed responsibility." And Zola resigned himself "because it seemed to him that his duty lay wherever the suffering was greatest. . . ." But the "flight," which was so hard to explain,[10] left some partisans bitter. Scheurer-Kestner's health was deteriorating. Picquart was in prison. Zola was in exile. The "party of justice" had lost three of its principal champions.[11]

And yet nothing seemed capable of stopping the momentum of the

* In France, the train stations, ports and borders would immediately be placed under surveillance as police agents were sent out to search for the fugitive. Under the name of Beauchamp, Zola would settle in July in Neighbridge, near the Thames, a dozen miles from the capital. In August he would find a house to rent, which was baptized Penn. His children would rejoin him in April and Mme. Zola in October. At the end of August, he would settle in Summerfield, then definitively in Queen's Hotel in Upper Norwood. His exile would last eleven months.

revisionists. Nor could anything impede the furious obstinacy of Cavaignac. He was obsessed with the idea that hidden powers, for money, had
undertaken to dishonor the Republic, whose champion he saw himself to
be. By now the revisionists were for him a veritable plot against the security
of the State. "He was," Reinach assures us, "the portrait of his father, the
General, but a poor copy—dry and blurred."* Stubborn, borne on by an
almost limitless confidence in himself, he entertained the ambition of
finishing once and for all with Dreyfus and the Dreyfusards. Losing all
sense of proportion, he was elaborating a plan to send before the Senate,
constituted as a High Court, those "responsible" for the revisionist movement on suspicion of engaging in a plot against the security of the State.
He would thus be able to rid France with a single stroke of all conspirators.
Cavaignac had already entrusted to a lawyer—no doubt President of the
Bar Ployer— the task of studying the juridical aspects of a vast legal action.
And on August 11, at a dinner that brought the ministers to the home of
the prime minister, he read a memorandum outlining his system. It would
entail depriving the customary jurisdictions of all the cases under way and
filing suit before the High Court with indictments against various jour-
nalists and politicians, including Auguste Scheurer-Kestner, Ludovic
Trarieux, Louis Leblois, Georges Picquart, Ernest Vaughan, Georges
Clemenceau, Urbain Gohier, Arthur Ranc, Victor Simond, Jean Jaurès,
Gérault-Richard, Yves Guyot, Joseph Reinach, Zola, and, of course,
Mathieu Dreyfus and the journalist Bernard Lazare. The ministers were
dumbfounded. Had Cavaignac gone mad? Brisson—who for once showed
firmness—declared curtly that he would never be party to such a trial.
Much put out, Cavaignac concealed his dissatisfaction. He would not insist
for the present, but he would not renounce his project.

   At least the civilian courts were to give Cavaignac some of the reparation he sought. On August 5, the grand jury of the Paris Court of Appeal,
convinced by the arguments of the public prosecutor, declared Judge
Bertulus incompetent to investigate the case against du Paty de Clam in
the forgery suit brought by Picquart. Du Paty, an officer on active duty, fell
under the jurisdiction of military justice.†

   On August 12, yielding to the pressures of the public prosecutor, the
grand jury quashed the order by which Bertulus had sent Esterhazy and
Marguerite Pays before the Court of Assizes for forgery. It declared that
the expert testimony attributing to her the handwriting of the "Speranza"

---

* Joseph Reinach quoted Mirabeau's line on Robespierre and applied it to Cavaignac: "He
will go far; he believes everything that he says."[12]
† The High Court of Appeal was to annul that ruling on September 2 and declare the
examining magistrate competent to proceed against du Paty. Any resultant satisfaction was
symbolic since the principals guilty of the crime, Esterhazy and Mme. Pays, could by then no
longer be brought to justice.

dispatch was not a "sufficient charge," that "fraudulent intention" did not appear in the composition of the telegrams, that the "clear, flagrant, and unjustifiable contradictions" of Christian Esterhazy discredited his testimony, that the young man, moreover, had "at the very end handed over, betrayed, and sold" the relative whose devoted friend he had claimed to be. That judgment, which satisfied the expectation of the Minister of Justice Sarrien, was no more than an impassioned plea on Esterhazy's behalf. The Court ultimately declared "that there were no grounds for proceeding against Walsin-Esterhazy and the woman named Pays." Judge Bertulus was thus defeated.

Esterhazy was freed that very evening, and sought his mistress at the Saint-Lazare prison. They were free, while Picquart remained incarcerated. This was no small satisfaction for the General Staff. As for Cavaignac, who was unflinchingly pursuing his plan, he was in the process of preparing a libel suit against Labori, Trarieux, Picquart, and Christian Esterhazy. And he could now finally bring Esterhazy on his own authority before an investigatory board. "Thank God that the Affair, despite all the remaining difficulties, has made it through this very difficult pass," wrote General de Boisdeffre, who was still ill, to his minister. "I hope that du Paty will understand the utility of keeping still, of remaining silent. . . ."[13] From London Zola wrote to Labori: "You would not believe the horror aroused in me by the echoes coming my way from France. We can no longer depend on the system of justice. My only hopes now are with the unknown, the unexpected. We need a lightning bolt falling from the sky. . . ."[14] On the evening of August 13, that lightning bolt would strike.

9

I Am Doomed; They Are Abandoning Me. . . .

On the evening of August 13, as on every other evening, Captain Louis Cuignet, serving with the minister of war's military staff, was at work in his office. On Godefrey Cavaignac's order, he was examining the documents in the secret file with meticulous care. Around 10 o'clock he was repeatedly examining in the light of his lamp the famous letter from Alessandro Panizzardi to Colonel Maximilien von Schwarzkoppen that Cavaignac had read before the Chamber and which had produced so decisive an effect, since Dreyfus's name appeared in its text: "I will say that I never had any relations with the Jew." Placing the letter under his lamp and observing it at length, Cuignet suddenly discovered that the rules of the paper were of two different shades. The heading and the signature appeared on paper whose lines were bluish gray; the body of the letter on fragments whose lines were pale violet. Cuignet was astounded. The letter which was by now so famous, that had been so exploited and so criticized, was actually made of pieces of two different letters. It was clearly a forgery. And this was the document that Commandant Henry pretended to have discovered in 1896 through Mme. Bastian via the "ordinary track"! Cuignet had been convinced of Dreyfus's guilt. He was also a friend of Henry. Suddenly he found himself in the presence of this terrible evidence. The principal document against Dreyfus was a fraud. It was Henry who had furnished the forgery. And that forgery, whose authenticity had been vouched for in Cavaignac's address, was posted all over France.

Cuignet would say later that at that point he felt very disturbed. He had the cruel obligation of denouncing both the forgery and the forger. "If it had to be done again," he would say, "I would do it still, but I would have wished never to have been mixed up in this horrible adventure." The next morning he rushed in to see General Roget, the head of the minister's cabinet. In broad daylight the difference in the letters was not so apparent.

The room was darkened and lamps brought in. The evidence was glaring. Cuignet and Roget immediately went to see the minister and repeated the experiment. Cavaignac in turn was convinced. It was to the credit of those three men, all committed to the struggle against revision, to have not for a moment thought of quashing their discovery. On that occasion there was no one to repeat General Gonse's words to Colonel Picquart: "If you do not say anything, no one will know."

Colonel Henry was not on duty; it was the day before his regularly scheduled leave. Cavaignac decided not to summon him immediately. General de Boisdeffre was also absent. The minister did not inform him either. Nor did he say a word to Prime Minister Henri Brisson or to Minister of Justice Sarrien. Was he trying to conceal the forgery? Future events would demonstrate the opposite. But Cavaignac was intent on retaining control of the situation. Had he been deceived as to the authenticity of a document? He would do himself honor by denouncing the error himself. He would declare that the document, which was dated much later than the Dreyfus trial, was secondary. He would be all the more effective in his pursuit of the Dreyfusards in that he would openly acknowledge his error.[1] On Roget and Cuignet he imposed the utmost secrecy: "The glory of having executed justice, which for the while belonged only to Cuignet's lamp, he would claim for himself." For himself alone.

On August 15, he traveled to Macon with the minister of justice. He did not breathe a word of what had transpired the previous day and allowed himself to bask in the crowd's acclaim. In a violent speech, he denounced the partisans of the revision as disloyal citizens. In Le Mans eight days later, he proclaimed, "In the presence of the impious attempts which have been made to discredit those working for the greatness of our country, patriots must affirm more forcefully than ever their love, their admiration for the Army. . . ."[2] He aroused great enthusiasm. More than twenty provincial assemblies expressed wishes "to honor the Army" and invited the government to take all possible measures to crush the "odious campaign." It was in Cavaignac that they trusted.

On the morning of August 16 Commandant Esterhazy, who had been out of prison for four days, learned that he was to be summoned to appear before an investigatory board. So the minister of war was keeping his promise. Esterhazy was losing his footing. His lawyer, Maurice Tézenas, advised him "to travel to other skies." Mlle. Pays caught him in the act of consulting a railway timetable. She made a terrible scene, accused him of being a "coward," a "scoundrel," and he renounced, for the while, his flight. Esterhazy pleaded his case before Edouard Drumont and obtained from him an article hostile to Cavaignac that was published in *La Libre Parole* of August 23. Cavaignac, the article claimed, "who knows the truth, is preparing to sacrifice the unfortunate Esterhazy to the rascals of the syndicate, the Jewish pack whose dogs can bark in every language." The article was threatening and lucid:

> The members of the investigatory board will do as they like, but it seems useful and necessary to me to show them what they will be doing. If they hand over Esterhazy to the Jewish and German syndicate, they will be bringing credibility to the campaign organized by Schwarzkoppen and Panizzardi, who are two confessed spies. . . . That is the logical progression; after Esterhazy, it will be du Paty de Clam, after du Paty, Henry, Lauth, and de Boisdeffre, and after de Boisdeffre, Mercier. . . . In abandoning their unfortunate colleague, the representatives of the Army will be betraying themselves.

But Cavaignac had decided to "execute" Esterhazy, and he was not a man to recoil. The investigatory board met in closed session on August 24 in the barracks of Château-d'Eau. Esterhazy immediately moved to the offensive. He would respond in political terms. He affirmed that he had committed all the acts that were delicately being qualified as "undisciplined" on orders from the General Staff. The Jews had offered him 600,000 francs to declare himself the author of the bordereau. He had refused that deal. And the indefatigable General de Pellieux, placing his authority in Esterhazy's service, confirmed that he considered him to be a "brave soldier." Was du Paty de Clam to be called as a witness? Esterhazy abruptly decided to discredit that "demi-dandified, demi-literate puppet caught up in a tale of highwaymen." He affirmed that his letters to Félix Faure had been dictated to him by du Paty, who protested, then acknowledged having furnished the "skeleton" of the first letter. Badgered by Esterhazy and the presiding officer of the investigatory board, the witness ended up making an ambiguous confession. "I don't know. . . . I don't dare make so bold as to confirm what the Commandant has said. . . . I am not saying the opposite. . . ." Exploiting his advantage, Esterhazy at this point maintained that everything he had done had been done on command, that he had never taken a single initiative that had not been in response to orders from the General Staff. Did they want proof? There existed a document in du Paty's handwriting; du Paty was General Gonse's right-hand man. General de Boisdeffre would be named in that document. Should they want it, they could find it in the hands of his lawyer. In a state of dismay, the investigatory board postponed the conclusion of its session.

On August 27 Esterhazy supplied the board with the "note in two handwritings"* that he managed to obtain—not without difficulty—from his lawyer. Du Paty was indeed obliged to acknowledge his authorship. "I have many more," Esterhazy assured them. "At present, I am restraining myself." He was not far from having won the entire match. The investigatory board concluded by discharging Esterhazy for "habitual misconduct," but judged him to be guilty of neither violations of honor nor violations of discipline. The procedure, so wished for by the minister of war, had become a disaster for the General Staff. In transmitting to Cavaignac the minutes and records of the investigatory board, General Zurlinden, military governor of Paris, drew the minister's attention to the fact that the minutes seemed to include "grave revelations concerning the role of certain officers in the Army General Staff in the first Esterhazy affair." "In keeping with the customs of the Army," Zurlinden concluded, "there would be grounds for exercising a certain indulgence toward Commandant Esterhazy." But one could not count on Cavaignac for indulgence; he discharged Esterhazy immediately. "A monstrous abuse of power," Esterhazy would comment, on the part of an Army that had made him do "its most confidential tasks." Cavaignac and his crowd were decidedly a pack of "cowardly and obscene scoundrels."[3] But the focus of the inquiry had shifted elsewhere. The investigation had revealed that the officers of the General Staff had been proceeding in a guilty manner. It remained for Cavaignac to light the fire. . . .

On August 30 the minister of war decided to interrogate Colonel Henry personally. General Gonse was ordered to escort Henry to the minister's office. General de Boisdeffre, who was still ailing, was also summoned urgently. Cavaignac, who received the general before questioning Henry, repeated the demonstration that Cuignet had performed for him. De Boisdeffre was dumbfounded. He refused to believe that Henry was a forger. But had it not in fact been a long time since he had had any illusions about the document Cavaignac was showing him?

The interrogation of Colonel Henry began on August 30 at 2:30 P.M. in the presence of Generals de Boisdeffre and Gonse. Colonel Roget, pen in hand, would keep extremely detailed minutes.† The minister went right to the target: examination of the two documents written in blue pencil—Alessandro Panizzardi's letter of December 31, 1896, and the item of June 1894 used for comparison—resulted in the observation that one of them contained words belonging to the other and vice versa.

"Given the materiality of the facts," the minister began, "the absence of

* See *supra* p. 226.
† The minutes were dated October 3, a circumstance permitting some, including Esterhazy, to contest their authenticity. Joseph Reinach regarded the document as beyond suspicion.[4]

an explanation would be as serious as an insufficient explanation. When and how did you reconstitute these documents?" Henry began his testimony by lying, but he was incapable of inventing a plausible explanation. Cavaignac decided to play his game. He would show these generals what it meant for a minister to want the truth. He repeated that the 1894 document contained "fragments belonging to the one from 1896." Henry equivocated: "How do I explain that fact? I can't simply say that I fabricated a document which I did not fabricate." De Boisdeffre and Gonse remained silent as Cavaignac badgered Henry with questions, like a hunter forcing his prey. Henry made a few concessions: "I arranged a few sentences. . . . I swear to you that I fabricated nothing." "Which are the words that you did fabricate?" "I don't remember any more." By then Cavaignac was looking for accomplices: "Who gave you the idea for those arrangements?" Henry responded that it was his idea alone. De Boisdeffre and Gonse remained silent. The luckless suspect explained: "My superiors were very worried. . . . I wanted to calm them, give them some serenity . . . I told myself: Let's add a sentence; if we only had proof in the situation in which we find ourselves. Moreover, no one knew anything about it. . . . I acted solely in the interest of my country."

Did he want to continue, as Cavaignac's daughter, drawing on her father's recollections, would write?[5] Did Cavaignac perceive a tremor, a quickly suppressed hesitation? Harried and disgusted, the minister ordered Henry to leave, then immediately called him back. "Now Henry, I am appealing to your honor as a soldier. Tell me the truth." Cavaignac wanted a complete confession. He badgered Henry with rapid-fire questions. In a state of desperation, Henry's resistance wore thin. He conceded, stammering out fragments of the truth. Finally, the minister summarized the accusation: "In 1896, you received an envelope with a letter inside, an insignificant letter; you suppressed the letter and fabricated another one?" Henry answered, "Yes." The ordeal was over. Henry had admitted his forgery. Cavaignac was victorious. De Boisdeffre and Gonse remained silent.

The minister ordered General Roget to escort Henry into a neighboring room and to keep him in view. De Boisdeffre took a sheet of paper from the minister's desk. Without pausing for a second, he wrote out his letter of resignation:

Mister Minister,
    I have just received proof that my trust in Colonel Henry, Chief of the Intelligence Services, was not justified. That trust, which was absolute, led me to be deceived, to declare authentic a document

that was not and to present it to you as such. Under these conditions, Mister Minister, I have the honor of asking you to be willing
to relieve me of my functions.

Cavaignac was surprised, and tried to make de Boisdeffre recant his
decision. "Anyone can be deceived . . . it is up to you to pursue the
investigation, to preside over the repression of the acts that resulted in the
error that you committed in all loyalty."* But Cavaignac knew only a small
part of the truth. He did not know that in a few minutes in his office, the
patient edifice constructed over the years by the General Staff had just
collapsed. He could not measure the extent of the disaster. "Anyone can be
led into error," replied de Boisdeffre. "But not everyone has had the
misfortune of affirming before a jury that a document was authentic when
it was not. . . . When one has found onself in such a situation, the only
thing left is to leave." Cavaignac had himself affirmed as much before the
deputies, and before the nation, but he was not insistent on that point. He
merely made public a communiqué that the Agence Havas published on
August 30, 1898. . . .

Today in the office of the minister of war, Lieutenant Colonel
Henry was acknowledged and acknowledged himself to be the
author of the letter dated October 1896 in which Dreyfus is named.
The minister of war immediately ordered the arrest of
Lieutenant Colonel Henry, who has been taken to the Fortress of
Mont-Valérien.

Alone with Henry, General Roget attempted to question him. Did he
have any accomplices? Henry repeated that no, he did not. Roget asked
him about Esterhazy. Did Esterhazy know Colonel Sandherr, head of the
Intelligence Service? Henry revealed that he had once seen, in 1895,
Esterhazy bringing documents to the colonel. And suddenly returning to
the bordereau, he assured Roget that the document had come to the
Intelligence Service "via the ordinary track. . . . Any other version is
contrary to the truth and materially impossible." Why the insistence on the
origin of the bordereau in just those circumstances?†

---

* Cavaignac was nevertheless alleged to have told an intimate on the evening of August 30:
"General de Boisdeffre has given me his resignation . . . he spared me the ordeal of asking
him for it."[6]
† It appeared suspicious—and revealing—to those (like Reinach) who maintained that the
bordereau did not arrive through the ordinary track. Until the very end, Henry would thus
have wanted to conceal his complicity with Esterhazy.[7] In any event, there was no other
witness of the conversation than General Roget.

Cavaignac arranged with the military governor of Paris to have Henry taken to Mont-Valérien where he would be kept under fortress arrest. Colonel Ferry, garrison adjutant of the fortress, arrived toward five o'clock in the afternoon in order to take Henry in a carriage to Mont-Valérien. * Just so, four years earlier, had Henry taken Dreyfus to the Prison of Cherche-Midi. Ferry first took Henry home to his small apartment at 13, Avenue Duquesne, so that he might gather a few belongings. Henry reassured his wife: "Everything will be all right. My conscience is serene." In the carriage, however, he broke down in despair. "What I have done I would be prepared to do again; it was for the good of the country and the Army. My poor wife, my poor little boy. Everything has collapsed in a moment. I will not be there for the opening of the hunt. What will they think. . . ." He sobbed and spoke of the "miserable wretches" who were the "cause of his misfortune." He was taken to the officers' wing, to the room that Colonel Picquart had occupied during the previous winter.

When the orderly serving him entered the room the next morning, he found him in a state of great prostration. Henry asked for writing materials. At 11 o'clock, he ate a light lunch and had a letter sent to General Gonse:

> General,
>   I have the honor of requesting you to agree to come see me here. I absolutely must speak to you.
>   Rest assured, General, of my respectful sentiments.

Then he wrote to his wife:

> My adored Berthe, I see that except for you everyone is going to abandon me and yet you know in whose interest I acted. My letter is a copy and contains nothing, absolutely nothing, of a forgery. It merely confirms verbal information I had been given a few days earlier. I am absolutely innocent, they know it, and everyone will know it later on; but right now, I can't speak. Take good care of our

---

* A declaration by General Gonse on September 5, 1898, attested that before leaving for Mont-Valérien, on orders from the minister, Henry would have accompanied General Gonse "by way of the interior of the Ministry's mansion" to the Service of Statistics in order to summarily hand his service over to him. After Henry's disappearance, General Gonse described as follows the conversation that the two accomplices would have had: "He spoke above all in abrupt sentences and monosyllables: 'What are they going to do with me? This is frightful! They're putting me in prison; they are going to take me to the Cherche-Midi and from there I'l be brought before a Court Martial! . . . I know what will happen to me! . . . And yet I have not acted wrongly; I have acted in the general interest! They're putting me in the hands of a police superintendant and they won't let me see my wife and our children.'"[8]

adored little Joseph, and continue loving him, as I love him and as I love you.

Good-bye, my darling; I hope you will be able to come see me soon. I embrace you both from the very bottom of my heart.

Henry was not telling the truth ("my letter is a copy. . . . It merely confirms verbal information. . . ."). He seemed to be defending his memory already. He had been drinking alcohol by the glassful for a few hours. He emptied half a bottle of rum.[9] His room, which was flooded with sunlight, was getting very hot. He began a second letter to his wife: "My beloved Berthe, I am like a madman; a frightening pain is gripping my brain. I am going to take a swim in the Seine. . . ."

He went no further. Either because of the heat or in order to be freer in his movements, he took off the civilian clothes that he had put on in the morning. He stretched out on his bed. It was toward three o'clock that Henry slit his throat with two strokes of a razor.* The blood gushed out in a violent jet that flowed over his hands, arms, sheets, mattress. Death was slow in coming: it took nearly a quarter of an hour. A little after 6 o'clock, an orderly brought Henry's meal. When he did not receive an answer, he informed the lieutenant on duty. They had to force the lock. Henry was stretched out on his bed, blood streaming from the corpse and onto the bed. The body was cold and stiff. His left hand had fallen back on the edge of the bed and strangely enough had closed the razor.[10] On the table, next to the bottle of rum, were found two final letters written to his wife, one opened, the other sealed. A Jewish physician, Dr. Léon Lévy, a young intern doing his military service at the fort, closed the eyes of the man who had done so much to send Dreyfus to prison and to keep him there. The next day, Dr. Lévy cleaned and prepared the corpse. Given the evidence of suicide, an autopsy appeared superfluous. In the officers' mess hall, a mortuary chapel was established. Gribelin and Lauth, friends and accomplices, sobbed while keeping vigil over the body. Then the remains were taken to Pogny in the Marne, the village of Henry's birth. The bishop of Châlons forbade the priest of Pogny from conducting a religious service. The local band, firemen, villagers, and numerous officers followed the coffin, which was draped in Henry's uniform. A soldier carried his decorations on a cushion. Neither Gonse nor de Boisdeffre attended. "I am doomed; they are abandoning me," the luckless colonel had confided

* In *La Gazette de France* of September 7, 1898, Charles Maurras wrote: "After a night and a day of meditation in solitude, exalted to the point of madness, Lieutenant-Colonel Henry, officer of the Legion of Honor, fourteen campaigns, two wounds, deemed it useful to inflict on himself two new wounds. He succumbed to them immediately. . . . In life as in death, he charged forward."

to his wife just before leaving for Mont-Valérien. Henry had been their executant, their instrument. He was now no more than a compromised agent, a dead one at that.

Henry had committed suicide. De Boisdeffre had resigned. Gonse no longer had the slightest authority. Du Paty de Clam had been gravely compromised by Esterhazy. Esterhazy had been discharged. For the members of the conspiracy, the debacle had taken place in a matter of days.

10

More Stupid than Cowardly, More Cowardly than Stupid

"You are not without knowing in whose interest I acted." Those last words from Commandant Henry to his wife have continued to fuel a controversy that many historians have claimed to resolve, each in his own manner. Had Henry acted in the interest of his old friend and confederate Commandant Esterhazy, as was the opinion of Mathieu Dreyfus, Joseph Reinach, and a number of other revisionists? Had he acted in the interest of the General Staff, Generals de Boisdeffre and Gonse, who had inspired or approved his criminal acts, and who had then left him to confess without so much as a single word? Was the final letter that Henry wrote to Gonse addressed to the architect of the forgery scheme, to whom Henry had been merely a loyal servant? Had he acted out of sheer military zeal, in order to "reassure" his worried superiors and defend, in his own way and with the means at his disposal, the Army's honor and the nation's interest? Or had he never been more than the docile instrument of a mysterious leader, the organizer of a vast betrayal whose name he had taken with him to the grave?

And how did he die? Several of the myths surrounding the Affair are rooted in the hypothesis that Henry was murdered. The very day after his death, Dr. Léon Lévy, who had examined Henry soon after his death, related that during the afternoon of August 31, at approximately the time of death, an officer of the General Staff had come to see the prisoner. A long conversation was alleged to have taken place between the two men. Upon leaving, it is claimed that the officer of the General Staff said to the officer on duty: "Do not disturb Lieutenant-Colonel Henry for a while. He has work to do. . . ." But there is no evidence attesting that such a visit took place. Several authors, in order to sustain the murder thesis, have insisted on a number of irregular details. Why, once Henry's crime was revealed, did General Cavaignac have him taken to Mont-Valérien and not to the Prison of Cherche-Midi as had been the case with Alfred Dreyfus?[1] What had become of the large sheets of paper that certain witnesses had seen on Henry's table? How could Henry have killed himself with a razor that was found closed? Why was an autopsy deemed pointless? These questions, along with the desire to add some mystery to an Affair that was already not lacking in drama, have fueled the accusation of murder. Even today numerous historians assume that Colonel Henry had been executed.[2] Executed by whom? By the General Staff, in the fear that he might tell more? By the true culprit, lest his name be revealed?

No doubt the possibility cannot be dismissed that Henry had been murdered, and that the murder was subsequently disguised as a suicide. But that appears no more than a fragile hypothesis and given the present state of the evidence, suicide remains the only convincing verdict. The tragic situation in which Henry found himself, his impassioned and melancholic character, the last words written to his wife, revealing as they do a mind beginning to lose its bearings, and the circumstances of his death grant plausibility to a suicide that reason itself might have dictated. Henry knew from experience that a compromised agent was an agent abandoned. The silence of de Boisdeffre and Gonse during Cavaignac's interrogation had confirmed to him, had he needed proof, that he was now a defeated man—alone and without hope.

It remains to determine whether on the night of November 2, 1896, Henry fabricated the forgery to which history has assigned his name, whether working out of his own zealous convictions, in order to reassure his superiors, or to satisfy wishes they did not dare express.* It is probable

---

* Léon Blum, in his *Souvenirs*, concludes that the General Staff's position becomes intelligible only "if one admits that Colonel Henry, from the very beginning, had all the strings and all the options in his hands. . . . He was both inspirer and implementor, instrument and agent." But that thesis, which assigns Henry the leading role, finds justification neither in the facts nor in his personality.[3]

that in serving the General Staff, Henry was an entirely subservient agent whose untiring, daring, and clumsy loyalty proved initially effective and then disastrous. It should not be forgotten that the Henry forgery, fabricated either on command or spontaneously (as claimed) in order to come to the aid of his superiors, was subsequently "authenticated" by Gonse, Henry, Lauth, and Gribelin, in hierarchical order.* They all knew that the document was counterfeit, yet vouched for its authenticity. Despite their efforts to prevent its use as evidence during the Esterhazy trial, Generals de Boisdeffre and Gonse had also vouched for it, when General de Pellieux had clumsily alluded to it in his testimony. The "Henry forgery" had thus become the collective forgery of them all.[4] They would henceforth walk hand in hand "and none was to let go of the others because they were bound thereafter by their complicity. Nothing would shake their perfect concert until the final catastrophe."[5] When Henry was confounded and urged to confess, he knew that he was being let go by those who were not only his superiors but his accomplices as well. And it was to General Gonse, who for two years had encouraged and covered up his crimes, that he wrote from his prison, "I absolutely must speak to you."

When the news of the day's events became known—Henry's confession in the minister's office, his death at Mont-Valérien, and General de Boisdeffre's resignation—it appeared for several hours that the revision was certain. Newspapers that had kept their distance from the fight now declared themselves in favor of examining the evidence once again. Most of the Catholic and nationalist newspapers seemed for a brief while to admit such a revision as though it were inevitable: "The Dreyfus trial will have to be begun anew," wrote Granier de Cassagnac on the extreme right, "and that trial can no longer take place in seclusion. . . . If Dreyfus is guilty, there is where it will be seen. That, in brief, is the risk. Without the revision, the Affair can know no end, but merely sink further into the mud." "All is changed," affirmed *L'Echo de Paris*, "the revision is a necessity. It is desired by a large number of officers. . . ." "It is better to have a revision provoked and accepted by the government," wrote *La Presse*, "than a revision belatedly imposed out of juridical scruples. . . ."[6] Henri Rochefort declared Henry's crime "at once odious and stupid." Edouard Drumont claimed in *La Libre Parole* "that whether or not there is a revision, at the point at which we are now, is not something that particularly concerns us." On the Dreyfusard side, the feeling was that the revision was henceforth inevitable: "Truth had triumphed," wrote Léon Blum. "The Cavaignac system had collapsed with one fell swoop. . . . No force in the

---

* Marcel Thomas treats that collective cautionary measure, later ratified by General Billot, as the act that sealed the conspiracy.

world could henceforth pose an obstacle to revision ... the affair was over. ..."[7]

But they would have to move quickly, profiting from the state of depression into which the revelation of Henry's forgery and death had plunged the anti-Dreyfusards. The prime minister, as was his wont, equivocated. He would claim to have been "overwhelmed" by the discovery of the forgery, by "repentance at having posted a forgery on all the walls of France." "I had dreams," he wrote, "in which I was tearing those wretched posters down with my nails."[8] He was henceforth convinced that the labor of reparation must be achieved and promised to pursue the revision himself. But prudence and hesitation were integral parts of Brisson's nature. And he had to take into account Cavaignac, who had quickly regained his second wind. When the ministers learned from Cavaignac how he had extracted a confession from Henry, one of them exclaimed, "So that means a revision." "Less than ever, Monsieur," retorted Cavaignac. Haughtily he resumed the assault.

During the day of August 31 the ministers held four official meetings. Their discussions bore on the events of the Affair, and in particular on General de Boisdeffre's resignation. On that same day, General de Pellieux offered his resignation as well.

> Mister Minister,
> Duped by men without honor, without hope of conserving that trust of my subordinates without which no command is possible, having for my own part lost trust in those of my superiors who had me work on forged documents, I have the honor of asking you to be willing to liquidate the retirement pension due me in reason of seniority of service.

The military governor of Paris held on to that resignation for a few days in order to give Pellieux "time to reflect," and Pellieux ended up retracting his resignation.* What was the prime minister to do? Initiate the revision procedure? Immediately modify Dreyfus's penal status? Caught between his conscience, fear of Cavaignac, and a concern for public opinion, Brisson hesitated. Not knowing exactly what to do, for three days he did nothing. He allowed the General Staff to regain courage, the anti-Dreyfusard press to recover, and Cavaignac to disseminate his conviction in all quarters. He lost precious hours.

It was only on September 3 that Brisson, through a mutual friend, Léon Bollack, advised Mathieu Dreyfus to file a request for revision. The

---

* It appears that Pellieux's resignation was concealed from the prime minister by Cavaignac.

government could have activated a Revision Commission on its own, but Brisson judged it more prudent to act upon request from Lucie Dreyfus.* A letter was immediately drawn up in Joseph Reinach's home in the course of a meeting that brought together Edgar Demange, Ludovic Trarieux, Fernand Labori, Gustave Mornard, Arthur Ranc, and Mathieu Dreyfus.[9] Once signed by Lucie Dreyfus, the letter was carried that very evening to the minister of justice. Léon Bourgeois, who rushed to see his friend Cavaignac, implored him to accept the revision procedure, which events had rendered necessary. Cavaignac was inflexible. "My credit has not been diminished by the discovery of the "Henry forgery." On the contrary, it was I who proved that the document was counterfeit." Today as before, assured Cavaignac, one needed to go after the syndicate itself, initiate a trial for high treason against all those who had made the cause of Dreyfus their own. Bourgeois was dismayed. Brisson and Cavaignac saw each other that evening. The prime minister maintained his position. The revision procedure could not be avoided. The minister of war countered that he would resign if the government did not follow his lead. Cavaignac was by then intent on rallying the anti-Dreyfusards, grief-stricken since the drama at Mont-Valérien. He would be their leader and their flag. Two hours after their talk, at about 9:00 P.M., Cavaignac sent a letter to the president of the Republic and made public his resignation, affirming proudly, "I remain convinced of Dreyfus's guilt."

The Dreyfus Affair had thus provoked a political crisis. Profiting from the respite, Esterhazy had prudently taken the train from Maubeuge on September 1. After shaving his mustache, he had crossed the Belgian border on foot. He then went to Brussels, and finally to London, where he settled under the name of de Bécourt.

Brisson was navigating as best he could in order to reach a revision while leaving his government intact. While the president of the Republic returned precipitously from Le Havre where he was staying, a new minister of war was being sought, who might help restore order. Félix Faure recommended General Emile Zurlinden, an Alsatian, a handsome man of impeccable reputation and an admirable horseman, who accepted eagerly, declaring "his regret at leaving the military governorship of Paris.† Zurlinden appeared prepared to go through with the revision. Appointed minister on November 5, he asked his new colleague, the minister of the Navy, to prepare forthwith to dispatch a ship to the Iles du Salut and to plan for the disembarkment of Alfred Dreyfus. He would meanwhile

* Jaurès protested in *La petite République* of September 8, 1898: "Why leave the initiative in the revision procedure to Mme. Dreyfus instead of taking it upon themselves in the name of France?"
† He had previously been minister of war after General Mercier.

study the Dreyfus case himself. On the following days, he saw General Roget, then Captain Cuignet. Each of them accused Commandant du Paty de Clam, whom they disliked, of wrongdoing but minimized the role played by Henry.* Henry, no doubt, committed forgery out of excessive zeal, but that forgery had been conceived of only in response to Colonel Picquart's forgery. Had not Picquart scratched out the address on the *petit bleu* in order to substitute for the actual addressee the name and address of an officer whom the syndicate had chosen to replace Dreyfus?† Yes, the Henry forgery had been the clumsy response of a good and brave soldier in order to confound Picquart and to save Esterhazy, whom he knew to be innocent. Cuignet had discovered an officer, Captain Tassin, who attested on September 8, 1898, to having spoken to Picquart the day after Dreyfus's ceremony of degradation and to having expressed astonishment in his presence at the revolting cynicism of Dreyfus observing "with interest" the removal of his stripes. "But of course," Picquart had replied to Tassin, "he was thinking of their weight. So many grams at such and such, that comes to. . . ." And Picquart, continued the witness, had even added these words, "There is not a Jew who doesn't have a few convicts in his family." How had Picquart, that fanatical anti-Semite, become Dreyfus's firmest supporter? Because he had sold his services to the syndicate, Zurlinden was quickly persuaded. No doubt he was yielding to pressure. On September 10 he transmitted his "negative recommendation" concerning a revision, which revived the courage of Cavaignac's partisans. Henry had indeed been guilty of a lapse in judgment. But that changed nothing concerning the center of the Affair, Dreyfus's guilt.

In the following days, Henry was transformed into a hero. On September 3 the Assumptionists related in several provincial editions of *La Croix* that Henry had been murdered by Jews who wanted to prevent him from speaking. But it was the writer Charles Maurras, in the royalist newspaper *La Gazette de France*, who invented the thesis of the "patriotic forgery." Maurras proclaimed Henry's virtue and transfigured him into a martyr for a just cause. He developed his thesis in two articles that appeared on September 5 and 6. "The energetic plebeian" had fabricated his forgery "for the public good, confiding his deed to no one, not even to the leaders whom he loved, consenting to run the risk entirely on his own. . . . Our poor half-Protestant upbringing is incapable of appreciating that

* Du Paty was a convenient culprit. General Zurlinden immediately charged General Renouard, the new chief of the General Staff with opening up an investigation of Colonel du Paty "for reason of his relations with Esterhazy." On September 1, General Renouard sent the minister a report recommending that du Paty be removed from active duty for "grave errors committed in the course of duty."

† It will be recalled that Henry had scratched out part of the *petit bleu* in order to give plausibility to the argument Roget and Cuignet were making at this juncture.

much moral and intellectual nobility." The criminal was Cavaignac, "the speculator in virtue," who had constrained Henry to death. And Maurras concluded his act of homage to the heroic servant of the great interests of the State:

> Colonel, there is not a drop of your precious blood, which does not steam still wherever the heart of the Nation beats. . . . We were not able to give you the great funeral that your martyrdom deserved. We should have waved your bloody tunic and the sullied blades down the boulevards; marched the coffin, hoisted the mortuary banner like a black flag. It will be our shame not to have attempted as much. . . . But the national sentiment will awaken to triumph and avenge you. Before long from the country's soil, in Paris, in your little village, there will arise monuments to expiate our cowardice. . . . In life as in death, you marched forward. Your unhappy forgery will be counted among your best acts of war.

On the following days, *La Libre Parole*, *La Croix*, *Le Petit Journal*, and *L'Eclair* adopted Maurras's themes, to which they added threats. "Revision means war," affirmed *La Libre Parole* of September 4 and 8. "For that war we are not prepared. Yes, it will be war and a debacle. And that is precisely the plan and the hope of the Jews."

Day by day, the anti-Dreyfusards were regaining hope. On September 8, when Fernand Labori requested that Picquart be temporarily paroled, the tide had already turned. His request was denied on September 22 by the correctional tribunal. At the meeting of the Council of ministers the same day, the government was plainly split. Zurlinden delivered an impassioned plea against revision. And he presented to the Council several "secret" items which helped him to arrive at his conviction.[10] The minister of justice, Léon Bourgeois, argued the opposite. He described the present situation: Henry was guilty of forgery; du Paty de Clam discharged; Esterhazy in flight; de Boisdeffre had resigned. How could they not appeal the case before the High Court of Appeal? Brisson and Zurlinden in turn threatened to resign. Félix Faure, who sensed that the majority sided with Brisson, and who was eager to preside over military maneuvers and then return to the hunt, postponed a decision until September 17. The meeting ended in an atmosphere of crisis.[11]

The Cabinet was dispersed. Acting on "secret" advice from Théophile Delcassé, the minister of foreign affairs, Colonel Picquart—on September 14 and 15—sent two letters intended to serve the cause of revision to Sarrien, one concerning the alleged charges retained against Dreyfus, the other concerning the "impression" the secret dossier could have produced on Dreyfus's judges. In a furor, Zurlinden responded on September 14 by writing a vindictive note on the "maneuvers employed by M. Picquart when he was head of the Intelligence Service in order to substitute another culprit for Dreyfus," and on September 16 he announced that he was ordering the governor of Paris to open an investigation to determine whether Picquart should be brought before a court-martial for "forgery and traffic in forgeries." This time, he had gone too far. The prime minister was secretly looking for a new minister to replace the increasingly excited Zurlinden. A personal friend of Brisson, Gachet, met with Joseph Reinach and paid a visit to Mathieu Dreyfus, asking whether they knew of a general favorable to revision who might serve as minister of war.[12] The government was thus reduced to taking advice from Dreyfus's entourage in order to find a minister who might help with the revision. Mathieu and Reinach suggested General Paul Darras. It was he who had presided over Dreyfus's degradation, and it was said that he remained stricken by the experience, and was prepared to atone. Reinach and Mathieu were asked to "sound out" Darras, which they did through a number of emissaries.[13] Meanwhile, Bourgeois had thought of General Charles Chanoine, a brave soldier, with a refined and cultivated mind, and who, when elected to the departmental assembly of the Marne, had on occasion voted with the left.

With a new minister in his pocket, Brisson was in a position to confront Zurlinden at the meeting of the Council of ministers on September 17. Zurlinden exhibited the *petit bleu*, which he called the "Picquart forgery," and asked the government for authorization to initiate legal action against Picquart. But this time Brisson appeared decisive. He countered that the question was not on the agenda. And at his request, the government decided to transmit to the Revision Commission Lucie Dreyfus's petition. Zurlinden stormed out, followed by the minister of public works who resigned along with him. Zurlinden's letter of resignation, like that of his predecessor Cavaignac, peremptorily affirmed Dreyfus's guilt. "Extensive study of the Dreyfus file has convinced me too profoundly of his guilt for me to be able to accept, as head of the Army, any other solution than that of respecting the judgment in its entirety." Whereupon arrived General Chanoine, the new minister who had promised to aid in implementing a revision.

But the new minister of war's first decision, made on September 20, was to reengage Zurlinden, who for lack of time had not been replaced in his post as military governor of Paris. Barely had he returned to his office at the Invalides than Zurlinden, after consulting with Chanoine, signed a mandate initiating legal proceedings against Picquart under a charge of forgery. It was in fact the case that Picquart was already scheduled to appear the following day, September 21, before a Court of Summary Jurisdiction. He and Louis Lebois had been charged with having divulged documents. Now it seemed there was a good chance that Picquart would be acquitted or in any event set free.* Zurlinden's intention, in demanding Picquart for military jurisdiction, was to force the Court of Summary Jurisdiction to postpone the civil case, but to keep Picquart in prison. Upon learning of this maneuver, Brisson was as dumbfounded as he was impotent. He discovered too late that he had been had by Chanoine and Zurlinden. At the session of the Eighth Chamber of the Court of Summary Jurisdiction, the public prosecutor asked for a postponement of the case since military proceedings had been initiated against Picquart on suspicion of forgery. Fernand Labori, who had become Picquart's impassioned attorney, objected to the postponement. Picquart asked to speak. Looking at Gonse and Pellieux—called as witnesses—who lowered their heads, he said simply with a voice barely affected by emotion:

> This evening I will perhaps go to the Cherche-Midi. This is perhaps the last time before the secret proceedings that I will be able to say a word in public. I want it to be known, should Lemercier-Picquart's noose or Henry's razor be found in my cell, that it will have been a murder, for a man such as myself would never for an instant think of committing suicide. I will go with my head held high before this accusation and with the same serenity that I have brought before my accusers. I have had my say.

After deliberating for a quarter of an hour, the Court of Summary Jurisdiction postponed the case and Picquart was returned to the Santé Prison. He spent his seventy-second night there. The following day, upon petition from the public prosecutor, he was brought to the Prison of Cherche-Midi and kept in isolation by order of General Zurlinden. This time military justice would prevail. The maneuvers of Zurlinden and Chanoine had been a success. As for the prime minister, he had demonstrated that he was incapable of imposing his will.

In *L'Aurore* during the following days, September 22-24, Georges Clemenceau insulted Brisson outright: "What can be said of Brisson, who is leading us, while lamenting over his destiny, to the worst catastrophes? More stupid than cowardly, or more cowardly than stupid? Both. Brisson, Sarrien, and Bourgeois, the whole Radical crowd, more Jesuitical than all the Jesuits combined. . . . Never has human trash of such lamentable

---

* In the preceding days, it appears that Labori had negotiated with the presiding judge a postponement *sine die* and Picquart's provisional release from custody. Chanoine and Zurlinden managed to dash that arrangement.

stamp been seen." Maneuvering, accommodating, absorbing every shock, Brisson was living through anxious and painful hours. He wanted a revision but could not find a way to achieve it.

The Revision Commission met at the Ministry of Justice for two full days, beginning on September 21. Composed of three judges from the High Court of Appeal and three directors from the Ministry of Justice,* it was manifestly divided, like the government itself, and was therefore unable to issue either a positive or a negative judgment.† Sarrien claimed that the division was tantamount to a negative recommendation and that there were grounds for heeding it as such. But at the ministerial meeting of September 24, Brisson, with the support of Delcassé and Bourgeois, finally revealed some determination. He recalled that the commission's recommendation was a consultation only, and that the initiative was entirely in the hands of the government. His role would not be a matter of proclaiming Dreyfus's innocence, but merely transmitting Lucie Dreyfus's request to the High Court of Appeal. There was no other way to free the Affair from politics and put an end to all the agitation. It was in the Republic's best interest. Brisson argued emotionally, but could not impose his will. It was decided to wait for the meeting of the Council of ministers of September 26 at which Félix Faure would preside.

In Paris, the agitation was mounting. The revisionists were organizing massive meetings. On the other side, Jules Guérin and Paul Déroulède were mobilizing their troops. "If Dreyfus returns to France," Déroulède predicted, "he will be torn to pieces." On September 26 the Council of Ministers deliberated for four hours. Sarrien, frightened at the prospect of transmitting Lucie's request to the High Court of Appeal, tendered his resignation, but then returned at once. Finally, the matter was put to a vote. Brisson won by six votes to four. The minister of war, who had not changed his mind, deemed it prudent to abstain. The same day, the minister of justice, constrained by the government, contacted the High Court of Appeal. It had taken approximately a month after Henry's confession for the revision procedure to be initiated. This was, nevertheless, a major step on the path to the truth, and an overwhelming change in the composition of the forces confronting each other, the Affair was no longer of concern solely to the executive and the military. They would henceforth have to take the judiciary into account.

But the Brisson government had made a show of its impotence. The

---

* The Revision Commission was empowered only to give a "recommendation" to the minister of justice, who remained free to forward (or not to forward) the request for a revision to the High Court of Appeal.
† It appears that the split opposed magistrates, who were favorable to revision, and functionaries of the Ministry of Justice, who were hostile to it.

nationalists derived encouragement from that display. Déroulède, an excellent leader, united in the Ligue des Patriotes* a considerable clientele of officers, tradesmen, petit bourgeois, and Catholics (although he affected not to be clerical). He was growing more and more active, and if he called himself a republican, he proclaimed lucidly that "the future lay with the first resolute republican who will put his hand in the hand of the first patriotic general."[16] Jules Guérin, the leader of the Ligue Antisémitique, "put the anti-Semitic idea into action just as Déroulède put the patriotic idea into action," placed himself at the service of the Duke of Orleans.[17] Guérin could be seen in the streets of Paris surrounded by strongmen, armed with clubs and iron bars, who would defend their faith. Toward August 1898, the duke promised monthly subsidies of approximately 25,000 francs in exchange for which Guérin offered the support of the four or five thousand persons alleged to belong to the Ligue Antisémitique. The Duke of Orleans, to be sure, was thinking only of defending France and the Army from Jews and foreigners. "It is the Army they want to destroy and France they want to doom. We will not allow it," he proclaimed on September 21. But Déroulède and Guérin were well aware of the fact that they could do nothing to shake the Republic without the support of the Army.

The unfortunate Brisson was plagued with every conceivable worry. In September, several hundred Parisian laborers, hired to work on the construction of the World's Fair, went on strike, demanding greater pay. Most of the construction workers' associations declared their solidarity. By the beginning of October, there were 20,000 strikers. Soon after, the railway employees announced a general strike. Brisson issued search warrants, had railroad stations occupied by the Army, and placed soldiers along the tracks. In October, there was, nevertheless, a rumor afloat of a plot against the Republic. It was said that General de Pellieux was serving as an intermediary between a group of officers and the Bonapartist pretender, a charge which Pellieux denied. Zurlinden was alleged to be part of the plot. It appeared that the coup d'état was scheduled . . . for October 16. There was great agitation among the revisionists. Several of them deemed it prudent to temporarily assume new addresses. In an atmosphere of "civic fear," meetings were held—in particular at *L'Aurore*—and plans were made. The revisionists Georges Clemenceau, Fernand Labori, Arthur Ranc, Jean Jaurès, Bernard Lazare, Mathieu Dreyfus and Alexander Millerand dined together. They decided to bring Brisson the alarming news they had received. Brisson, who was already apprised, promised that

---

* Founded in May 1882. Its initial objectives were purely patriotic: to keep alive the memory of Alsace-Lorraine and the cult of national virtues. It was only gradually that the Ligue became nationalist and anti-Parliamentarian.[15]

he would be vigilant.[18] On the fatal day, nothing happened . . . but for eight days the military plot had dominated all political activity.

Along with so many causes of agitation was the added scare of war with England.[19] The ministers of foreign affairs Gabriel Hanotaux and Théophile Delcassé had conceived the plan of cutting off England's route of access from Cairo to the Cape. This policy had now led to a standstill in the village of Fachoda on the Nile, where both the British and French flags had been planted. Two rights of conquest, two usurpations, were thus in a situation of confrontation. During September and October, negotiations proceeded between France and England amid an atmosphere of high drama. Russia declared itself prepared to mobilize, but advised France to yield. English public opinion was unfettered against France. Faure and Brisson, who had no other choice beside war, exhausted themselves in negotiating the provisions of a humiliation that might not be construed as such, while a "hostile and mocking" Europe looked on. [20]

Both Chambers were convened until October 25. On October 22 Déroulède invited the Parisian population to protest in front of the Palais-Bourbon and to demonstrate their confidence in the Army, and their aversion for traitors. He warned that "no outrage against France would be tolerated," while the Ligue Antisémitique, beneath the signatures of Drumont and Guérin, called on patriots to shout "Down with the Jews," "Long live the Army," "Down with traitors." On October 24, the Committee of the League of the Rights of Man requested republicans "to respond with contempt to the swaggering and perfidious meetings of an association of felons."[21] The Socialists formed a "watchdog committee" grouping all factions, including Jules Guesde, Jean Jaurès, Aristide Briand, Alexandre Millerand, and Réne Viviani. On the 25th, an unruly crowd invaded the approaches to the Palais-Bourbon. Cavalry regiments blocked the neighboring streets and occupied the Tuileries. At the very start of the session, the nationalists, with Déroulède at their head, demanded Brisson's resignation with shouts of "Long live the Army!" Whereupon Déroulède called, as though by chance, the name of General Chanoine. Had they coordinated their interventions? Chanoine asked to be allowed to speak, and in a few scathing sentences offered his resignation.

My comrades, the leaders of the Army approved me when I accepted the portfolio of War; I exposed myself at the time (and I knew it) to suspicions and to an unpopularity which I did not deserve; I resigned myself to them out of devotion to the Army, to my country, and to the Republic. . . . A moment ago, there was talk of that pernicious affair before which my predecessors opted to withdraw. I have the right to my opinion; it is the same as theirs. Today the Parliament is joined together; I can speak to you, the representatives of the Nation, and say to you: "I am placing in your hands the trust committed to me of the Army's interests and honor." From this tribune I hereby resign as minister of war.

There was thus no longer a minister of war. And Chanoine, before disappearing, had proclaimed—like his two predecessors—Dreyfus's guilt. Stabbed in the back, the prime mininster protested, "The Chamber will support me in my will to have the supremacy of civilian authority prevail." He asked for an adjournment while the left applauded. The session was halted, as Brisson and Sarrien sought out the president of the Republic. During that intermission, the offices of the republican groups, from the Socialists to the moderates, drafted a motion "affirming the supremacy of the civilian authorities" and the Chamber's confidence in the "Army's loyal obedience to the laws of the Republic." When the discussion resumed, Count Albert de Mun and Godefroy Cavaignac—as sure of himself as ever—were heard: "I have no need to affirm here the supremacy of the civilian authorities. I affirmed it as a minister of war." A unanimous Chamber nevertheless voted for adoption of the republican motion affirming the supremacy of the civilian authorities." But the crisis was not over yet. Louis Barthou—a deputy of the center—asked to speak, and declared he and his colleagues had no further confidence in the government. The prime minister saw this as the fatal blow. He was tired. He responded in a few vague words. He knew that if the center abandoned him, he was defeated. He lost a vote of confidence by 286 votes to 254. The former prime ministers (Jules Méline, Alexandre Ribot, and Charles Dupuy), and almost all the former ministers (including Cavaignac, Barthou, and Raymond Poincaré) voted against him. Spontaneously or by design, the Chanoine maneuver had produced its effect. The government of the left was struck down. *La Libre Parole* extended the resigning general its "patriotic thanks." The General Staff appeared to triumph. It was, as Clemenceau wrote in *L'Aurore* of October 27, the "return of Esterhazy's ashes."

It was, however, a short-lived victory that the nationalists, as though astonished by the facility of their success, did not dare to exploit in the streets.* Two days later on September 27, the Criminal Chamber of the High Court of Appeal convened to decide whether Lucie Dreyfus's request was admissible. Beneath the gilded ceilings of the High Court of

---

* Jules Guérin was arrested for having struck a police superintendent on the Place de la Concorde. Anti-Semitic demonstrations continued into the night in Paris.

Appeal, amid the solemnity of ermines and robes, the Dreyfus Affair appeared to be a different matter entirely. There was no apparent passion, with the exception of respect for the law. Drumont and a hundred of his supporters wanted to attend the hearing, but the police kept them at a distance. Justice Bard was assigned the task of reporting on the case by the presiding judge of the Criminal Chamber, Justice Loew, a magistrate of Alsatian origin who was as rigorous as he was courageous. Reinach described Bard as "still young, a vigorous jurist, a man of logic and ardor, a weathered republican, who was unmarried, and consequently less vulnerable to invective and threats of death. . . ."[22] In a monotone, he read his report, which demonstrated that the Affair was far from ready for a hearing, that an inquest was necessary.

> To bring the truth to light, that is the mission the law imposes on you. It would be superfluous for me to say just how delicate that task is. But that that might be a pretext for evasion will be admitted by no one, and you would admit it less than anyone. There have been enough lapses. Removed from every other consideration than that of justice, invulnerable to any suggestion, insensitive to threats and to outrage, you have before you a great task. You will appreciate what it requires and you will do what your conscience dictates.

At the session on the following day, the old public prosecutor Manau delivered an address, suppressing the sobs rising in his throat. He spoke vividly, with a pathos of eloquence already out of style. This great old man was in a sense an illustration of his own speech: "O! Sacred laws for the protection of the accused, and even of the convicted, what have they done to you . . . let the Republic's justice then proceed; let it cross the seas!" He too concluded in the affirmative concerning the admissibility of the request for revision. Arguing next on behalf of Lucie Dreyfus, the lawyer Henri Mornard demonstrated the necessity of a revision with implacable precision and an elegant clarity unadorned by rhetorical flourish.* After extremely long deliberations, on October 29, the Criminal Chamber issued the decision that initiated the procedure allowing for a revision.[24] "The Court declares the request admissible in its present form; says that it will proceed to a supplementary judicial investigation; says that it has no

* Mornard "had accepted to enter into the Affair during its most critical phase, when all hope seemed lost, in the wake of Zola's conviction. And he continued to perform his duty with great simplicity, without seeking to push himself into the fore, without any grandiloquent gestures or phrases, as modest as he was valourous." These duly merited words of praise by Joseph Reinach were also a veiled indictment of Labori.[23]

reason to decide at present as to the public prosecutor's request for a suspension of sentence."

From the depths of his sickbed, old Auguste Scheurer-Kestner, who had been immediately informed by Reinach, allowed his joy to burst forth: "Your dispatch has moved me so that I have been short of breath from the happiness. It has not killed me, because one does not die of joy. We are still France." And Zola wrote from London, "For me this supplementary inquest means the certain acquittal of an innocent man."[25] Such had become the complexity of the Affair. In less than two days, the revisionists, defeated in Parliament, had triumphed in the High Court of Appeal.

11

To Roast the Jews

B y the end of the year 1898, the boundaries separating the Dreyfusards and the anti-Dreyfusards were clearly drawn. And they would barely change during the years that followed.

For the Dreyfusards, the time in which the fight was solely to prove Alfred Dreyfus's innocence and secure his release from prison was now over. The first to devote themselves to the cause of an innocent man unjustly convicted—Mathieu Dreyfus, of course; Ferdinand Forzinetti, the director of the Prison of Cherche-Midi; the writer Bernard Lazare; and the politician Auguste Scheurer-Kestner—were now swept up, willingly or not, in a struggle far transcending Dreyfus's return and the revision of an iniquitous sentence. "We were no longer fighting," observed Léon Blum, "for the reparation of a judicial error, to save a single man."[1] Many Dreyfusards wanted to generalize their gains, propagating a series of shock waves around the jolt produced by the Affair. For a large number, the battle for Dreyfus had become a battle against the guardian institutions of traditional France—the Church and the Army—which seemed linked to the defense of an older France. The Dreyfusard camp tended to group all the forces of intellectual and political contestation: "true" republicans, antimilitarists, anticlericals, Freemasons, Jews, frequently Protestants, the marginal elements in every social group; in brief, all those who felt rejected or excluded by "traditional France," all those as well who dreamed of the advent of a free and just society. The League of the Rights of Man, founded on June 4, 1898, by Ludovic Trarieux, embodied many of the principles that would henceforth unify and guide most Dreyfusards. In "the person" of Dreyfus, it claimed to defend the interests and rights of all citizens, the principles of tolerance, and the humane ideals of 1789.

But within a few months, there would be division among the Dreyfusards: between those like Mathieu Dreyfus and Edgar Demange, who were concerned solely with the defense of an innocent man in his martyrdom; those, like the writers Bernard Lazare and above all Charles Péguy, who had elevated the fight for Dreyfus to the level of an ideological struggle for justice and truth and who would claim to have embodied—at considerable distance from the politicians—the soul of Dreyfusism in its purity and in its honor;[2] and those like Georges Clemenceau, Léon Blum, and Jean Jaurès, for whom the Dreyfus Affair had become a political struggle against the organizations and forces of conservatism. The day would come when the politically minded would reproach those who sought only the release of the prisoner and abandoned the struggle whose symbol he had become. And the ideologues would not forgive the politicians for having dragged the moral cause of Dreyfusism "into demagogy and Radical, anticlerical agitation," for having degraded the Affair and having led it astray.[3] It would also be necessary to distinguish among the politically minded those who, throughout the Affair, wanted to defend the legacy of the Enlightenment and the French Revolution, the spirit of tolerance, secular democracy, and public freedoms, and those, like Jaurès, Blum, and a number of Socialists soon after, who hoped that the confrontations of the Affair would assist in the development of a new society. But on the eve of the year 1899, because revision was still an immediate and imperative aim and because the traditional forces had themselves united to prevent the revision, such differences were as yet barely visible. The Dreyfusard camp had common principles and, in the short run, a clear goal.

Inversely, the anti-Dreyfusards had also regrouped. The anti-Dreyfusard army included monarchists, anti-Semites, the large majority of military personnel, most priests, a near totality of the congregations, the mass of practicing Catholics, and, generally, all those who wanted to defend traditional France, its morality, virtues, institutions, even its economy against the rot of the Republic, rampant secularism, capitalism, and all that the Jews had brought with them. Nationalism and anti-Semitism were the common ground of the anti-Dreyfusard block. It cannot be contested that "the political forces of the Church," were a principal

agent engaged against Dreyfusism.[4] The fact that the hierarchy remained
discreet, and that a few Catholics militated in support of Dreyfus cannot
mask the blatant evidence that the Church and the congregations, fearing
the development of a new society hostile to the Church, if not entirely
atheist, a society with neither morality nor virtue, clutched fast to the
Dreyfus Affair as if to a life buoy amid a tempest.[5] For the anti-
Dreyfusards too Dreyfus became a symbol. The debate over Dreyfus's
innocence was in the last analysis secondary. "His worst crime," Maurice
Barrès would say, "was to have served for five years to disrupt the Army
and the entire Nation."[6] Might Dreyfus not be in fact the most harmless of
the Dreyfusards? It was they who were guilty. "They insult everything that
is dear to us: the nation, the Army. . . . Their plot is dividing and disarming France." Barrès laid down the principles which, whatever the circumstance, exonerated the anti-Dreyfusards: If Dreyfus were not a
traitor, his shame lay in arousing such sympathies. Even if Dreyfus were
innocent, his supporters remained criminals. Good conscience inspired
the entire anti-Dreyfusard struggle.

Within that struggle, the "leagues" contributed an original style. They
constituted, according to René Rémond, "a first attempt at a mass movement."[7] They had neither a precise program nor a permanent organization. They sought to regiment their members, to keep them constantly
alert, to bring their action into the streets. The Ligue des Patriotes,
founded in 1882, dissolved in 1889, and officially reconstituted at the end
of 1898, had found in Paul Déroulède the popular and theatrical leader it
needed, who had succeeded in arousing the fervor and loyalty of his troops
and also in attaining a rare measure of prestige on the streets of Paris. In
1889 the Ligue contained about 60,000 "patriots." Most of its strength was
in Paris, where Déroulède, with the aid of Marcel Habert, gave of himself
immeasurably in demonstrations, meetings, and—when there was
need—fistfights. His tall silhouette, large gesticulating arms, huge outmoded frock coat, and shrill voice, all contributed to give him the sympathetic allure of a half-theatrical, half-military Don Quixote. But ultimately the government was obliged to take quite seriously, if not his
speeches, then his actions, notably the staking out of Paris into sections,
block by block, which he entrusted to his subordinates.* Noisier but less
active was Jules Guérin's Ligue Antisémitique, which claimed to count
11,000 adherents throughout the whole of France in July 1898. Its weekly,

* Zeev Sternhell has written that the "Ligue des Patriotes was the first mass party in France
structured around a nationalist and authoritarian ideology—at once militarist, populist, and
anti-Marxist—the first also to implement modern methods of recruitment, propaganda, and
street action."[8]

L'Antijuif, issued 40,000 copies during the same period, selling half as many.[9] The building Guérin rented at 59, rue de Chabrol had been converted into a veritable fortress with a high iron fence, steel-lined shutters, alarms, and telephones in every corner.[10] Guérin was a fearful adversary, less because of the number of his followers than because of his violent methods. He was a specialist in punitive expeditions, and when he descended into the street with his bodyguards, Jews and Dreyfusards did well to disappear.

It was in December 1898 that a group of men of letters and professors founded the Ligue de la Patrie Française, in order to counter the Dreyfusard "intellectuals": François Coppée, Ferdinand Brunetière, Jules Lemaître, and Maurice Barrès were its founders, along with Gabriel Syveton, Henri Vaugeois and Louis Dausset. The Ligue, whose president was Coppée, then Lemaître, immediately achieved an immense success. Nearly 1,200 persons attended its first general meeting on January 19, 1899. Twenty-three members of the Académie Française, numerous members of the Institute, hundreds of university professors, and numerous practitioners of the liberal professions all became members. But the Ligue, whose membership swelled to 40,000 in a few months, suffered from the ambiguities of its ideology. It found neither the nationalism of Barrès and Déroulède nor the anti-Semitism of Guérin to be fully congenial. Like the Dreyfusards, it tended to invoke justice and truth. In extremely vague terms, it claimed to defend "the fundamental pacts of human society," which specifically implied the acceptance of judgments delivered by competent authorities. It posited on principle that an officer judged guilty by a competent tribunal could not be innocent. It awaited the solution of social problems from Christian charity. It attacked the corruption and irresponsibility of Parliament, but refused all authoritarianism. Socialism and collectivism were denounced as the principal enemies, but so were all forms of government dominated by an individual personality. It thus ran the risk of appearing confused, soft, and a good deal less exalting than the aggressive nationalism of Déroulède. Lacking any clear ideology, rather poorly organized, and too moderate for many of its adherents, the Ligue de la Patrie Française would soon find itself in jeopardy. By 1902, it would be dissolved.[11]

But at the end of 1898, anti-Dreyfusard passion and intransigence were at their high point. The Ligue des Patriotes and the Ligue Antisémitique supplied shock troops for the struggle. The Ligue de la Patrie Française gathered the "serious" individuals who were less inclined to resort to their fists. And above all, a large part of the regular and secular clergy, numerous officers, and all those who continued to see the Republic

as an accident of history saw in the eddies of the Affair the opportunity for
a return to traditional forms of life and thought. A powerful Catholic press
was blowing on those embers of hope—or nostalgia.

The contribution campaign initiated by *La Libre Parole* in December
1898 that allowed Colonel Henry's "widow and orphan" to file suit against
Joseph Reinach, who had accused Henry of being Commandant Esterhazy's accomplice in treason, helps explain the dimensions of the anti-
Dreyfusard exaltation. The campaign's goal was to defend the honor of
the "French officer killed, murdered by the Jews. . . . However small the
amount offered, it will be a slap in ignoble Reinach's obscene face."* The
campaign was a triumph. In less than a month there were 25,000 contributions, bringing in 131,000 francs. These were particularly numerous
among workers and craftsmen,[12] especially in the clothing industry, which
was presumed to be "invaded" by Jews; the Army contributed 4,500
donors,[13] among whom were 3,000 officers. Twenty-eight retired generals, including General Mercier, the former minister of war, signed up. A
percentage of 8.6 students[14] on the list reveals the existence of anti-
Semitism within the universities, which may correspond in part to the
temptation of extremism, in part to the strength of the antibourgeois
Socialist trend. The liberal professions supplied 8.25 percent of the
donors.[15] The medical and legal professions, where the competition and
presence of Jews was strongest, furnished the largest contingents. Note as
well, 433 signatures preceded by the aristocratic particle, including 336
titled members of the nobility, 7 dukes and duchesses, 2 princes, 50
marquesses, and more than 200 counts, viscounts, and barons. The nobility of the Empire, on the other hand, was for all purposes absent. Three
hundred fifty priests signed up in the campaign, and while only 100
acknowledged their support, many others contributed anonymously. A
crippled priest, sending in 8 centimes, wished he could wield a sword as
well as he could an aspergillum. Another prayed he might have a "bedside
carpet made of kikeskin" so that he might step on it morning and night. A
third signed himself "a poor priest disgusted that no Bishop in France has
made a contribution." A local priest in Poitou, who sent one franc, claimed
he would be happy to sing a requiem for the last of the kikes. On the other
hand, one finds few industrialists and executives (0.9%), rather few lower
level employees (6%),† and—contrary to all expectations—few small
businessmen (2%).‡ Geographically, there was a higher proportion of
contributors in the urban centers, a low—and frequently very low—
proportion in the countryside. The 18 departments revealing a higher

---

* *La Libre Parole,* December 17, 1898.
† For 13% of the population.
‡ For 3% of the population.

rate of contributions may be assembled in three groups: the East, where there was a long-standing tradition of anti-Semitism linked to the large Jewish presence therein; the departments of the South (where there were a number of very old Jewish communities), where an agricultural crisis was resulting in outbursts of anti-Semitism; and finally Paris and its surrounding departments. What has been called the Henry monument thus gives a rather faithful image of the structures of anti-Semitism in France.

But what is still more revealing are the commentaries accompanying a large number of contributions. They reveal both the violence of the anti-Semitic hatred and the deliberate or unconscious bases of that passion. Jewish exploitation, Jewish money, and Jewish financial power were the reasons given by all those who felt oppressed or humiliated: "a concierge for Jews who is disgusted by kikes"; "Jeanne, ex-maid for kikes"; "three embroiderers from Bains-les-Bains Vosges, who in working for a Jew make 14 sous in 15 hours"; "a laborer without work"; "a noble woman ruined by the Jews"; "an eighty-year-old royalist consigned to an asylum by Jews"; "a small industrialist ruined by the Jews"; and "a native of the Vendée who would be happy to take down the rifle of his ancestors of 1793 to fire at the kikes who are poisoning France." Abject poverty, exploitation, and unemployment were thus blamed on the Jews. They were perceived as agents of social upheaval, frequently resembling in this, Protestants, Freemasons, and intellectuals. They were destroying sure moral values, fixed and reassuring traditional categories. To be sure, the eager contributors were defenders of France, the Church, and the Army, and it was their Jewish enemy that linked them. There were exhortations of "Long live the Army, death to the Jews"; "Long live the saber that will rid us of all the vermin"; "A patriot awaiting the saber to avenge us"; "For God and country"; "For God, for his country and the extermination of the Jews"; "God's goodness ends where the Jew begins."

Numerous contributors lumped the Jews together with Protestants, politicians, and republicans: "a group of farmers against the Republic of Jews and Freemasons that is dishonoring France," "a French Catholic out of hatred for the Jews and Freemasons who are dishonoring France." Similarly, intellectuals were associated with the coalition of France's enemies: "Out of France with the kikes and their pimps, the intellectuals"; "muzzle the pedants and the Jews, who have the same soul"; "a proletarian of letters," "an academic fallen victim to the intellectuals."

Finally, the Jew was described by numerous contributors as a stinking and dangerous animal, a plague, a centipede, a microbe, a mite, a cancer, an ugly spider, and synagogue lice. Reinach the slanderer was a toad, a reptile, a monkey, a pig. The Jews were unclean, as stated "a cesspool drainer who would not dare touch Reinach for fear of dirtying himself."

The Jew was threatening, polluting, ambiguous, marginal, shapeless. He inspired horror, as claimed "a young woman who gets sick to her stomach at the sight of a Jew." He was capable of anything, specifically because of his monstrous sexual appetite according to "a working woman seduced and deceived by her Jewish boss," and "a man of Roubaix who wants to contribute his modest share to snatch a Frenchwoman out of the hands of a Jew."

What remained was how to get rid of them. A military physician proposed "vivisection of Jews rather than harmless rabbits." A cook contributed in order "to roast the Jews." An officer in the reserves asked to "massacre the filthy kikes." A denizen of Baccarat would have liked to see "all the kikes and kikettes and their kiddy-kikes placed in glass furnaces." Another signed up "to convert the flesh of the kikes into mincemeat." Another offered .25 francs "to rent a deportation car." The historian Stephen Wilson has correctly observed that anti-Semitism thus had the function in French society of "freeing from repression a contained violence and giving expression to an aggressiveness born of a feeling of inferiority. The logic of extermination remained at the level of ritual gestures and psychological compensation."[16] The Jew was most often perceived in mythical terms, without precise definition, as the incarnation of evil, the person responsible for suffering and misery. He helped the anti-Semite to define and situate himself. He exonerated him. In a sense, he consoled him. In France in 1898 "it was impossible to act out these fantasies," Wilson observes at the conclusion of his study. "The will to transcribe into acts a final solution," he writes, "was not necessarily implied or sought."[17] But there remains at least the latent justification of genocide—if not its actual implementation—which runs through the Henry monument.

The overall impression left by the 18 lists of contributors published by *La Libre Parole* is that of a popular, clerical, and jingoistic anti-Semitism.[18] But it was not merely the "little" people who enrolled, contributing their few farthings. The rich bourgeoisie, numerous aristocrats, lawyers, physicians, professors, and intellectuals participated, including Paul Valéry, who contributed "only after hesitating." François Coppée pitched in with 20 francs; Count Albert de Mun sent 50 francs "to defend our beloved Army." Numerous politicians insisted on participating, most of them ardent Catholics. Not to mention Maurice Barrès, who donated 50 francs.

Abbé Caperan wanted to see in the Henry monument a "memorial of pity" that Frenchmen, and specifically Catholics, were inspired to contribute to by a widow and an orphan reduced to indigence. It is more, observes the historian Pierre Pierrard lucidly, a "moment of Catholic consciousness or unconsciousness in France, the basest and least debatable expression of an aberrant and collective blindness."[19] What was remarkable was not simply the savage expression of collective anti-Semitism, but also the manner in which it was celebrated by the entire anti-Dreyfusard press. Henry had become a national hero, a martyr of the Jews. And *La Croix* wrote that "this demonstration of respect and sympathy, that spans the great and small, the rich and the poor, old men and children, men of science and the uneducated . . . is a great, comforting, and consoling spectacle. . . . I believe that out of this will come one of those rays of light destined to restore peace to France."[20]

Instead of peace, henceforth the Affair would be opposing "two Frances," that which adhered fiercely to the principles of *J'Accuse* and that symbolized by the Henry monument. "We were no longer fighting," wrote Léon Blum, "for or against Dreyfus, for or against revision; we were fighting for or against the Republic, for or against militarism, for or against the secularism of the State." As for the actual Dreyfus Affair, to many Dreyfusards, it seemed to be moving irresistibly toward the proclamation of his innocence, which henceforth appeared certain. "The enchantment had ended, because the truth had been established. One could still fight against Dreyfus and the Dreyfusards. But one could do nothing against the logical and historical fact that Dreyfus's innocence had been demonstrated."[21] In fact, that would take another seven years; at the end of 1898, Alfred Dreyfus was still enduring his torture.

12

And So We Arrive at the Last Stage

From the Iles du Salut, Alfred Dreyfus wrote long letters to his wife during June and July 1898. She would receive only a few of them. "All that I have written you these last months can be summarized quite simply. My honor belongs to me; it is the patrimony of my children. I have demanded that honor from my country . . . your right, your duty is to demand it tirelessly from our country, from the supreme magistrate of the nation, until it is returned to us."[1] He spoke at length of his children, who still believed him to be away on a trip, of their sensibilities, of the proper methods of raising them: "One must act above all through moral influence." "Every minute away there has been a heart beating only for you, for our children; in the distance there has been a soul that has gradually freed itself from everything in order to watch day and night in thought over you, over them. . . ." But over all else must prevail the "cult of honor. . . . Bravely, tirelessly, without boasting and without flinching, I have insisted on my honor."[2] Dreyfus's letters continued to express familiar sentiments: that honor is a patrimony; that it is the supreme value; that one has to do one's duty, love one's family, have faith in justice and truth. They also betrayed an immense fatigue and by now repeated not merely words, but entire sentences. The requests for a revision that he would tirelessly send off remained unanswered. In order to know his rights, he asked for a copy of the penal code; it was refused him. In September he declared that he would put an end to all his correspondence until he received an answer. That decision would be conveyed somewhat imprecisely to Lucie, who would experience deep despair at the thought that he had resolved no longer to write to anyone, even herself.[3] He was by then in a state of extreme weakness, and knew long periods of despair during which he would remain prostrate, without moving, eating, or drinking. He implored still again that his requests be answered. On October 27, unaware that Lucie herself had filed a request, he was informed that he was going to receive "a definitive answer" to the petitions for revision that he had sent to the chief of state. That announcement restored his hope. And during the first days of the month of November, the censor passed on a letter of September 26 from Lucie in which she explained to her husband that she had filed a request and that the Council of Ministers had transmitted his case to the High Court of Appeal.

> And so we arrive at the last stage, the final crisis that will return to us what we unjustly lost, our honor, that will bring you back to all your dear ones who are beside themselves with joy at the thought of seeing you, of hugging you in their arms, of showing you how they love you. To describe our emotion is impossible. As for myself, I live only in the thought of the profound joy that you will have in learning the news, and I wish for myself the strength, the superhuman power to see you in this moment of supreme satisfaction. Provided, my God, that this great shock not be deleterious to you and that your poor weakened body not suffer from the effects of such a jolt!

I haven't dared say anything to the children. They haven't been aware of anything. They haven't known our pain. They don't have any idea of our joy. They will know of your return only once you are free, close to coming to embrace them. So long as they are small, I don't want them to know of life's sadnesses. They will have the happiness of seeing you again and will only learn later on, when they will be old enough to understand, to appreciate what you have suffered for them, the heroism, the greatness of soul of their admirable father. . . .[4]

Dreyfus experienced wild emotion. Finally, he could hope for a moment of happiness. "It is in our mutual affection, in that of our dear and adored children, in the satisfaction of our consciences and of a duty accomplished that we will find how to forget our great sufferings. . . ."[5]

On November 16 he received a telegram worded as follows:

Governor to deportee Dreyfus
via high command of Iles du Salut

To inform you that the Criminal Chamber of the High Court of Appeal has declared admissible in present form request for revision of your verdict and decided that you would be informed of this decision and invited to produce your means of defense.

He then asked to be put in contact with his lawyer. Of all that had transpired since 1894, he knew next to nothing. He still believed his case was entirely dependent on the bordereau, that it was limited to a debate over handwriting.

It appears that it was at this point that the director of the penitentiary decided that Dreyfus was no more than a simple prisoner. The stockade was taken down. On November 28 he was authorized to walk about in the morning from 7 to 11 o'clock and in the afternoon from 2 to 5 o'clock "within the enclosure of the entrenchment," an enclosure of dried stones, less than a meter high, which surrounded the guards' barracks. Finally, he could see the ocean again, which he had not seen for two years. He could see the islands. He was permitted an "officer's" diet. He seemed to be returning to life.

Then the communications stopped. No letters from his wife in December. None of the letters his wife would have sent him in October ever reached him. He asked the prison authorities when the proceedings before the High Court of Appeal were to take place, but they knew nothing. On December 28 he finally received a letter from Lucie written in

November. She knew that he had learned, in a telegram from the governor, that the request for a revision had been judged admissible. She thought he had received her preceding letters, and knew more. Above all she was sad at the resolution he had taken to write to her no longer:

> Fifteen days ago, I learned of a letter from you in which you announced your resolution not to write anymore, even to me. Whatever impulse you were obeying, be it impatience, grief, or despair, I beg you, my darling, do not deprive me of the only thing that was sweet in my life. . . .

Alfred Dreyfus was indignant. So they had shown his wife an excerpt from his letter. They had allowed Lucie to believe that he no longer wanted to write to her. They had made his wife suffer. He protested to the governor: "There is a duty of conscience incumbent on whoever—and I do not know nor do I wish to know who—committed that act and who is under obligation to make reparation." And the day after Christmas, he wrote to Lucie to reassure her:

> If my voice were no longer heard, it would be that it had been extinguished forever, for if I have lived, it has been in order to insist on my honor, which belongs to me, the patrimony of our children, in order to do my duty, as I have always and everywhere done it and as it must always be done, when right and justice are on one's side, without ever fearing anything or anyone.[6]

So he was—in suffering as in joy: intransigent in relation to principles, rigid, imperious, implacably virtuous, perpetually repeating the words that oriented his life and his martyrdom: "my honor," "my duty," "my children," "justice," and above all else, "my country." He and Lucie shared the same themes and emotions. The resolution, the bravery of each enforced that of the other. Perhaps in Lucie, the signs of a more tormented sensibility may be intuited. For Dreyfus was, as he said, a rigorous soldier who placed his country "above individuals," a man of high principle who was intent on always being able to examine himself in his conscience "with the knowledge of having always and everywhere done his duty."

IV

TRUTH ON THE MARCH*

* Such was the title given to Zola's publication (on February 16, 1901) of the articles he had written throughout the Affair.[1]

1

Bar Girls

President Félix Faure, who had a taste for military parades, had become increasingly enamored with "his" Army and was less and less inclined to conceal his hostility to the revision of the Dreyfus trial. In forming his new government, he called on Charles Dupuy, who had been prime minister at the time of Dreyfus's conviction. In difficult circumstances Dupuy's mediocrity would have made him an unlikely choice, but Faure remained grateful to him, for it was Dupuy, in selecting him as a minister years earlier, who had launched Faure's political career.

The Republicans were intent on seeing a civilian put in charge of the Ministry of War. The Chanoine "blow" had taught them a lesson. Dupuy named Charles de Freycinet, who had been in retirement for six years and had been devoting his time to scientific philosophy. Freycinet was a Protestant "who did not worry Catholics."[2] It was known that he rather inclined toward Dreyfus's cause. After allowing himself to be sufficiently implored, he accepted the post. For the Ministry of Justice, whose role would be crucial in any revision procedure, there was talk of Alexandre Ribot, a former prime minister, who had come out in favor of revision. But Dupuy chose instead an obscure deputy, Le Bret, a law professor from Caen, who had taken a stand against Dreyfus, and whom Drumont immediately saluted as "an honest man and a good citizen." Received well by the center, with distrust by the Radicals, and with hostility by the Socialists, the new prime minister delivered a vague speech, promising to govern only with republican support, but managed to please the left by speaking of "clerical influences" at work within the Army. He was approved by a vote of 413 to 68.*

The Criminal Chamber of the High Court of Appeal began its preliminary investigation—an immense task that it decided to pursue in

---

* Socialists and a few royalists. "Assemblies are like women," J. Cornély wrote, commenting on the vote in *Le Figaro* of November 5. "One can impose oneself on them, or, more precisely, they submit to their conquerors for very diverse reasons, among which nervous irritation and fatigue occupy a considerable place."[3]

plenary session.* From November 8 to 14, it first heard the five ministers of war who had succeeded each other since Dreyfus's arrest: Auguste Mercier, Jean-Baptiste Billot, Godefroy Cavaignac, Emile Zurlinden, and Charles Chanoine. Four were generals. They all had affirmed Dreyfus's guilt. Mercier, Cavaignac, and even Zurlinden attempted to prove it. The judges appeared quite surprised to learn of Commandant du Paty de Clam's bizarre visit to Dreyfus, on orders from Mercier, the day after his conviction. "Why did you not keep minutes?" they asked Mercier. "It was a closed case," Mercier responded, "it was impossible to foresee that an entire race would later declare its solidarity with Dreyfus." Asked by the presiding judge of the Criminal Chamber about the communication of secret documents, Mercier replied curtly that the request for a revision was limited to consideration of whatever might ensue from the forgery committed by Commandant Henry and the contradictory evaluations of the experts. "I don't believe it behooves the Court to concern itself with that question."

As for Cavaignac, he proposed the thesis—which had now become dear to him—that Dreyfus had had the bordereau copied by his accomplice Esterhazy. And he delivered an expert lecture demonstrating that the documents mentioned in the bordereau "were a transcription of the very life of the General Staff during the months of July and August 1894." Dreyfus had known them all, Esterhazy had not. From November 21 to 23, the Criminal Chamber heard General Roget, chief of the Fourth Bureau, who performed the same demonstration. "Esterhazy could not have known the documents enumerated in the bordereau." Then, from November 23 to December 5, Colonel Picquart, removed from his prison, was heard; he told in detail all that he knew. His calm, his precision, and his moderation, in stark contrast with the passions apparently agitating the preceding witnesses, made a deep impression on the magistrates.

Receiving on November 10 a letter from Alfred Dreyfus dated September 24 and transmitted by the Ministry of Colonies, Lucie Dreyfus learned that her husband had not been informed of the Criminal Chamber's decision declaring her request admissible. She protested to the minister of justice. Joseph Reinach vented his indignation in *Le Siècle;* Yves

* In October, Justice Atthalin, delegated by Presiding Justice Loew, had received from an officer of the court two decisive items to be used for purposes of comparison. They were two letters written by Esterhazy on near-transparent graph paper identical to that used for the bordereau. The first, dated August 17, 1894, began with the words: "I received, upon returning from the Châlons camp, where I have been for fifteen days . . ." The second, dated August 11, bore the heading: "Firing school of the 3rd Artillery Brigade. Châlons Camp." Esterhazy wrote: "I am leaving the camp in five days . . ." Same near-transparent paper, same handwriting. And the two documents bore dates very close to that of the bordereau.[4]

Guyot, in *Le Soleil*, denounced "the ferocity of fear."[5] But the government did not flinch. The Criminal Chamber deliberated and decided that Alfred Dreyfus would be informed "through swift channels" of the decision it had taken, that its text would be transmitted to him along with that of the request for revision.* Moreover, Dreyfus would be "invited to prepare his defense." In this the High Court of Appeal exposed itself to the obloquy of the nationalists. Through that decision, they believed they could discern which way it was leaning. Paul Déroulède and Godefroy Cavaignac wanted to challenge the government not to defer to the order of the High Court of Appeal. Mercier let it be known that the Criminal Chamber had been "bought" by the syndicate already three years earlier. Edouard Drumont and Henri Rochefort called Presiding Justice Loew "the Jew Lévy." On October 28, *La Libre Parole* published the addresses of the judges of the Court of Appeal. "What precious lives are sheltered at these mysterious addresses?" In *Le Gaulois* of November 16, Arthur Meyer, a Jew whose anti-Semitism knew no bounds, claimed that "the judges of the Court of Appeal have undertaken . . . to cast aspersions on the Army out of hatred for the sabre."[6] The "criminal" magistrates were seeking only to open the borders to foreigners, and then to withdraw—with their "fortunes made."† Rochefort stigmatized them as "bar girls" available to the highest bidder, and suggested that the judges' eyes be gouged out before the "hideous blindmen" be taken off to be pilloried.‡

While civilian justice was performing its duty, military justice chose to perform its own. But the two bore no resemblance. Captain Tavernier, examining magistrate with the Court-Martial, strained ingeniously to demonstrate that Picquart, after suitable scratching, had added Commandant Esterhazy's name and address to the *petit bleu*. That hypothesis had received some plausibility from Henry, who had crudely scratched

---

* The Criminal Chamber, convoked as an "investigatory commission," ruled on November 14, 1898, "that the minister of colonies would be requested to inform the convict Dreyfus through swift channels . . . of the ruling of the 29th of last October."

† *La Libre Parole* and *L'Intransigeant* of October 17, 1898.

‡ *L'Intransigeant* of October 18, 1898: "We would line up all the members of the High Court of Appeal as is done in county jails. A duly trained torturer would first cut off their eyelids with a pair of scissors . . . . When they would thus be reduced to the absolute impossibility of closing their eyes, large spiders of the most poisonous variety would be placed into nutshells which would then be affixed over their eyeballs and carefully held in place by solid laces tied behind their heads. The famished spiders (who are not very demanding as to their food) would gradually gnaw away the pupils and crystalline lenses until there were nothing left in the cavities now devoid of sight. Then, all the hideous blindmen would be brought to a pillory erected before the Palais de Justice in which the crime was committed and this sign would be placed on their chests: 'This is how France punishes traitors who try to sell her to the enemy!'"

Esterhazy's name and address on the *petit bleu*. Thus it could be thought that the document had been doctored, and by none other than Picquart. The thesis was all the more fragile in that Lauth's photographs of the *petit bleu*, which Henry had been negligent enough not to destroy, of course bore no trace of any scratches. The indefatigable Captain Lauth, then General Roget himself, who had become one of the champions of the fight against revision, repeated that the *petit bleu* had all the signs of a fraudulent and counterfeit document, and that in addition, its handwriting remained unidentified. After being kept in absolute isolation for three weeks, Picquart was finally heard. On November 13, through the personal intervention of the minister of justice, the lawyer Fernand Labori was authorized to see his client. By then, Picquart had spent 122 days in prison, 49 of them in solitary confinement. On November 16, Tavernier delivered his ruling, concluding that Picquart should appear before the Court-Martial. His ruling was, in fact, an indictment. It took up all the accusations of Henry, Lauth, and Roget. Picquart had "had the *petit bleu* fabricated." The proof was that in the packet of papers coming in through the ordinary track, Henry had never noticed "this document of such great interest." Picquart had long concealed the *petit bleu* from his hierarchical superiors, and "undoubtedly he had his reasons for doing so." He had undertaken all sorts of operations: negatives, touch-ups, photographs. Thus, even with Henry dead, all his lies had survived him. The General Staff's thesis was correct. Neither knowledge of Henry's forgery nor knowledge of Esterhazy's dealings with du Paty de Clam had changed anything. The true culprit was Picquart; the others had done nothing but defend the honor of the Army. On November 24, Military Governor Zurlinden ordered Picquart to stand trial; he would appear before the Second Court-Martial on December 12, accused of forgery and the communication of secret documents to an unauthorized person. The protracted machination pursued in order to eliminate Picquart was at last achieving its goal.

That vicissitude demonstrated that the revision of the Dreyfus trial was far from a certainty. But in its very absurdity, it aroused a vast protest. Lists were circulated, which contained the signatures of already committed "intellectuals," but with new names as well. Public meetings were organized, notably by the League for the Rights of Man and the Grand Orient. Jean Jaurès, Francis de Pressensé, and the Socialist Allemane (who was by then mobilized) spoke out on several occasions, in Paris and in the provinces. Other prominent intellectuals (Duclaux, Reclin, Buisson, Huvet, and Paul Meyer) made speeches. People jostled each other in an effort to hear them. Anatole France abandoned his customary moderation. "Let only the language of reason be heard," he said, "but with a boom

On April 21, 1890,
Captain Alfred Dreyfus married
Lucie Hadamard.

Mathieu Dreyfus (left)
beside his younger
brother Alfred. He
devoted twelve years of
his life to establishing his
brother's innocence.

Commandant of the military prisons of
Paris, Commandant Forzinetti (above)
received Dreyfus at the Cherche-Midi
Prison. Immediately convinced of his
innocence, Forzinetti never ceased his
efforts to have it proclaimed.

Colonel Picquart (right), who became head
of the Intelligence Service in July 1895,
discovered that Esterhazy was the author of
the bordereau. Removed from the scene,
persecuted, and arrested in July, 1898, he
had but one goal: to have the truth
proclaimed and the culprits punished.

+ où sera interné Ullmo dès son arrivée — Cette petite mai-
sonnette que j'ai pue ayant d'arriver à   12 — ILES DU SALUT
Cayenne est celle ou a été enfermé   L'île du DIABLE et le Bain des Forçats à l'île ROYALE
Dreyfus pendant si longtemps! —

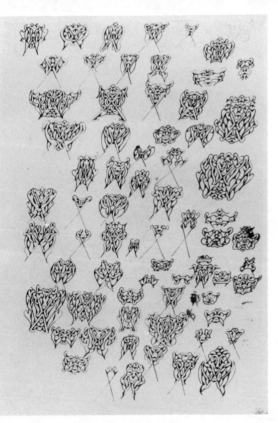

Postcard showing a view of Devil's Island from Royal Island. The anonymous sender marked the location of Dreyfus's primitive hut.

A page from the "notebook" composed by Alfred Dreyfus in November 1898 on Devil's Island. The penned motif is reproduced hundreds of times, interspersed with notes on readings and reflections. In like manner, Dreyfus, in his letters, repeated the same words and sentences to the point of obsession.

Bernard Lazare. The publication in November 1896 of his brochure *Une erreur judiciaire: La vérité sur l'Affaire Dreyfus* invigorated the struggle for revision.

A former collaborator of Léon Gambetta, Joseph Reinach "early on had an intuition of innocence" and committed himself courageously.

Auguste Scheurer-Kestner, deputy from Alsace, was the first influential political personality to proclaim Dreyfus's innocence.

A Catholic and a conservative, Edgar Demange (above) became Alfred Dreyfus's attorney in 1894. He argued before the Paris and Rennes Courts-Martial and was tirelessly devoted to his client.

If Edgar Demange was Dreyfus's own lawyer, Fernand Labori (left), represented Dreyfusism itself. He argued on behalf of Emile Zola before the Court of Assizes, but refused to speak at Rennes because he disapproved of the "conniving" strategy adopted by Demange and Mathieu Dreyfus.

au capitaine Alfred Dreyfus
admiration et affection
Emile Zola

Photograph of Emile Zola dedicated to Alfred Dreyfus. By the summer of 1897, Zola plunged vigorously into the battle for revision, publishing notably in Dreyfus's favor a "letter to the young" and a "letter to France."

On January 1898, the day after Esterhazy's acquittal, under the heading *J'accuse* (chosen by Clemenceau), *L'Aurore* published Emile Zola's famous letter denouncing publicly the crimes of the General Staff. "We felt our confidence rising anew and welling forth within us," wrote Léon Blum. "*J'accuse* turned Paris on its head in a single day."

Anti-Semitism was brought to its jubilant expression in this popular song lampooning Zola's *J'Accuse.*

A courtroom incident between Picquart and Henry.

The High Court of Appeal annuls the prior verdict of the Court of Assizes who had condemned Zola on April 2, 1898.

In January 1898, Colonel Picquart is arrested and punished with 60 days of fortress imprisonment (as seen in *Le petit journal illustré*).

The verdict of February 23, 1898: a joyous crowd welcomes the sentence condemning Zola to a year in prison. An officer (no doubt Henry) proclaims the victory (April 1898).

On the day of General Mercier's testimony at Rennes, Réné Waldeck-Rousseau arrested and had charges preferred against several nationalist leaders, including Paul Déroulède. Jules Guérin, the founder of the Ligue Antisémitique, barricaded himself on rue Chabrol into the headquarters of the Grand Occident of France, which he transformed into a fortress. The police here begin their siege of "Fort Chabrol."

A bonus offered by *La Libre parole* to its readers: the card shows Drumont elected deputy from Algiers in May 1898. "Cosmopolitan Jewry…that's the enemy!…France for the French."

A bas les juifs
et les judaïsants

EDOUARD DRUMONT
Député d'Alger.

La Juiverie cosmopolite voilà
l'ennemie ! unmissons nous tous
et soyons pour cette devise
la France aux Français !

Edouard Drumont

318

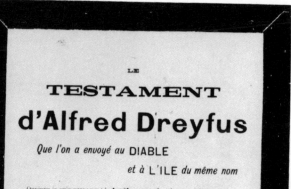

An announcement of the "death" of Alfred Dreyfus. "For the demise of the traitor, it is requested that a jolly time be had by all," and Alfred Dreyfus's "testament" was hung in the lavatory of Devil's Island. These publications express with frightening vulgarity the hatred for Jews and Germans together.

SUPPLÉMENT GRATUIT

Le Siècle

PRIX DE L'ABONNEMENT

Directeur politique : YVES GUYOT

RÉDACTION ET ADMINISTRATION

LES MENSONGES DE LA PHOTOGRAPHIE

Photographic montages published by *Le siècle* in January 1899. Mortal enemies Edouard Drumont and Joseph Reinach appear to be joined in friendship.

Similarly one finds together Esterhazy and Schwarzkoppen. But their meeting was not merely a photographic mirage…

A Dreyfusard cartoon by Couturier putting into the mouths of the principal officers involved in the Affair the admission of their abuses. Du Paty de Clam is in the arms of the notorious "veiled lady." As for General Mercier, his crimes here seem to be rather diminished.

The calling of an opposition meeting in favor of the revision, September 1, 1898.

In Rennes, the "hedge of dishonor": soldiers turn their backs and form a barrier as Dreyfus passes, walking stiffly.

The auditorium of the Rennes Lycée at the opening of the proceedings on August 7, 1899.
On the right, defendant Dreyfus may be seen, standing in front of his lawyers.

During a recess, in the courtyard of the
Rennes Lycée, the lawyer Fernand Labori
chats with Colonel Picquart (in civilian dress
due to his discharge in February 1898). They
would become friends.

General Mercier and General de Boisdeffre
(left) in consultation. They bore "the honor
of the Army" and that honor demanded
Dreyfus's condemnation.

July 21, 1906: in the courtyard of the École Militaire, Commandant Dreyfus receives the Cross of the Legion of Honor. He embraces his wife after the ceremony.

Commandant Dreyfus wears the Cross of the Legion of Honor on his chest, a broad smile on his face.

Free at last with his family, no
doubt at Carpentras. Dreyfus is at
the center, his wife at his right.
Their children, Pierre and Jeanne,
are in front.

Commandant Dreyfus returned to
service during World War I. He
was 55 years old, prematurely
aged by the ordeals of Devil's
Island.

of thunder."* Jaurès proposed that Picquart go to prison "for the sake of the absolute perfection of the General Staff's crime,"† but Georges Clemenceau responded: "We will not tolerate the iniquity against Dreyfus to be redeemed at the price of a still greater iniquity against Picquart."‡ The Dreyfus Affair now encompassed Picquart.

In his prison, Picquart remained serene. To a friend who was authorized to visit him, he said: "I don't understand why I am being exalted by some and insulted by others. I did nothing but my duty."[7] Deputies and senators announced imminent interpellations. The left wanted the government to adjourn—as law permitted—the sessions of the Court-Martial. On November 28 before the Chamber, Alexandre Millerand, with the rigor of an excellent jurist, developed the argument which allowed the government to stay the proceedings: "If you do not exercise your right and if the military judges do not exercise theirs, which is to impose a stay, the responsibility will be yours." Whereupon Raymond Poincaré asked to speak. He had been a minister at the time of Dreyfus's conviction and had always kept silent concerning the Affair. He was known to be as intelligent as he was prudent, an extremely diligent worker of unlimited ambition and capable of infinite patience. For the first time, he took a stand: "The silence of some of us at the present time would be a true act of cowardice." He named his former colleagues, his fellow ministers in 1894: "My friend Dupuy ... my friend Barthou ... my friend Leygues. ..." those who, like himself, had remained silent until then. And he warned Dupuy, who was again prime minister, "If it were true that a judicial error had been committed, those of us who were in charge in 1894 would have the imperious obligation not to do anything or let anything be done that might impede its discovery." Louis Barthou, the leader of the group of progressivist republicans, declared his solidarity with the attitude of "his friend Poincaré." Poincaré was interrupted: Why had he waited so long to speak? Whereupon, as planned, he unburdened himself of a number of thoughts. He declared that none of his colleagues had ever heard of any other charge than the bordereau, that none of them had ever known of any secret or diplomatic file, that they had never known anything of the convict's "admissions" to Captain Lebrun-Renault, that General Mercier had never spoken to any of his colleagues of the confession that Cavaignac had seized upon in his famous address. And accusing himself of having remained silent for so long, he concluded: "I am well aware that today, in breaking this silence which weighed on me, I am

* December 1, 1898, at the Grand Orient.
† *La Petite République* of November 22, 1898.
‡ *L'Aurore* of November 28, 1898.

exposing myself to attacks, insults, and slander. That does not concern me. I am happy to have taken from this tribune the all too long awaited opportunity of freeing my conscience."

Poincaré's "confession" had a considerable effect on the Assembly.[8] Minister of War Freycinet intervened to explain that the government could not prevent the Court-Martial from holding its session (which would be tantamount to "embarking on the path of the arbitrary"), but that the Criminal Chamber, were it to solicit for its own investigation the originals of the documents in the Court-Martial's file, could in effect impose a postponement by taking the materials of the case out of the hands of the Court-Martial. There could be no more cowardly resolution to the problem—entrusting it to the maneuvers of the Criminal Chamber. "Within the government, the habit of bravery has been lost," wrote *Le Figaro* of November 29. The prime minister murmured a few words about respecting the workings of justice; his sole concern was not to lose electoral support. By a vote of 338 to 83, the Chamber rejected the Socialist motion inviting the minister of war to order a postponement. It was clear that a very large majority of the Chamber remained fiercely opposed to a revision. Ought Picquart then to prepare to join Dreyfus in jail?

Things were more difficult in the Senate for the simple reason that the upper chamber was far less sensitive to electoral concerns. And it counted in its membership a large number of jurists. In its session of December 1, the Senate passed a motion according to which cross-examination would be extended to the preliminary investigations of Court-Martials. That reform, which came too late for Picquart, indicated in which direction the Senate was leaning. It was then that René Waldeck-Rousseau asked for the floor.

A well-known corporate lawyer, with numerous cases at the Palais de Justice, a senator from the Loire, elected in 1894 then reelected in 1897, he had never intervened in the Senate. A former collaborator of Léon Gambetta and Jules Ferry, he enjoyed great authority, which was based on his rectitude and intelligence. He had prudently oscillated from the center-left to the center-right, but had never suffered any decline. He was known to be shy, proud, and secretive. Outside of Parliament he had built a career which was the envy of all (he was perhaps the greatest civil lawyer of his time), and was regarded as aloof, a judgment confirmed by his slightly haughty demeanor. For him to have intervened in this circumstance, the "measure of iniquity and stupidity" must have reached a new high.[9] Above all, he must have felt that the moment was particularly opportune to take a stand. He defended before the Chamber legislation allowing the High Court of Appeal to order the suspension of legal action it deemed related to matters already in its purview. He would thus shield

Picquart from the Court-Martial. Why had Waldeck-Rousseau, who never did anything without careful consideration, chosen that moment and that pretext to abandon the silence he had maintained since 1894? Was it juridical scruples that impelled him to intervene, even as they had influenced Poincaré in the Chamber?[10] Was he searching amid the storm for a legalistic solution that might satisfy both camps? More probably, he had judged that the time was then right for him to move forward. His speech to the Senate produced a great effect. The legislation he argued for was barely defeated by a vote of 113 to 113. For Waldeck-Rousseau, who had succeeded in carrying half the Senate, that failure was a personal success. Whether he wanted it or not, he was now counted in the Dreyfusard camp. Like Alexandre Millerand, who had converted to Dreyfusism after Henry's suicide. Like Raymond Poincaré, who had finally abandoned his silence. The three famous lawyers consulted with each other. To them was added Louis Barthou. Their meetings thus assembled all the shades of republicanism—from the socialist Millerand to the progressivist Waldeck-Rousseau. Neither the Parliament nor the press could fail to see what was happening. The rallying of these men, who cultivated their careers with utmost care, was a sign of the future.

December 12 was approaching. What else could be done to shield Picquart from the Court-Martial? Carried away by his zeal, Zurlinden had sent Picquart before the Court-Martial not merely for forgery but for violation of the espionage law. Now Picquart, along with his lawyer Leblois, was still to be tried before the Court of Summary Jurisdiction for "communication of the secret Esterhazy file." The same facts were thus simultaneously being submitted to both military and common-law jurisdiction. The lawyers representing Picquart and Leblois consulted. They hastily brought before the High Court of Appeal on December 2 a request for a ruling. The High Court of Appeal agreed to consider the case immediately and the matter came before the Criminal Chamber on December 8. There were only four days left before the military Court-Martial convened. The reporting judge concluded that it would be wiser and more practical, before reaching a decision, to take the Court-Martial's dossier into custody. Public Prosecutor Manau approved, scolding that "it was necessary to rise above passions that had grown fierce."[11] The shrewd ruling by the High Court of Appeal merely ordered the transmission of the military file. That ruling effectively imposed a stay: Picquart remained in prison, but for the while at least, he was safe from military justice. Just in time. The furor of the adversaries of revision had grown explosive. It was clear that the Criminal Chamber was "on the side of the Jews." It was to become a matter of urgency to get the dossier of the Dreyfus Affair back from those "dishonest or imbecilic" judges.

2

To the Elysée, General

The Criminal Chamber was conducting its investigation, divided like all of France. But conflicts in the High Court of Appeal tended to be hidden in the folds of judicial robes. Opinions were expressed only cautiously and with moderation. Reserve was more than a duty; it was a style shared by all, consisting of prudence, but professional custom as well. Whatever their beliefs, the work of justice tolerated neither outbursts nor demonstrations of emotion.

Legal knowledge, respect for the law, and for many a veneration for written rules (be they of law or procedure) could not but have an effect on men's characters. Most of the Court's judges had behind them a long past devoted to the study of legal theory and practice. The juridical spirit had formed them. It had given them a method, which was half-scientific, half-literary, in which inventiveness and imagination had their place, but were accompanied by meticulous attention to detail, rigor of examination, and coherence of argumentation. Most of the magistrates in the High Court of Appeal were conservatives. Almost all were republicans.* The Combined Chambers of the High Court of Appeal, in addition to the Criminal Chamber, included the Civil Chamber and the Chambre des Requêtes, each of which examined appeals filed in civil cases. It appears that the spirit of traditional France was stronger in Civil Chambers than in the Criminal Chambers. Their social milieu, upbringing, education, even their discipline, inclined them to be respectful of institutions and authorities. But unlike Army officers, they could not easily admit that the

---

* Starting in 1897, the Republic had undertaken a major effort to bring the judiciary to heel, resorting to a variety of means which showed little respect for judicial independence. A law of July 1883, which suspended the irremovability of judges for a few months, had permitted a vast purge: 609 "sitting" magistrates had been eliminated. Nearly 300 magistrates resigned in solidarity. Thus were the Bonapartists, royalists, and "clerical conservatives" chased from the judiciary in a purge that was conducted in a manner as brutal as it was arbitrary. Fifteen years later the French judicial system was still feeling its effects, and above all still retained a memory of what had happened. (On the great purge of 1883, see J.-P. Royer, R. Martissage, P. Lecocq, *Juges et notables au XIXme siècle*, PUF, 1982, pp. 365ff.)

honor of an institution required a judicial error. Neither the secret communication of documents during court deliberations, nor the fabrication of a forgery, nor the execution of a crime out of obedience or zeal could be easily tolerated by these men. An exasperation of the juridical spirit tended to find all irregularities repugnant, regardless of the principle in which they were clothed. The High Court of Appeal was neither revolutionary nor "radical"—merely republican. A sizable number of the judges were predisposed against Dreyfus. For *res judicata*, the authority of a prior verdict—delivered even by a military tribunal—was one of the rules of law they held sacred. Many of the judges were anti-Semites, but incapable of accepting any random infraction of the law in the service of their prejudice. Several of them were in addition spirits imbued with a sense of justice, for whom the word designated not merely an institution, but a duty and an ideal. And some of them were simply trying to determine which way the wind was blowing and were prepared to become Dreyfusards if the government chose that course.

It was known that Judge Sevestre, who had numerous relatives in the Army, was the leader of the minority that was hostile to revision. He reproached Presiding Judge Loew, who was plainly favorable to revision, with unduly "letting his opinions be known," and falling short of his dual duties as judge and as presiding officer of the Court. Several of the judges seemed indifferent, either because they had not yet formed an opinion or because they had decided to keep it to themselves. All of them labored diligently on the case. In December the Criminal Chamber heard General Gonse, as fierce as ever, but increasingly confused, and General de Boisdeffre, who had retired to an old ancestral manor in Normandy, and who seemed daily more depressed and fatigued. It heard all those who had direct or indirect knowledge of the alleged confession, the principal ministers in 1895, and former President of the Republic Casimir-Périer himself. Maurice Weil, the Jewish officer, was heard at length on the subject of his relations with Commandant Esterhazy. Esterhazy, who had left London for Rotterdam, where he was living under an alias, wrote to the Chief Presiding Justice of the High Court of Appeal, Charles Mazeau, to offer to testify, but he insisted that he be granted protection. He feared, he said, that Judge Bertulus, who was still investigating the swindling charge brought by his nephew Christian, might collar him. He knew that his prerequisite was impossible to fulfill, and consequently did not come. He continued to grant interviews to all the newspapers of Europe, endlessly inventing stories and contradicting himself, despite the fact that the market value of his revelations was gradually declining.[1]

The focus of attention remained the secret file. The High Court of Appeal had asked the government for it on November 14. Charles de

Freycinet, the minister of war, had initially promised that he would with-
hold nothing from the High Court of Appeal, and then began posing his
conditions. The Criminal Chamber would have to commit itself to publish
nothing of the secret file without his consent, and Captain Cuignet would
present the file to the Court personally, bringing it with him in the
morning and returning with it in the evening. Several judges, who were
shocked by the procedure, protested, but then the Criminal Chamber
agreed. What else could they have done?

Beginning on December 30, Captain Cuignet thus came every day to
the Palais de Justice to present and explain the contents of the "secret
file"—which by then consisted of nearly four hundred documents—in the
presence of the public prosecutor and Maître Mornard, Lucie Dreyfus's
attorney. Everything concerning the bordereau, all the testimony accumulated around Dreyfus's confession, and, finally, all the documents collected
or fabricated by Colonel Henry and General Gonse were examined in
succession. The judges read, commented on, and passed the documents to
each other. Gradually, it dawned on the majority of the judges that the
secret file was as bereft of hard evidence as the official judicial dossier.
Cuignet perceived their misgivings and was worried; the civilian justices
simply did not understand the need to uphold the honor of the Army.

The counteroffensive came from within the High Court of Appeal
itself. On Christmas day 1898, L'Eclair and La Patrie abruptly published
the confidential statements of Jules Quesnay de Beaurepaire, presiding
justice of the Civil Chamber of the High Court of Appeal. After a rather
dull career as a lawyer, he had become a magistrate in 1878, where he
demonstrated a rare audacity. As advocate general of Paris, he had prosecuted General Boulanger at a time when the public prosecutor refused to.
In 1892, he was appointed presiding justice of the Civil Chamber. Severely
criticized by the Socialists during the Panama scandal trial, he insisted on
personally presenting his defense before the Combined Chambers of the
High Court of Appeal. Exonerated of any infraction against honor,[2] he
had retained from the entire affair a certain bitterness, but also a violent
desire to be a center of public discussion. Courage also came naturally to
him, and he was bored by the Civil Chamber, plunged deep into unre-
warding paperwork. That the progress of the Dreyfus Affair should take
place without his participation was something he found intolerable.

Already, in early December, he expressed his opinion that the Criminal
Chamber was a pack of politicians and fools. He had been witness to some
"revealing" scenes, which he soon shared with the nationalist press. When
Colonel Picquart had been taken from prison in order to testify before the
Criminal Chamber, he was lead to the office of the presiding justice of the
Civil Chamber, for lack of another room. It was there that Beaurepaire

heard Judge Bard, reporting the case, say to the prisoner, "My dear Picquart, give me your opinion of the testimony of . . ." Bard did not have time to finish his sentence. Beaurepaire rose up before him. He had indeed heard the words, "My dear Picquart." It was an admission of collusion between the reporting judge and the principal agent of the Jewish syndicate. The press exploited the story. Beaurepaire became the man of the day and the Criminal Chamber was plunged into anguish. Emboldened, Beaurepaire revealed new details to the press every day. He had heard Bard say to Picquart: "Here is Gonse's testimony. I think we've got him." Chief Presiding Justice Mazeau was asked to investigate, but on December 28, Beaurepaire, encouraged by the mounting success of his revelations, sent Mazeau a memorandum enumerating seven acts of "favoritism" by Justice Loew and Judge Bard benefiting Picquart and Dreyfus's lawyers, Henri Mornard and Fernand Labori. On one occasion, they served Picquart a beverage; on another day, a hot toddy. Bard had been seen conversing with Labori. And Presiding Justice Loew, embarrassed at having kept Picquart waiting, had asked the court clerk to convey "all the Court's regrets."

Presiding Justice Loew and Judge Bard of the Civil Chamber were thus constrained to respond, point by point, to the accusations. The Council of Ministers deliberated on the matter, which became an affair of State, for the anti-revisionists perceived the profit they might derive from it. Beaurepaire was growing exasperated. On January 6 he issued a threat and demanded an investigation: "I will establish that because of the behavior of several magistrates, the High Court of Appeal has been singled out for public scorn; that we are obliged to say in society that we belong to the civil chambers." Abruptly, on January 8 upon failing to receive any answer to his ultimatum, he sent to the minister of justice—without explanation—his resignation as presiding justice of the High Court of Appeal. And he informed the press.

This time the hapless minister was at a complete loss. He hesitated for three full days. As a replacement for the resigning justice, Judge Ballot-Beaupré was chosen, and it was decided that Chief Presiding Justice Mazeau himself would preside over the Criminal Chamber with the option of selecting his own reporting judge. Loew was thus forced to submit to what public opinion regarded as a singular humiliation. As for Beaurepaire, he became an indefatigable journalist. In January 1899 *L'Echo de Paris* published his most recent revelations: Judge Dumas had frequent conferences outside the Palais de Justice with Dreyfus's friends and relatives; a second judge had had "premeditated meetings" with Picquart by the urinals of the High Court of Appeal.

Parliament was by this time proceeding according to the clock of the

High Court of Appeal. On January 12, Émile Deschanel, reelected president of the Chamber, made one of the resplendent speeches which constituted the larger part of his function. "How could it come to pass that those two noble loves of France, Justice and the Army, were pitted against each other at the risk of tearing her heart apart?" Several deputies insulted various magistrates. From the tribune, a deputy denounced Justices Manau, Bard, and Loew, that "trio of scoundrels." The minister of justice was called on to dismiss the public prosecutor. In order to appease the Chamber, Le Bret pledged to ask Mazeau for a new judicial inquiry into the facts brought to light by Beaurepaire. The Chamber debated the hot toddy served to Picquart. The minister affirmed that Generals Billot and Roget had also had a pitcher of water and a flacon of rum at their disposal. This absurd conflict was only mildly distracting from a rather different one: Edouard Drumont and Henri Rochefort were openly accusing Jewish money of having corrupted the High Court of Appeal.

In order to pursue his investigation, the majestic chief presiding justice called to his side two magistrates chosen for their seniority, deans of the judiciary: Judges Dareste and Voisin. For ten full days, the three magistrates heard the accuser and various witnesses. They descended into the most minuscule of details. There was great difficulty in identifying the judge who had communicated with Picquart at the urinals, but finally a policeman was found who claimed to have been on the scene at the time. During a public hearing of the Criminal Chamber, he recognized and identified Judge Chambareaud. It was a matter of notoriety that Chambareaud was stricken with a disease of the bladder. Finally, the deans' inquest ended without substantiating any of Beaurepaire's charges. On January 27, Chief Presiding Justice Mazeau and Judges Dareste and Voisin sent Minister Le Bret a letter whose terms had been carefully calculated. It was intended simultaneously to exonerate their colleagues and to open the path toward "dispossessing" the Criminal Chamber of the case:[3]

> We have the honor of submitting to you, along with the recommendation you requested, the testimony taken during the informal inquiry entrusted to us and bearing on the recent elements brought to light by M. Quesnay de Beaurepaire.
>
> As a result, we are left with the impression that it would be wise, given the exceptional circumstances the country is at present traversing, not to allow the Criminal Chamber sole responsibility in arriving at a definitive sentence. For three months, our colleagues have been undertaking a laborious investigation amid an unprecedented unleashing of contrary passions that have penetrated even

into the courtroom. Is it not foreseeable that a judgment reached under such conditions would be impotent to effect an appeasement of minds and would lack the authority necessary for all to respect it?

We suspect neither the good faith nor the honorability of the magistrates of the Criminal Chamber; but it is our fear that disturbed by the insults and outrages, and carried away for the most part by contrary feelings out of prejudices of which they are not aware, they will no longer be able, once the preliminary investigation is completed, to maintain that tranquillity and moral freedom indispensable to their function as judges.

Thus while the Criminal Chamber—slandered,* sacrificed by the highest authorities of the State to the clamor of the anti-revisionists—patiently proceeded with its investigation, the procedure for dispossessing it of the case had already been initiated. On January 28, the government submitted legislation applicable to the proceedings underway, attributing to the Combined Chambers of the High Court of Appeal power of decision in all cases of revision. Whereas the majority of the Criminal Chamber seemed favorable to Dreyfus, Mazeau had indicated to the government that the majority of the two other Chambers, the Civil Chamber and the Chambre des Requêtes, was tending in the opposite direction. It thus appeared improbable that the combined Chambers would authorize a revision. What remained was to find a formula for saving face. For such a dispossession of a high court, a few days before its expected judgment, was without precedent and in defiance of the law.† On February 6, the Criminal Chamber informed the minister of justice that it was reaching the conclusion of its investigation. If the case were to be removed from its jurisdiction, swift—indeed, very swift—action would have to be taken. The debate over dispossession took place in the Assembly on February 10. The reporting member of the parliamentary commission, Renault-Morlière, a former lawyer with the High Court of Appeal, delivered a critique of a law that trampled on all principles, a law drummed up for the occasion, an odious law. "You are killing in this nation the very idea of

* The violence of the slander to which the Criminal Chamber—and specifically Justice Bard and Presiding Justice Loew—were subjected on a daily basis is well described in the book that Loew would publish in 1910: *La Loi de déssaisissement par un déssaisi* (Fischbaches). "Lévy-Loew" was accused of having sold out to the syndicate, and at a steep price. His brother, a notary who remained in Strasbourg, was accused of being a German agent. His son also was attacked in his family life and his business relations. Caricatures showed Lévy-Loew receiving his sacks of coins from the Jews or wearing his judicial robes and a German helmet.
†By a vote of 9 to 2, a commission appointed by the Chambre des Députés, voted against passage.

justice." Then the Socialist Alexandre Millerand rose to assail the infamous document. "To Caesar it is permitted to display contempt for the law and to debase the judiciary; it is the honor and the strength of a democracy not to tolerate such arbitrariness." Next it was Pelletan's turn to intervene: "We have here neither a Republican law nor a French law. If it is passed, there will be no more party of the Republic because there will be no more justice. And since there is much talk of the French Nation, I dare say that a great nation deserves its Chamber—at the end of this century—*not* to inflict this shame on its history."

But the prime minister and the minister of justice dug in behind the shelter provided by the chief presiding justice's opinion. "Who could object?" Charles Dupuy asked. "The defendant? The premature—or overweening—partisans of Dreyfus's innocence? They believe in the self-evidence of their cause. But is that self-evidence of so special a nature that it can be appreciated only before the Criminal Chamber?" Minister of Justice Le Bret was less adept, but more convincing. Sinking unusually low to obtain a favorable vote, he advised the deputies to "sound out your districts." The legislation was passed by a vote of 324 to 207. Almost the entire center and two thirds of the Radicals voted along with the right.

The vote was going to be more difficult, it appeared, in the Senate. On the very day, however, on which the upper house designated the commission that would examine the projected dispossession, February 16, President Félix Faure awoke in a state of fatigue. He nevertheless kept to his schedule of meetings and lunched quite heartily. Around 5 o'clock the officers on duty heard shouts appearing to come from the president's study. They rushed in and found him lying inert and immobile on his bed, his face fixed in an expressionless stare. The state of the room left little doubt as to the circumstances in which the cerebral hemorrhage had struck the president. A doctor who happened to be present at the Elysée came running, but Faure was already emitting a death-rattle. The house physicians were called in while the "disorder of persons and effects" was tidied up.[4] The president's mistress was escorted out a side door. Toward 5:30 P.M., Faure lapsed into a coma. He died at 10:00 P.M. after receiving the sacrament of penitence. The holy oils arrived too late for extreme unction.*

For the revisionists, the sudden death of Faure came as a relief, for he had joined the anti-Dreyfusard camp and was countering the revision with all the resources of his authority. The fact that he had died in a woman's arms was a source of amusement if not outright celebration. It was a great

* On February 18, *La Patrie* insinuated that Félix Faure had been murdered by the Jews or by a Jewess.

boon to the gossip mills. What remained was the hope that Émile Loubet, president of the Senate, would be elected president of the Republic. Loubet had been prime minister at the time of the Panama scandal, a circumstance that did not help his candidacy. But he was a "true republican" and a convinced revisionist. The Dreyfus Affair was by then at the center of political life.

The republican groups in the Senate and in the Chamber immediately proclaimed Loubet's candidacy. Radicals and even Socialists came to his home in a delegation in order to declare their support. The progressivists, on the contrary, stubbornly stuck to a Méline candidacy. Jules Méline hesitated and allowed himself to be implored. Quite quickly, Loubet found himself showered with insults. He was the candidate from Devil's Island! The Ligue de la Patrie Française was agitating in every direction. On the very morning of the election, Quesnay de Beaurepaire and Jules Lemaître published articles denouncing Loubet's seedy interventions in the Panama Affair. Nevertheless, on February 29 the preferred candidate of the "Panamists" and "Dreyfusists" was elected in the first round with 483 votes. Méline, who was not officially a candidate, received 279 votes, and the remainder were lost on Godefroy Cavaignac, Paul Deschanel, and Charles Dupuy.

The Dreyfusards were exultant. But the nationalists had had sufficient time to "prepare" for the big day. Jules Guérin recruited additional troops ("longshoremen, dockworkers, assorted loiterers from the outskirts and other vagabonds"), and Paul Déroulède, mobilized the members of his Ligue. Charles Dupuy, who had been forewarned, chose to do nothing, "either out of negligence, or because it was not unpleasant to this portly man . . . to disgust Loubet with his new role during his very first day in office."[5] The new president of the Republic took the train from Versailles to Paris. When he disembarked at the Gare Saint-Lazare, hundreds of demonstrators were waiting to heckle him. Amid shouts of "Resign!" and "Panama!" his car was mobbed. He had great difficulty in making it to the Elysée.

During the same period, Déroulède and his troops, who had arrived from Versailles, were running through the streets in a state of great excitement. Déroulède was implored to march on the Elysée. At the Place des Pyramides, leaning against the statue of Joan of Arc, he pledged to "boot out of France a foreign Constitution—just as Joan of Arc had done to the English. . . . Today's election is a provocation. It is up to the people to choose the President of the Republic."[6] While shouts of "To the Elysée!" continued, he protested, "Let us not do anything this evening; there is in the Elysée a dead man whom I loved . . . on Thursday, I will do my duty."

On Thursday, the Republic would bury Félix Faure. Déroulède's pledge was not a vain threat. The police reported a plan by Ligue members to march on either the Elysée or the Palais Bourbon after the funeral.

The Chambers had voted for a state funeral. The religious ceremony was to take place at Notre-Dame. Émile Loubet, who was troubled by the nationalist agitation, sent the Chambers a message seeking to establish some equilibrium. "There must be respect for both the judiciary, which applies the laws, and the Army, which assures the nation's independence." He also warned "that he would not allow the rights conferred upon him by the Constitution to be diminished while in his hands."

With the help of his aide Marcel Habert, Déroulède was preparing to act. What he wanted was a "military 4th of September without bloodshed." The people—that is, the members of the Ligue—were to carry off a general already sympathetic to their cause and, followed by a brigade, take off for the Hôtel de Ville and the Elysée. The Elysée and the Ministry of the Interior were to be occupied. Déroulède, the liberating general, and, if need be, a civilian accomplice—who might be Cavaignac if he accepted—would proclaim to the nation the abrogation of the usurpatory Constitution of 1875 and announce that the people would soon be convened in its electoral committees. Déroulède prepared the text of his message to his countrymen: He would end up reading it—after the affair turned sour—to the High Court.[7]

What remained was to find a general who could manage to gain the support of the Army. There was talk of General de Pellieux, for whom anti-Dreyfusism had become a justification for living, and who was lashing out at the Jews and the Criminal Chamber which had sold out to the Jews. When approached, Pellieux was hesitant, and made a few vague promises. Déroulède, who had learned that the site at which the troops were to be dispersed after the funeral was the Place de la Nation, informed 25,000 members of the Ligue by summonses, telegrams-letters, and even posters, that they were to appear at 3 o'clock at the Bastille. The pretext—which would fool no one—was that from there they would go to the Père-Lachaise Cemetery to place a wreath on Faure's grave. Déroulède was hoping that between 5,000 and 6,000 Ligue members would come to the Bastille, a number sufficient for his plans. He harangued his troops on September 21 in a huge meeting held in Salle Charrasse, which ended with shouts of "Long live the Republic; down with Parliament." For their part, but with less specific plans, Guérin's bands were preparing to act. The Duke of Orleans was increasing his contacts in the hope that the whole affair might be of some profit to him.

The effort was an almost comic failure. The funeral proceeded in an atmosphere of perfect calm. Then General de Pellieux, followed by his troops, leaving the square in front of Notre-Dame en route to Place de la Nation, was either overcome by scruples or undone by fear. He decided not to go to the meeting place where Déroulède awaited him. Invoking a somewhat vague "concern" that had just occurred to him and the risk of being "noisily acclaimed" at the Place de la Nation, he asked the military governor, Émile Zurlinden, to replace him. Pellieux was obliged to bargain at great length in order to obtain satisfaction.* Meanwhile, Déroulède was waiting at the Place de la Nation, his deputy's sash over his shoulder and his pockets stuffed with proclamations, decrees, gold coins, and cash in the hope of being able to meet any needs as they arose. His aide Habert assured him that all was going well. Members of the Ligue were lining the path that went from the Place de la Nation to the Hôtel de Ville and from there to the Elysée. Toward 4:30 the awaited brigade was seen approaching. Déroulède, followed by two hundred of the faithful (since fewer had shown up than expected), prepared to greet it. A general on horseback was marching at the head of the brigade, beneath a black plumed hat. But it was Roget instead of Pellieux.

Déroulède tried to make the best of this blow struck by fate. He rushed up to a surprised Roget. "Follow us, my General, have pity on the Nation, save France and the Republic. To the Elysée, General." Barrès and Habert spoke vociferously, attempting to lead him away with them. Roget's horse reared, and Roget violently thrust Déroulède aside. With his sword, he indicated Boulevard Diderot to his troops—the way back to the Reuilly barracks. At that point, the members of the Ligue, realizing that their operation had failed, attempted to block his path. Roget forced his way through the barrier and stormed back to the barracks with his men. At the threshold of the barracks, Déroulède again attempted to grab hold of the horse's reins. He and Habert were dragged into the courtyard, while the majority of the rioters, along with Barrès and Guérin, remained in the street.

The conspirators thus found themselves trapped within the barracks. Roget, by this time frankly embarrassed by his prisoners, invited them to withdraw. They refused. "Go tell Paris," Déroulède shouted, "that I am a prisoner of the Army." He began shouting in the barracks courtyard, challenging the officers: "The Army has betrayed me. . . . You are no longer soldiers. You are Parliamentarians." Roget, unable to eject them, informed Zurlinden, who informed Dupuy. It was near midnight when the police superintendent Armand Cochefert arrived at Reuilly to tell Roget that he was to "keep" the deputies and to consider them under

---

* Maurice Barrès, who was at Déroulède's side at Place de la Nation, would maintain that the carefully planned *coup d'état* had failed because of a series of indiscretions, but above all because of General de Pellieux's "betrayal."[8]

arrest. At 1:00 A.M. Cochefert escorted the conspirators to jail under suspicion of "having entered military barracks at the head of a group of demonstrators and having refused to leave the premises despite orders from military authorities." Déroulède was indignant. The terms of the arrest warrant were an insult. He managed to insert into the official record "that he had gone to the Place de la Nation in order to enlist military troops in an insurrection and overthrow the Parliamentary Republic." For fear of being arrested, Guérin, along with about sixty men, retreated to his fort on Rue Chabrol. No sooner was he informed than the Duke of Orleans sadly went to bed. Despite this doomed failure, the danger of Caesarism would continue to make its presence felt thereafter in French political life—and to inflect its course.*

Forewarned of the plot as very few governments have been, the Dupuy goverment acted with a distinct lack of vigor to defend the Republic. When the prime minister asked the Chamber to suspend parliamentary immunity for deputies under arrest, he invoked only a violation of the press law and the misdemeanor of provoking soldiers to disobey orders. There followed a rather bizarre judicial inquiry during the course of which the defendants obstinately maintained that they had attempted to incite the people and the Army and to overthrow the Republic. Meanwhile, the examining magistrate and public prosecutor strained to demonstrate that they had committed no more than benign offenses. In an effort to demonstrate his republican zeal, Dupuy nevertheless decided to instigate generalized legal action against the Ligues for violation of an antiquated law covering unauthorized associations of more than twenty persons. Suit was filed jointly against the Ligue des Patriotes, the Ligue Antisémitique, and the Ligue des Droits de l'Homme. The court was to impose a fine of 16 francs with suspended sentence.[10]

The aborted coup and the nationalist agitation might have resulted in relegating the dispossession law to oblivion. That, however, was by nc means the case. Dupuy and Le Bret obstinately stuck to their plan as though nothing had happened. Parliamentary debate on the issue was discussed first in the Senate on January 27. After several impassioned speeches, René Waldeck-Rousseau ascended the tribune. "No eloquence," related Joseph Reinach, "was ever less obtrusive. . . . One is tempted to say that the man, who does not make a single gesture, who is cold, serene, and virtually immobile, does not speak to understanding through the sense of hearing, but rather through that of sight; it is not noise but light that

---

* It is possible that this aborted plot was later "exaggerated" by Waldeck-Rousseau to suit the implementation of his domestic policies.[9]

passes by."[11] Waldeck-Rousseau denounced the suspect and feeble law as a violation of legal principle and an outrage to conscience:

> Yesterday there was an appeal made to that French sentiment which enjoys recalling its past, what it has been, its diverse glories; what worries me is not seeing our institutions under attack. The very character of the nation is being threatened.
>
> We have always been a people enamored of reason and the ideal. We were eager for equality and now preachers, in a fury, are exhuming—in order to vaunt them—memories which are the shame of history, and are attempting to set a whole fraction of the populaton against another one. We were eager for justice, and they were able to say—without the entire populace trembling—that against the laws of individuals might be pitted reasons of State.
>
> Certain words have lost their meaning: to fear lest an error had been committed is not to obey the most noble duty and most noble sentiment of humanity. No, in the jargon of a certain nationalism it is to misperceive the reality of the country.
>
> To want to correct that error is an abuse. And now we are being asked for exceptional and extraordinary tribunals.
>
> It seems, in truth, that certain acts have been forgotten and that certain memories no longer gnaw at the hearts—as once they did—of the sons or descendents of the refugees of 1851.
>
> I will not allow myself to amnesty the past; we will not accord the reactionaries of the future a republican precedent.
>
> There has been talk of public opinion . . . . I respond: let us speak about justice; I say, moreover, that the public opinion of France must not be confused with the clamor of a few professionals.
>
> I say, in turn: men in politics must never consider the present moment; they should always be looking toward the future. Yes, public opinion is quite movable! Yes, it undergoes abrupt and irresistible turns. . . . And what it forgives the least are the mistakes it made because its representatives allowed it to make them. I know of only one way not to err and not to deceive it, and that is, first, to listen to one's conscience, and, then, to obey it.

The celebrated attorney succeeded in producing a great impression, but not in changing the vote. By a margin of 155 to 125, the Senate declared itself in favor of the law and proceeded to a discussion of its provisions.* But Waldeck-Rousseau had achieved his goal. He had been speaking "beyond the Affair." It was a political message that he had been delivering from the tribune, calling the Dupuy Ministry to account. He wanted to appear as the inflexible defender of the Republic and its freedoms. He was already thinking of the next election. . . .[12]

3

Appealed and Annulled

No sooner had the dispossession legislation been promulgated on March 1, 1899, than the Criminal Chamber made a show of its independence—or its dissatisfaction. Two days later, it welcomed Lieutenant Colonel Picquart's petition for a ruling determining under whose jurisdiction his case would fall. Most of the elements retained against Picquart by military strictures, and specifically the falsification of the *petit bleu*, were declared by the High Court of Appeal to be "continuous" with the "illicit" communications made to Louis Leblois, which fell under common law jurisdiction. Picquart had thus managed to escape the Court Martial once and for all, and the nationalist press denounced the latest victory of the Jews, which confirmed the Criminal Chamber's extreme docility to the interests of the syndicate.

As a result of the "judicial *coup d'etat*," in Alexandre Millerand's phrase, constituted by the dispossession law, the Criminal Chamber's case was to be transferred to the Combined Chambers. But the dispossession came at a time when the Criminal Chamber had already completed its investigation. In order to replace Judge Bard, Chief Presiding Justice Mazeau was looking for a new recording judge who might perform the same task for the Combined Chambers. It seemed appropriate or prudent to him to

---

* The Chief Presiding Justice of the High Court of Appeal, Mazeau, nevertheless voted for the law which, in defiance of all principles of jurisprudence, removed the case from the Criminal Chamber.

It was not until June 11, 1908—with the revision achieved—that the government would propose legislation abrogating the dispossession law. The law restoring its powers to the Criminal Chamber of the High Court of Appeal was promulgated on March 5, 1909.

name a presiding justice from one of the Chambers. Mazeau eliminated Presiding Justice Tanon of the Chambre des Requêtes, who was notoriously favorable to a revision, and named Presiding Justice Ballot-Beaupré, who had replaced Beaurepaire in presiding over the Civil Chamber, and whose feelings about the Affair were completely unknown. He was a man of rather ponderous appearance who seemed to be a worthy and well-nourished burgher, living with his mother in circumstances of rigorous austerity. He was reputed to be an excellent jurist as well as a magistrate of integrity and generosity, whose career owed nothing to intrigue. In Nancy he had been public prosecutor and then chief presiding justice. He had now been sitting on the highest Court for seventeen years. Ballot-Beaupré immediately set to work. On March 27 the Combined Chambers received the secret file, which was brought to them by General Chanoine, with the assistance of the indefatigable Captain Cuignet. In April they ordered an "additional investigation." They could well have spared themselves the effort, but it seemed to the Combined Chambers that in declaring their satisfaction with the work of the Criminal Chamber they would have been remiss in their functions. They would thus hear ten more witnesses during the months of April and May, while Dreyfusards and anti-Dreyfusards busily speculated, based on the proceedings, on how individual judges would cast their votes in the final judgment.* *L'Aurore* counted 24 magistrates for revision and 23 against. Others calculated that 12 swing votes would prove decisive at the final instant. But the large majority of the judges, disturbed by the campaign against the Criminal Chamber, kept their silence.

Maître Mornard, Lucie Dreyfus's lawyer, had obtained copies of the minutes of the sessions of the Criminal Chamber. It seemed to Mathieu Dreyfus—and this was also the opinion of Clemenceau, Bernard Lazare, Ludovic Trarieux, and Joseph Reinach—that in order to move public opinion, it would be necessary to publish the minutes, even though such a move would be in defiance of the law. Mornard, who regularly kept Mathieu Dreyfus abreast of their contents, could not take it upon himself to authorize their publication. They invented a subterfuge which played fast and loose with norms of professional secrecy. The lawyer Fernand Labori, who had the documents copied by his secretaries at Mornard's home, agreed to transmit his copies to Mathieu, insisting on utmost secrecy, on condition that Mathieu would have them copied and then return them. In the event of an investigation, it was imperative that their

---

* "The new investigation," wrote presiding Justice Loew, "which was initiated by the Combined Chambers, in fact merely confirmed all the data (of the Criminal Chamber); not one of its findings was contested; not a single witness came to object that his testimony had been poorly interpreted or imprecisely recorded . . ."[1]

origin not be discovered. Bernard Lazare found a few indigent Russian Jews who worked day and night at the immense scribal labor. And on March 31, *Le Figaro* began publication of the investigation of the Criminal Chamber, which lasted through the end of April.

It was a scandal, but an effective one, and the circulation of the newspaper increased dramatically. Diverse rumors spread to explain the leak. It was Mlle. de Freycinet, daughter of the minister of war, one suggested, who had informed the newspaper. A "masked man," another claimed, had been seen carrying documents to Sardou, the editor of *Le Figaro*. The file had been stolen from a judge. There was no doubt, *La Libre Parole* assured, "that a scoundrel in hermine had betrayed."[2] The government ordered an investigation, or "the appearance of an investigation,"[3] which yielded no results. But the publication had a considerable effect. From that point on, the public was aware of the case in its entirety. To most observers—and even to numerous anti-Dreyfusards—it seemed that the revision could no longer be prevented.

During this period, Commandant Esterhazy was relentlessly fueling a press campaign that was growing increasingly chaotic. On March 5, he gave *L'Aurore* and *The Daily Chronicle* (which paid him 5,000 francs) a detailed account of his collusion with the General Staff, the mysterious meeting in the Parc Montsouris, and the pressures exerted on experts and witnesses during his trial. Edouard Drumont, in order to diminish the effect of his statements, claimed in *La Libre Parole* of March 9 that he had sold out to the syndicate. Esterhazy responded: "No, Monsieur, and you know this better than anyone else, the syndicate has not bought me. I am not for sale." Esterhazy insulted everyone involved. "Gonse? A fool." "Pellieux? A decent man who is in a perpetual state of fear when confronted with civilian authority." "Billot? A politician." "Cavaignac? A narrow-minded mouthpiece for the military, completely grotesque." "Picquart? An ambitious fop, a paper-pushing Napoleon." "Déroulède is a madman." Only Henry deserved any respect: "A true soldier; we were very close and concealed nothing from each other. His forgery? But will you French never understand that an Intelligence Service is and must of necessity be a hotbed of forgery? . . ." Esterhazy was tired of living at such a time, surrounded by marionettes: "I've had enough of it. I shall probably leave for the Sudan. The French have not understood me. So much the worse for them."*

The politicians too seemed caught up in the current. In the corridors of the Assembly, then before the High Court of Appeal, the prime minister conveyed his impression: "I wonder whether we were not the victims of

---

* *Le Matin*, March 16 and 17, 1899; *The Observer* of April 9, 1899; *Le Temps* of April 10, 1899.

a mystification in 1894." During its return to business in May, the Chamber itself, sensing which way the wind was blowing, vigorously attacked Minister of War Charles de Freycinet, who had deemed it wise to suspend Professor Georges Duruy at the École Polytechnique, whose sole sin was having published in *Le Figaro* a series of articles—which were later assembled under the title, "Pour la Justice et pour l'Armée"—in which he implored the Army not to take up Esterhazy's cause as its own. Violently attacked from the tribune, in particular by his Radical friends, the minister of war submitted his resignation on May 5, pleading that after the welcome he had received from the Chambers he no longer had the necessary authority. Yet another minister of war had abandoned his office. . . . Charles Dupuy named as his replacement the minister of public works, Camille Krantz, who immediately ordered the resumption of Duruy's courses. Barely had he arrived in his office than Krantz learned that Cuignet was supplying various newspapers with documents and information. Cuignet, by then actively involved in the conflict, proudly assumed responsibility for his "error." Krantz withdrew him from active duty.* All this occurred a few days before the judgment by the High Court of Appeal. These minor governmental outbursts were not without significance. Even the prime minister was vacillating. He explained to the Chamber that "the dispossession law was not the cornerstone of his policy." Why might not he, after all, be the leader of the government that would undertake the revision?

The three Chambers of the High Court of Appeal met in solemn session on May 29. By an odd coincidence, Paul Déroulède and Marcel Habert, who were being tried for their abortive coup, appeared the same day before the Court of Assizes in a neighboring room. The judges listened, for several hours, to the report of Presiding Justice Ballot-Beaupré whose meticulous rigor and very austerity accounted for its forcefulness. The courtroom was filled with lawyers, intellectuals, politicans, combatants from both sides, and high society. But in that forum, "the atmosphere of battle had evaporated; what prevailed was respect, something almost religious."[4] After having presented in detail the opposing arguments, the reporting judge ran through the essential aspects of the Affair once again in order to reveal his opinion. He demonstrated that the alleged confession was not a confession at all. At last he came to the bordereau, "the principal basis for the accusation and conviction of Dreyfus." He asked the single question on which everything depended: "Is it or is it not written in Dreyfus's hand?" He paused for a moment as

* But—to display his objectivity—he imposed the same punishment a few days later on a Jewish officer, Commandant Mayer, who was criticizing the French Army in foreign journals.

though he were still considering the question. And his answer, which opened the path to revision, came slowly, almost solemnly: "Gentlemen, after an examination in depth, I have, for my part, reached the conclusion that the bordereau was written not by Dreyfus but by Esterhazy." He added: "No, the Army is in no way being called into question by us. It is not the Army which falls under our jurisdiction. Thank God, it is well above these proceedings which cannot affect it, and its honor assuredly does not require an innocent convict to be kept on Devil's Island." And he concluded by asking the Court not to proclaim Dreyfus's innocence but to decide that "a new element had emerged which was capable of establishing" such a verdict.

Public Prosecutor Manau reached the same conclusion, but lacked Ballot-Beaupré's moderation. He affirmed "that there was a multitude of new elements." In order to move the judges, he read letters from the deportee of Devil's Island. Like the reporting judge, he asked the High Court of Appeal to annul the verdict of 1894 and to send Dreyfus before a new Court-Martial.* Then Lucie Dreyfus's lawyer spoke. Mornard repeated the admirable demonstration of his written memorandum. As he had agreed with Lucie and Mathieu, he asked in turn for Captain Dreyfus to be judged by his peers. "It is with joy in their hearts that the military judges, proclaiming an error committed in all sincerity and loyalty, will declare that their unfortunate brother in arms, so great in the midst of his ordeal, has never fallen afoul of the law of honor. . . . I await your decision as though it were the blessed dawn of the day that will allow the great light of concord and truth to shine over the nation."

The Combined Chambers withdrew to deliberate. On the previous day, May 31, Déroulède and Habert had been acquitted by the Court of Assizes after a few minutes of deliberation. Within the Palais de Justice and later in the street, Déroulède had been carried aloft in triumph. The nationalist press was exultant. And as the High Court of Appeal began the most celebrated deliberations of its history, General Zurlinden, on orders from Minister Krantz, had Commandant du Paty de Clam arrested and placed in the cell recently vacated by Picquart, who was taken to La Santé, a common law prison.

The deliberations were long and frequently violent. They lasted the evening of June 1 and throughout the following day. The judges did not

---

* In principle, the High Court of Appeal, upon observing the existence of "new elements capable of establishing the convict's innocence," was to annul the extant conviction and send the accused before a new Court-Martial. In certain exceptional cases, "if it is no longer possible to hold new proceedings or if the annulment of the verdict leaves nothing standing that might be qualified as a crime or misdemeanor," it could pass judgment itself without further trial. This last option would be utilized in 1906. See *infra* pp. 478–79.

consider the "Henry forgery," since it had not been used against Dreyfus in 1894. They agreed without difficulty that the legendary confession was, on principle, unacceptable. The Court retained the secret communication of the "scoundrel D." document, which it declared to be "inapplicable to Dreyfus." Finally, the Court essentially retained the new expert evaluations which appeared to establish that the bordereau itself was insufficient proof, "given that these facts, which were unknown to the Court-Martial delivering the conviction, tend to demonstrate that the bordereau would not have been written by Dreyfus. . . ." On the other hand, no majority was willing to formally attribute the bordereau to Esterhazy.

On June 3, Chief Presiding Justice Mazeau, before opening the solemn session, delivered a speech to his colleagues. The terrible affair, which had torn the country apart, had also troubled the High Court of Appeal, and it was now time to put aside all quarrels in the celebration of justice accomplished. He spoke in particular to the Criminal Chamber. It must not brood over any of the rancor of the past. Presiding Justice Loew, who had been so harshly slandered, rose and took Mazeau's hand. "In the name of the Criminal Chamber, Mr. Chief Presiding Justice, I forget and I pardon."*

Slowly, heavily robed in scarlet and ermine, covered with decorations, the high magistrates walked into the courtroom. And amid a "frightening silence," Chief Presiding Justice Mazeau read in a grave voice, that cracked at times with emotion, the judgment that authorized the revision.

> For these reasons and without need to recur to any additional means, the Court hereby rescinds and annuls the verdict rendered on December 28, 1894, against Alfred Dreyfus, and sends the accused before the Court Martial of Rennes, designated for this task by extraordinary deliberations taken by the Court, to be judged on the following question: "Is Dreyfus guilty for having, in 1894, resorted to machinations or entered into intelligence with a foreign power or one of its agents in order to engage it to commit hostilities or wage war against France, or in order to procure for it the means of so doing by conveying to it the notes and documents mentioned in the aforementioned bordereau?"

Jean Jaurès, Georges Clemenceau, Bernard Lazare, Mathieu Dreyfus, and Louis Leblois, the principal architects of the revision, were present. As the judges withdrew, the victors embraced each other and wept. Lucie

---

* Presiding Justice Loew, upon retiring in 1903, would be named Honorary Chief Presiding Justice and made an Officer of the Legion of Honor that same year.

Dreyfus, who was informed immediately, let her joy overflow. The news was announced to the children. The long voyage was over. Papa was coming home.

The weaknesses of the decision, its hesitations, the doors it left open for chicanery and hatred, went unremarked. That evening in Mathieu Dreyfus's home, there was a celebration. Alfred was coming back; he would be acquitted in triumph. The Affair was over, and it had ended in victory. Mathieu was smiling, calm, joyous. He had accomplished his mission.

On the same day, *Le Matin* published an interview with Commandant Esterhazy in which he acknowledged being the author of the well-known document.*"Yes, it was I who wrote the bordereau, at the request of Colonel Sandherr, my superior and my friend. I am revealing the secret that no one has ever been able to extract from me for the price of gold. . . . Billot, Boisdeffre, and Gonse knew that I was the author of the bordereau."

But for the moment, Alfred Dreyfus's family and supporters did not need Esterhazy's elucubrations. The prisoner of Devil's Island was coming back and he was going to be acquitted.

4

Panama the First

As might have been expected, the decision of the High Court of Appeal provoked an explosion of anger in the anti-Dreyfusard press. Ballot-Beaupré was portrayed as "a scoundrel who will go down in the history of human ignominy." The magistrates of the High Court of Appeal were no more than "old macaques who had bled the cashboxes of the syndicate dry." Edouard Drumont was virulent: "An Army which does not know how to defend its honor against a band of Jews will not know how to defend the nation against a foreign army." "It is the Army that will have the last word," warned Granier de Cassagnac. Maurice Barrès feigned

---

* *Le Matin*, June 3, 1898. The interview was signed "Paul Ribon," a pseudonym of Serge Basset. It would be authenticated on June 8 in a signed statement by Esterhazy.

disgust: "The Dreyfus anecdote, that obscene and confused affair, does not interest me; what does is civil war."* The president of the Republic was insulted from all sides. "Panama the First," as he was called in the press, became the bête noire of the nationalists. Paul Déroulède's acquittal had given them back a measure of hope. "Déroulède acquitted means Loubet condemned," *La Libre Parole* of June 1 assured. Loubet was called on to resign if he did not want to be "chased out of the Elysée like a valet." Once again rumors of a coup began to spread. On Sunday, June 4, President Emile Loubet was to go to the racetrack at Auteuil to attend the steeple-chase. As a precautionary measure, the minister of the interior stationed troops along the road the president was scheduled to travel.

No sooner did Loubet—who had reached Auteuil without incident—step forward to ascend the presidential platform than shouts began to resound from all sides: "Down with Loubet," "Down with Panama," "Re-sign." The demonstrators numbered several hundred, "society people and stable boys," according to Joseph Reinach.[1] The president pretended not to notice them and took his seat. Suddenly, an elegantly attired blond young man climbed the steps of the presidential podium and began thrashing vigorously with his cane at Loubet, who remained untouched except for his hat. As the attendant officers rushed to seize the assailant, the president quite calmly offered his apologies to his neighbor, the Countess Tornielli, who had been slightly ruffled. The aggressor, the Baron Fernand Chevreau de Christiani, was quickly brought under con-trol. A group of royalist demonstrators, most of whom wore either a white carnation or an anti-Semite's bluet in their lapels, began scuffling with the police. The fighting lasted half an hour. About fifty individuals, almost all of them titled or from the aristocracy, were arrested. The prime minister, who was present at Loubet's side, offered his apologies. Loubet replied curtly: "I am not hurt. But this is a lesson."[2]

Déroulède's plot, his acquittal, the incident at Auteuil, and the atmos-phere of an impending coup d'état felt by all were beginning to provoke extreme dissatisfaction among the republicans. Charles Dupuy's lack of vigor, and his inability to maintain order, appeared all the more unbeara-ble in that Drumont and several others were calling on the people "to start up again," to take to the streets to chase out "Panama the First." On the other side, certain of Dreyfus's partisans, encouraged by the judgment authorizing a revision, were beginning to demand justice. Urbain Gohier lashed out in *L'Aurore* at the "band of scoundrels and rogues in ostrich feathers the prisons were now awaiting," while Jean Jaurès and Georges

* *La Libre Parole*, May 29, June 2 and 4; *L'Autorité*, May 31, June 1 and 3, 1899; *L'Intransigeant*, June 1 and 3.

Clemenceau asked in turn for the immediate arraignment, even the arrest of General Mercier.[3] In the Chamber on June 5, after the republicans protested the Auteuil scandal, the "Mercier case" was brought up for discussion. Alexandre Millerand and then René Viviani, who by this time were flying quite high, vigorously supported bringing charges against the former minister of war. The former prime minister, Alexandre Ribot, felt obliged to oppose them, and invoked juridical reasons to that effect. There was much discussion of legal issues. Henri Brisson, Raymond Poincaré, and Jean Barthou remained silent. By a vote of 277 to 228, the Chamber found the most convenient solution: it postponed any action on the charges. On the other hand, the republicans regained their ardor in order to support a Socialist proposal to have the decision of the High Court of Appeal posted in all the communes of France. Brisson took on the role of sponsor of that symbolic project, saying, "as prime minister who had the misfortune of having forgeries posted by order of the Chamber, today I ask for the posting of the judgment. . . ." The posting was approved despite the opposition of the right and the nationalists.

But the Army, which was to judge Dreyfus once again, was showing signs of agitation. "I am an accuser, not an accused," warned General Mercier. In Angers and in Rennes, military officers were making public demonstration—through their orders to their staffs or letters published in the press—of their intention to defend the Army against the Dreyfusard clan. At the École Militaire, Lieutenant Colonel de Coubertin harangued his cuirassiers: "Should the situation call for it, I order you to use your arms against the Army's insulters."[4] The minister of war did not object. On June 11, the Sunday following the incident at Auteuil, the republicans organized a huge demonstration to defend the Republic and to pay homage to Emile Loubet. Nearly 100,000 people marched, including many workers and students. The crowd headed toward Longchamp, singing "La Marseillaise." Numerous demonstrators were armed with canes and clubs. On that day, the nationalists were not to be seen. The prime minister, however, ordered a huge deployment of soldiers and police. Seemingly indifferent when the Republic was under threat, he demonstrated extraordinary zeal when it was being defended. Toward evening, several scuffles broke out between demonstrators and the police. On June 12 in the Chamber, Edouard Vaillant, a Socialist, a former member of the Commune, and a deputy from Charonne, rose to "execute" a government so lacking in soul or strength. Dupuy, who realized that he was doomed, assumed full responsibility for the actions of the police. He decided that at least he would fall proudly. He was abandoned by the center, by the Radicals, and even by his friends, who all rushed to join the wave of negative opinion. And at the suggestion of the Radical Ruau, the Chamber passed a motion in which it declared itself "resolved to support only governments intent on defending vigorously the institutions of the Republic and on maintaining public order. . . ." By a vote of 296 to 159, Charles Dupuy was overthrown. The Dreyfus Affair had thus displayed its political effects. The defense of the institutions of the Republic was henceforth at the center of the debate between the partisans and enemies of Dreyfus.

During this period, Dreyfus's cause was making swift progress. Zola had returned to Paris on June 4. He had immediately organized an opposition to the judgment by the Court of Assizes which had convicted him in absentia. The case was postponed until . . . November 23. The same day on which Zola entered his petition, the court chamber in charge of indictments, faithful to the changing requirements of the public prosecutor, ordered Colonel Picquart freed from prison. On June 13, it dismissed all charges against him and against Louis Leblois. Two of the principal combatants of the Affair, Zola and Picquart, were thus free and in Paris. By this time Alfred Dreyfus had embarked for France, abandoning the accursed island.

On June 10, Ludovic Trarieux hosted a large dinner in honor of Picquart, who had spent 384 days in prison. He had never complained, never hesitated to do his duty. Hundreds of friends came to salute him at Trarieux's home. He received thousands of telegrams. The anti-Dreyfusards protested that they were witnessing the apotheosis of Picquart. The League of the Rights of Man charged Trarieux with addressing public thanks to "Dreyfus's champions, Scheurer, Zola, and Picquart." BernardLazare was saddened by the omission of other supporters. In *L'Aurore*, he issued a protest on behalf of those whom the League of the Rights of Man had forgotten, the combatants of the first months: Ferdinand Forzinetti, the director of the Prison of Cherche-Midi, "who had suffered the daily sufferings of the innocent"; Louis Leblois, who had worked silently on Picquart's behalf; Edgar Demange, who was "absolutely unforgettable," and who was the first to have suffered himself for his position; and Lazare himself, who "had stretched out his hand to the victim of misfortune in the days of solitary struggle," and who had withdrawn only at Mathieu Dreyfus's request, because he was too committed, too Jewish, too proud of being so:

I belong to the race of those, in Renan's words, who were first to introduce the idea of justice in the world. . . . All, every one of them, my ancestors and my brothers, had the fanatical wish that everyone receive his due and that the scales of the balance never be made to tip unjustly. For that, for centuries now, they have shouted, sung, wept and suffered, despite the outrages, despite the insults, despite being spat upon. I am one of them and I wish to be one. Being as I am, do you not think me right to speak of those you did not think of?

Lazare appealed to Mathieu Dreyfus, "an admirable brother and a true hero." Picquart, for his part, felt attacked by Lazare's protest, mistreated. Thus there began with the limited victory an assessment of relative merit and an awarding of prizes among the combatants. Individual pride was already creating rifts. Distinctions were made between the soldiers of the first days and the workmen of the final hour.

On Monday, June 5 at 12:30 P.M. the chief-guard entered precipitously into Dreyfus's hut and handed him the following message:

Kindly inform Captain Dreyfus immediately of appeal decision as follows: "The Court rescinds and annuls the judgment rendered on 22 December 1894 against Alfred Dreyfus by the first Court-Martial of the Military Command of Paris and sends the accused to appear before the Court-Martial of Rennes, etc."

Say that the present judgment will be imprinted and transcribed on the records of the First Court-Martial of the Military Command of Paris in the margins of the annulled decision; by virtue of this decision, Captain Dreyfus is no longer subject to deportation, becomes a simple suspect, is returned to his rank, and can again don his uniform. Have the penitentiary administration complete his release and withdraw the military guards from Devil's Island. At the same time, have the suspect taken into custody by the commandant of troops and replace the surveillance team by a brigade from the gendarmerie, which will keep guard on Devil's Island as required by military prison regulations.

The cruiser *Sfax* is leaving Fort-de-France today with orders to find the suspect on Devil's Island in order to bring him back to France.

Communicate to Captain Dreyfus the terms of the decision and the departure of the *Sfax*.

"My joy," Alfred Dreyfus wrote, "was immense, unspeakable. I was at last escaping the rack where I had been nailed for five years. . . . The dawn of justice was rising for me."[5]

He knew next to nothing about his case. He had only just heard of Commandant Esterhazy, of Colonel Henry's forgery, and of the forger's suicide. With Picquart he had had only official dealings. Of the battles joined on his behalf, the struggle of the intellectuals, the agitation surrounding the revision, he knew only vague rumors which had come to him through his guards. In the Court's decision, he had read only that the author of the bordereau was not he. His innocence was thus acknowledged. All that remained for the Court-Martial of Rennes was "the honor of rectifying a frightening judicial error."[6]

That evening there arrived from Cayenne the brigade of gendarmes to whose custody he would henceforth be consigned. Dreyfus bid his guards farewell, and distributed his books among them as mementos. The mayor of Cayenne sent him a suit and linen, which he would need for the crossing.

The *Sfax* cast anchor rather far from the island during the evening of June 8, too late for Dreyfus to embark before nightfall. He slept for the last time in his hut. On the morning of June 9 a launch came to get him and to take him aboard the *Sfax*. The sea was so violent that Dreyfus, who was exhausted, became sick. He went aboard the ship, where he was received by the officer second in command. He was taken to a cabin for noncommissioned officers, which had been modified especially for him—with bars on the porthole, and a glass door onto the corridor. Thereafter he was treated like an officer under close arrest, circumstances that did not surprise him. They conformed to regulations. On June 9 the *Sfax* weighed anchor. Devil's Island soon disappeared into the mist. Captain Dreyfus's detention had lasted four years and three months.

Considering himself the equal of any aboard, he spoke to no one. During a stop in the Caribbean from June 18 to 20, an officer loaned him books and a copy of *The Times*. He read in it that du Paty de Clam had been arrested and transferred to the Prison of Cherche-Midi, the prison in which he himself had been held. The report confirmed to him that his innocence was now definitively acknowledged. On June 30 the *Sfax* arrived within sight of the French coast.

It was then that his disillusionment began. For an entire day, the ship didn't move. The landing was repeatedly postponed. It was only at 9 P.M. that Dreyfus was informed that a dinghy was waiting for him at the foot of the *Sfax*'s ladder to take him to another boat that would bring him ashore. The sea was so turbulent that Dreyfus had a great deal of difficulty in climbing into the dinghy, rocked by the waves and bouncing around violently. He injured both legs and was taken with a high fever. He then had difficulty climbing onto the steamboat that was to bring him to the landing site. He was transferred once again—to a lifeboat. It was 2:15 A.M. when—in darkness and under falling rain—he reached the French coast. He would later learn that he had landed at Port-Haligan. By lantern light, Dreyfus could distinguish the soldiers stationed on the dock as well as the local inhabitants who had come out of curiosity. Three gendarmes pushed him into a carriage which took off on a path lined with soldiers on either side. No one spoke to him, nor did he speak to anyone. He was taken to a train station—at Quiberon, he would later learn. He was put on a special train which stopped in the night at a railroad crossing in the middle of the countryside. The prefect was waiting, with a squad of gendarmes. He was raised into a carriage and soon entered a city which he understood to be Rennes. At 6 A.M. the gate of the military prison was opened. He was locked into a cell. At 9 A.M. he was informed that he would see his wife for a few moments in a neighboring cell. The small room was furnished with a table and two chairs, closed by an iron gate encased in wood. From within, it was impossible to see out into the courtyard. He waited several minutes. It was increasingly painful for him to remain standing.

The door opened. Lucie threw herself into his arms. They wanted to speak, but no words came to their lips. They looked at each other, saw on their faces, their bodies, the signs of their suffering. They were overcome with joy and pain. The infantry lieutenant present at their meeting withdrew as much as possible. He too was holding back tears. They remained like that for a short time, close yet separate, huddled against each other, incapable of speech. Her face had been ravaged with suffering. His was unrecognizable.

5

Silence in the Ranks

Once Charles Dupuy was overthrown, the president of the Republic called on Raymond Poincaré to form a cabinet. "He remained," Reinach wrote, "at the head of his political generation, but was at once an enigma and a source of hope. No one knew exactly what he lacked in the way of the qualities and shortcomings required of a statesman."[1] He was known to be a diligent worker and a man of eminent seriousness. It was assumed that he would be as skillful in managing the affairs of state as he was in crafting his career. He was known to have few friends, but even fewer enemies. Although he was a lawyer, he had managed to raise to a new perfection the art of remaining silent. He had come late to

Dreyfusism, "in order to relieve his conscience." He wanted power, yet was frightened by it, intent on not making a single blunder on the road that was to take him to the Elysée.

Poincaré could not succeed in forming a government. According to Georges Clemenceau, he applied all his intelligence to assuring the failure of his own arrangements. The Radicals wanted nothing to do with Louis Barthou, on whom Poincaré insisted. Personal rancor and ambition were to count more than the Republic's interest. Poincaré consequently withdrew and advised the president of the Republic to call on René Waldeck-Rousseau. Waldeck-Rousseau was to the center-left what his colleague Poincaré was to the center-right: a parliamentarian whose intelligence, seriousness, and—most rare of all—integrity, were widely recognized. But unlike Poincaré, he was not driven by overweening ambition. He seemed, on the contrary, distant, almost detached, situated above the common run of parliamentary destinies, an attitude that added to his prestige. Waldeck-Rousseau thought first of forming a homogeneous cabinet of moderate republicans, then inclined toward a cabinet of republican unity. Reinach claimed that it was he himself who had advised Waldeck-Rousseau to bring Alexandre Millerand, leader of the parliamentary Socialists, into the goverment. The duel which had pitted him against Millerand was behind him, and it appeared to Reinach that Millerand was the symbol of the evolution of the Socialists toward that defense of republican society whose impetus had been provided by the Dreyfus Affair. "For fifteen months the Socialists had been fighting side by side with the members of the bourgeoisie on behalf of a man who was bourgeois." Since Millerand would unite the republicans, it would be possible to carry along the Socialists. It was also known that Millerand had dreams of entering the government and that there were numerous Socialists who supported him in his ambition.

Waldeck-Rousseau first offered the Ministry of War to Jean Casimir-Périer, who chose not to accept. He then approached his old friend General Gaston de Galliffet, the former architect of the Commune "massacre," who was dying of boredom in retirement. He was sixty-nine years old, and lived in the pride of his past, flaunting his glory as a soldier, his reputation as an executioner, and attempting to quench his thirst for pleasure. During the previous months, he had not concealed his sympathy for Dreyfus's cause. But quarrels quickly erupted. The progressivists would not accept a Socialist in the government at any price, and the Socialists refused any mention of Galliffet. Disheartened, Waldeck-Rousseau ceased his efforts on June 19. The president of the Republic renewed his request to him on June 22. At that point, Waldeck-Rousseau decided to move swiftly, extremely swiftly, in order to overcome all resistances. He ignored the progressivists, who made too many demands, and the small group gathered around Poincaré, who were too ambitious and too complicated. And that evening, he constituted a strange government in which "the head dominated and absorbed all the rest."[2] Galliffet was named minister of war; Alexandre Millerand, minister of commerce; Joseph Caillaux, who had entered the Chamber only a year earlier and was known to very few, minister of finances. Ernest Monis, a lawyer totally devoted to Waldeck-Rousseau, was installed in the Ministry of Justice. Theophile Delcassé remained minister of foreign affairs. All that the ministers had in common was a personal bond linking them to the prime minister. In addition, they were almost all, either openly (like Millerand) or discreetly (like Caillaux), favorable to Dreyfus's cause.

As soon as it was revealed, the composition of the new goverment was received as an insult to common sense and a scandal. It was the "Dreyfus Ministry," the nationalists objected indignantly, "the government of treason." "Loubet is sinking into crime. . . . Waldeck, lawyer to Eiffel and Dreyfus, is presiding over the Witches' Sabbath. And all in order to save an ignoble Jew," wrote *L'Intransigeant.* "Galliffet and Reinach have the same soul, a soul of baseness and filth," wrote *La Libre Parole.* In *Le Gaulois,* François Coppée opined: "This new-born is a monster. When will the Terror begin?" And Jules Lemaître in desperation wrote, "They want to terrorize an adored Army." But among the Socialists and in the case of many Radicals, there was no less indignation, albeit for different reasons. Camille Pelletan protested the "act of infamy" of entrusting the Republic to the executioner of the Commune, and Edouard Vaillant let it be known that he would break with any Socialists who supported such a cabinet. On June 23, along with twelve supporters (including Marcel Sembat and Lassalle), he founded a separate group calling themselves "revolutionary socialist." Jules Guesde, Paul Lafargue, Edouard Vaillant, Dubreuilh, Landrin, and Alexandre Zevaès would together prepare the manifesto, written for the most part by Guesde and published in June, which would condemn in explosive terms "the allegedly socialist policies consisting of the compromises and deviations that had all too long been made to substitute for a politics of class," and the "scandal" constituted by the presence of Millerand in the cabinet, "hand in hand with the gunman of May."*

* The text of the manifesto, which denounced Jaurès without naming him, was published in *Le Socialiste* of July 16, 1899: "The Socialist Party, a class party, cannot be or become a cabinet-affiliated party lest it risk suicide. It has no need of sharing power with the bourgeoisie, in whose hands the State can be only an instrument of social conservation and oppression. Its mission is to seize power from it to make of that power the instrument of liberation and social revolution.[3]

The opening session would not be held until June 26. The delay would allow the prime minister sufficient time to demonstrate his firmness. Within twenty-four hours, the prefect of police was replaced and the public prosecutor relieved of his functions. Several generals were transferred to different posts, and General Roget learned to his astonishment that he had been reassigned to Belfort. Prefects and heads of Army divisions received circulars of extraordinary vigor. His words to the Army, said Galliffet, were "silence in the ranks." The politics of republican defense had begun.

That vigorous style was useful to Waldeck-Rousseau, whose situation remained all the same rather difficult. When the government was introduced to the Chamber, it was greeted by shouts, jeers, and animal noises. "Murderers, killers, long live the Commune," came shouts directed at Galliffet. "The murderer is here," responded Galliffet, taking his seat on the bench reserved for the cabinet. Waldeck-Rousseau had the impression that he was entering into a cage of wild beasts.* He was insulted personally as "a lawyer for scum, swindlers, and murderers." He attempted to speak, but his voice was drowned out by shouting. René Viviani attempted to come to his aid: "There are not three different policies represented here; there is a policy of defending the Republic and a policy of treason. Take your choice." But Waldeck-Rousseau seemed already defeated. A Radical deputy chose not to speak "in order not to step on a corpse." Then suddenly, with brutal resolution, Henri Brisson saved the government. With his voice cracking with emotion, he spoke of his anguish for the threatened Republic. "The government proposes to defend the Republic. I give it my vote. I invite all those on whom I may have had, in the course of my career, any influence in this Chamber, to vote, I am not saying for the government, but for the Republic."[4] Brisson's speech had a great effect. Fatigue and perhaps genuine concern took care of the rest. The government triumphed with a majority of twenty-five votes. Eight days later the parliamentary session was ended. Waldeck-Rousseau would govern for three years.

He would govern almost by himself, keeping the president of the Republic, whom he regarded as a trifler, at a distance, and demanding of his ministers an unprecedented degree of submission. "Everything concerning the policies of the cabinet," he told the Council of Ministers, "belongs to the prime minister and to him alone." He made an exception only for Galliffet, who was his close personal friend, and whom he needed in order to keep the Army in hand.

* "He needs as his adversaries men and not wild beasts," wrote Clemenceau in *L'Aurore* of June 27.

The disciplining of the Army was begun forthwith and pursued with all due vigor. A number of officers who had made their career in the ministry were transferred to garrisons. In June and July, the principal leaders—including General Emile Zurlinden and General de Pellieux— were removed. Several generals were retired. The nationalist press waxed indignant in vain, claiming that the High Command had been over- thrown, that France would henceforth be unable to wage war. Waldeck- Rousseau and Galliffet pursued their efforts at regaining control, which the Army submitted to without protest. Structural reforms, regarding the composition of the High Military Council and rules of advancement, would follow, in order that the Army remain subordinate to civilian authority. Perhaps out of traditional loyalty, surprise, or the absence of any recourse, the "holy Ark," which only recently had been so active and so powerful that the civilian authorities did not dare oppose it, was submit- ting without rebellion or discussion to the demands of the republican government.

That was not all. On July 7, Waldeck-Rousseau asked the new prefect of police to undertake an investigation to determine whether all the demonstrations that had recently taken place, from Reuilly to Auteuil, had been organized in concert. Although very little was found to sustain that suspicion, Waldeck-Rousseau seized on what little evidence there was, presented the matter to the Council of Ministers in dramatic terms on August 10, and persuaded the Council to agree to a series of arrests. On August 12, Paul Déroulède, Marcel Habert, and the principal nationalists were arrested. Jules Guérin and several of his anti-Semitic friends would attempt to escape arrest by locking themselves into the "fortress" on rue Chabrol.[5]

There remained the Church and the congregations. Waldeck- Rousseau was not anticlerical. Rather, it seemed to him, that religion was condemned to wither away because it did not satisfy the needs of the modern mind.[6] He believed that the progress of civilization would gradu- ally do away with religious notions. On the other hand, he was convinced that the Catholic Church should be subordinated to the power of the Republic. It would be a source neither of resistance nor reaction. For Waldeck-Rousseau, a priest was merely a functionary to whom it was imperative to apply the same rules as to any other agent of the state, and a minister of religious cults would treat religious questions as simple ad- ministrative matters. At bottom, Waldeck-Rousseau remained a partisan of a concordat. The separation of Church and State seemed to him a goal that was no doubt desirable, but far off. At present, it would be necessary to impose some discipline on priests and on members of the religious orders. During the first year of his government, the prime minister suspended the salaries of nineteen priests who had expressed opinions unfavorable to the government. Through the minister of religious cults, he cast blame on the bishops supporting—however discreetly—leaders hostile to his policies. Within a few months, no voice dared be heard in the Church expressing the slightest hostility to the republican government.

The project of republican defense also entailed imposing submission on the congregations, specifically on the Assumptionists, whom Waldeck-Rousseau, not without reason, took to be unrelenting foes of the Republic. On November 14, 1899, he proposed to the Chamber legislation relating to contracts of association. Its principal provision was devoted to the congregations. A second proposal required that candidates to public office pass their three final school years at a public school. On November 11, he requested legal action against the Assumptionists. The trial would take place in January 1900 and the congregation would be disbanded. But Waldeck-Rousseau dreamed of going further still. He wanted to destroy the "clerical invasion," which followed the path of religious schooling, and to break the financial and social power of the congregations. For this, he needed time.

Thus proceeded the shy, rather cold and distant man, who had come to power almost by chance, in his defense of the Republic. Within a few months, the balance sheet of his "republican defense" was impressive indeed.[7] The Army, the Church, and the congregations were submitting without protest to the harsh law that Waldeck-Rousseau's Republic was imposing on them. The nationalists, taken by surprise and dismantled in their organization, were losing their vigor. The members of Parliament were astonished. It had been a long time since republican authority had been exercised so strongly. It remained to put an end to the Dreyfus Affair.

That Waldeck-Rousseau was a Dreyfusard—out of reason rather than passion—was doubted by no one. His friendship with Edgar Demange—whom he had recommended to Mathieu Dreyfus to represent his brother—and his ties with Joseph Reinach were known. He had taken a stand on two occasions in the Senate, and did not hide his sympathies for a cause that had merged in his mind with that of the defense of the Republic. But now, as prime minister, he was aware of the impassioned atmosphere surrounding the Affair. Any government initiative would arouse resentment and would satisfy neither camp. And if he was intent on disciplining the Army, he had no wish to either exasperate or humiliate it.

As soon as he took office, Waldeck-Rousseau attempted to acquaint himself more thoroughly with the Affair. Unfamiliar with its details, he was discouraged by the scope and complexity of the various dossiers. His friend Joseph Reinach overwhelmed him with information. Finally, he asked Commissioner Tombs, the sole civilian directly acquainted with the Affair, to prepare a clear and precise report on the case and on the maneuvers and actions of the members of the military involved since 1894. Tombs's report convinced Waldeck-Rousseau of Dreyfus's innocence.

For his part, Galliffet requested the secret file. The minister of war quickly came to the conclusion that it was without force; the trial at Rennes would be a mere formality. "His scorn for the Generals was such that he could already see them reduced to ridicule by the defense."[8] And no doubt he was already savoring the outcome. "I believe," Galliffet wrote to his friend Princess Radziwill, "that poor Mercier's testimony will be quite simply ridiculous." General Eugène Chamoin, whom Galliffet had sent to Rennes to "follow" the trial, sent back numerous reassuring reports. Everything would be simple. Out of optimism about the verdict, in order to give the appearance of respecting the prerogatives of the public prosecutor, the government decided not to insist that the military prosecutor drop all charges against Dreyfus. Millerand and Reinach pleaded in vain to Waldeck-Rousseau, pointing out the dangers of such a strategy. But Galliffet objected that dismissing all charges would be seen as an indictment of the military judges, and that the acquittal would come as a matter of course. Waldeck-Rousseau himself was more pessimistic. At the beginning of the trial, the prime minister told his friend Reinach "that he could see only a very slight chance of getting Dreyfus acquitted." Waldeck-Rousseau no doubt gauged better than Galliffet, who believed himself more influential than he was, the strength of the Army's esprit de corps.[9] The prime minister secretly charged the prefect of Ille-et-Vilaine with the singular mission of contacting the military prosecutor, even the judges, with the purpose of influencing them. During the trial, Waldeck-Rousseau would demonstrate his sympathy to Dreyfus's cause by intervening with the German embassy to obtain documents useful to Dreyfus's case, specifically the "items enumerated in the bordereau."* Later, Colonel Picquart, and especially Fernand Labori, who disliked Waldeck-Rousseau for professional reasons, would accuse the government of having disarmed them with false promises, of having traded off—with the lawyer, Edgar Demange, as intermediary—a promise of acquittal against a "moderate defense," and of having thus betrayed the Dreyfusards, preventing them from demonstrating and denouncing the Army's crimes. Waldeck-Rousseau and Galliffet would thus have been shrewdly keeping guard over the Army's honor without any true commitment to an acquittal.[10] But those reproaches would also serve to excuse the errors in strategy commit-

---

* He would intervene on four occasions with the embassy between August 12 and 19, without informing the government or even Galliffet of his actions. He would go so far as to visit the embassy personally, on August 12, without obtaining satisfaction.

ted by the Dreyfusards throughout the trial at Rennes. It does not appear that Waldeck-Rousseau ever concealed the difficulties he saw of a trial before a military tribunal in which he had no confidence. Could he have done more, ordered the military prosecutor to drop all charges, bring all of his weight to bear on the course followed by the trial? But Waldeck-Rousseau's principal concern at the time was not acquittal, but appeasement. His thoughts were of preserving national unity while bringing the Army under control. What certain Dreyfusards did not see in the fever of the battle was that he was the head of the French government and not an agent of Dreyfus's defense.

6

To Rennes, to Rennes, Gentlemen of the Army

Two days after Dreyfus was committed to the military prison of Rennes, his lawyer, Edgar Demange, came to visit him. He was accompanied by Fernand Labori. Mathieu Dreyfus, who had admired Labori greatly at the Zola trial, judged that the aged Demange—almost too prudent, and occasionally timid—would be usefully assisted at Rennes by his impassioned colleague. Demange, who had seen a good number of his clients forsake him since he had defended Dreyfus, knew no other duty in life than the forceful defense of his client.* A Christian and a conservative, he had no wish to know everything about his client's case. For numerous Dreyfusards he had no sympathy at all. Labori, on the other hand, had never met Dreyfus, and identified wholly with the cause. His courage and his talent had made him the Dreyfusards' champion. The two lawyers might thus complement each other, in both conviction and temperament.

---

* See the eulogy of Edgar Demange delivered at the opening of the Conférence des Avocats by its first secretary, Maître René Bondoux, on January 14, 1933: "His clients deserted his practice, his friends became fewer, but his conscience reassured him: he was following his course without deviation."

In the visitors' room, Dreyfus embraced his old lawyer, and was introduced to Labori, of whom he knew almost nothing. The two lawyers returned the next day and handed Captain Dreyfus the essential material pertaining to his case, namely the court record of the 1898 trial and the investigation of the High Court of Appeal. Dreyfus spent the whole night reading the summary of the Zola trial, then, on the following days, those of the Esterhazy trial and the High Court of Appeal's investigation. Although he was suffering from high fever and constantly shivering, he spent his days and nights working. He now wished to have some say in his defense. He questioned his lawyers and ordered them to perform specific tasks. He felt manifestly closer to Demange than to Labori. A painful scene occurred during one of the early visits to the prison, after Demange had explained that there could be no question of "reconducting the Zola trial." "And as for me, I will not reconduct the 1894 trial," was Labori's furious response. He threatened to leave the case, to resign from the defense. Alfred Dreyfus was obliged to calm him. "Labori," Joseph Reinach explained, [1] "had imbibed too early of too strong a wine. . . . The striking success that he had known quite young, the adulation and the attacks, which were equally intoxicating for a mind insufficiently prepared for them, had persuaded him that the Zola trial had been his [triumph] and that after victory, there would be but a step from the bar to the tribune, and from the Chamber to the most elevated of destinies."[2]

Labori was finding it increasingly difficult to put up with Demange. Everything seemed to oppose the two lawyers: their ages, their temperaments, their conceptions of defense, the idea each had of his destiny.* Labori was convinced that René Waldeck-Rousseau was abandoning Dreyfus, that Demange was no more than an instrument in the hands of his friend Waldeck-Rousseau, and that General de Galliffet was no more than an instrument in the hands of the Army. In the notes that he left behind, Labori claimed that if his illness—he had typhoid fever—had allowed him to participate in the formation of a government, he would have "dictated his conditions."[3] He would not have let Waldeck-Rousseau choose Galliffet without extracting a formal commitment. "My influence was considerable. . . . As of the beginning of 1898, it had always been predominant. . . . I had all the strands in my hand. . . . Zola and Picquart did nothing without me. . . . I was the center of the Affair. . . ."[4] By this juncture, he was convinced that he was being betrayed on all sides, by those who wanted to save the generals and to accommodate General Mercier and the General Staff. The government had promised a mediocre acquittal to "the minority it favored." In exchange, Dreyfus's defense would be dis-

---

* "It was Labori who thundered and Demange who argued," according to *bâtonnier* René Bondoux. "If Labori was 'the defense,' Demange was 'the lawyer.'"

creet and moderate. He, Labori, refused to go along with such a shameful transaction. Everything would have to be revealed, demonstrated—without accommodating anyone. The gap was growing between those who, counting on the government's support, wanted a measured and moderate trial and those who, following Labori, were intent on conducting a trial devoid of compromise and precaution, which would force the judges to acquit Dreyfus.[5]

In the preparations for the Rennes trial, General Mercier quickly emerged as the leader of the anti-Dreyfusards, even as he had been the leader of the conspiracy against Dreyfus in 1894. He gave numerous interviews, announced that in Rennes, he would tell all that he knew. He confided to *Le Journal* and *La Libre Parole* that he would present formidable evidence, even if war should break out as a result.[6] The nationalists regained hope. "We want to stare the truth in the face," wrote François Coppée, "no matter how hideous and terrible it be, and if that means war, perhaps it will be our rebirth and salvation." Mercier leaked to the press the various truths he would unleash on the court. The bordereau written on tracing paper, the bordereau of 1894, was only a copy—or a reproduction—of the original bordereau. And the original had been annotated by hand by none other than the emperor of Germany. It was said that there was a photograph of it in Mercier's possession and that he would reveal it at the trial. That would be the hour of truth, and Dreyfus would be confounded by the secret and conclusive documents that no one had dared to produce thus far. Quesnay de Beaurepaire was also quite active. He appointed himself judge and decided to try Dreyfus on his own, since official justice was in the hands of the Jews. He announced to the press that a witness had categorical proof of Dreyfus's crimes. The witness turned out to be a swindler, and *Le Figaro* of July 5 related in copious detail the lamentable mystification to which the former Presiding Justice of the Civil Chamber had fallen victim. But it was Maurice Barrès who, in a series of articles in *Le Journal*, posed the terms of the trial and locked the military judges dangerously into the consequences of their own ideals. "The choice is clear," he wrote on July 4, "Dreyfus or our principal leaders."[7] Dreyfus's friends were the Nation's enemies. "They insult everything that is dear to us, the Nation, the Army . . . their plot is dividing and disarming France, and they are delighted at the prospect." The trial at Rennes was quite simple: "On the one hand, there is Dreyfus's honor; on the other, there is the honor of all the ministers and generals who have sworn to Dreyfus's guilt." And he threatened:

> We are several million decent people who have never been under
> obligation to have any acquaintance with the Affair and who have

trusted—as reason and duty dictated—the legitimate authority of
the Courts Martial and the leaders of the Army. If Generals Mercier, Billot, Chanoine, Zurlinden, and MM. Cavaignac and Méline
have deceived us, if they have associated us with the infamous
effort of keeping an innocent man in jail, no punishment will be
too harsh for them.[8]

Barrès warned that if Dreyfus were acquitted, there would be reprisals.
It was thus no longer a matter of deciding whether Dreyfus was innocent
or guilty. Nationalist ideals, military solidarity, and simple prudence all
dictated that he be convicted. Barrès encouraged and prodded the officers: "At Rennes, the truth must shine forth with the clarity of self-
evidence. . . . To Rennes, to Rennes, gentlemen of the Army! Cavaignac
and Mercier have given you their example. There is no escape possible.
March on!"[9]

The revisionists listened to such speeches with distracted ears, as if
they were a sign of nothing more serious than rearguard skirmishes. And
they were divided in their preparation for the trial. There were endless
debates as to whether the Court-Martial was bound by the decision of the
High Court of Appeal, whether there were any "acquired and conclusive"
truths which had been definitively established by the High Court of
Appeal—such as the matter of the alleged confession. Georges
Clemenceau warned in *L'Aurore* of July 21 that it would be imperative to
"hear everyone and to pose all the questions" lest the trial sink to the level
of such "unspeakable judges" as Chief Presiding Justice Mazeau. The
nationalist journalists applauded the suggestion: "What we need is a major
housecleaning." The government, which had asked the military prosecutor, Major Carrière, in a semiofficial communication not to speak to
any one of the points ruled on by the High Court of Appeal thus found
itself disavowed by one of the most ardent revisionists. Labori, who did not
want to declare himself satisfied with the authority of the High Court of
Appeal's judgment, affirmed his solidarity with Clemenceau. He decided
to call on Captain Lebrun-Renault and to confront him with Dreyfus in
order to "put a definitive end" to the legend of a confession. Hesitating
among several diverse strategies, the defense chose none of them. The
prosecution listed seventy witnesses, and specifically all those who had
testified against Dreyfus before the High Court of Appeal. The defense
listed twenty. And while Mathieu Dreyfus, with Alfred Dreyfus in prison,
attempted to reconcile their lawyers and friends, who were growing increasingly divided, Carrière chose to assist him in the case a monarchist
lawyer, Jules Auffray, who had previously counseled Commandant du
Paty de Clam and who was publicly known for his ties to the General

Staff.* The Dreyfusard team which assembled at Rennes during the days preceding the trial arrived in an atmosphere of incoherence and division.

The friendship, the enthusiasm, and the febrility of combat were still present. Meetings were held at the Auberge des Trois Marches, in the countryside, approaching Rennes. The local Guillet couple and a Mme. Jarlet prepared for the Dreyfusard clan and their guests, friendly journalists, meals of "middle-class cooking—simple and healthy." Colonel Picquart's former orderly helped to serve the food.[10] The pseudonymous journalist Séverine described the Auberge des Trois Marches as follows:[11]

> Comments—witty or impassioned, happy or grave—fly in all directions, gradually rising toward higher conceptions. Jaurès's fine voice sounds like a clarion; his laughter reverberates throughout the room. Georges Picquart is arguing softly. A scientist is making a speech, establishing the relation of effects to causes in the matter under debate. . . .
>
> Ugliness, hatred, deception, and might marching against right are all exposed to mockery. Those who have defected and those who have given up are dispatched in a few words.
>
> Often they all fall silent before the eloquence of a single individual. He speaks as the apostles must have spoken, when the first Christians, under suspicion, huddled in the Catacombs. They listen: the faith, the wish for heroism swell your heart.
>
> There is a knocking at the door: coming from the South or the North, the East or the West, it's some pilgrim who has made his way to this inn table where the bread of truth is broken.
>
> He comes in, sits down, remains silent. . . . But the sermons are all short. A Parisian gibe breaks the spell, gives the battle a modern touch.
>
> And then they leave. The most threatened are taken off together.[12]

Zola, Clemenceau, and Reinach remained in Paris in order to avoid "any pretexts for passion and trouble." But they were constantly consulted. Auguste Scheurer-Kestner was dying at Luchon. Ludovic Trarieux and Louis Leblois, along with many others who contributed information, gave advice, and frequently attempted to aggrandize their role. Between Labori and Demange, relations were growing increasingly tense. Mathieu Dreyfus "employed all his diplomatic skills and his painful experience of men"[13] to calm both sides. He was only barely succeeding.

---

* It was he who had "done the courtroom" for the General Staff during the Zola trial.

On Sunday, August 6, Mathieu spent a long period with his brother. He found him calm, quite serene, and extremely confident. But Mathieu was concerned. Captain Dreyfus expressed himself extremely slowly. He had not yet regained the habit of speech. The loss of several of his teeth caused a slight whistle when he spoke. He was extremely thin. How would he bear up under the emotions and fatigues of the hearings? And who would know—so effectively was he concealing his physical ills—that this was a man cruelly affected by the tortures of his years in prison who was appearing before his peers?

7

Living Mauled Flesh

On Monday, August 7, at 6:00 A.M. Mathieu Dreyfus went on foot to the Rennes lycée where his brother's trial was to take place.* He observed an astonishing spectacle: "Rennes looked like a city under siege."[1] The streets leading to the avenue on which the lycée was located were guarded by troops on foot and on horseback. To get to the lycée it was necessary to pass through several roadblocks and show one's pass each time. Gendarmes paced back and forth in every direction, officers rode by, saber in hand. "There was a great clamor from the movement of the horses, the rattling of sabers, the noises of rifle butts."

The lycée's auditorium, extremely high, huge and rectangular in shape, had been transformed into a courtroom. On the stage which dominated the auditorium, a large table and chairs were placed for the judges of the Court-Martial and, behind them, for General Eugène Cha moin, representing the minister of war, Maurice Paléologue, representing the minister of foreign affairs, and several others. To the right of the tribunal, down in the auditorium, was the defense's bench, in front of which were two chairs, one for the accused and one for the gendarme captain accompanying him. To the left, facing the defense's bench, was a table and chairs for the military prosecutor, Major Carrière, his deputy,

---

* The first Dreyfus trial had lasted for three days. The second would last for five weeks (from August 7 to September 9).

and the clerk. There were benches, somewhat recessed, for representatives of the press, both national and foreign. The rest of the room was divided into two parts separated by barriers, the first reserved for witnesses, the second for those privileged enough to have gained entrance cards. The gendarmerie was everywhere.

The judges of the military tribunal already had in their possession the case file of the 1894 trial and the investigation record of the High Court of Appeal. They had studied them for a month. They were all former students of the École Polytechnique. None had ever expressed an opinion on the case, with the exception of Commandant Lancrau de Bréon, a fervent Catholic, who had joined his wife in contributing five francs to the "Henry monument." Colonel Albert Jouaust, who was presiding, had "a splendid head, though somewhat harsh, his face scarred by a thick mustache," and was regarded as a decent man and a fine soldier. He was on the verge of retirement. Lieutenant Colonel Brogniart was director of the École d'Artillerie. Commandants Maurice Merle and Profillet had been classmates of Cavaignac at Polytechnique. Captain Parfait, cold and attentive, and Captain Beauvais "the most intelligent of the seven soldiers,"[2] completed the tribunal. The judges appeared to be serious men, who were no doubt still undecided.

On the opening day of the trial, August 7, *Le Matin* began publication of a long letter that Commandant Esterhazy had sent to the military prosecutor, Commandant Carrière. Esterhazy affirmed that he would not attend because he knew that the Court-Martial was resolved to acquit Dreyfus and, in addition, he was without the material resources to pay for the trip. He took up one of his preferred themes: "Before God and the sacred memory of my father, I swear that I entered into relations with Schwarzkoppen only on orders from Sandherr." General Mercier and the General Staff were greatly relieved by his absence. Far better that Esterhazy not appear at the hearings.

At 7:00 A.M. the courtroom was jammed. Newspapers sent their best journalists: Maurice Barrès, Jean-Bernard, André Chevrillon, Jules Clarétie, Séverine, Maizières, Marcel Prévost, Serge Basset, and Gaston Salles. Juan Juarès and René Viviani were also present and would write almost every day. Foreign journalists jostled each other for places. There were more entry cards than seats. In the section of the room reserved for witnesses, Mathieu Dreyfus observed the actors of the tragedy that had engulfed his brother. General Mercier, "sinister in his ugliness, his sea-green eyes half covered by thick, wrinkled lids,"[3] was in the first row, in a reserved seat. Godefroy Cavaignac, tall and thin, looked lugubrious, pacing back and forth. General Billot seemed to be enjoying himself observing the public. Strapped tight into his uniform, with a monocle affixed to his eye, General Zurlinden seemed to be preoccupied with his own appearance. General Roget fluttered about among the other generals as though he were a messenger. General Gonse and Captain Lauth, one more somber than the other, were conversing in a corner. General de Boisdeffre kept apart, frozen into an attitude that betrayed his fatigue. Former President Casimir-Périer sat beside General Mercier without looking at him. Colonel Henry's widow, "enveloped in a long veil of mourning," was there.[4] And then the court usher announced the Court-Martial with the call to "Present arms." Amid a stir of spurs and sabers, the members of the tribunal entered, followed by their deputies. All, standing erect, raised their hand to their cap, then with a second order to "Lay down arms," the judges assumed their places. Colonel Jouaust declared the Court in session. "Bring in the accused."

All eyes were turned toward the door behind the defendant's bench. Mathieu closed his eyes. He did not have the courage to watch his brother come in. The door opened. Alfred Dreyfus appeared. The whole audience stood to get a better view. Wearing an artillery captain's uniform, he stepped forward briskly, with a deliberately automatic stride. His legs faltered and he feared being unable to mount the steps to his seat. He made an effort to appear firm, impenetrable, "more solid than a wall." He stood still, saluted the Court in military fashion. Then, at the presiding judge's invitation, he removed his cap and sat down.

He looked like a statue.[5] His hair was white, cut short, contrasting with his fine mustache, which had remained brown. His very pale complexion would turn red for short intervals. "From time to time, blood would rush to give color to his skin and then leave it livid again."[6] His trousers flapped about his legs, which had neither muscle nor flesh, as though they were sticks. He had his uniform padded to give himself a semblance of stature. He had plied himself with stimulants. Above all, he did not want to be pitied. "I had but one duty: to appeal to the reason and the conscience of the judges. It is I who have pity for the men who dishonored themselves by condemning an innocent man through the most criminal methods." For a moment, Maurice Barrès appeared to be moved:

> The whole courtroom swayed with combined horror and pity when Dreyfus appeared.
> His thin and contracted face! His sharp stare from behind the pince-nez! Oh! how young he seemed to me at first, this young man who, weighed down by so much commentary, stepped forward with prodigious swiftness. At that moment we felt nothing but a thin wave of pain breaking over the auditorium. A miserable

human rag was being thrown into the glaring light. A ball of living flesh, fought over by the players of two teams and who has not had a minute's rest for six years, comes rolling from America into the midst of our battle. But Dreyfus had already climbed the steps of the podium, this next station in his calvary. . . .[7]

This description would not be confirmed by the journalists of *La Libre Parole*, *L'Eclair*, and *Le Journal*. They would note that the traitor "had in no way suffered from either the climate or the warders of his distant retreat," that "his face was resplendent with health," that he appeared "as though ashamed in the military uniform that had been returned to him."[8]

The charges of 1894 were read; Dreyfus seemed not to comprehend them. There followed the roll call of witnesses: Esterhazy was in flight; Commandant du Paty de Clam indisposed; Maurice Weil, the Jewish officer, was ill. Colonel Jouaust began the questioning. The Dreyfusards were stunned by the abrupt and almost brutal tone with which the presiding judge asked his questions or interrupted the defendant. Jouaust was plainly trying to harden his voice, to shake up the accused. He passed the bordereau to Dreyfus, who was standing as stiffly as ever. He questioned him concerning its contents. Dreyfus burst out: "I affirm again that I am innocent. I have tolerated so much for five years, my Colonel, but one more time, for the honor of my name and that of my children, I am innocent." Most of his words were lost.[9] "Honor . . . children . . . innocent" were heard. His face lost all color; he was overcome with dizziness. His eyes were moist with tears. "So you deny it," the presiding judge summarized. "Yes, my Colonel." The words "my Colonel" seemed to Barrès "like the two arms of a desperate man on his knees, clutching his all-powerful judge." But "his characterless voice added to the disastrous effect of his unemotional demeanor." He seemed to speak "like a phonograph."[10] Mathieu, "frightfully pale, would have liked to cry out for him."[11] The pathetic phrases uttered by Dreyfus—"I am innocent, I swear that I am innocent"—were recognized by Maurice Paléologue, sitting behind the judges. He had heard them on "the sinister morning of the ceremony of degradation. . . . Why do they still ring so false in my ear. . . . Why is the man incapable of any warmth? Why, in his strongest protests, does nothing of his soul manage to emerge in his choked voice. There is something indefinably incomprehensible and fateful about him, like the hero of an ancient tragedy."[12]

Jouaust questioned Dreyfus with increasing harshness. He brought up the old accusations, gambling, women, the indiscreet questions asked by Dreyfus of other officers.

Did you not bet on horses?

Never.

Why was your presence in Alsace tolerated?

For seven years I was refused a passport.

And yet you went there.

On three occasions, clandestinely, passing through Switzerland.

He was questioned about the confession to Captain Lebrun-Renault. Once again, he grew indignant. His hands were shaking continuously. He was finding it difficult to hold back tears:

> The conversation [with Lebrun-Renault] was a broken monologue. I said to him: "I am innocent. . . ." I felt outside a whole people in turmoil to whom would be shown a man who had committed the most abominable crime that a soldier can commit; I understood the patriotic anguish gripping that people and I said: "I would like to cry out to the people that it is not I who am guilty. I would like to be able to transmit to the crowd something of the tremor I am experiencing. I would like to make them understand that the man they believe to have committed the crime is not the one who has been convicted. I am going to shout out my innocence to the people." I added: "The Minister is well aware of this." That referred to what I had said to Lieutenant Colonel du Paty de Clam during his visit; I told him: "Tell the Minister that I am not guilty."[13]

The accused often replied with simple denials, without any commentary. "No, my Colonel," "Never, my Colonel." If he responded at length, Jouaust interrupted him. "That is unnecessary talk. Do you deny it or don't you?" One observer would comment, "He doesn't speak; he barks."[14] Another would write: "For him, the only humiliation is having been caught. . . . he splits hairs with the dexterity of a wily attorney.[15] "He is lying like a schoolboy. . . . As obstinate as the lowest of scoundrels, he has but one method: denial." His partisans would have liked him "to allow his heart swollen with so many miseries to burst," wrote Séverine, overwhelmed that he was bringing so little emotion to the proceedings. But he could not, nor did he wish to. "What was needed was an actor," concluded Joseph Reinach, "and he was a soldier."[16]

At a recess, the judges chatted with the representatives of the minister of war and the minister of foreign affairs, in order to sketch out what they called their "collaboration."[17] Colonel Brogniart and Commandant de Bréon walked "a stretch" with Maurice Paléologue along the Vilaine. They did not conceal the unfavorable impression Dreyfus had made on them during that first day. "Our task is difficult," commented Brogniart. Despite himself, Maurice Barrès recorded his initial reaction: "As for me, may my friends forgive me, I was looking at the man, the distant face, the ghost who was throwing France into crisis, and I felt that the hated name of Dreyfus all the same represented living and mauled flesh."[18]

Barrès evoked the liturgy of Good Friday. "Let us pray for the perfidious Jews." But he recovered rather swiftly. "If what were at stake were merely a man, we would have covered his shame with a shroud. But what is at stake here is France."[19]

8

The Final Battle

The Court-Martial ruled, by a vote of 5 to 2, to meet in closed session "in the interest of national defense" when General Chamoin presented the secret file. Almost immediately, the tactics that had riddled the earlier proceedings began. Chamoin spontaneously "added" to the secret file an item that had been confided to him by General Mercier* "as a private document" intended for his own information. Found out by Fernand Labori, Chamoin confessed his error and apologized to the Court Martial "for his ignorance in matters of judicial procedure."† But Dreyfus's lawyers understood thereafter that Chamoin was in the hands of General Mercier, a fact that was confirmed by the resolutely favorable bias toward the General Staff that informed his manner of presenting the contents of the file. This took up three sessions on August 8, 9, and 10. Dreyfus seemed to be almost absent from the proceedings, as though the

---

* This was a note from Commandant du Paty de Clam concerning the translation of a message from Alessandro Panizzardi, which had been circulating in different versions throughout the Affair.[1]

† Commissioned by Trarieux, Labori, and Picquart, the publisher Stock traveled to Paris to request from Waldeck-Rousseau an exemplary sanction against General Chamoin. Waldeck-Rousseau refused. "General Galliffet," he told Stock, "does not wish to go beyond the severe reprimand he has given Chamoin. I have discussed the question of an arrest with him, and he told me that if I acted on that idea, he would resign. . . . I will not have General Chamoin arrested. Make that clear to your friends."[2]

dossier did not concern him, and the presiding judge seemed to forget the accused was present.

"My file had no effect on the judges," Chamoin confided to Maurice Paléologue on the paths of the Park of Mont-Thabor where they strolled to discuss the case.[3] But Chamoin told Paléologue that Mercier was going to make a decisive revelation, deliver a "staggering blow." The phrase "staggering blow" worried Paléologue. Henry had said the same about his own famous document.

Mathieu Dreyfus, for his part, was disturbed because of the closed sessions. On August 8, he wrote to Joseph Reinach that he "feared the worst,"[4] that it would be imperative to obtain at whatever price from the German government indisputable proof of Commandant Esterhazy's crime—for example, the "notes" accompanying the bordereau. On August 10 and 11, still in closed session, Paléologue presented to the military judges the diplomatic dossier. Dreyfus remained silent. "Not a word came to his lips; not a feature of his face moved." The judges asked numerous questions, fascinated.[5] While leaving the courtroom, one of the judges asked Paléologue his opinion of the proceedings. He responded, "If I simply told you that after having been firmly convinced of Dreyfus's guilt, I now believe in his innocence, you would not derive much profit from our conversation. . . ." And Paléologue offered the judge several bits of advice: "You have to elucidate the arrival of the bordereau . . . obtain from Henry's widow that she knew whom her husband was alluding to when he wrote 'you know in whose interest I have acted'; you must stage a confrontation between Esterhazy and Weil. . . ."* A strange dialogue indeed. After which, Paléologue dined with his friend Casimir-Périer, who was scheduled to testify the following day. . . .

During the session of August 12, Casimir-Périer stepped forth to testify. He explained that throughout the trial he had been kept in the dark concerning the communication of the secret file, that never had a word been breathed to him concerning the alleged confession to Captain Lebrun-Renault, and finally that never at any moment had any risk of war with Germany existed. He then told how Waldeck-Rousseau and Joseph Reinach entreated him in 1894 to request that the Affair not be adjudicated in closed session: "I replied to them that I could do no more than convey their desire to the Council of ministers."† The nationalist press seized on the anecdote. So, in 1894 Waldeck-Rousseau was intervening on

---

* On the basis of vague leads, Paléologue would elaborate the thesis of a complicity between Esterhazy and Weil, both manipulated by a "third individual." See *infra* p. 508.
† That declaration provoked an incident with Edgar Demange, whom Casimir-Périer forced to apologize in public. At the time, the lawyer had misinformed Dreyfus about their discussion, allowing him to believe that the president of the Republic had committed himself.[6]

Dreyfus's behalf! "That alliance of Reinach and Waldeck was the alliance of Blücher and Wellington for a new Waterloo."[7]

General Mercier and his devastating revelation were eagerly awaited. He arrived in full military dress and took the oath. Then in a low and casual voice, a voice that could barely be heard, he began a long account of the Affair, which he went through methodically and with remarkable precision.[8] He recounted once again the tragic night "during which we were two steps away from war,"* on which General de Boisdeffre, at the Ministry, was awaiting mobilization orders, and how the minister had decided—in order to avoid a war that would be lost before it began, and "out of devotion to his country"—to let Dreyfus's judges know in secret the devastating charges against the accused. He did not show the decisive item that had been so awaited, but he spoke allusively of the "annotated bordereau." "His Majesty the Emperor of Germany took a personal interest in these espionage matters. . . . At the castle in Potsdam everyone knew the name Dreyfus."[9] He told the tribunal that "the denials that foreign diplomats might issue (for reasons of state) had to be examined with the greatest skepticism." Thus did Mercier proceed, through vague insinuation combined with specific detail, to make a great impression.† He spoke for four hours without once looking at Dreyfus, who was seated two feet away from him. "He looks at the traitor as though he were an object," Maurice Barrès would write. Then he came to his conclusion, finally turning toward his victim:

> I have not reached my age without having come to the sad conclusion that everything human is subject to error. As a result, I have followed with poignant emotion all the arguments of the revisionist campaign. If the slightest doubt had crossed my mind, gentlemen, I would be the first to tell you so, for I am an honest man and the son of an honest man; I would come before you to say to Captain Dreyfus: "I erred in good faith. . . ."

At that point, Dreyfus sprung up, his arm outstretched toward Mercier, and shouted, "That is what you should do." It looked as though he was about to fling himself on the witness. Applause erupted. The gendarme returned Dreyfus to his seat. The former minister of war, quite pale, began again, "I would come to say. . . ." Dreyfus shouted again, "It's your duty." The applause and the jeers were by now drowning out Mercier's voice. He nevertheless finished the text that he had learned by heart:

---

* *Supra* p. 83 and pp. 108–09.
† In the course of the trial, General Mercier would have a revised version of his recorded testimony published and forwarded to each of the judges.

I would come before you to say to Captain Dreyfus: "I erred in good faith; I recognize that fact with the same good faith, and I will do everything humanly possible to make amends for a frightful error." Except . . . no! My conviction since 1894 has not been modified in the slightest; it has deepened through a more thorough study of the case; and it has been fortified by the inanity of the results obtained in the effort to demonstrate the innocence of the convict, despite the enormous sum of millions squandered to that end! . . .

And he withdrew quietly, as though borne by the serenity of his belief. Barely had he left the stand than Casimir-Périer rose up. "General Mercier has made several declarations concerning my role in 1895 that I would not want my silence to confirm and that I, in fact, cannot tolerate. I ask to confront him." Colonel Jouaust decided that the confrontation would take place on Monday morning and called the session to a close.

That Saturday, August 12, had been a good day for the revisionists. In Paris during the morning, about fifteen "conspirators"—including Paul Déroulède—had been arrested. Marcel Habert had taken to flight. Jules Guérin had bolted himself into his fort on Rue Chabrol. The Republic was well defended. In Rennes, General Mercier had not said anything that was not already known. His decisive proof did not exist! Jean Jaurès, Georges Clemenceau, and Joseph Cornély exulted in the Dreyfusard press. Mercier lost the battle and Dreyfus would be acquitted.

In the adverse camp, the sense of disappointment was brutal. On August 14 *Le Gaulois* published an open letter to Mercier: "You have told a great deal of the truth, but have you told it all?" And speaking of the annotated bordereau, the newspaper specified: "You have in your possession a photograph of it and you brought it with you to Rennes. If your affirmation is serious and accurate, confirm it. If it is in part erroneous, correct it." Mercier kept his silence, but was quite busy on another front. Mutual friends were skillfully besieging Judges Parfait, Profillet, Beauvais, and Brogniart daily. As for Bréon, he could be seen going to church every day at the close of the court session. He was vigorously attacked by the Dreyfusard press as a hypocrite and a fanatic fallen into the hands of his brother, the abbé de Bréon.

On Monday morning, August 14, shortly after 6:00 o'clock, Colonel Picquart and Fernand Labori headed toward the courtroom along the banks of the Vilaine, still deserted at that hour. A young man, dressed in a black jacket with white sleeves and a flat cap, followed them at a distance of three or four meters. Picquart suggested that Labori speak more softly when suddenly, they heard a gunshot. Labori, hit in the back, slumped to the ground. Picquart rushed off after the murderer, who had quickly disappeared from sight. At 6:30, just after the court session began, a growing clamor was heard. A man burst into the auditorium, proclaiming "Labori has just been assassinated." The prime minister suspended the proceedings.

Miraculously, the bullet had stopped a few millimeters from Labori's spine. Moved into Professor Victor Basch's home, Labori was to regain his strength rather swiftly. The physicians, after some consultation, opted not to remove the bullet. "How can one remove a bullet," *La Libre Parole* commented, "that is as evasive as the murderer?" His convalescence was brief. There was a rumor that if all went well, Labori would return to his place in Court by August 21. Telegrams by the thousands expressed support for the lawyer. "My dear, my great, my valiant friend, get better and complete our victory," Emile Zola wrote on August 16.[10] Even notorious anti-Dreyfusards like Léon Daudet manifested sympathy for him. The attack was condemned in all quarters. Without any proof, Labori's colleagues accused General Mercier of having armed the assassin. Others suspected the government. "Rest assured," wrote Maurice Barrès, "the Dreyfus family and the government are better off for the eight days that the impetuous lawyer has been forced to spend in bed." Barrès added cynically, "Oh, my old comrade Labori, for a Frenchman who wants to wage war, the least disagreeable option still remains to serve in the armed forces of France." He continued: "In the sinister group composed of Dreyfus, who sells our generals, Demange, who ridicules them, and Labori, who dishonors them, it is Labori, who was born an Alsatian and a decent fellow, who is the worst. . . . He is the clarion of all the foreigners and mercenaries assaulting France."

While Labori was recovering from his wound, his foul humor grew worse. The police, of course, had been unable to get their hands on the assassin. And Waldeck-Rousseau and Edgar Demange were taking advantage of his absence. On August 14, Jouaust ordered a resumption of the proceedings. Alfred Dreyfus personally requested an adjournment of the trial until Labori was fully recovered—presumably, on August 21. The Court-Martial unanimously declined the request.* Labori was informed that his colleague had not backed up the request for a temporary suspension very vigorously, and Mathieu Dreyfus immediately brought in Henri Mornard, a lawyer at the High Court of Appeal, to replace him. Labori was increasingly convinced that they were trying to get rid of him—by any means.

At the last session of August 14, which had been interrupted by the

---

* The Military Code stipulated categorically that the proceedings could not be interrupted for more than 48 hours without having to be started over again.

attack against Labori, the confrontation between Casimir-Périer and Mercier had proved inconclusive. Mercier had continued to affirm, in opposition to the former president of the Republic, that during the "tragic" night of January 6, everyone awaited the results of the telegrams between Count Münster von Derneberg and Emperor Wilhelm—to know "whether it was war or peace that would emerge from the crisis." It was Labori who was to question Mercier. With Labori now absent, Demange was constrained to improvise a few questions quickly, to little effect. Labori's supporters let it be known that Mercier would not have gotten off so easily had he been questioned by the great lawyer.

The former ministers of war Billot, Chanoine, and Zurlinden were called next. Each in turn affirmed his unshakable conviction: the author of the bordereau and Colonel Maximilien von Schwarzkoppen's informer was Dreyfus.[11] With heads held high, they repeated their absolute confidence in the evidence accumulated by the Intelligence Service. Then Godefroy Cavaignac, "with his emaciated body, his deep-set eyes, glistening pupils, and greenish skin," summarized the arguments of the General Staff in a powerful synthesis. He had the mien and the skill of a grand inquisitor. According to Paléologue, the judges were fascinated.[12] "Pale, horrified, his open mouth gaping, Dreyfus listened in mournful stupor to the irrefutable demonstration of his guilt . . . drops of sweat came to his temples; his whole face expressed frightful distress." Former Minister of Colonies Lebon explained the "double shackles" to which the deportee had been subjected, the odious system of punishment that had been conceived for him. But Dreyfus interrupted, "I am not here to speak of the atrocious forms of torture inflicted on an innocent man, but to defend my honor." He would not tolerate the slightest appeal to emotion.

The testimony continued, after a recess for the religious holiday of Assumption, without casting any new light. There was no more talk of the bordereau, which was precisely what Waldeck-Rousseau had feared. Dreyfus himself seemed increasingly absent from the proceedings. The various legal procedures, intrigues, deceptions, and forgeries were brought up and examined with difficulty. Attention wandered as the witnesses paraded through. Colonel Henry's widow, questioned by one of the judges, affirmed that it was "in the Army's interest" that her beloved husband had committed his mistake. She repeated, "In the interest of the Army . . . in the interest of whom else could you believe that he was acting?" General Roget delivered an eloquent indictment. He demonstrated to the judges, who were suitably impressed, that Esterhazy was an adventurer who had sold out to the Jews, that Dreyfus and Esterhazy were conspirators. Paléologue observed that General Roget seemed to have the judges in the palm of his hand, as though he were dictating their maneuvers.[13] Judge Bertulus then related at length his investigations. He seemed "equivocating and servile, furtive and nebulous" to Paléologue. Finally Picquart's testimony was to be heard, much awaited by the Dreyfusards.

"Monsieur Picquart," the clerk announced. He appeared in civilian dress, seeming almost embarrassed in the presence of his former comrades in uniform. He told all that he knew, with firmness and moderation. But his testimony as a defrocked soldier inevitably inspired skepticism on the part of the officers. "During the whole time that he was at the stand," Paléologue wrote, "he made me think of a heresiarch, an apostate, appearing before an ecclesiastical tribunal."[14] Then came Captain Louis Cuignet, who had gradually risen to a state of exaltation in the wake of his disgrace and the disciplinary measures to which he had been subjected. The man who had discovered the "Henry forgery" and who allowed for the revision was now borne on by his hatred of the Dreyfusards. He offered as certainties inventions of such mean-spirited paltriness that Dreyfus could not keep from interrupting him: "I cannot spend all this time listening to such lies." Presiding Judge Jouaust asked the accused to remain silent.

On August 19, General de Boisdeffre testified. Not yet sixty years old, he looked much older. He spoke in a slow, almost shattered voice. He affirmed sadly, firmly, his belief in Dreyfus's guilt. He expressed assurance that Esterhazy had been only the Dreyfus family's straw man. His words were as categorical as his voice was weary. Dreyfus listened to him in despair. He had so admired Boisdeffre. He had had so much confidence in him. He suffered a loss of faith and great pain.[15] When the presiding judge asked him whether he had anything to say, Dreyfus could not find the words: "I do not wish to respond to General de Boisdeffre."

There followed a stampede. General Gonse, who had been relieved of his functions on July 29, stumbled, lost the thread of his thought, and retracted what he had said, all the while lashing out at Dreyfus and Picquart.[16] Dreyfus's former classmates, Lieutenant Colonel Bertin-Mourot in particular, had gathered to destroy him once again and described him as pretentious, prying, a gambler, a libertine, and perennially in search of secret information. Dreyfus could not bear it any longer. "That is false; I love the Army; I love my country." But, Barrès observed: "There was nothing of sincerity to be found in him. . . . He was a machine that had been started up. . . . His sole hope? That the assembled public would support him. They were obscenely rich, reeking of perfume, secretly rotten with every form of corruption."[17] All of Dreyfus's friends, "the mournful squadron of rebels presided over by Picquart's sinister smile" and "the university faction whose maneuvers were being called by Jaurès," all of them along with the lawyer Edgar Demange, who asked his questions "with the solemnity of a head waiter passing the turbot," were enemies of

France. And now Barrès could see Dreyfus's face "dripping with betrayal."
"He and his partisans have committed the worst of crimes: which is not to
have handed over the documents enumerated in the bordereau, but to
have served the function, for five years, of casting the Army and the
Nation into turmoil."[18] The officers who had known Dreyfus, whom he
had served under, with the single exception of General Ducros, all claimed
to have been suspicious of him. All were certain of his crime. Could the
whole Army be wrong?

On August 22, Fernand Labori resumed his place in the courtroom.
Numerous witnesses, in particular Billot and Mercier, came to congratu-
late him. Presiding Judge Jouaust greeted him with a few brief words to
which the lawyer responded with an impassioned speech.[19] Would things
change? No doubt Demange had neither Labori's talent nor his exuber-
ance. He had allowed many an opportunity to slip by. No doubt the
defense was handicapped by far too many absences. Sandherr was dead.
Henry was dead. Du Paty de Clam had not come and asked to be heard by
a rogatory commission. Esterhazy was in England. Maurice Weil claimed
to be ill. No doubt, moreover, all the useful witnesses had not been called.
One of the judges of 1894, Captain Martin Freystaetter, came to tell of his
recollection of having read "several documents" in the course of the
deliberations leading to Dreyfus's conviction. He acknowledged the impression that those documents had made on him. In this he contradicted
Colonel Maurel, who had presided over the Court-Martial and who was
certain of having read only one document and of not having offered any
commentary. He contested the impression made by the secret file. The
defense called none of the other judges. Out of prudence? Out of incom-
petence? Many had thought that with Labori's return, they would march
on to victory, but Labori was exhausted and rather dissatisfied. His hostility toward Demange was now manifest. The defense now had two contradictory strategies, which frequently neutralized each other. Labori
seemed "eager for battle." He sought out occasions for conflict, less, it
appears, in order to profit his client than to reclaim his turf. At every
session, he clashed with the presiding judge, whom he found increasingly
difficult to tolerate:

> I beseech you to speak with moderation.
>   I have not said a single immoderate word.
> But your tone is not moderate.
>   I am not in control of my tone.
> Well you should be. Every man is in control of his own person.
>   I am in control of my person, but not of my tone.
> I am going to withdraw your permission to speak.

Go ahead and withdraw it.

Sit down.

I will sit down. But not on any orders.

Every day offered a new pretext for confrontations between Jouaust and Labori, and also between Demange and Labori. The nationalists were delighted. "It appeared to me," Barrès commented, "that there was a priest's hatred between those two robes."[20] Under Labori's guidance a witness acknowledged that in the General Staff Demange was considered a specialist in the defense of foreign agents. Demange did not conceal his displeasure. Neither the defendant nor Mathieu Dreyfus, who suffered through such scenes uneasy at the idea of any remonstration, dared to intervene in a decisive manner. All the while, General Mercier, seated in his armchair, dominating the troop of military witnesses, followed the proceedings with due composure and acumen. He passed messages, dispatched emissaries, and asked to intervene whenever an officer got bogged down or threatened to yield. Even as he was the leader of the conspiracy in 1894 which led to Dreyfus's conviction, so, in Rennes, was he the head of the force that would prevent his acquittal. Before his eyes, Dreyfus's defense was caught in the mire of its contradictions and resentments.

As the depositions tirelessly continued, Alphonse Bertillon, the handwriting expert, "like some astrologer from the sixteenth century,"[21] paraded once again before his blackboard, displaying his fantastic diagrams with the gestures of an exorcist. One expert followed another amid a growing tedium as the trial dragged on, uneasiness spreading through the Dreyfusard camp. General Chamoin continued to predict an acquittal "for lack of evidence" to the minister of war, but he was alone in his optimism. Maurice Paléologue, who had daily conversations with the judges, informed the minister of foreign affairs that unless there were some startling development—"which could come only from either Rome or Berlin"—it appeared certain that Dreyfus would be convicted.[22] The Dreyfusards Arthur Ranc and Ludovic Trarieux did not conceal their concern. Jean Jaurès, who was increasingly pessimistic, wrote in *La Petite Republique* of August 27, "Given this irremediable moral collapse and definitive fall into stupidity, France may have no other resource than revolution."[23] At other times, he regained hope. A conviction seemed to be "a physical impossibility." Only Picquart retained his obstinate confidence. Dreyfus would be acquitted because he was innocent.

Mathieu Dreyfus, Joseph Reinach, and Edgar Demange were convinced that their only chance would be to force the Court-Martial to return to the narrow case that concerned Dreyfus alone, that is, to the bordereau, and to definitively prove Dreyfus's innocence by obtaining from Germany an accusation against Esterhazy as well as the notes appended to the bordereau that were transmitted by Esterhazy to Schwarzkoppen.[24] For once Labori and Demange seemed in agreement, and Labori wrote to Waldeck-Rousseau on August 24 to implore him to intervene personally with the German government. "If something from outside of the Affair does not transpire, the production of the documents pertaining to the bordereau and subsequent items (a simple declaration will no longer suffice) or some legal action against the conspirators, with General Mercier at their head, I consider the success of the cause of justice to be impossible. I will fight to the end, but, will do so, once again, without hope. . . ."[25] On August 12 the prime mininster saw Ambassador Münster von Derneberg, who had just been named a prince, and asked him personally for the help so eagerly awaited by the Dreyfusards. He renewed his initiative on August 24 with the greatest urgency.[26] On August 25, von Bülow, the secretary of state for foreign affairs, replied:

> The German goverment is sincerely desirous of satisfying the French government. But the manner in which the official French agencies have ignored my declaration to the Reichstag, as representative of the Imperial government, that Germany has never had either direct or indirect dealings with Dreyfus excludes, in accord with the will of His Majesty the Emperor and King, any possibility that the German government intervene hereafter in this internal French matter in any manner at all.[27]

Waldeck-Rousseau insisted once again on August 28, and this time Minister of War Galliffet joined him in his endeavor. To no avail. Von Bülow answered him on August 29 in an extremely polite disclaimer:

> His Majesty's government willingly acknowledges that the present French government is in all respects and at all times motivated by the proper point of view. German policy, nevertheless, must take into account not only the French government today but those national forces that are at present troubling the country with their mutual hostility and their efforts to impose their point of view—all that might be encapsulated by the collective notion of "public opinion." Concerning that public opinion, and however contradictory it may be on other matters, Germany and specifically the person of the monarch, as soon as they were mentioned in connection with the Dreyfus Affair, have been discussed in a manner that makes it imperative for the Imperial goverment, in so far as possi-

ble, to avoid any further implication of Germany and her Emperor in it. For after all that has happened up until now, we must consider it impossible for any fact or person thrown into the debate by Germany to be appreciated with any objectivity. The Imperial goverment is thus in no position to examine whether—outside of the declaration I have made, as is known, to the Reichstag—it might furnish other materials to clarify the Dreyfus case. His Majesty the Emperor, who is following attentively the frequently curious phases of the Dreyfus trial, has thus been brought to the position presented above.

Your Excellency will kindly transmit this information to M. Waldeck-Rousseau's intermediary or to himself personally and express at the same time my deep personal regrets at not having the good fortune to second the efforts of a government whose intense struggle for legality and truth I support with my most sincere sympathies. I nevertheless believe that that struggle can be waged usefully solely by exclusively French forces and that the introduction of foreign elements, whose ultimate usefulness would be neutralized by a general suspicion, cannot at all be calculated in its consequences before the fact.

A singular situation: the French government was petitioning the German government in vain for help in facilitating Dreyfus's acquittal. Galliffet would tirelessly pursue his efforts right up until the verdict to arrange at least for the appearance of Colonel von Schwarzkoppen. And until the end, he would be met with such courteous refusals. And Emperor Wilhelm II, annotating his minister's report suggesting that Schwarzkoppen not be authorized to speak, even though such an intervention "would facilitate the return of peace and quiet in France," would write in his own hand: "How does this concern me? I am not Emperor of the French."[28] The notes appended to the bordereau would never be transmitted—nor, it seems, even located. There would be no assistance expected from Germany.

The balance sheet of points scored by the defense was, nevertheless, hardly negligible. The expert Chavray had gone back on the conclusions of his evaluation—one of those that had resulted in Dreyfus's conviction in 1894. He had solemnly acknowledged that the bordereau was not written by Dreyfus but by Esterhazy.* In his testimony, General Deloye, director of

* "I insist on declaring that in 1894, abused by a resemblance in handwriting, I erred in attributing the document known as the bordereau to the author of an anonymous specimen of handwriting that was by Captain Dreyfus. Having discovered a new written element, I have acknowledged my error, and it is a great relief for my conscience to be able to come before you, Gentlemen, and above all before the victim of that error, to declare that I was wrong in 1894."

artillery for the Ministry of War, had established that Dreyfus could not have known the secret mechanism of the 120 short gun and particularly not its hydropneumatic brake. Captain Lebrun-Renault had stumbled and contradicted himself, and the legend of a confession had emerged quite wounded after his deposition. Labori had ridiculed General Gonse. One of Dreyfus's former classmates, Fonds-Lamothe, who had long been quite hostile to Dreyfus, had attested that those serving temporarily with the General Staff in 1894 had been informed in May 1894 through a circular from Boisdeffre that they would not be going on maneuvers. Dreyfus could thus not have written the last sentence of the bordereau. During the last week of the trial, it might have seemed that the balance was tilting in favor of acquittal.

It was at that juncture that the prosecution discovered a new witness, Eugène Lazare de Cernuski, an Austrian and former dragoon lieutenant, who had introduced himself successively on September 3 to Roget, Mercier, and Cavaignac, claiming to be in possession of proof of Dreyfus's guilt. All three had dismissed him. More audacious than they, Carrière, the military prosecutor, asked the Court-Martial to hear him. The rumor soon spread that a major development was in the offing. Heard on Monday, September 4, at the discretion of the presiding judge, Cernuski, who claimed to speak French only with difficulty, had his testimony read by the court clerk. He affirmed that one of his friends, "section head of the Ministry of Foreign Affairs in Vienna, had confided to him in August 1894 the names of four persons engaged in espionage in France on behalf of the Germans. The first of the four names was Dreyfus." A month later a high officer with the German General Staff had confirmed that information. Cernuski made a rather troublesome impression on the Court Martial. "With the face of a scoundrel and swindler," Paléologue noted, "his very appearance was enough to discredit him."[29]

As though he sensed onto what dangerous ground he was headed, the military prosecutor suddenly interrupted his witness and asked for the remainder of his deposition to be heard in closed session. The judges were dumbfounded. Labori saw the profit to be derived from the incident. He mentioned his reservations as to the witness's honorability. And without consulting Demange, he announced that if it was the presiding judge's will that a witness of foreign nationality be included in the proceedings, he proposed that the notes appended to the bordereau be requested of the appropriate authorities through diplomatic channels. The tribunal found itself in an awkward situation. The judges consulted Paléologue, who assured them that Minister of Foreign Affairs Delcassé would never agree to transmit such a request to Berlin. The Court-Martial then rejected Labori's motion, and he announced, quite furiously, that he would have

Colonel von Schwarzkoppen and General Alessandro Panizzardi heard as witnesses. The military prosecutor perceived the defense's blunder and replied that he had no objection. Labori dispatched forthwith telegrams to Schwarzkoppen and to Panizzardi phrased as follows:

> A serious incident that has just taken place before the Rennes Court-Martial obliges Captain Dreyfus's defense to call for your personal testimony. Your testimony has been officially requested by me during today's session. The military prosecutor has received the standard notification. This request will be transmitted to you officially through diplomatic channels. Given the urgent situation, I find it imperative to inform you personally before my request reaches you by diplomatic channels and so that you may take measures in order that your testimony be received in the shortest time possible.

The closed session scheduled to hear Cernuski on September 6 lasted only a few minutes. In the interim, the police had discovered that the witness had numerous debts, was afflicted with mental problems, and had lied on numerous points. Cernuski took the oath, gave the names of his alleged informers, and then, upon being pressed with questions by lawyers, broke down. That afternoon he didn't appear in court, claiming to be ill. He never came back. Plainly, this last minute witness had been useful to the defense.* But Labori, at the risk of compromising the advantage he had just gained, persisted in his claim. He urged the presiding judge to make use of his discretionary powers to order that Schwarzkoppen and Panizzardi be heard and made a motion to that effect, which the Court-Martial rejected as beyond its competence.[31] It was then learned that Labori, carried away by his scheme, had telegraphed the emperor of Germany and the king of Italy to insist on their being heard! The nationalist press inveighed that Labori was a madman, that the party of treason this time had showed its hand. On September 7 Labori moved that the two attachés be heard by a rogatory commission. The question was becoming an affair of state. Emperor Wilhelm II informed his ministers that it was impossible to meet the lawyer's request. Von Bülow, who had consulted with the emperor in Stuttgart, telegraphed the Wilhelmstrasse:[32]

> His Majesty the Emperor and King, our most gracious master, considers it naturally and totally impossible to accede in any man-

---

* "He's a scoundrel and a false witness," Presiding Judge Jouaust had confided to Paléologue on September 4.[30]

ner to Maître Labori's strange suggestion. For His Majesty's government and insofar as Germany is concerned, the matter is completely elucidated and definitively ended by the declarations of Prince von Münster in Paris in 1894 and of myself to the Reichstag last year. We are further confirmed in this manner of seeing things by the fact that the Rennes Court-Martial has, in the interim, rejected the defense's request for an intervention of the French government with foreign governments. It is in the light of this unshakable decision of His Majesty that I ask you to rein in the language of the press you have any control over.

Paléologue, for his part, let Minister Delcassé know the inconvenience that a hearing of Schwarzkoppen, given the present atmosphere of the trial, would entail.[33] Berlin replied simply with a note, phrased as follows, at the top of the official section of the *Monitor of the Empire* of September 8:

We are authorized to renew the declarations which, concerning the French Captain Dreyfus, the Imperial government, even while retaining the reserve dictated by loyalty in an internal affair of a foreign power, but in order to safeguard its own dignity, has made in order to fulfill its duty toward humanity. By order of the Emperor, in December 1894 and January 1895, Ambassador Prince von Münster transmitted to M. Hanotaux, Minister of Foreign Affairs, to M. Dupuy, prime minister, and to the president of the Republic, M. Casimir-Périer, repeated declarations that the German embassy in France had never had any relations, either direct or indirect, with Captain Dreyfus.

Secretary of State von Bülow expressed himself in these terms on January 24, 1898 before the Reichstag commission: "I declare as formally as possible that between the French ex-Captain Dreyfus, presently imprisoned on Devil's Island, and any German agency, there has never existed any relation or connection of any sort whatsoever."

Paléologue took the precaution of bringing the note to the judges himself. It contained nothing which they did not already know. "But the tone was new," Reinach observed, "and its timing made it doubly important. Germany was clearing its conscience one last time."[34]

The trial was drawing to a close. Cuignet was heard again, bringing with him a new secret file, which had to be examined before its insignificance was ascertained. Trarieux offered testimony which seemed to Reinach "admirable in its clarity and logic,"[35] but Paléologue, on the contrary, found him "waxing rhetorical, without for a moment realizing the disastrous effect he was producing."[36] Finally, taking as his pretext an article in the September 6 evening edition of *La Libre Parole* which maintained that "diplomatic considerations prevented the photograph of the real bordereau, annotated by the Emperor, from being communicated to the judges," General Mercier asked to take the stand one last time. He delivered a stinging indictment of Dreyfus's former judge, Captain Freystaetter, whose deposition concerning the communication of the secret file, he feared, might influence the judges. Mercier described Freystaetter as a mentally distraught soldier, with strong Jewish connections, and who now seemed strangely scrupulous for a man who had ordered thirty-five natives shot in Madagascar without trial. Freystaetter, who had already left Rennes, was not present to reply. Then Mercier marshaled anew and summarized the arguments proving treason and posed one last time the dilemma of favoring "either Dreyfus or myself." One last time he asked the judges to consider well his testimony, how he had had "the honor of bringing to this stand a degree of trust and moral authority." Up until the very end, he presented himself as a spokesman, expressing the beliefs of the Army in its entirety.

Colonel Jouaust declared the public proceedings over. Suddenly all the military witnesses and officers rose in unison to leave the courtroom. Such was the order they had received from Galliffet. They marched out together, in rhythm, heads held high, as though they were on maneuvers. One could almost hear their orders. "Their entire attitude," Paléologue noted, "seemed to say: our task is accomplished; we have won the Army's cause; the verdict is a mere formality."[37] The Army had waged this final battle with closed ranks, behind its former chief, General Mercier.

9

Yes, the Accused Is Guilty

Commandant Carrière delivered his summation on September 7. It was as lacking in substance as the Dreyfusards could possibly have wished, consisting of a long series of undeveloped arguments, embryonic hypotheses, all of them unconnected and delivered in barely comprehensible jargon.* But the theses of the General Staff—however deformed by the mediocrity of Carrière's thought and expression—were clearly audible in his presentation. "Esterhazy undoubtedly served as Dreyfus's intermediary, but of this we have no proof. . . . Everyone is free to think what he wants of the *petit bleu*, it is not worth discussing. . . . When Dreyfus wrote to his wife from Devil's Island, he always made drafts of his letters; he was, then, an extremely careful, extremely intelligent man, who did not write the bordereau as a normal document. He necessarily took precautionary measures. He imitated his brother's handwriting, Esterhazy's handwriting. . . ." "It was," in Maurice Paléologue's words, "an indescribable spectacle offered by this poor man with his shifty head, his open-eyed gaze, his voice alternately sepulchral and shrill, his clownish gestures. The twaddle he inflicted on us for an hour and a half was so obscure, amorphous, incoherent, sloppy, and inconsequential that on twenty occasions the stenographers laid down their pens in incomprehension. The judges looked humiliated."[1] As a conclusion, Carrière pronounced these few words: "Gentlemen of the Court, I tell you: Dreyfus is guilty. I therefore request the application of Article 76 of the Penal Code." The government's representative had thus come to the conclusion—contrary to the conviction of most of the members of the government—that Dreyfus was guilty. René Waldeck-Rousseau and General de Galliffet had permitted an all too well disciplined conscience to express itself.[2]

It was now up to the defense. The internal difficulties that had been troubling it had increased since the failed assassination attempt against

---

* Cornély commented: "We heard some protracted and more or less incomprehensible drivel which—according to Colonel Jouaust—was supposed to be the military prosecutor's summation . . ." (*Le Figaro* of September 8).

Labori. They had reached a degree of extreme violence when Labori, on his own, had decided to request Colonel von Schwarzkoppen's testimony and had telegraphed the emperor of Germany. It was not simply a conflict in strategy, but a personal quarrel in which Colonel Picquart, Ludovic Trarieux, Joseph Reinach, Bernard Lazare, and George Clemenceau had by then become involved. Mathieu Dreyfus was no longer able to arbitrate among them. Reinach and Lazare strongly desired that Labori renounce pleading for the defense: Since the Zola trial, after the extravagance of his questions, Labori had wisely tempered his final statement, but it was plain that the lawyer was alienating the military judges. His relations with Colonel Jouaust were frankly hostile. It was feared that his mere presence at the stand would assure Dreyfus's conviction. Inversely, Picquart and Clemenceau had confidence in no one but Labori. They denounced the prudent and enervated strategy—which had been formed by Demange and which had been advised by Waldeck-Rousseau—whose first results they saw in Carrière's odious summation.

The manner in which events then transpired has given rise to contradictory interpretations. It appears that Mathieu, who was in charge of his brother's defense, was hesitant. It appears as well that Labori—because he felt there was nothing more to be hoped for, because there was a wish to "accommodate the criminals" in order to please the government—had expressed his intention of leaving the case on several occasions. On September 6 in any event, Mathieu, declaring himself "indignant at the events of the morning session," implored Labori, in the name of his brother and himself, to remain at the defense bench.* On September 7, Picquart left Rennes. Labori felt himself rather isolated. On September 8, an extremely encouraging letter from Zola was brought to him: "If Dreyfus can be saved, you will save him. My confidence is with you. . . ."

On the morning of September 8, the day of the defense's final statement, Bernard Lazare came to see Labori at 5:45 A.M., accompanied by Jean Jaurès and Professor Victor Basch. Jaurès spoke: "I'll come right to my point. Mathieu Dreyfus is going to ask you to renounce making the final argument." Labori was to claim that Jaurès added: "It's at the request of the government† . . . acquittal is certain if you don't take the floor. The situation is lost, on the other hand, if you speak." According to his own version, Labori is alleged to have demonstrated to his three visitors the trap into which Mathieu was about to fall. From the very first session, every

---

* Following, it appears, incidents surrounding the request for Schwarzkoppen to be heard that had been addressed to the German Emporor by "Labori, Captain Dreyfus's lawyer."
† It appears that the government—encouraged in particular by General Chamoin—had hoped until the end that acquittal was possible with "a minority in favor." Acquittal before a Court-Martial could in fact be achieved with "a minority in favor" (3 votes out of 7).

error that had been committed was the result of overconfidence and pusillanimity, all in the hope of winning over one or two judges, in particular Captain Beauvais, who was in fact, according to Labori, one of Dreyfus's staunchest adversaries. And now they were about to submit to the will of the General Staff. "Your initiative liberates me," was Labori's alleged comment. "Not only is Captain Dreyfus doomed, but in silencing me, you are casting on him the last shovelful of earth." "You must deliver the final statement," replied Jaurès, convinced, in this version at least, by the force of Labori's arguments. It was too late.

In the courtroom, which was already invaded by the public, Labori met Mathieu, who had two letters with him. One, for Labori, came from Joseph Cornély, political editor of *Le Figaro*, who maintained that "the duty of lawyers intent on arguing usefully for their client was to accommodate the generals," and, according to Labori, to lace their interventions with variations on the theme "Long live the Army";* the other, from Joseph Reinach to Mathieu, revealed between the lines his wish to see Labori remove himself from the case:

> Thursday, 4 o'clock. My dear friend, the bearer will bring you a letter from Cornély for Labori to the effect that Bernard Lazare and Victor Simond telephoned me that Clemenceau should be made to write him. Clemenceau, who has just left me, refuses to write to Labori. He feels that there is only one person who has the necessary authority and the right to ask Labori either to desist from speaking or to restrict himself within certain limits and that that person is you. When Clemenceau does not wish to do something, you know that there is no way to constrain him to do it. In addition, I believe that he is right. . . .

Reinach's letter ended with these words: "Personally, I have not lost hope, and I maintain until the very end the belief that an infamy that so dishonors France will not be committed. But I owe it to the truth to acknowledge that I am alone in maintaining this belief or this illusion. I embrace you."[4] The letter included a postscript formulated as follows: "Whether or not you transmit Cornély's letter to Labori is your own decision, but my personal feeling is to let Labori proceed. In this, I am in agreement with Clemenceau, Calmette, and Arène."

The intent of the two letters was ambiguous. They let it be understood that Labori's presence before the Court complicated things, but they preferred to "let him proceed." As hesitant as Jaurès and Lazare, Mathieu

* Cornély, who became a convinced Dreyfusard late in the day, had an on-going relation with General Galliffet.[3]

showed the letter to Labori, who kept it. No sooner had he read it than Labori shouted: "I will not address the Court. I will remain silent." Mathieu, who appears to have transmitted the letter without conviction, tried to get the lawyer to change his decision. Labori was obstinate: "If I speak and if, as I no longer doubt, your poor brother is convicted, they will say that it is my fault, that everything was saved without me. I shall remain silent." He took his seat beside Demange as the Court entered into session. "Do you know what I have just been told?" he asked Demange. "It is a great misfortune," Demange replied. "I am against it. I had no part in it. You must address the Court." Their dialogue was interrupted by the presiding judge: "Maître Demange, the floor is yours."

Demange began his address to the court at 7:35 A.M. on Saturday, September 9. His speech would last five hours. "A fine plea," Maurice Paléologue would write, "without concern for gratuitous eloquence or adornment, but solid, clear, prudent, moderate, imbued with honesty, common sense, and pity."[5] An "admirable" plea, Jaurès wrote in *La Petit Republique* of September 10, "because of the decisive light with which it clarified the entire Affair." "A masterpiece of logic and clarity," *L'Aurore* would claim. Labori, seated alongside Demange, admired his fine demonstration. But with Demange's very first words, "I am sure that doubt will at least have entered your minds, and doubt is enough for you to acquit Dreyfus," Labori could sense the abyss that separated him from his elder colleague. Demange accommodated "the very distinguished high officers" and the ministers of war who had followed each other to the stand. Their conviction had impressed him, even troubled him, he said. He was profuse in his homages to the Army, "loyal officers, old warriors, who have shed their blood for their country," and even managed to "understand" those who had attacked Dreyfus through the worst of means. The judges were quite attentive and gradually seemed won over by emotion. Colonel Brogniart was overcome with grief. Commandant de Bréon did not take his eyes off Dreyfus. Commandant Merle, who was said to be hostile to Dreyfus, had tears in his eyes. Demange arrived at the end of his statement:

> You are about to enter the chamber to begin your deliberations, and there, what are you going to ask? Whether Dreyfus is innocent? No! I myself can attest to his innocence, but you yourselves have only to ask whether he is guilty. . . . You will say to yourselves: "We don't know! Someone else may have committed treason; but him, no . . . there are things that he could not have done . . . that handwriting is not his. . . . There is a man over there on the other side of the English Channel who may have committed the

crime. . . ." At that moment, I swear to you, there will be a doubt in your mind. That doubt is enough for me; that doubt is an acquittal!

"That doubt is enough for me!" The words horrified Labori. No, he would not address the Court. He would not speak. Demange finished, addressing the judges, who were plainly overwhelmed: "I will say to all of you: we are French; consequently we commune in our love of our country, our love of the Army." The audience burst into applause. Labori remained frozen, immobile. Upon being prompted by the presiding judge, Carrière replied that he would respond in the afternoon. During the break, Mathieu and Demange implored Labori to change his mind. His address, after all, was already prepared.* "It saddens me to think that after having suffered the hardships for so long," Demange told him, "you will not be there later on for the honor." "We'll see what honor, . . ." mumbled Labori. He would not be persuaded.[7]

When the session resumed, Commandant Carrière took the floor. He read a text prepared for him by his colleague Jules Auffray. He told the judges that they did not need proof, that their inner conviction was enough:

> The law does not ask jurors to account for the ways in which they have reached their beliefs. It does not prescribe rules to which they are obliged to submit their sense of the sufficiency of evidence. It asks them only one question, which comprises the full measure of their duty: Are you intimately convinced?

And in order to encourage the judges to bring in a verdict of guilty, he "proceeded to grease," in Reinach's words, "the slope of iniquity,"[8] by suddenly invoking attenuating circumstances. Exhausted by his efforts of the morning, Demange begged Labori to respond. Labori refused. Whereupon Demange spoke a few words—which were in fact quite insufficient—containing a last homage to the Army:

> Gentlemen,
> Mr. Military Prosecutor, in reading the text of the law, you recalled what we all know: that you owe an account of your judgment only to your conscience and to God. What I also know, and this is my last

* Labori would publish it in the February 1, 1900, issue of *La Grande Revue*. While firmer than Demange's concluding remarks, Labori's were no less measured and moderate. But how can one compare a written text published a year later with words that would have been uttered in the heat of the combat?[6]

word on the subject, is that men of the loyalty and rectitude of these military judges will never raise to the level of proof possibilities and presumptions such as those that have been brought here. Consequently, my last word is the one I have uttered before all of you.

I have confidence in you because you are soldiers.

Possibilities? Presumptions? Labori was indignant. One last time Demange was accommodating the General Staff, flattering the judges. Labori confided to his collaborator Maître Hild: "With the tactics that have been followed, defeat was inevitable. But Demange has just finished off the job."[9]

"Captain Dreyfus, have you anything to add in your defense?" For the first time the presiding judge had acknowledged Dreyfus's rank. Dreyfus, extremely pale, seemed in a state of extreme distress. He said a few words which died away in a hoarse murmur: "I am innocent . . . the honor of the name my children bear. . . . Your loyalty. . . ." He made a gesture, as though he had something to add, and then fell back into his seat. The presiding judge seemed surprised: "Is that all you have to say?" "Yes, my Colonel."

The judges withdrew for their deliberations. It was 3:15 P.M. The wait continued. Both Dreyfus's friends and enemies were speculating how the judges would vote. Three "nos" would be enough to acquit Dreyfus with a minority in his favor. What value could be attributed to the tears of Commandant Merle, who was believed to be hostile? They had seen an overwhelmed Commandant de Bréon staring uninterruptedly at Dreyfus, as if to read his mind: what choice did his conscience dictate? The rumor spread that Colonel Jouaust had treated Dreyfus harshly only to counteract his own conviction. He believed him to be innocent. Captain Parfait and Commandant Profillet were intent on condemning him. But what of Brogniart, who took copious notes during Demange's address? And what of Beauvais, who was said to be vacillating?

At 4:45 P.M. there was a ringing of bells. In front of the podium, a line of gendarmes faced the public. Each door was guarded by an Infantry detachment. The tribunal was called to order. Dreyfus's chair remained empty. In accordance with the Military Code, he was not to be present at the reading of the verdict. Demange, his eyes closed and his hands clasped, seemed to be praying. Labori, his arms crossed, stiffened his posture in order to appear impassive. Amid a crushing silence, Colonel Jouaust began, "In the name of the French people"—the words came slowly—"by a majority of five votes to two, yes, the accused is guilty. By a majority, there are attenuating circumstances." In consequence thereof, the Court-Martial condemned Alfred Dreyfus to ten years of detention. There was no protest, simply an overwhelming and mute pain, some poorly contained sobs. And while the livid judges remained in the courtroom, the crowd flowed out into the street without a disturbance.[10]

Demange was in tears, slumped over in his seat, his head in his hands. He said to Labori: "Go tell him. I can't bring myself to do it." Labori entered the small room reserved for Dreyfus, who upon seeing him, immediately understood. He embraced his lawyer. "Two votes for you, plus attenuating circumstances, is a conviction. But you won't return to Devil's Island, I promise you." Steeling his nerves, Dreyfus attempted to remain impassive: "Take care of my wife and my children," he asked Labori.[11]

In the corridor, the judgment was read to Dreyfus. He stood at attention, rigid as a corpse. For the second time, a court of justice had decided that he had betrayed France. For a second time, he would be stripped of his rank.

Maurice Barrès was about to leave Rennes, like the other journalists, the witnesses, the audience. The human beast, the ball of mauled flesh no longer inspired any emotion in him. The victory of the Army was being celebrated:

> Let us no longer remember the traitor except to love those who punished him. Let us express our gratitude to those officers, the Merciers, the Rogets, the Deloyes, who are now the object of immense popularity, who gave us some magnificent examples of clear French reason. Let us place our trust in this young Army, whose representatives we saw mounting the steps of the podium of the lycée at Rennes. They have intensified and justified our fraternity as Frenchmen. . . .
>
> The national conscience of France has been irritated and ruffled because foreigners both inside and outside of France wanted to "put one over on us." We acknowledge with immense hopefulness the victory of Rennes.[12]

There had nevertheless been two officers voting for acquittal. Commandant de Bréon, "a mystic," according to Barrès, "more a Christian than a soldier, and a man obsessed with scruples." And Colonel Jouaust, the presiding judge, who "had sold his soul to the devil." Barrès claimed that "the price promised for his betrayal was a general's stars,"* and that, now that he had committed his abuse, he would live in remorse. He had

---

* In fact, Colonel Jouaust was retired on January 28, 1900.

betrayed the Army: "The sight of a uniform will hereafter be a living reproach to him." And Barrès related that he had been seen the day after the verdict, destroyed by the dishonor of having voted for acquittal, walking slowly along the banks of the muddied Vilaine, "as though looking for a place in which to drown the life that was killing him."[13]

10

The Incident Is Over

The absurd verdict, which had transformed the judges' hesitations into attenuating circumstances, shocked and saddened the revisionists. But it did not plunge them into despair. It was not, wrote Emile Zola, the "fifth act" which they expected. "It was the sacred terror of the man who watches the impossible come to pass, rivers flowing backward toward their source."* "Iniquity is recoiling," Georges Clemenceau proclaimed in *L'Aurore*. In the first trial, the judges had condemned Dreyfus unanimously. This time there were two votes proclaiming his innocence. The struggle would have to continue, still longer, forever. . . .

But how was the odious sentence to be executed? By sending Dreyfus back to prison? By restaging the ceremony of degradation? Mathieu Dreyfus, when he saw his brother again the day after the conviction, found him ravaged by suffering. "His features were as though convulsed, and the painful grimace of his mouth had become still more pronounced."[1] At the mere mention of degradation, Dreyfus reacted with a violent start: "I will never tolerate a new condemnation. I will not put on my uniform again. They will have to drag me out. They will take me there by force."

The sentence was a source of consternation for the prime mininster, but it had come as no surprise. René Waldeck-Rousseau had expected the worst. A few days before, he had explained to General de Galliffet that he would activate the High Court of Appeal if Dreyfus were convicted and that he would prevent the sentence from being carried out. On September 8, Galliffet had taken the precaution of writing to the prime minister in order to inspire him to prudence: "There is in the Army a prejudice that

* Emile Zola, "Le cinquième acte," *L'Aurore* of September 11.

has taken hold, and taken hold absolutely, against the acquittal of Dreyfus." The government must not enter into combat "against the entire Army frozen into a posture of moral resistance." It was imperative to avoid the following situation: "on one side the entire Army, a majority of the French, and all the agitators; on the other, the cabinet, the Dreyfusards, and the international community."* Waldeck-Rousseau was aware of those difficulties. The day after the verdict, he consulted again with Galliffet, then with Theophile Delcassé, later with the president of the Republic, concerning his plan of initiating a petition to the High Court of Appeal in the interest of the law.† During the day of the 10th, Waldeck-Rousseau received at length Maître Henri Mornard. As experienced jurists, they evaluated the prospects for such a petition, and found them rather slim. And what would be Dreyfus's fate, sent back, after the annulment of the verdict, to a third Court-Martial? Mornard explained to Waldeck-Rousseau that Dreyfus was neither in a physical nor moral state to remain in prison. "A pardon is possible," Waldeck-Rousseau told him simply. No doubt he was already considering it.

On the same day, the judges of the Court-Martial, as though they were not content with their own decision, held a meeting. They unanimously decided to request that Dreyfus be spared a ceremony of degradation, and asked that their request be submitted to the president of the Republic. It was a strange initiative on the part of judges who were thus expressing their wish that their sentence not be carried out. But that request indicated a conceivable direction that might be taken—toward a pardon.

Newspapers the world over expressed their reprobation.[3] Several asked that France be quarantined, that the World's Fair about to open in Paris, "that sinister place," in the spring, be boycotted. There were demonstrations in Antwerp, Milan, Naples, London, and New York. The police intervened to protect the French embassies. France's honor was denounced for the collective crime in relation to which all the other crimes of French history paled into insignificance. There were calls for a revolt of the world's conscience.[4] But it was not such outbursts, which subsided rather swiftly, that worried Waldeck-Rousseau. What concerned him was Dreyfus's fate, and above all the restoration of public tranquillity. He was looking for a solution that would put an end to the Affair, reconcile Frenchmen, and satisfy justice. Would not a pardon mean that Dreyfus was guilty? Would it be a defiance of justice? How would the party of

---

* Letter from Galliffet to Waldeck-Rousseau, September 8, 1899.[2]
† He concluded that the Court-Martial had gone beyond its mandate by trespassing, in the course of its proceedings, the limits to which it had been restricted by the ruling on revision. In particular, there had been extensive discussion of the question of a confession, on which, according to Waldeck-Rousseau, the High Court of Appeal had passed sovereign judgement.

revision, which was venting its distress and its indignation, be able to bear that all should end with a "pardon" granted to an innocent man?

It was Joseph Reinach, in *Le Siècle* of September 11, who publicly proposed an immediate pardon, "shredding a military judgment as soon as it was rendered, before the ink could dry." A pardon would be the executive power's response to an unjust verdict. France, through her government, would be exonerated of the crime. Reinach asked for a pardon, not as a conclusion to the Affair, but as a "transitional measure, a preface to rehabilitation."[5]

Mathieu Dreyfus was quickly convinced. His first duty was to save his brother's life. "Later, we will look for ways to reverse the unjust conviction."[6] Mathieu asked Reinach to see his friend Waldeck-Rousseau, to obtain a pardon. He then saw Clemenceau, who seemed of two minds: "My heart says yes; my reason says no." Jean Jaurès was in a similar state of mind. Bernard Lazare, on the other hand, was favorable to a pardon. They could not let Dreyfus die in prison. What was certain was that "the pardon ended the heroic phase of the Affair." Dreyfus returning to his wife and his children, living peacefully . . . would put an end to the Affair.[7] But what else could be done?

On September 11, Reinach paid a visit to the prime minister. "With my very first words," Reinach would write, "his face brightened."[8] Waldeck-Rousseau was already convinced. But he intuited a number of difficulties. President Emile Loubet, timorous by nature, might fear a disavowal of the judges of Rennes as an affront to the Army. Might they not wait a few weeks. "In a month," Reinach shot back, "a pardon will be no more than a measure enacted out of pity. The pardon of this innocent man must have a different meaning. I am not asking you for a pardon, but for an immediate pardon." Waldeck-Rousseau acquiesced, and gave his word.

The prime minister then undertook to persuade the ministers individually, specifically Galliffet. The latter was already thinking of Dreyfus's pardon as the means toward a general amnesty that would definitively bury the Affair.* The difficulty came from Alexandre Millerand, the most ardent of Dreyfus's defenders in the government, who discovered, as a good jurist, that no pardon was juridically possible unless Dreyfus first withdrew the petition for a revision which Mornard had automatically— and without any hope—had him sign on September 9. The withdrawal of the petition would not deprive Dreyfus of any real succor, but it would

---

* Studying the letters exchanged between Waldeck-Rousseau and Galliffet, Pierre Vidal-Naquet, in his introduction to *Cinq années de ma vie*, shows the objections offered by Galliffet, who invoked the Army, but also the middle class, the Catholics, and the members of Parliament. Vidal-Naquet describes in detail the events surrounding Dreyfus's pardon and the positions taken by each of the actors involved.[9]

force him to take an initiative. Dreyfus would appear to be asking for a pardon, not merely submitting to one. Already the victory cry of the adversaries of the revision could be heard: Dreyfus, in renouncing a request for appeal, was thus acknowledging that he was guilty.

The minister of commerce insisted: Dreyfus would have to withdraw his petition immediately. If by some impossibility the petition were accepted, the Revision Council might well rule without debate, rectify the verdict solely in regard to technicalities by eliminating several elements. It would appear that Dreyfus had been convicted a third time. By this time Jaurès and Clemenceau were openly hostile to a pardon. It did not seem possible to them for Dreyfus to take an initiative without dishonoring himself—and his cause. They had reached a standstill. For in the interim, the president of the Republic, yielding to the entreaties of the prime minister, had given his accord. He would pardon Dreyfus as soon as Dreyfus withdrew his petition.

A meeting was called to debate the insoluble problem, late in the afternoon of September 11 in the office of the minister of commerce on rue de Lille. Millerand insisted vigorously to Mathieu Dreyfus, who was hesitant. "If I were Dreyfus's lawyer," said Millerand, "I would advise him to withdraw his request." Reinach attempted to persuade Mathieu in the gardens of the Ministry: "In two days, if you like, you can be far away with him in some tranquil spot; he'll regain his wife, his children, a measure of happiness. . . ." Mathieu knew that from his prison, Alfred had asked to see his children again. But was it possible that at the end of this long and terrible struggle, Alfred Dreyfus should leave prison asking to be pardoned? Never could such a conclusion to the Affair have been imagined. . . . And how might one assume so frightful a responsibility? Mathieu was overwhelmed, he could not bring himself to make a decision. He demanded that Jaurès and Clemenceau be called in: "I can't decide anything without them."

It was an extraordinary meeting which assembled and opposed the principal combatants of Dreyfus's cause in Millerand's office. For a full hour, with moments of true ferocity, Clemenceau argued that Dreyfus could not withdraw his request for revision and ask for a pardon. "You are humiliating the Republic before the saber. . . . It's his honor that you are asking Dreyfus for." The discussion grew violent. "I do not want to let myself be guided by my sentiments," said Clemenceau, "and yet, this morning I wept upon seeing Mathieu." "That proves," Reinach replied curtly, "that you can't cry twice in the same day."[10] The minister deployed all his talents for persuasion. "What interest do you have in making of us the jailers of an innocent man?" Little by little, yielding to the arguments of Millerand and Reinach, Jaurès consented, on the condition that they promise to continue the fight. "You have the majority," Clemenceau said to Mathieu, who remained unsatisfied. "If you persist in recommending against the withdrawal of the petition, I will not give my consent." Clemenceau reflected for a lengthy moment, then said the words which provided a seal of unanimity: "If I were his brother, I would accept."

By then Jaurès was seated at the minister's desk. He composed in a firm hand the text that Alfred Dreyfus would make public the day after his pardon:

> The government of the Republic grants me my freedom. It means nothing to me without my honor. Beginning today, I shall persist in working toward a reparation of the frightful judicial error whose victim I continue to be. I want all of France to know through a definitive judgment that I am innocent. My heart will be at rest only when there is not a single Frenchman who imputes to me the crime committed by another.

It was decided that Mathieu would leave immediately for Rennes with Jaurès's text and with a letter from Galliffet in order that he be immediately authorized to see his brother. One last time, Millerand reassured him, "I give you my word, Monsieur Dreyfus, that if a pardon is not granted tomorrow, I will tender my resignation." Thus did the government of the Republic and Dreyfus's supporters deliberate in order to thwart the decision imposed by the Army. Yes, the times had changed.

Mathieu took the evening train, arrived at dawn, and rushed to see his brother. It took him more than an hour to persuade Dreyfus to agree. Mathieu was obliged to take up one by one all of Millerand's and Reinach's arguments. Above all, he repeated: you will be free, happy with Lucie and the children. Finally, Alfred gave in. He consented to sign the withdrawal of his petition.[11] Mathieu rushed off to telephone Millerand.

New difficulties arose. With the support of Delcassé, the president of the Republic decided it would be preferable to wait awhile in order to preserve the honor of the Court-Martial and, beyond it, that of the Army. Millerand, who had given his word of honor to Mathieu, offered to resign, as did Waldeck-Rousseau and Galliffet. Negotiations were reinitiated on all fronts. Mathieu, through the intermediary of René Viviani, was obliged to absolve Millerand from his pledge lest the government dissolve. An agreement was reached by compromise: they would wait a week. A doctor was dispatched to examine the convict. Dr. Delbet observed that Dreyfus's condition was very serious, threatened by further detention. The president of the Republic now had a reason to grant immediate pardon. At the ministerial meeting of September 19, Emile Loubet, responding to General de Galliffet's proposal, signed the decree which pardoned Alfred Dreyfus.* That same morning, Auguste Scheurer-Kestner died.

Alfred Dreyfus was free. The following night, the director of the Criminal Investigations department—*La Sureté*—came to fetch him from the prison and to bring him by car, then by train, to Nantes, where Mathieu was waiting for him. At Nantes, the two brothers took the train to Bordeaux, then to Sète. They changed at Tarascon and got off at Avignon. The trip was complicated extraordinarily by police measures taken to prevent the slightest incident. In Bordeaux, the crowd invaded the area surrounding the station and the Hotel Terminus, where Alfred, accompanied by his brother, took his first meal as a free man. The din rose from beneath the windows as Alfred, who was quite calm, contemplated the tablecloth, the reflections of the crystal, the luster of the silver, "all things to which he was no longer accustomed."[12] The two brothers had difficulty getting on the next train without incident. When they arrived in Avignon on September 21 at 7:00 A.M., two cars were waiting for them. They were driven to the home of Dreyfus's sister and his brother-in-law Joseph Valabrègue in Carpentras. Lucie and the children were waiting. He saw Pierre and Jeanne again. The long voyage was over. His martyrdom had lasted four years and ten months.

That same day, September 21, General de Galliffet—without consulting Waldeck-Rousseau—sent the Army orders that were to become famous:

> The incident is over! The military judges, enjoying the respect of all, delivered their judgment in all independence. Without mental reservations, we submitted to their decision. We will also submit to the act which a deep feeling of pity has dictated to the president of the Republic. There can no longer be any question of reprisals of any sort. I thus repeat, the incident is over.
>
> I ask you and, should it be necessary, I would order you to

---

* The decree was preceded by a report to the president of the Republic by the minister of war, who recalled that Dreyfus had renounced any appeal, affirmed respect for the decisions of the courts, and concluded by invoking Dreyfus's state of health and the general interest. "Beyond these considerations, of a nature to arouse our solicitude, still others, of a more general order, tend toward the same conclusion. A higher political interest, the necessity of restoring all its energies have always commanded governments, after difficult crises, concerning certain orders of realities, to resort to measures of clemency and amnesty. The government would be responding poorly to the wishes of the country, which is eager for pacification, if, through its acts, either by its own initiative or by a proposal to Parliament, it did not attempt to remove all traces of a painful conflict. It is up to you, Mister President, through an act of high humanity, to perform this first act in the work of bringing peace, which public opinion demands and the good of the Republic dictates."

forget the recent past and think only of the future. With all my comrades, I shout out with all my heart: "Long live the Army!" which belongs to no party, but only to France.

Irritated by such orders, Waldeck-Rousseau reprimanded his minister and refused to have the text printed in the *Journal Officiel*. The revisionists were furious. The Dreyfus Affair was by no means over. But Galliffet was doing his job. He was appeasing the Army, rendering the government's disavowal of the military tribunal acceptable. Beyond that, he was speaking to public opinion—and preparing the way for amnesty.

During the following days, the pardon—which, at the time, most of Dreyfus's partisans had tolerated, if not quite accepted, out of fidelity or respect—became the occasion of quarrels that would gradually divide the revisionists. On September 14, in *L'Aurore*, Clemenceau had written that he regretted there was not a second ceremony of degradation. "Well as for myself, if I were able to bracket the issue of martyrdom, I should miss— for its fine emblematic quality—the matchless procession. . . . It goes without saying, of course, that they would bring in Esterhazy for the celebration." On September 18, when the rumor of a general amnesty began to spread, Clemenceau was indignant. "They are accomplices. Now they require amnesty. Amnesty for them, to be sure. The innocent man will rest content with his dishonored pardon." And on September 24 the unyielding Dreyfusard summarized his thoughts in extremely harsh terms: "Dreyfus is taking care of Dreyfus, which is fine. As for us, we are thinking of our country succumbing beneath the implacable iniquity of the Roman sect and the imbecile brutality of the sword in its powerlessness against foreign enemies." Clemenceau, Labori, Picquart, and, more hesitantly, Jaurès and Zola, linking irreducibly Dreyfus's pardon and the amnesty that was to follow, would accuse Mathieu, Reinach, and Alfred himself of having cut a deal with Waldeck-Rousseau, the shrewd politician, of having exchanged a pardon for freedom to grant amnesty to Mercier and to the other criminals.[13] "The Dreyfus family" would thereafter be guilty of allowing the Affair to end on terms that were humiliating if not shameful. Unhappy at not having been consulted about the pardon, increasingly embittered with Waldeck-Rousseau, Labori would take his place at the head of the "group of true Dreyfusards, . . . those who had never kissed the flag,"[14] who had ultimately accepted a pardon, since, Labori would write, "it was not given to everyone to be a hero."[15] But he would never tolerate an amnesty that lumped together Picquart and Mercier, and treated identically the heroes and the criminals. Labori, with Picquart's approval, would accuse Reinach of having been Mathieu's "agent," Alfred of having been a toy in the hands of his brother, and all of them of having been manipulated by Waldeck-Rousseau. Later,* Picquart would write in order to sort out the "pure," those who saw in Dreyfus's rehabilitation the triumph of the idea of justice and who thought that "so splendid a cause, that had survived such enormous crimes, should have achieved a decisive victory through the sole force of truth," and the others, "intimidated by the violent conflicts through which they had suffered" and who were "trembling within," or "who, adept in the practice of political and other affairs, told themselves it was better to restrict the arena of combat and strengthen a cabinet composed of friends." For the incorruptible Picquart, the Dreyfus Affair had sunk into the mire of political—and politicians'—maneuvers.

By that time, Alfred Dreyfus would no longer be spared. "The pardon was inseparable from the amnesty. By accepting the former, Dreyfus rendered the latter possible,"[16] according to Picquart, who would not forgive him for consenting to that deal, for having renounced his role as a symbol. Labori would judge his former client as beneath the cause he embodied, incapable of fulfilling the heroic role to which he was destined. As a deportee, Dreyfus could cause displeasure to no one. As a free man, he accumulated the rancor of many. To this one or that, he did not show sufficient gratitude.† He was not a persecuted innocent, protected by his martyrdom, but a man who lived, wrote, and spoke, and all of whose behavior was subject to evaluation. "What is tragic, fatal," Charles Péguy would later write, "is precisely that he does not have the right to be a private individual, that we have the perennial right to call him to account, to call him to the most severe and rigorous of accounts."[18] In accepting the pardon and allowing the amnesty, Dreyfus revealed that he did not have the stature of a "Dreyfusard." And all those close to him, who wanted him not to die in prison, to regain his freedom and, if possible, his happiness, all those were not worthy of having served his cause.

But who indeed was worthy? Picquart denied that quality to Joseph Reinach. Labori denied it to Mathieu Dreyfus. Péguy in turn would deny it to Picquart, Clemenceau, and Jaurès.[19] Jaurès's and Clemenceau's fight for the revision "was merely a squandering of the spirit into politics," the "degradation of an eminent crisis." Picquart's battle was "an impure affair," Jaurès's a politician's betrayal. The only true Dreyfusards were the heroes, the mystics, those who lived as heroes and martyrs the last adven-

* *Gazette de Lausanne*, May 2, 1903.
† When Joseph Reinach met Alfred Dreyfus for the first time in the country near Carpentras, at the Valabrègue home, Dreyfus shook his hand, and without apparent emotion, simply said: "Thank you." "I was proud enough," wrote Reinach, "to find that equally worthy of him and of myself." To others, that much modesty verged on coldness: "they declared empty a heart that was full, but failed to overflow."[17]

ture of the republican mystique: Of that handful the symbol was Bernard Lazare. . . .

Thus, with the passage of time, the Dreyfusards would divide and tear each other apart. For once Dreyfus was free, his cause was no longer a struggle that could blur rivalries and conceal fundamental differences. Each returned to his convictions and to his temperament. Soon the politics of anticlericalism, the aborting of social reforms, the repression of worker agitation, the pacifist propaganda of some and the will to seek revenge of others, would separate those whom the defense of an innocent man, the cause of justice, had temporarily assembled.[20] Issues of caste, prejudice, opinion, and ambition would sweep up into opposing currents the Dreyfusards now bereft of Dreyfus himself. To be sure, some would continue to fight for revision, for the juridical proclamation of Dreyfus's innocence. But those who were still so engaged were rare indeed. Moreover, who could doubt his innocence, and what importance could be attributed to a juridical consecration of what was self-evident? Dreyfus was free, living peacefully. He came to Paris, received friends, occasionally lunched in the city.* As a group the Dreyfusards were no more than war veterans warming over their memories of heroism. Many were nostalgic for the Affair. At bottom, they reproached Dreyfus for leaving Devil's Island, deserting the role which had kept them marching in step together, sharing their courage and their pride. Now, the revolutionaries, the politicians, the mystics, even the faithful, had nothing in common. They were teachers, lawyers, journalists, parliamentarians. They were Radicals, Socialists, Opportunists. They were Jews or Protestants or even Catholics. They were rich and poor. The Dreyfus Affair was over—even the nationalists seemed to be forgetting it.

Waldeck-Rousseau knew it. The time had come to disarm the Dreyfus Affair definitively with a grant of amnesty.

---

* He would frequently participate in the Thursday lunches that attempted to assemble—in the home of the Marquise Arconati-Visconti—leading Dreyfusard personalities. But with the passing of years, absences proliferated.[21]

11

Forgetting

Emile Loubet felt that his task as president of the Republic assigned to him the mission of reconciling the French to the outcome of the Affair. By temperament he was inclined to accommodation. General de Galliffet was meanwhile seeking to reassure the Army even as he was subjecting it to republican discipline. And Waldeck-Rousseau was about to wage a harsh battle against the congregations; to appease the Catholics. Thus all had good reason to want a general amnesty blanketing all infractions linked to the Dreyfus Affair.

Driven by his hatred for Edgar Demange and Waldeck-Rousseau, Fernand Labori imagined that Dreyfus's conviction, the withdrawal of his petition of appeal, the pardon, and the amnesty together had been no more than the perfect execution of a diabolical plan fomented by Waldeck-Rousseau, to which Joseph Reinach, with enthusiasm, and Mathieu Dreyfus, out of resignation, had contributed their aid. The accusation does not appear to be founded. It appears, on the contrary, quite probable that Waldeck-Rousseau did everything—with the exception, perhaps, of forcing the military prosecutor to drop the charges—to facilitate an acquittal he desired without having much confidence that it would come to pass. The prime minister played no role in the signing of the petition of appeal, which was introduced by Dreyfus's lawyers and which in the opinion of a number of jurists consulted at the time, constituted an insurmountable obstacle to any pardon. What was certain, on the other hand, and Reinach was obliged to acknowledge as much, was that "the revision and the reparation of the injustice were rather distant preoccupations for Waldeck-Rousseau."[1] The prime minister's principal concern thereafter was to be the defense of the Republic, with its corollary: the appeasement and reconciliation of the French people.

The time was propitious. After Dreyfus's pardon, the agitation had been brief and extremely localized. There were protests reported only in the South. A few demonstrations were held in Cahors and Alès. In the region surrounding Marseille, the Dreyfusards organized a few meetings which were rather sparsely attended. Most of the departmental assemblies in their autumn sessions approved the way in which the government had settled the Affair.[2] In Paris, the agitation persisted for some time. Through September and October, the insults continued, but the furor was waning. When the trial of Paul Déroulède, Buffet, and Jules Guérin opened before the High Court on November 9, the public showed scant interest.* In vain did the nationalists attempt to rouse public opinion for the trial. *L'Echo de Paris* and *L'Eclair* acknowledged in December that nationalism seemed to be losing steam. On November 19, on the occasion of the launching of Jules Dalou's journal, *Triomphe de la République*, "citizens' groups, unions, professional societies, all officially invited, joined with official agencies to consolidate the success, under the government's leadership, of a public demonstration." It was a joyous Republican celebration, unmarred by any signs of hostility.[3] France, fatigued by its battles, appeared prepared to forget. The World's Fair would bring grandeur to Paris; it was the right time for forgetting.

When the Chambers went into session in November, it was quickly apparent that Waldeck-Rousseau enjoyed the Parliament's confidence. When the Rennes trial was evoked from the tribune, Galliffet found words to reassure the left: "The Army has no right to complain. . . . Never had greater freedom been accorded to a Court-Martial. I will go still further and say: I proceeded with deliberate weakness in not using all my rights and privileges in relation to the military prosecutor."† Waldeck-Rousseau presented his program to the deputies. His plan was no longer merely the defense of the Republic, but the secularization of the State, the old republican battle against the clerical party and the congregations. The prime minister knew that such a speech would regroup the left. In vain did Jules Méline reproach him with laying the groundwork for social revolution: "In granting the Socialists a place, you have lodged the enemy inside the fort on the pretext of defending it." On November 16, Waldeck-Rousseau obtained a large majority of 317 votes to 211. Almost half of the progressivists—including Louis Barthou and Raymond Poincaré—voted for the government. The vote appeared to offer the basis of a new majority.

With the Chamber's confidence, Waldeck-Rousseau revealed to the Senate on November 17 his proposed legislation, entailing amnesty "for all

* When Buffet and Déroulède would be condemned (on January 8, 1900) to ten years of exile, and Guérin to ten years of detention, the severity of the verdicts would go more or less unnoticed.
† In September Galliffet, pursuing his policy of "bringing the Army to heel," had the government issue a decree removing from the High Council of War and the High Commissions of Promotion the prerogative of naming generals. Thereafter such appointments would be under the jurisdiction of the minister alone (decree of September 29, 1899).

criminal acts or misdemeanors connected with the Dreyfus Affair or comprised in any lawsuit relative to any of those acts." A single verdict was to stand, that delivered at Rennes, so that Dreyfus not be deprived of the right to pursue a revision.

That precaution was taken because there were still numerous trials under way that might reactivate the Affair and its passions. The Zola trial was scheduled to be called before the Court of Assizes of Versailles on November 21, and Commandant Henry's widow's suit against Reinach was slated for December 21 in Paris. Lieutenant Colonel Picquart was still liable to appear before the Court-Martial for minor misdeeds.[4] His hope was to be acquitted and to relaunch the Affair. On November 17, he had made public his protest against any amnesty. "I am eager to demonstrate that the charges brought against me are based on fraud and deception. . . . I protest against an amnesty with all my energy. To grant amnesty to a man who has been unjustly accused is to deprive him of the moral reparation which is his right."[5] Picquart demanded a judicial investigation to be initiated against General Gonse "for his sinister role in the affair of the 'Henry forgery' " and Félix Gribelin, from the Section of Statistics, "perennially charged with confidential tasks in the Ministry of War." Georges Clemenceau and Jean Jaurès asked that legal action be initiated against General Mercier, "the first of the criminals," and his appearance before the High Court. They called for retributive verdicts: "Waldeck-Rousseau's ministers," wrote Clemenceau in *L'Aurore* of November 17, "are turning into the bandits' accomplices. They are putting off every act of will, every act of courage, and that is what they call governing France." Despite such protests, all the trials under way were placed in abeyance in expectation of the amnesty—with the exception of Labori's suit against *La Libre Parole*, accused of having "organized" the assassination attempt of Rennes. On December 13, Edouard Drumont, who was incapable of supplying any defense, defaulted and was condemned. Now Henry's widow protested: How had Labori been able to convict Drumont while justice was denied to her in her suit against Reinach?[6]

The projected amnesty law came before the Senate in the course of an extremely orderly parliamentary session. It appeared that with the approach of the first springtime of a new century there was general agreement to observe a "World's Fair truce." Paul Deschanel, reelected president of the Chamber, chose to salute in his tirelessly lyrical style "the noble spirits, the righteous consciences, the generous hearts" which, on both sides, had struggled and suffered. Waldeck-Rousseau had little difficulty defending his legislation before the Senate's legal commission. "It is not a matter of judging or absolving acts already accomplished, but merely of rendering various parties incapable of reviving a painful conflict."* He refused to include in his amnesty the nationalists convicted by the High Court, whose conviction, he claimed, "has assured public order." It was not clear why public order required the impunity of General Mercier.

From Carpentras, where he was slowly recovering, Alfred Dreyfus addressed to the Senate a vigorous protest on March 8, 1900:

> This legislation stifles public actions from which I hoped to see emerge the revelations, perhaps even the confessions, which would have allowed me to bring my case before the High Court of Appeal. It deprives me of my most cherished hope. . . . I asked for no pardon. The right of the innocent is not clemency but justice. . . . No one more ardently than myself wants an allaying of tensions, a reconciliation of all good Frenchmen, an end to the horrible passions whose first victim has been myself. But only justice can allay tensions. Amnesty is a blow to my heart; the sole person to profit from it would be General Mercier. . . . I implore the Senate to accord me my right to the truth, to justice.[7]

Zola also protested: "I want to be judged and to complete my work."[8] Reinach, for his part, railed against the amnesty, but in finely nuanced articles; his ties to Waldeck-Rousseau were well known. There was indignation as well among the anti-Dreyfusards. Edmond Lepelletier expressed the opinion of many of them, who joined the Dreyfusards in rejecting the proposal, in *L'Echo de Paris* of March 14. "The amnesty is perfidious and shameful. It was prepared by Waldeck-Rousseau with the Dreyfus confederates as traitors-in-chief and the apprentice traitors Picquart, Reinach, and Zola. That trio of scoundrels is sweating with fear at the thought that the amnesty might be rejected." But such protests left the public indifferent.[9] At the opening ceremony of the World's Fair, Emile Loubet celebrated the reconciliation of all Frenchmen as well as concord among peoples. Waldeck-Rousseau saluted in the event "testimony to our regained moral tranquillity." And he pursued his course with renewed vigor.

But on May 28, an incident in the Chamber came close to ruining his efforts. A confused debate had called into question the acts of a number of officers. General de Galliffet had courageously shielded his subordinates at the risk of receiving some of the blows himself.[10] Waldeck-Rousseau in

---

* "I refuse to amnesty the past," Waldeck-Rousseau had proclaimed from the tribune of the Senate during the debate over the dispossession law (*supra*, p. 377). But now he was prime minister. . . .

turn mounted the tribune and for once his words would betray him. He spoke of "an officer's felony." The right and a part of the center rose and began shouting in protest. Perhaps feeling that he was being disavowed by the prime minister, his friend Galliffet left the auditorium in a state of extreme irritation. Pale and visibly mortified, Waldeck-Rousseau asked to explain what he had meant. He spoke of his affection for Galliffet and his respect for the Army. There was a hasty attempt to find Galliffet, but he had already written his letter of resignation, invoking reasons of health. That brutal exit was admirably suited to his temperament; for months, Galliffet had ceased to conceal how unbearable political life was becoming for him. He was exhausted and dreamed of returning to private life. The government was barely rescued through an intervention by Léon Bourgeois, stigmatizing the maneuvers of the right to weaken the Republic.[11] Waldeck-Rousseau immediately replaced Minister of War Galliffet with General Louis André. The new general, as courteous as he was obstinate, an alumnus of the École Polytechnique who thirsted for science and method, and who had so little the bearing of a warrior that he always seemed to be a civilian in uniform, had the reputation of being an intransigent republican and a notorious anticleric. Upon being appointed by Galliffet the previous year to command an infantry division in Paris, he had forbidden the reading of clerical and anti-Semitic newspapers in the barracks.[12] André did not have Galliffet's prestige, but was at least able to pursue the efforts of the aged marquis, who had returned to his *château* and his loves.

The proposed law was debated in the Senate on June 1 and 2. On the eve of the proceedings, Zola sent to the senators an impassioned letter:

> You had done no more than change judges; now you are being asked to say that there will be no more judges. . . . In being sent off back to back with bandits, we are being sullied. . . . We are not the ones who are starting up the Affair afresh and using it to suit our electoral needs, drumming it into the ears of the crowd until they are dazed. . . . What we want is for the Affair to be over. I am writing this letter quite simply for the immense honor of having written it. I am doing my duty and I doubt that you are doing yours.

But was anyone still listening to Zola? Everyone knew that the amnesty would be voted through. But there was now a further insult to all those defending Dreyfus's cause because it seemed to them an affront to justice; by a margin of 700 to 300, General Mercier had been elected senator from the Loire-Inférieure on January 28, 1900. Once elected, Mercier had studiously avoided going to the Senate. He made his first appearance there during the debate over amnesty. As Ludovic Trarieux, who was speaking, described in legal terms the odious effects of an amnesty—Zola and Reinach transferred from the criminal court to the civil court, Picquart deprived of the judgment he had been seeking, and above all the principal culprits left unpunished—Mercier, the most guilty of them all, listened, as motionless as a dead man. He asked to be allowed to speak. That much bravery or cynicism was a surprise, he was listened to in silence. He argued that what he had "done in 1894, he had done with the deep-seated conviction that he was rendering a service to his country." He added that he would not discuss the amnesty, "since it was of no interest to him." And he returned to his seat, impassive again.

Waldeck-Rousseau responded. Mercier's intervention, the elevation of the subject, and the confidence he had in his own political strength opened up large vistas to his talent. Waldeck-Rousseau paid homage to those who refused the amnesty because such revolts of conscience were "among the most legitimate reflexes of the human soul." But the amnesty, he said, "does not judge, nor does it accuse, nor does it exonerate, nor does it condemn. It chooses not to analyze and it draws its inspiration from the public interest." He explained why on the morrow of the verdict in Rennes "the government had to determine wherein lay its duty from the point of view of humanity and from that of politics as well"; how it had no other solution, in its desire to efface all the traces of so painful a conflict, than a pardon for the innocent man and an amnesty for the country. And without acknowledging Mercier, he demolished him in his conclusion:

> To those who think this law too indulgent and that we risk debilitating the Nation in the sentiment of its responsibilities, I shall limit myself to observing that there are punishments more severe than some that are meted out by law, and that the justice of courtrooms is not the only justice. There is another, formed by public awareness, which traverses the ages, is the teaching of peoples, and is already entering into history.

Overwhelmed by an address that raised the debate to such heights, by a vote of 231 to 32, the Senate quickly passed the amnesty law.

The Chamber delayed its examination of the proposed law and the summer recess ensued with the World's Fair in full swing, and Paris, which had become the capital of Europe, abounding with spectacles and celebrations. The festivity saddened Clemenceau: "There are shows everywhere. . . . Repentant revolutionaries are discovering that there are occasions for joy within the social order. . . . Everything illuminated the sound of brass, dancing. It is the Republic celebrating its own death."[13] Rather, it was enjoying its life. The World's Fair projected the image of a hardworking France that was taken with technology and science, but also joyous, alive to the arts and all forms of amusement. On September 22, to commemorate the anniversary of the proclamation of the First Republic, twenty thousand mayors, deputy mayors, and municipal delegates were gathered at the Tuileries for an immense banquet presided over by Emile Loubet. The president of the Republic spoke of reconciliation and concord. "This anniversary is a festival of patriotism as well as a festival of liberty." Beneath the lights, liberty, patriotism, and concord danced together. Who could oppose a general pardon?

Meeting in Paris, the International Socialist Congress discussed endlessly the Millerand "case": the problem, that is, posed by the participation of a Socialist in a bourgeois government.[14] Jules Guesde raised the question: "Can a Socialist be simultaneously an agent of conservation and of social revolution?" Jean Jaurès defended Millerand's participation courageously:

> Yes, the Socialist party is a party of sustained and profound opposition to the entire capitalist system. That is, all our acts, all our thoughts, all our propaganda, and all our votes ought to be aimed at the most rapid suppression possible of capitalist iniquity. But because the Socialist party is fundamentally and essentially a party opposed to the entire social system, it does not follow that we should not distinguish between the different bourgeois parties and the different bourgeois governments that succeed each other.
>
> To be sure, society today is divided between capitalists and proletarians; but at the same time, it is threatened by the offensive return of all the forces of the past, by the offensive return of feudal barbarism and the omnipotence of the Church; and it is the duty of Socialists, whenever republican freedom is at stake, when freedom of thought is threatened, when the ancient prejudices which revive the racial hatreds and the atrocious religious quarrels of past centuries seem to be being reborn, it is the socialist's and proletarian's duty to march with those fractions of the bourgeoisie that do not wish to return to the past.[15]

Finally a compromise was found: it was a matter, it seemed, "not of principles, but of tactics." But the Millerand ministry was obliged to harden its positions. In October Millerand spoke at Lens on the right to strike, obligatory arbitration, and salary, "which will be no more eternal than the systems of slavery and serfdom were." He announced the evolution of private property toward social property. Louis Barthou, the leader of the progressivists (i.e., the center), responded: "One does not accord socialism a place without incurring serious risks . . . the collectivist doctrine, were it to succeed, would mean the triumph of inequality in servitude and the most detestable of tyrannies. The country cannot pay for the defeat of nationalism at such a price." Many Radicals approved his harsh language. With the Affair over, was the governmental coalition about to come undone? But Waldeck-Rousseau delivered a major address at Toulouse on October 28 in order to reassemble his troops, and it was the politics of anticlericalism that provided him with a vehicle. He spoke to the hearts of the Radicals and Socialists. He initiated an attack against the teaching congregations and showed the Church herself to be increasingly "threatened by the Chapel." He denounced the political organization of the congregations, their immense wealth, "the peril of a growing mortmain that threatened the principle of the circulation of goods." The harvest he was preparing would surprise Waldeck-Rousseau himself . . . but for the while he retained his majority.[16]

There was no longer any talk of the Affair. Alfred Dreyfus, after spending the winter and the spring at Carpentras, settled in Switzerland, at Coligny on the banks of Lake Geneva. He was attempting to regain his strength. While Joseph Reinach wrote his history of the Affair, Dreyfus was beginning to assemble his recollections with the intention of publishing them. They saw each other in September in Coligny, where Reinach told Dreyfus that the amnesty would certainly be voted through during the fall session. "We have to remain alert," Reinach advised, "prowling around the revision. Chance, one day, will come to our aid."[17]

By the fall, Dreyfus's presence in Switzerland had become the occasion of malevolent remarks. Comments like "Esterhazy in London, Dreyfus in Switzerland" seemed to condemn the two together.[18] Mathieu thought it better for his brother to return to Paris, which he did at the beginning of the winter, moving into the home of his father-in-law, Hadamard, on rue de Chateaudun. When Mathieu informed Labori of his brother's arrival, the lawyer's only reaction was an unpleasant remark: "You have no doubt apprised M. Waldeck-Rousseau." And he wrote in his notes, "It is clear that this return is designed—in accord with the government—to assure the passage of the amnesty law."[19]

The estrangement was virtually complete. Labori saw everywhere the concerted action of Demange, Waldeck-Rousseau, and Reinach, for whom, he felt, Mathieu Dreyfus remained only an instrument. He asked the family to break with Demange, something they were neither capable nor desirous of doing. Labori and Mathieu met on December 14. They had nothing more in common but memories. Labori showered the Dreyfus family with so many reproaches, that Mathieu, beside himself, finally exploded: "All is over between us. Au revoir, Monsieur." In a long letter to Mathieu, written on the evening of their break, Labori felt impelled to send him an account of the incident, which ended as follows:[20]

The amnesty "covering all deeds relating to the Dreyfus Affair" is perhaps the most deplorable and scandalous measure that has been taken in three years. Especially since it is the work, I'm not saying of the republican party, but of the government of republican defense which the Dreyfus Affair brought to power. Certainly, no one more than myself, if I were simply considering my personal interest, would derive material advantage from amnesty. But to allow the passage of this law of iniquity, impotence, and deception without doing everything possible to oppose it, and whatever, moreover, the result of such effort be, seems to me not only an unjustifiable attitude, but an unpardonable error.

Then, evoking the past, the manner in which he was prevented from pleading at Rennes, the reserve in which he remained, all the same, a "slave to his professional duty," Labori concluded:

You have given me my freedom today. To the extent that there still remain things for me to do, I will proceed on my own schedule and under my own responsibility; and I will be all the more excessively devoted to the idea of justice for which I have always been ready to incur all sacrifices. I will not conceal from you the sadness that I feel at the end of so many efforts. May the emotion you caused me today prepare me a little more for the ordeals of the future. I expect still worse. No man, I believe, can flatter himself with knowing the limits of ingratitude.
It is my honor, Monsieur, to salute you.
Labori, 14 December, Midnight.

Mathieu answered him with a letter, still cordial in tone, intent on correcting the "errors" of Labori's account, but seeking to efface all memory of the incident.[21]

15 December 1900

My dear friend,

I will continue to call you so every chance I have, since that designation corresponds to the feelings that I have had, that I still have for you, and if yesterday I allowed myself to call you "Monsieur," it was because I was seized with an extreme anger. . . . It seems to me that a simple divergence of views should not have caused such an incident. I was perhaps wrong to respond to you as I did. The gratitude, the longstanding affection that I bear you should have led me to overlook the bitterness, unfairness, and violence of some of your words. But I myself was a bit nervous, and the extreme tension of my nerves, so long stretched toward a single aim, has made me more sensitive than I thought. And then, too, what exasperates me is your persistent belief in clandestine relations with the government, despite my statements to the contrary.

But let us leave aside such vain recriminations. In what I said yesterday, I engaged no one but myself. My brother has nothing to do with this incident, which concerns me alone.

Rest assured, dear Friend, of my most cordial sentiments.
Mathieu Dreyfus

Alfred Dreyfus himself intervened in order to try to ward off a quarrel that was causing him great sadness. He wrote to Labori, "Dear Lawyer and Friend, . . . I would be quite happy to have a frank, clear, and complete conversation with you on the subject." He asked to be received by Labori, who let him know that he was about to leave on a trip. On December 20 Labori answered, refusing the meeting, because Alfred's letter "did not contain any expression of regret" concerning the incident that had opposed Mathieu and himself. Alfred Dreyfus insisted on December 20:[22]

I deeply regret that we have not yet been able to talk together; I regret it all the more in that I have a deep admiration for the courage and talent you showed in the terrible circumstances that occurred, I continue to count on your admirable loyalty, and I thought that if at times tactical differences might present themselves, there would never arise any disagreement between us.

I hope then, dear Sir, that you will be willing to accord me this meeting, convinced as I am that after we will have talked together, our union will be all the stronger.

Labori finally agreed to the meeting on the condition that it take place in Colonel Picquart's presence. It was a strange and painful meeting in which Alfred Dreyfus listened to the reproaches of his lawyer in the presence of Picquart, acting as arbitrator and witness. But Labori refused to listen. "The break has occurred. As a man, my devotion to you is intact.

As a lawyer, I can no longer continue giving you my advice." Dreyfus
protested, "Such a break would be an abominable thing." He took Labori's
hand. "Look, that's not your last word, is it? Look, stay, do it for me, do it for
me." He uttered those last words, according to Picquart, who was keeping
minutes at Labori's request, "in a very odd insinuating tone."* Mathieu's
version was different. It was Picquart who, upon realizing that the divergence of views was irremediable, put an end to the meeting. "It's best to
leave it at that. Let each do his duty in his own way."[24] Dreyfus left. Labori
noted that he wept in the vestibule. Alfred Dreyfus would write two more
letters to Labori, assuring him in the last "of the eternally grateful memory
of your admirable devotion."[25] They would never see each other again. A
year later Labori would also quarrel with Reinach, when the lawyer,
editor-in-chief of *La Grande Revue*, would break with his collaborator
Joseph Cornély, a circumstance which Reinach, a stockholder in the *Revue*
and a friend of Cornély, would interpret as an issue of principle. Reinach
would withdraw the files he had given Labori, who would draw up a
detailed account of fees paid and fees due, debts incurred because of the
Affair—a creditor at the end. Their friendship was thus to end amid
sordid calculations.[26] Labori would also break with Bernard Lazare. Picquart would refuse Demange's hand, and the lawyer would long nurse the
wound. Later on he would refuse to shake Mathieu's hand. Thus was the
heroic crew of the days of combat and turmoil to disperse—amid the most
mediocre of resentments. On December 4, 1901, Labori would explain in
Le Journal what Captain Dreyfus, in his eyes, had become:

> In accepting his pardon, Alfred Dreyfus did in no way acknowl-
> edge his guilt. For reasons it is not up to me to judge, he preferred
> his immediate freedom to the uninterrupted, heroic continuation
> of the effort to achieve his juridical rehabilitation. Although he
> owes his salvation solely to a group of men joined by their interest
> in justice for all and concerned above all with pursuing a labor of
> social progress, it is his right as a private individual. An individual
> can place himself above the justice of men, and who would deny
> that Alfred Dreyfus was well placed to find such justice contempt-
> ible? He may—satisfied with the judgment of his conscience and
> whatever be the interest of all—prefer his freedom to his legal
> honor. But in so doing he is acting as an isolated and independent
> individual, not as a man gripped by humane concerns and aware of
> the beauty of social duty. He is acting purely as an individual, not as

* This singular "account by Colonel Picquart of the meeting with Dreyfus on 22 December
1900" may be found in Labori's handwritten notes.[23]

a member of the human collective, in solidarity with his fellow men. At the same time, however great the role he played may have been, he is no longer representative of anything.*

While such cruel breaks were being consummated among the Dreyfusards, Waldeck-Rousseau pursued without difficulty the vote for the amnesty law in the Chamber. To Drumont he refused the amnesty accorded to Déroulède and Guérin. "It would be an act not of Republican defense, but Republican defection." When a deputy asked him to exclude Mercier from the amnesty, he replied that "the amnesty was made for the guilty, whoever they might be, but on one condition: that the public interest require it." He felt close to the amnesty's adversaries: "I will not condemn impulses which I myself have experienced. . . . But there are times when it is necessary to turn toward the future and look less where guilt seems to lie than at a state of things that produced such guilt."[28] The amnesty would put an end to "that state of crisis which is the vital medium in which only nationalism can thrive." During the night of December 18 to 19 the law was passed by a vote of 155 to 2 in an open ballot which was demanded by the right. The wording of the legislation, revised by the Chamber, was returned to the Senate. One more time, Trarieux asked that Picquart be exempted from the amnesty, even as he paid homage to the prime minister's "protective and benevolent intention." Waldeck-Rousseau refused and the law was finally adopted by an overwhelming majority of 194 to 10. It was a major victory for Waldeck-Rousseau, but a victory that entailed few risks since on all sides the Affair seemed to have been forgotten. Throughout the month of December, Rochefort published numerous venomous articles in the hope of starting up the conflict anew; but there was little response.[29] The prime minister knew that he was satisfying public opinion, which was by now fatigued with the endless battle that grew ever more complex. And with Dreyfus free, what had the Affair become if not a quarrel among jurists, a focus of vain and outmoded agitation?

But for Colonel Picquart the Affair was still alive and painful. Since it was announced that his appeal to the Council of State in protest of the decision removing him from the military would in all probability be well received and that the government was even thinking of giving him a post of command, Picquart abruptly withdrew his appeal to the courts. And on December 25, 1900, he advised Waldeck-Rousseau, in a courteously insult-

* He would publish several articles in the same tone on his former client in response, it appears, to attacks from Bernard Lazare that were allegedly reported by a journalist in *L'Echo de Paris*.[27]

ing letter that he also had published, that he did not wish to receive anything from the present government.[30] He would appeal to history.[31]

A day will come when the truth will be understood by all and when it will be realized that under the pretext of saving the Republic, you misled public opinion through a more or less justified diversion against your political enemies, while you left unpunished the criminals who were the true enemies of the country and whom you did not dare to touch because, no doubt, you would have been obliged to strike too strongly against crimes that were too great. And during this time, our prisons are filled with people whose greatest offense is not having means of subsistence!

Zola, sad and dignified, wrote to Loubet, "I have fulfilled my role as honestly as I could, and I now am entering definitively into silence."[32] Clemenceau fulminated against a politics of cowardice and abandonment. And since Henri Rochefort, in his articles, was reviving the legend of the annotated bordereau, Alfred Dreyfus wrote to Waldeck-Rousseau on December 26, 1900, a letter in which he recalled his innocence in vigorous terms and requested a judicial inquiry:

My innocence is absolute; I will pursue the juridical recognition of that innocence through revision until my dying breath. I am no more the author of the bordereau annotated by the Emperor of Germany, which is no more than a forgery, than of the original authentic bordereau, which was written by Esterhazy. With the exception of Henry, all the principals responsible for my unjust conviction are still alive. I have not been stripped of all my rights. I retain the right of every man, which is to defend his honor and to have the truth proclaimed. I retain the right, then, Mister President, of asking you for an investigation, and I have the honor of soliciting it.

But Waldeck-Rousseau had ceased listening to such voices, which brought with them the risk of perturbing the salutary silence. He did not go to the effort to respond to either Dreyfus or Picquart. So ended the year 1900, in which a century began and the Affair ended. Commandant Esterhazy was living in London and peddling his secrets to whoever would buy them. Withdrawn in his manor, General de Boisdeffre was sinking into depression. General Gonse had retired. Commandant du Paty de Clam was pursuing his desire to sink into oblivion. General Mercier sat alone and scorned in the Senate. Henry alone had paid for his crimes—by his own

himself out in his efforts and was visibly weakened.* He also claimed that
he had accomplished the program that he had traced out upon coming to
power, and that a political individual ought not to perpetuate himself at
the head of the government. His Ministry, which came close to lasting no
longer than a day, had remained for three years. No cabinet in the Third
Republic was to know a comparable longevity.

Léon Bourgeois, then Henri Brisson, refused the difficult task of
succeeding him. Perhaps it was on Waldeck-Rousseau's recommendation
that the president of the Republic offered the task of forming a government to an obscure senator from the Charente, Dr. Emile Combes, who
had played an important role in the debate over associations. Born in Tarn
to a family of poor artisans, Dr. Combes was a diminutive old man, was
very alert, very authoritarian, enamored of combat, as stubborn in his
hatreds as in his friendships. In Pons, the city of his wife's birth, he had
enjoyed an unexceptional and discreet political career. He had been
educated at a seminary, yet anticlericalism had become his religion. He was
about to make of it, for three years, the policy of France.

Eight years had elapsed since the first Dreyfus trial, four since the Zola
trial. The actors of the protracted tragedy had begun to disappear.[11]
Auguste Scheurer-Kestner, the purest of politicians, was first to pass away.
Edouard Grimaux, the man of science whose involvement was rooted in an
intransigent conscience and a scruple for truth, had died on May 2, 1900.
General Billot, the former minister of war, had gone into an unrelenting
decline, as though the source of life within him had dried up. Ludovic
Trarieux and Bernard Lazare were each afflicted with cancer which would
prove fatal. On September 30, 1900, Zola and his wife lit a fire in the
fireplace of their bedroom in their small townhouse on rue de Bruxelles.
Mme. Zola awoke during the night, went into the next room to breathe
some fresh air, then returned to bed. In the morning the door would have
to be broken down. Mme. Zola was gasping in the bed. Emile Zola was
stretched out, dead from asphyxiation, his body still warm.†

Alfred Dreyfus came to meditate before the body of the man to whom
he owed so much. Mme. Zola and the prefect of police urged him not to
attend the funeral lest there be demonstrations. He hesitated, but Anatole
France let it be known that he would not speak at Zola's grave if Dreyfus
were absent. The last night, from October 4 to 5, Dreyfus kept vigil with

* Stricken with cancer of the pancreas, he was to take to bed in December 1903 and begin a
painful period that would end with his death on August 10, 1904.
† Rochefort and Drumont would write that he had committed suicide. Certain of Dreyfus's
supporters would maintain that he had been murdered. A judicial investigation would be
initiated that failed to turn up any conclusive evidence.

Mme. Zola. The burial took place on October 5. As a sign of the changing times, the government was represented by the minister of public education, who paid homage not only to the great writer, but to the courageous citizen. And in the name of Zola's friends, Anatole France delivered at his grave a farewell speech that has remained famous:

> Given the obligation which befalls me to recall the struggle waged by Zola on behalf of justice and truth, is it possible for me to remain silent concerning those men so passionately bent on destroying an innocent man and who, feeling themselves doomed were he to be saved, attacked him with the desperate daring of fear? How might I remove them from your sight when it is mine to show you Zola rising up, weak and unarmed, before them? Can I silence their lies? That would amount to silencing his heroic rectitude. Can I silence their crimes? I would be silencing his virtue. Can I silence the outrage and the slander with which they pursued him? I would be silencing his recompense and his honors. Can I silence their shame? I would be silencing his glory. No, I will not speak.
>
> Let us envy him: he has honored his country and the world with an immense body of work and a great deed. Let us envy him; his destiny and his courage combined to endow him with the greatest of fates. He was a moment in the conscience of humanity.

Alfred Dreyfus attended the ceremony. Not a word, no sign of hostility, marred the tribute.

13

On Punctured Drums

Mathieu Dreyfus now divided his time between Paris and Mulhouse, where he had resumed control of the family's business. Alfred Dreyfus lived alternately in Paris and in Switzerland. Neither ceased looking for the "new element" that would allow them to initiate a second revision procedure to reverse the judgment of the Rennes Court-Martial.

Lieutenant Colonel Picquart suspected Dreyfus of stalling for time, "shielding himself behind the specious pretext that it was difficult to find a new element,"[1] and Fernand Labori continued to maintain that the two brothers were indifferent to a revision. The fact was that the disastrous verdict in Rennes did seem to counsel prudence. Henri Mornard and Edgar Demange, who knew the scrupulous formalism of the High Court of Appeal, advised against filing any request if there was the slightest risk of failure. In order to open up the path, new elements, unknown to the judges of Rennes, would have to be discovered. But at Rennes it seemed all the facts had already been entered into the proceedings.

Mathieu Dreyfus was convinced that General Mercier's unscrupulous maneuver in the Paris trial of 1894 had been renewed at Rennes; he believed that secret documents had been shown to the judges during their deliberations. Those, no doubt, that Mercier had claimed to have in his possession and which he had not dared to produce at the open session. According to the existing rumor, which consisted of confidential information bruited about in various salons and newsrooms, the documents were letters from the emperor of Germany referring to "his agent" Dreyfus, and above all the "imperial bordereau," the bordereau on heavy paper stock, annotated by Wilhelm II, of which the bordereau on tracing paper was merely a copy. That "annotated bordereau," it was said, had been returned to the German embassy during the first trial by Casimir-Périer, then president of the Republic, in order to avoid war. Photographs of it were alleged to have been taken. Several persons claimed to have seen them.

It did not suffice for Mathieu Dreyfus to establish that photos of the annotated bordereau were being circulated.* He also had to prove that they had been presented to the judges during their deliberations. He needed to question the judges.[2] Commandant de Bréon and Colonel Jouaust, who had voted for acquittal, were locked into absolute silence. Mathieu thought of sounding out Commandant Merle, whose confidences might be of interest since it appeared that at Rennes he had changed his mind at the last moment, no doubt in the course of the final deliberation. A friend of Mathieu's, Dr. Dumas, proposed to approach the commandant through mutual friends. The meetings took place in Avignon and Montpellier during October 1902. Dumas felt he had culled a sizable harvest, which he offered in a letter of November 12, 1902, to Mornard. He said that he had pressured the former judge with his questions. "So it's true then, the abominable story of a bordereau bearing annotations

---

* For Mathieu Dreyfus, the annotated bordereau was itself a forgery, fabricated on orders from the General Staff, by Henry or someone else, during the period that false documents were being collected to indict Dreyfus.

signed by the Emperor of Germany, a bordereau on thick paper in which Dreyfus would be named in the notes?" Merle was alleged to have appeared "dumbfounded," "frightened," pleading "We must not talk about such matters, they could resurface . . . don't talk about it, I don't want to discuss it." But Merle would later deny such a conversation. He would say that he felt that Dumas was baiting him to speak about the Affair. "I did not confide the slightest thing to him. . . . I did not say a word to him on the subject of the Rennes trial."[3] The attempt thus ended in failure, but it succeeded in leaving Mathieu and Alfred with the conviction that the annotated bordereau had been the secret proof Mercier and his supporters had held throughout the Rennes trial and had introduced into the final deliberations.[4]

Mathieu and Alfred Dreyfus, Mornard, and Demange concerted with their friends, with Trarieux, with Clemenceau, and with Leblois as to how best to relaunch the Affair. But it was Jaurès, who had been elected deputy from Carmaux in May, who would intervene most decisively. Jaurès thought that the Combes government—of which he was a principal supporter in Parliament—must be made to feel that the republican party was in favor of revision not to inflame passions, but to establish the truth and to put an end to the Affair. Jaurès wanted to bring the Affair before both Chambers. He would take as his pretext the debate over the "invalidation" of Deputy Gabriel Syveton, an impassioned adversary of Dreyfus whose election was being contested by the left. He would obtain from the government an investigation—notably on the subject of the annotated bordereau—that would clear the way toward revision. Clemenceau, who was consulted on the plan, at first disapproved, and then allowed himself to be convinced. Jaurès paid a visit to Waldeck-Rousseau, who gave him ample advice on questions of law and the usefulness of prudence.[5] He then informed the prime minister, who would have preferred not to add to the difficultes of the struggle against the congregations. But Combes, convinced of Dreyfus's innocence and combative by nature, ended up giving his agreement. Henri Brisson, who was also informed, promised his support. Thus did Jean Jaurès prepare his reentry into Parliament. Joseph Reinach evoked his rationale as follows: "As an artist, he could envision the fine speech resounding around the world and throughout history as well as the handsome gesture. As a politician, he calculated the consequences of his act: nationalism definitively defeated, dishonored, and what a blow to the heart of the ecclesiastical parties!"[6] And "with his crude schoolboy's handwriting," Jaurès began to write the immense address that would open the road to a second revision. "On February 6," wrote Alfred Dreyfus, "Jaurès developed for me the outline of his speech from the tribune of the Chamber. It was perfect."[7]

Intervening in the debate over Syveton's election, Jaurès occupied the tribune during the entire session of April 6, 1903, and for more than two hours on April 7. After saying a few words about Syveton, he began an implacable demonstration of Dreyfus's innocence and the crimes committed to send and keep him in prison. Hour after hour, he pursued his course, resisting interruptions, indifferent to insults, as though borne on by an irresistible force. He interspersed his address with lyrical appeals to justice and truth, as well as accusations against the Church, a tactic that allowed him to unite the republican majority. "The immense majority of the secular and regular clergy considered that the acquittal of the Jew convicted by the authorities would be a defeat for the Church itself and for the principle of authority." Speaking of Henry's confession, Jaurès read from General de Pellieux's letter asking Godefroy Cavaignac for authorization to retire: "Duped by men without honor, having lost confidence in those of my superiors who had me working on forgeries. . . ."* At that point, Brisson interrupted Jaurès. Had they prepared the presentation together?† "That letter from General de Pellieux, you say, is dated August 31, 1898?" "Yes," answered Jaurès. "As prime minister at that time," shouted Brisson, "I declare that the government was not informed of its existence." The left exploded in applause. Cavaignac, more livid than usual, asked to speak. Amid the storm raging on the left, he spoke with the same authoritarian tone he had used as minister. He claimed full responsibility for the events that had taken place under his administration. "I bring to the men on whom suspicion has been cast, Gonse, Boisdeffre, the superiors who had instructed Pellieux to work on forgeries, the testimony of my total trust." Whereupon Brisson and Cavaignac proceeded to settle old scores. "Count the amnesty among your blessings, M. Cavaignac. For had it not been voted through, you would be deserving of an indictment." Dramatically, Brisson evoked Jean Baptiste Cavaignac's tomb in the Montmartre cemetery. "I wonder whether the bronze figure is not about to rise before you and shout, 'You are no longer in the Republic, you are no longer part of our lineage.'" Cavaignac, attempting to respond, was interrupted, insulted by the left. "You sent the razor to Henry," Aristide Briand yelled. "If this were the Convention," shouted Deputy Breton, "you would be guillotined."

The next day, Cavaignac mounted the tribune and took the offensive. He attacked the revisionist enterprise, the resurrection of the syndicate,

* The text quoted by Jaurès is not quite precise. See *supra* p. 335.
† That in any event is what Dreyfus related.[8] "Brisson was to create an incident in the Chamber during Jaurès's intervention in order to ask Cavaignac how it was that he, Brisson, the head of the government at the time, had not been kept informed by his minister of war in the midst of a major crisis."

and above all the policies of the coalition. His passion and his hatred were so sincere that they attained a measure of furious eloquence.* "Our conscience is worth every bit as much as yours . . . you are not judges. You are not here as servants of the truth: you are the slaves of your passions. . . . Your enterprise is a cause of disorganization and national renunciation. . . ." The Socialists jeered him. He stared them down. "You actually think that we will assume the posture of defendants in your presence? Are you all cowards like M. Jaurès?" "M. Cavaignac," shouted back Jaurès, "has aroused in me no other emotion than contempt." The leftists had gone too far. By the end of Jaurès's major address, General André, the minister of war, had intervened in the name of the government to accede to Jaurès's request. "The government, eager to facilitate the search for the truth in this matter, fully accepts the charge of proceeding administratively with an investigation." The intended aim had been achieved without any difficulty; and no doubt Jaurès and Emile Combes had reached an agreement before the proceedings began. But the left, carried away in its fervor, had made numerous errors. It unseated Syveton, even though he had been elected by a large majority. Jaurès—who had obtained satisfaction—wanted to press his advantage. He offered a motion whereby the Chamber would acknowlege the government's declarations, a motion which Combes accepted. But Alexandre Ribot, the former prime minister, ascended the tribune and delivered a hypocritical speech in which he admonished Cavaignac, Jaurès, and Combes as well, whom he reproached with simply following Jaurès blindly. Combes, out of prudence, broke with Jaurès's motion, which was rejected by the Assembly who declared "the Chamber confident in the government and resolved not to allow the Dreyfus Affair out of the realm of the judiciary."

Did the Chamber's vote mean that the inquest promised a few moments earlier by General André had been rejected? Over the following days, there were numerous discussions among Buisson, Reinach, Mornard, Clemenceau, and Jaurès. How was the Assembly's vote to be understood and respected? Should Alfred Dreyfus immediately ask the government to initiate the investigation offered by André from the tribune of the Chamber? The prime minister saw Francis de Pressensé, who saw Dreyfus. Let Dreyfus be patient, advised Combes, and wait a few days. . . . Or was Dreyfus to present the minister of justice with a petition for revision? . . . Mornard, perennially prudent, counseled against doing anything while the ministers continued to debate the exact bearing of the motion passed by the Chamber. But Alfred Dreyfus, tired of waiting, decided to take action at the risk of displeasing the government and

---

* "He carried death within him," wrote Joseph Reinach. Cavaignac was suffering from liver cancer and he knew that he was doomed.[9]

Jaurès, who would reproach his initiative. He sent the minister of war a request for an investigation based on new elements that had come to his attention. The prime minister was in an awkward situation. He chose a rather subtle option: at Dreyfus's request, General André would proceed not with the administrative inquest proposed by Jaurès from the tribune, but with a "personal" investigation intended to serve the cause of truth.* The minister of war would begin his investigation after the close of the parliamentary session. He would thus be spared any interpellations. He would be assisted by M. Crétin, in charge of disputed claims at the Ministry of War, and Captain Targe his aide-de-camp. The Affair had started up anew.

General André was without prejudice; he was not convinced of Dreyfus's innocence and with Captain Targe he was intent on performing a thorough, serious, and honest investigation. Whatever the truth might be, Targe would later say, "we were resolved to make it known to all."[11]

The first order of business was reassembling the various files that had been dispersed in the wake of the trial at Rennes. Targe undertook a veritable excavation and managed to gather not only all the documents submitted to the military tribunal, but in addition important documents which first Commandant Henry, then General Gonse had concealed because they seemed to favor Dreyfus. These included three notes from Colonel von Schwarzkoppen establishing that the traffic in master plans had begun in 1892, long before Dreyfus came to the Ministry, and had continued after his conviction. Aided by Targe, André studied the entire case personally, document by document. And he called in the archivist Félix Gribelin—who was still at the Ministry—to assist him. Gribelin, who had founded a "veritable cult" to Henry's memory and remained convinced of Dreyfus's crime, nevertheless decided to conceal nothing of what he knew. "He had become truthful with age," Reinach commented, "as one becomes obese or bald."[12] Since there was much that he knew, after having been one of the artisans of the crime he now became one of the artisans of the revision.

André and Targe quickly discovered that two important items in the secret file had been falsified by Colonel Henry.† One was Panizzardi's letter to Schwarzkoppen: "I tell you that I will have the organization of the

---

* In May, Alfred Dreyfus had met Clemenceau, who had intervened with the Prime Minister. Clemenceau had declared himself ready to undertake any effort that might prove useful and had assured Dreyfus of his assistance.[10]

† Studying the celebrated "Henry forgery" discovered by Cuignet by the light of his lamp, André observed the anomaly of differences in tint by daylight. He concluded too hastily that Cuignet's account of the conditions under which he had made his discovery were inaccurate. And André long believed that someone had falsified the "Henry forgery" to make the forgery more apparent.[13]

railroads. . . . "* It was dated March 28, 1895: at the time Dreyfus was on Devil's Island. Henry had ripped off the upper portion of the letter, which bore the date, and inscribed in his own hand the date April 1894, which would compromise Dreyfus. A copy made by Gribelin at the time and bearing the original date (March 28, 1895) was found. Gribelin had no difficulty recognizing that the words *April 1894* were in Henry's script. The second forgery was one that Cavaignac had read from the tribune of the Chamber: the letter in which Panizzardi wrote to one of Schwarzkoppen's collaborators that "P . . . had brought him many interesting things." Henry had scratched out the *P* and replaced it with a *D*. The fraud was obvious, demonstrated conclusively by the discovery of a copy— customarily made by the Intelligence Service—which Gribelin discovered and submitted to Targe. The copy bore the letter *P*. Finally Gribelin revealed that on orders from Henry he had falsified all the accounting records concerning Val-Carlos.† Plainly in a confessional mood, Gribelin went on to tell how Henry had also augmented certain expenses incurred by Picquart to create the impression that the latter was squandering secret funds, and explained several minor frauds in which he (at the behest of his venerated chief) had been a scrupulous accomplice. Indeed new elements were not lacking!

The investigation lasted almost six months. General André delivered his report to the prime minister on October 19, 1903, presenting without commentary his principal findings and the seriousness of the facts that had been uncovered. It appears that at the time Jaurès had unofficial knowledge of the results of the inquiry and that he informed Dreyfus, who then called a meeting of friends—including Pressensé, Buisson, Reinach, Leblois, and Demange—at Mornard's home to decide how to proceed. The results of the investigation would have to be transmitted to the minister of justice. At each meeting of the Council of ministers, André unsuccessfully requested such action; he would obtain it only in November. On November 22 Jaurès conveyed the good news to Dreyfus: the results of the investigation had just been transferred to Minister of Justice Valle, who was empowered to activate the Revision Commission without delay. But the government preferred Dreyfus to file his own request. Revision had become politically desirable.

On November 25, 1903, Alfred Dreyfus and his lawyer, Mornard, together composed the text of a petition for revision of the judgment of the Court Martial of Rennes. They based the petition on the "revelation" to the Chamber by Deputy Jaurès that an "audacious forgery had affected the awareness of certain judges," on the results of the investigation con-

* *Supra* p. 195.
† *Supra* p. 88–89.

ducted by the minister of war, concerning which Dreyfus "believed he knew"—since he was assumed to have no knowledge of the investigation—that it justified a revision, and on several instances of false testimony, including that of Eugène Cernuski, an Austrian lieutenant, which had been heard during the final hours at Rennes. Finally they invoked a letter from Count Münster von Derneberg to Joseph Reinach, attesting that Colonel von Schwarzkoppen had confessed to his former ambassador that the spy informing him had been Commandant Esterhazy.[14]

Alfred Dreyfus concluded his petition in these terms:

My conviction, so painfully extracted from judges whose doubts were expressed in the form of attenuating circumstances, is thus the result of forgery and deception.

I request the revision of my trial, because I require all of my honor, for my children and myself, because I have never been remiss in any of my duties as a soldier and a Frenchman.

Just as he was to file the petition, Mornard was summoned by the minister of justice. Suddenly, there was some hesitation as to how to proceed. The government feared an interpellation. How was General André's "personal" investigation to be explained? The prime minister, it appeared, was concerned. The equivocations continued; it was only on the evening of November 26 that the request for revision was officially registered in the Ministry of Justice.[15]

On November 27, the Council of ministers decided that the minister of justice would transmit the request to the Revision Commission, retaining as new elements, for legal purposes, the two forgeries for which André's investigation had supplied evidence. On December 24, the commission stated unanimously that there were grounds for revision. On Christmas day, the minister of justice referred the judgment at Rennes to the High Court of Appeal. Nine years had passed since Dreyfus's conviction.

The revision was moving forward. Henri Rochefort and Edouard Drumont issued rather spiritless protests. "The stormy sea" of the first revision, observed Reinach, "had calmed into a peaceful lake."[16] The nationalists were aware of their defeat; they were resigned to it. A single hope remained for Mercier's supporters: that the High Court of Appeal send Dreyfus before a third Court Martial, and that he be convicted a third time. But that hope seemed rather fragile. This time the minister of war was the staunchest architect of revision, and the government was negotiating the successive phases of the procedure with Alfred Dreyfus himself. Edouard Drumont and Charles Maurras might still wax indignant, invoke the honor of the Army, and denounce the syndicate of treason. They were no longer heeded. "They were beating on punctured drums."[17]

On September 2 Bernard Lazare had died. He was thirty-eight years old. For months he had been enduring the cruelest of agonies. His death passed unnoticed; there were few mourners.* Dreyfus was absent. Until the end, Lazare had remained a loner, almost suspect. "His eyes were too clear," his friend Charles Péguy would write.† Lazare had always been "elsewhere." "To be elsewhere, the great vice of this race, its great secret virtue; the great vocation of this people. . . ." He was a hero; he was a saint; he had taken his leave. "He was not intended to be on the side of the victors."[19]

14

Marching in Step

The president of the Criminal Chamber was no longer the aged Louis Loew, who had been so mistreated during the first revision. He had reached the age of mandatory retirement and was succeeded by a former friend of Léon Gambetta, Justice Chambareaud. He too had been showered with abuse during the months preceding the dispossession legislation. To report the case he designated Justice Boyer, who had not participated in the first revision and passed for a rigorous jurist.

Manau was no longer public prosecutor. He had been replaced in September 1900 by Laferrière, who had died on July 3, 1901, and was succeeded by Manuel Achille Baudouin. He belonged to an old family of magistrates: his father had been a judge of the High Court of Appeal and his wife's father a judge of the Court of Appeal of Rennes. Baudouin had had a brilliant career in the jurisdiction of the Court of Appeal of Lyon,[1] and had then become presiding justice of the civil court of the Seine. In

* *Supra* p. 139
† "Working in the same manner, evolving through a single matter, there were at least two Dreyfus Affairs, elaborating the same story. Bernard Lazare's—ours—was innocent and need not be defended. In another sense as well there were two Dreyfus Affairs, one issuing from Bernard Lazare, one issuing from Colonel Picquart. That which issued from Colonel Picquart was very good indeed. That which issued from Bernard Lazare was infinite."[18]

Paris he had shown himself to be a scrupulous magistrate, with a passion for justice, whose inexhaustible verve on occasion was deemed to be excessive. Public Prosecutor Baudouin did not yet believe in Dreyfus's innocence when he was assigned to plead the government's case. He was prepared, he would later say, to submit to the instructions of the government (which was manifestly favorable to revision), but to keep his distance from the official canon during his oral argument—as was his right—if the case convinced him of Dreyfus's guilt. He worked with extreme diligence, became fully acquainted with the immense file, and was gradually persuaded of Dreyfus's innocence. His conscience was thus happily free to enter into accord with the government's will.

In January 1904, the judges of the Criminal Chamber received Baudouin's charge. Its conclusion left no room for doubt.

In summary, Alfred Dreyfus was convicted on September 9, 1899, by the Rennes Court Martial by virtue of a group of accusations not one of which appears to resist scrutiny (which would not be enough to authorize revision), but also, through the introduction of documents, which, after the conviction, were acknowledged to be forged and whose fabrication was as much intended to create against the accused the direct charges lodged against him as to invalidate the authority of the witnesses for the defense whose depositions he might invoke.

And we are convinced that the High Court of Appeal will honor our requests, which tend, by order of the minister of justice, toward a revision of the judgment and that its decision will prepare for the triumph of truth and justice, which, however veiled or misconstrued by reason of the limitations of the human mind, at least never die.

Dreyfus himself composed a long statement concerning his Affair. Mornard corrected the text, which was filed on February 1.

The public hearing had been scheduled for March 3. In the days preceding it, Fernand Labori let Mornard know that he was prepared to "reenter" the Affair and that if he did not take part in the revision, he would be obliged to explain publicly the roles of Waldeck-Rousseau and Joseph Reinach. But Labori had published in *La Grande Revue* and in *Le Journal* several articles that were openly hostile toward Dreyfus, whom he accused of having negotiated his pardon with Waldeck-Rousseau and of not pursuing the revision diligently. That was more than Dreyfus would tolerate. He refused to entrust his interests to Labori. They had nothing in common but the past.[2]

The session of the Criminal Chamber of March 3, 1904, began with
Justice Boyer's report—precise, austere, attentive to the slightest details,
all the more convincing in that it appeared free of prejudice. Boyer
eliminated the thesis, to which Mathieu and Alfred both subscribed,
positing the communication of the annotated bordereau or some other
document to the judges during their deliberations, citing lack of evidence.
On the other hand, the reporting judge retained as new evidence Panizzardi's doctored letters, concerning which "it was not excessive to think
that they might have had a sufficient influence on the judges to bring
about the conviction." He concluded that a supplementary investigation
would be necessary. Public prosecutor Baudouin addressed the court for
two full sessions to promote the same conclusion. But he went further still,
affirming Dreyfus's innocence on several occasions, refusing to conceal his
distrust of the military courts, and already appearing to favor revision
without benefit of a new trial.[3]

Finally Mornard argued his case. Seated at his side were Edgar Demange and Fernand Labori, who had come, finally, to demonstrate his
solidarity. Lieutenant Colonel Picquart was present. Mornard attempted
to convey Dreyfus's personality to the magistrates of the High Court.

> This spirit described as haughty and imperious . . . is in fact that of
> a shy man fighting his own timidity; I know what lies behind this
> allegedly unfeeling heart that has suffered so cruelly in obeying a
> self-imposed rule not to show its suffering; and on this point, my
> colleagues Demange and Labori would be able to bring you tes-
> timony that is truly poignant. They could tell you. . . .

Upon hearing his name pronounced, Labori rose, donned his lawyer's
cap, and left the courtroom. "Well done, well done," Picquart praised him
as Labori passed by, with sufficient volume to be heard by all. Labori,
pacing the galleries of the Palais de Justice, was already expounding that a
distinction had to be made between "the man and the cause," that Mornard should not have appealed to his testimony to describe Alfred
Dreyfus's sensibility, that he wanted neither to confirm those declarations
by his silence, nor to contest them by protesting, "I walked out and that is
all."*

---

* That at least was Joseph Reinach's description.[4] Labori did not mention the incident in his
handwritten notes. But like Picquart, he accused Reinach of having systematically distorted
the truth. "M. Reinach's book is no more than a biased work, written in bad faith," he wrote of
the fourth volume on March 15, 1904.[5] "The work is strictly Semitic in inspiration," Labori
maintained.[6] "No work is as well suited to mislead future historians as M. Joseph Reinach's
work, which he has called pretentiously *Histoire de l'Affaire Dreyfus*."[7] Picquart and Labori
collaborated in drawing up an inventory of "errors" committed by Reinach.[8]

A few hours after that incident, the High Court of Appeal delivered its judgment. It declared the petition for revision admissible in its present form and ordered a supplementary judicial inquiry to be conducted. Dreyfus wanted to become "legally innocent, completely innocent."[9] But that procedure seemed in public opinion a matter of indifference. The news was reported in the press with little emotion.

The Criminal Chamber's investigation began on March 7, 1904. The Court called for all the files relevant to the Affair. Since General André had deemed it advisable to remove the secret file of love letters between Colonel von Schwarzkoppen and Mme. Weede, the Criminal Chamber insisted on having it. The Court demanded to know everything. But invoking the precedent of the Combined Chambers, by a ruling of March 7, the Criminal Chamber allowed the public prosecutor and Mornard to be present at the plenary sessions. It was prepared for its preliminary procedures to be marked by contradictory testimony.

The investigation was to proceed, breaking only for judiciary recess, until November 19, 1904, the day on which the Chamber delivered its final judgment. All the actors of the Affair were interrogated with scrupulous care. In particular, the Court heard the former ministers of war, the chiefs of the former General Staff, and the principal officers. It seemed that by now even the most impassioned of Dreyfus's accusers had lost some of their fire. General Mercier lacked his former vehemence. He no longer spoke of evidence or presumptions—with the exception of Bertillon's "irrefutable" demonstration, which he persisted in clinging to. General Billot claimed not to have attached particular importance to either the "Henry forgery" or to the "liberating document," and his memory on most occasions failed him. General Roget subtly altered his opinions. He now paid homage to Picquart's probity; at Rennes, he had accused him of squandering secret funds. Captain Lauth handled Picquart gently and kept his distance from Henry's memory. General de Boisdeffre was no more than a shadow of his former truculent self. General Gonse appeared, in Alfred Dreyfus's words, "pitiful, a luckless wretch crushed beneath the weight of all the infamies he had committed."[10] He denied everything or sought refuge in amnesia. Only the "venomous and perfidious" Commandant du Paty de Clam[11] and Captain Cuignet, who had become a fanatic, showed any ardor or imagination. But the first was plainly unstable and the latter was to all appearances carried away by hatred. Picquart's deposition was, as always, a masterpiece of precision. But he felt obliged to add an account of the disagreements at Rennes, to explain how Mathieu Dreyfus and Demange had transmitted to him "orders to remain silent," had asked him not to attack the generals, not to pronounce the words *false testimony* and *fraud*, how they had advised him "to appear to believe in the good faith of their adversaries." He spoke in praise of Labori, "fettered by his client's will." He explained, moreover, his reasons for regarding Commandant Esterhazy as Maurice Weil's associate: the link between the two men, the "two vile profligates," as de Boisdeffre had once called them, seemed to him too longstanding and too close for them not to have collaborated in espionage. Weil was heard, interrogated, and treated quite roughly by Baudouin. He grew angry and refused to allow himself to be treated as a defendant. Nothing was learned from him.

Toward the end of the investigation, after the Court had heard the witnesses—including Brücker and Mme. Bastian—Alfred Dreyfus asked to be allowed to speak. The Court consented and was eager to hear him. He introduced himself on June 22, 1904. He was, as on every other occasion, apparently cold, careful to conceal any emotion. He claimed to be astonished to have read in one of General Chamoin's letters to former Minister of War Galliffet, written during the Rennes trial, "Dreyfus has not been able to move people; he has not spoken from the heart." Dreyfus commented: "I am dumbfounded. I believe in reason, I believed that reason in such matters, in which the heart's emotions can never contribute any explanation, any attenuation, was supposed to be the judge's sole guide."[12] And he withdrew, leaving the judges of the Criminal Chamber as astonished as General Chamoin had been at Rennes. No anger was displayed. No sign of indignation. Alfred Dreyfus seemed almost a stranger to his own case.

Before closing the investigation, there remained two reports solicited by the Criminal Chamber. The first, requested of the General Staff, concerned technological questions raised by the Affair. The report, prepared by several superior officers, including the commandant of the École Supérieure de Guerre, refuted point by point the accusations brought against Dreyfus on the basis of the bordereau. The famous phrase "the way in which the 120 piece performed" would have been an "utterly abnormal" expression on the part of an artilleryman. The three notes in the bordereau dealing with artillery concerned the three "innovations" tried out in 1894 at the Écoles de Châlons, precisely during Esterhazy's stay there. The *Manuel d'artillerie* was in no way confidential. The difficulties in procuring the manual invoked by the author of the bordereau indicated merely that he was trying to gain recognition for himself. The General Staff had thus enumerated with meticulous care the arguments exonerating Dreyfus. It had taken it ten years to discover them.

The second report had been assigned to three men of science, Professor Appel, dean of the Faculté des Sciences, Jean Gaston Darboux, permanent secretary of the Academy of Sciences, and Henri Poincaré, professor at the Sorbonne, with the aim of examining once again the "Bertillon system." The conclusions of their report were unequivocal: "The absurdity of the system is evident." Bertillon's reconstitution of the bordereau was in error, the result of shameless tinkering. The bordereau was plainly not a forged document, it had been written in a fluent hand. Thus, "of the mass of hypotheses and fabrications accumulated around Dreyfus, there was nothing left."[13] Henceforth, the government, the judiciary, the General Staff, and the experts would march in step with unanimous zeal.

With the preliminary investigation over, on November 19, 1904, the Criminal Chamber forwarded the case to the Combined Chambers, as had been ruled earlier by the dispossession law. Judge Ballot-Beaupré, who had become chief presiding justice in 1900, designated successively three reporting judges who were unable to pursue or to accept the immense task. It was only on May 14, 1905, that Justice Clément Moras was appointed. Public Prosecutor Baudouin had more or less written his conclusions and Mornard his final statement.* But there was unanimous agreement to delay the proceedings. It would be better, before playing the final act, to let the general elections pass. . . .

15

France's Premier Cop

For three years, the great debate that would culminate in the separation of Church and State had dominated French political life. Emile Combes had stayed his course with an obstinacy that the difficulties he incurred only reinforced. The decrees of June 27, 1902, had ordered the closing of a hundred twenty establishments of religious education in France. The law of July 7, 1904, had banned all teaching by the religious congregations. Since Pope Pius X had reacted violently to the acts of the Combes government, France had broken off diplomatic relations with the Vatican in July 1904. During the winter of 1904–1905 the Socialist Aristide Briand was preparing to advance his career by presenting to the

---

* Maître Henri Mornard's written statement on behalf of Alfred Dreyfus, "ex-Captain of the Artillery, residing in Paris at 101 Boulevard Malesherbes," was the most complete, precise, and clear document drawn up in Dreyfus's defense. It comprises more than seven hundred printed pages in the edition of the Ligue française des Droits de l'homme (Paris, 1907).

Chamber the separation law, which would not be passed until July 1905, after the fall of the Combes government.

It was the minister of war who provoked that fall. General André had already devised numerous measures, extremely resented by the nationalists, intended to democratize Army life* and to "repair" the careers of those republicans who had suffered in their advancement.[1] A law of March 1905 had reduced military service from three to two years and eliminated the exemptions enjoyed by students and ecclesiastics. Carried away by his republican zeal, General André kept the advancement of officers under closer control by using a card-index held by his aide-de-camp Captain Mollin, a Freemason who had agreed to send a circular to all masonic lodges, asking to be informed—"from a philosophical and political point of view"—about the officers stationed in their cities. Soon the cards —25,000 in four years—swelled the two files labeled "Carthage" and "Corinth" which allowed the minister of war to advance or delay an officer's career. This new form of Army "regimentation" created an immediate scandal.

The right-wing press published several lists of such "cards" and there was soon an impassioned polemic on the subject. "Masonic delation," the harm done to the Army, and the fanaticism of the Republic were denounced. Georges Clemenceau, who hoped for Combes's downfall, perceived the profit he might derive from the situation: if General André were to begin anew—with or without Freemasonry—"the secret files of the Dreyfus Affair," we would be faced with nothing but "reverse Jesuitism." Jaurès, on the other hand, opted to defend André and to accuse those venting their indignation of "Pharisaism." The League of the Rights of Man, caught between its sympathies and its principles, was hesitant to take a stand against the system of filecards. Joseph Reinach resigned from the league, arguing that it was thereby abdicating "its moralizing function."[2]

André held fast for a while, protesting the minister of war's right to keep informed by all possible means.[3] Impassioned debate in the Chamber on October 28 and November 4 left the government with a majority of . . . two votes. The insulted and exhausted André, having won his difficult victory, had returned to his place on the ministerial bench when Deputy Syveton flung himself on André. "I slapped him not from behind, but in the face," Syveton would tell the examining magistrate, "in order to outrage him, to avenge the Army surrendered and the country betrayed." Paul Déroulède congratulated Syveton for having "slapped an

---

* Suspension of obligatory mess, of obligatory dowries, tolerance of concubines, etc.

entire regime," Maurice Barrès for having "accomplished one of those acts which, far more than any speech, act on the soul of the parties." On the eve of his appearance in criminal court, Syveton would be found dead in his study with the gas on. "A new Masonic crime," Jules Lemaître and Francois Coppée proclaimed. The Combes government had died as well. On November 15, 1904, André submitted his resignation to Combes, who implored him in vain to remain in his post. Combes, disheartened, surrounded by enemies, began imagining sinister intrigues launched by Waldeck-Rousseau's former ministers and by Clemenceau. He continued in office through a series of diminishing majorities. His coalition was gradually disintegrating. A variety of factors contributed to the process: the proposed income tax, which worried the wealthy because it seemed to bear within it the seed of proportionality; the development of unionism; the rise of workers' demands and strikes; the difficulties experienced by Russia, the preferred ally; and the antimilitarism of the extreme left. Radicals in increasing numbers were taking their distance from the Socialists and moving closer to a more reasonable center. A sign of the times: Paul Doumer, a Radical supported by the right, was elected president of the Chamber against Brisson, the coalition's candidate. In January 1905, Combes resigned, no doubt to avoid being overthrown.

The coalition was falling apart, but as yet there was no other majority.[4] President Emile Loubet called on Pierre Maurice Rouvier to replace Combes. A wily old politician, previously compromised in the Panama Affair, Rouvier pledged to put an end to the practices of the preceding Ministry. "I will form a government out in the open," he announced. In point of fact, he formed an opportunist cabinet, closely tied to the world of business. Parliament terminated its discussion of the separation law, which was passed on July 3, 1905, by a leftist coalition which reassembled its former unity for that occasion. But little remained to unite the Radicals and Socialists now that the fight for secularity had been won—and exhausted.

There existed difficulties, moreover, stemming from relations with Morocco. Emperor Wilhelm II visited Tangiers on March 31, 1905, to demonstrate his desire to undermine the French effort to incorporate Morocco into the French Empire. Should the leftists stand up to Germany as Théophile Delcassé, minister of foreign affairs, wanted, or attempt to negotiate, as preferred by Rouvier? Rouvier forced Delcassé to resign and negotiated with Germany the Algesiras accord, "a grotesque text," Joseph Caillaux would later say, intentionally ambiguous, a false agreement which recognized simultaneously the territorial integrity of Morocco and the "historic rights acquired" by France and Spain as "civilizing nations." The

Algesiras accord merely prepared the way for new conflicts. The Franco-German rivalry became once more a pressing concern, bearing with it the threat of a new war dreaded by some and desired by others.[5]

But it was social issues which began to dominate political life, now that it was no longer enough to declare one's hatred for priests. The Radicals barely had a clear policy: a few vague ideas—on liberty and progress—and an overwhelming prudence took the place of a clear agenda. What the Socialist Alexandre Millerand had attempted under Waldeck-Rousseau's government* had received only resigned support on the part of the Radicals. Combes replaced Millerand with a small-minded champion of anticlericalism, Trouillot, who accomplished nothing. For him as for the head of the government, monk-baiting took the place of a social program. A conservative by temperament, worried about displeasing big business, Rouvier was repelled by the idea of social reform. And strikes were growing more numerous and more serious as the Rouvier government's majority, vote by vote, was growing weaker and weaker.

On January 17, 1906, the left was still sufficiently united to carry to the presidency of the Republic Armand Fallières, candidate of the various lefts, who defeated Paul Doumer, recently emerged as the hope of the conservatives. In his inaugural address, Fallières expressed sympathy for all those deprived of wealth, saluted in the Army the "devoted guardian of our institutions and our laws," and issued an appeal to all republicans. The left was satisfied. And in order to execute the separation law, it began taking complete inventory of all ecclesiastical holdings: statues, chandeliers, ciboria, chalices, and chasubles. Tabernacles were to be opened, their objects counted and weighed. In several churches, Catholics soon ran interference. The police intervened; some of the faithful were wounded. A Catholic was killed near Hazebrouck. Parliament sought refuge in oratory. Aristide Briand lamented over those Catholics whom deception had driven to fanaticism. Abbé Lemire stood up against the inventories on behalf of all Catholics. Rouvier stubbornly persisted: the inventories would be completed at whatever cost. But he continued to lose support, simultaneously disappointing the Radicals and the Socialists. On March 7, 1906, he was overthrown.

It was former Minister of Justice Jean Sarrien, as courteous as he was colorless, whom Fallières designated to succeed Rouvier. Combes described him as "indecisiveness raised to the highest power. Every action seemed repugnant to this flaccid spirit who feared equally any cause of satisfaction or dissatisfaction. Sarrien's character was not to have any."[6] But many of the most ambitious figures of the Republic were assembled in his

---

* Opportunities offered to the syndicalist movement, laws on government arbitration of social conflicts, improvement of working conditions.

government: Louis Barthou, Aristide Briand, Raymond Poincaré. Above all, Georges Clemenceau, senator from the Var since 1902, was named minister of the interior. For the first time, at age sixty-five, the old demolisher of cabinets was a minister, and it was clear that this was merely a way station. The courageous struggle that Clemenceau had waged for Dreyfus thus received its compensation.

Soon after it was installed, the Sarrien government ran into serious difficulties with labor. While the cabinet ministry was being formed, a fire-damp explosion in the coal mines of Courrières caused more than a thousand deaths. A strike was spreading among the workers. Clemenceau wasted no time in revealing his temperament. He traveled to Lens, harangued the workers, then, unable to persuade them, called in gendarmes, hussars, and dragoons. The strike immediately spread. In the Pas-de-Calais the Army was called in to repress the riots. In Paris, the postal workers went on strike: Clemenceau immediately fired the strikers; the government had no intention of tolerating a strike by public employees. On the eve of May Day 1906, anticipating trouble, Clemenceau received the workers' leadership and warned them that he would be pitiless. "You are behind a barricade. I am in front. Your means of action is disorder. My duty is to ensure public order." May Day passed without disturbance, but numerous strikes prolonged the symbolic work stoppage. And as the former champion of Dreyfus's cause forged his image as "France's premier cop," the fear of the middle class began to rise. To many, syndicalism now appeared as a threat to the Republic, socialism as an attempt to destroy the social order. On the other hand, Clemenceau showed greater flexibility in the secularist struggle. On March 16—a month and a half before elections—he invited prefects to suspend their inventories. "The fact of knowing whether or not the chandeliers in a church will be counted is not worth a human life," he affirmed. A portion of the left found it hard to accept such a lapse in their sacred struggle.

Radicals and Socialists were thus gradually diverging. The Dreyfus Affair, the defense of the Republic, and the fight for secularity had temporarily brought them together against the common enemy: the forces of reaction as supported by the Army, the Church, and the congregations. But now the division between social classes was breaking that fragile union. The Army was engaged in defense of the Republic, and the congregations and the Church enjoyed supervised freedom. For most, the true threat now was the rise of the working class, collective bargaining, and disorder in the streets.* That Clemenceau should take charge—and with

* See, however, Alfred Dreyfus's restrained reactions concerning the Socialists in his letters to Marquise Arconati-Visconti.[7] Even though he felt distant from them, he could not forget the role they had played, Jaurès's ardent loyalty in the fight for revision.

such ardor—of the repression of the working class clearly symbolized that the Dreyfus Affair was now over.*

The threat of war and the anticipation of revenge would consolidate the growing division. After the "patriotic alert" of 1905, the majority of moderate Dreyfusards would rally to a staunch and intolerant patriotism, which would frequently allow them to shuck off with little effort those aspirations for social change and a belief in universal progress which they had at times entertained during the duration of the Affair. "I don't give a damn," the very republican and Dreyfusard Marquise Arconati-Visconti would proudly declare, "for the liberties of the proletariat. I would give anything for perfected cannons." She wrote to Jaurès: "Order in the street, a strong national defense. I believe, dear friend, that like myself, you are of the opinion that for any people those are the two vital necessities, the two irresistible platters that must be served."[9] Such vigorous exhortations might well have recalled others which had served to keep Dreyfus in prison. But Clemenceau was now proclaiming the "vital necessities" and would become the implacable champion of the national cause.

In April 1905 the congress intended to unify the Socialists was held in Paris. The break-up of the coalition of republican defense was consummated. The motions passed did not forbid voting with or for the Radicals, but they eliminated any participation by a Socialist in a bourgeois government, and even structural or stable alliances. The Socialists thus united and hardened their stance while the Radicals looked on with anxiety at the threats foreseen from the working class. Considering the "roots of the post-Dreyfusard coalition," the Socialist Léon Blum observed that the "foundations of the Affair had disintegrated." Its resources for exaltation and renewal were exhausted.[10]

---

* "It is frightening," the former Dreyfusard Roujon would exclaim. "The social revolution has begun. We sowed the wind and we're reaping the whirlwind."[8]

16

Innocence Proclaimed

At the end of the year 1905, the High Court of Appeal was still awaiting Justice Moras's report. Alfred Dreyfus found it difficult to accept such slowness in the revision procedure: his request was more than two years old! But successive governments had agreed to put off the final flourish until after the legislative elections of 1906. A bit more time would be needed before the Affair was finally broached in the Combined Chambers. In order to justify the wait, the Court's case overload, "the imperious exigencies of the Court's service," were invoked. Dreyfus suffered from the delay: "I awaited the end of my torture."[1] Lieutenant Colonel Picquart, on the other hand, waxed indignant and fulminated against the former warriors of the revision who, he wrote, "are no longer too intent on fighting since they have taken to collecting booty." Official justice seemed to him to be maddeningly attentive to governmental strategy.[2]

The general elections took place in May. Abstentions numbered only 20 percent. Republican discipline—which survived the disintegration of the parliamentary block—still benefited the left, which strengthened its majority, obtaining 420 seats. The defeated right lost 60 seats. The old right, with its base in *châteaux* and the Church, was dying and survived only in the fiefdoms of the West.[3] The left, despite the hemorrhage occasioned by the appearance of "independent Socialists," won 59 seats. Above all, the Radicals and Radical-Socialists and the group adjacent to the democratic alliance swept up more than 250 seats. They had plainly benefited from an impressive influx of votes from the right, a circumstance that would not be without influence on their political behavior. The Radicals could thus govern without the Socialists, who no longer wanted to govern with them. Jaurès threw out this challenge to his recent allies, "We will now see what you are capable of." Clemenceau emerged as the strong man, who had maintained social order and who won the elections. A few months later, Sarrien would fall ill and leave the prime minister's role to Clemenceau.

As for the Dreyfus Affair, it played virtually no role in the campaign. But the most noted revisionists, Jaurès, Pressensé, Labori, Viviani, and

Reinach himself, were either elected or reelected, carried in by the surge of the left. Now the revision procedure could resume its progress before the High Court of Appeal. The session of the Combined Chambers was fixed for June 15. Crushed by the elections, the right seemed to be prostrate. Déroulède, Rochefort, and Drumont had almost given up their insults, as though they had lost all energy—or hope. The inflexible Cavaignac died in September 1905. General Mercier was no more than a phantom haunting the Senate. The hour of justice could be sounded. It would disturb no one.

On June 15 and 16, the justices of the Combined Chambers met in closed session to examine the secret file. On June 18, the Chambers held a public hearing. And the proceedings which seven years earlier had been invaded by an impassioned crowd were now followed only by the Dreyfus family and a small number of former militants and lawyers. Death too had thinned out the ranks: Ludovic Trarieux and Emile Duclaux died in 1904, without having known this day of victory for which they had given much of their strength. "No security precautions were taken," observed Reinach. "The calm of an ordinary day prevailed."[4] But those tranquil days that concluded twelve years of combat could not dissipate a number of resentments. The aged Edgar Demange came to sit beside Mornard; Labori did not. On the day of the last session, Mathieu Dreyfus would make a move to shake Picquart's hand. Picquart would reject his outstretched hand and turn away. To Mme. Zola, a stunned witness to the insult, Mathieu Dreyfus would simply say, "He has all the rights; I have all the duties."[5]

The presiding justices of the three Chambers surrounded Chief Presiding Justice Ballot-Beaupré: Judge Tanon, presiding over the Chambre des Requêtes; Albert Sarrut, who was formerly an advisor to Auguste Scheurer-Kestner and was now presiding over the Civil Chamber; and Alphonse Bard, the courageous reporting judge in 1898, who had become presiding justice of the Criminal Chamber. From June 18 to 22 Clément Moras read his report. He remained seated and spoke in a voice that never faltered. His report, like Ballot-Beaupré's in 1898, was a remarkable example of precision and integrity. Moras retained three new elements which sufficed to open the path to revision. Then he summarized the entire Affair, with implacable care, discussing every document, every instance of testimony, and concluded that revision was justified. He did not speak to the question of whether or not the case should be sent before a new Court-Martial.

After him, Public Prosecutor Baudouin addressed the Court for eight sessions. Speaking in a strong, often emotional voice, alternately reading and improvising, he excommunicated in passing all those who at one time or another, had impeded the work of truth.* The prosecutor's endless phillipic seemed to awaken, day by day, a somewhat drowsy public opinion. Captain Cuignet wrote to the minister of justice to protest. Commandant du Paty, although "extremely honored by the insults of the public prosecutor," published in *La Libre Parole* a letter to the chief presiding justice, and filed a complaint with the minister of justice. Félix Gribelin, who had become a journalist, wrote to Ballot-Beaupré to protest the slander he felt himself subjected to. General Zurlinden and General Gonse issued public protests. Gonse accused Picquart of having lied,† and Picquart replied that Gonse's word was without value. On July 9, they faced each other in a duel; Gonse missed Picquart, who did not fire. Commandant Esterhazy fulminated in a long letter to Drumont published in *La Libre Parole* of June 29, 1906. No, he had never been a traitor. Yes, he had written the bordereau. "Yes, I wrote it, everyone knows it, and more than any others those who imprudently deny it, be they from Normale, from Polytechnique, or from Charenton. But I was obeying orders from Sandherr." *La Libre Parole* of July 6 called on General Mercier, who was silent, to say all that he knew: "General, the time is short, the High Court of Appeal is going to pass judgment and you have said nothing. . . ." Obliged to do something, Mercier sent an embarrassed and insignificant letter to Presiding Justice Ballot-Beaupré in which he merely said that he now situated on December 12, 1894, and no longer on January 6, 1895, the night "during which the question of war or peace was in suspense." One last time he affirmed the guilt of the officer who had betrayed his country. "You have not spoken," Drumont would respond in *La Libre Parole* of July 16. "You have merely pretended to speak." Through the vehemence of his address, Public Prosecutor Baudouin had thus managed to raise a last and brief tempest. And he concluded his address by asking the Combined Chambers to annul the decision of the Rennes Court-Martial without sending Dreyfus before a third Court-Martial.‡ "Baudouin," commented Reinach, "with his impassioned argumentation, his lack of indulgence, his fresh hatred, is the voice of all those latecomers who are now rushing in, that immense rearguard joining up with the small victorious army."[8]

---

* "The court session was quite beautiful," Mme. Mathieu Dreyfus wrote to her mother Mme. Emile Schwob on the day of the first hearing. "Baudouin decimated du Paty and Mercier with great energy. . . . He gets quite excited when speaking of Mercier's crime, banging on his desk and saying that his place is in jail. It did us good to hear it."[6]

† In reporting Gonse's famous remark: "If you don't say anything, no one will know . . ."

‡ "There is an incredible crowd since the prosecutor has begun his summation," Mme. Mathieu Dreyfus wrote to her mother. "Maître Baudouin demonstrates very clearly that there are grounds for annulling the verdict without ordering a new trial, since there is no charge against Alfred: he is innocent and Esterhazy, who is guilty, has been acquitted."[7]

Then Henri Mornard spoke. It was the fourth time that he had
intervened on Dreyfus's behalf before the High Court of Appeal. For
three days, on July 5, 6, and 7, calmly, with the natural seriousness that
never left him, he went through his implacable demonstration one last
time. He was tempted now to make some additions. He speculated that
Esterhazy had perhaps been a counterspy even as Baudouin had speculated that the author of the bordereau had been an accomplice in a vast
anti-Semitic plot. One of the dangers that came with studying the Affair,
Reinach observed, was to inspire the most insane hypotheses. "Since it was
extraordinary, there is a desire to make it more extraordinary still. . . ."[9]

But Mornard's principal effort—which he had not undertaken in 1898
at the request of Mathieu and Lucie—was to demonstrate that the High
Court of Appeal should order a revision without sending Dreyfus before a
new Court-Martial. The risk entailed by a new trial was obvious. Mornard
developed two arguments to which Baudouin had already subscribed in
his remarks. The first—which was rather dubious—was that with Commandant Henry dead and Esterhazy acquitted, a new trial became juridically impossible since oral debate could not be engaged against all "parties
concerned."* The second argument, which was less fragile, appealed to
the provision instructing the High Court of Appeal to pronounce judgment without a new trial "when the annulment of a verdict does not leave
any extant charges against the convict that might be defined as criminal."
Mornard went to great pains to demonstrate that such was indeed the case
in the present situation. Once the bordereau was eliminated, the legend of
a confession dissipated, and the forgeries denounced, no criminal charges
remained pending against Dreyfus. Mornard let it be known that Dreyfus
wanted nothing but his honor, that he claimed no monetary compensation. He simply requested that the judgment be published in the *Journal
Officiel* and in a number of newspapers.

Mornard had argued for three days. "Maître Mornard," wrote Mme.
Mathieu Dreyfus, "argued admirably yesterday. . . . His voice had grown
firmer; one could hear him very well even though at times he was quite
moved. The judges listened to him with great attentiveness and apparent
sympathy, and we were told from various quarters that his plea had
produced a great effect on them."[11] He concluded by saluting the officers
who had shattered their careers in order to speak the truth: Picquart, that
superior instance of human conscience, and Freystaetter, the judge of
1894, who had dared to tell the truth about the deliberations and who had

* But could Henry and Esterhazy be regarded as "parties" in the case against Dreyfus?
Several juridical studies had been assembled to enlighten the High Court of Appeal on the
difficult problem of a revision without further trial.[10]

been harassed to the point of being constrained to leave the Army. And he paid homage to those, all those who had been the worthy servants of justice—Scheurer-Kestner, Trarieux, Zola, Lazare, Duclaux, Grimaux, Giry, Molinier—and who had been unable to travel to the end of the road.

The deliberations of the Combined Chambers were short and calm. "No further passions, no further anger, no more gusts coming in from without," wrote Reinach. "No longer any doubt, not a single doubt as to Dreyfus's absolute innocence. No more Dreyfus Affair."[12] "Maître Mornard's conclusion," wrote Mme. Dreyfus to her mother,

> was superb. . . . Everyone was moved. The public prosecutor, M. Baudouin, asked Mathieu to come to his office after the end of the session. He wanted to make his acquaintance. He was very cordial and told him that his impression was that we would get an annulment of the verdict without any new trial. We don't know how long the deliberation will take. Will it be one, two, or three days? We won't go to the Palais de Justice. We'll wait—how impatiently!—at Alfred's home for them to come in an automobile and tell us the verdict. . . . How long it takes, dearest Mother.[13]

The only discussion was over the eventuality of a new trial. Abiding by a strict interpretation of the law, Judge Moras was of the opinion that the High Court of Appeal had no other option than to refer the case to a new Court-Martial. The three presiding justices judged otherwise: annulment without a new trial was called for. Chief Presiding Justice Ballot-Beaupré sided with this interpretation, even though—as reporting judge in 1898—he had professed the opposite opinion. There was unanimity on the question of Dreyfus's innocence. And a majority decided for annulment without a new trial. On the basis of Moras's recommendations, Ballot-Beaupré wrote up the judgment that would be read at the session of July 12, 1906.*

On that day, before a standing audience, Chief Presiding Justice Ballot-Beaupré—heavyset, massive in stature, draped in ermine, surrounded by the presiding justices and judges of the three chambers—slowly read the judgment, annuling the verdict of the Rennes Court-Martial and rehabilitating Alfred Dreyfus. Upon concluding his reading (which had lasted more than an hour), Ballot-Beaupré paused for a

---

* See the critical analysis of the judgment, clause by clause, in Dutrait-Crozon's *Précis de l'Affaire Dreyfus.*

The High Court of Appeal, wrote Georges Sorel, "resorted to an extravagant application of Article 445." " . . . its mood was one of Dreyfusard generosity . . . and it did not take umbrage at one more irregularity in order to please the powerful."

moment, as though to isolate the words that had put an end to the Affair. Then, solemnly, controlling his emotions only with difficulty, he continued:

> Given that in the final analysis, of the accusation against Dreyfus there is nothing that remains standing,
>
> And that the annulment of the Court-Martial's verdict leaves no charge that may be qualified as a crime or a misdemeanor against him,
>
> Given, then, that by application of the final paragraph of Article 445 of the Penal Code, no referral to further adjudication is in order; For these reasons,
>
> The Court annuls the verdict of the Court-Martial of Rennes which, on September 9, 1899, condemned Dreyfus to ten years of detention and dishonorable discharge from the Army by virtue of Articles 76 and 463 of the Penal Code and Article I of the law of June 8, 1850;
>
> Declares that it was wrongfully and by error that that conviction was pronounced;
>
> Acknowledges Dreyfus's statement that he renounces any claim to monetary compensation, which Article 446 of the Code of Criminal law permitted to award to him;
>
> Orders that in conformity with that Article, the present judgment be posted in Paris and in Rennes and be inserted in the *Journal Officiel*, as well as in five newspapers to be chosen by Dreyfus;
>
> Authorizes Dreyfus to have it published at the expense of the Treasury and at the rates of legal insertion in fifty Parisian and provincial newspapers of his choice;
>
> Orders that this judgment be entered into the registers of the Court-Martial of Rennes and that mention of it be made in the margins of the annulled decision.

A shameful decision, the nationalists would maintain and one that defied the law. The High Court of Appeal could not quash the Rennes verdict without sending the Affair before another Court-Martial.[14] But the judgment, in Reinach's words, proclaimed that "day had come at a time when the sun was already high on the horizon."[15] The outcome had been inevitable and merely "relieved France's national conscience from a cumbersome burden of remorse."

Friends and relatives rushed to the Dreyfus home. A table with twenty-four places was quickly set at which the family and closest friends would soon be seated. Flowers in joyous profusion were delivered. Mathieu received the journalists arriving at the apartment and gently ushered them away. "Excuse my brother. Today he is entirely at the disposal of his friends." There was much embracing and weeping. "I had never doubted this triumph of justice and truth over error, deception, and crime," Dreyfus would write.[16] "What sustained me . . . was the unshakable faith that France would one day proclaim my innocence to the world. . . ."*

It had taken twelve years for France to vindicate an innocent man.

17

I Name You Knight of the Legion of Honor

With justice rendered, the time for reparation had come. In the Senate, on behalf of the leftist groups, Minister of Justice Monis immediately filed a proposed resolution paying homage to the civic courage of Auguste Scheurer-Kestner and Ludovic Trarieux, both of whom had died. He proposed "that busts of those two great citizens be placed in the gallery leading to the auditorium." The resolution was passed that very day by a vote of 181 to 29. General Mercier abstained.

On the same day, July 13, the Chamber was presented with two proposals by the government; one concerned Dreyfus, the other, Picquart. The High Court of Appeal's decision, which revoked the verdict at Rennes, restored Dreyfus to his rank as Captain with seniority of . . . seventeen years.† The proposal filed by Minister of War Etienne would

---

* Dreyfus wrote immediately to Picquart, who sent him the following response: "My dear Dreyfus, I thank you for your note. I can imagine your joy and that of those close to you. I would have preferred, as you know, a Court-Martial, but I won't be stubborn. Perhaps it is better like this."

† He had been a captain since September 12, 1889. Dreyfus, had he not been convicted, would have been decorated "for at least six years already," Etienne affirmed in his speech to the Chamber on July 13.

confer—through an exceptional law—the rank of squadron chief on Alfred Dreyfus "which he would assume on the day of the promulgation of the law" and award him the Cross of the Legion of Honor. The second proposal would reintegrate Picquart into the Army, and establish that "the period he had spent out of service would be counted as active duty." It recommended as a result that he be awarded the rank of brigade general, effective July 10, 1903.

The two proposals treated Picquart and Dreyfus differently.* Whereas Picquart regained all of his seniority and became a general retroactively as of 1903, Dreyfus plainly suffered damage to his career. For had he not been convicted, he would already have been a squadron chief for four or five years, and he would accede to that rank, according to the terms of the proposal, only at the time of the law's enactment. The government's proposal thus deprived him of any chance to attain those higher ranks of the Army which had once been his life's ambition. Even if Dreyfus, in his exhaustion, had no intention other than ending his days in retirement, he might have seen, in such treatment, a fresh injustice.† And the minister of war, in fact, had a difficult time persuading several of his colleagues to propose a law in favor of the rehabilitated officer. Clemenceau took no government action to prevent that iniquity, which only strengthened Alfred Dreyfus's decision: he would stay in the Army for no more than a year and then retire.

The Chamber, either moved by the occasion or anxious to begin its recess, voted through the two proposals on July 13. No one asked to speak. There were only 32 votes opposed, including Barrès and the remaining aristocrats and superior officers still in the Assembly. Concerning Picquart's reintegration,‡ a vigorous debate ensued, in which Louis Barthou and Maurice Barrès intervened, but only 26 votes were cast in opposition. The Chamber paid homage to Henri Brisson for having been "the most foresighted and courageous artisan" of the revision. Whereupon Pressensé intervened and injected an element of passion into an otherwise restrained debate.[1] He requested disciplinary sanctions against those officers "concerning whom the revision procedure had revealed fraudu-

---

* Some have detected in this the hand of Clemenceau, who was a great friend of Picquart.
† It appears that Reinach informed Etienne of Alfred Dreyfus's disappointment: "I understand nothing of the bitterness Dreyfus feels," Etienne wrote to Reinach on July 19, 1900. "It was with his agreement that I designated him in charge of Vincennes" (unpublished letter consulted courtesy of Dr. Jean-Louis Lévy).
‡ "The Army that marches today at Longchamp," wrote Judet in *L'Eclair* of July 14, "is now apprised of the fate awaiting it and of future reprisals. It includes today one more squadron chief and one more general. Picquart's case is even more curious than Dreyfus's. Advancing two ranks at once is, to say the least, original. . . . I wonder what military campaign in a foreign war would have brought in that many stripes and stars."

lent or criminal maneuvers posterior to the amnesty of 1900." For Pressensé, who had made the transition from Christian mysticism to socialism, this was the occasion for a solemn speech. A nationalist deputy, Pugliesi-Conti, cut him short, shouting that a government that allowed its Army to be insulted in such manner was no more than a government of cowards. Albert Sarraut, undersecretary of state with the Ministry of Interior, sprang on to him. Blows were exchanged.* Maurice Barrès intervened, denouncing the reprisals of the left "against the great institutions to which we are all attached, against the General Staff, against the Court-Martial—that is, against discipline and our military forces." The motion was finally rejected, but the Chamber paid "homage to the artisans of the revision" and "withered those responsible for the crimes denounced in the judgment of the High Court of Appeal." There were still many in that Assembly who, eight years earlier, had lashed out at "the leaders of the odious campaign undertaken to trouble the public conscience." Before dispersing amid an atmosphere of retributory enthusiasm, the deputies found time to order the High Court's judgment to be posted and—following a recommendation from Jaurès and Allemane—to vote for the transfer of Zola's ashes to the Pantheon.

In the Senate, General Mercier had the audacity to intervene in the debate over Dreyfus's reintegration and to accuse the High Court of Appeal of having resorted to an "irregular" procedure. At first the senators were dumbfounded; there followed an explosion of indignation. The senators hurled in his face the communication of the secret file in 1894 and the crimes he had either committed or covered up thereafter. Mercier stood his ground. "I am not presenting my defense. I am explaining my vote." He tried to speak amid the shouts, to complete his intervention: " . . . In these circumstances the conviction that I acquired in the course of the proceedings of 1899 is in no way shaken, and my conscience does not allow me . . . " The word "conscience" provoked a wave of jeers. The aged Senator Delpech, one of the earliest Dreyfusards, recalled to Mercier the debate over amnesty and threatened: "Were we, however, to press our need for justice still further, there exists a man who should replace the honorable victim in jail, whose innocence—after such protracted suffering!—was proclaimed yesterday: that man is you, Sir." Barthou intervened in turn, abusing Mercier, seeming to forget his own silence during those long years. Mercier attempted to respond in vain; he could

---

* That very evening the deputy and the minister had a swordfight on the property of Gast, a deputy from Seine-et-Oise and a relative of Picquart. The minister of the interior was a witness for his undersecretary of state. Sarraut was wounded and then fainted. This was the last of the 31 principal duels occasioned by the Affair.[2]

barely speak. By a crushing majority, the Senate voted for the reintegration of Dreyfus and Picquart.[3]

On July 20, the *Journal Officiel* announced Dreyfus's designation as Knight of the Legion of Honor. Reinach and General André had asked that Dreyfus receive the honor in the presence of troops assembled in the principal courtyard of the École Militaire where, twelve years earlier, the atrocious procession had occurred. Dreyfus feared he would be unable to bear the memory of the prior ceremony, and the minister of war proposed that the Legion of Honor be bestowed upon him in the small courtyard, in the presence of a restricted number of guests. At Dreyfus's side, Captain Targe, who had done so much for the revision, would receive an officer's rosette.

The military ceremony occurred on July 21. The day was gray and overcast. It was hoped that the occasion would be discreet: the Dreyfus family, Georges Picquart, Manuel Baudouin, Anatole France, and a number of journalists and photographers were present. Mornard, Demange, Reinach, Jaurès, and General André were not informed of the event.

Toward 1:30 P.M., Commandant Dreyfus arrived in full military dress: the four-braided black hussar's dolman and grenade-adorned cap of unassigned officers. The officers present greeted him and engaged him in conversation.[4]

The troops assembled in Dreyfus's honor—two batteries on horseback and two squadrons of cuirassiers—lined up parallel to the three sides of the courtyard. At 1:55 the trumpets were sounded. The captain of the first battery stepped forth to face Dreyfus, who crossed the line of cuirassiers. He had assumed the stiff, automaton-like posture that he had had on the day of his degradation. Upon reaching the end of the battery, Commandant Dreyfus snapped to attention, unmoving, his head high, his body continuously straining to remain erect. His terrible memories returned. He did not see the regiments there in his honor, but only those present at his degradation. General Gillain, Commandant of the 1st Cavalry Division, arrived, in ceremonial dress. With large strides, he passed before the troops. Dreyfus and Targe stepped forward, took their position in front of the General. To Dreyfus the difficult silence seemed endless: "My mind, disoriented, took flight, reawakening the dormant memories of twelve years before, the roaring crowd, the atrocious ceremony, my decorations stripped from me, my saber broken and lying in pieces, scattered at my feet . . . my heart was beating as though it would break . . . sweat covered my forehead . . ."[5]

Disturbing the silence, the General's voice first called Commandant Targe. From the rear of the courtyard a few cries of "Long live the

Republic, long live the Army!" resounded. Then the General stepped toward Dreyfus: "In the name of the president of the Republic, and by virtue of the powers invested in me, I hereby name you Knight of the Legion of Honor." His sword descended three times on Dreyfus's shoulder. General Gillain pinned the cross on the black dolman and embraced the soldier before him. "Commandant Dreyfus, I am happy to have been charged with decorating you." From windows overlooking the courtyard Lucie Dreyfus and Colonel Picquart viewed the ceremony. Someone shouted: "Long live Picquart"; "No, no, long live Dreyfus," Picquart protested. By then the troops were amassed in the rear of the courtyard, and slowly, to the sound of the brass band, they marched before General Gillain, before Commandant Dreyfus. At the moment they passed before him, they saluted him with their sabers, the traitor Dreyfus, the innocent martyr, the deportee of Devil's Island, the squadron chief of the French Army.

As the last of the troops disappeared beneath the vault, those attending surrounded Commandant Dreyfus. They shook his hands, embraced him. There were cries of "Long live Dreyfus!" He protested: "No, gentlemen, I beg you." He shouted "Long live the Republic! Long live the truth!" Lucie, his children Pierre and Jeanne, and his brother Mathieu were close by. He felt "the delicious embrace of all those I loved, for whom I had had the courage to go on living."[6] Dreyfus made his way toward General Picquart and expressed his gratitude. Picquart shook his hand warmly. Finally, broken by so many emotions, Dreyfus felt ill, and had to be escorted home.

The Republic had thus compensated Dreyfus for his years in prison, the worst suffering, with the Legion of Honor. In a few months Clemenceau would be prime minister, and Picquart minister of war. Zola's ashes would be transferred to the Pantheon. Alfred Dreyfus himself was squadron chief and Knight of the Legion of Honor. On July 25, he was presented to the president of the Republic by Joseph Reinach. He told the chief of state his intention to take his retirement the following year. On July 14, 1907, Commandant Dreyfus petitioned General Picquart, the minister of war, to liquidate all his pension privileges upon retirement. Dreyfus felt that he had nothing more to ask for, nothing more to gain. It was enough for him that France had restored his honor.

18

I Was Only an Artillery Officer

I n July 1906, Dreyfus had been appointed head of artillery in Vincennes. His retirement pension was liquidated by a decision of October 25, 1907; it had amounted to 2,350 francs for 30 years, 10 months, and 24 days of service. Since he had not been a squadron chief for two full years, he was retired at the rank of captain. His stay on Devil's Island was not counted, although legally, his time in prison could have been considered spent "under orders." Dreyfus did not protest. By a decree of October 12, 1907, he was named reserve squadron chief, and assigned to the military command of Paris.

Upon retiring, he was able—as he had so hoped on Devil's Island—to retreat into family life, devote himself to Lucie, to his children, to all those close to him, and attempt, as he had written, "to forget in calm all the sadnesses of the past and be born again to life."[1] His health was ruined beyond repair. He had brutal bouts of fever, long days of infinite fatigue. His nights were racked by nightmares; Lucie could hear his shouts. He began, patiently, to collect stamps—for he would receive hundreds of letters each year, until he died. He helped Lucie with her sewing. He read, classified, and annotated with meticulous care the newspaper articles thoughout the world that continued to evoke the "Affair."

However great his efforts to live in silence, he insisted in remarking on every possible occasion his loyalty to those who had helped him retrieve his life and his honor.* On June 4, 1908, he went to the official ceremony in the Pantheon celebrating the transfer of Zola's ashes. Aristide Briand, the former Socialist, was now prime minister. Georges Clemenceau, Jean

---

* Some, however, would reproach him with "ingratitude." He would be criticized for not attending Bernard Lazare's funeral even though he was in a state of exhaustion and recuperating in Switzerland at the time. The publisher Stock, who had taken great risks throughout the Affair, would not forgive him for having offered *Cinq années de ma vie* to another publishing house.[2]

Jaurès, and General Picquart were present. The Dreyfusards were reassembled for a moment in memory of Zola and the famous text that had restored their strength and their trust at a desperate time.* At the close of the ceremony, the journalist Gregori fired two shots at Dreyfus, who suffered a slight wound in his arm. *L'Action Française*, which was now the torchbearer of the defeated anti-Dreyfusards, exalted "this gesture for France." Before the Seine Court of Assizes, where he appeared in September 1908, Gregori proclaimed that he had wanted to protest "against Dreyfusism," to accomplish a symbolic gesture against a government that dared to "bestow military honors on Dreyfus's treason and Zola's antimilitarism."† Gregori was acquitted!‡ *L'Action Française* found in the event the wherewithal to launch a new and violent campaign against the Jews and the traitors who were now in power. Commandant Louis Cuignet—the man who had discovered the "Henry forgery"—became the most ardent spokesman of the anti-Dreyfusards. In a letter published in *L'Action Française* of September 16, 1908, he showered Chief Presiding Justice Ballot-Beaupré with abuse. "If in the High Court of Appeal, you are pre-eminent in dignity, you are also pre-eminent in breach of duty and infamy." The nationalists had the text posted in Paris and numerous other cities as a response to the posting of the vile judgment which had exonerated Dreyfus. On October 4, 1908, on the occasion of the dedication in Nîmes of a monument in memory of Bernard Lazare, *L'Action Française* organized a large demonstration. Léon Daudet and Commandant Cuignet were among the speakers. To a crowd of 4,000, they lashed out at the traitor Dreyfus, the magistrates who had sold out to the Jews, and the infamous Ballot-Beaupré. Clemenceau, on the other hand, was handled with felt gloves, for he had governed in 1906 and 1907 with the vigor of a true leader. He had brought the working class to heel. He was exalting the Nation in every quarter. Perhaps he was not as alien as the Dreyfus Affair had led them to believe. . . .

Alfred Dreyfus kept as far from these last waves of agitation as he could. When war came, he was mobilized as reserve artillery squadron chief, stationed first with the artillery officer staff of the fortified area of Paris, then, in 1917, with the artillery park of the 168th Division. He followed that division in its various displacements, and participated in the battles of the Chemin des Dames and of Verdun. Commandant Dreyfus

* A few days before the ceremony, Lieutenant Colonel du Paty de Clam felt obliged to send *L'Aurore* a refutation of Zola's attacks against him in *J'accuse*. "The planned ceremony," he concluded, "is the apotheosis of calumny."

† Du Paty de Clam and Lebrun-Renault, indefatigable anti-Dreyfusards, testified in criminal court on behalf of Gregori.[3]

‡ "This is the revision of the revision," Gregori would proclaim before the courthouse. He would dedicate his account of the "Pantheon trial" to "his great comrade Edouard Drumont."

attempted to be a French officer like any other. But those serving under him remembered his celebrated cause. Whatever he might do to be forgotten, in the Army he would remain the hero of the Affair. He was surrounded by hatred, curiosity, or deferential sympathy. In September 1918, he was promoted Lieutenant Colonel in the reserves. In July 1919, he was named an Officer of the Legion of Honor.

He was now a colonel in the reserves, prematurely aged, whose ordeals had ruined his health, and who was attempting to end his life peacefully. Suffering had transformed the diligent, ambitious, and active officer into a withdrawn and unoccupied old man. In his small and regular handwriting, revealing no trace of imagination or fantasy—but which so resembled that of the bordereau—he endlessly annotated the newspapers and books which spoke of his affair, his martyrdom.[4] In his apartment on rue des Renaudes, he spent long hours at his desk. Silently, smoking his pipe, he would be bent over a book, over the stamps he handled and classified with great care. He received his children, Pierre and Jean, and his grandchildren, on whom he bestowed ample attention. When they were invited, they knew they were to arrive on time; their grandfather could not tolerate the slightest delay. He took long walks to protect his fragile health. "I can still see him," wrote his grandson, Dr. Jean-Louis Lévy, "on Boulevard Courcelles—fragile, stooped over, nervous, walking rapidly, his large pocketwatch always within reach."[5]

Neither at meals nor during the vacations the family spent at the seaside was there talk of the Affair or of the time spent on Devil's Island. But the stooped figure of the old retired colonel, with his sudden bouts of fever, the vacant stare that would lose its focus, his life in isolation from the world, were eloquent. When darkness came, Lucie would help him to dispel his nightmares, the double shackle, the giant spiders, the cries of hatred, his broken saber cast at his feet. Death claimed Alfred Dreyfus in July 1935. He had been suffering for several months, went to Switzerland for an operation, returned, and took to the bed from which he was never to rise. Until the very end, he was cared for by his son-in-law, Dr. Pierre-Paul Lévy, and by Professor Marion. On July 11 his son Pierre came to see him as he did every day. Alfred Dreyfus held his hand for a long time, without saying a word, as though he wanted to transmit to him, in that silent gesture, his energy and his thoughts. The next day, about five o'clock in the afternoon, calmly, surrounded by his family, he died. Pierre placed his head on the silent heart that had loved and suffered so much. Lucie gave a last kiss to the companion who was leaving her. Both together and apart, they had shared everything. Until death she had been the light toward which, day and night, he turned.[6] "I can still see him on his death bed," wrote Dr. Jean-Louis Lévy, "with a tender and vulnerable look that I will never forget. A blue steadfast stare of wrenching tenderness: an inward stare."[7]

His cruel life thus ended as it had begun, amid the peaceful intimacy of middle-class order. Alfred Dreyfus had summarized it himself in these unassuming words: "I was only an artillery officer whom a tragic error prevented from following his course."[8]

Those who hated the Jew, the traitor, have preferred—for the convenience of their hatred—for him to appear mediocre, unpleasant, unintelligent, and soulless. During the ceremony of degradation, he appeared curt, stiff, agitated by convulsive gestures, a true marionette. Even to Maurice Paléologue, who was restrained in style and upbringing, Dreyfus in tatters seemed "as grotesque in appearance as he was pitiful. The traitor might shout: 'I am innocent,' but his voice remained dry, toneless, mechanical. There was no emotion in it."[9] "He is incapable of a movement of revolt, of a cry of horror. All his protests ring false." When Dreyfus reappeared at Rennes, he had not changed. To be sure, he was "worn out, emaciated, a miserable vestige of a human being."[10] But his voice was still hoarse, monotonous. It sounded as false as it had before. When he collapsed into his chair, he was still "like an automaton." He was incapable of warmth. "Nothing of his soul can emerge from that choked voice." It was as though he felt nothing.

That portrait sketches the features that can be found underscored and caricatured in numerous studies of the Dreyfus Affair. The anti-Dreyfusard tradition, which continues to perpetuate itself in a number of texts,[11] needed to entertain the image of an antipathetical and wily Dreyfus lacking in sincerity and humanity. In many respects, that image merely reproduces that of the stereotypical Jew. Dominique Jamet points out a sketch of Dreyfus by Georges Roux, who, upon meeting Dreyfus as an old man, claimed that he had the physiognomy of a vile scoundrel and that he was truly repulsive, almost repugnant.[12] Henri Giscard d'Estaing described "the cohabitation in a single individual of a distinguished mind and a glacial and shrunken soul. . . . His entire being, his way of holding himself, his gestures, his voice all exuded an invincible antipathy that not only his judges and adversaries experienced, but also his warmest advocates."[13] Armand Lanoux saw him as "so flat, so commonplace, so well reproduced in hundreds of thousands of copies, so physically lacking in any personality that one can understand that he has no existence as an individual."[14] But it is not only anti-Dreyfusards—who, unable to reproach him his treason, unwittingly accuse him of his innocence—that sketch this caricature. Numerous Dreyfusards have maintained it, though in a different manner. They have judged Dreyfus unworthy of his cause: "In his official role as hero and martyr," Péguy was already to write, "he has acquitted himself lamentably.[15] A major Dreyfusard current thus rids itself of Dreyfus by declaring him unable to serve his cause. He is seen as rather foolish, uncultivated, naively obsessed with a cult of honor and love of country, incapable of imagination, almost a simpleton. He looked "like a pencil salesman," Clemenceau is alleged to have said.[16] Many who regard the Affair as a heroic struggle for the values of truth and freedom thus eliminate Dreyfus, whom they ridicule or "annihilate."[17] In the last analysis, Dreyfus would have been a mere pretext, at best a symbol. An immense conflict over ideas and feelings would have been born of a man undeserving of anyone's attention.

No one was more convinced that the Affair transcended his own person than Dreyfus himself.[18] The day after the decision of the High Court of Appeal restoring his honor, he elected to isolate himself in the silence of his retirement. He wanted neither to assume the role of the hero he did not claim to be nor to be regarded as a symbol. "Dreyfus as symbol of justice is not me," he wrote to Victor Basch. "That Dreyfus was created by you."[19] Nor did he want his martyrdom to make of him a public personality or fuel any sort of notoriety. For him the Dreyfus Affair was over. For others, it continued, was only a brief incident in the struggle for justice or a stage in the transformation of a society. Many Dreyfusards who had never met or befriended Dreyfus, merely the cause he incarnated and the struggles at whose center he found himself, could not accept his refusal to uphold the role for which he had been marked: "Whoever is designated must march," proclaimed Péguy. "Whoever is called must respond. That is the law; that is the rule. That is the level attained by heroic lives, the level of lives of holiness."[20] But Dreyfus failed to heed that law:

> What did he proceed to do amid that world reputation, celebrity, and glory? A victim in spite of himself, he betrayed his glory. . . . There was a man who was a captain. He was hoping to be promoted to colonel or perhaps general. He was promoted to Dreyfus.
> Designated a hero in spite of himself, designated a victim in spite of himself, designated a martyr in spite of himself, he was unworthy of that triple designation. Historically and authentically unworthy. Insufficient, lacking, incapable, unworthy of that triple consecration, that triple investiture.[21]

But who had conferred on Dreyfus those "capital roles," that "triple investiture"? Who had "designated" him to march if not his executioners? It is true that he may have disappointed the devotees of the mystique, the politicians, all those who were serving ends for which he was a mere pretext. He had disappointed Clemenceau and Labori. He had disappointed Lazare and Charles Péguy. But Dreyfus had never asked for more than his due, never anticipated anything but his freedom, his honor and the proclamation of his innocence. He never saw or described himself as "designated a hero," "designated a martyr." "We would have died for Dreyfus," Péguy proudly affirmed, "and Dreyfus did not die for Dreyfus." But his struggle had been precisely not to become a martyr. On July 12, 1906, his struggle ended, Dreyfus disappeared from the scene. The fight was thus over for all those who had fought only for the innocent victim—Mathieu's fight, Demange's fight, the fight of the very small crew who were inspired by neither the mystique nor politics, and who had never struggled for anything other than the reparation of an injustice.

But the fact that Alfred Dreyfus restricted his role in such manner, that he disappointed those who asked more of him, is no license to distort our perception of him. He was in no way the disarticulated marionnette, the narrow-minded soldier, the alternately grotesque and odious character whom Dreyfusards and anti-Dreyfusards have often described, united at least in observing the discordance between the immensity of the Affair and the mediocrity of its hero.

There is no doubt that Alfred Dreyfus was the child of a solemn, somewhat limited and even petty provincial bourgeoisie. He was comfortably nourished on the edifying sentiments entertained by his family: a taste for privacy, respect for work, a sense of honor, love of country, devotion to truth and justice. He received as a legacy the principles of order and exactitude and a faithfulness to rites and customs. He hated the unexpected and distrusted everything that upset his habits, schedules, established customs and approved hierarchies. The new bourgeoisie, to which he belonged, was comfortable, thrifty. In a thousand sundry details of Alfred Dreyfus's life, an attitude toward money harmonious with that of his social class may be observed. He was satisfied to have it, and quite careful not to waste it.

It is probable that his upbringing, the fact also that he was the last born of a large family, at once spoiled and isolated, encouraged in him an almost neurotic modesty, a real difficulty in contracting social relations, and even a sense of solitude which seem to have been a source of both suffering and pride. He spoke little, expressed himself with difficulty, feared those whom he did not know. A shy man, he seemed pretentious. Reserved, he seemed haughty. He was said to have few friends in his life. He kept others at a distance, out of fear, out of modesty, or because he did not require them. That he was quiet, discreet, and even secretive did not prevent him from being impassioned and quite emotional. Many of his letters reveal extreme and even violent feelings, and emotions of brutal intensity. But he strained to control—or at least conceal—them. He was intent never to reveal anything of himself for fear of being indiscreet or ridiculous. From that self-control, which was certainly exacerbated by his military training, he derived true pride. Pride, in fact, is what Alfred Dreyfus found it hardest to conceal. He was proud of his family, proud of his position in society, proud of his profession, proud of his solitude, proud also of his character. In the depth of his worst ordeals, when he was shackled with irons on his feet, he retained pride in dominating his suffering, proving to himself that he was stronger than his agony.

It is not the least paradox of this drama, François Mauriac would write, that the victim of the General Staff was "the most soldierly of all those soldiers."[22] Dreyfus said that his military vocation was influenced by the occupation of Alsace by the Germans, but even before encountering the Army, he had numerous sympathies with it. A sense of honor and familial tradition appear to have been pressed in his case to the point of paroxysm: the honor of his name, the honor of his family, the honor of his children. The word honor was undoubtedly the one that flowed most frequently from his pen. He valued his honor more than his freedom, more perhaps than his life. A respect for hierarchy, moreover, came naturally to him. He loved and respected his superiors, even as he took his distance from those who were lower in rank than himself. He never called into question the hierarchies around him; they seemed to him immutable. Instinctively, he was a conservative with regard to the social order. An officer, he was confident in the Army because it had given him his place, because his rank revealed his merits, because organization and discipline were the cornerstones of the military. Until his return from Devil's Island, he would remain stubbornly convinced that his superior, General de Boisdeffre, was working toward the revision of his trial. Those who have seen in this a sign of his naiveté forget what the hierarchical feeling in the French Army at the end of the nineteenth century was like. The military hierarchy was not only perceived by officers as a hierarchy of functions dictating obedience, but also as a true hierarchy of merits imposing respect and even admiration for one's superiors. Concerning that hierarchy, Alfred Dreyfus had no other ambition than to rise within it by perpetually showing himself to be the best. If it took him so long to admit that the General Staff had wanted his conviction, that it had committed crimes in order to keep him in prison, it was because he felt he deserved, if not the sympathy, at least the esteem of his superiors. The exalted idea he had of the Army would collapse at Rennes, when he would come to know the details of his case and would discover the role played by the General Staff. That was a decisive and undoubtedly painful break about which he spoke very little. The day after the proclamation of his innocence, he would request his retirement, less to resume a peaceful life than because he could no longer truly serve the Army which had so hated him.

Pierre Vidal-Naquet has properly taken note of Dreyfus's silence concerning his affiliation with the Jewish tradition.[23] Neither in his writings nor in his letters does Dreyfus make the slightest reference to *La Libre Parole*'s campaign against Jewish officers in the Army in 1892, nor even to the anti-Semitism which he had, however, encountered. Not once, in his letters to Lucie from Devil's Island, did he say or indicate that his condemnation, his martyrdom, was influenced by the fact that he was Jewish.* It cannot, however, be maintained that he wanted to renounce his Jewish heritage. He married a Jewish woman in a Jewish ceremony: on April 21, 1890, Chief Rabbi Zadoc Kahn declared Alfred and Lucie joined in marriage according to the law of Moses and Israel. In the Santé Prison, on December 23, 1894, he wrote to the Chief Rabbi: "I would be very happy if you would be good enough to come see me and comfort me with your warm and eloquent words." Authorization was refused.[24] In the Paris trial, he asked Rabbi Dreyfuss to testify on his behalf. He assumed his heritage, even as he was proud of the name whose honor he defended. But he was the heir of a bourgeoisie which wanted to be completely assimilated. The fact that he was of "Israelite" persuasion concerned his private life. It was a matter of religion and family tradition concerning which he was not accustomed to speak. We run the risk of misunderstanding that silence if we view it with our contemporary eyes. The members of the assimilated Jewish bourgeoisie were not unaware of the fact that they were Jewish. They were not ashamed. But they did not believe that that singularity was in need of affirmation. Jewish tradition and belief belonged to the most intimate core of each individual, a core concerning which bourgeois discretion and modesty made it imperative not to speak. We are today the children of more garrulous times. We find it hard to admit that pitiless form of censorship, to understand that what is essential may be kept silent.

But it is also true that Dreyfus felt no solidarity with the Jews of France and of the world. The struggle for the recognition of Jewish originality, that waged by Bernard Lazare in favor of a Jewish nation, did not interest him. Even after hearing, on the day of his degradation, the cries of "death to the Jews!", and after reading all the newspapers in which the Jewish traitor was denounced, he did not really believe that what was being condemned in him was a Jew. No doubt he would later see what was patent:

* It is true that modesty played an important role in his case. And the deportee of Devil's Island knew that his letters were read and reread by the Prison Administration.

that anti-Semitism had played a decisive role in his case. But he would not speak about it any more then than he had before. Every source of suffering for the assimilated Jew, Michael Marrus has observed, only reinforced his will to assimilation.

It has been repeated that Dreyfus, had he not been Dreyfus, would have been an anti-Dreyfusard. There is little basis to believe this. No doubt, he was inclined to trust his superiors, the General Staff. The Army's honor was dear to him. He was prepared to defend it at all times. He loved his country to the point that the very idea of treason horrified him.* In his worst moments on Devil's Island, he nevertheless wrote that the ignoble treatment he was subjected to would still have been too gentle if he had been a traitor. But he would undoubtedly have been incapable of admitting that the honor of the Army required the condemnation of an innocent man or that anyone would have to be sacrificed for reasons of State. He would not have understood Maurice Barrès's point that the interest of France was the sole law, before which all others must bend. For France, in his mind, merged with an extremely demanding moral law. Being Jewish undoubtedly played a great role in his exalted notion of the nation. Like many republicans, he believed in the unending progress of the human species, in the irresistible spread—through space and time—of the cardinal virtues borne by the Republic. That France's interest or the Army's honor should dictate any abuse would have seemed absurd to him. In this he was closer to Picquart—also an Alsatian, also implacably virtuous—than to officers like de Boisdeffre or Pellieux for whom the "holy Ark" had the mission of defending old France against a changing world.

It is possible that Alfred Dreyfus, in his rigid and distant bearing, aroused antipathy. From his social class, he inherited a narrow view of the world. He never called into question the order into which he was placed, the virtues he had been taught, or the morality of his milieu. He contested nothing in the society in which he lived and suffered. He had little sense of humor. He was methodical to the point of being meticulous, rigorous and precise to the point of mania. He loved uniforms, decorations, hierarchies, military order, and never took them lightly. Amid the worst suffering, he seemed careful to maintain appearances. He exalted his various duties without ever questioning their content. His private life also revealed its limitations. He cherished his wife and children and those close to him, but we do not find in him any spontaneous sympathy for those who were different, strange, or foreign. Never did his sufferings in prison provoke a

---

* Jean-Louis Lévy has qualified his intransigent patriotism as "maternal." "He loved and did not judge his country. Whence, between France and Dreyfus, that wrenching lover's quarrel: Dreyfus loved France, who rejected and cursed him."[25]

greater reflection on prison as an institution, and the society that organizes so savage a repression. His honor, country, and family were the limits of his horizon. Even his conception of women revealed how he was a prisoner of his bourgeois and military context. Until his marriage he appears to have accepted distractions in the company of women of easy virtue. Once married, he exalted the family. He was a good son, a good husband, a good father, and a good Frenchman. What he did not know barely interested him. His culture was traditional, without daring or fantasy. What he said or wrote concerning the authors he read reveals that he retained only what was useful for him. His model was Napoleon. Throughout his correspondence, we do not find in him any imagination or spaciousness of thought. His ideas remained self-directed and repetitious. Julien Benda, who met Dreyfus after his liberation from prison, was stupefied by his will to "objectify" everything. Dreyfus always strained to be precise. He wanted to describe events and people as though he were outside them.[26] "That generation of rhetoricians," Mauriac has observed, "has as its hero the man most alien to all rhetoric."[27] He censored his feelings, even his ideas in order to retain only the facts and present them as though they did not concern him. There was much modesty in that stubborn will, an immoderate respect for method, perhaps the deformation of a scientific mind, but also a posture that reduced and severely limited him.

And the paradox was that that stance, combining morality and esthetics, cost him and caused him such suffering. He was obliged to remain impassive, almost detached, at a time when sentiments of rare violence were burning within him. His love of country was not a vague idea, a faint obligation he assumed half-heartedly. It was a veritable passion, which inspirited and energized him. He believed in the irresistible triumph of the truth, the final proclamation of his innocence, with a force that neither his suffering nor his failures could breach. That quasi-religious faith in the virtues of his country, in the victory of justice and truth, may seem odd today, a sign of naive obstinacy. But if Dreyfus had not been possessed by such powerful certitudes, he undoubtedly would not have survived the treatment to which he was subjected. More lucid and more skeptical, he would not have "held out." Without the assistance of chance, without Picquart's discovery of the *petit bleu*, without Cuignet's lamp, Dreyfus would probably have died a deportee on Devil's Island where many had succumbed to exhaustion or illness. Such was his trust in France, his obstinacy in believing in the forces of good, that he kept hope when most others would have given up. In order for Dreyfus to survive, a combination of fantastic human courage and invincible convictions was needed, which is not a bad definition of a hero. What would have been Captain Dreyfus's destiny, if the coincidence of a resemblance in handwriting had not resulted, one day in 1894, in his being summoned to the Ministry of War, then sent from prison to conviction, to deportation? He was reduced to that inglorious form of heroism consisting in no more than surviving, his considerable virtues marshaled to do no more than fight against death.

19

The Last Survivor

When Dreyfus died on July 12, 1935, he was, through some defiance of destiny, the last survivor of the principal actors in the affair whose hero he had been.

General Picquart, after having served as minister of war until July 20, 1907, had been appointed commander of the 2nd Army Corps by Minister Briand. He died on January 19, 1914, as a result of complications following a horseback riding accident, and received a state funeral.* After the ceremony of rehabilitation, he had not seen Dreyfus again.

A few months later, on the evening of July 31, 1914, with the German government having just decreed a "state of danger of war," Dreyfus learned of Jean Jaurès's assassination—struck down by Villain with two

---

* P.-V. Stock reproduces the obituary Jean Jaurès devoted to him: "General Picquart's death arouses in me a poignant melancholy. It is the sudden evocation of an already distant past with its ardent and painful struggles, its generosity, suffering, and hope. How incomplete this man's destiny was! When M. Clemenceau called him to the Ministry of War, I told our friends how much I deplored the appointment. Who could be sure that the moral nobility and penetration of mind that Lieutenant Colonel Picquart was to display in the course of the drama of the Dreyfus Affair endowed him with the requisite qualities for administering and reforming the Army? I feared that he would lose in a task for which he was not prepared a share of the sympathy and the merits that his heroism had earned him. Events were to prove me right, and his ministry was a cruel disappointment for many.

"But after all, what matter those errors of fate and those poorly chosen paths in a life! A few fervent and luminous hours are sufficent to give meaning to an entire existence, to perpetuate through history its reflection and example. Good citizens at this hour will remember only the calm words with which, throwing his life in the balance, he became the worker of justice: 'I will not take this secret to the grave.' As for me, I evoke the memory of our protracted conversations in the witness's chamber of the Palais de Justice during the Zola trial, of our familiar chats on the roads of Brittany after the sessions of the Rennes trial, in the twilight where at times it seemed to me I was hearing once again the death throes of justice."[1]

pistol shots. He experienced enormous sadness. Not only had Jaurès been the force who had gradually rallied the Socialists in support of his cause, but he had also been the shrewd and vigorous architect of the revision of 1906. More than Clemenceau—who had never accepted Dreyfus's acquiescence to a pardon—Jaurès had understood that the innocent victim refused to die in prison, a consequence not only of his generous and intelligent sympathy, but also of the fact that Jaurès placed the human individual above every other value:

> For Socialists, the value of every institution is relative to the human individual. It is the human individual, affirming his will to be free, to live, and to grow who henceforth is to bring life to institutions and ideas. It is the human individual who is the measure of all things, of country, family, property, humanity, and God. That is the logic of the revolutionary idea. That is socialism.[2]

Jaurès had succeeded in being devoted simultaneously to Dreyfus and to Dreyfus's cause. Gradually, the Socialist leader, whose vast culture and broad philosophical perspective nourished the project of changing the world, and the old officer in retirement had grown close. Beyond their differences, the distance that may have been created by Jaurès's support after 1906 for a pacifist and antimilitarist brand of socialism, bonds of esteem and sympathy continued to hold them together. Jaurès's assassination, the revenge of the nationalist spirit, henceforth identified with patriotic fervor, the subordination of considerations of justice and law to the higher interest of the nation at war, all seemed to mark the end of Jaurès's dream. It was a dream that Dreyfus had never shared.

Edgar Demange, the aged conservative, who, amid the tumult, had defended Alfred Dreyfus, the completely loyal and occasionally awkward lawyer, remained a close friend of the family until the end of his life. From the Affair he had derived no other profit than the satisfaction of having accomplished his duty and the respect of his colleagues who had so mistreated him during the period in which, courageously, he was alone in rendering Dreyfus a lawyer's services. In 1919, Joseph Caillaux, being tried before the Senate constituted as a High Court for communications with the enemy, asked Demange to defend him. One last time Dreyfus's attorney, by now stooped with age, his gaze still fiery beneath a shock of white hair, was seen raising in vain the eternal protest of law and justice against the arbitrariness cloaked in the folds of *raison d'Etat*. Until his death, Demange went daily to the Palais de Justice, dividing his life between his apartment on the Quai de Tournelle and his small house in

Monfort-l'Amaury. Very old and very poor, he died at his worktable on
February 10, 1925.

Elected deputy from the district of Fontainebleau in 1906, Fernand
Labori intervened in the Chamber in all major debates over questions of
justice: in 1908, in the debate over the abolition of the death penalty, to
ask that it be maintained; in 1907 and 1908, at Clemenceau's request, to
oppose the suppression of Courts-Martial, and to propose that they simply
be corrected by the addition of professional magistrates to the military
magistrates. He was quickly disgusted with the Parliament: "Parliamentary initiative is approximately nil . . . the work of Parliament is done
without any rule or order and frequently without any sincerity. Votes are
snatched up by vested interests. Parliamentary control is impossible. The
Deputies are subordinates of the Ministers."[3] In 1910, he elected not to be
a candidate. On June 30, 1910, his colleagues chose him to be their future
bâtonnier, president of the French Bar, and he had the pleasure of defeat-
ing Maître Raymond Poincaré in that competition. It was to be the sole
defeat of Poincaré's life. "You were the defense," proclaimed *bâtonnier*
Busson-Baillaut, an old anti-Dreyfusard, upon bestowing the accolade on
Labori in the name of all the assembled lawyers. In March 1914, Labori
exchanged with Mathieu Dreyfus letters of reconciliation, but the quarrel
flared up anew when Labori read a manuscript written by Mathieu, who
had judged him rather severely. Labori contined to argue a number of
"great cases." On the eve of the Great War, he argued magnificently for
the wife of Joseph Caillaux, who had struck down Gaston Calmette, the
director of *Le Figaro*, with six bullets.* She was acquitted. Once again
Labori proved he was undoubtedly the greatest criminal lawyer of his day.
He died on March 14, 1917 of complications from a long and painful
illness. He too had never seen Dreyfus again.

Nor did Georges Clemenceau come any closer to the innocent victim
for whom he had fought so valiantly. If Dreyfus owed much to
Clemenceau, Clemenceau owed much to Dreyfus. Sullied by the Panama
scandal, defeated for reelection in 1893, surrounded by hatred,
Clemenceau appeared to be written out of political life when the Affair
erupted.[4] For him it was the starting point of a new rise that would take
him to the leadership of the government in 1906. Clemenceau, who
remained quite close to Picquart and Labori, accepted neither the way in
which the Rennes trial had been conducted—to please Waldeck-
Rousseau, he thought—nor the acceptance of a pardon, nor the ties that
developed—through Joseph Reinach—between the Waldeck-Rousseau

---

* Undertaken to put an end to the press campaign waged by *Le Figaro* against her husband,
then minister of finance, to stop the publication of personal letters, to "do justice."

government and the Dreyfus family. However devoted and courageous he may have been in the service of an innocent man, Clemenceau remained above all a politician. The Affair for him was first of all a political struggle, and Dreyfus a symbol to help shake up political life and overthrow governments.

When the Tiger, as he was called, came to power in November 1917, appointed by Poincaré, he issued an inaugural statement that remained famous, exalting the Army and the nation to become one, and promising to punish traitors:

> In your presence and in the presence of the nation which demands justice, we take the pledge that justice will be done in accordance with the rigor of the law. Neither the considerations of individuals, nor flights of political passion will either divert us from our duty or inspire us to exceed it. Too many abuses have already been paid for on the battlefront with a surplus of French blood. Weakness would be complicity. We will be without weakness, even as we will be without violence. All the indicted will be court-martialed. The soldier in the courtroom will feel solidarity with the soldier on the front. No more pacifist campaigns, no more German plots. Neither treason nor demi-treason. War. Nothing but war. Our Armies will not be caught between two lines of fire. Justice will be passed. The country will know it is being defended. . . .

Thus did Clemenceau arouse the enthusiasm of the nationalists. And the new prime minister began legal action against all those whom he suspected or detested. Louis Malvy, the former minister of the interior and Joseph Caillaux, the former prime minister, were arrested and detained. The fragility of the accusations mattered little. Clemenceau invoked "the anxiety of the *poilus*, our soldiers, who can sense that while they fight, there are people betraying them." "It is imperative," he affirmed, "that those who are about to be killed have confidence in the government behind them." "The Army must be defended. . . . The public cause must be served."[5] Guilt and innocence, for Clemenceau the warrior, were jurists' quibbles. The nation, public opinion, and the Army's morale were in need of some exemplary convictions. The words now pronounced by Dreyfus's intractable defender were those that he had hated and denounced. In different circumstances, he was repeating what Mercier, Boisdeffre, and Barrès had claimed: above individual men and laws stood France, the Army. In the ditches of Vincennes, soldiers were being shot in the name of *raison d'Etat*. But the times had changed. No one, amid the enthusiasm of the Sacred Union, recalled the principles to which Clemenceau had clung twenty years earlier. France and Clemenceau were waging war. The Dreyfus Affair was a memory of more tranquil times. Clemenceau died in 1929 without having seen Alfred Dreyfus again.*

Mathieu Dreyfus had fulfilled his mission. He had given everything, six years of his life, his intelligence, his shrewdness, his fortune, without ever flinching, without ever complaining. He asked nothing but the proclamation of his brother's innocence. With his duty accomplished, he returned to direct his businesses in Mulhouse. Like Alfred, he retreated into silence. The War of 1914 tested him cruelly: his son Émile, seriously wounded on the front, died in October 1915. His son-in-law, Adolphe Reinach, was killed in 1917.† After the War, Mathieu Dreyfus moved to Paris and devoted himself to raising the three children of his daughter Marguerite and Adolphe Reinach. He was the most attentive of grandfathers, applying himself to cultivating in his grandchildren firmness of character and intransigent patriotism: the traditional Dreyfus qualities. He died in October 1930, leaving a will three pages in length, written in his fine, oblique, precise hand, and ending with the words "I ask forgiveness of those I have offended," and the luminous example of a life that knew no other guides than duty, tenderness, and courage. His grandson Jean-Pierre, who enlisted with the Free French forces, was parachuted into France in 1942 and killed in the course of accomplishing his heroic mission.

Lucie Dreyfus lived in Toulouse, then in Valence, throughout the years of war and occupation. She who had been a radiant model of courage and fidelity survived the man to whom she had given all by ten years. Until her death, she was a perpetual example of energy and loyalty, devoting her last strength to her family and to Jewish charity efforts. From so much suffering, she had retained an immense sadness. Lucie rejoined her companion in the family tomb in the Montparnasse Cemetery in December 1945.

Pierre Dreyfus was a heroic combatant in the Great War. He died accidentally in 1946. In 1936, he had published recollections of his father, paying filial homage "to the man who will be for future generations one of the purest heroes of the history of our beloved France."[6] Jeanne Dreyfus died in 1981. Stooped with age, at the end of her life, she was still the very image of her father: the same proud gait, the same "tender and vulnerable" gaze. Everything about her evoked the presence of her father, who had left on an all too long voyage when she was not yet two years old.

---

* They had seen each other, as Alfred Dreyfus's unpublished correspondence attests, in Clemenceau's apartment, on Rue Franklin, before the definitive revision. Thereafter their relations seem to have dissolved.

† Concerning the relations between the Dreyfus and Reinach families, see *supra* p. 236

Those who had committed Dreyfus to jail, and whose impunity had been ensured by the amnesty, had for the most part already died when Dreyfus passed away. General de Boisdeffre, who had retreated into a desperate solitude, had died on August 24, 1919. Colonel du Paty de Clam, wounded several times during the war of 1914, a glorious combatant cited on the Army rolls as "having given the most beautiful examples of courage and authority," was to die of complications from those wounds on December 3, 1916 at the age of 63. General Mercier remained a senator until 1920. He died in his eighty-eighth year on March 3, 1921.

In August of 1923, *The Daily Express* announced that on May 21 of the same year "Count Jean de Voilemont" had died in Harpenden in Hertford County. He was a traveling salesman, according to the newspaper, who had grown rich.* A very few neighbors followed the old aristocrat's remains to the grave. His solitude, it was said, concealed a thoroughly appalling past.

* The anti-Dreyfusards would maintain that such was the "compensation" paid by the Jews to Esterhazy, their employee.[7]

EPILOGUE

IN THE MIRROR
OF THE AFFAIR

1

From Legend to Legend

as the Affair yielded all of its secrets? Most of those who have written recently on the Affair have made clear the number of enigmas it continues to hold, which they have attempted to decipher as though the interest of the Affair still lay in solving its enigmas.* Joseph Reinach had already perceived the temptation that swiftly grips those who approach "the fascinating and captivating study of the Affair," that of allowing free rein to one's imagination.

> Because it was so extraordinary, they wanted it still more extraordinary; only complicated explanations would charm the reader; so they added to the drama, taking clear, simple, and brutal elements, and making them mysterious and confused. . . . In order to resist the temptation, it would have been necessary, like Ulysses, to tie oneself to the mast, and remain interested only in the facts.[2]

From the discovery of the bordereau to Commandant Henry's suicide, the Affair was the arena of so many crimes, collaborations, novelistic or absurd episodes that the temptation to add to them remains strong. The ruses of espionage and the intrigue of detective work perpetually meshed in new combinations throughout six long years, and they inevitably appeal to the imagination. Throughout the Affair, legends arose one after the other, invented in their entirety or fabricated on the basis of doctored clues: the legend of Dreyfus's confession the day after the ceremony of degradation; the legend of the "historic night" during the first revision; the legend of the bordereau annotated by Wilhelm II at the time of the Rennes trial; the legend of the veiled lady; of the syndicate of treason; of Henry's masked assassin; and of the forger Lemercier-Picard. The Affair was strewn with mysterious meetings, concealed plots, secret characters, centered, for the most part, on the Intelligence Service. Staging, masks,

---

* Marcel Thomas, at the end of a work executed with exemplary rigor, is one of the few authors to conclude: "It would be vain, in our opinion, to hope to resolve in an entirely new manner a 'mystery' which in fact has no longer been one for quite some time."[1]

and deception were all part of the "ordinary track" in that context. The drama began with a cleaning woman picking crumpled papers out of the wastebasket of a German diplomat and ended when an officer was discovered with his throat slit, a closed razor in his hand. Esterhazy, the traitor, was an adventurer, a blackmailer, a seducer, a superb and wretched lunatic. The principal criminal, Henry, was simultaneously a secret agent, a glorious soldier, a cynical police agent, and a mediocre forger. Given all this raw material, how could one not be tempted to add to so fabulous a tale?

In addition, the various theses promulgated find ample support in the very accumulation of testimony and statements. Esterhazy, in the innumerable interviews he gave, perpetually oscillated between the fantasies of a megalomaniac and the inventions of a skillful liar. In the end he clung to the version which "moralized" his role, but conceded to the evidence that he was the author of the bordereau: he had written it on orders from Colonel Sandherr, a circumstance which the deceased Sandherr was in no position to refute. Count Maximilien von Schwarzkoppen, whose *Notebooks* have the poised ring of truth, nevertheless took considerable liberties in his statements about the case. He systematically diminished the importance of the "ordinary track" because his negligence would have earned him a legitimate rebuke. He denied having received the bordereau, having thrown it into the wastebasket. But how could a diplomat who was also a secret agent acknowledge having acted so thoughtlessly? And of course Henry, General Mercier, General Gonse, Captain Lauth, and Commandant du Paty de Clam never ceased lying—first to accuse the suspect, later to exculpate themselves. In their innumerable depositions at the six successive judicial proceedings, they defended theses which were often at variance with each other, and on occasion openly contradictory.

Already Public Prosecutor Baudouin—in his remarks in 1906— allowed his inventive ardor to wander. He saw Colonel Sandherr, in an anti-Semitic rage, commanding Esterhazy to write the bordereau in order to obtain, through the similarity of their handwriting, material evidence against the Jew Dreyfus. And the very sage lawyer Henri Mornard, arguing in 1906 before the High Court of Appeal, admitted that Esterhazy might have been functioning as a double agent, with the acquiescence of Henry, if not Sandherr. Joseph Reinach himself, who denounced so effectively the temptation to fabricate the sensational, devoted a number of pages to demonstrating—on the basis of very flimsy evidence—a complicity between Henry and Esterhazy: from the moment of the bordereau's arrival, Henry would have recognized the handwriting of his former comrade and would subsequently have committed all his abuses in order to protect him.* Marcel Thomas, completing the argument proposed at the time by Colonel Picquart, has shown the fragility of the thesis that already in 1894 would make of Henry Esterhazy's active accomplice. That accusation requires us to assume that Henry continued to see Esterhazy after the latter had already left the Section of Statistics in 1880 and also that he would have "recognized" Henry's handwriting at the time of the bordereau's arrival. It asks us to imagine that Henry would have found it impossible to destroy the bordereau—which would have been the simplest solution for him—and thus to assume that other officers would have seen the document before him. It requires us to admit that Henry would have remained silent concerning that complicity when he "cracked" in front of Cavaignac, and above all to believe that Esterhazy, who furnished so many contradictory explanations, would have concealed— against his interest—the only one which was true. Moreover, is it essential to our comprehension of the Affair to determine whether Henry became Esterhazy's accomplice in 1894, at the time of the bordereau's arrival, or later in 1896, after Picquart had showed him the *petit bleu*? In proposing that Henry and Esterhazy were already accomplices in 1894, Joseph Reinach's thesis, which was taken up by Mathieu and Alfred Dreyfus, and after them by numerous others,† expands Henry's role. It aggravates his crimes. Henry becomes, as Léon Blum thought, Esterhazy's superior, the man in the General Staff who was both the "fomentor and the animator," who held in his hand from the very first "all the strings and all the switches."[6] When Henry pointed to Dreyfus in the 1894 trial and said "There is the traitor," he would appear even more monstrous if he were shielding the true traitor and were attempting to substitute one culprit for another. Is it necessary to make so dubious an addition to the burden of administrative abuse weighing down his memory and demonstrating the criminal behavior of the General Staff? And would not Reinach's thesis, on the contrary, have the unjust consequence of reducing General Mercier's guilt by exaggerating Commandant Henry's?

* Labori drew up a balance sheet of Joseph Reinach's errors and "inventions" in a note of March 15, 1904, on the morrow of the publication of the fourth volume of *L'Histoire de l'Affaire Dreyfus*.[3] Several of Labori's observations were approved by Picquart, who wrote in particular concerning the arrival of the bordereau: "The account of the arrival of the bordereau given by M. Reinach is completely incorrect."[4] Beginning on May 2, 1903, Picquart published in *La Gazette de Lausanne* several articles which contradict Reinach's positions on essential questions.[5] With convincing precision, Picquart set out the reasons why, in his opinion, it was completely implausible for Henry to have been Esterhazy's accomplice and inspirer from the outset.

† "Without absolutely adopting as our own such a hypothesis, we acknowledge that it is the one we find most attractive," writes Léon Lipschitz in the preface to his *Bibliographie thématique et analytique de l'Affaire Dreyfus*, Fasquelle, 1970.

Publishing in 1955 the *Journal de l'Affaire Dreyfus** that he had kept for
five years, from October 16, 1894, to the end of the Rennes trial, Maurice
Paléologue proposed a new version of the Affair based on his personal
knowledge of the case. There would not have been one culprit, Esterhazy,
but three: Esterhazy, Maurice Weil, and the third, "an extremely high
ranking officer."†

The accusation against Maurice Weil was not without precedent.
Throughout the trials, Esterhazy's links with Maurice Weil had been
brought up and during the proceedings of the second revision, Picquart
had vigorously called into question that friendship, which may have concealed a complicity. Maurice Weil, an extremely intelligent, brilliant officer
had had a turbulent career. He had served a term with the Intelligence
Service under orders from Colonel Samuel. There he had known Henry as
a young lieutenant. Later he had managed to get himself appointed to the
staff of the minister of war, General Berthault. He profited from that
experience by forging ties with several high ranking officers, including
General Félix Saussier. Most of his time was spent studying history,
speculating at the Bourse, attending race tracks, or in the company of
pretty women. An elegant Viennese lady, who was Jewish (as he was),
became his wife. He was seen in numerous salons, at the homes of the
Rothschilds, the equally prominent Ephrussis, and the Cahen d'Anvers.
In 1881, it was discovered that he had been cheating at the races. He was
obliged to resign from the Army and go into hiding for a brief period. In
1890, he managed to get himself reintegrated into the Army with the
support of General Saussier, a notorious homosexual, who had become or
pretended to be the lover of the lovely Mme. Weil. The indulgent husband
immediately reestablished his fine career at the Staff Headquarters of the
Military Governor of Paris. Two or three times each week he dined at the
Saussier home, as all Paris knew. In 1892, the Marquis de Morès had
begun a violent campaign in *La Libre Parole* against the thieving Jewish
officer "who had his major and minor entries into our national defense."
At the time Weil was constrained to leave Staff Headquarters, but General
Saussier, Maurice Paléologue maintained, "remained an intimate of the
Jewish couple."[10]

It happened that Maurice Weil was also a friend of Esterhazy to whom

* Maurice Paléologue was assigned to follow the Affair from its beginnings for the Ministry
of Foreign Affairs. Gabriel Hanotaux and then Théophile Delcassé renewed his mission.[7] It
was Paléologue who in 1899 presented the "diplomatic file" to the magistrates of the High
Court of Appeal and the judges of the Rennes Court Martial. The text of the *Journal*, given by
Maurice Paléologue to Librairie Plon in 1942 with orders to publish it four years after the
author's death, was manifestly corrected and revised by Paléologue.[8]
† The accusation is raised on several occasions in Paléologue's account and is once explicitly
formulated.[9]

he had loaned money, and whom he had recommended insistently when Esterhazy sought to be appointed to a ministerial staff. The commander-in-chief of the French armed forces was an intimate of Weil, who was an intimate of Esterhazy. But is this relationship sufficient to constitute complicity? That Weil was an intriguer, a cheater, without scruples, indulgent, and perpetually in need of money may have created a propitious climate for espionage. But there is not a single shred of evidence pointing to an act of treason.* And yet the temptation to close the circle is strong: Esterhazy and Weil would have worked together with the protection (if not the complicity) of General Saussier. In the most indulgent hypothesis, the two accomplices would have allayed the commander-in-chief's suspicions and profited from the secret information at his disposal. The thesis has been taken up on several occasions, after Paléologue, and in various versions. For some, it presents the advantage of replacing a Jew with a Jew. Dreyfus was innocent, but Weil was guilty. He was, moreover, a true Jew, as Maurice Paléologue observed, a Jew who had married a "voluptuous and Jewish" Austrian, who frequented the world of Jewish high finance, who could be found visiting the Rothschilds. General Mercier, in the last analysis, would simply have chosen the wrong Jew.

But who would the third party be? Maurice Paléologue refers to him without name[12] as an "extremely high ranking officer, who, after having occupied important posts at the Ministry of War, today is engaged in commanding troops."† That man could not be General Saussier. There is general agreement that Maurice Paléologue was denouncing General Rau, who had been General Mercier's chief of staff at the Ministry of War in 1893 and who had been appointed in 1895 to command the Twenty-third Infantry Brigade. General Rau, from 1886 to 1893, would thus have acted at times in concert with the two other spies, at times on his own, while organizing large scale treason for the benefit of the German, Italian, and Austrian General Staffs. "It was in Commandant Lauth's interest," Paléologue wrote, "for reasons of a private order to shield the third traitor." It was in fact the case that General Rau had married Mlle. Marie-Mathilde Lauth, which might explain why Lauth would have taken so active a role as soon as the bordereau had arrived.

On what had Maurice Paléologue's thesis been based? Henri Guillemin, denouncing the adventurous hypothesis,[13] properly remarked that it may have received fragile support from the text of the *petit bleu*, in which

---

* Concerning the legend of the "third man" and the accusations—particularly from Maurice Paléologue—against Maurice Weil, see Marcel Thomas's demonstration in Appendix II of his *L'Affaire sans Dreyfus*.[11]
† Maurice Paléologue wrote these lines, if the chronology of his *Journal* is accurate, on Tuesday, January 3, 1899.

Schwarzkoppen asked Esterhazy for a written explanation to determine, he wrote, "whether I can continue my relations with the R. house or not." *R* would designate Rau, as *D* seemed to designate Dreyfus. The thesis would also have been fueled by vague suspicions circulating in the Ministry of War at a certain point, though without leaving any trace, since General Rau pursued a brilliant career which he ended as general of an Army Corps and Grand Officer of the Legion of Honor. Marcel Thomas [14] discovered the minute clue on which Maurice Paléologue undoubtedly constructed his accusation, a note from Commissioner Tombs, dating from considerably before the Dreyfus Affair, and relating that a German adventurer accused of espionage had defended himself by claiming to have been in close contact with Commandant Rau.* In order to accuse General Rau of treason, Maurice Paléologue thus did not even need a similarity of handwriting. In five lines, the eminent diplomat strung together a frightening accusation (against a dead man, it is true) without proposing the slightest justification.

In his extremely well documented work of 1962, Henri Guillemin applied himself to demonstrating that the third man was . . . General Saussier himself. [15] Guillemin recalls the tight links joining Esterhazy and Weil and the suspicions which—already in the Rennes trial—were shared, notably by Picquart, concerning Maurice Weil. Guillemin then specifies, and rightly so, that Weil was plainly being protected by his wife's lover, to whom he owed his second career in the Army. He also observes that on at least two occasions Saussier's protection extended from Weil to Esterhazy. And Guillemin assembles the essential facts which might, in his opinion, lead to an accusation against General Saussier.

> Esterhazy, a regimental officer, was incapable of obtaining on his own the highly-valued intelligence that he furnished for months to Germany. He was not at the source of such information. Consequently, he had nevertheless found a way of entering into contact with that source. Someone was communicating to him what he was selling to the Germans. Someone who must inevitably be sought in a very small high ranking group.
>
> Saussier, the commander-in-chief, the highest military personality in France, the all-powerful Saussier, as Picquart writes, knew Esterhazy. Above all he knew Weil, a tainted individual, suspected of espionage by Sandherr and whom Saussier nevertheless had

---

* The accusation merited no credit and was not taken seriously, although enough to fuel gossip. Can it, moreover, be imagined that Esterhazy, if he had been General Rau's accomplice, would have silenced his name, he who up until the end tried to pass himself off as an agent of the General Staff?

taken on at one point as aide-de-camp. Saussier dined at Weil's home and slept with his wife, who was Austrian.

In 1894, Saussier attempted to prevent any legal action—indeed any investigation—when the bordereau surfaced.

Saussier shielded Esterhazy in 1897 to the point of allowing him his freedom at a time that he was already being charged with treason.

From the day that Saussier, at age 70, left his post, disarray began to spread through the General Staff, and Esterhazy, "discharged" by Cavaignac, began his revelations—which were not deceitful but truthful—concerning the support he had received from higher ups in order to dupe the judges before whom he had appeared in January 1898 and concerning the bordereau which he had indeed written.[16]

Saussier's guilt would clarify Henry's mysterious words to his wife: "You know in whose interest I acted. . . ." Guillemin is prepared to admit that his thesis "is only a hypothesis . . . an attempt at elucidation offered with all due reservations."[17] He does not specify whether he regards General Saussier as an active traitor or a traitor in spite of himself, from whom Weil and Esterhazy would have extracted the information they were selling to the Germans without his knowledge. Taking up Colonel Picquart's testimony before the High Court of Appeal on May 7, 1904,* Guillemin proposes that Esterhazy, through Weil's intermediation, would have obtained the documents he was selling on rue de Lille by blackmail;[19] and in addition, that Mme. Weil, something of a "veiled lady," would have supplied Esterhazy with information she overheard or pilfered from her lover.

But Henri Guillemin offers additional hypotheses as well. Perhaps it *was* Colonel Sandherr, as Esterhazy claimed, who had dictated to him— whose activities he had uncovered—the mysterious bordereau whose text is unintelligible and which never reached Schwarzkoppen. Perhaps in this way Colonel Sandherr hoped that a photo of the document would be transmitted to General Saussier, that Saussier would recognize the handwriting of his protégé, and that he would be inclined, as a result, to be more prudent in the future. Sandherr would thus have manipulated the spy in order to put an end to the espionage. The maneuver would have failed because of Albert d'Abboville, who noted the similarity of the script to Dreyfus's handwriting. A second culprit would have been invented—

---

* Picquart had declared: "A question which has always preoccupied me a good deal is that of knowing whether at a given moment Weil and Esterhazy had not attempted to blackmail someone who was highly placed."[18]

who was Jewish. Sandherr's anti-Semitism would have been satisified even though his diabolical plan had failed.

Thus do talent and inventiveness take their leave of the facts as the most complicated paths begin to seem the most natural. "A reverie, all this," Henri Guillemin concludes, "a hypothesis I have floated and whose fragility I can well see. By no means would I insist on it."[20] But in the interim, the Jew Weil has been convicted *in absentia* of espionage, and Mme. Weil and General Saussier of complicity. No doubt the trials of the dead are less cruel than those of the living. The Dreyfus Affair thus still bears its burden of hasty accusations and quickly packaged verdicts. It is still rife with convictions and degradations.* Undoubtedly the legend of the third party will resurface sooner or later, designating a new culprit.

Other historians have taken the opposite tack. They do not accuse, but exonerate the General Staff, the Army, and at times even Esterhazy himself. Thus Michel de Lombarès,[22] observing the oddities of the bordereau, reflecting on the conditions of its arrival at the Section of Statistics, and resituating the few unexplained details, claims that the bordereau would be a document fabricated by German counter-espionage from notes that Esterhazy had given to Schwarzkoppen, through imitation of Esterhazy's handwriting and on paper that he was accustomed to using. German counter-espionage is alleged to have wanted to guarantee that Esterhazy, who was offering his services to the German military attaché, was not a double agent. If the French Intelligence Service "reacted" upon receiving the bordereau, they had proof that Esterhazy was an authentic spy whom Germany could trust. Esterhazy was indeed a French agent, according to Michel de Lombarès, but he belonged not to the Intelligence Service, which was unaware of his activity, but to a small team of agents that had been constituted by General Saussier, specifically with the help of Weil. Weil would have recruited Esterhazy, who would have gone "on a mission" to the German embassy to sell a few documents, and lure the military attache in the hope of finding out—for this was General Saussier's major preoccupation—what the Germans knew of the 75 gun and the degree of real interest they had in it, Esterhazy would have kept up his dealings with the Germans for his own advantage. . . .

This complicated version is based on a few particularities of the bordereau. The paper was alleged to have been manufactured in Germany by Varinard, an expert who testified at the Esterhazy trial. The bordereau contained Germanic turns of phrase, German letters and syntax. Its con-

---

* Marcel Thomas writes: "There is not much to be derived today from those vague second or third hand assertions, embellished or distorted at will, dating from a period when the intoxicating procedures of the Section of Statistics began to be glimpsed only through a haze conducive to every misunderstanding."[21]

tradictions could not be explained if the document were the work of Esterhazy. "In all the letter's details," maintains Michel de Lombarès, "the hand of the German Intelligence Service is to be found."[23] Michel de Lombarès thus presents a thesis precisely the opposite of Henri Guillemin's, since it ends by exonerating Weil and Esterhazy, who would have been nothing more nor less—at least at the time of the bordereau—than agents of Commander-in-Chief Saussier's exploits in serving his country, and Esterhazy would have died without revealing the patriotic mission he had accomplished. In the last analysis, it would be the Germans, the true authors of the bordereau, who would bear responsibility for the matter; the French would be innocent.

Another volume published by Henri Giscard d'Estaing[24] exonerates Esterhazy, as well, posing him as a double agent. D'Estaing also undertakes to justify General Mercier and the entire General Staff. His starting point is quite close to Michel de Lombarès's: at the time that the technical services of the French Artillery were perfecting the 75 gun, General Mercier sought to divert German attention by intoxicating them with true or false information intended to channel their investigations and defend the "vital secret" of the French arsenal. Esterhazy would thus have been employed as a double agent in order to abuse the Germans by giving them false or useless information. Alas, the French Counter-Espionage Service was too efficient and the German military attache in Paris too irresponsible. Once the bordereau was discovered and Dreyfus suspected, General Mercier could not reveal the existence of his secret network. He had no other choice, given the national interest, than to allow an innocent man to be accused. Henri Giscard d'Estaing thus manages to absolve everyone: Captain Dreyfus, since it is hardly possible to do otherwise; Esterhazy, whose acts were performed in the service of France; General Mercier, who was constrained to submit—in a silence imposed by the national interest—to the "dreadful stroke of fate" which had thwarted his plans; and finally the entire Army, which retrieves its dignity and emerges cleansed by the author "of the accusations lodged against it by those who have judged in the name of philosophy, unaware of the true grounds of the Affair."

As Jean-Pierre Peter has correctly observed, in the course of his meditation on the dimensions of the Dreyfus Affair,[25] Henri Giscard d'Estaing takes up Mercier's enterprise "as though it were his own." On the other hand, he condemns pell-mell the anti-Semitic press, whose relentlessness was to provoke the revisionists' investigation; Esterhazy's venality, since he began to traffic in documents for his private advantage; Schwarzkoppen's irresponsibility, the initial cause of the Affair; and the ill-determined mystique of the anti-Dreyfusards. But he also condemns Dreyfus's lies and contradictions, the bad faith or intellectualism of his defenders, and the shady maneuvers of the Jewish syndicate. By the conclusion of Henri Giscard d'Estaing's study, there is nothing left of the Dreyfus Affair, nothing but an unfortunate turn of events, a misunderstanding, "an impossible dialogue between two parties who were not speaking about the same thing." And Dreyfus? He had—at least according to d'Estaing—the good fortune to be a Jew and thus to benefit from the solidarity of Jewish high finance.* An indigent Christian would have remained in jail. Moreover, d'Estaing agrees that Dreyfus was not a German agent, but offers the hypothesis that he may have been engaged in intelligence work for France and also for Russia; that like Esterhazy he had become a double agent who would have been "liquidated" without regret.

Henri Giscard d'Estaing's hypotheses clarify, in their way, the permanence of the conflict of ideas and beliefs to which the Dreyfus Affair, in its time, gave expression. For the author pursues an idea, if not a mission: to demonstrate that the General Staff—with General Mercier at its head—was serving throughout this drama the most noble of ends, that it was concerned solely with the clearly understood interest of the nation. And if the Affair overran its bounds, it was because Dreyfus was a Jew; because "a large section of the good people of France, legitimately exasperated by the hypocritical intrusion of France's enemies (under cover of a fallacious humanitarianism) was driven to regrettable excesses"; because the Jews, with their enormous finances, and the intellectuals who flocked to their service, exploited the Affair and prevented it from remaining what it would have been had it involved only true Frenchmen, Christians, "a family affair."

There has thus persisted—without our having to examine the efforts of the militants of anti-Dreyfusism†—a tradition revealing, in Jean-Pierre Peter's phrase, "the existence of a long cycle which has not yet produced all its effects." Esterhazy is rehabilitated and elevated to the dashing role of a double agent. General Mercier is exonerated for never having done anything but his patriotic duty. Henry himself was no more than an overzeal-

---

* "People took a stand for Dreyfus," explains Henri Giscard d'Estaing, "the way they subsequently did for Sacco and Vanzetti, for example. Some, and not the least, were Dreyfusard out of intellectualism as though it were a matter of resolving a debate on Cubist art or existentialism."[26]

† Among which, let us note Andre Figuéras's *Ce canaille de D . . . reyfus*, which revives pell-mell all the accusations of the General Staff against Dreyfus, but which has the additional interest of expressing the persistence of an anti-Dreyfusard tradition indifferent to history.[27] Henriette Dardenne's study,[28] written by Cavaignac's daughter with the help of her father's notes and archives, is a moving homage inspired by filial piety but is blinded, alas, by anti-Dreyfusard hatred.

ous aide serving the most noble of ends. And the Dreyfus Affair, in ardent, virtuous France, was no more than an insignificant accident, due to the carelessness of a German diplomat, the coincidence of a resemblance in handwriting, and—alas—the shortcomings and excesses of the Jews.

2

The Long Wave . . .

It remains to be determined what role the Affair played in French social history at the turn of the century. What did it change or consolidate? Major contradictions may be observed among those who have attempted to draw up a balance-sheet of the Affair, totalling differently with each point of view. Some see in the Dreyfus Affair a crisis with lasting effects which dictated or precipitated a large-scale shift in society. Others maintain that that long wave touched only the surface. "Once the Affair was over and the fever subsided, society, its political institutions, groups, and individuals found themselves much as they had been before, as though nothing had happened," concluded Léon Blum in his *Souvenirs de l'Affaire*.[1] Distinctions between social classes had not been blurred, social relations had not been altered, "nothing had affected the human condition." As an "evenemential" crisis, the Affair would ultimately have "left less of a mark . . . than a simple crisis of industrial overproduction."

One of the difficulties involved in summing up the Affair is that there are in fact several different Dreyfus Affairs. First, there was a judicial affair that lasted for twelve years, from Captain Dreyfus's arrest until his rehabilitation. But even that episode can be divided into several affairs, interrupted by extended parentheses. The first affair ended in January 1894 when Captain Dreyfus, convicted of treason, disappeared in his prison on Devil's Island. The second began in 1896 with the efforts of Mathieu Dreyfus, Auguste Scheurer-Kestner, and Georges Picquart. It continued until Henry's suicide in August 1898, "after which," wrote Léon Blum, "the Affair, the true Affair, was over."[2] There then occurred the protracted period that began with the first revision procedure and continued through the Rennes trial up until Dreyfus's pardon in September 1899, when the "incident" was finally over. Still a later affair would take us—from 1900 to 1906—to the decision by the High Court of Appeal establishing Dreyfus's "juridical innocence."

No doubt the political Affair was shorter. It went from Mathieu Dreyfus's denunciation of Esterhazy to the presidential pardon, from November 1897 to September 1899.[3] But it cannot be maintained that in the years preceding and following that violent two-year explosion the Affair was a matter of indifference to French political life. And were there not still other Affairs, press campaigns, intellectual confrontations, ideological, mystical, and ethical involvements which do not necessarily mesh with the series of legal procedures and the political struggle? All those who entered into the Dreyfus Affair on one side or the other did not do so at the same time or for the same reasons. They did not live the same Affair—so much so that they frequently could not understand each other. How can one channel into a single river water flowing down such different slopes?

The very duration of the Affair—or the Affairs—is a source of difficulty. Two years? Six years? Twelve years? If one concentrates on the most extensive period, running from the discovery of the bordereau to the judicial proclamation of Dreyfus's innocence, how can one isolate the Affair in order to verify its effects? In twelve years the forces confronting each other, their behavior and their relations, changed a great deal. Those twelve years saw the collapse of monarchist hopes, the decline of the Church's influence, the disciplining of the Army, the consolidation of the Republic, the rise of workers' demands and workers' movements, and the unification and then the dispersal of the various lefts. How might one perceive the role of the Affair over so long and tumultuous a period? How could one determine when it provoked various developments, when it encouraged them, and when it remained indifferent? Inversely, twelve years is a short time, as Jean-Pierre Peter has observed,[4] over which to observe the shifts within a society: "Only a certain density of time endows societies with their consistency, constructs them before our eyes in their coherence and their evolution." Within French history, the Dreyfus Affair was perhaps something in the order of an "abscess," the symptom of a more general problem. But can one claim to "reconstitute the entire social organism" from an examination of that exception? And in the fever that racked a whole society, how might one determine whether the abscess is a cause or an effect? In what respects was it both? The Affair, to the extent that one attempts to isolate it, to extract it in order to better our comprehension, inevitably runs the risk of evading our grasp. And there is yet a great temptation to yield to the lures of the imagination. Our devotion to the ideas and ethical principles which were deployed in the Affair and the great debate it initiated may inspire us to exaggerate its historical importance. Inversely, we risk diminishing its effects on the pretext of reacting against such an exaggeration, seeing it as a mere "ripple" on the surface lest we be mystified by a confrontation that was bourgeois, Parisian, intellectual, and superficial.

Where all observers seem to agree is the role the press played in the Affair.[5] For the first time the press exercised a major influence on the political life of the nation, dramatizing and fueling the event, supporting or denouncing the authorities, exercising pressure and various forms of blackmail. "The Dreyfus Affair is first of all an affair of public opinion," writes Pierre Miquel. "At every phase of its evolution the press was more or less to be found. . . . It took the place of official justice, the police, and Parliament itself. It engaged in every form of blackmail, lashed out at every reputation, focusing society's energies, or if need be dispersing them, amusing them, in order to remarshal them indefinitely later on. It was the press which made of the Dreyfus case the Dreyfus Affair and then the Dreyfus myth."[6] And Patrice Boussel has usefully drawn up an inventory of the principal interventions by the press which made and unmade the Affair:[7] *La Libre Parole*'s campaign of 1892 against Jews in the Army; in October and November 1894, the articles in *La Libre Parole*, then in *Le Soir*, announcing the arrest of Captain Dreyfus; the campaign waged against the traitor on the eve of his trial; the article in *L'Eclair* of September 15, 1896 revealing the introduction during the deliberations of the military judges of a secret document "in which Dreyfus was named"; the publication of the text of the bordereau in *Le Matin* of November 10, 1896; the "Vidi" and "Dixi" articles; the publication by *Le Figaro* of Mathieu Dreyfus's letter denouncing Esterhazy on November 17, 1897; Zola's important articles in *Le Figaro* and the celebrated *J'accuse* published in *L'Aurore* of January 13, 1898; the publication in *La Libre Parole* starting in December 1898 of the lists of contributors to the fund for Colonel Henry's widow; *Le Figaro*'s publication, organized by Mathieu Dreyfus, of the results of the investigation of the Criminal Chamber. . . . There would be no end to an enumeration of the writings which played a role in the evolution of the Affair, both to help send Dreyfus to prison and to assist in getting him out, and of the multitude of articles in which Henri Rochefort, Edouard Drumont, Maurice Barrès, Georges Clemenceau, Jean Jaurès, Jules Lemaître, Ferdinand Brunetière, Lucien Herr, and Emile Zola appealed to public opinion, for the journalists of the Affair were most often writers or committed politicians who found in the press the most effective means of reaching their public. "The Dreyfus Affair," Pierre Miquel has written, "historically constituted the appearance, within the liberal framework of a restored parliamentary regime, of the press as a power linked—but also equal—to that of wealth. . . . It was the press in its entirety, of the left and of the right, which was the great victor of the Affair. In striking fashion, it succeeded in demonstrating its power."[8]

That the press played a decisive role first in sending Dreyfus to prison (by exploiting anti-Semitism and a hatred for traitors inherited from the War of 1870), then in the revision of the trial (by helping to reveal the shameful conditions of his conviction and the crimes committed against the deportee of Devil's Island) is beyond doubt. In commenting on the new power of the press, Pierre Miquel is right to assert: "Jaurès the journalist was stronger than Jaurès the Deputy; Clemenceau, defeated in the elections, was more formidable in *L'Aurore* than in Parliament. As a Deputy, Drumont had no audience at all in the Chamber." It is true that during those years the principal public forum shifted from Parliamant to the press. The fear aroused by newspapers in republican governments could already be observed. The fact that General Mercier wanted to please *La Libre Parole* explains in part Dreyfus's trial and the communication of the secret documents. Charles Dupuy and Jules Méline were perceived as trembling before the newspapers of the right. And it was the left-wing press which pressured Henri Brisson, the reluctant revisionist, and constrained him to commit himself.

But we should also take note of the limits of the press. First of all, its influence was a function of circulation. In 1898 and 1899, the years most jolted by the Affair, *La Libre Parole* was publishing editions of 100,000, *Le Figaro*, a newspaper of the center, editions of 40,000; and *L'Aurore*, which was left republican, editions of 25,000.* The larger printings were those of the Catholic press—*La Croix* alone printed editions of 170,000—and above all the press intent simply on divulging information and which devoted scant space to the Affair: *Le Petit Journal* claimed to print editions of more than a million, *Le Petit Parisien* of more than 700,000, *Le Journal* of 450,000.[9]

Moreover the press, despite its influence on public opinion, could not fully control that opinion.[10] It amplified its movements; it could not create them.[11] At times it was impotent. When Waldeck-Rousseau pardoned Dreyfus and proposed an amnesty, the Dreyfusard press and a large sector of the anti-Dreyfusard press, for opposite reasons, condemned his policy. "The reduction of the sentence and the pardon," Janine Ponty has observed, "were obtained in spite of the views of the majority of the press."†

* Except immediately after the publication of *J'accuse*: for a few weeks *Le Journal* had printings of nearly 150,000.
† The Dreyfusard press, with 11 dailies in Paris and 17 in all of France, at the time reached only 11% of the readers in Paris, and 15% of those in France.[12]

But the public had tired of the Affair, a circumstance that Waldeck-Rousseau, who was indifferent to the press, had perfectly understood. During the second revision procedure, Drumont and Rochefort tried once again to arouse public opinion against the traitor of Devil's Island, the High Court of Appeal, and the Jewish syndicate. They were no longer heeded. Anti-Semitism itself, after 1902, despite the efforts of the right-wing press, seemed exhausted and in decline. The press could hardly prevail against popular sentiments to which it ultimately submitted.

Next it is imperative to gauge the influence not of the editorially-oriented, opinion-forming press—which regularly intervened in the Affair and which was essentially Parisian—but of the provincial press, which while it spoke little of the Affair, all the same managed to influence its readers, and above all of the Catholic press, specifically the publications of La Bonne Presse, which played an essential role in the diffusion of anti-Semitism.* And undoubtedly the global role of that press—nurturing and cultivating the state of mind of the impoverished or irritated middle classes, stirring up the anti-Judaic traditions of Christianity, encouraging a hatred for foreigners, Jews, members of Parliament, all those who disturb the traditional balance and its peaceful order—is in the last analysis more important in explaining the evolution of the Affair. Its action went deep and was more insidious than the brutal explosions of the intellectual press, which tended to affect procedure rather than public opinion.

Finally it is necessary to investigate just who were the various "publics" the press was addressing, at times in order to inform, at others to move. What is called public opinion is perhaps, writes Jean-Pierre Peter, "in a world of clearly defined interests and overt conflicts, the mass of those who believe that by not committing themselves, they have retained their freedom, who are satisfied merely to keep informed of events—the unorganized, with their confused stands and poorly defined interests."[14] "Public opinion," in that light, would above all be the domain of the middle classes.† "Justice and Truth rising against intolerance and *raison d'Etat*: that debate concerned only a small number of lucid and privileged individuals."[16] Beyond them, Jean-Pierre Peter has proposed the hypothesis that from the beginning to the end of the Affair, the middle classes had no other aspiration than order and tranquillity. The revision would have been

---

* There were about a hundred provincial supplements to *La Croix*. Danielle Delmaire has studied the anti-Semitism of *La Croix du Nord*—with editions of 25,000—during the years 1898 and 1899. "The anti-Semitism" disseminated on a daily basis by the paper "impregnated and contributed to mislead many minds." On the other hand, it devoted very little space to the Dreyfus Affair itself.[13]

† If there was a "public opinion affair," writes Jean-Pierre Peter, it was in the sense that public opinion was toyed with and that the press experienced its strength in the process. Peter gives his study of the role of the press the title: "L'Opinion spectatrice."[15]

an impossibility as long as it was perceived as a form of disorder. It would have become easier to implement once social order seemed to dictate it: "What in fact triumphed was public order and a certain form of the Republic."[17] That public order was the true victor throughout the Affair is probable, but why did that order require successively Dreyfus's guilt, his innocence, his deportation and his liberation? And did not the press play an essential role in amplifying those contradictory impulses, augmenting in addition the share of irrationalism which inevitably enters into the turbulent phases of a society's existence?

A further consequence of the Affair, inseparable from the role of the press, was the coming together of intellectuals into a collective involvement with the life of the *polis*. Throughout the eighteenth and nineteenth centuries, contemplatives, artists, and poets had become involved in public life; it may even have appeared to be one of the original features of French society. But it was in the Dreyfus Affair that for the first time they intervened as a group, in a massive and concerted show of commitment. "It was striking testimony to the fact that it was becoming impossible to govern while abusing the laws of the human mind. Thought itself was becoming aware that in a democracy it too was powerful."[18] The organized involvement of the intellectuals, as an influential group, expressing a shared authority, would henceforth be one of the constants of French political life.[19] What was remarkable in the Dreyfus Affair was not simply the gathering of intellectuals—on the left, immediately after *J'accuse*; on the right, with some delay, in the Ligue de la Patrie Française behind Jules Lemaître, François Coppée, and Maurice Barrès—but also that the Dreyfusard involvement comprised numerous intellectuals who were resolutely removed from any political action and indeed any political concerns, specifically on the part of scientists who seemed not to take any interest in public affairs. The involvement of Edouard Grimaux, Emile Duclaux, Paul Painlevé, and many others thus took on a specific meaning. It signified not merely the moral imperative of truth and justice, but the demands of free inquiry against blind fanaticism, scientific method against impassioned improvisation, scruples against arbitrariness. It was, in a pure state, a revolt of intelligence, aware of its own authority. That public intervention of uncommitted intellectuals—in the name of freedom of inquiry and logical rigor in order to defend truth and justice— would recur in the twentieth century at a few rare junctures.

How did the Affair modify the history of the Republic, the balance of political forces in France? Most observers[20] acknowledge that it ultimately served the cause of the Republic, strengthened parliamentary democracy, ensured the defeat of the forces of reaction, and ruined the hope for a restoration of the old order.[21] The fusing of a common hatred of Jews,

Dreyfusards, Parliament, and the Republic; the excesses of anti-Semitism, from the fanaticism of its speeches to the violence of its acts; the brutality of a nationalism wrapping the values of the *ancien regime* in the folds of the flag; and the attempts at a *coup d'état* all had as their counter-effect the unification of the partisans of the Republic. There thus resulted a dislocation of the rather flabby center on which Jules Méline had depended for his base of support. And Waldeck-Rousseau's government marked at the beginning of the twentieth century the decisive victory of the Republic over those forces—the Army and the Church—entertaining the hope of a return to "traditional France." Would that path have been trodden without the Dreyfus Affair? Would the reactionaries have found other ways of threatening the Republic, thus provoking the same defenses? It is true that nationalism was merely renewed and exacerbated by the passion of the anti-Dreyfusards. It could be situated as the heir of Boulangism. That aggressive right, bruised by its contacts with the modern world, was not born of the Affair. Contesting the role normally attributed to the Affair,[22] Rudolph Winnacker has observed that the political realignments that occurred during the Affair were already found in the results of the elections of 1893, which consecrated the victory of the Republic. Only 78 monarchists had been elected, as opposed to 503 republicans. The 1898 elections thereafter did no more than maintain the republican majority, and in that the Dreyfus Affair played virtually no role. Thus the breakup of the center in June 1898, the fall of the Méline government, and the constitution of a government of the various lefts would owe (almost) nothing to the Affair. The Waldeck-Rousseau government was already programmed into the natural evolution of the forces confronting each other. "The Dreyfus Affair had simply indicated the political weakness of the anti-republicans who, if left to themselves, would normally have withered away."[23]

But should we not be cautious about underestimating—as well as exaggerating—the role played by the Affair during the six decisive years for the Republic that ended the nineteenth century. The Dreyfus Affair opened up to the anti-republican right—defeated at the polls since 1893—an arena for propaganda and activity into which it plunged with great ardor. It allowed nationalism to clothe itself with a mystical aura. It helped a good deal in furnishing the movement with a doctrine, notably by fueling it with anti-Semitism. It justified the struggle against the Republic and all but endowed it with a sacred mission. As a result it supplied justification and energy to the cause of defending the Republic, without which it is not clear that the Republic would have been as strenuously upheld. Without the turbulence of the Affair, would Déroulède's plot, the agitation of the nationalists, the commitment of numerous officers to reaction, the crimes of high-ranking officers to keep Dreyfus in jail, and the "Holy Ark" itself have been crushed and brought to heel as they were by Minister of War Galliffet and André after him? If the teaching congregations and the Church itself had not joined in the nationalist agitation, if the quasi-religious battle against Jews had not succeeded in enlisting the clerical forces, would the Republic have achieved a majority around policies of such unrelenting anti-clericalism? The Army and the Church, the two great anti-Dreyfusard forces, were thus also the victims of the Affair. Because they plunged into it and fought what they saw as the united threats of Dreyfus and the Republic, they forced the Republic to impose its will on themselves.

Madeleine Rebérioux attributes yet a further role to the Affair in the history of French society. It would have marked the entry into public life of new strata expressing themselves through new means.[24] The absolute reign of committees of *notables* and elected intermediaries came to an end during the years of the Affair. Not only the press, the organized intellectuals, and the *ligues* of the left and the right, but also unions, cooperatives, professional societies, and academic associations were henceforth to regard themselves as active participants in public life. "Permanent headquarters were established, posters plastered on walls, tracts distributed."[25] Here and there, women were beginning to get involved in public life.* The Republic was thus no longer merely the restricted arena of rivalries between elected officials, but the affair of citizens who organized and expressed themselves through various channels. Was not that progress in democracy due more to the development of media of expression, to the evolution of a whole mentality than to the Affair itself? But it is true that the violence of the feelings aroused and the force and rivalry of the clashes provoked by the Affair contributed a great deal to the process.

It cannot, however, be maintained that the political tally of those years can be summarized as a strengthening of the Republic and a progress in democracy; reality was no doubt more complicated. First, the press, in discovering its own power, quickly demonstrated that such power was capable of manipulation. Without *L'Aurore* and Zola, Dreyfus might have remained in prison. But without Drumont and *La Libre Parole*, would he ever have even been found there? The emerging press already revealed what it would become in the history of democracy, the best and the worst of its traits: a rampart against the arbitrary, a weapon for truth, but also a vehicle for slander, a means of stultification, a school of fanaticism, in brief

---

* The first group of socialist women was constituted during the Affair. Several women became part of the central committee of the League of the Rights of Man. Marguerite Durand founded *La Fronde*, an ardently Dreyfusard feminist newspaper. At René Viviani's initiative, the law of June 30, 1898, opened the profession of law to women.

the docile instrument of all those guiding it. Already the submissiveness of the political powers to the power of the press, presumed to express or form "public opinion," was manifest. The Dupuy government, the Méline government, and the Brisson government were already suffering from the congenital weakness of republican regimes: to govern with one eye on the newspapers, perpetually intent on charming its supporters, terrified of causing displeasure, and most frequently diverted from action for fear of judgment.

Similarly, it is far from certain that the prestige of parliamentary institutions emerged strengthened from these eventful years.[26] Throughout the Affair, Parliament showed itself to be incapable of seriously disposing of the matter. It remained a captive of electoral interests, vulgar prejudices, abruptly responding to the mood of the moment or the fleeting impression produced by a resounding speech. The clashes between orators, the gossip, and the duels could not conceal the reality: that the members of Parliament had their eyes riveted on their districts, that they were working in a fashion that was already outmoded, that they had neither method nor long-term perspective, that they were concerned solely with acquitting themselves as best they could, at minimal cost, of short-term difficulties. During the crucial phase of the Affair, Parliament obstinately refused to take notice of it. Méline's phrase—the matter has been adjudicated—expressed the convenient consensus. On the other hand, when the Affair was virtually over (without Parliament having played any role), the Chambers latched on to it. And the Dreyfus Affair, once the Dreyfusards had won the match, became an inexhaustible theme of fruitless discussion. Until the War of 1914, the Affair would be a source of heat in both houses, and members of Parliament would often take refuge in the nostalgic evocation of the Dreyfusard battle in order to avoid the real problems emerging from the evolution of French society. That perpetual gap between Parliamentary rhetoric and real life, in ideas and methods, was to find in the Dreyfus Affair a medium in which it emerged with growing clarity. And the lucid politicians whose ambition was to govern (Waldeck-Rousseau, Poincaré, Caillaux, and Millerand) already observed the impotence of the Parliamentary regime and reflected on what means might be used to remedy it.

The major confrontation, in which means were not considered, and the manner in which the republicans used their victory were not without effect. In several circumstances, the law served as an instrument of political passion; the law of dispossession was one of the last maneuvers of the anti-Dreyfusards to attempt to keep Dreyfus in prison. The laws voted through on July 13, 1906, in order to rehabilitate Picquart's career and to partially rehabilitate Dreyfus, remedied injustices, but were reminders

that the legislative majority made its own laws. Convictions were sufficiently strong that the perversion of legislative activity appeared legitimate
to both camps. In like manner, the judiciary was constantly made to submit
to the political pressures. The dispossession of the case from the Criminal
Chamber at the point at which the investigation was nearly concluded was
a blatant sign of the contempt in which the government and Parliament
held the judicial system. But the Dreyfusards nevertheless expected favorable judgments from the judiciary when they gained some measure of
influence. No doubt Georges Sorel was excessive when he termed "judicial
domestics" the magistrates of the High Court of Appeal who on July 12,
1906, annulled without further trial the judgment at Rennes and—"in a
mood of Dreyfusard generosity"—exercised their genius in devising "cer-
tificates of honorability" to award to Dreyfus.[27] But it is true that under the
Waldeck-Rousseau government, then under those of Combes and Sarrien,
the executive and the judiciary were proceeding in perfect harmony. The
High Court of Appeal delayed the revision as long as the government
opposed it; later it annulled the judgment without any further adjudica-
tion as the government then desired. If the High Court of Appeal was
divided in 1899, as the government itself was, that was no longer the case in
1906, when the regime was openly Dreyfusard. From those twelve years,
the left and the right risked emerging with a common belief, which
merged with an old tradition of the *ancien regime*: that the judiciary should
be impeded from opposing the political powers that be.[28] Thus the Affair
did not simply strengthen democracy. It did not clearly oppose authoritarian vice, on one side, and democratic vice on the other. It revealed on
occasion the ability to manipulate the mechanisms of power in accordance
with criteria of greater convenience, to submit means to ends, to deny
democracy its power in order to respect its appearance. This chronic strain
on institutions, which affect all political forces, would grow worse amidst
the turbulence of the twentieth century.

Did the Affair at least transform the left in a lasting manner? The
Dreyfus Affair, according to Claude Willard, had posed "more forcefully
and in a new context" the problem of the unification of the worker's
movement.[29] It had also forced the Socialists to question their methods:
ought they to ally themselves with the democratic forces and take charge of
the defense of the Republic? Zeev Sternhell maintains that the essential
result of the Affair was to have made the Socialists become involved,
through Parliamentary support or participation with the government, in
the conduct of the affairs of the bourgeois Republic, to have integrated the
proletariat into the national collectivity.[30] For Rudoph Winnacker, on the
contrary, this trend had begun before the development of the Affair and

would continue without it. In willingly (or grudgingly) accepting the minimal program laid out by Millerand at Saint-Mandé, the Socialists had already "lost their revolutionary stigma" and—without fully admitting it—taken their place within the parliamentary Republic. At century's end, the trend toward unity was irresistible, and the alliance with the republican parties inevitable.

By integrating the working class into the Nation, the Affair had served to defeat the reaction and to ensure the victory of the Republic. In the long run, did it denature French Socialism? "Just prior to 1914," Sternhell has written,[31] "it was clear that the national sentiment was emerging as the dominant force in history, that the Nation embodied the society's fundamental values, and left-wing extremists like Gustave Hervé and Hubert Lagardelle could denounce the immense mystification the Dreyfus Affair had been for the working class." In order to counter the nationalist and clerical wave, the workers had joined in a common front with the liberal bourgeoisie. Sternhell has returned to that provocative analysis in his last work.[32] "Each, in its individual way and at a time of its choosing, of the various Socialist movements took on the voice of social-democracy, which is that of a compromise with the established order. In France, the Dreyfus Affair only confirmed that evolution by forging an alliance between Socialism and the bourgeois center for the defense of the liberal order. In choosing to collaborate with the liberal bourgeoisie, French Socialism in its entirety was laying the bases for a policy that would persist through the twentieth century."[33] For Gustave Hervé and Hubert Lagardelle, "the Affair in the final analysis had been a debacle."* For the result was not the triumph of Socialism, but the rise of Radicalism, which was victorious already in 1902, and the transformation of the Socialist Party into a parliamentary party like the others, the "advent of a Socialism which very quickly took on the appearance of its renegades, Millerand, Briand, and Viviani." "The hate-filled break" between a Radical government, using the Army to effect a bloody repression of strikes, and a proletarian world frustrated of its victory would have marked the "bankruptcy of

---

* The theme was to be developed by Hubert Lagardelle in several issues of *Le Mouvement Socialiste*. Once again the proletariat, duped by its political leaders, had become the watchdog of the bourgeoisie, the zealous servant of its own oppressors. Gustave Hervé and Georges Sorel would exalt an intransigent socialism that refused all class collaboration. And since democracy and the bourgeoisie were inextricably bound together, in order to shatter bourgeois society, it would be necessary to destroy democracy, the mortal enemy of socialism. Georges Sorel would drift without difficulty toward nationalism and anti-Semitism. Lagardelle, after passing through Bergery's "frontism," would become a minister under Pétain. Thus would the extreme French left evolve along with the extreme right an anti-democratic, anti-capitalist, anti-Semitic ideology, renouncing the legacy of the Enlightenment and the Revolution, and in which Sternhell detects the first stirrings of fascism.[34]

Dreyfusism" in the years 1906 and 1907: the sinister fruit of an alliance which had, for a time, drawn together the Socialist proletariat and the liberal bourgeoisie.* In 1914 the *union sacrée* and the entry of Sembat and Guesde into the government would mark the Socialists' definitive submission to the national ideology and to bourgeois reformism. The Dreyfus Affair would paradoxically have prepared the way for the victory of a nationalist conservatism, hypocritically masked under the cloak of the Dreyfusard ideology. Defense of the nation in danger would do the rest.

Writing in 1905, Léon Blum did not draw up so pessimistic a balance-sheet for French Socialism. But Blum was in solidarity with Jaurès, who placed a humane ideal of Socialism above the interests of the working class. Jaurès and Blum were convinced that the victory scored over individual injustice would in the long run serve the struggle against social injustices: "By abstaining from taking action, or even by moderating its actions, Jaurès felt, "Socialism would have become diminished and debased; but by making the triumph over injustice its own, by imprinting its mark on that victory, what an aura of attraction it endowed itself with for the future."† Léon Blum acknowledged that events were only partially to confirm his generous optimism: "Jaurès's campaign clothed Socialism in a new moral grandeur, endowed it with glory, but in the last analysis did not manage to provoke that tidal wave of agreement and conviction which had been hoped for." It was nevertheless the case, according to Blum, that "thanks to Jaurès's ingenious prescience, the Party had achieved its unity and augmented its strength." Jaurès had undoubtedly given his personal imprint to the Affair and decisively served the cause of justice and truth.[37] But had he served Socialism? Had not the "victory over injustice" ultimately accrued to the benefit of the bourgeois Republic?

Even if its rise were inevitable, the Socialist Party's aspiration to govern the Republic swelled with the Affair; and it was Jaurès who had supplied the theoretical reasons for its momentum.‡ The Socialists had fought alongside other republican movements. They had achieved unity among

---

* Sternhell makes much of the violence of the repression visited on the workers by Clemenceau the Dreyfusard and Briand the former Socialist.[35]

† Jaurès expressed himself as follows in 1900 during his famous controversy with Jules Guesde: "Well, may he allow me to tell him this: on the day that a crime is committed against a man, on the day that it is committed by a bourgeois hand, but while the proletariat, by intervening, might have stopped the crime, it is no longer the bourgeoisie alone that is responsible, but the proletariat itself. For by not stopping the hand of the murderer ready to strike, it becomes the murderer's accomplice. And then it is not a blot on the setting capitalist sun, but a blot on the rising socialist sun. We have wanted none of that shameful stain on the dawn of the proletariat."[36]

‡ Positing notably that "socialism is a morality,"[38] and that proletarian egotism is nothing but the sacred egotism of humanity itself.

themselves. The years of the Affair, François Mitterand has written, marked the first steps toward a unification of the various lefts, toward a union of the left. "The great French democratic trend" had been born and would give its *élan* to the new era."[39]

Thus, in whatever arena one looks, the long-term effects of the Affair appear uncertain. Once the cyclone had passed, Léon Blum maintained, France resumed its former identity. "A strange spectacle indeed, which might inspire many an embittered reflection . . . , which might almost discourage one from taking action at all. Imagine! For years an unprecedented passion had possessed and overwhelmed individual lives and the collective life. . . . Everything in the environment had seemed so different."[40] But everything had ultimately remained the same. The Republic was consolidated, the Army and the Church brough to heel; the Socialists had gained, if not in strength, at least in their influence over the bourgeois Republic. The defeat of the reactionaries was "neither more lasting nor more substantial than the victory of the adverse camp." Their real strength was not destroyed, merely altered. What had died was the monarchist dream, the nostalgia for a return to the *ancien regime*. But nationalism was opening up new vistas to the forces of traditionalism. After Clemenceau, power would pass to those who had been the most "prudent" in the Affair, who had rallied only once the revision had become inevitable: Aristide Briand, Louis Barthou, Raymond Poincaré, and Eugène Caillaux, oscillating between the center-left and the center-right, always seeking their base of support in the middle classes, governing France much as Méline and Rouvier had. "Ten or twelve years after the suicide at Mont-Valérien and the trial at Rennes, Parliamentary life had recovered—almost exactly—its former complexion."[41]

France seemed to have assimilated the Affair. Had the Jewish community at least retained any memory of its passions? Léon Blum has harshly judged the French Jews. At first, he recalled, the dominant sentiment was captured in the formula: "This is something that Jews should not get involved with." There was some degree of patriotism in that response and a true respect for the Army, but also "a kind of selfish and fearful prudence."[42] Commenting in 1899 on the role of Jews in the Affair, the historian Levasseur wrote: "I believe they are wrong to form a block to defend one of their own." The Jews did not want to fuel the passion of the anti-Semites by defending a Jew; "after excommunicating the traitor, they repudiated the embarrassing zeal of his lawyers." And it was above all the rich Jews, those of the upper and middle bourgeoisie, the Jews of Dreyfus's own class and social standing who shunned him. "They imagined that the passion of the anti-Semites could be diverted through a cowardly neutrality. They secretly cursed those among them who in taking a public stand were exposing them to the adversity that had lasted so many centuries."*

The Jews would thus have sought to avoid the Dreyfus Affair, but Léon Blum's analysis undoubtedly underestimates the difficulty of any minority to overcome a defensive reflex, to withdraw and shrink back, a normal symptom of adaptation to a hostile social environment. Moreover, it neglects the essential fact that during the worst anti-Semitic excesses, the French government and administration continually condemned anti-Semitism. The excesses were not committed by France itself but by an agitated minority, and were disavowed by the public authorities. As French citizens, Jews thus had reason to feel reassured.[44] It remains the case that the Affair did not call into question the will to assimilation which inspired the general behavior of the the French Jewish community.[45] In addition, as Annie Kriegel has correctly observed, the Jews of France had good reasons, specific to the French political culture by which they were influenced, not to experience the Dreyfus Affair as their experience. Within the logic governing the perception of the Jews that had been transmitted by the Revolution, there was no Jewish entity, no Jewish collectivity, no Jewish minority, and, most assuredly, no Jewish vote or syndicate. There were merely scattered "French citizens of the Mosaic persuasion."[46] At best, they tolerated the existence of "Jewish *milieux*," "the term *milieu* designating the vaguest degree of social interaction." The Jewish dimension of the Affair was not that of Frenchmen of an Israelite traditon: it was that of the anti-Semites.

But for all that, it cannot be maintained that the Dreyfus Affair was without influence for French Jews.[47] First, it should be noted that the Jews involved in the Affair were more numerous than Léon Blum admits: Bernard Lazare, the Reinach brothers, Marcel Proust, Daniel Halévy, Victor Basch, Paul Meyer, Lucien Lévy-Bruhl, Emile Durkheim, Arthur Lévy, the Natanson brothers, and Léon Blum himself, to mention only the most famous. No doubt they did not commit themselves out of mere solidarity with Dreyfus, but the fact that they were Jews prompted them to get involved, as was acknowleged by Joseph Reinach, who became a militant of the Affair early on even though he was quite representative of the assimilated bourgeoisie. "We are each of us being attacked as Jews, Monsieur," Bernard Lazare had written to Joseph Reinach. "That is why we can forget our economic or philosophical differences and agree on the fight to be waged against anti-Semitism." They had not forgotten them, but temporarily transcended them. Blum, moreover, overlooked the various forms assumed by the Jewish reaction: challenges to duels, which were

* Péguy maintained that three quarters of the Jewish upper bourgeoisie and a third of the Jewish petty bourgeoisie were anti-Semites.[43]

frequent between 1892 and 1896 (Edouard Drumont had to submit to three duels against Jews, Raphaël Viau to at least five) and numerous demonstrations of support organized with the participation of rabbis and Jewish notables between 1898 and 1900. However restricted and cautious, such reactions do not allow one to conclude that there was merely indifference (and still less cowardice) on the part of French Jews.[48] The examination of Jewish behavior during the Affair seems only to have considered the Jewish bourgeoisie, and often the wealthy bourgeoisie.[49] That bourgeoisie, however vilified by the right-wing press, continued its assimilation into French society. Its economic power and the many influential connections forged by marriage and friendships assured a large sector of the Jewish bourgeoisie privileged access to assimilation. The most restricted circles of the right opened their clubs and castles and gave their children in marriage to this financial bourgeoisie, whose power in society commanded respect. But what of the poor Jews, and the Jewish proletariat, which had formed in the 1890's as a result of the exodus from Russia? How were they influenced, if not by the Affair, which barely concerned them, at least by the outbreak of anti-Semitism in 1898, the pillaging and violence occasioned by the Affair (or for which it served as a pretext)? And can it be said that assimilation was the only perspective open to them?

It cannot be denied, in any event, that the notion of a Jewish specificity—consisting initially of shared misfortunes—and even the idea of a Jewish organization, a Jewish Nation, were fostered a great deal by the Affair.[50] It is known that the spectacle of Dreyfus's degradation played an important role in the evolution of Theodore Herzl's thinking. It was then that he perceived the limitations and illusions of the dream of assimilation and began to reflect on a Jewish Nation. The path of Bernard Lazare—who was not at all enthralled by a mystique of Judaism when he wrote his *Histoire de l'antisémitisme* in 1894—is quite indicative of an evolution on the part, if not of the middle class, at least of the intellectuals. Because of the Affair, even more than through Herzl's influence, Bernard Lazare moved from advocating assimilation of the Jews, conceived as a necessary progress of revolutionary society, to a defense of the Jews, united as a persecuted community. Before his death, amid the indifference of the Jews of France, he too conceived the project of a Jewish Nation. Dreyfus's martyrdom had persuaded him that a Jew would never be able to live in complete happiness and tranquillity anywhere other than in a Jewish State. When Bernard Lazare died—suspect, isolated, and infinitely poor—that seed was not lost. The idea of the Jewish Nation, much debated in other countries, in all oppressed or persecuted Jewish communities, had already attained a public in France which cannot be seen as negligible, however limited it may have been to intellectuals and extremists. And in a certain sense, as Annie Kriegel has observed, the nationalist idea itself, whose victims the Jews had been, would served the dream of a Jewish Nation. The French idea of the Nation-State, often defended against the Jews, would in part inspire a collective emancipation of the Jewish people.*

The lasting effect of the Dreyfus affair was at least to have discredited anti-Semitism in left-wing organizations, be they parties or unions. No doubt popular anti-Semitism survived the Affair. It would be used between the wars by an extreme left-wing and an extreme right-wing anti-Semitism, and under the German occupation, it would supply the Vichy government with themes and slogans.† The myth of the Jew, exploiting the populace, ruining the little people, despoiling the weak, growing rich on the misery of France, and destroying the social order, had not yet produced its last effects. Hatred of the Jew would continue to be fueled by hostility to capitalism. Later, the alliance between the State of Israel and the United States would furnish new arguments. But beginning with the Dreyfus Affair, left-wing parties and workers' unions would never again invoke the "wisdom" of an anti-Semitic stance, for the Affair had definitively linked anti-Semitism with reactionary ideology. Fascism, the Franco-German War, the anti-Jewish policies of the Vichy government, and above all the Hitlerian genocide would complete the dishonor in France of anti-Semitic doctrines. Anti-Zionism would at times pick up where a discredited anti-Semitism left off, but the latent anti-Semitism of many of the French would be obliged thereafter to seek expression in other, more complicated, ways.

---

* This is the thesis also defended by François Furet: "It was the French Revolution which invented the two responses to the Jewish question: the individual one and the national one."[51]
† Through a natural channel in which Sternhell sees the continuity of French fascism over fifty years of French history.[52]

3

The Dividing Line

"The Affair is to the trial what the sea is to a ship. It exceeds it infinitely."[1] Thus did Ernest Lavisse, who hesitated to involve himself in the struggle, express the immensity of the horizons opened to the observer by the Dreyfus Affair. And no doubt it is less fascinating to elucidate the last mysteries the Dreyfus "case" may still conceal than to reflect on what it means beyond its own era, to look at French society at the end of the nineteenth century and also in the twentieth century in the mirror of the Affair. With the "temporal thickness" given us by almost a century's distance, does the "abscess" referred to by Jean-Pierre Peter[2] allow us to reconstitute the entire social organism? Beyond the tragic adventure of Alfred Dreyfus, was the shock indicative of enduring conflicts essential to this people which would recur in other forms on other occasions?

That prognostic function is generally attributed to the Affair, particularly by the spritual heirs of the former Dreyfusards. In his Preface to *Cinq années de ma vie*, François Mauriac claimed that "the Dreyfus Affair is a mirror whose fidelity is terrifying and which recaptures us in our eternal traits: the noble ones and the basest ones."[3] This incident contained the seed of the history of the twentieth century: "The Dreyfus Affair is no more than an episode, but the most significant one, of a civil war that is still going on." In the conclusion of his work on the Dreyfus Affair, Pierre Miquel similarly maintains that it would be impossible to explain the evolution of contemporary public opinion without taking this episode into account: "The Dreyfus Affair . . . created two ways of thinking, two attitudes, two political philosophies."[4] Had it created them or simply revealed them? Extending the influence of the Affair, Dr. Jean-Louis Lévy wrote that it gave the values of truth and freedom "an opportunity to deploy themselves, to be expressed and to emerge from repression." It bore witness concerning human nature. "Prodigiously complex in its development . . . , it was luminously simple on the ethical level. It was a divider. It traced in filigree the crested line on either side of which citizens would be sorted out, distributed (according to subtle lines of force) and counted. Posing the question of conscience to every individual, it constrained each one to react, to know and to acknowledge himself."[5] Two ways of thinking, two systems of values, two ethics. Most meditations on the Dreyfus Affair are governed by that perspective: the legacy of the Affair would be to "separate" men of freedom from those of order, those of justice from those of *res judicata*. The "two Frances" referred to by Lavisse would be endlessly engaged in new episodes—be they violent or restrained—of an interminable conflict.

That notion of the Dreyfus Affair—as an "episode" indicative of an eternal civil war—should be considered with caution. The society in which the Affair erupted, after all, was still close to that of the eighteenth century. Current ways of life, mentalities, and the surrounding environment have changed enormously in less than a century.

To begin with, the role played by chance in the Affair cannot be forgotten, even if to say that chance is one of the artisans of history, and even if what is essential is to perceive the forces which exploited fortuitous occurrences.[6] If Esterhazy had not needed money? If Schwarzkoppen had burned the bordereau? If Dreyfus's handwriting had not resembled Esterhazy's? If Mme. Bastian had not gathered up the *petit bleu*? If it had fallen into other hands than Picquart's? The pursuit of such strokes of fortune—or misfortune—which helped convict Dreyfus and then to exonerate him might be carried on without end.

But the fruits of that fortune, in the guise of Colonel d'Abboville entering Colonel Fabre's office on October 6, 1984,[7] could only grow on very favorable terrain. That an Alsatian Jewish officer was accused of treason in France in 1894 was undoubtedly an opportunity for a major crisis. Since 1871, defeated France was living its relation to victorious Germany in humiliation and animosity. That mentality was a nearly unanimous sentiment crossing classes and ideologies, and was one which the Republic took up and cultivated with pride. At the time not a single voice was to be heard (unless completely isolated and without a public) casting doubt on patriotic fervor and the moral, quasi-religious obligation to love and to serve the Nation. A pathological obsession with spies and xenophobia was the natural consequence of that painful and exacerbated love of a defeated country, and the general opinion was that France had lost the war not because it was victim of the balance of forces, but because it had been betrayed. Republicans and monarchists competed in the zeal with which they went about tracking down traitors. Treason was the ultimate crime, which nothing could excuse or expiate. When Dreyfus was convicted, Jaurès waxed indignant from the Assembly tribune that he had not been shot. Clemenceau deplored the all too gentle fate which the weakness of the authorities had reserved for the criminal. Dreyfus—who shared the common view—would never cease writing from Devil's Island that were he a traitor, his treatment would be insufficiently harsh.

Now the spy, it happened, was Alsatian and a Jew. Alsatians such as Dreyfus, whose family had opted in 1871 for French citizenship, suffered from an ambiguous status. Their patriotic choice, the sign of their devotion to the nation, was undoubtedly respected; but it remained that those Alsatians were born on land that had become German, even if by annexation, that they often spoke German, that many of them, like Dreyfus, had relatives who continued to live in Alsace. French Alsatians could not escape a German "climate." They often traveled to Alsace, that is, to Germany, to visit their relatives or their lands. In addition, the German and French intelligence services counted numerous agents of Alsatian origin. For Allan Mitchell, Dreyfus's Alsatian origin fueled the suspicions against him from the very first.[8] Several of the witnesses in the 1894 trial reproached Dreyfus with speaking German, having an accent, retaining interests and relatives in Alsace, willingly crossing the border. As an Alsatian, he was a Frenchman of a particular stamp. The rampant xenophobia in the France of 1894 created against him an unfavorable prejudice.

Above all Dreyfus was a Jew. The fact that he was Jewish, Marcel Thomas has observed, played no role at the beginning of the Affair.* It was chance and stupidity which designated an officer temporarily serving with the General Staff as the culprit. But from the moment his name was mentioned by d'Abboville and his handwriting compared with that of the bordereau, the fact that he was a Jew became—complementary or conclusive—grounds for presuming his guilt. "I should have thought of it," exclaimed Colonel Sandherr, an Alsatian and an anti-Semite, and he undoubtedly expressed the sentiment of a majority of officers. Even before anti-Semitic rhetoric, through the press campaign that would begin on November 1, 1894, took up the Affair, Dreyfus's "name" had become a decisive factor persuading the General Staff of his guilt, nullifying any evidence favorable to his defense and clarifying anything that, like his handwriting, worked against him. We have mentioned the vast campaign which (starting in 1892) denounced the presence of Jews in the Army as potential traitors. Self-proclaimed or unwitting anti-Semites, the officers of the General Staff could not have been insensitive to this sentiment. Many of them read *La Libre Parole* or *La Croix*. If they occasionally disapproved of their excesses, they frequently shared their convictions. When Dreyfus was suspected, then arrested, his name and beliefs were no

---

* Marcel Thomas has studied quite rigorously the "mechanism of error" that led to Dreyfus's arrest.[9]

substitute for proof—and as a precaution, the secret file would have to be constituted—but they cast a rather dazzling light onto the case. They transformed the flimsiest leads—his handwriting, his service with diverse branches, the questions he asked, his habits, his appearance, his character—into damning evidence.

And yet it is impossible to understand the contagion which every day pitted a growing number of officers against Dreyfus if one does not situate the Army in the France of the time. On the morrow of the War of 1870, the Army seemed to be inseparable from the bruised and humiliated Nation.[10] The Army was the necessary instrument of revenge needed to restore to France her integrity.* The republicans did not question the alliance of the Army and the Nation, they merely dreamed that military service, like obligatory education, would become a school of virtue and patriotism.[11] To criticize the Army's leaders was to prevent the country from defending itself, a form of treason. By 1890, that cast of mind had evolved very little. No doubt the Army gradually aroused the distrust of the republicans: the high-ranking officers of the General Staff constituted an oligarchy of aristocrats, who were frequently students of the Jesuits and did a poor job of concealing their sympathy for the France of the *ancien regime* and their distrust of the republican values threatening to replace traditional ones. No doubt the Boulangist adventure brought to light the danger of a military *coup d'état*. At the end of the century anti-militarism would become one of the points on which diverse Socialist tendencies could fuse. Many became involved in the Affair, having come from the extreme left, because their hostility toward the Army was greater than their distrust of the bourgeois cause. Moreover, the colonial expeditions continued to "widen the gap between the Army higher-ups and the foot-soldiers."[13] But in 1894, the "holy Ark" remained an "order" with its own laws, rules, and jurisdictions, founded on the "military spirit," which consisted of a cult of the nation, a sense of honor, respect for superiors, and a rigorous loyalty to hierarchical order. The mentality that would unite most of the officers, first in sending Dreyfus to prison, then in keeping him there, was quite well expressed in a letter sent to Dreyfus after the revision by one of his comrades at the General Staff:

> When the Deputy Chief of the General Staff gathered us in 1894 to
> tell us that you were guilty and that they had undisputable proof,

---

* "The esteem enjoyed by officers," writes William Serman, "was first of all a function of the nature of their service. Leaders in war, they took up the heritage of chivalrous virtues: courage, loyalty, disinterest, a sense of sacrifice. To be sure, the nineteenth century had made functionaries out of them, but functionaries obeying the power of death. Their swords and their lives were at the disposition of the Nation-State for the defense and glory of the country, for revenge after 1870."[12]

we accepted that certainty without discussion since it came to us from a superior. In that context, we immediately forgot all your qualities, the friendly relations we had with you, in order to search in our memory only for what might corroborate the certitude that had just been inculcated in us. There was nothing that could not be used.[14]

Such was the strength of hierarchical feeling, which Alfred Dreyfus would also share—to the point of obstinately placing his trust in his superior officer General Boisdeffre until he discovered the sad truth in the prison at Rennes, not because Boisdeffre was his friend, but because he was his superior. "We accepted the certainty without discussion." Thus for hundreds of officers throughout the Affair, Boisdeffre, Gonse, Mercier, Billot, Pellieux, and Roget would necessarily be followed in their convictions. Thus may be clarified the mental processes that might lead an honest officer to regard Dreyfus as a traitor. His qualities and virtues were to be forgotten. Everything about him that might nourish the evidence of his betrayal was to be sought. The subservience of judgment, dictated in this case by the "military spirit," in another by religious faith, in another still by party loyalty, turned an innocent man into a guilty one. No doubt some of the officers who were relentless in their hostility to Dreyfus were fanatics, like Bertin-Mourot, or illuminati, like du Paty de Clam. Others, like Mercier or Henry, became criminals. But many were men of great moral virtue, and contrary to the portrait frequently drawn of them, some exercised their influence by virtue of remarkable qualities of mind. Boisdeffre, Pellieux, and Mercier himself dominated the trials by virtue not only of their uniform and their duties, but of their intellectual authority as well. Almost all of them were burdened by their prejudices, blinded by their sense of hierarchy, and captives of the order to which they belonged. Even the best of them, in whom a sense of duty, unyielding virtue, or the demands of Christianity provoked rebellions, had long periods of blindness. Captain Freystaetter, who would shatter his career by testifying at Rennes how the secret file had been revealed to him, was no more astonished than any of the other judges by that communication, which violated the law and simple justice. Commandant Picquart, who was also informed of the communication, at the time showed no indignation. He was the "dupe of men without honor," General de Pellieux would write the day after Henry's suicide; but however "duped" he may have been, he had conducted the Esterhazy trial under disgraceful conditions, and in order to better defend the Army, he had become the confidant and friend of a German spy. Cuignet, who discovered the "Henry forgery" did not detect in it reason for suspicion; the officer who "made the revision" later became

the most fanatical of anti-Dreyfusards. Dreyfus's innocence was believed
by most French officers neither in 1894, nor in 1898, nor even in 1900.*
Every piece of evidence persuaded them that he was a traitor, and every
legend—be it of the historic night of the confession, or of the annotated
bordereau—provided new and "useful material."

Does it matter that Dreyfus was innocent? At Rennes, did Comman-
dant Merle, who wept while listening to Demange, and Commandant
Beauvais, who hesitated, it was said, until the last moment, believe that
Dreyfus was innocent? It is not improbable, but his innocence was not
sufficient to make them change their judgment. "I am convinced of
Dreyfus's innocence," a French officer said to Emile Duclaux, "but if his
verdict were up to me, I would convict him again for the honor of the
Army." Because the nation required it, because those gathered on
Dreyfus's side were the enemies of the Army and were weakening France,
Dreyfus was guilty in three consecutive manners. First, he was guilty
because he had been designated for the role. Once charged, his guilt was
ratified because he had already been declared so; France's interest and the
Army's honor required that he remain convicted. Finally, he was guilty
"for having served for five long years as a source of turmoil in the Army
and the entire Nation," for having been the symbol and the instrument of
the forces of evil.[16]

The Dreyfus Affair was thus well rooted in its times. There is a risk of
denaturing it by extrapolation. The "two ways of thinking," the "two
systems of values" confronting each other in the Affair were expressions at
the time of two social orders which were pitted against each other during
the last decade of the nineteenth century. "The order being called into
question," Pierre Miquel has observed, "was that of the nineteenth
century—the world of *châteaux* and ecclesiastical residences."[17] The traditional nobility and the French upper middle class still exercised a burden-
some influence over political life, through departmental councils and
parliamentary assemblies. They were supported by the Church. Local
priests, living off the largesse of *châteaux*, were their aides, out of either
conviction or necessity. Church and *château* quite properly saw themselves
as threatened by the progress of capitalism, the development of industry
and the growth of cities. No doubt the old caste still managed on
occasion—through wealth or marriage, through the places it secured on
boards of directors, through a network of relations and influences—to
partially penetrate the new system. No doubt Pope Leo XIII, worried by

* See in Robert Gauthier, *Pourquoi l'Affaire*, the letter to his colonel from officer Louis
Bruyèrre—which earned him a dismissal—in which the officer expressed his disagreement
with the prevalent conception of the Army's honor and of the military mind.[15]

the Church of France's loyalty to the old order, incited priests and Catholics in general to rally to the Republic in order to conquer it. But on the eve of the Dreyfus Affair, the large majority of the aristocracy and the upper middle class had irritably and defensively retreated into the society of the Old Regime, its hierarchies and its values. And amid the economic upheaval of the end of the century, the Army had become both an opportunity and a shield, the refuge of a threatened caste, and the guarantor of values whose loss it feared.

In addition, the great depression of the 1890's, unemployment, reconversion to industry, credit difficulties, and the intransigence of banks made all sorts of "little people" viciously defensive: ruined businessmen, unemployed workers, and peasants forced off the land randomly accused Jews, financiers, urbanization, Parliament, and often the Republic for their demise. All had in common the experience of being shunted aside by the "new strata" and their solidarity was above all a function of their anxiety.[18] The Boulangist coalition, Pierre Miquel has observed, had already revealed this curious alliance—of provincial aristocrats, garrisoned soldiers, shopkeepers, artisans, and peasants from the anti-Republican regions—against the France of railroads, banks, and big cities, the France of Rothschild, the France which had been opened up to foreign forces.[19] That alliance can be traced throughout the Affair, and the campaign for the "Henry monument" even allows one to formulate it statistically. The Church, which was afraid of the progress of secular society, supported all who were excluded from the new world, or who felt themselves to be. Under the guise of self-defense, it helped them to preserve the nostalgically enshrined images of an old society: dogma, authority, hierarchy, honor, ancient institutions, *res judicata,* and the unity of the national entity, shattered by the destruction of the monarchy, the refusal of the "reign of money" which symbolized the new world. Nationalism—a new concept—endowed those values with the philosophical link they were lacking, and the memory of defeat nourished them. Without foreigners, without the Germans, without the Jews, without cosmopolitan capitalism, without international socialism, the French would be pious, orderly, patriotic, prosperous.

The years of the Affair were those in which French society was shifting from one era to another. Capitalism became entrenched, large-scale businesses were developing, and with them a new bourgeoisie—which was active, enterprising, daring, at times Jewish, and often international—was taking over most of the levers of command in both the economy and the administration. In the Army of 1894, one can perceive the distance separating Alfred Dreyfus, the son of a recently arrived member of the bourgeoisie, who was rich, proud, happy, from many of his comrades, young men coming from an aristocracy or an ailing bourgeoisie. Rather quickly, the young Jew struck them as insolent.

On another front, the working class was expanding, gaining awareness of its strength, becoming organized into parties and unions, and beginning—through union propaganda and strikes that were increasing in severity, but also through its power in Parliament, and soon through its participation in bourgeois governments—to make its influence felt in the life of the nation. The elections of 1894, 1898, and 1902 revealed a constant shift toward the left. By 1898, Radicals and Socialists formed a majority of the government. In 1902, the right was virtually decimated: a sign that the change was all but complete, and that the old order, supported by the two pillars of the Army and the Church, no longer dominated French society. The Affair was thus a confrontation, at the close of the nineteenth century, between two societies, two systems of values. The struggle ended with the victory of what Lavisse called the society of the Revolution over the society of the Old Regime.

But by placing the Dreyfus Affair in its own time, we can also see its limits. First, that this conflict of values was for the most part located within the dominant class. The peasantry seems to have been indifferent to a battle it perceived as middle-class and urban. If the influence of the working class, the rallying of Jaurès and then of the Socialist Party, played a decisive role in the revision, it was nevertheless the case that most workers stayed at a great distance from the Affair. The decisive confrontation never went beyond the bounds of the middle class, or the middle classes, if one chooses to separate the upper bourgeoisie from the petty bourgeoisie. In addition, it must be acknowledged that it was less the courageous voices of truth and justice than the evolution of political and social forces which reversed the course of the Dreyfus Affair and allowed for the revision. When Méline shouted "There is no Dreyfus Affair," he wanted, primarily, to preserve the public peace and order so important to the middle classes on which he depended for support. Disorder, at that point, was the struggle waged on behalf of revision.[20] When the century ended, the balance of forces was no longer the same. Déroulède's abortive *coup d'état*, the fanatical involvement of the religious congregations, the progress of the working class, the rise of the left in the legislative elections, and the press campaigns gave Brisson the daring that he lacked. In allowing the revision procedure to begin, in obliging Cavaignac to step down, he was following the republican forces rather than leading them; revision had come to signify republican order. On the morrow of Rennes, Waldeck-Rousseau's perspicacity lay in having understood that French society at the beginning of the century had cast off its mooring to the Old Regime, that the new social and

economic order and the nation's tranquillity demanded Dreyfus's liberation and amnesty, even if morality might find itself frustrated in the
process. In 1906, it was a refusal of revision that would have been a
ferment of disorder.[21]

The twentieth century would prove that the boundaries between the
two opposing systems of values, the two contrasting moralities, were not all
that clearly defined. The apparently defeated values were not the
monopoly of a privileged caste, but had been the foundation of the
mentality of an entire people. The Dreyfusards would waste no time
revealing that respect for reasons of State, the exaltation of hierarchies,
and the cult of the Army were part of the shared heritage of a traditional
culture on which they in turn would draw.[22] In 1906 Georges Clemenceau,
the most fiery of the Dreyfusards, organized the repression of the working
class and maintained public order by mobilizing the Army. He reminded
all that the victory of the Dreyfusards had not been the victory of the
working class. Later, the great majority of Dreyfusards could also be found
preparing for the war of revenge and exalting the Nation. In 1913, the
leftist majority, in its patriotic fervor, voted for the return of military
service. It was the Socialist René Viviani who was in power when war broke
out in 1914. The *union sacrée* dictated by the war once again exalted the
values adored by the nationalists; Dreyfusards and anti-Dreyfusards were
now joined in the same cult. Amid the unanimous fervor, Barrès attended
Jaurès's burial. Jules Guesde and Marcel Sembat entered the government.
The Socialist Millerand, now minister of war, composed "confidential
notes" authorizing execution within twenty-four hours of death sentences
passed by Courts-Martial. Drumont and Maurras were astonished. The
Nation, the Army, Honor, order, and hierarchy were now unanimously
embraced values. A few months later, innocent soldiers, presumed spies,
would be shot, simply because the morale of the Army demanded it and in
order "to set an example." Had the Dreyfus Affair exhausted its resources
that swiftly?

And yet it would be unduly reductive to restrict the Affair narrowly to
its own time on the pretext of avoiding a caricature, to deny what was
enduring or "eternal," in Mauriac's phrase: what continues to help us
know ourselves and acknowledge what we are almost a century after
Dreyfus's conviction. It is true that the Dreyfus Affair can only be understood within its own time, in terms of the economic, social, and cultural
forces of the end of the nineteenth century. It is also true that dramatic
opposition between two moralities, two mentalities, is not only of the past.
For what were the anti-Dreyfusards fighting? For the Nation, the Army,
and Honor, and often for God himself. What was at stake, said Barrès, was
the house of our fathers, our land, our dead.[23] For Cavaignac, it was "the

Nation's greatness," "the heritage of the defenders of the country."[24] It was also, proclaimed Déroulède, "the spirit of abnegation, the spirit of discipline, the spirit of solidarity."[25] And behind the exaltation of the nation, the ancestral heritage, and traditional virtues could be found the popular sentiments diversely formulated in the comments of the contributors to the "Henry monument": love of order, respect for work, devotion to country, rejection of foreigners, demands for security, and anxiety in the face of a changing world.

With what did the Dreyfusards oppose this? They never called into question loyalty to the Nation. Speeches hostile to the Army, were rare even if hostility to the Army helped a good deal, beginning in 1898, in recruiting Dreyfusards from the Socialist ranks.[26] But the Dreyfusards claimed that neither order, nor respect for authority, nor institutional might, nor even the national interest were to stand in the way of the higher principles of justice and freedom. There were ethical values higher than all interests, higher even than the law, expressed by Péguy as follows: "The passion for Truth, the passion for Justice, the impatience with falsity, the intolerance of deception occupied all our hours, all our energies."[27] On one side, encapsulating the clash, we find the principle that every act is to be judged in relation to France. On the other, that the rights of man are placed above every institution and every conviction.[28]

In point of fact, within the Affair itself, the divisions were neither so simple nor so clear cut. For men are not simply a function of their culture and morality, their convictions and prejudices. In the course of their lives, they are affected and occasionally transformed by their class, their social milieu, their friends, the social fabric within which they live and grow old. On the Dreyfusard side, one would be hard put to attribute the same attitudes to Auguste Scheurer-Kestner and Georges Clemenceau, to Bernard Lazare and Joseph Reinach, to base their involvement in the Affair on the same grounds. What relation was there between Picquart's implacable sense of duty and the higher philosophical doubt which brought men such as the scientist Grimaux to Dreyfusism? And how might one subsume under the same dogmas, on the anti-Dreyfusard side, General Mercier and Godefroy Cavaignac, Commandant Henry the forger and Captain Louis Cuignet who discovered his crime? How also can one fail to note, specifically in the case of the politicians, all those whose commitment was slow in forming, amid hesitations and retreats, those who, like Henri Brisson, long oscillated between a respect for order and the attraction of truth, those also who, like Barthou or Poincaré, only entered the Affair when they were assured that their conscience and their career could walk the same path together?

If it is thus true that one should be cautious about explaining the Affair summarily as a systematic confrontation between two moralities, a clear division between men of Truth and men of dogma, it is also the case that it revealed in its time and in its way enduring distinctions: on the one hand, those who, in Jaurès's phrase, make of "the human individual the measure of all things, of the country, the family, human property, and God,"[29] and on the other, those who posit and serve values higher than the individual: God, the Nation, the Army, the State, the party; those who do battle for Justice, an undefinable ideal of freedom, truth, and generosity, and those who fight on behalf of prejudices, in the etymological sense of the word: the established order, recognized organizations, prior verdicts; those who look toward the ancient cemetery and those who dream of leaping the wall; those taken with memory and those driven by sympathy.

And no doubt, in the mirror of the Dreyfus Affair, one can perceive, however deformed, the permanent features of a people whose ways of life have changed more swiftly than its attitudes. There has never been an end to the signs of that congenital unsuitedness for democracy that Barrès theorized about and Déroulède attempted to exploit. At every agitated phase of their history the French have experienced the temptation of awaiting a pure and severe leader who would clean out the Parliamentary stables and put the nation's house in order. General Boulanger has never ceased exercising his allure . . . any more than the country has lost its fascination with monarchical order, the deeds and glories of kings, the comforts of entrusting oneself to a sovereign.*

Similarly, the French have continued to enjoy an agitated relationship with the issue of private and public freedoms. The two wars, the foreign occupation, the purge, the Algerian war, the revolt of the Army, then the repression of its subversion have been so many jolts in which an old country, athirst for order, has found an opportunity to reduce freedoms experienced as a luxury of happier times, a privilege of those rare peaceful moments in an overly turbulent history.[30] Exceptional procedures, extraordinary laws, frivolous accusations, premature arrests, precipitously prosecuted cases, and instances of torture are yet not entirely unfamiliar in France. At the time of the Dreyfus Affair, it was the national interest and the Army's honor which dictated the deportation of the Jewish captain. Later, reasons of State, national defense, exceptional circumstances, the need to set examples, and the rules of war necessitated injustice and occasionally criminal acts. Throughout the twentieth century it has been as though the anti-Dreyfusards regained their public and their authority

---

* Founding the presidential monarchy on universal suffrage, General de Gaulle may have achieved a harmonious combination of two apparently contrary traditions. It is remarkable that today, and for the first time perhaps in the history of the Republic, there seems to be virtually unanimous agreement on the question of institutions.

as soon as the country felt itself to be endangered, as though, better than the intransigent defenders of freedom, it was they who expressed the national temperament. The Algerian War, whether waged by governments of the left or the right, evoked the aberrations of the Dreyfus Affair in many respects. The honor of the Army was seen to absolve summary executions and national interest to excuse torture. Those who dared to cast doubt on the nation's exigencies were accused of treason. It was also observed that the intellectuals committed themselves collectively, claiming to exercise anew their moral calling, to influence Parliament and the government, demanding that democracy recognize the "power of the mind." The leaders of the government, eager for calm, were heard to evoke the national interest and the authority of prior verdicts. And Parliament, whose incapacity to work seriously had already been observed by Labori, continued to content itself with vain speeches, concealing its abdications. Only the great rhetorical stars have disappeared. And duels have gone out of style.

There might thus be observed, in crudely simplified outline, the continuity of a society in which the Dreyfus Affair still has effect, resurfacing every time the State crushes the individual, *raison d'état* locks up whoever—Jew, Christian, or Arab—causes displeasure, or a judge convicts a presumed culprit without evidence. But the Dreyfus Affair, thus construed, is not fixed in space and time. The combat of the individual against society, truth against deception, is specific neither to France nor to the end of the nineteenth century. Alfred Dreyfus bears witness for millions of innocent victims of persecution even as they bear witness for him. The fact that the revision of his trial was possible might well, in the world of today in which three quarters of humanity is enslaved, be regarded as an anachronism, the luxury of a liberal society. A free press was needed. A system of civil justice that had not been domesticated was needed. The pressure of the working class, the right to strike, freedom to organize, and Parliamentary representation were needed. Democratic elections capable of ensuring a Dreyfusard majority were needed. As were irrepressible energies, like those of Mathieu Dreyfus, and unfailing virtues, like those of Colonel Picquart.

It is true, then, that the Affair continues to affect us. Nationalist sentiment, the worship of hierarchies, the fear of foreigners, and the hunger for security are permanent features of the French mentality, which the twentieth century has not effaced. It is not an exaggeration to say that nationalist sentiment has even gained, if not in strength, at least in legitimacy: two wars, the Resistance, the betrayal of a part of the right, which sacrificed its ideology to its class interests, have resulted in a left, the Socialist and even the Communist left, that has taken up where the right left off. Patriotic fervor and the exaltation of national defense have become the common legacy, achieving in peace as in war a *union sacrée*, constituting an undivided heritage. Barrès's discourse on the land and its dead, on ancient cemeteries, on the cult of France, is a source of unanimous comfort to the nation, perhaps because it satisfies the ancestral mentality of a people of peasants and warriors: the speeches of Boulanger, Déroulède, Cavaignac, and Barrès continue to resound for our benefit. The Nation's defense, the greatness of France, the salute of the flag, respect for reasons of State, the exigencies of order and security, even the surge of *La Marseillaise*, the haunting stride of the Army on July 14, celebrate an old ideology joining together Joan of Arc and Léon Gambetta, caricatured by Cavaignac, sublimated by Barrès, put to work by Clemenceau, renewed by de Gaulle, and celebrated today by all parties and all statesmen.

But the dividing line referred to by Jean-Louis Lévy,[31] which constrains each individual to know himself and to acknowledge who he is, does not separate—as might be convenient—men of truth and freedom on one side, men of *raison d'Etat* and national interest on the other. Convictions may have been for a brief while in the Dreyfus Affair "luminously simple on the ethical level" because a conspiracy of criminals driven by a hatred for Jews and their pride of caste had been organized in order to keep an innocent man in jail.* But the line separating Dreyfusard from anti-Dreyfusard most frequently was drawn within each individual. The sector that sacrifices innocence to prejudice, that condemns without proof, hates difference, fabricates accusations, clothes personal interest in the garb of higher interests, and loves only its own freedom is in each of us. An anti-Dreyfusard existed in Picquart, but his virtue was greater than his prejudices. Cavaignac, who was possessed by a hatred for Dreyfus, had a brutal passion for the truth and forced Henry to make the confession that brought about the revision. In the Zola trial, Labori was the splendid lawyer of Dreyfus's cause, yet he was taken with a hatred of Edgar Demange and Mathieu Dreyfus that would abound in summary accusations. Péguy, who aspired to the purity of a heroic Dreyfusard, lashed out at Jaurès in the most unjust terms; and he excommunicated Dreyfus himself, accused of having been Jaurès's accomplice. Clemenceau, who could not tolerate the conviction of an innocent man, grew indifferent to such isssues

---

* And even then it is our hindsight of today that allows us to see the Affair in its "ethical simplicity," to denounce the criminals, Mercier the organizer, Henry the forger, Gonse and Lauth the perpetrators of dirty tricks, and inversely to extoll those who fought for the innocent martyr, Picquart the "hero," Bernard Lazare the "saint," the very virtuous Scheurer-Kestner, and all those who out of moral fervor or intellectual rigor joined their struggle. At the time in which they were lived, the episodes of the "eternal civil war" were not, for the most part, either so clear or so simple.

when he became a statesman. Even today eminent writers, in order better to defend Dreyfus, send Maurice Weil, General Rau, and General Saussier (all fortunately dead before sentencing) off to prison. Such is perhaps the ambiguity of this people of Latin culture, Catholic tradition, apprehensively attached to its customs, its heritage, fanatical, intolerant, resolutely hostile to all that is different, perpetually eager to punish and repress; and also moved by great emotions, quick to be carried away at freedom's behest, capable of shooting an innocent one day and of being shot for the sake of an innocent the next. A people that could keep Dreyfus in prison, to the amazement of the entire world, when his innocence was certain, and then proclaim his defense without shame, as though a complete reversal were the natural order of things. They were Frenchmen who on January 5, 1895, in the courtyard of the École Militaire stripped off Captain Dreyfus's galloons. They were Frenchmen who on July 21, 1906, bestowed on him, in the same setting, the Cross of the Legion of Honor. These were not the actions of two Frances, following each other in succession, but merely two movements of a single people.

Perhaps Captain Dreyfus was one of the rare individuals of his era in whom that "dividing line" may not be detected. One finds in him no trace of that contradiction which, depending on circumstance, was apt to nourish in each individual the very best and the very worst of which he was capable. By what appears to have been natural disposition, he was the man of both French traditions in every sense. And that, no doubt, is what made for his aloofness, almost his absence, in his own Affair. It was also what made for the fact that he was nowhere recognized, nowhere loved. He cherished the Army as he did his family. He was happy in a hierarchy, in every hierarchy in which he found himself placed. Similarly, without any discord, he made of freedom and truth, republican virtues, French virtues, his honor and his idea. The patriot's nation and the rights of man converged for him—and in him. Little conflict can be detected within Captain Dreyfus between the passions which were clashing around him. Alfred Dreyfus had all the same indicated the limits of that agreement, writing: "My life belongs to my country; my honor does not." He experienced the clash of values which were equally dear to him and their separation into hostile forces with great pain. "It was because he was a man of both traditions," Dr. Jean-Louis Lévy has written, "that Dreyfus was obliged to mobilize incredible defensive resources without which he would have disintegrated. And he was forever broken as a result."

What was France for him if not the most exalted site of freedom and truth? What was the Army if not the sanctuary of honor, devotion, and generosity? What was the family if not the domain of essential affections, the refuge of the sweetest intimacy? My Affair, he wrote, upon concluding the book of his *Souvenirs* was "one of the most extraordinary efforts at rehabilitation the world has ever witnessed, an accomplishment that will resound into the most distant future, because it will have marked a turning point in the history of humanity, a grandiose stage on the road to an era of immense progress for the ideas of freedom, justice, and social solidarity."[32] There is no hatred, no trace of the slightest bitterness on the part of Alfred Dreyfus. He seemed to reproach no one. His martyrdom was as yet for him the tragic expression of his duty. The physical and moral ordeals he endured, the humiliation of the parade, the cries of hatred, the insults, the years of prison, the shackles on his feet, his destiny destroyed, his health ruined, all that he saw as "a grandiose stage on the road to an era of progress." He did not doubt that universal freedom was at the end of the road.

It remained simply that this Frenchman, who suffered so much from France, now looked beyond its borders. He would have liked his "Affair" to serve humanity.

NOTES
BIBLIOGRAPHY
INDEX

NOTES

PROLOGUE

Judas on Parade

1. Letter to Lucie Dreyfus, Thursday at noon. *Lettres d'un innocent* (Paris: P. V. Stock, 1898), p. 48.

2. Letter to Lucie Dreyfus, Thursday, 11 P.M. *Lettres d'un innocent*, p. 50. Alfred Dreyfus wrote four letters to his wife that day, January 3, 1895.

3. Letter to Edgar Demange, January 3, 1895, Thursday at noon. *Lettres d'un innocent*, p. 276.

4. Alfred Dreyfus, *Cinq années de ma vie* (Paris: Maspero, republished in 1982), p. 80, Introduction by Pierre Vidal-Naquet.

5. Maurice Paléologue, *Journal de l'Affaire Dreyfus* (Paris: Plon, 1955), p. 37.

6. Maurice Barrès, "La parade de Judas," in *Scènes et Doctrines du nationalisme* (Paris: Félix Guven, 1902), pp. 132ff.

7. *Ibid.*, p. 134.

8. Léon Daudet, "Le châtiment" in *Le Figaro* of January 6, 1895.

9. These were the words reported by Alfred Dreyfus in his *Souvenirs et correspondence* (Paris: Grasset, 1936). See also *Cinq années de ma vie*, p. 81, Maurice Paléologue, *op. cit.*, p. 39; Bruno Weil, *L'Affaire Dreyfus*, (Paris: Gallimard, 1930), p. 64; Jean France, *Autour de l'Affaire Dreyfus* (Paris: Rieder, 1936), p. 42, which give similar versions or change only a few words.

10. Barrès, "La parade de Judas," *loc. cit.*, p. 135.

11. Joseph Reinach, *Histoire de l'Affaire Dreyfus,* (Paris: Fasquelle, 1929), p. 501.

12. Daudet, "Le châtiment," *loc. cit.*

13. Paléologue, *op. cit.*, p. 39.

14. "In a cold, metallic voice, in which no emotion resonated," wrote witness Paléologue, *Ibid.*, p. 39.

15. It appears that there were separate sections reserved for officers' wives and celebrities, from which Dreyfus was spat upon. Raphaël Viau, *Vingt Ans d'antisémitisme.* France, *op. cit.*, p. 42.

16. Daudet, "Le châtiment," *loc. cit.*

17. Barrès, "La parade de Judas," *loc. cit.*, p. 135.

18. Paléologue, *op. cit.*, p. 38.

19. Alfred Dreyfus, *Cinq années de ma vie*, p. 81.
20. Barrès, "La parade de Judas," *loc. cit.*, p. 137.
21. *Le Figaro*, January 6, 1895.
22. Paléologue, *op. cit.*, p. 40.
23. Barrès, "La parade de Judas," *loc. cit.*, p. 135.
24. *Ibid.*, p. 135.
25. Letter of January 5, 1895, to Lucie Dreyfus, *Cinq années de ma vie*, p. 82.
26. Letter of January 5, 1895, Saturday, 7:00 P.M., *Ibid.*, pp. 82–83.
27. Saturday evening, January 5, 1895, *Ibid.*, p. 83.
28. Letter to his lawyer Edgar Demange, *Lettres d'un innocent*, p. 278.
29. Letter of January 7, 1895, to Lucie Dreyfus, *Ibid.*, p. 60.

1. THE TRAITOR DREYFUS

1. *A Child's Pledge*

1. Michael Marrus, *Les Juifs en France à l'époque de l'Affaire Dreyfus* (Paris: Calmann-Lévy, 1972), coll. Diaspora. Preface by Pierre Vidal-Naquet.
2. See Alfred Dreyfus, *Souvenirs et correspondances,* published by his son (Paris: Grasset, 1936), pp. 40ff.
3. See Henri Villemar, *Dreyfus intime* (Paris: Stock, 1898).
4. Dreyfus, *Cinq années de ma vie* (Paris: Maspero, 1982), p. 57.
5. Dreyfus, *Souvenirs et correspondances*, p. 42.
6. Dreyfus, *Cinq années de ma vie*, p. 57.
7. Dreyfus, *Souvenirs et correspondances*, p. 42.
8. Villemar, *op. cit.*, pp. 10ff.
9. Dreyfus, *Souvenirs et correspondances*, p. 42.
10. Marrus, *op. cit.*, pp. 246ff.
11. Concerning Alfred Dreyfus's attachment to the Republic and to secular values, see Pierre Vidal-Naquet, Introduction to *Cinq années de ma vie*, pp. 13ff.
12. See French National Archives, BB 19101.

2. *The Army of Revenge*

1. Charles De Gaulle, "Vers la revanche," *La France et son Armée* (Paris: Plon, 1938), pp. 197ff.
2. *Ibid.*
3. J. Monteilhet, *Les institutions militaires de la France, 1814–1932* (Paris: Félix Alcan, 1932), p. 220.
4. William Serman, *Les Officiers français dans la Nation, 1848–1914* (Paris: Aubier-Montaigne, 1982).
5. Raoul Girardet, *La Société militaire dans la France contemporaine 1815–1939* (Paris: Plon, 1953), pp. 132ff.
6. De Gaulle, *op. cit.*, p. 205.
7. *Ibid.*, p. 205.
8. Girardet, *op. cit.*, p. 183.

9. De Gaulle, *op. cit.*

10. "Rugged, powerful, firing far, consecrating the system of the rifle-bolt," Girardet, *op. cit.*, p. 185.

11. Michel de Lombarès, *L'Affaire Dreyfus. La clef du mystère* (Paris: Robert Laffont, 1972), p. 23.

12. *Ibid.*, p. 23.

13. Girardet, *op. cit.*, p. 185.

14. *Ibid.*, p. 185. The Army of revenge in fact benefited from an added measure of esteem: it embodied the heritage of ancient virtues, was the bearer of the nation's pride, and in addition offered a refuge to those who were ill at ease in the modern world. But Raoul Girardet undoubtedly exaggerates the social prestige enjoyed by officers. It remains that in 1890 officers, whose salary was quite meager, were losing respect in a society in which hierarchies based on monetary wealth were growing in importance, that political and intellectual antimilitarism were not without influence, and finally that the rigor of military discipline— "imposing on officers a behavioral model so demanding that the man in each case was to be obliterated by the soldier"—discouraged many a would-be soldier's vocation. William Serman presents a far more nuanced evocation of officers' prestige at the end of the nineteenth century (Serman, *op. cit.*, pp. 14 ff.)

On the other hand, it is probable that the military career offered educated youth, whose numbers were growing, a reasonable vocational outlet. The number of candidates for the École at Saint-Cyr rose from 1,144 in 1884 to 2,079 in 1894: guaranteeing long-term employment as much, or more, than the attractiveness of the Army's prestige.

15. François Bedarida, "L'Armée et la République," *Revue historique,* September 1964.

16. *Ibid.*, p. 131.

17. Paul-Marie de La Gorce, *La France et son Armée* (Paris: Fayard, 1963), p. 34.

18. Serman, *op. cit.*, pp. 8 ff.

19. de La Gorce, *op. cit.*, p. 36.

20. Girardet, *op. cit.*, p. 200.

21. Bedarida, *op. cit.*, pp. 119 ff.

22. Concerning the social world of officers, studied through their marriages and lifestyles, see Serman, *op. cit.*, pp. 145 ff. A majority of officers came from the middle classes, and thanks to the scholarship system, a proportion that was not negligible came from the poor. At Saint-Cyr from 1891 to 1900, there were more than 50% scholarship-holders. The Army thus kept its system of promotion under the control of its most conservative and clerical elements.

23. Girardet, *op. cit.*.

24. Concerning the political opinions of officers, see William Serman, *op. cit.*, pp. 20 ff. The law of July 27, 1872, stripped them of the right to vote, and that of November 30, 1875, of their eligibility for election to the Chamber of Deputies. Although eligible for the Senate, their number there would grow smaller and smaller.

The majority of officers did not at all voice their political opinions or even their religious beliefs, largely out of prudence, but also because the principles of passive obedience and hierarchical subordination seemed incompatible with any political opinion—or at least with its expression.

25. Bedarida, *op. cit.*, p. 159.

26. *Ibid.*, p. 159.

27. *L'Armée et la démocratie.*

28. Quoted by Bedarida, *op. cit.*, p. 162.

29. Concerning the rituals and isolation of military life, see Serman, *op. cit.*, pp. 125ff.

30. Bedarida, *op. cit.*, p. 164.

3. *Intelligent, Zealous, Conscientious, Quite Active*

1. Concerning the casual love affairs of French officers, see William Serman, *Les Officers français dans la Nation* (Paris: Aubier-Montaigne, 1982), p. 180. In a study composed on the eve of the trial at Rennes (whose unpublished text was communicated to us by Alfred Dreyfus's grandson, Dr. Jean-Louis Lévy) concerning d'Ormescheville's report which had accused Dreyfus in 1894 of having frequented women of questionable morals, if not outright spies, Alfred refuted the attack by denying most of the adventures with which he was reproached, and by situating those that he acknowledged before 1888.

2. Dreyfus, *Cinq années de ma vie*, Preface by François Mauriac (Paris: Fasquelle, 1962), p. 26.

3. On the development of soldiers' salaries at the end of the nineteenth century and the poverty of unmoneyed officers, see William Serman, *op. cit.*, pp. 128ff.

4. Michael Marrus, *Les Juifs de France à l'époque de l'Affaire Dreyfus* (Paris: Calmann-Lévy, 1972), p. 228. An extremely complete bibliography concerning anti-Semitic campaigns against Jewish officers and duels may be found in Marrus. Serman (*op. cit.*, p. 101) observes that over twenty years, the proportion of Jewish officers in the Army had risen from 2% to 10%.

5. Marrus, *op. cit.*, p. 230.

6. At the time of the trial, his wife and brother would not receive help from a single high-ranking officer. Concerning patronage in the French Army, see Douglas Johnson, *France and the Dreyfus Affair* (London: Blanford Press, 1966).

7. Jacques Kayser, *L'Affaire Dreyfus* (Paris: Gallimard, 1946), p. 29.

8. Archives of the Ministry of War. "Secret File." File C, item 97. Mathieu Dreyfus would attempt in vain to get General de Dionne to testify on Dreyfus's behalf before the Court-Martial. The general would refer him to the "excellent grades" given Dreyfus, which, in his opinion, sufficed. And he would enter those grades into the case file, supplemented by a malevolent commentary.

9. See the portraits assembled by Dr. Jean-Louis Lévy, Dreyfus's grandson, in "Alfred Dreyfus, antihéros et témoin capital," postface to *Cinq années de ma vie* (Paris: Maspero, 1982), pp. 239ff.

10. Dreyfus, *op. cit.*, p. 11.

4. *A Jew*

1. Concerning this problem, among countless studies, see in particular, Michael Marrus, *Les Juifs de France à l'epoque de l'Affaire Dreyfus* (Paris: Calmann-Lévy, 1972); Hellmut Andics, *Histoire de l'antisémitisme* (Paris: Albin Michel, 1967); Léon Poliakov, *Histoire de l'antisémitisme: l'Europe suicidaire, 1870-1933* (Paris: Calmann-Lévy, 1973); Michel Winock, *Edouard Drumont et Cie. Antisémitisme et fascisme en France* (Paris: Seuil, 1982); Samuel Trigano, *La République et les Juifs après Copernic* (Paris: Presses d'Aujourd'hui, 1982); "Les Juifs en France," *Revue trimestrielle d'Histoire*, no. 3, November 1979, Hachette; *De l'antijudaïsme antique à l'antisémitisme contemporain*, Études de l'Université de Lille III (Presses universitaires de Lille, 1979); Patrick Girard, *Les Juifs de France de 1789 à 1860, de l'émancipation à l'égalité* (Paris: Calmann-Lévy, coll. Diaspora). See François Furet's studies of several of these books, collected in "Les juifs et la démocratie française," *L'Atelier de l'Histoire* (Paris: Flammarion, 1982), pp. 276ff.

2. Marrus, *op. cit.*, p. 108; Furet, *op. cit.*, p. 278.

3. Ernest Crémieu-Foa, *La Campagne antisémitique. Les duels. Les responsables* (Paris: Alcan Lévy, 1892).

4. Isidore Cahen, "Le cinquantenaire des archives israélites" in *La Gerbe*, Paris, 1890, p. 9, quoted by Marrus, *op. cit.*, p. 109.

5. Annie Kriegel ("Révolution francaise et judaïsme," *L'Arche*, March 1975) has shown how the Revolution was also able to open the way to the idea that the emancipation of an oppressed people might take a collective or national form. "The conquest of juridical equality," writes François Furet *(op. cit.),* "and of individual freedom by the Jews of France, in exposing them to the values of the surrounding society, certainly secularized them, but it also contributed to make them cherish the ideas of democracy, the nation, or socialism, which were also not alien to the Jewish national awakening of the end of the nineteenth century."

6. Quoted by Marrus, *op. cit.*, p. 113.

7. Quoted by Marrus, *op. cit.*, p. 113. See also Chief Rabbi Zadoc Kahn's sermon of September 19, 1876: "The nation has tremendous claims on us, and we must never feel ourselves to be absolved of them . . . we must learn how to sacrifice our tranquillity, our wealth, and even our life when interest demands it."

8. Marrus, *op. cit.*, p. 144.

9. Pierre Pierrard, *Juifs et Catholiques français* (Paris: Fayard, 1970), p. 20.

10. As in 1840, the murder of a Capuchin monk in Damascus, erroneously attributed to the Jew David Harari. In 1846, the Catholic publisher Gaume published a two volume indictment of the Jews on this subject under the signature Achille Laurent (see Pierrard, *op. cit.*, p. 21).

11. Quoted by Pierrard, *op. cit.*, p. 21.

12. See in particular the book by Fourier's disciple Alphonse Toussenel, *Les Juifs rois de l'époque*, published in 1845.

13. Concerning forced conversions, see Pierrard, *op. cit.* These involved Jewish children baptized without the authorization of their parents in order to "snatch a soul from Satan," according to Louis Veuillot in *L'Univers.*

14. Bernard Lazare, *L'antisémitisme. Son histoire et ses causes*, Paris, 1894, p. 227.

15. See Marrus, *op. cit.*, p. 181.

16. Jeannine Verdès-Leroux, *Scandales financiers et antisémitisme catholique* (Paris: Le Centurion, 1969), pp. 121ff.

17. Pierrard, *op. cit.*, p. 25.

18. Concerning scorn for the poor and filthy Jew, see Verdès-Leroux, *op. cit.*, p. 135.

19. See Zeev Sternhell, *Maurice Barrès et le nationalisme français*, Cahiers de la Fondation nationale des sciences politiques, 1972; See also by the same author: *La Droite révolutionnaire en France, 1885–1914: les origines françaises du fascisme* (Paris: Seuil, 1978), and *Ni droite ni gauche, l'idéologie fasciste en France* (Paris: Seuil, 1983).

20. "It was thus conjointly that throughout all of Europe the same fears and the same passions attained expression, that men from extremely diverse backgrounds and quite distant disciplines contributed to the formulation of a common ideology. It is hard not to be struck by the similarities between the nationalism of a Barrès, a Déroulède, and a Rochefort, and that of a d'Annunzio, a Carducci, a Corradini, a Karl Lueger and his Social-Christians, of Georg von Schönerer and of the German National Party in Austria, of the pan-Germanist and anti-Semitic parties in Germany or of the various pan-Slavist movements." Zeev Sternhell, *Maurice Barrès et le nationalisme français*, pp. 18-19.

21. "It is the characteristic of 'right-wing' historians," writes Michel Winock ("Edouard Drumont et l'antisémitisme en France avant l'Affaire Dreyfus," *Esprit*, May 1971), "to explain everything by conspiracy. For Edouard Drumont, the French Revolution was largely a Jewish plot: 'the only one who profited from the Revolution was the Jew. Everything derived from the Jew. And everything accrued to him.'"

See as well by the same author: *Edouard Drumont et Cie. Antisémitisme et fascisme en France* (Paris: Seuil, 1982). But the idea that for every misfortune and every anxiety there is a responsible party is not restricted to the right. The sufferings of all those crushed by industrial society at the end of the nineteenth century would find in anti-Semitism a convenient explanation and compensation, both on the left and on the right.

22. Maurice Barrès, *Scènes et Doctrines du nationalisme* (Paris: Félix Guven, 1902), p. 152.

23. *L'Action française*, March 28, 1911.

24. See the works referred to above in Note 1.

25. Verdès-Leroux, *op. cit.*, p. 117. Three anti-Jewish weeklies—*L'Antijuif*, launched in 1871, *Le Syndic révolutionnaire* (in 1882), and *L'Antisémitique* (in 1883)—disappeared almost immediately.

26. Pierrard, *op. cit.*, p. 29.

27. It would excite, nevertheless, the lasting admiration of Georges Bernanos, notably in *La Grande Peur des bien-pensants*: "No analysis can convey an idea of this magical book." Jules Lemaître would see in it "a work of genius" and Alphonse Daudet would write: "His pillory is the equal of Dante's."

28. Michel Winock, "Edouard Drumont et l'antisémitisme en France avant l'Affaire Dreyfus," *loc. cit.*, p. 1097.

29. *Ibid.*, p. 1099.

30. Quoted in Joseph Jurt, "L'Affaire Dreyfus: le rôle de l'opinion," *Bulletin de l'Amitié judéo-chrétienne*, No. 4, 1981, pp. 75 ff. Concerning the rise of anti-Semitism in the Army after 1890, see William Serman, *Les Officiers dans la Nation* (Paris: Aubieu, 1982), pp. 100 ff.

31. By the end of 1890, *La Libre Parole* had printings of 500,000 and *La Croix*, 170,000. See also Stephen Wilson, "Antisemitism and Jewish Response in France during the Dreyfus Affair," *European Studies Review*, 6, 1976.

32. This is the classification offered notably by Jeannine Verdès-Leroux in her work, *Scandales financiers et antisémitisme catholique*. It is the customary classification.

33. The standard—though earlier—work was Gougenot des Mousseaux's celebrated book, *Le Juif, le judaïsme et la judaïsation des peuples chrétiens,* published in 1869. Edouard Drumont would claim that Gougenot had been murdered by the Jews.

34. The first works appear to have been the book by Fourier's disciple Toussenel, *Les Juifs, rois de l'époque,* (1845), which Drumont would salute as an "imperishable masterpiece," and an article bearing the same title by Pierre Leroux (1846). Those texts appear not to have had a wide readership at the time of their publication. A Jew, for Toussenel, is "any trafficker of money, any unproductive parasite living from the substance of other people's work." Pierre Leroux denounced "the Jewish spirit," that is: the will to profit, to wealth, the "banker's mentality."

35. The four volumes of Arthur de Gobineau's *Essai sur l'inégalité des races humaines,* published from 1853 to 1855, had few readers. Gobineau complained of this to Tocqueville. The courses given by the theorist of racism, Vacher de Lapouge—"Les Sélections sociales" (1888) and "L'Aryen, son rôle social" (1889)—hardly exercised more influence at the time than had Gobineau, but in the course of time they were to have repercussions. The writings of Ernest Renan (notably the texts recently regrouped under the title *Judaïsme et Christianisme* (Paris: Copernic, 1977), when read superficially, frequently fueled anti-Semitic racism.

36. Verdès-Leroux, *op. cit.*, p. 114.

37. See in particular Danièle Delmaire, *"L'Antisémitisme de la Croix du Nord pendant l'Affaire Dreyfus, 1898–1899"* in *De l'antijudaïsme antique à l'antisémitisme contemporain* (Presses universitaires de Lille, 1979).

38. Edouard Drumont, *La France juive: Essai d'histoire contemporaine,* (Paris: Flammarian, 1886), p. 35.

39. Verdès-Leroux, *op. cit.*, p. 126.

40. *Ibid.*, pp. 127 ff.

41. A theme later taken up by Guy de Maupassant.

42. Maurice Barrès, *op. cit.*, pp. 140 ff.

43. Verdès-Leroux, *op. cit.*, pp. 140 ff.

44. *Ibid.*, pp. 140 ff. The economic measures proposed in order to punish or despoil Jews were, of course, quite varied.

45. *La Juiverie*, Gautier, 1887, p. 107.

46. *Le Mystère du sang chez les Juifs de tous les temps,* Savine, 1889.

47. Georges Meynie, *Les Juifs en Algérie,* p. 322.

5. *The Republic of Opportunists*

1. Jacques Chastenet, "La République des républicains," *Histoire de la IIIe République*, vol. II (Paris: Hachette, 1954), pp. 207ff.

2. *Ibid.,* p. 246.

3. Concerning the gradual rise of the middle classes, see in particular J. Lhomme, *La Grande Bourgeoisie au pouvoir, 1830–1880* (Paris: PUF, 1960) pp. 288 ff. Lhomme has studied the "doctrine" of the middle classes—an egalitarianism looking upward, not downward, and anticlericalism—and their behavior in relation to power, a blend of concern for their interests and taste for ideas, of zeal for business and idealism.

4. There were twenty cabinets between February 1879 and April 1893. Because of the sinister precedent of May 16, 1877, no one dared to invoke the dissolution procedure.

No doubt there was always lacking—in both the Senate and the Chamber—a coherent and organized government majority. If men such as Jules Ferry and Charles Freycinet managed to remain at the head of their governments long enough to accomplish major acts, the customary situation during the period was that of a Parliament lacking in continuity and discipline, perpetually overthrowing compromise governments. The corruption of a few members of Parliament—denounced during the Wilson Affair and the Panama scandal—which was magnified and exploited beyond all proportion, Parliament's inability to achieve a stable majority, the insults and commotion characterizing a number of sessions, and the ceremonial duels all managed to discredit in the public's eyes a Parliament which all the same had worked during difficult years more seriously and more diligently than its reputation suggests.

5. Chastenet, *op. cit.,* p. 332.

6. M. Lévy Leboyer, "La Croissance économique en France au XIXe siècle" in *Annales ESC,* July–August 1968. Comp. Jean Bouvier: "Le Mouvement d'une civilisation moderne" in Georges Duby, *Histoire de la France* (Paris: Larousse, 1970) and T. J. Makovitch's conclusions in his major investigation of "French industry from 1789 to 1964." Bouvier notes that all the historic forms of industrial production coexisted in the latter half of the nineteenth century in France: "The industrial world was a museum in which the ancient and the new could be found side by side."

7. 66% in the decade 1855–1864; 65% in the decade 1863–1874; 64% in the decade 1875–1884; 61% in the decade 1885–1894 (Bouvier, *op. cit.,* p. 420).

8. 46.8% from 1885 to 1864; 46.9% from 1865 to 1874; 43.8% from 1875 to 1884; 41.1% from 1885 to 1894; 39.2% from 1895 to 1904 (Bouvier, *op. cit.,* p. 420).

9. Concerning the shortcomings of an educational system that reproduced social stratifications and tended to indulge privilege rather than combat it, see Antoine Prost, *Histoire de l'enseignement en France 1800–1967* (Paris: A. Colin, 1968).

10. Chastenet, *op. cit.*, p. 303.

11. *Ibid.*, p. 304.

12. Pierre Sorlin, *Waldeck-Rousseau* (Paris: A. Colin, 1966), p. 356.

13. Except in the public services and in several major firms.

14. Speech to the Chamber of November 21, 1897.

15. Chastenet, *op. cit.*, pp. 305ff.

16. The French continued to deposit in savings accounts. The annual amount saved rose from 2 million for the period between 1875 and 1893 to three and a half million for the period from 1893 to 1911. Guy Palmade, *Le Capitalisme français* (Paris: A. Colin, 1961). A long-term monetary stability maintained the value of revenues based on accumulated capital. A slow tendency toward lower prices—due specifically to technical progress and the development of production—worked in the same direction. The State treasury—a secure investment—perpetually attracted the mass of small investors.

17. This increased the imbalance in relation to the population of Germany. In 1893, Germany enjoyed an advantage of 13,000,000 inhabitants. The circumstance is not unrelated to the search for an alliance with Russia, which was an inexhaustible reservoir of men.

18. Bouvier, *op. cit.*, p. 417.

19. Chastenet, *op. cit.*, p. 341.

20. From 1878 to 1893, the proportion of the population living from industry went from 28% to 32%.

21. Concerning the slow evolution of social structures in France and the hierarchy of conditions, see Adeline Daumard, "L'evolution des structures sociales en France à l'epoque de l'industrialisation (1815–1914)" in *Revue historique*, April 1972. Concerning the fusion—beyond any prejudices—of the aristocracy and the capitalist bourgeoisie, see Guy Palmade, *Le Capitalisme français au XIXᵉ siècle* (Paris: A. Colin, 1961), and Lhomme, *op. cit.*

22. *Op. cit.*, pp. 423ff.

23. Concerning the "refusal of industrial civilization," see Bouvier, *op. cit.*, p. 433. Bouvier notes that the delay of the "mental" in relation to the social, of the social in relation to the economic is a matter of general observation. But in France, the enormous weight of structures (specifically of property) and the play of mentalities worked strongly in this direction.

24. Sorlin, *op.cit.*, p. 355.

25. Pierre Miquel, *L'Affaire Dreyfus* (Paris: PUF, 1959), p. 11.

26. Chastenet, *op. cit.*, p. 241.

6. *The Ordinary Track*

1. In *La France juive*, Drumont was to denounce the colonial expeditions as conquests desired and organized by Jews, exclusively for their own profit.

2. Jacques Chastenet, *Histoire de la IIIᵉ République* (Paris: Hachette, 1954), p. 336.

3. Michael Marrus, *Les juifs de France à l'époque de l'Affaire Dreyfus* (Paris: Calmann-Lévy, 1972) pp. 145ff. In 1899, Jean Jaurès was denouncing the risks

France was running because of its alliance with the Czar. See *La Petite République* of October 15, 1893; quoted in the Jaurès *Anthologie* edited by Louis Lévy, preface by Madeleine Rebérioux (Paris: Calmann-Lévy, 1983), pp. 116ff.

4. Not even Joseph Caillaux, who would attract so much hatred for having dealt with Germany in 1911 and who dreamed of a Franco-German alliance as the cornerstone of Europe. Jean-Denis Bredin, *Joseph Caillaux* (Paris: Hachette-Littérature, 1980), and Jean-Claude Allain, *Joseph Caillaux, le défi victorieux* (Paris: Imprimerie nationale, 1978).

5. Among the numerous works dealing with espionage and intelligence services (specifically in the context of the Dreyfus Affair), see in particular Marcel Thomas, *L'Affaire sans Dreyfus* (Paris: Fayard, 1961), pp. 66ff and also Allan Mitchell's "The Xenophobic Style: French Counter-Espionage and the Emergence of the Dreyfus Affair," article in the *Journal of Modern History* of September 1980 (University of Chicago), pp. 489-499.

6. The Prefecture would also employ an odd assortment of "freelance" spies, who sold their information. In 1870, the Prefecture of Police could identify 165 German spies. It appears that the excellence of the German espionage services had long been the object of the admiration of the French specialists.

7. The date of the creation of the Section of Statistics is uncertain: between 1872 and 1876. See Guy Chapman, *The Dreyfus Case* (London: Rupert Hart-Davis, 1955), p. 48. Allan Mitchell, *op. cit.*

8. Thomas, *op. cit.*, p. 68.

9. Numerous intelligence agents came from Alsace. Able to speak German, they had retained useful relations there. Thus it was that after Sandherr, Colonel Picquart—who was also Alsatian—would direct the Intelligence Service.

10. Thomas, *op. cit.*, p. 69.

11. During the years preceding the war, Notebook B would grow to include pacifists and extreme left-wing militants. Concerning Notebook B, see Jean-Jacques Becker, *Le Carnet B. Les pouvoirs et l'antimilitarisme avant la guerre de 1914* (Paris: Klincksieck), 1973).

12. Mitchell, *op. cit.*, p. 499.

13. Thomas, *op. cit.*, p. 71.

14. Sandherr's father, a functionary in the commercial court of Mulhouse and a Protestant converted to Catholicism, overtly professed his anti-Semitism. The colonel himself was openly anti-Semitic. Cf. Armand Charpentier, *Les côtés mystérieux de l'Affaire Dreyfus* (Paris: Rieder, 1977), pp. 148ff.

15. *Ibid.*, p. 151.

16. Thomas, *op. cit.*

17. An extremely positive portrait of Henry may be found in Henri Giscard d'Estaing, *D'Esterhazy à Dreyfus* (Paris: Plon, 1955), pp. 4ff.

18. Joseph Reinach, *Histoire de l'Affaire Dreyfus*, vol. I, *Le Procès de 1894* (Paris: Charpentier & Fasquelle, 1929), pp. 20ff. Often accused of being biased, because of the abundance and precision of its sources and also because Reinach was a privileged witness of the Affair, Reinach's *Histoire* remains the fundamental work. Reinach, moreover, was a remarkable writer.

19. Thomas, *op. cit.*, p. 76; Bruno Weil, *L'Affaire Dreyfus,* translated from the German (Paris: Gallimard, 1930), p. 24.

20. The German Emperor, Wilhelm II, would lapse into a fury when he was to learn in 1899 of that degree of negligence. He would annotate in such terms the report by the minister of foreign affairs, Prince von Bülow: "Incomprehensible irresponsibility . . . a fine disorder prevailed at the embassy."

21. Paléologue, *Journal de l'Affaire Dreyfus,* pp. 4 ff.

22. Thomas, *op. cit.*, p. 79.

7. *Maximilien and Alexandrine*

1. Prince von Bülow would nevertheless write in his *Memoirs:* "Until the World War, Germany spent much more on its intelligence and espionage services than the other great powers and behaved far more moderately than they in this crucial but unclean domain." Quoted by Maurice Baumont, *Aux sources de l'Affaire Dreyfus* (Paris: Productions de Paris, 1959), p. 16.

2. Baumont, *op. cit.*, pp. 62 ff; Bruno Weil, *L'Affaire Dreyfus (Paris: Gallimard,* 1930), pp. 24 ff; Marcel Thomas, *L'Affaire sans Dreyfus,* pp. 64 ff. Concerning the nature of the numerous documents intercepted and the "leaking" of master plans, see Joseph Reinach, *Histoire de l'Affaire Dreyfus,* vol. I, pp. 30 ff.

3. Weil, *op. cit.*, p. 26; Baumont, *op. cit.*, p. 17, Thomas, *op. cit.*, pp. 60 ff.

4. Baumont, *op. cit.*, p. 58.

5. *Ibid.*, p. 59.

6. Weil, *op. cit.*, p. 26; Thomas, *op. cit.*, p. 62.

7. But they frequently exchanged surnames, a circumstance which often complicates the problem of identifying their letters. See Reinach, *op. cit.*, p. 31; Thomas, *op. cit.*, pp. 63 ff.

8. Archives of the Ministry of War, Secret File, nos. 236 to 317, letters of February 1894.

9. Archives of the Ministry of War, Secret File, letter of October 5, 1894.

10. October 1895.

11. February 1896.

12. Archives of the Ministry of War, Secret File, nos. 247 to 286.

13. July 1893, Document 254.

14. End of 1893, Document 255.

15. October 1894, Document 256.

16. November 1894, Document 260.

17. Received April 27, 1897, Document 277.

18. Intimate correspondence with Mme. de Weede. Archives of the Ministry of War, Documents 159 to 239.

19. Thomas, *op. cit.*, p. 65.

20. *Ibid.*, p. 63.

21. *Ibid.*, p. 66.

8. *A Mysterious Visitor*

1. Comte Maximilien von Schwarzkoppen, *Les Carnets de Schwarzkoppen* (Paris: Rieder, 1930), p. 10.

2. Marcel Thomas, *L'Affaire sans Dreyfus*, p. 84.

3. Esterhazy's successive lies have complicated the task of historians. Thomas has established (*op. cit.*, pp. 90ff) that Esterhazy had left Châlons on August 9 and that he was in Paris on August 12 and 13.

4. Schwarzkoppen, *op. cit.*, p. 14.

5. Schwarzkoppen, who was quite cautious, also dispatched a second observer to the Châlons camp to gather information concerning that piece of artillery. But Marcel Thomas has established that Schwarzkoppen's German "agent," Alex, alias R. B., was in fact a double agent working for the French Intelligence Service. It was thus the Section of Statistics which—through a double agent—would inform Schwarzkoppen . . . falsely. Thomas, *op. cit.*, pp. 91–92.

6. Schwarzkoppen, *op. cit.*, p. 15.

7. *Ibid.*, p. 15.

9. *The Dictation*

1. Alfred Dreyfus, *Cinq années de ma vie*, p. 27. It appears that the year 1894 had been the happiest year in Dreyfus's life. In 1893, he had lost his father and his wife had been seriously ill. His son Pierre, during his first year, had been a very fragile child and had caused great disquiet to his parents. In 1894, the clouds seemed to disperse. See Henri Villemar, *Dreyfus intime* (Paris: Stock, 1898).

2. Du Paty would claim this in his "report" to General Auguste Mercier, minister of war; he would no longer say so in his testimony at the Rennes trial. The document written by Dreyfus does not reveal any sign of "trembling."

3. Dreyfus, *op. cit.*, p. 29. Subsequently several successive and contradictory versions of Dreyfus's "alleged agitation" would be given. In his report of October 31, 1894, du Paty would write that Dreyfus had answered him "with a sort of nervous grimace."

4. Dreyfus, *op. cit.*, p. 29.

5. *Ibid.*, p. 30.

6. Du Paty, in his report to the minister, did not mention this "proposition." But it is established by Cochefort's deposition and by du Paty's subsequent testimony.

7. 1894 Report.

8. See Joseph Reinach, *Histoire de l'Affaire Dreyfus*, p. 120.

9. Du Paty would maintain that it was not possible to show Dreyfus the original of the incriminating bordereau, which was in the hands of the Deputy Chief of the General Staff. There had not been sufficient time to prepare a copy.

10. Dreyfus, *op. cit.*, p. 31. He was treated as a convict, an illegal measure which was later reported.

10. *The Bordereau*

1. A Catholic, Mercier was married to an Englishwoman, who was Protestant. (See Joseph Reinach, *Histoire de l'Affaire Dreyfus*, vol. I, pp. 1ff.)

2. *Ibid.*, pp. 5ff.

3. Quoted by Joseph Reinach, *Ibid.*, p. 12, Note 1.

4. Henri Guillemin, *L'Enigme Esterhazy* (Paris: Gallimard, 1962), pp. 75ff.

5. Reinach, *op. cit.*, vol. I, p. 38.

6. *Ibid.*, p. 39.

7. *Ibid.*, p. 108.

8. Reinach, *op. cit.*, vol. I, p. 45. Reinach's thesis is the one most frequently adopted. See in particular Jean France, *Autour de l'Affaire Dreyfus* (Paris: Rieder, 1936), pp. 122ff and Armand Charpentier, *Les Côtés mystérieux de l'Affaire Dreyfus* (Paris: Rieder, 1937), pp. 10ff, as well as Michel de Lombarès, *L'Affaire Dreyfus; la clef du mystère* (Paris: Robert Laffont), pp. 69ff. There is also a subsidiary version: Mme. Bastian would have stolen the bordereau from the concierge and then transmitted it to Brücker.

9. "The dangerous missive had been purloined by Agent Brücker from the concierge's stall in the embassy," Alfred Dreyfus would write (*Souvenirs et correspondances*), p. 68.

10. Baumont, *op. cit.*, p. 35.

11. Comte Maximilien von Schwarzkoppen, *Les Carnets de Schwarzkoppen* (Paris: Rieder, 1930), p. 24.

12. Archives of the Ministry of War. Secret File.

13. Thomas, *op. cit.*, p. 86.

14. *Ibid.*, p. 114.

15. Marcel Thomas has established (*op. cit.*, p. 118) that it was between September 25 and 29, and probably on the 27th, that the bordereau was inserted in an "information bulletin" (no. 109) intended for the minister, to which was appended a report by Sandherr that did not figure in any official file.

16. *Ibid.*, p. 122.

17. On Artillery Captain Dreyfus's report sheet prepared after the six-month training period he had spent in the 4th Bureau, from July 1 to December 31, 1893. Then a second, more complete specimen of Dreyfus's handwriting was located in the archives of the Eastern Military Commission where he had worked.

18. Reinach, *op. cit.*, vol. I, p. 62.

19. A "secret" memorandum, prepared in 1898 by the Intelligence Service at Minister of War General Zurlinden's behest, tells of the conditions in which "the first suspicions of Dreyfus's guilt emerged" (French National Archives, B B 19 105, d.1, p. 11). It concludes: "It was Colonel Fabre and not the Intelligence Service who nourished the first suspicions of Dreyfus's guilt. There was thus no preconceived idea on the part of those who first had the idea that Dreyfus might be the culprit."

20. Thomas, *op. cit.*, p. 130. Sandherr was from Mulhouse, like Dreyfus.

21. Statements of General Mercier at the Rennes trial. Reinach, *op. cit.*, p. 64.

22. Thomas, *op. cit.*, p. 132.

23. Guillemin, *op. cit.*, p. 99.

11. *The Conspirators*

1. Marcel Thomas, *L'Affaire sans Dreyfus*, p. 137.

2. There was a file on Maurice Weil at the Section of Statistics. Poorly stocked

on the espionage activities with which Weil had vaguely been reproached, the file was more informative on his financial malpractices—and, to be sure, on his relations with his "protector," General Saussier.

3. Casimir-Périer's deposition at Rennes. Mercier, on the contrary, would claim to have shown the bordereau and the items used for comparison to the president of the Republic. This was categorically denied by Casimir-Périer. Their recollections were irreducibly opposed.

4. Joseph Reinach, *Histoire de l'Affaire Dreyfus,* vol. I, p. 79.

5. Maurice Paléologue, *Journal de l'Affaire Dreyfus,* pp. 1ff.

6. A promise which—according to Marcel Thomas—would be the origin of the constitution of the secret file (*op. cit.,* p. 141).

7. He himself would discover the suspected officer by comparing the military register and information relative to Dreyfus's career in one of the items used for purposes of comparison.

8. Quoted by Marcel Thomas, *op. cit.,* pp. 143ff.

9. Reinach, *op. cit.,* vol. I, p. 92.

10. He had ten hours in which to do his job during the day of October 13. Bertillon was already noting "that the writing contained a few touch-ups here and there, a few moments of vacillation, such as ordinarily characterize tracing" of another script. The onion-skin paper, so light as to be almost transparent, on which the bordereau was written encouraged such thoughts: Bertillon would later defend the hypothesis of a "forged document."

11. Thomas, *op. cit.,* p. 146.

12. *The Capers of Bertillon*

1. Henri Villemar, *Dreyfus intime* (Paris: Stock, 1898), p. 20.

2. Mathieu Dreyfus, *L'Affaire telle que je l'ai vécue* (Paris: Grasset, 1978), p. 19.

3. Joseph Reinach, *Histoire de l'Affaire Dreyfus,* vol. I, p. 153.

4. Forzinetti, *Lettres d'un innocent,* pp. 259ff.

5. Minutes of October 24, 1894.

6. Alfred Dreyfus, *Cinq années de ma vie,* p. 32.

7. Saussier reproached Forzinetti with having received a prisoner without informing him: "If you were not my friend, I would have given you two months of prison for having received a prisoner without my order."

8. Reinach, *op. cit.,* vol. I, p. 166.

9. *Ibid.,* pp. 195ff.

10. Marcel Thomas, *L'Affaire sans Dreyfus,* pp. 150ff.

11. Mathieu Dreyfus, *op. cit.,* p. 21.

12. Reinach, *op. cit.,* vol. I, p. 173.

13. See the full-scale analysis of Bertillon's diagram by Joseph Reinach, *op. cit.,* vol. I, pp. 308ff.

14. *Ibid.,* p. 311.

15. Maurice Paléologue, *Journal de l'Affaire Dreyfus* (Paris: Plon, 1955), p. 28.

16. Reinach, *op. cit.,* vol. I, p. 178.

17. *Ibid.,* pp. 128ff.

18. Forzinetti's notes of October 27.

19. Concerning the role of the press in "encouraging" Mercier, see Bruno Weil, *L'Affaire Dreyfus* (Paris: Gallimard, 1930), pp. 40ff.

20. Thomas, *op. cit.*, p. 155.

21. Reinach, *op. cit.*, vol. I, p. 210.

22. Mathieu Dreyfus, *op. cit.*, p. 24. Minutes of the conversation were recorded by du Paty. See Reinach, *op. cit.*, vol. I, p. 212, note 1.

23. Reinach, *op. cit.*, vol. I, p. 324. Pierre Sorlin, *Waldeck-Rousseau*, p. 392, note 8.

24. Paléologue, *op. cit.*, p. 35.

25. Reinach, *op. cit.*, vol. I, p. 324.

13. *This Jew Protected by Germany*

1. Joseph Reinach, *Histoire de l'Affaire Dreyfus*, vol. I, p. 223ff. The statistic for readers of *Le Petit Journal*, advanced by Joseph Reinach, seems exaggerated.

2. *La Libre Parole*, November 14, 1894.

3. *La Croix*, November 7, 1894, quoted by Pierre Sorlin, *La Croix et les Juifs* (Paris: A. Colin, 1966), p. 111.

4. *La Croix*, November 14, 1894.

5. *La Croix*, November and December 1894, quoted by Sorlin, *op. cit.*, pp. 112ff.

6. Joseph Reinach quotes numerous passages from the "nationalist" press of November and December 1894. Several articles, in particular those by Drumont, Rochefort, and Judet, were reprinted in the provincial press.

7. *Petit Journal*, November 3, 1894.

8. Reinach, *op. cit.*, vol. I, pp. 228–229.

9. *La Libre Parole*, November 3, 1894.

10. *Soleil du Midi*, November 12, 1894, signed by Oscar Havard. The article was entitled "Atavisme."

11. Mathieu Dreyfus, *L'Affaire telle que je l'ai vécue*, p. 26.

12. *La Libre Parole*, November 5, 1894 article by Drumont.

13. *La Libre Parole*, November 6, 1894, article by Drumont.

14. *La Libre Parole*, November 7, 1894.

15. *L'Intransigeant*, November 5, 1894.

16. Marcel Thomas, *L'Affaire sans Dreyfus*, p. 170.

17. *La Libre Parole*, November 22, 1894.

18. Reinach, *op. cit.*, vol. I, pp. 242ff.

19. Mathieu Dreyfus, *op. cit.*, p. 25.

20. Maurice Baumont, *Aux sources de l'Affaire Dreyfus*, pp. 95ff.

21. *Ibid.*, pp. 96ff.

22. *Ibid.*, p. 98.

23. Telegram of November 28, 1894.

24. Maurice Paléologue, *Journal de l'Affaire Dreyfus* (Paris: Plon, 1955), pp. 22ff.

25. Baumont, *op. cit.,* p. 99.

26. *Le Temps* of November 30. Paléologue, *op. cit.,* p. 22; Baumont, *op. cit.,* pp. 100ff.

27. See Paléologue, *op. cit.,* p. 26, note 1; Baumont, *op. cit.,* p. 102.

14. *I Am Approaching the End of My Suffering*

1. See Joseph Reinach, *Histoire de l'Affaire Dreyfus,* vol. I, p. 288.

2. See French National Archives BB 19 101, pp. 28ff.

3. Cherche-Midi Prison, letter of December 5, 1894 to Lucie Dreyfus, *Lettres d'un innocent,* p. 21.

4. Cherche-Midi Prison, letter of December 7, 1894 to Lucie Dreyfus, *Ibid.,* p. 22.

5. Cherche-Midi Prison, letter of December 8, 1894 to Lucie Dreyfus, *Ibid.,* p. 25.

6. Appendix to *Lettres d'un innocent,* pp. 264ff.

7. Mathieu Dreyfus, *L'Affaire telle que je l'ai vécue,* p. 35.

8. Maurice Paléologue, *Journal de l'Affaire Dreyfus* (Paris: Plon, 1955), p. 9.

9. Marcel Thomas, *L'Affaire sans Dreyfus,* pp. 162ff.

10. *Ibid.,* p. 163.

11. *Ibid.,* p. 166. Concerning the constitution of the secret file, see Reinach, *op. cit.,* vol. I, pp. 330ff.

12. Thomas, *op. cit.,* p. 168.

13. *Ibid.,* Joseph Reinach regarded it as certain.

14. Reinach, *op. cit.,* vol. I, p. 134.

15. *Ibid.,* p. 137.

16. *Ibid.,* p. 137.

17. Mathieu Dreyfus, *op. cit.,* p. 36.

18. *Ibid.,* p. 38.

19. *Ibid.,* p. 35.

20. Friday December 15, 1894, letter to Lucie Dreyfus, *Lettres d'un innocent,* p. 29.

21. Tuesday December 19, 1894, letter to Lucie Dreyfus, *Ibid.,* p. 33.

15. *This Man Is the Traitor*

1. Joseph Reinach, *Histoire de l'Affaire Dreyfus,* vol. I, p. 387.

2. *Ibid.,* p. 387.

3. The remarks are signed by Dreyfus. In them may be read: "Given on the one hand, that the sole piece on which the accusation is based in its entirety is an unsigned letter, attributed to Captain Dreyfus, but staunchly denied by him and on whose authenticity the experts are far from unanimous . . ." (French National Archives BB 19 101, d4), p. 4.

4. Reinach, *op. cit.,* vol. I, p. 400.

5. *Ibid.,* vol. I, p. 401.

6. Picquart would nevertheless say before the High Court of Appeal: "He protested with utmost energy against the accusation weighing against him, but in a

somewhat theatrical manner, which did not make a good impression on the court."

7. Reinach, *op. cit.*, vol. I, p. 403.

8. French National Archives, BB 19 101, d4, p. 4.

9. See Armand Charpentier, *Les Côtés mystérieux de l'Affaire Dreyfus* (Paris: Rieder, 1930), p. 69.

10. Reinach, *op. cit.*, vol. I, p. 417; Charpentier, *op. cit.*, p. 70.

11. Reinach, *op. cit.*, vol. I, p. 418.

12. Charpentier, *op. cit.*, p. 70.

13. Reinach, *op. cit.*, vol. I, p. 420.

14. Alfred Dreyfus, *Cinq années de ma vie*, p. 39.

15. Reinach, *op. cit.*, vol. I, p. 498.

16. Maurice Paléologue, *Journal de l'Affaire Dreyfus* (Paris: Plon, 1955), p. 36.

17. Reinach, *op. cit.*, p. 435.

18. Alfred Dreyfus, *op. cit.*, p. 40.

19. "I was no more than a secretary," du Paty would later say. "The commentary was written by me . . . as dictated by Colonel Sandherr." Du Paty's "commentary" is in the form of a memorandum—four large pages long—analyzing the documents in the secret file and attributing them to Dreyfus. General Mercier would not deny having ordered the preparation of the text to accompany the secret file. See Marcel Thomas, *L'Affaire sans Dreyfus*, p. 173, and Reinach, *op. cit.*, vol. I, p. 276.

20. Reinach, *op. cit.*, vol. I, pp. 442ff.

21. *Ibid.*, p. 450.

16. *The Affair Is Over*

1. Maurice Paléologue, *Journal de l'Affaire Dreyfus* (Paris: Plon, 1955), p. 30.

2. *Ibid.*, p. 32.

3. Joseph Reinach, *Histoire de l'Affaire Dreyfus*, vol. I, p. 476.

4. November 9, 1894.

5. Charles Péguy, *Notre Jeunesse* (Paris: Gallimard, 1933), pp. 101–102. Cf. Michael Marrus, *Les Juifs en France à l'époque de l'Affaire Dreyfus* (Paris: Calmann-Lévy, 1972), p. 236.

6. Alfred Dreyfus, *Cinq années de ma vie*, pp. 41ff.

7. December 24, 1894, letter to Lucie Dreyfus, *Lettres d'un innocent*, p. 35.

8. December 26, 10 P.M., letter to Lucie Dreyfus, *Ibid.*, p. 40.

9. December 27, 6 P.M., letter to Lucie Dreyfus, *Ibid.*, p. 41.

10. French National Archives, BB19 75, d1, p. 50.

11. Reinach, *op. cit.*, vol. I, pp. 481ff.

12. According to du Paty this mission was the subject of a detailed report to the Section of Statistics, which has not been rediscovered. (Reinach, *op. cit.*, vol. I), p. 485.

13. Alfred Dreyfus, *op. cit.*, p. 48.

14. *Ibid.*, p. 50.

15. French National Archives, BB19 75, d1, p. 67.

16. Alfred Dreyfus, *op. cit.*, p. 63.

17. Maurice Barrès, *Scènes et Doctrines du nationalisme* (Paris: Félix Guven, 1902), p. 146.

18. Alfred Dreyfus, *op. cit.*, pp. 67ff and Reinach, *op. cit.*, vol. I, pp. 562ff.

19. Reinach, *op. cit.*, vol. I, p. 569.

20. January 21, 1895, Ile de Ré, letter to Lucie Dreyfus, *Lettres d'un innocent*, p. 82.

21. Alfred Dreyfus, *op. cit.*, p. 85.

II: LONG LIVE ESTERHAZY

1. *The Legend of a Confession*

1. *Le Figaro*, January 6, 1895.

2. Joseph Reinach, *Histoire de l'Affaire Dreyfus*, vol. I, pp. 494ff and 513ff.

3. Telegram from Colonel Guérin to the Military Governor of Paris, French National Archives BB19 75, d6, p. 3.

4. *Le Figaro*, January 6, 1895.

5. Reinach, *op. cit.*, vol. I, p. 530.

6. *Ibid.*, vol. I, p. 536.

7. *La Libre Parole* had accused the German ambassador of having requested a closed session.

8. Reinach, *op. cit.*, vol. I, p. 536.

9. Maurice Paléologue, *Journal de l'Affaire Dreyfus* (Paris: Plon, 1955), p. 47; Maurice Baumont, *Aux sources de l'Affaire Dreyfus* (Paris: Productions de Paris, 1959), pp. 114ff.

10. *Ibid.*, p. 119.

11. Reinach, *op. cit.*, vol. I, p. 544.

12. Reinach, *op. cit.*, vol. I, p. 544.

13. *Le Petit Journal* of January 13. Article by Judet entitled "Les Privilèges de l'avocat: Pour la France ou pour Dreyfus."

14. *Le Soleil* of January 9, 1895.

15. Article by Judet, *Le Petit Journal* of January 13, 1895; Reinach, *op. cit.*, vol. I, pp. 552–553.

2. *The Retirement of Mercier*

1. Maurice Paléologue, *Journal de l'Affaire Dreyfus* (Paris: Plon, 1955), p. 50.

2. Joseph Reinach, *Histoire de l'Affaire Dreyfus*, vol. I, p. 553. Reinach, a friend of Casimir-Périer, reveals his admiring loyalty to him in his history of the case.

3. *Ibid.*, p. 553.

4. *Ibid.*, pp. 556ff.

5. Paléologue, *op. cit.*, p. 51.

6. Marcel Thomas, *L'Affaire sans Dreyfus*, p. 182.

7. Marcel Thomas argues on the basis of a statement by Boisdeffre to du Paty in March 1898: "General Mercier alone can absolve you from your pledge." But Marcel Thomas undoubtedly is too trustful of statements made by du Paty at a time

he was attempting to exonerate himself. There was in fact no need for the "conspirators" to take a pledge before the minister. Their complicity entailed their solidarity without any—in fact, quite implausible—recourse to a formal oath. Cf. Thomas, *op. cit.*, p. 183.

3. *Don't Do That; It's Not Nice*

1. Mathieu Dreyfus, *L'Affaire telle que je l'ai vécue* (Paris: Grasset, 1978), p. 47.

2. The feeling that the affair had been adjudicated and definitively closed was general in 1895, in particular among Jews. See Léon Blum, *Souvenirs sur l'Affaire* (Paris: Albin Michel, 1965), pp. 517ff.

3. Mathieu Dreyfus, *op. cit.*, p. 53.

4. See the account of the "traps" set for Mathieu Dreyfus in *L'Affaire telle que je l'ai vécue*, p. 55.

5. *Ibid.*, p. 57.

6. *Ibid.*, p. 58.

7. *Ibid.*, p. 61.

8. *Ibid.*, p. 75.

9. Concerning Léonie, see Joseph Reinach, *Histoire de l'Affaire Dreyfus*, vol. II, pp. 172ff.

10. Mathieu Dreyfus, *op. cit.*, p. 49.

11. *Ibid.*, p. 51.

12. *Ibid.*, p. 67.

13. Recounted to the author by Mme. France Beck, granddaughter of Mathieu Dreyfus, on June 2, 1983.

14. In order to move the president of the Republic, Mathieu had confided to him the letter in which Alfred Dreyfus told his wife of the frightful scenes at La Rochelle.

15. Called as a witness at the Zola trial, Dr. Gibert, who was quite ill, would prepare in writing an account of his conversation with Félix Faure. But could Faure at the time do anything other than deny it? In order to spare the aged physician that ordeal, Mathieu would forego his testimony and burn Dr. Gibert's testimony. Gibert would die on March 18, 1899, a month after Félix Faure, after having fought to the limit of his strength for the revision of the Dreyfus trial. It appears that Félix Faure was indeed preparing to deny the comments he had made to his friend, Dr. Gibert.

16. Mathieu Dreyfus, *op. cit.*, p. 52.

17. Newspaper edited by Arthur Meyer, a fiercely anti-Semitic Jew.

18. Reinach, *op. cit.*, vol. II, p. 176.

19. Reinach, *op. cit.*, vol. II, p. 176. There was in fact no need for the indiscretions committed by the judges and reported by Joseph Reinach. Du Paty and Picquart knew of the existence of the secret file, as did Fabre and d'Abboville, no doubt, as well. The entire Section of Statistics—which was discreet, to be sure, by trade—also knew of it.

20. Reinach, *op. cit.*, vol. II, p. 178.

21. Mathieu Dreyfus, *op. cit.*, p. 75.

4. *A Fabulous Gambler*

1. Maurice Baumont, *Aux Sources de l'Affaire Dreyfus* (Paris: Productions de Paris, 1959), p. 104.

2. Marcel Thomas, *L'Affaire sans Dreyfus*, p. 97.

3. Comte Maximilien von Schwarzkoppen, *Les Carnets de Schwarzkoppen* (Paris: Rieder, 1930), p. 20.

4. *Ibid,,* p. 26.

5. *Ibid.,* p. 127.

6. Marcel Thomas, *op. cit.,* p. 205.

7. *Ibid.,* p. 210.

8. *Ibid.,* p. 210.

9. Quoted by Marcel Thomas, *Ibid.,* p. 214.

10. *Ibid.,* p. 189.

11. *Ibid.,* pp. 194 ff.

12. *Ibid.,* p. 194.

13. *Ibid.,* p. 197.

14. *Ibid.,* p. 41.

15. *Ibid.,* pp. 54 ff.

16. *Ibid.,* p. 199.

5. *Dreyfus the Deportee*

1. Alfred Dreyfus, *Cinq années de ma vie* (Paris: Fasquelle, 1901), pp. 86 ff.

2. It was transmitted to us by Mme. Beck, the granddaughter of Mathieu Dreyfus and Joseph Reinach.

3. Joseph Reinach, *Histoire de L'Affaire Dreyfus* (Paris: Fasquelle, 1929), vol. II, p. 123.

4. *Ibid.,* p. 124.

5. *Ibid.,* p. 126. Remarks made to the Director of the Prison Administration by High Commandant of the Isles Bouchet.

6. Dreyfus, *Cinq années de ma vie,* pp. 87–88.

7. In May 1895, chief-guard Lebars would be sent from Paris to replace the head of surveillance, Pouly, who had accompanied Dreyfus from the Ile Royale. The latter was assisted by Agents Papaud, Leblanc, Arboiseau, and Battesti-Leblanc. Lebars was sent from Paris in order to intensify surveillance. Minister Chautemps received him before his departure: "If he tries to flee," the minister told him, "blow his brains out." Faithful to his mission, Lebars would be an implacable jailer.

8. *Ibid.,* pp. 93 ff.

9. Reinach, *op. cit.,* vol. II, p. 134.

10. Letter of May 8, 1895. Dreyfus, *Cinq années de ma vie.*

11. Letter of June 21, 1895. *Ibid.*

12. Letter of August 2, 1895. *Ibid.*

13. Letter of October 4, 1895. *Ibid.*

14. Journal, May 9, 1895. *Ibid.*, p. 113.

15. Journal, June 29, 1895. *Ibid.*, p. 121.

16. Journal, July 14, 1895. *Ibid.*, p. 124.

17. Letter to Lucie Dreyfus, January 4, 1897.

18. Letter to Lucie Dreyfus, April 24, 1897. Alfred Dreyfus, *Souvenirs et correspondances* (Paris: Grasset, 1936), p. 153.

19. Letter of October 16, 1895.

20. Letter to Lucie, March 20, 1895.

21. Journal, September 27, 1895. Dreyfus, *Cinq années de ma vie*, p. 132.

22. Journal, September 29, 1895. *Ibid.*, p. 133.

23. Journal, October 26, 1895. *Ibid.*, p. 136.

24. Reinach, *op. cit.*, vol. II, p. 139.

25. Journal, April 25, 1895. Dreyfus, *Cinq années de ma vie*, p. 105.

26. Journal, December 30, 1895. *Ibid.*, p. 146.

27. Reinach, *op. cit.*, vol. II, p. 180.

28. Letter to Lucie Dreyfus, October 5, 1895. Alfred Dreyfus, *Lettres d'un innocent* (Paris: Stock, 1898), p. 151.

29. Dreyfus, *Cinq années de ma vie*, pp. 160-161.

30. A. B. Marbaud, *Dreyfus à l'île du Diable* (unpublished, 1960), p. 28.

31. Journal, April 19, 1895. Dreyfus, *Cinq années de ma vie*, p. 99.

32. Marbaud, *op. cit.*, p. 29.

33. Journal, April 21, 1895. Dreyfus, *Cinq années de ma vie*, p. 102.

34. Journal, April 26, 1895. *Ibid.*, p. 106.

35. Journal, April 28-29, 1895. *Ibid.*, p. 107.

36. Marbaud, *op. cit.*, p. 46.

37. Journal, May 11-13, 1895.

38. Marbaud, *op. cit.*, p. 46.

39. *Ibid.*, p. 53.

40. Journal, December 7, 1895. Dreyfus, *Cinq années de ma vie*, p. 140.

41. Journal, December 30, 1895. On December 30 he received "a variety of commercial articles from Cayenne, foodstuffs from Potin, 29 letters and magazines."

42. Journal, January 27, 1896. On March 4, Jules Bravard replaced Bouchet as High Commandant of the Isles. Dreyfus had already been on Devil's Island for a year. . . . It appears that several modifications favorable to Dreyfus went into effect at that time.

43. Journal, September 6, 1895.

44. Marbaud, *op. cit.*, p. 73.

45. Journal, September 8, 1896. Dreyfus, *Cinq années de ma vie*, p. 157.

46. On the other hand, he improved Dreyfus's diet. But Bravard would be replaced in November, at Minister Lebon's orders, by Deniel, chosen in France for his brutality. During the same period, Lebars departed, replaced by the chief of surveillance Kerbrat.

47. Dreyfus, *Cinq années de ma vie*, p. 160.

48. *Ibid.*, p. 163.

6. *The First Jew to Rise on Behalf of the Jew*

1. Joseph Reinach, *Histoire de l'Affaire Dreyfus* (Paris: Fasquelle, 1929), vol. II, p. 188. In July 1895, Mathieu Dreyfus rented a house in Saint-Cloud under the name of his sister Valabrègue. He and his wife called themselves "M. and Mme. Mathieu" in order to avoid curiosity.

2. Léon Blum, *Souvenirs sur l'Affaire* (Paris: Fasquelle, 1929; Gallimard, 1982). Concerning Bernard Lazare, see Nelly Wilson, *Antisemitism and the Problem of Jewish Identity in Late 19th Century France* (Cambridge University Press, 1978).

3. *La Libre Parole*, January 10, 1895.

4. Bernard Lazare, *L'antisémitisme. Son histoire et ses causes* (Paris: Editions de la Différence, 1982), pp. 182ff.

5. "In the vast movement which brings every people to the harmony of the elements composing it, the Jews are refractory. They are still the stiff-necked nation against whom the lawmaker hurls his anathema; they are associated with abolished social forms whose autonomy has long since been destroyed. To a certain extent, they are a Nation that has survived its nationality. For centuries they have been resisting death.

"Why? Because everything has contributed to maintain their characteristics as a people: because they possessed a national religion which had a perfect logic when they formed a people, ceased being satisfactory after the dispersion, and kept them apart; because throughout Europe they have founded colonies jealous of their prerogatives, attached to their customs, rites, and mores; because they have lived for years under the domination of a theological code which has immobilized them; because the laws of the numerous countries in which they planted their tents, the prejudices and persecutions prevented them from mixing; because ever since the second exodus and their departure from the land of Palestine, they have erected—and there have been raised around them—uncrossable and rigid barriers. Such as they are, they have been slowly created and they have created themselves; their intellectual and moral being was forged; attempts were made to differentiate them and they have applied themselves to that task on their own." Lazare, *op. cit.*, p. 193.

6. *Ibid.*, pp. 198ff.

7. Michael Marrus, *Les Juifs en France à l'epoque de l'Affaire Dreyfus* (Paris: Calmann-Lévy, 1972), p. 207.

8. P.-V. Stock, *Mémorandum d'un éditeur: l'Affaire Dreyfus anecdotique* (Paris: Stock, 1938), p. 18.

9. Marrus, *op. cit.*, p. 210.

10. *Ibid.*, pp. 212ff.

11. *Ibid.*, p. 212. Concerning the deliberate discretion of Mathieu's efforts (since he still believed that discreet initiatives with the public authorities were the best path to follow), see Blum, *op. cit.*, pp. 528ff.

12. Marrus, *op. cit.*, p. 212.

13. Without any conclusive evidence, Hannah Arendt maintains that the Dreyfus family treated Bernard Lazare, "one of the noblest figures of the Affair, as

a paid agent in their employ." Hannah Arendt, *Sur l'antisémitisme* (Paris: Calmann-Levy, 1973, p. 231).

14. Reinach, *op. cit.,* vol. II, p. 196.

15. Quoted by Reinach, *ibid.,* p. 194.

16. Bernard Lazare, "Contre l'antisémitisme," *Le Voltaire,* May 20, 1896.

17. Marrus, *op. cit.,* p. 212.

18. *Ibid.,* p. 214.

19. Quoted by Marrus, *ibid.,* p. 214.

20. Blum, *op. cit.,* p. 518.

21. Quoted by Marrus, *op. cit.,* p. 219.

22. Similarly, the Alsatian Jew Louis Lucien Klotz denigrated Bernard Lazare and wrote that there was not a shred of anti-Semitism in the Dreyfus Affair: "A Bernard Lazare," *Le Voltaire,* November 10, 1896.

23. Bernard Lazare, open letter to M. Trarieux, *L'Aurore,* June 7, 1899.

24. Charles Péguy, *Notre Jeunesse* (Paris: Gallimard, 1933), pp. 103ff.

25. *Ibid.,* p. 79.

26. *Ibid.,* p. 82.

27. *Ibid.,* p. 94.

28. *Ibid.,* p. 163.

7. The "Petit Bleu"

1. Marcel Thomas, *L'Affaire sans Dreyfus* (Paris: Fayard, 1961), p. 203.

2. His family was from Lorraine. His great-grandfather was president of the Lorraine Parliament. It was his grandfather who settled in Lorraine.

3. All observers agree in acknowledging in Picquart an exalted sense of duty and exceptional firmness of character. F. de Pressensé celebrated his personality in a volume of 1899 entitled *Un héros.* Henri Guillemin offers a curiously severe portrait of him: a prudent man, an intriguer, "gifted with a police-like mentality." *L'Enigme Esterhazy* (Paris: Gallimard, 1962), p. 114. Mathieu Dreyfus, when he was estranged from Picquart, would describe him as vain and easily offended, endowed with invincible self-confidence. Stock, the publisher, who knew him quite well, saw him as intelligent, perspicacious, a cultivated man of letters. Picquart spoke German flawlessly, as well as English, Italian, and Spanish. In prison, he would learn Russian. P. V. Stock, *Mémorandum d'un éditeur: l'Affaire Dreyfus anecdotique* (Paris: Stock, 1938), p. 205.

4. Joseph Reinach, *Histoire de l'Affaire Dreyfus* (Paris: Fasquelle, 1929), vol. II, p. 209. Concerning Picquart's anti-Semitism, see Henri Guillemin, *op. cit.,* pp. 115ff.

5. Reinach, *op. cit.,* vol. II, pp. 216ff.

6. Du Paty and Schwarzkoppen met in the home of that officer.

7. Reinach, *op. cit.,* vol. II, p. 229.

8. Louis Leblois, *L'Affaire Dreyfus: L'Iniquité; La Réparation* (Paris: Librairie Aristide Quillet, 1929).

9. Thomas, *op. cit.,* p. 227.

10. Reinach, *op. cit.,* vol. II, p. 241.

11. Thomas, *op. cit.*, p. 229.

12. Reinach, *op. cit.*, vol. II, p. 245.

13. Thomas, *op. cit.*, p. 217.

14. *Ibid.*, p. 216.

15. Comte Maximilien von Schwarzkoppen, *Les Carnets de Schwarzkoppen* (Paris: Rieder, 1930), p. 139.

16. Maurice Paléologue, *Journal de l'Affaire Dreyfus* (Paris: Plon, 1955), p. 67.

17. Thomas, *op. cit.*, pp. 217ff.

18. *Ibid.*, p. 222.

19. *Ibid.*, p. 224.

20. Schwarzkoppen, *op. cit.*, p. 140.

21. In *D'Esterhazy à Dreyfus* (Paris: Plon, 1950, p. 222), Henry Giscard d'Estaing, basing his argument on Schwarzkoppen's *Notebooks,* has conceived of another thesis: the *petit bleu* would have been pilfered intact from the post office by Dreyfus's supporters. Simultaneously they organized the burglarizing of Schwarzkoppen's apartment. Making off with his personal correspondence, they were able to verify that the *petit bleu* had been written by his mistress, Mme. de Weede. After that, the Jewish syndicate would have fraudulently introduced the document, after tearing it up in a thousand pieces, into the "ordinary track." The clandestine initiatives of the "syndicate" would thus have accomplished the "rather handsome *tour de force* of removing the *petit bleu* from Schwarzkoppen's pocket and bringing it into Lauth's hands" (*ibid.*, p. 113). The Jewish syndicate is denounced as "the originator and beneficiary of the operation." This account, which is sustained by no evidence, is merely a renewed version of the theses advanced by the General Staff when the *petit bleu* was used to exculpate Dreyfus.

22. "Without delay, Henry warned Esterhazy," wrote Joseph Reinach, who lists his reasons in support of this argument, affirming "that there is no lack of evidence that Esterhazy was warned by Henry." Joseph Reinach notes in particular that Esterhazy abruptly ceased all dealings with Schwarzkoppen. That, however, was not quite the case (See *infra* p. 506). Was not the *petit bleu* sufficient reason? Thomas, *op. cit.*, p. 234.

8. *I Was Terrified*

1. Marcel Thomas, *L'affaire sans Dreyfus* (Paris: Fayard, 1961), pp. 237ff and Joseph Reinach, *Histoire de l'Affaire Dreyfus* (Paris: Fasquelle, 1929), vol. II, p. 248.

2. Reinach, *op. cit.*, p. 250.

3. French National Archives, BB19 88, d.1, p. 28.

4. Reinach, *op. cit.*, vol. II, p. 251.

5. *Ibid.*, p. 249.

6. Thomas, *op. cit.*, pp. 240ff. and Reinach, *op. cit.*, vol. II, pp. 265ff.

7. Louis Leblois, *L'Affaire Dreyfus: L'Iniquité; La Réparation* (Paris: Librairie Aristide Quillet, 1929), p. 26.

8. Reinach, *op. cit.*, vol. II, p. 286.

9. Thomas, *op. cit.*, p. 254.

10. *Ibid.,* p. 259.

11. Reinach, *op. cit.,* vol. II, p. 290.

9. *An Idealist?*

1. Joseph Reinach devoted a long chapter to the history of the Esterhazy family. He was of the opinion that such a history helped to explain the individual. The adventures of the Esterhazys were inexhaustible. It is known that in 1818, then in 1824, a Count Esterhazy invited Schubert (who was in a state of severe poverty) to give music lessons to his daughters. Schubert fell in love with the younger of the two, Caroline Esterhazy, age 17, and composed the "Unfinished Symphony" for her. Joseph Reinach, *Histoire de l'Affaire Dreyfus* (Paris: Fasquelle, 1929), vol. II, pp. 1ff.

2. *Ibid.,* p. 7.

3. Marcel Thomas, *L'affaire sans Dreyfus* (Paris: Fayard, 1961), p. 26.

4. Reinach, *op. cit.,* vol. II, p. 19.

5. Thomas, *op. cit.,* p. 32.

6. *Ibid.,* p. 32.

7. *Ibid.,* p. 33; Reinach, *op. cit.,* p. 36.

8. Thomas, *op. cit.,* pp. 36-37.

9. *Ibid.,* p. 57.

10. On July 7, according to Marcel Thomas, Esterhazy deposited 5,000 francs in his account at the Crédit Lyonnais. But he was drowning in debt at the time— including 2,500 francs owed in mortgage (*op. cit.,* p. 56).

11. Reinach, *op. cit.,* vol. II, pp. 25ff.

12. *Ibid.,* p. 40.

13. *Ibid.,* p. 24.

10. *The Serenity of France*

1. Léon Blum does not specify the date of the meeting: no doubt during the summer of 1896. *Souvenirs sur l'Affaire* (Paris: Gallimard, 1982), p. 519. In *Au signe de Flore* (Paris: Grasset, 1933), Charles Maurras wrote: "It was in mid-June 1897, five full months before the Dreyfus Affair broke out." According to François Goguel: "It was from 1897 to 1900 that the Dreyfus Affair exercised a profound influence on the development of politics and public opinion in France." *La Politique des partis sous la IIIe République* (Paris: Seuil, 1958), p. 69. From January 1895 to the end of 1896, there was virtually no more discussion in France of the Dreyfus Affair.

2. The Bourgeois government counted several "new faces," including Paul Doumer at Finance and Emile Combes at Public Education. Eight cabinet members were Freemasons. Jean-Marie Mayeur, *Les Débuts de la IIIe République* (Paris: Seuil, 1973), pp. 214ff.

3. The project, taken up again by Joseph Caillaux, would pass the Chamber only in 1907, the Senate in 1914.

4. The conflict posed a constitutional dilemma. In resigning, Bourgeois appeared to be acknowledging the Senate's power to overthrow the government.

The Senate would make use on several occasions of the power created by this precedent.

5. Méline's centrist majority attracted a number of remarkable orators who cultivated their careers while oscillating around the center: Louis Barthou, Paul Deschanel, Raymond Poincaré, René Waldeck-Rousseau.

6. "The Church is infiltrating all over the place," Léon Bourgeois would exclaim at Château-Thierry in 1897. Brisson outlined all the forms taken by the "clerical Hydra." Jean-Marie Mayeur, *op. cit.*, p. 298.

7. The rural population went from 67.5% in 1876 to 61% in 1896. It still constituted a majority political force. Concerning the political importance of the countryside in 1896, see Mayeur, *op. cit.*, p. 219.

8. Waldeck-Rousseau, who supported the Méline government, was of the opinion at the time that the social problem had been resolved in France, a country in which wealth stemmed "not from the accumulation of the major capitalists, but from the labor of the humble." Pierre Sorlin, *Waldeck-Rousseau* (Paris: Rivière, 1911), p. 375.

9. The term designated the various groups interested in the development of colonization. The *Union Coloniale,* which assembled businessmen and "practitioners of economic life in the colonies," was founded in 1895.

10. Mayeur, *op. cit.*, p. 228.

11. Jean Chastenet, *Histoire de la IIIᵉ République* (Paris: Hachette, 1955, vol. III), p. 102.

12. Funds loaned to Russia by French banks amounted to 5.7 billion by January 1, 1892. They reached a level of 10.6 billion on January 1, 1895. Cf. R. Girault, "Sur quelques aspects de l'alliance franco-russe," *Revue d'histoire moderne et contemporaine,* January 1961, and Mayeur, *op. cit.*, p. 229.

13. Concerning the dispersion and then the unification of French socialists and their hesitant rally to the Republic, see in particular Claude Willard, *Les Guesdistes* (Paris: Éditions sociales, 1981). Guesde's followers would later say that they had adhered to the Saint-Mandé "Credo" only because they believed that "its elasticity and vagueness might be useful in attracting to the socialists a part of the middle class elite" (*Le Socialiste,* July 30, 1899). Claude Willard casts lights on the "fluid and hesitant tactics" of the Guesdists in relation to the Dreyfus Affair and the temptations of republican concentration.

11. *Keep the Two Affairs Separate*

1. Marcel Thomas, *L'Affaire sans Dreyfus* (Paris: Fayard, 1961), pp. 260ff.

2. Joseph Reinach, *Histoire de l'Affaire Dreyfus* (Paris: Fasquelle, 1929,) vol. II, p. 296.

3. See Henri Dutrait-Crozon, *Précis de l'Affaire Dreyfus* (Paris: Librarie d'Action française, 1924), p. 67; Thomas, *op. cit.*, p. 265.

4. *Ibid.*, p. 267.

5. Reinach, *op. cit.*, vol. II, p. 298; Thomas, *op. cit.*, pp. 271ff.

6. *Ibid.*, p. 279.

7. Reinach, *op. cit.*, vol. II, p. 230.

8. Hannah Arendt, *Sur l'antisémitisme* (Paris: Calmann-Lévy, 1973), p. 230.

9. Mathieu Dreyfus, *L'Affaire telle que je l'ai vécue* (Paris: Grasset, 1978), p. 80.

10. André Lebon would later maintain that he had long hesitated to order Dreyfus to be shackled on the basis of an inaccurate news story, but his cablegram was dated September 4, 12:30 P.M. Lebon, age 37, a minister for the second time, was, it seems, devoured by ambition. A professor at the École des Sciences Politiques, he published annually a volume devoted to the "Political Year" under the pseudonym André Daniel.

11. Reinach, *op. cit.*, vol. II, p. 331.

12. Thomas, *op. cit.*, p. 309.

13. Reinach, *op. cit.*, vol. II, p. 356.

14. *Ibid.*, p. 335.

15. At the High Court of Appeal, he would claim to have "hesitated" about Dreyfus's guilt and spent "several sleepless nights." *Ibid.*, p. 336.

16. Dutrait-Crozon, *op. cit.*, p. 72.

17. Reinach, *op. cit.*, vol. II, p. 359; Thomas, *op. cit.*, p. 313; Dutrait-Crozon, *op. cit.*, p. 73.

18. Thomas, *op. cit.*, p. 315.

19. *Ibid.*, p. 315.

20. Mathieu Dreyfus, *op. cit.*, p. 83.

12. *The Patriotic Forgery*

1. Joseph Reinach, *Histoire de l'Affaire Dreyfus* (Paris: Fasquelle, 1929), vol. II, p. 379.

2. Marcel Thomas, *L'Affaire sans Dreyfus* (Paris: Fayard, 1961) p. 318.

3. *Ibid.*, p. 316.

4. Reinach, *op. cit.*, vol. II, 399.

5. *Ibid.*, p. 399, note 7.

6. Comte Maximilien von Schwarzkoppen, *Les Carnets de Schwarzkoppen* (Paris: Rieder, 1930), p. 149.

7. Thomas, *op. cit.*, p. 329.

8. *Ibid.*, p. 329.

9. Upon confessing his forgery to Godefroy Cavaignac, the minister of war, he would say in his distress: "I saw that my superiors were quite worried; I wanted to relieve them; I wanted to restore calm to the situation.... I told myself: 'Let's add on the sentence that will bring tranquillity to everyone.' What if war were declared in the state in which we now find ourselves! ... Whereas, in doing this, peace will return...." (Thomas, *op. cit.*, p. 331). It was Charles Maurras who would call the forgery, executed to serve the nation and confound a traitor, a "patriotic forgery."

10. In the inventories of the secret file drawn up as of 1897, the letter would be described as dated by Henry June 14, 1894—no doubt a fictitious date. Otherwise the document, however ambiguous, would have been used against Dreyfus. "The plainly false date was undoubtedly affixed to the letter the day on which Henry fabricated his forgery" (Thomas, *op. cit.*, p. 334).

11. According to Joseph Reinach, Henry entrusted the material execution of the forgery to secret agent Lemercier-Picard, a mysterious individual who was a former butcher in Thionville, frequently convicted, and a past master in the art of forgery (*op. cit.*, vol. II, pp. 412ff and p. 518). Marcel Thomas regards that thesis as a "legend" (*op. cit.*, p. 337). The mediocrity of the "Henry forgery" makes it quite improbable that any expert forger was implicated in its confection.

12. According to Reinach, *op. cit.*, vol. II, p. 412.

13. Thomas, *op. cit.*, p. 339.

14. *Ibid.*, pp. 340ff.

15. Only *Le Temps* and *Les Débats* gave an analysis of the text. The other newspapers either ignored it or vented abuse at the maneuvers of the Jewish syndicate (Reinach, *op. cit.*, vol. II, p. 498).

16. That same day, Gribelin and Henry, in a great rush, rediscovered a copy of the bordereau at the Section of Statistics (Thomas, *op. cit.*, p. 355).

17. *Ibid.*, p. 359.

18. Henri Dutrait-Crozon, *Précis de l'Affaire Dreyfus* (Paris: Librairie d'Action française, 1924), pp. 79–80.

19. Mathieu Dreyfus, *L'Affaire telle que je l'ai vécue* (Paris: Grasset, 1978), pp. 87ff.

20. Schwarzkoppen, *op. cit.*, p. 162.

21. *Ibid.*, p. 162.

22. The day after the publication of the article in *L'Eclair* (September 20), Schwarzkoppen had written to his superiors in these terms:
"We can only derive profit from renewed discussion of the Dreyfus Affair, provided that it results in a true clarification of the mysterious affair in accordance with the truth—a circumstance that can only be to our advantage. In the almost two years that have elapsed since the event, I have not been able to obtain any clarification relating to it. The only thing I can imagine is either that a falsified document entered into the case or that Dreyfus actually did attempt to enter into relations with us and a document pertinent to that attempt was discovered before reaching its destination. Whatever the case, the affair is quite enigmatic and the deportee's guilt is at present the subject of increasing doubt."

23. Maurice Baumont, *Aux sources de l'Affaire Dreyfus* (Paris: Productions de Paris, 1959), p. 150.

24. *Ibid.*, p. 144.

25. *Ibid.*, p. 145.

26. Reinach, *op. cit.*, vol. II, p. 450.

27. *Ibid.*, p. 452.

28. Mathieu Dreyfus, *op. cit.*, p. 84.

13. *Speranza*

1. Marcel Thomas, *L'Affaire sans Dreyfus* (Paris: Fayard, 1961), p. 371.

2. Letter from General Gonse, quoted by Thomas, *op. cit.*, p. 373.

3. Thomas's translation, *op. cit.*, p. 376.

4. *Ibid.*, p. 378.

5. *Ibid.*, p. 380.

14. *From Colonel to Lawyer, Lawyer to Senator*

1. Joseph Reinach, *Histoire de l'Affaire Dreyfus* (Paris: Fasquelle, 1929), vol. II, p. 473.

2. Marcel Thomas, *L'Affaire sans Dreyfus* (Paris: Fayard, 1961), p. 387.

3. *Ibid.*, p. 387.

4. Reinach, *op. cit.*, vol. II, p. 254.

5. Thomas, *op. cit.*, p. 391.

6. Reinach, *op. cit.*, vol. II, p. 519.

7. Reinach is often harsh, too harsh, regarding Leblois. *Ibid.*, p. 523.

8. Thomas, *op. cit.*, pp. 396–397. Reinach, *op. cit.*, vol. II, p. 526.

9. Reinach, *op. cit.*, vol. II, p. 528.

10. *Ibid.*, p. 529.

11. Thomas, *op. cit.*, p. 398.

12. Reinach, *op. cit.*, vol. II, p. 530.

13. *Ibid.*, p. 530.

15. *I Have a Closetful*

1. Quoted by Marcel Thomas, *L'Affaire sans Dreyfus* (Paris: Fayard, 1961), pp. 415–416.

2. *Ibid.*, p. 417.

3. *Ibid.*, p. 417.

4. Henri Guillemin, *L'Énigme Esterhazy* (Paris: Gallimard, 1962), pp. 126ff.

5. Thomas, *op. cit.*, pp. 290ff.

6. Joseph Reinach, *Histoire de l'Affaire Dreyfus* (Paris: Fasquelle, 1929), vol. II, p. 568.

7. Thomas, *op. cit.*, p. 424.

8. *Ibid.*, p. 425.

9. Reinach, *op. cit.*, vol. II, pp. 469ff.

10. *Ibid.*, p. 590.

11. Thomas, *op. cit.*, p. 430.

12. *Ibid.*, p. 430.

13. Reinach, *op. cit.*, vol. II, p. 292 and Schwarzkoppen, *op. cit.*, pp. 173ff.

14. Reinach, *op. cit.*, vol. II, p. 594.

15. Thomas, *op. cit.*, p. 431.

16. Thomas, *op. cit.*, p. 173.

17. See Reinach, *op. cit.*, vol. II, p. 596.

18. Schwarzkoppen, *op. cit.*, p. 176.

19. Du Paty or Henry according to Thomas, *op. cit.*, p. 435.

20. Thomas, *op. cit.*, p. 436.

21. Reinach, *op. cit.*, vol. II, p. 577.

22. Maurice Paléologue, *Journal de l'Affaire Dreyfus* (Paris: Plon, 1955), p. 58.

23. *Ibid.*, p. 60.

16. *My Dear Friend, Just Listen to Me*

1. The first appears to have been performed by Gabriel Monod, a member of the Institut de France, who would play an important role in the battle for revision. Mathieu Dreyfus, *L'Affaire telle que je l'ai vécue* (Paris: Grasset, 1978), pp. 88ff.

2. Léon Blum, *Souvenirs sur l'Affaire* (Paris: Fasquelle, 1929; Gallimard, 1981), pp. 83ff.

3. *Ibid.*, p. 81.

4. *Ibid.*, p. 83ff.

5. *Ibid.*, p. 81.

6. Robert J. Smith, "L'Atmosphère politique à l'École normale supérieure à la fin du XIXe siecle," *Revue d'Histoire moderne et contemporaine*, 1973, pp. 258ff.

7. Blum, *op. cit.*, p. 80.

8. Léon Blum wrote that Jean Jaurès was a Dreyfusard "of the oldest contingent" and that he would have been so "as naturally as he breathed," even if the authority of Lucien Herr had not come into play. In point of fact, Jaurès had to overcome his prejudices as well as those of his friends, who long attempted to restrain him. He came slowly to Dreyfus's cause. Allemane, who was convinced before Jaurès, played an important role in Jaurès's total commitment, which would not have been realized, according to Madeline Rebérioux, before July 1898. *Ibid.*, pp. 77ff.

9. *Ibid.*, p. 77.

10. For others, Léon Blum maintained, such as Jaurès and Clemenceau, there was nothing to be expected from the reactionary government: "Dreyfus's fate would depend on who struck the first blows." "Instead of dealing with the two sharpsters Méline and Billot, we should have marched forward without warning. . . . We should have shouted out the whole story, disrupted everything." Such a defense was imaginable long after the event, but in 1897, what means were at hand to tell "the whole story?"

11. French National Archives BB 18 88, d3.

12. Joseph Reinach, *Histoire de l'Affaire Dreyfus* (Paris: Fasquelle, 1929), vol. II, p. 624.

13. *Ibid.*, vol. II, p. 625.

14. Marcel Thomas, *L'Affaire sans Dreyfus* (Paris: Fayard, 1961), p. 443.

15. Joseph Reinach "follows step by step" the account of this meeting given by Scheurer-Kestner in his *Memoirs* and on numerous occasions in testimony. The conversation lasted four hours. Reinach, *op. cit.*, vol. II, p. 629.

16. *Ibid.*, p. 630.

17. In *L'Intransigeant* of November 3, Juliette Adam revealed Scheurer-Kestner's "German relations." Camille Pelletan scolded him in *La Dépêche* of October 31. *Ibid.*, p. 631.

18. Thomas, *op. cit.*, p. 447.

19. *Ibid.*, p. 449.

17. *Help Me, My Prince, to My Rescue!*

1. Marcel Thomas, *L'Affaire sans Dreyfus* (Paris: Fayard, 1961), p. 451.

2. *Ibid.*, p. 451.

3. Joseph Reinach, *Histoire de l'Affaire Dreyfus* (Paris: Fasquelle, 1929), vol. II, p. 462.

4. Thomas, *op. cit.*, p. 455.

5. French National Archives BB 19 88, d3, p. 23.

6. Thomas, *op. cit.*, p. 459.

7. *Ibid.*, p. 465.

8. Mathieu Dreyfus, *L'Affaire telle que je l'ai vécue* (Paris: Grasset, 1978), p. 99.

9. Thomas, *op. cit.*, p. 469.

10. *Ibid.*, p. 469.

11. *Ibid.*, pp. 470ff.

12. *Ibid.*, p. 471.

13. *Ibid.*, p. 475.

14. Reinach, *op. cit.*, vol. III, pp. 10ff.

18. *I Speak to You as from the Grave*

1. Joseph Reinach, *Histoire de l'Affaire Dreyfus* (Paris: Fasquelle, 1929), p. 321.

2. Alfred Dreyfus, *Souvenirs et correspondances*, (Paris: Grasset, 1936), p. 143; letter dated September 1896.

3. In November, prison guard Lebars was replaced by Chief of Surveillance Kerbrat, and Bravard, High Commandant of the Islands, was replaced by Deniel, come from France "to take charge" of the deportee. Deniel "was quick to flaunt the trust that the minister had shown him in appointing him High Commandant." His first effort consisted of a total revision of scheduled rounds of surveillance, which were now complicated with day-time and night-time rounds throughout the island. (A. B. Marbaud, *Dreyfus à l'île du Diable*, unpublished, p. 89.)

4. After the revision, Commandant Dreyfus would attempt to retrieve from the Ministry of Colonies the originals of the letters which had been received only in copy as well as a number of letters which had not been received at all. Alfred Dreyfus, *Cinq années de ma vie* (Paris: Fasquelle, 1901), p. 176.

5. Dreyfus, *Souvenirs et correspondances*, p. 146.

6. Dreyfus, *Cinq années de ma vie*, p. 191.

7. September 4, 1897. Alfred Dreyfus, *Lettres d'un innocent* (Paris: Stock, 1898), p. 235.

8. Marbaud, *op. cit.*, p. 92.

9. Letter from Lucie Dreyfus dated December 4, 1897, received in February 1898. Dreyfus, *Cinq années de ma vie*, p. 200.

10. *Ibid.*, p. 202.

11. Dreyfus, *Souvenirs et correspondances*, p. 163.

12. *Ibid.*, p. 164.

13. January 26, 1898, *ibid.*, p. 165.

14. Letter to Lucie Dreyfus of August 10, 1897. Dreyfus, *Lettres d'un innocent,* p. 282.

19. *Let Us Not Allow Ourselves to be Devoured*

1. Mathieu Dreyfus, *L'Affaire telle que je l'ai vécue* (Paris: Grasset, 1978), p. 101.

2. French National Archives, BB 19, 123 d, p. 67.

3. Marcel Thomas, *L'Affaire sans Dreyfus* (Paris: Fayard, 1961), pp. 481ff.

4. *Ibid.*, p. 482.

5. *Ibid.*, p. 483.

6. Joseph Reinach, *Histoire de l'Affaire Dreyfus* (Paris: Fasquelle, 1929), vol. III, p. 90.

7. *Ibid.*, vol. III, p. 91.

8. French National Archives, BB 19, 123 d, p. 91.

9. Dreyfus, *op. cit.*, p. 102.

10. Thomas, *op. cit.*, p. 487.

11. Reinach, *op. cit.*, vol. III, p. 105.

12. French National Archives, BB 29 94, d1, p. 1. Reinach, *op. cit.*, vol. III, pp. 108ff.

13. *Ibid.*, vol. III, p. 107.

14. Joseph Reinach described in particular the traps allegedly set by Lemercier-Picard, an agent frequently used by Henry and a skillful forger (*ibid.*, vol. III, p. 108).

15. *Ibid.*, vol. III, p. 114.

16. *L'Echo de Paris,* December 1, 1897.

17. *L'Intransigeant,* November 30, 1897.

18. *Ibid.*

19. *La Libre Parole,* December 1, 1897.

20. Reinach, *op. cit.*, vol. III, p. 119.

21. *Le Jour,* November 29, 1897.

22. January 15, 1898.

23. Reinach, *op. cit.*, vol. III, p. 121.

24. *Ibid.*, vol. III, p. 121.

25. *Ibid.*, vol. III, pp. 126ff.

26. Thomas, *op. cit.*, p. 491.

27. *Ibid.*, p. 492.

28. Reinach, *op. cit.*, vol. III, p. 127.

29. Thomas, *op. cit.*, p. 494.

30. *Ibid.*, p. 393.

31. Quoted by Joseph Reinach, *op. cit.*, vol. III, p. 133.

32. *Ibid.*, vol. III, p. 133.

33. Maurice Paléologue, *Journal de l'Affaire Dreyfus* (Paris: Plon, 1955), p. 23.

34. Reinach, *op. cit.*, vol. III, p. 141.

35. *Ibid.*, vol. III, p. 143.

36. from 881-882.

37. Quoted by Maurice Baumont, *Aux sources de l'Affaire* (Paris: Productions de Paris, 1959), p. 162.

20. *They Would Not Have Done as Much for a Poor Man*

1. Joseph Reinach, *Histoire de l'Affaire Dreyfus* (Paris: Fasquelle, 1929), vol. III, p. 170.

2. *Ibid.*, vol. III, p. 171.

3. *Ibid.*, vol. III, p. 185.

4. French National Archives, BB 19-124 d1, p. 30.

5. Testimony of December 30, 1897.

6. French National Archives, BB 19 79.

7. Marcel Thomas, *L'Affaire sans Dreyfus* (Paris: Fayard, 1961), p. 499.

8. Maurice Baumont, *Aux sources de l'Affaire* (Paris: Productions de Paris, 1959), p. 169.

9. *Ibid.*, p. 176.

10. Comte Maximilien de Schwarzkoppen, *Les Carnets de Schwarzkoppen* (Paris: Rieder, 1930), pp. 187ff.

11. *Ibid.*, p. 190.

12. Thomas, *op. cit.*, p. 500.

13. Léon Blum, *Souvenirs sur l'Affaire* (Paris: Fasquelle, 1929; Gallimard, 1981), pp. 100ff.

14. *Ibid.*, pp. 108ff.

15. Quoted by Léon Blum, *op. cit.*, p. 556.

16. *Ibid.*, p. 556.

17. However different they were in temperament and social milieu, they would become friends and the two families would unite. Mathieu's daughter, Marguerite, would marry Adolphe Reinach, Joseph's only son. Adolphe Reinach, a young archeologist, would fall in battle during the 1914 war. He would leave behind an already considerable record of scientific accomplishment. His three children— Suzie, France, and Jean-Pierre—would then be raised by their grandfather Mathieu. Jean-Pierre Reinach, who joined the Free French forces, would be parachuted into France and killed in the course of his mission.

18. Specifically by Lemercier-Picard, who would be discovered a few months later hanging from a window hasp.

19. Mathieu Dreyfus, *L'Affaire telle que je l'ai vécue* (Paris: Grasset, 1978), p. 116.

21. *Long Live Esterhazy*

1. Joseph Reinach, *Histoire de l'Affaire Dreyfus* (Paris: Fasquelle, 1929), vol. III, p. 195.

2. Concerning Fernard Labori, see the volume prepared by his wife, Marguerite Fernand-Labori, from notes and manuscripts left at the time of his death. *Labori. Ses Notes. Sa vie* (Paris: Victor Attinger, 1947).

3. *La Grande Revue*, 1901.

4. Maurice Allehault, "Eloge de Fernand Labori," address delivered at the opening of the Lawyers' Conference of December 3, 1927.

5. Mathieu Dreyfus, *L'Affaire telle que je l'ai vécue* (Paris: Grasset, 1978), p. 123.

6. *Ibid.*, p. 123.

7. See the article by Dr. Jean-Louis Lévy in *Le Monde* of October 15, 1981.

8. Dreyfus, *op. cit.*, p. 125.

9. *Ibid.*, p. 125.

10. *Ibid.*, p. 127.

11. Reinach, *op. cit.*, vol. III, pp. 205ff.

12. *Ibid.*, vol. III, p. 215.

13. French National Archives, BB 19 79.

14. Reinach, *op. cit.*, vol. III, p. 213.

15. *Ibid.*, vol. III, p. 214.

16. *Ibid.*, vol. III, p. 214.

III. TWO FRANCES

1. *J'Accuse*

1. Léon Blum, *Souvenirs sur l'Affaire* (Paris: Gallimard, 1982), p. 114.

2. *Ibid.*, p. 115.

3. *Ibid.*, p. 116.

4. *Ibid.*, p. 117.

5. See Emile Zola, *L'Affaire Dreyfus: la vérité en marche,* preface by Colette Becker (Paris: Garnier-Flammarion, 1969), pp. 34ff.

6. *Ibid.*, p. 89.

7. Jacques Kayser, *L'Affaire Dreyfus* (Paris: Gallimard, 1946), p. 128.

8. *Ibid.*, p. 128.

9. Zola, *op. cit.*, pp. 112ff.

10. Joseph Reinach, *Histoire de l'Affaire Dreyfus* (Paris: Fasquelle, 1929), vol. III, p. 226.

11. *Ibid.*, vol. III, pp. 226ff.

12. Marcel Thomas, *L'Affaire sans Dreyfus* (Paris: Fayard, 1961), p. 501.

13. Blum, *op. cit.*, p. 118.

14. Reinach, *op. cit.*, vol. III, p. 227.

15. Blum, *op. cit.*, vol. III, p. 119.

16. Maurice Barrès, *Scènes et Doctrines du nationalisme,* "Les intellectuels ou logiciens de l'absolu" (Paris: Felix Guven, 1902), pp. 40ff.

17. Kayser, *op. cit.*, p. 130.

18. Blum, *op. cit.*, p. 120.

19. Quoted by Thomas, *op. cit.*, p. 120.

20. Reinach, *op. cit.*, vol. III, p. 231.

21. *Ibid.*, vol. III, p. 235.

22. *Ibid.*, vol. III, p. 236.

23. *Ibid.*, vol. III, p. 238.

24. Lucie Dreyfus would send Cavaignac a public letter of protest on January 14. Cavaignac would reply on January 15 that the written testimony was in the hands of the minister of war. Lucie Dreyfus would renew her protest, recalling to Cavaignac on January 16 that Forzinetti and others had it from Lebrun-Renault—for it was undoubtedly he to whom Cavaignac was alluding—that Dreyfus had not confessed anything to him.

25. Cavaignac's motion to place the blame with the government received 183 votes against 299. The vote of confidence in the government was decided 312 to 122.

26. Reinach, *op. cit.*, vol. III, p. 296.

27. In December 1897. Quoted by Thomas, *op. cit.*, p. 502.

28. Reinach, *op. cit.*, vol. III, p. 309.

29. *Ibid.*, vol. III, p. 309.

30. Maurice Paléologue, *Journal de l'Affaire Dreyfus* (Paris: Plon, 1955), pp. 90ff.

31. *Ibid.*

32. Letter of December 25, 1897. Alfred Dreyfus, *Lettres d'un innocent* (Paris: Stock, 1898), p. 252.

33. Letter of January 26, 1898. Alfred Dreyfus, *Souvenirs et correspondances* (Paris: Grasset, 1936), p. 165.

34. Letter of January 25, 1898. *Ibid.*, p. 164. During the month of January, Alfred's letters to Lucie frequently repeated the same sentences.

2. *The Question Will Not Be Raised*

1. Concerning the Zola trial, see in addition to the trial transcript published by the League of the Rights of Man, the excerpts from the transcript selected with commentaries by Marcel Thomas (*Le Procès Zola*, Geneva: Idégraf, 1980).

2. In a criticism of Joseph Reinach's *Histoire de l'Affaire Dreyfus*, Labori maintained that if Barboux and du Buit were approached, it was without Zola's authorization. Marguerite Fernand-Labori, *Labori. Ses Notes. Sa vie* (Paris: Attinger, 1947), p. 354.

3. Jean France wrote that Fasquelle, the publisher of *La Revue du Palais*, edited by Labori, introduced Labori to Zola, who was looking for a lawyer. But Labori had been Lucie Dreyfus's lawyer in the Esterhazy trial, and in a few weeks, he had become a familiar figure in Dreyfusard circles. Jean France, *Autour de l'Affaire Dreyfus* (Paris: Reider, 1936), p. 89.

4. In his memoirs, Labori deplored the fact that Mathieu Dreyfus had taken on Joseph Reinach as his confidant: "He went off to Avenue Van-Dyck (where Reinach lived) virtually every morning."

5. Léon Blum, *Souvenirs sur l'Affaire* (Paris: Gallimard, 1982), p. 123.

6. The defense was subsequently to give up its attempt to hear them.

7. Joseph Reinach, *Histoire de l'Affaire Dreyfus* (Paris: Fasquelle, 1929), vol. III, p. 340.

8. *Ibid.*, vol. III, p. 342.

9. *Ibid.*, vol. III, p. 343.

10. Labori, in his notes, protested vehemently against this judgment by Reinach: "It would have been a pleasure to behold, such a petition! First of all, what fate would it have had? . . . Should we have exhausted public opinion with a wait that ran the risk of dissipating all interest? This Reinach, who is no fool, is a wretch." *Ibid.*, vol. III, pp. 343 and 359.

11. Mathieu Dreyfus, *L'Affaire telle que je l'ai vécue* (Paris: Grasset, 1978), p. 140.

12. Blum, *op. cit.*, p. 123.

13. Marguerite Fernand-Labori, *op. cit.*, p. 360.

14. Reinach, *op. cit.*, vol. III, p. 352.

15. Maurice Paléologue, *Journal de l'Affaire Dreyfus* (Paris: Plon, 1955), p. 110.

16. Paléologue, who attended the trial, described witness du Paty as follows: "a disquieting individual, a morbid mind, a shady and perverse mind, a bizarre blend of fanaticism, extravagance, and foolishness." *Ibid.*, p. 111.

17. Reinach, *op. cit.*, vol. III, p. 368.

18. Jacques Kayser, *L'Affaire Dreyfus* (Paris: Gallimard, 1946), p. 152.

19. Paléologue described all the experts as though they were puppets "hurling their extraordinary doctrines at each others' heads, denigrating each other and insulting each other like the physicians in Molière." He saw Bertillon as "prone to hallucinations, a madman." Paléologue, *op. cit.*, p. 112.

20. P.-V. Stock, *Mémorandum d'un editeur* (Paris: Stock, 1938), p. 66.

21. Paléologue, *op. cit.*, p. 112.

22. Quoted by Reinach, *op cit.*, vol. III, p. 378.

23. *Ibid.*, vol. III, p. 379.

24. *Ibid.*, vol. III, p. 417.

25. Paléologue, *op. cit.*, p. 112.

26. Mathieu Dreyfus, *op. cit.*, p. 141.

27. Marcel Thomas, *L'Affaire sans Dreyfus* (Paris: Fayard, 1961), p. 504.

28. *Ibid.*, p. 504.

29. *Ibid.*, p. 506.

30. Kayser, *op. cit.*, pp. 155ff.

31. Paléologue, *op. cit.*, pp. 114ff.

32. Reinach, *op. cit.*, vol. III, p. 454.

33. *Ibid.*, vol. III, p. 470.

34. Fernand-Labori, *op. cit.*, p. 36.

35. Reinach, *op. cit.*, vol. III, p. 481.

36. Quoted by Kayser, *op. cit.*, p. 153.

37. Mathieu Dreyfus, *op. cit.*, p. 144.

38. Blum, *op. cit.*, p. 144.

39. *Ibid.*, p. 125ff.

40. Maurice Baumont, *Aux sources de l'Affaire* (Paris: Productions de Paris, 1959), pp. 194ff.

41. *Ibid.*, pp. 194ff.

42. *Ibid.*, p. 198.

43. *Ibid.*, p. 200.

44. Mathieu Dreyfus, *op. cit.*, pp. 144.

45. Letter of December 22, 1898. Comte Maximilien von Schwarzkoppen, *Les Carnets de Schwarzkoppen* (Paris: Rieder, 1930), p. 234.

3. *Logicians of the Absolute*

1. Concerning student demonstrations at the time of the Zola trial, cf. Eric Cahn, "Les étudiants de Paris en janvier 1898," *Bulletin de la Société d'études jaurésiennes,* October–December 1878.

2. Concerning the involvement of writers in the Dreyfus Affair, particularly after the Zola trial, consult the contributions to the colloquium, "Writers and the Dreyfus Affair," held in Orléans on October 29 and 31, 1981, by the Centre Charles-Péguy.

3. Maurice Barrès, *Scènes et Doctrines du nationalisme* (Paris: Félix Guven, 1902), pp. 40ff.

4. In his communication to the colloquium at Orléans in October 1981 devoted to "Writers and the Dreyfus Affair," Jacques Suffel has studied the reasons behind Anatole France's involvement in the Affair. Suffel demonstrates the imprecision of the theses of those—like Maurras and Tharaud—who subsequently attempted to "co-opt" France for the anti-Dreyfusard cause and maintained that France had only committed himself half-heartedly or that he had been submitting to the influence of his friend Mme. de Caillavet, a converted Jewess. Suffel notes that it was France, on the contrary, who was behind her involvement—a circumstance that brought with it the inconvenience of abruptly "depopulating" her salon. Contribution to the Orléans colloquium, *Les écrivains et l'Affaire Dreyfus.*

5. Maurice Barrès, *op. cit.*, p. 50.

6. Christophe Charle, "Champ littéraire et champ du pouvoir: Les écrivains et l'Affaire Dreyfus," *Annales ESC,* March–April 1977.

7. *Ibid.*, p. 249ff.

8. *Ibid.*, p. 253.

9. Madeleine Rebérioux pays stricter attention than does Christophe Charle to the specificity of "disciplines" in her article, "Histoire, historiens, dreyfusisme" (*Revue historique,* 1976). Cf. also by Madeleine Rebérioux, "Zola, Jaurès, et France, trois intellectuels devant l'Affaire" (*Cahiers naturalistes,* 1980, no. 54).

10. *Revue bleue,* July 2, 1898.

11. See Christophe Charle, *op. cit.*

12. Robert Gauthier, *Dreyfusards!* (Paris: Julliard, 1965), pp. 137–138.

13. Preface to the re-edition of Jaurès's *Les Preuves* (Paris: Éditions le Signe, 1981).

14. The weekly *La Croix du Dimanche, Le Pèlerin,* and all the publications of La Bonne Presse represented a figure of nearly 130 million pages a year, according to the Catholic historian abbé Caperan. Louis Caperan, *L'anticléricalisme et l'Affaire Dreyfus* (Toulouse: Imprimerie régionale, 1948).

15. Robert Smith, "L'atmosphère politique à l'École normale supérieure à la

fin du XIXe siècle" in *Revue d'histoire moderne et contemporaine,* 1973, pp. 248–268.

16. Péguy would write those lines at the time of his break with Herr. *Notre jeunesse* (Paris: Gallimard, 1913), p. 95.

17. Toward the close of 1898, Romain Rolland would break with Herr: "You are well aware of it, I am not hiding my anti-Semitic feelings from anyone. I would be willing to put those feelings aside and think only of justice, if justice did not occupy a very secondary place in the preoccupations of those defending Dreyfus" (Letter of December 13, 1898). Romain Rolland at the time was in the process of breaking with his first wife, who belonged to a family of Jewish intellectuals. Robert Smith, *op. cit.*

19. A. B. Jackson, *Les Origines de la Revue Blanche, 1889–1891* (Paris: Lettres modernes, 1960).

20. Auguste Anglès, *André Gide et le premier groupe de la Nouvelle Revue Française* (Paris: Gallimard, 1978), pp. 28 ff.

21. Léon Blum, *Souvenirs sur l'Affaire* (Paris: Gallimard, 1982), pp. 93 ff.

22. Charles Péguy, *op. cit.,* pp. 64 ff.

23. It was after the Rennes trial that Blum situated that political commitment on his part. But it was already to be seen in many Dreyfusards during the year 1898. Blum, *op. cit.,* pp. 147 ff.

24. Christophe Charle, "L'Affaire Dreyfus et la lutte des classes en littérature," contribution to the aforementioned colloquium on *Les écrivains et l'Affaire Dreyfus.*

25. Blum, *op. cit.*, p. 97.

26. Charle, *op. cit.*, pp. 242 ff.

4. *The Fury of France*

1. Joseph Reinach, *Histoire de l'Affaire Dreyfus* (Paris: Fasquelle, 1929), vol. III, pp. 274 ff.

2. Pierre Pierrard, *Juifs et catholiques français* (Paris: Fayard, 1970), pp. 144 ff.

3. *Ibid.,* pp. 144 ff.

4. Reinach, *op. cit.,* vol. III, p. 279.

5. Zeev Sternhell, *La droite révolutionnaire 1885–1914, les origines françaises du fascisme* (Paris: Seuil, 1978), pp. 230 ff.

6. Preface to *Cinq années de ma vie* (Paris: Fasquelle, 1962), p. 13.

7. *Les Fleurs de l'histoire* by Théodore Valentin.

8. Pierre Sorlin, *La Croix et les Juifs* (Paris: Grasset, 1967), pp. 118 ff.

9. *Ibid.,* p. 28.

10. *Ibid.,* p. 216.

11. *Ibid.,* p. 216.

12. *Ibid.,* pp. 60–61.

13. *Ibid.,* p. 223.

14. *Ibid.,* p. 229.

15. See in particular Danièle Delmaire's study, "L'antisémitisme du journal *La Croix du Nord* pendant l'Affaire Dreyfus, 1898–1899," *De l'antijudaïsme antique à l'antisémitisme contemporain* (Lille: Presses Universitaires de Lille, 1979).

16. See Janine Ponty, "La presse quotidienne et l'Affaire Dreyfus en 1898–

1899, essai de typologie," *Revue d'histoire moderne et contemporaine*, XXI, 1974, pp. 193–220.

17. Pierrard, *op. cit.*, pp. 166ff.

18. And beyond that, on the ideology of Vichy France. On the continuity of anti-Semitic ideologies, see Zeev Sternhell, *Ni droite ni gauche: l'idéologie fasciste en France* (Paris: Seuil, 1983).

19. Pierrard, *op. cit.*, p. 121.

20. *Ibid.*, p. 126.

21. *Ibid.*, p. 129.

22. *Ibid.* Pierre Pierrard and Jean-Marie Mayeur have drawn up the balance sheet of those initiatives—as important as they were courageous—which attempted to oppose the Catholic anti-Dreyfusard trend.

23. *Ibid.*, p. 187.

24. *Ibid.*, p. 191.

25. *Ibid.*, p. 197.

26. See Anatole Leroy-Beaulieu, *Israël chez les nations* republished by Calmann-Lévy (Paris: 1983).

27. According to Pierrard, separate treatment should be accorded Léon Bloy whose confused and hyperbolic book *Le Salut par les Juifs* is an amalgam of insulting opinions against the Jews, but also a superb (and isolated) effort to raise the Jewish question to the religious level: "The history of the Jews obstructs the course of human history the way a dike obstructs a river—in order to raise its level." Bloy was little heard during the Dreyfus Affair, and only resumed his dark dialogue with the Jewish people much later: "Be it known that every morning I devour a Jew named Jesus Christ, that I spend part of my life at the feet of a Jewess with pierced heart whose slave I have elected to become, that I have placed my trust in a pack of kikes, one offering a lamb, another carrying the keys to heaven, a third charged with instructing the nations . . . and I know that one can be a Christian only with such sentiments. All the rest is banal contingency and has absolutely no existence. Léon Bloy, *Le Salut par les Juifs* (Paris: Demay, 1892), p. 393.

28. See François Gerbod, "Le représentation de l'Affaire Dreyfus dans *Notre Jeunesse*," contribution to aforementioned colloquium, "Les Ecrivains et l'Affaire Dreyfus."

29. Charles Péguy, *Notre Jeunesse* (Paris: Galimard, 1933), p. 195.

30. Sternhell, *op. cit.*, p. 177.

31. *Ibid.*, pp. 186ff.

32. Quoted by Sternhell, *ibid.*, p. 187.

33. Quoted by Sternhell, *ibid.*, p. 189.

34. Auguste Chirac, *Les Rois de la République* (Paris: 1883), p. 394.

35. Boulangism, which was not anti-Semitic in its inception, had nevertheless drawn on it. In 1889, several Boulangist candidates—including Barrès in Nancy, Laur and Rochefort in Paris—had developed violently anti-Semitic themes in their campaigns. Barrès had waged his campaign in Nancy on the theme of social anti-Semitism: "To shout down with the Jews is to shout down with social inequalities. . . . State socialism is the indispensable corrective to the anti-Jewish

formula. State socialism is our whole hope." "Credit is a terrible weapon that the kike invented in order to multiply his power tenfold, a hundredfold."

36. Quoted by Sternhell, *op. cit.*, p. 211.

37. Maurice Barrès, *Scènes et Doctrines du nationalisme,* "Le programme de Nancy" (Paris: Félix Guven, 1902), pp. 430ff.

38. Karl Marx, *La Lutte des classes en France* (Paris: Pauvert, 1964), p. 76.

39. Sternhell, *op. cit.*, p. 188.

40. Léon Blum, *Souvenirs sur l'Affaire* (Paris: Gallimard, 1982), p. 108.

41. Michael Marrus, *Les Juifs de France à l'époque de l'Affaire Dreyfus* (Paris: Calmann-Lévy, 1972), p. 239; Claude Willard, *Les Guesdistes* (Paris: Éditions sociales, 1981).

42. Blum, *op. cit.*, p. 108.

43. For the working class, "the Affair in the last analysis was a fiasco." Such was the thesis that would be passionately defended by Gustave Hervé in his newspaper *La Guerre sociale* and by Hubert Lagardelle in *Le Mouvement socialiste.* Cf. Sternhell, *op. cit.*, pp. 318–338.

44. Concerning Barrès's doctrine, see the standard work by Zeev Sternhell, *Maurice Barrès et le nationalisme français,* Cahiers de la Fondation nationale des sciences politiques, no. 182.

45. Barrès's, *op. cit.*, p. 80.

46. *Ibid.,* p. 152.

47. *Ibid.,* p. 153.

48. There is not even freedom of thought. . . . We are not the masters of our own thoughts. They do not come from our intelligence. They are ways of reacting in which very ancient physiological dispositions are conveyed." *Ibid.,* pp. 40ff.

49. *Ibid.,* pp. 40ff.

50. *Ibid.,* p. 33.

51. *Ibid.,* p. 130.

52. *Ibid.,* p. 433.

53. The expansion of communal freedoms and municipal referendums were part of Barrès's platform: "Give every individual two homelands." *Ibid.,* pp. 437ff.

54. *Ibid.,* pp. 134ff.

55. *Ibid.,* pp. 134ff.

56. Blum, *op. cit.*, pp. 42ff.

57. Marrus, *op. cit.*, p. 255.

58. Quoted by Marrus, *op. cit.*, p. 256.

59. *Ibid.,* p. 261.

60. *Ibid.,* p. 275.

61. *Ibid.,* p. 272.

62. *Ibid.,* p. 327.

63. *Ibid.,* p. 219.

64. *Ibid.,* p. 221.

65. Published in France by the *Nouvelle Revue internationale,* December 31, 1896, and January 15, 1897.

66. Helmut Andics, *Histoire de l'antisémitisme* (Paris: Albin Michel, 1967), p. 190.

67. Marrus, *op. cit.*, pp. 295ff, p. 237.

5. *Thou Shalt Not Follow the Multitude*

1. Marcel Thomas, *L'Affaire sans Dreyfus* (Paris: Fayard, 1929), p. 509.

2. Joseph Reinach, *Histoire de l'Affaire Dreyfus* (Paris: Fasquelle, 1929), vol. III, p. 553.

3. *Ibid.*, vol. III, p. 551.

4. *L'Echo de Paris, La Libre Parole, L'Intransigeant*, April 13–15, 1898.

5. Reinach, *op. cit.*, vol. III, p. 559.

6. *A Republican Majority*

1. Pierre Miquel, *L'Affaire Dreyfus* (Paris: PUF, 1973), p. 66.

2. *Ibid.*, p. 66.

3. Joseph Reinach, *Histoire de l'Affaire Dreyfus* (Paris: Fasquelle, 1929), vol. III, p. 571.

4. *Ibid.*, vol. III, p. 583.

5. Pierre Sorlin, *Waldeck-Rousseau* (Paris: A. Colin, 1966), p. 388.

6. Reinach, *op. cit.*, vol. III, p. 570.

7. François Goguel, *La Politique des partis sous la IIIᵉ République* (Paris: Seuil, 1958), p. 106.

8. Reinach, *op. cit.*, vol. III, p. 629.

9. Miquel, *op. cit.*, p. 67.

10. Reinach, *op. cit.*, vol. III, p. 632.

11. Goguel, *op. cit.*, p. 92.

12. Reinach, *op. cit.*, vol. III, p. 632.

13. *Ibid.*, vol. III, pp. 634ff.

7. *All This Is Going to End Badly*

1. Léon Blum, *Souvenirs sur l'Affaire* (Paris: Gallimard, 1982), p. 102.

2. Marcel Thomas, *L'Affaire sans Dreyfus* (Paris: Fayard, 1961), p. 513.

3. *Ibid.*, p. 514.

4. Concerning Cavaignac's accomplishments, see the impassioned book by his daughter, Henriette Dardenne-Cavaignac, *Lumières sur l'Affaire Dreyfus* (Paris: Nouvelles Éditions latines, 1964), pp. 136ff.

5. Thomas, *op. cit.*, p. 515.

6. Joseph Reinach, *Histoire de l'Affaire Dreyfus* (Paris: Fasquelle, 1929), vol. IV, p. 25.

7. Dardenne-Cavaignac, *op. cit.*, p. 143.

8. Blum, *op. cit.*, p. 130.

9. *Ibid.*, p. 131.

10. *Ibid.*, p. 132.

11. Reinach, *op. cit.*, vol. IV, pp. 28–29.

12. Mathieu Dreyfus, *L'Affaire telle que je l'ai vécue* (Paris: Grasset, 1978), p. 148.

13. Reinach, *op. cit.*, vol. IV, p. 31.

14. *Ibid.*, vol. IV, p. 28.

8. *We Need a Lightning Bolt*

1. Joseph Reinach, *Histoire de l'Affaire Dreyfus* (Paris: Fasquelle, 1929), vol. IV, p. 33.

2. Mathieu Dreyfus, *L'Affaire telle que je l'ai vécue* (Paris: Grasset, 1978), p. 161.

3. Henri Dutrait-Crozon, *Précis de l'Affaire Dreyfus* (Paris: Librarie d'Action française, 1924), p. 155.

4. Reinach, *op. cit.*, vol. IV, p. 37.

5. Marcel Thomas, *L'Affaire sans Dreyfus* (Paris: Fayard, 1961) p. 517.

6. Reinach, *op. cit.*, vol. IV, p. 47.

7. *Ibid.*, vol. IV, p. 118.

8. *Ibid.*, vol. IV, p. 76.

9. *Ibid.*, vol. IV, p. 58.

10. See J. Cornély's article in *Le Figaro* of July 21: "When one is dealing with an individual or a limited group, one can afford gestures that need to be explained because there can be some hope of convincing people. When one is dealing with a crowd, one can be understood only through acts of extreme and even excessive simplicity. . . ."

11. Reinach, *op. cit.*, vol. IV, p. 61.

12. *Ibid.*, vol. IV, p. 118.

13. Quoted by Thomas, *op. cit.*, p. 519.

14. Quoted by Jacques Kayser, *L'Affaire Dreyfus* (Paris: Gallimard, 1946), p. 180.

9. *I Am Doomed; They Are Abandoning Me . . .*

1. Joseph Reinach, *Histoire de l'Affaire Dreyfus* (Paris: Fasquelle, 1929), vol. IV, p. 160.

2. *Ibid.*, vol. IV, p. 161.

3. *Ibid.*, vol. IV., p. 181.

4. *Ibid.*, vol. IV., p. 184.

5. Henriette Dardenne-Cavaignac, *Lumières sur l'Affaire Dreyfus* (Paris: Nouvelles Éditions latines, 1964), p. 178.

6. *Ibid.*, p. 180.

7. Reinach, *op. cit.*, vol. IV, p. 195.

8. French National Archives, BB 19 75, d2, p. 16.

8. Reinach, *op. cit.*, vol. IV, p. 211.

9. Report by Medical Major 2nd Class Pauzat on the Decease of Lieutenant-Colonel Henry at Mont-Valérien (French National Archives, BB 19 75, d2, p. 9.)

10. *More Stupid than Cowardly, More Cowardly than Stupid*

1. Henriette Dardenne-Cavaignac maintains on the contrary that the Code of Military Justice required the procedure that was followed. *Lumières sur l'Affaire Dreyfus* (Paris: Nouvelles Éditions latines, 1964), pp. 180ff.

2. Thus Pierre Miquel, in his excellent *L'Affaire Dreyfus* (Paris: PUF, 1973), writes: "It is thus quite probable that Henry was executed either by poison or by moral pressure" (*op. cit.*, p. 75).

3. Léon Blum, *Souvenirs sur l'Affaire* (Paris: Gallimard, 1982), p. 66.

4. Marcel Thomas—like most of the historians of the Affair—admits that General de Boisdeffre was aware from the beginning that the document produced by Henry was a forgery. The relentlessness with which the Chief of the General Staff prevented the document from being made public does indeed tend to support the thesis that he knew the whole truth. But it cannot be excluded that the chain of complicity may have stopped at General Gonse. Boisdeffre, who was aloof and perhaps suspicious, would simply have allowed the others to proceed without attempting personally to know what precisely was transpiring, as is suggested by his letter of resignation.

5. Marcel Thomas, *L'Affaire sans Dreyfus* (Paris: Fayard, 1961), pp. 342ff.

6. Joseph Reinach, *Histoire de l'Affaire Dreyfus* (Paris: Fasquelle, 1929), vol. IV, pp. 223ff.

7. Blum, *op. cit.*, p. 142.

8. Quoted by Reinach, *op. cit.*, vol. IV, p. 201.

9. *Ibid.*, vol. IV, p. 234, note 5.

10. *Ibid.*, vol. IV, pp. 256ff.

11. Dardenne-Cavaignac, *op. cit.*, p. 196; Mathieu Dreyfus, *L'Affaire telle que je l'ai vécue* (Paris: Grasset, 1978), p. 182.

12. Reinach, *op. cit.*, vol. IV, p. 267.

13. Dreyfus, *op. cit.*, p. 183.

14. *Ibid.*, p. 184.

15. René Rémond, *Les Droites en France* (Paris: Aubier-Montaigne, 1982).

16. Reinach, *op. cit.*, vol. IV, p. 306.

17. *Ibid.*, vol. IV, p. 303.

18. Dreyfus, *op. cit.*, p. 188.

19. Reinach, *op. cit.*, vol. IV, p. 312.

20. *Ibid.*, vol. IV, p. 315.

21. Members included Ludovic Trarieux, Emile Duclaux, Professor Giry, Edouard Grimaux, Louis Havet, Paul Mayer, Yves Guyot, Joseph Reinach, Lucien Herr, Ranc, Isaac, Pressensé, Reclin, Séailles, Siegnobos, etc. Reinach, *op. cit.*, vol. IV, p. 331.

22. Justice Bard was born in Paris in 1850. He had been public prosecutor in Marseille in 1884 and in charge of the Criminal Division in 1888. He had been a Justice of the High Court of Appeal since 1892. *Ibid.*, vol. IV, p. 324.

23. *Ibid.*, vol. IV, p. 347.

24. By a vote of ten to four. Reinach gives the names of the magistrates with their votes. The secrecy of the deliberations was apparently amply violated (*ibid.*, vol. IV, p. 348, note 1).

24. *Ibid.*, vol. IV, p. 348.

11. *To Roast the Jews*

1. Léon Blum, *Souvenirs sur l'Affaire* (Paris: Gallimard, 1982), pp. 147ff.

2. Charles Péguy, *Notre Jeunesse* (Paris: Gallimard, 1913, 1933), pp. 91ff.

3. *Ibid.*, p. 121.

4. Adrien Dansette, *Histoire religieuse de la République* (Paris: Flammarion, 1965, pp. 200ff.

5. See abbé Louis Caperan, *L'Anticléricalisme et l'Affaire Dreyfus* (Toulouse: Imprimerie régionale, 1944), which contests the global accusation brought against the Church in its entirety. The author usefully demonstrates how that accusation served the anti-clerical policies initiated under Waldeck-Rousseau and which reached fruition under the Combes government.

6. Maurice Barrès, *Scènes et Doctrines du nationalisme* (Paris: Félix Guven, 1902), p. 209.

7. René Rémond, *Les Droites en France* (Paris: Aubier-Montaigne, 1982), p. 165.

8. Zeev Sternhell, *La Droite révolutionnaire*, "Anatomie d'un mouvement de masse: la Ligue des patriotes" (Paris: Seuil, 1978), pp. 77ff.

9. Pierre Pierrard, *Juifs et Catholiques français (1886–1945)* (Paris: Fayard, 1970), p. 146.

10. *Ibid.*, p. 149.

11. Sternhell, *op. cit.*, pp. 131ff.

12. 39.25% for a population of 20%. See Stephen Wilson, "Le monument Henry; la structure de l'antisémitisme en France, 1898–1899," *Annales, ESC*, March–April, 1977.

13. 28.6% for an active population of 3%.

14. 0.6% of the population.

15. 2.6% of the active population.

16. Stephen Wilson, *op. cit.*, p. 285.

17. *Ibid.*, p. 287.

18. Pierrard, *op. cit.*, pp. 102ff.

19. *Ibid.*, p. 107.

20. Quoted by Pierrard, *ibid.*, pp. 107ff.

21. Blum, *op. cit.*, p. 148.

12. *And So We Arrive at the Final Stage*

1. Letter of July 16, 1898. Alfred Dreyfus, *Souvenirs et correspondances* (Paris: Grasset, 1936), p. 169.

2. Letters of August 7 and August 28, 1898. *Ibid.*, p. 174.

3. Alfred Dreyfus, *Cinq années de ma vie* (Paris: Fasquelle, 1901), p. 213.

4. Letter from Lucie Dreyfus of September 26, 1898. Alfred Dreyfus, *Souvenirs et correspondances,* p. 175.

5. Letter of November 5, 1898 to Lucie Dreyfus. *Ibid.,* p. 177.

6. Alfred Dreyfus, *Cinq années de ma vie,* p. 214.

IV. TRUTH ON THE MARCH

1. *Bar Girls*

1. Emile Zola, *L'Affaire Dreyfus, la vérité en marche,* preface by Colette Becker (Paris: Garnier-Flammarion, 1969).

2. Joseph Reinach, *Histoire de l'Affaire Dreyfus* (Paris: Fasquelle, 1929), vol. IV, p. 353.

3. Joseph Cornély, *Notes sur l'Affaire Dreyfus* (Paris: Société française d'éditions d'art, 1900), p. 90.

4. Reinach, *op. cit.,* vol. IV, p. 362.

5. See also Cornély's article in *Le Figaro* of November 16, "A l'Ile du Diable," *op. cit.,* p. 163.

6. Reinach, *op. cit.,* vol. IV, p. 374.

7. *Ibid.,* vol. IV, p. 394, note 3.

8. Cornély, "Un témoignage," vol. IV, p. 409.

9. According to Reinach, who was a great admirer of Waldeck-Rousseau. *Op. cit.,* vol. IV, p. 409.

10. This is Pierre Sorlin's thesis in his important work, *Waldeck-Rousseau* (Paris: A. Colin, 1966), p. 394.

11. Reinach, *op. cit.,* vol. IV, p. 412.

2. *To the Elysee, General*

1. Joseph Reinach, *Histoire de l'Affaire Dreyfus* (Paris: Fasquelle, 1929), vol. IV, p. 454.

2. *Ibid.,* vol. IV, p. 482.

3. *Ibid.,* vol. IV, p. 511.

4. *Ibid.,* vol. IV, p. 550.

5. *Ibid.,* vol. IV, p. 566.

6. *Ibid.,* vol. IV, p. 518.

7. *Ibid.,* vol. IV, p. 573.

8. Maurice Barrès, *Scènes et Doctrines du nationalisme* (Paris: Félix Guven, 1902), pp. 249ff. Cf. Zeev Sternhell's meticulous study of the failed *coup d'état* in *La Droite révolutionnaire, 1885–1914* (Paris: Seuil, 1978), pp. 120ff.

9. René Rémond, *Les Droites en France* (Paris: Aubier-Montaigne, 1982), p. 168, note 10, which draws on Pierre Sorlin's "thesis."

10. Reinach, *op. cit.,* vol. V, p. 9.

11. *Ibid.,* vol. V, p. 20.

12. Pierre Sorlin, *Waldeck-Rousseau* (Paris: A. Colin, 1966), p. 398.

3. *Appealed and Annulled*

1. Loew, *La Loi de désaisissement, op. cit.*, p. 167.
2. Joseph Reinach, *Histoire de l'Affaire Dreyfus* (Paris: Fasquelle, 1929), vol. V, p. 44. Mathieu Dreyfus, *L'Affaire telle que je l'ai vécue* (Paris: Grasset, 1978), pp. 202ff.
3. *Ibid.*, p. 203.
4. Reinach, *op. cit.*, vol. V, p. 93.
5. See the detailed critique of Ballot-Beaupré's report in Henri-Dutrait-Crozon, *Précis de l'Affaire Dreyfus* (Paris: Librairie de l'Action française, 1924), pp. 235ff.

4. *Panama the First*

1. Joseph Reinach, *Histoire de l'Affaire Dreyfus* (Paris: Fasquelle, 1929), vol. V, p. 115.
2. *Ibid.*, vol. V, p. 117.
3. *Ibid.*, vol. V, p. 126.
4. *Ibid.*, vol. V, p. 139.
5. Alfred Dreyfus, *Cinq années de ma vie* (Paris: Fasquelle, 1962), pp. 218ff.
6. Reinach, *op. cit.*, vol. V, p. 198.

5. *Silence in the Ranks*

1. Joseph Reinach, *Histoire de l'Affaire Dreyfus* (Paris: Fasquelle, 1929), vol. V, p. 156.
2. Pierre Sorlin, *Waldeck-Rousseau* (Paris: A. Colin, 1966), p. 401.
3. Claude Willard, *Les Guesdistes*, "La crise millerandiste" (Paris: Éditions sociales, 1981), pp. 422ff.
4. Reinach, *op. cit.*, vol. V, p. 193.
5. Zeev Sternhell, analyzing in particular the archives of the legal proceedings, maintains that Déroulède had again attempted a coup d'état. General Négrier, who had recently been relieved of his functions, was to march on the Elysée. A government of public salvation was to be constituted with Pellieux and Quesnay de Beaurepaire. Habert, Déroulède's aide, was to be named Chief of Police *La Droite révolutionnaire en France, 1885-1914* (Paris: Seuil, 1978), pp. 125ff.
6. Sorlin, *op. cit.*, p. 425.
7. *Ibid.*, pp. 410ff.
8. *Ibid.*, p. 412.
9. See, on the other hand, the recollections of P.-V. Stock, who paid a visit to Waldeck-Rousseau during the trial in order to request the arrest of General Chamoin. Waldeck-Rousseau seemed quite optimistic to him: "I am well informed.... Dreyfus will be acquitted." *Mémorandum d'un éditeur: L'Affaire Dreyfus anecdotique* (Paris: Stock, 1938), p. 111.
10. The reproach is renewed in part by Pierre Vidal-Naquet in his introduction to *Cinq années de ma vie* (Paris: F. Maspero, 1982), pp. 20ff.

6. *To Rennes, to Rennes, Gentlemen of the Army*

1. Joseph Reinach, *Histoire de l'Affaire Dreyfus* (Paris: Fasquelle, 1929), vol. V, p. 213.

2. But in the notes he left behind, Labori denounced the "infamies" and "perfidies" of Reinach's *Histoire*. Marguerite Fernand-Labori, *Labori. Ses Notes. Sa vie* (Paris: Attinger, 1947), p. 360.

3. *Ibid.*, p. 76.

4. *Ibid.*, pp. 99ff.

5. *Ibid.*, pp. 99ff.

6. Reinach, *op. cit.*, vol. V, p. 220.

7. *Le Journal*, July 4 and 7, 1899. The articles written by Maurice Barrès during the trial were assembled under the title "A Rennes" in *Scènes et Doctrines du nationalisme* (Paris: Félix Guven, 1902), pp. 129ff.

8. *Ibid.*, pp. 132–133.

9. *Ibid.*, p. 134.

10. P.-V. Stock, *Mémorandum d'un éditeur: L'Affaire Dreyfus anecdotique* (Paris: Stock, 1938), p. 100.

11. Quoted by Stock. Séverine would baptize the house in Pierrefonds (where she died at 64 on April 22, 1929) "les Trois Marches" (*op. cit.*, pp. 101ff.)

12. In 1899, Edmond Gast, a relative of Picquart, and P.-V. Stock would have the idea of organizing a "Trois Marches banquet" to gather all the "veterans" of the Rennes Trial. The inaugural banquet took place on November 8, 1899, at the Restaurant Champaux at Place de la Bourse in Paris. Most of the "major" Dreyfusards were present, including Mathieu Dreyfus, Bernard Lazare, Joseph Reinach, Georges Picquart, Gabriel Monod, Ludovic Trarieux, Octave Mirbeau, Marcel Prévost, Jean Psichari, Arthur Ranc, and Paul Bertulus. There were fewer and fewer people at subsequent banquets and the tradition "died" in 1902. P.-V. Stock, *op. cit.*, pp. 115ff.

13. Mathieu Dreyfus, *L'Affaire telle que je l'ai vécue*, (Paris: Grasset, 1978), pp. 297ff.

7. *Living Mauled Flesh*

1. Mathieu Dreyfus, *L'Affaire telle que je l'ai vécue* (Paris: Grasset, 1978), pp. 206ff.

2. Joseph Reinach, *Histoire de l'Affaire Dreyfus* (Paris: Fasquelle, 1929), vol. V, p. 210.

3. Dreyfus, *op. cit.*, p. 210.

4. Reinach, *op. cit.*, vol. V, p. 280.

5. *Ibid.*, p. 281.

6. Maurice Barrès, *Scènes et Doctrines du nationalisme*, "A Rennes" (Paris: Félix Guven, 1902), pp. 138ff.

7. *Ibid.*, pp. 129ff.

8. Reinach, *op. cit.*, vol. V, p. 283.

9. *Ibid.*, p. 287.

10. Barrès, *op. cit.*, p. 139.

11. Reinach, *op. cit.*, p. 286.

12. Maurice Paléologue, *Journal de l'Affaire Dreyfus* (Paris: Plon, 1955), p. 195.

13. Reinach, *op. cit.*, vol. V, p. 293.

14. Quoted by Reinach, *op. cit.*, vol. V, p. 294.

15. *L'Echo* of August 9.

16. Reinach, *op. cit.*, vol. V, p. 295.

17. Paléologue, *op. cit.*, pp. 196ff.

18. Barrès, *op. cit.*, p. 140.

19. *Ibid.*, p. 141.

8. *The Final Battle*

1. Joseph Reinach, *Histoire de l'Affaire Dreyfus* (Paris: Fasquelle, 1929), vol. V, pp. 240ff. and pp. 297ff.

2. P.-V. Stock, *Mémorandum d'un éditeur: L'Affaire Dreyfus anecdotique* (Paris: Stock, 1938), pp. 110ff.

3. Maurice Paléologue, *Journal de l'Affaire Dreyfus* (Paris: Plon, 1955), pp. 200ff.

4. Reinach, *op. cit.*, vol. V, p. 307.

5. Paléologue, *op. cit.*, p. 201.

6. *La Libre Parole*, August 13 and 14.

7. Reinach, *op. cit.*, vol. V, p. 317.

8. Paléologue, *op. cit.*, p. 205.

9. Reinach, *op. cit.*, vol. V, pp. 324ff.

10. Marguerite Fernand-Labori, *Labori. Ses Notes. Sa vie* (Paris: Attinger, 1947), p. 117ff.

11. Paléologue, *op. cit.*, p. 210.

12. *Ibid.*, p. 211.

13. *Ibid.*, p. 218.

14. *Ibid.*, p. 218.

15. Reinach, *op. cit.*, vol. V, p. 388.

16. Paléologue, *op. cit.*, p. 218.

17. Maurice Barrès, *Scènes et doctrines du nationalisme* (Paris: Félix Guven, 1902), pp. 200ff.

18. *Ibid.*, p. 209.

19. Reinach, *op. cit.*, vol. V, p. 39.

20. Barrès, *op. cit.*, p. 165.

21. Paléologue, *op. cit.*, p. 229.

22. *Ibid.*, p. 233.

23. Reinach, *op. cit.*, vol. V, pp. 416ff.

24. *Ibid.*, p. 461.

25. Fernand-Labori, *op. cit.*, p. 146.

26. Maurice Baumont, *Aux sources de l'Affaire Dreyfus* (Paris: Productions de Paris, 1959), p. 248.

27. *Ibid.*, p. 249.
28. *Ibid.*, p. 256.
29. Paléologue, *op. cit.*, p. 245.
30. Reinach, *op. cit.*, vol. V, p. 492.
31. Paléologue, *op. cit.*, p. 248.
32. *Ibid.*, pp. 253ff.
33. Reinach, *op. cit.*, vol. V, p. 495.
34. *Ibid.*, p. 498.
35. Paléologue, *op cit.*, p. 251.
36. *Ibid.*, p. 256.

9. *Yes, the Accused Is Guilty*

1. Maurice Paléologue, *Journal de l'Affaire Dreyfus* (Paris: Plon, 1955), p. 256.
2. Joseph Reinach, *Histoire de l'Affaire Dreyfus* (Paris: Fasquelle, 1929), vol. V, p. 510.
3. Marguerite Fernand-Labori, *Labori. Ses Notes. Sa vie* (Paris: Attinger, 1947), p. 156, p. 163.
4. *Ibid.*, p. 163; Reinach, *op. cit.*, vol. V, p. 521.
5. Paléologue, *op. cit.*, p. 527.
6. Concerning the incidents surrounding the publication by Stock of Labori's written remarks in the transcript of the Rennes trial in 1900 and the intervention of the League of the Rights of Man insisting that Stock publish Labori's notes, see Stock, *Mémorandum d'un éditeur: L'Affaire Dreyfus anecdotique* (Paris: Stock, 1938), pp. 90ff.
7. Fernand-Labori, *op. cit.*, p. 178.
8. Maurice Barrès, *Scènes et Doctrines du nationalisme* (Paris: Félix Guven, 1902), p. 211.
9. *Ibid.*, p. 219.

10. *The Incident Is Over*

1. Mathieu Dreyfus, *L'Affaire telle que je l'ai vécue* (Paris: Grasset, 1978), p. 237.
2. Joseph Reinach, *Histoire de l'Affaire Dreyfus* (Paris: Fasquelle, 1929), vol. V. Appendix 4.
3. *Ibid.*, pp. 543ff.
4. *Ibid.*, p. 544.
5. *Ibid.*, pp. 544ff.
6. Dreyfus, *op. cit.*, p. 236.
7. Reinach, *op. cit.*, vol. V, p. 546.
8. *Ibid.*, p. 544.
9. Pierre Vidal-Naquet, Introduction to *Cinq années de ma vie* (Paris: Fasquelle, 1962), pp. 20ff.
10. Dreyfus, *op. cit.*, p. 241.
11. *Ibid.*, p. 243.
12. *Ibid.*, p. 248.

13. Cf. on this question the thoughts of Pierre Vidal-Naquet (*loc. cit.*, pp. 29ff). Vidal-Naquet criticizes the strategy he attributes to Waldeck-Rousseau quite harshly: "it was a contemptible bit of shrewdness to have manipulated the prisoner Dreyfus in order to make of him a means of putting an end to the Affair."

14. Marguerite Fernand-Labori, *Labori. Ses Notes. Sa vie* (Paris: Attinger, 1947), p. 242.

15. *Ibid.*, p. 243.

16. *Ibid.*, p. 375.

17. Reinach, *op. cit.*, vol. VI, p. 10.

18. Charles Péguy, *Notre Jeunesse* (Paris: Gallimard, 1933), p. 191.

19. *Ibid.*, pp. 110ff.

20. On the gradual disintegration of the Dreyfusards, see Gerard Baal's richly documented article: "Un salon dreyfusard, des lendemains de l'Affaire à la grande guerre: la marquise Arconati-Visconti et ses amis." *Revue d'histoire moderne et contemporaine*, July–September 1981, pp. 433ff.

21. *Ibid.*, pp. 435ff.

11. *Forgetting*

1. Joseph Reinach, *Histoire de l'Affaire Dreyfus* (Paris: Fasquelle, 1929), vol. VI, p. 22. Cf. in the same vein the opinion of Pierre Vidal-Naquet in his Introduction to *Cinq années de ma vie* (Paris: Maspera, 1982). Vidal-Naquet has partially adopted the thesis which accuses Waldeck-Rousseau, by admitting that he would have "constrained Dreyfus, in withdrawing his appeal, to put an end to the Affair himself." He concludes that this was "a fine example of Machiavellian politics." *Op. cit.*, pp. 39ff.

2. Pierre Sorlin, *Waldeck-Rousseau* (Paris: A. Colin, 1966), pp. 419ff.

3. *Ibid.*, p. 420.

4. Reinach, *op. cit.*, vol. VI, p. 50.

5. *Ibid.*, p. 52.

6. *Ibid.*, p. 55.

7. *Ibid.*, p. 82.

8. *Ibid.*, p. 83.

9. *Ibid.*, p. 86.

10. *Ibid.*, p. 118.

11. *Ibid.*, p. 126.

12. General Mercier had formerly called him to head the École Polytechnique with instructions "to resist the invasion of clerical gangrene." André, *Cinq ans de ministère*, p. 220.

13. Quoted by Reinach, *op. cit.*, vol. VI, p. 132.

14. The congress, which assembled the diverse tendencies within socialism, met at Salle Japy. It ended to the sound of *L'Internationale* on December 8, 1899, after difficult and confused discussions. Concerning "Millerandism," Claude Willard has observed, the two motions adopted—one by Guesde and one by Delesalle—were contradictory and left room for ambiguity. Jean Jaurès, *Anthologie*

prepared by Louis Levy, Preface by Madeleine Rebérioux (Paris: Calmann-Lévy, 1982), pp. 132ff.

15. Claude Willard, *Les Guesdistes* (Paris: Éditions sociales, 1981), p. 437.

16. Reinach, *op. cit.*, vol. VI, p. 137.

17. *Ibid.*, p. 138.

18. Mathieu Dreyfus, *L'Affaire telle que je l'ai vécue* (Paris: Grasset, 1978), p. 263.

19. Marguerite Fernand-Labori, *Labori. Ses Notes. Sa vie* (Paris: Attinger, 1947), p. 246.

20. Dreyfus, *op. cit.*, p. 272.

21. *Ibid.*, p. 273.

22. *Ibid.*, p. 276.

23. Fernand-Labori, *op. cit.*, pp. 261ff.

24. Dreyfus, *op. cit.*, p. 277.

25. *Ibid.*, p. 278.

26. Fernand-Labori, *op. cit.*, pp. 276ff.

27. *Ibid.*, pp. 277ff.

28. Reinach, *op. cit.*, vol. VI, p. 145.

29. Sorlin, *op. cit.*, p. 420.

30. Reinach, *op. cit.*, vol. VI, p. 152.

31. *Ibid.*, p. 156.

32. *Ibid.*, p. 157.

33. *Ibid.*, p. 154.

34. *Ibid.*, p. 175.

12. *A Moment in the Conscience of Humanity*

1. Julien Benda, *Revue franco-allemande*, August 1901.

2. This unpublished letter from Louis Leblois to Reinach was shown to us courtesy of Dr. Jean-Louis Lévy.

3. Joseph Reinach, *Histoire de l'Affaire Dreyfus* (Paris: Fasquelle, 1929), vol. VI, p. 180.

4. Pierre Sorlin, *Waldeck-Rousseau* (Paris: A. Colin, 1966), p. 443.

5. "Few elections," according to Madeleine Rébérioux, "were prepared over as long a time and as passionately fought as those of 1902." *La République radicale, 1898–1914* (Paris: Seuil, 1975), p. 56.

6. Jean-Thomas Nordmann, *La France radicale* (Paris: Gallimard-Julliard, 1977), pp. 42ff and Rebérioux, *op. cit.*, p. 51.

7. Rebérioux, *op. cit.*, p. 58.

8. *Ibid.*, p. 54.

9. Sorlin, *op. cit.*, p. 481.

10. The nationalists enjoyed an upsurge only in Paris, in the central districts, where Brisson, Allemane, and Viviani were defeated. Madeleine Rebérioux notes that the success of the left should not mask the electoral stability of France. During the first round, barely 200,000 votes separated the two camps. *Op. cit.*, p. 58.

11. Reinach, *op. cit.*, vol. VI, p. 197.

13. *On Punctured Drums*

1. Joseph Reinach, *Histoire de l'Affaire Dreyfus* (Paris: Fasquelle, 1929), vol. VI, p. 200.

2. Mathieu Dreyfus, *L'Affaire telle que je l'ai vécue* (Paris: Grasset, 1978), pp. 279ff.

3. Reinach, *op. cit.*, vol. VI, p. 214.

4. Jean Jaurès, *Preuves: L'Affaire Dreyfus* (Le Signe, 1981), pp. 275ff.

5. Alfred Dreyfus, *Souvenirs et correspondances* (Paris: Grasset, 1936), p. 347.

6. Reinach, *op. cit.*, vol. VI, pp. 215ff.

7. Dreyfus, *op. cit.*, p. 347.

8. *Ibid.*, p. 353.

9. Reinach, *op. cit.*, vol. VI, p. 242.

10. Dreyfus, *op. cit.*, p. 363.

11. Reinach, *op. cit.*, vol. VI, p. 250.

12. *Ibid.*, vol. VI, p. 250.

13. *Ibid.*, vol. VI, p. 265.

14. *Ibid.*, p. 280. See Dreyfus, *op. cit.*, p. 366.

15. *Ibid.*, p. 379.

16. Reinach, *op. cit.*, vol. VI, pp. 279ff.

17. *Ibid.*

18. Charles Péguy, *Notre Jeunesse* (Paris: Gallimard, 1913), p. 94.

19. *Ibid.*, pp. 102ff.

14. *Marching in Step*

1. The evaluation prepared in 1881 by the Chief of the Lyon Court of Appeal commented on his knowledge of the law, firmness of judgment, and "brilliant and easy" delivery. It specified: "His financial situation is quite fine." The Chief Presiding Justice of the Lyon Court judged him as follows: "His age and the talents with which he has been gifted already allow one to anticipate that M. Baudouin will climb to the highest stations of the magistrateship: I would not make so bold as to claim that he is unaware of this, but he is preparing for it in a most worthy, conscientious, and honorable manner."

2. Alfred Dreyfus, *Souvenirs et correspondances* (Paris: Grasset, 1936), p. 303.

3. Joseph Reinach, *Histoire de l'Affaire Dreyfus* (Paris: Fasquelle, 1929), vol. VI, p. 291.

4. *Ibid.*, p. 294.

5. Marguerite Fernand-Labori, *Labori. Ses Notes. Sa vie* (Paris: Attinger, 1947), p. 343.

6. *Ibid.*, p. 345.

7. *Ibid.*, p. 344.

8. *Ibid.*, pp. 346ff.

9. Léon Blum, *Souvenirs sur l'Affaire* (Paris: Gallimard, 1982), p. 145.

10. Dreyfus, *op. cit.*, p. 388.

11. *Ibid.*, p. 388.

12. *Ibid.*, p. 391; Reinach, *op. cit.*, vol. VI, p. 371.

13. Reinach, *op. cit.*, p. 375.

15. *France's Premier Cop*

1. "Misguided by a newly prevalent mysticism," writes William Serman, "nearly 2,000 Free-Mason officers abandoned the customary paths of tolerance and strict secularism in order to move from anti-clericalism to anti-Christianity." William Serman attributes the consolidation of the alliance between the Army and the Church to the extravagance of the policies pursued by André with the support of Free-Masonry. Many officers, who until then had regarded themselves as apolitical, swung over—out of conformity—toward nationalism and clericalism. William Serman, *Les Officiers français dans la Nation, 1848–1914* (Paris: Aubier, 1982), pp. 107–109.

2. Joseph Reinach, *Histoire de l'Affaire Dreyfus* (Paris: Fasquelle, 1929), vol. VI, pp. 412ff.

3. "I am of the opinion that André—and this is the opinion of Monod as well, who is not a Jacobin like myself—should have forcefully invoked his right to be informed and shown that he always checked and verified any information received. But the Jesuits, in truth, are less stupid than the Free-Masons" (unpublished letter of November 14, 1904, from the Marquise Arconati-Visconti, daughter of A. Peyrat, a former president of the Senate, to Alfred Dreyfus). Marquise Arconati-Visconti's correspondence is extremely revealing of the "republican" mentality under the Combes government and of the strength of anti-clerical sentiment (see the excerpts published by Gérard Baal in the aforementioned article, "Un salon dreyfusard: la marquise Arconati-Visconti et ses amis"). Dr. Jean-Louis Lévy has been kind enough to give us access to the letters (recopied in Alfred Dreyfus's hand and annotated by him) sent him by the Marquise from the time of the Rennes trial until the war. They also shed light on the social and political reasons for the dispersion of the former Dreyfusards.

4. Madeleine Rebérioux, *La République radicale* (Paris: Seuil, 1975), p. 107.

5. The attitude of the Socialists to the Army and their choice in time of war would henceforth be at the center of political debate. The former Dreyfusards would be split. Beginning in July 1905, one can detect a rising anger against the Socialists and particularly against Jaurès in Marquise Arconati-Visconti's letters: "Ah! I leap up in anger and contempt at such fine optimism, which feigns belief in some world-wide embrace. Ah! As though one could indeed declare war on war. What's at stake is staying free and alive in a world which knows nothing but force. Jaurès is losing all sense of things, that's his sole excuse. . . . He will come to a sorry end between Hervé, who is betraying him, and Guesde, who has contempt for him. It's sad, very sad. . . . And for myself, henceforth I refuse to get excited for anything except the defense of the country, its dignity and its strength vis-à-vis the world" (unpublished letter to Alfred Dreyfus, September 25, 1905).

6. Jean-Denis Bredin, *Joseph Caillaux* (Paris: Hachette, 1980), pp. 58ff.

7. Gérard Baal, "Un salon dreyfusard: la marquise Arconati-Visconti et ses amis," *Revue d'histoire moderne et contemporaine*, July–September 1981, pp. 445ff.

8. Quoted by Baal, *ibid.*, p. 448.

9. Letter to Jaurès, quoted by Baal, *ibid.*, p. 444.

10. Léon Blum, *Souvenirs sur l'Affaire* (Paris: Gallimard, 1935), pp. 150–151.

16. *Innocence Proclaimed*

1. Alfred Dreyfus, *Souvenirs et correspondances* (Paris: Grasset, 1936), p. 420.

2. "In the eyes of the Dreyfusards," wrote Georges Sorel in *La Révolution dreyfusienne*, "servility, stupidity, and bad faith are the principal qualities of the magistrates given us by the Republic." The book is a violent indictment of the High Court of Appeal, accused of having submitted to orders from the government in its progress toward revision. *Op. cit.* (Paris: Riviere, 1911), p. 51.

3. Madeleine Rebérioux, *La République radicale* (Paris: Seuil, 1975), p. 110.

4. Joseph Reinach, *Histoire de l'Affaire Dreyfus* (Paris: Fasquelle, 1929), vol. VI, p. 437.

5. Mathieu Dreyfus, *L'Affaire telle que je l'ai vécue* (Paris: Grasset, 1978), pp. 291ff.

6. Unpublished correspondence consulted courtesy of Dr. Jean-Louis Lévy.

7. Aforementioned unpublished correspondence.

8. Reinach, *op. cit.*, vol. VI, p. 445.

9. *Ibid.*, p. 440.

10. French National Archives. Study by Jean Appleton, BB 19 117, d2, p. 1, and unsigned study BB 19 117, d2, p. 8.

11. Aforementioned unpublished correspondence.

12. Reinach, *op. cit.*, vol. VI, p. 468.

13. Aforementioned unpublished correspondence: Sunday morning, 9 A.M.

14. See the critical analysis of the judgment, clause by clause, in Henri Dutrait-Crozon's *Précis de l'Affaire Dreyfus* (Paris: Librairie d'Action francaise, 1924), pp. 518ff. The High Court of Appeal, wrote Georges Sorel, "resorted to an extravagant application of Article 445. . . . its mood was one of Dreyfusard generosity . . . and it did not take umbrage at one more irregularity in order to please the powerful." *Op. cit.*, p. 53, pp. 518ff.

15. Reinach, *op. cit.*, vol. VI, p. 431.

16. Alfred Dreyfus, *op. cit.*, p. 431.

17. *I Name You Knight of the Legion of Honor*

1. Joseph Reinach, *Histoire de l'Affaire Dreyfus* (Paris: Fasquelle, 1929), vol. VI, p. 496.

2. That very evening the deputy and the minister had a swordfight on the property of Gast, a deputy from Seine-et-Oise and a relative of Picquart. The minister of the interior was a witness for his undersecretary of state. Albert Sarraut was wounded and then fainted. This was the last of the thirty-one principal duels occasioned by the Affair. P.-V. Stock, *Mémorandum d'un editeur* (Paris: Stock, 1938), pp. 50ff. Concerning the rite of duels, particularly in the Army, see William Serman, *Les Officiers francais dans la Nation* (Paris: Aubier, 1982).

3. Dreyfus's reintegration was passed by a vote of 182 to 30. Picquart's was passed by a vote of 182 to 26.

4. See Joseph Reinach's account based on the recollections of several guests (*op. cit.*, vol. VI, p. 501) as well as Alfred Dreyfus's version in *Souvenirs et correspondances* (Paris: Grasset, 1936), pp. 434ff.

5. Dreyfus, *op. cit.*, p. 435.

6. *Ibid.*, p. 436.

18. *I Was Only an Artillery Officer*

1. Alfred Dreyfus, *Cinq années de ma vie* (Paris: Fasquelle, 1962), p. 228.

2. P.-V. Stock, *Mémorandum d'un editeur* (Paris: Stock, 1938), p. 244.

3. Cf. Henri Dutrait-Crozon, *Précis de l'Affaire Dreyfus* (Paris: Librairie d'Action française, 1924), p. 567.

4. See the analysis of Dreyfus's handwriting by his grandson. Dr. Jean-Louis Lévy, in his postface to *Cinq années de ma vie* (Paris: Maspero, 1982), p. 251.

5. *Ibid.*, pp. 251ff.

6. Alfred Dreyfus, *Souvenirs et correspondances* (Paris: Grasset, 1936) Pierre Dreyfus's account, p. 446.

7. Lévy, *op. cit.*

8. Quoted by Jean-Louis Lévy, who draws a profound and undoubtedly faithful portrait "of a man infinitely less complicated than the Affair bearing his name."

9. Maurice Paléologue, *Journal de l'Affaire Dreyfus* (Paris: Plon, 1955), pp. 37ff.

10. *Ibid.*, pp. 194ff.

11. Under the title *Ce canaille de D...reyfus,* Andre Figueras published in 1981 a book which took up (while simplifying) the theses of the General Staff. Without manifesting the slightest interest in the facts of the case, the book is a reservoir of anti-Dreyfusard hatred.

12. Text by Dominique Jamet reported by Lévy, *op. cit.*, p. 246.

13. Henri Giscard d'Estaing, *D'Esterhazy à Dreyfus* (Paris: Plon, 1950), p. 57.

14. Quoted by Lévy, *op. cit.*, p. 247.

15. Charles Péguy, *Notre Jeunesse* (Paris: Gallimard, 1913), p. 195.

16. Comment made to Bruno Weil by Clemenceau's secretary. Bruno Weil, *L'Affaire Dreyfus* (Paris: Sphinx, 1931) p. 307.

17. Concerning the "annihilation" of Dreyfus by numerous authors, see Lévy, *op. cit.*, pp. 245ff.

18. *Ibid.*, *loc. cit.*

19. Lévy, *ibid.*

20. Péguy, *op. cit.*, p. 195.

21. *Ibid.*, pp. 196ff.

22. Preface to *Cinq années de ma vie* (Paris: Fasquelle, 1962), pp. 18ff.

23. Pierre Vidal-Naquet, Introduction to *Cinq années de ma vie* (Paris: Maspero, 1982), pp. 11ff.

24. Unpublished correspondence deposited with the Paris City Archives, consulted courtesy of Jean-Louis Lévy.

25. Lévy, *op.cit.*, p. 277.

26. See Vidal-Naquet, *op. cit.*, pp. 7ff., and Lévy, *op. cit.*, pp. 245ff.

27. François Mauriac, "L'Affaire Dreyfus vue par un enfant," preface to *Cinq années de ma vie* (Paris: Fasquelle, 1962), p. 19.

19. *The Last Survivor*

1. P.-V. Stock, *Mémorandum d'un editeur* (Paris: Stock, 1938), pp. 202ff.

2. "Socialisme et liberté," published in *La Revue de Paris* of December 1, 1898. Cf. *Jaurès: Anthologie* prepared by Jean-Louis Lévy, Preface by Madeleine Rebérioux (Paris: Calmann-Lévy, 1982), p. 240.

3. Marguerite-Fernand Labori, *Labori. Ses notes. Sa vie.* (Paris: Attinger, 1947), pp. 290ff.

4. Robert Gauthier, *Dreyfusards!* (Paris: Gallimard-Julliard, 1965), p. 271.

5. Jean-Denis Bredin, *Joseph Caillaux* (Paris: Hachette Littérature, 1980), pp. 170ff.

6. Alfred Dreyfus, *Souvenirs et correspondances*, Preface by Pierre Dreyfus (Paris: Grasset, 1936).

7. Henri Dutrait-Crozon, *Précis de l'Affaire Dreyfus* (Paris: Librairie d'Action française, 1924), p. 657.

EPILOGUE: IN THE MIRROR OF THE AFFAIR

1. *From Legend to Legend*

1. Marcel Thomas, *L'Affaire sans Dreyfus* (Paris: Grasset, 1978), p. 524.

2. Joseph Reinach, *Histoire de l'Affaire Dreyfus* (Paris: Fasquelle, 1929), vol. VI, pp. 440ff.

3. Marguerite-Fernand Labori, *Labori. Ses notes. Sa vie* (Paris: Attinger, 1947), pp. 342ff.

4. *Ibid.*, p. 346.

5. *Ibid.*, pp. 373ff.

6. Léon Blum, *Souvenirs sur l'Affaire* (Paris: Gallimard, 1982), p. 66.

7. Maurice Paléologue, *Journal de l'Affaire Dreyfus* (Paris: Plon, 1955).

8. See the publisher's note preceding Maurice Paléologue's book.

9. Paléologue, *op. cit.*, pp. 69ff, 140 and 204.

10. *Ibid.*, p. 72.

11. Thomas, *op. cit.*, pp. 535ff.

12. Paléologue, *op. cit.*, p. 156.

13. Henri Guillemin, *L'Enigme Esterhazy* (Paris: Gallimard, 1962), pp. 218ff.

14. Thomas, *op. cit.*, Appendix II, p. 535.

15. Guillemin, *op. cit.*, pp. 218ff.

16. *Ibid.*, p. 227.

17. *Ibid.*, p. 228.
18. *Ibid.*, p. 228.
19. *Ibid.*, p. 228.
20. *Ibid.*, p. 231.
21. Thomas, *op. cit.*, p. 540.
22. Michel de Lombarès, *L'Affaire Dreyfus: La Clef du mystère*, (Paris: Robert Laffont, 1972).
23. See Lombarès's detailed analysis. *Ibid.*, pp. 241ff.
24. Henri Giscard d'Estaing, *D'Esterhazy à Dreyfus* (Paris: Plon, 1955).
25. Jean-Pierre Peter, "Dimensions de l'Affaire Dreyfus," *Annales ESC*, November-December 1961, p. 1141.
26. Giscard d'Estaing, *op. cit.*, p. 162.
27. Publications André Figueras, BP 575.
28. Henriette Dardenne, *Lumières sur l'Affaire Dreyfus* (Paris: Nouvelles Editions latines, 1964).

2. The Long Wave . . .

1. Léon Blum, *Souvenirs sur l'Affaire* (Paris: Gallimard, 1982), p. 151.
2. *Ibid.*, pp. 144–145.
3. *Ibid.*, pp. 942–943.
4. Jean-Pierre Peter, "Dimensions de l'Affaire Dreyfus," *Annales ESC*, November–December 1961, p. 1167.
5. Among the numerous works concerning the role of the press in the Dreyfus Affair, see Patrice Boussel, *L'Affaire Dreyfus et la Presse* (Paris: Armand Colin, 1960), and (in collaboration with Jean A. Chérasse) *Dreyfus ou l'intolérable vérité* (Paris: Pygmalion, 1975); Janine Ponty, "La presse quotidienne et l'Affaire Dreyfus en 1898–1899. Essais de typologie" (article cited *supra*); Maurice Manevy, *La Presse sous la IIIᵉ République* (Paris: Grasset, 1955); Pierre Sorlin's essential work, *La Croix et les Juifs* (Paris: Grasset, 1967); and numerous shorter studies, including Joseph Jurt, "L'Affaire Dreyfus, le rôle de l'opinion" (*Bulletin de l'amitié judéo-chrétienne*, No. 4, 1981); Danielle Delmaire, "L'antisémitisme de *La croix du Nord*," *De l'antijudaïsme antique à l'antisémitisme contemporain* (Lille: Presses Universitaires de Lille, 1979).
6. Pierre Miquel, *L'Affaire Dreyfus* (Paris: PUF, 1973), pp. 16ff.
7. Boussel, *Dreyfus ou l'intolérable vérité*, pp. 31ff.
8. Miquel, *op. cit.*, p. 8.
9. Ponty, *op. cit.*, pp. 194ff.
10. Miquel, *op. cit.*, p. 120.
11. "Newspapers could model, arm, and constrain public opinion only insofar as it was already prepared to be influenced and submissive. How can it be maintained that the press determined the choice of particular men or ideas that became the focus of public passion? It merely appealed to a series of ideological substrata already in place. Those ideologies are the true subject of the important studies that remain to be done." Peter, *op. cit.*, p. 1163.
12. Ponty, *op. cit.*, p. 220.

13. Delmaire, *op. cit.*, p. 235.

14. Peter, *op. cit.*, p. 1163.

15. Jean-Pierre Peter, "L'Affaire Dreyfus" in *Encyclopedia Universalis.*

16. *Ibid.*

17. Peter, *op. cit.*, p. 1163.

18. Miquel, *op. cit.*, p. 8.

19. René Rémond, *Revue française de science politique*, December 1959, pp. 860ff. Régis Debray, *Le Pouvoir intellectuel* (Paris: Ramsay, 1980).

20. See in particular Miquel, *op. cit.*, pp. 120ff and Madeleine Rebérioux, *La République radicale* (Paris: Seuil, 1975), pp. 36ff.

21. Blum, *op. cit.*, p. 15.

22. Rudolph Winnacker, in *Papers of the Michigan Academy of Science, Arts and Letters*, XXX, 1936, pp. 465ff.

23. *Ibid.*

24. Rebérioux, *op. cit.*, p. 40.

25. *Ibid.*

26. *Ibid.*, p. 40.

27. Georges Sorel, *La Révolution dreyfusienne* (Paris: Rivière, 1911), p. 51.

28. Concerning the relations between judges and political power in the nineteenth century, see the excellent works by Jean-Pierre Royer, *La Société judiciaire depuis le XVIIIᵉ siècle* (Paris: PUF, 1979) and by Royer, R. Martissage, and P. Lecocq, *Juges et Notables au XIXᵉ siècle* (Paris: PUF, 1982). The different means employed by the emergent Third Republic to subjugate the judiciary are studied in detail (*ibid.*, p. 365ff).

29. Claude Willard, *Les Guesdistes* (Paris: Editions sociales, 1981), pp. 439ff.

30. Zeev Sternhell, *La Droite révolutionnaire, 1885–1914* (Paris: Seuil, 1978), pp. 401ff.

31. *Ibid.*, p. 402.

32. Zeev Sternhell, *Ni droite ni gauche, l'idéologie fasciste en France* (Paris: Seuil, 1983).

33. Concerning Jaurès's reasons for choosing to promote this policy, see his celebrated texts on the "two methods." Louis Levy, *Jaurès: Anthologie* (Paris: Calman-Lévy, 1982), pp. 131ff, 284ff. Cf. also, Zeev Sternhell, *Ni droite ni gauche*, pp. 30ff.

34. Sternhell, *ibid.*, pp. 29ff and 66ff.

35. Sternhell, *La Droite révolutionnaire*, pp. 321ff.

36. Jean Jaurès, *Etudes socialistes*, vol. II, pp. 196–199 (in Levy, *op. cit.*).

37. Jaures's *Les Preuves*, which he published at the end of September 1898, constitutes a monument of intelligence in the service of truth.

38. Levy, *op. cit.*, pp. 261ff.

39. Chérasse and Boussel, *op. cit.*, p. 26.

40. Blum, *op. cit.*, p. 151.

41. *Ibid.*, p. 150.

42. *Ibid.*, p. 43.

43. Klotz reacted to the publication of Lazare's pamphlet with regret "that our

friend and former collaborator had so compromised himself" and waxed indignant: "How can you allow yourself to believe that in France, if Dreyfus had not been Jewish, he would not have been convicted?"

44. Stephen Wilson, "L'Attitude juive face à l'antisémitisme durant l'Affaire Dreyfus" in *European Studies Review,* VI, No. 2, pp. 223ff.

45. "Les Juifs et la democratie française" in *L'Atelier de l'histoire* (Paris: Flammarion, 1982), pp. 273ff.

46. Annie Kriegel, *Les Juifs et le monde moderne* (Paris: Seuil, 1971), pp. 173ff.

47. Stephen Wilson, *op. cit.*

48. *Ibid.*

49. Which Péguy would denounce in *Notre jeunesse:* "Money is everything, dominates everything in the modern world—to such an extent, so entirely, so totally, that the horizontal separation of rich and poor has become infinitely more serious, more cutting, more absolute, if I may say so, than the vertical separation of race between Jews and Christians." *Op. cit.,* p. 189.

50. See the aforementioned articles by François Furet, particularly "Israël, sionisme, et la diaspora," pp. 303ff.

51. Furet, *loc. cit.,* p. 278. See also Annie Kriegel, *op. cit.,* pp. 178ff.

52. Sternhell, *Ni droite ni gauche,* pp. 26ff.

3. *The Dividing Line*

1. Ernest Lavisse, "La réconciliation nationale," *Revue de Paris,* October 1899, pp. 648ff; cf. Pierre Nora, "Ernest Lavisse, son rôle dans la formation du sentiment national," *Revue historique,* July–September 1962, pp. 73ff.

2. Jean-Pierre Peter, "Dimensions de l'Affaire Dreyfus," *Annales ESC,* November–December 1961, p. 1167.

3. Alfred Dreyfus, *Cinq années de ma vie* (Paris: Fasquelle, 1901), p. 20.

4. Pierre Miquel, *L'Affaire Dreyfus* (Paris: PUF, 1973), p. 126.

5. Postface to *Cinq années de ma vie* (Paris: Maspero, 1982), p. 257.

6. Observing after others the role of the fortuitous in the Affair, Edgar Faure wrote that "it raises the question of the role of chance in history." Jean-A. Chérasse, *Dreyfus ou l'intolérable vérité* (Paris: Pygmalion, 1975), p. 22.

7. Marcel Thomas, *L'Affaire sans Dreyfus* (Paris: Fayard, 1961), p. 124.

8. Allan Mitchell, *Journal of Modern History,* Univ. of Chicago, vol. 52, no. 3, September 1980.

9. Thomas, *op. cit.,* pp. 104ff.

10. William Serman, *Les Officers français dans la Nation* (Paris: Aubier, 1982), pp. 101ff and Robert Gauthier, *Dreyfusards!* (Paris: Gallimard-Julliard, 1965), pp. 257ff.

11. See Gauthier's reflections, "Pourquoi l'Affaire?," *op. cit.*

12. Serman, *op. cit.,* p. 14.

13. Gauthier, *op. cit.,* pp. 257ff.

14. Letter cited by Dr. Jean-Louis Lévy in his postface to *Cinq années de ma vie.*

15. Gauthier, *op. cit.,* p. 262.

16. Maurice Barrès, *Scènes et Doctrines du nationalisme* (Paris: Félix Guven, 1902), p. 209.

17. Introduction to *Une enigme? l'Affair Dreyfus*, Dossier Clio (Paris: PUF, 1972).

18. See Jean-Pierre Peter, "L'Affaire Dreyfus," *Encyclopedia Universalis.*

19. Miquel, *op. cit.*, p. 7, and aforementioned article in *Encyclopedia Universalis.*

20. Peter illuminates this theme of "order triumphant."

21. Concerning this see Jean-Pierre Peter, "Dimensions de l'Affaire Dreyfus," aforementioned article.

22. See on this subject the previously mentioned article by Gérard Baal, which illuminates the itinerary of a large number of Dreyfusards after 1906 amid fear of social danger and preparation for the war of revenge. "You see," confessed the Dreyfusard Roujon, bearing witness for many others, "after the Dreyfus Affair, we went too far." "Un salon dreyfusard," *Revue d'histoire moderne et contemporaine*, July–September 1981, pp. 144ff.

23. Barrès, *op. cit.*, pp. 15ff.

24. Address to the Ligue des Patriotes, July 16, 1899.

25. Lecture delivered at Nancy on December 1, 1901. Concerning anti-Dreyfusard ideology, see Raoul Girardet, *Le Nationalisme français* (Paris: A. Colin, 1966).

26. See the aforementioned article by Gérard Baal. Certain of Jaurès's antimilitarist speeches after the Affair and the support he appeared to be giving Gustave Hervé alienated a large majority of former Dreyfusards. For that very reason—Jaurès's "subservience" in the face of Hervé's antimilitarism—Péguy excommunicated him in a series of pitiless pages: "He allowed it to be said—and done—that France was to be renounced, betrayed, and destroyed, thus creating the political illusion that the Dreyfusard movement was an anti-French movement." *Notre Jeunesse* (Paris: Gallimard, 1913), pp. 147ff. Concerning the depiction of the Affair in *Notre Jeunesse*, see Françoise Gerbod's contribution to the Orleans Colloquium on "Les écrivains et l'Affaire Dreyfus," October 1981.

27. Quoted by François Goguel, *La Politique des partis sous la IIIme République* (Paris: Seuil, 1958), p. 103.

28. Adrien Dansette, *Le Boulangisme 1886–1890* (Paris: Perrin, 1946), pp. 269ff.

29. Jean Jaurès, *Etudes socialistes*, vol. II, pp. 94–95.

30. On the gnawing away of freedoms during the so-called exceptional periods in French history, see Roger Errera, *Les Libertés à l'abandon* (Paris: Seuil, 1975) and the previously mentioned preface of Pierre Vidal-Naquet in *Cinq années de ma vie* (Paris: Maspero, 1982), pp. 16ff.

31. Jean-Louis Lévy, Postface to *Cinq années de ma vie* (Paris: Maspero, 1982), p. 257.

32. Alfred Dreyfus, *Souvenirs et correspondances* (Paris: Grasset, 1936), pp. 436ff.

BIBLIOGRAPHY

The bibliography of the Dreyfus Affair, both in France and internationally, is quite considerable, and there can be no question of drawing up an exhaustive list of works in this context. In French, there have been two attempts at such an inventory. The first, at the tail end of the Affair, was undertaken by Paul Desachy: *Bibliograhie de l'Affaire Dreyfus* (Paris: Cornely, 1905). More recently, Léon Lipschutz has published a *Bibliographie thématique et analytique de l'Affaire Dreyfus* (Paris: Fasquelle, 1970).

Among the innumerable texts—books as well as articles—devoted to the Dreyfus Affair, two works deserve pride of place in this bibliography, since they each draw on a considerable amount of documentation: Joseph Reinach's *Histoire de l'Affaire Dreyfus*, seven volumes (Paris: La Revue blanche, 1901–1911; Fasquelle, 1929), and Marcel Thomas's *L'Affaire sans Dreyfus* (Paris: Fayard, 1961).

Archives

The documents used in the proceedings of 1894, the "secret file" constituted at the time and then "augmented" over the years until the trial in Rennes, are now in the Archives of the Historical Service of the Ministry of Armed Forces (ministère des Armées) in the Fort of Vincennes.

The French National Archives contain numerous documents connected with the Affair. Specifically, the files used by the High Court of Appeal in its two judicial reviews may be found under filing code BB 19 73 to 191.

The Bibliothèque nationale houses the "papers" of several persons who played an important role in the Affair: Joseph Reinach, Mathieu Dreyfus, Émile Zola, Auguste Scheurer-Kestner. Esterhazy's personal papers, donated by Paul Desachy, also belong to the Library.

Finally, the Bibliothèque historique de la Ville de Paris possesses a rich collection of press clippings relating to the events of the Dreyfus Affair.

Proceedings

1. The revision of the Dreyfus trial

Judicial Inquiry of the High Court of Appeal

- Preliminary investigation of the Criminal Chamber (October 31, 1898 to February 1899)
- Preliminary investigation of the Combined Chambers (April 17–29, 1899)
- Supplementary documents

2 vol. (Paris: Stock, 1899)

The revision of the Dreyfus Trial
Proceedings of the High Court of Appeal

1 vol. (Paris: Stock, 1899)

2. The Dreyfus Trial before the Court-Martial at Rennes
Verbatim transcript of the trial

3 vol. (Paris: Stock, 1900)

3. The revision of the Rennes Trial
- Inquiry of the Criminal Chamber (March 5–November 19, 1904)

3 vol. (Paris: Ligue des droits de l'homme, 1908–09)
- Proceedings of the High Court of Appeal (March 3–5, 1904)

(Paris: Société nouvelle de librairie et d'édition, 1904)
- Memorandum of Maître Henry Mornard (1905)

(Paris: Ligue des droits de l'homme, 1907)
- The plea composed by Public Prosecutor Baudouin (1905)

(Paris: Ligue des droits de l'homme, 1907)

4. Proceedings of the High Court of Appeal
Combined Chambers (June 15–July12, 1906)

2 vol. (Paris: Ligue des droits de l'homme, 1906)

5. The Zola trial
Verbatim transcript and supplementary documents

2 vol. (Paris: Librairie du Siècle, 1898)

Works by Alfred Dreyfus

Léttres d'un innocent (Paris: P.-V. Stock, 1898).

———. *Cinq Années de ma vie* (Paris: Fasquelle, 1901; reedition with preface by François Mauriac, 1962).

Ibid., with a preface by Pierre Vidal-Naquet and a postface by Dr. Jean-Louis Lévy, grandson of Alfred Dreyfus (Paris: F. Maspero, 1982).

———. *Souvenirs et correspondances* published by Pierre Dreyfus (Paris: Grasset, 1936).

The Affair as Seen by its Participants

Blum, Léon. *Souvenirs sur l'Affaire* (Paris: Gallimard, 1935, reed. preface by Pascal Ory, Gallimard, 1982). The works of Léon Blum (Paris: Albin Michel, 1965, vol. I).

Brisson, Henri. *Souvenirs de l'Affaire Dreyfus* (Paris: Cornély, 1908).

Clemenceau, Georges. *L'Iniquité* (Paris: Stock, 1899).

———. *Vers la réparation* (Paris: Stock, 1899).

———. *Contre la justice* (Paris: Stock, 1900).

———. *Des juges* (Paris: Stock, 1901).

———. *Justice militaire* (Paris: Stock, 1901).

———. *Injustice militaire* (Paris: Stock, 1902).

———. *La Honte* (Paris: Stock, 1903).

Cornèly, Joseph. *Notes sur l'Affaire Dreyfus* (Paris: Société française d'éditions d'art, 1900).

Esterhazy, Fernand Walsin. *Les dessous de l'Affaire Dreyfus* (Paris: Fayad frères, 1898).

Dreyfus, Mathieu. *L'Affaire telle que je l'ai vécue* (Paris: Grasset, 1978).

Guyot, Yves. *La Révision duj procès Dreyfus* (Paris: Grasset, 1898).

Jaurès, Jean. *Les Preuves. L'Affaire Dreyfus,* reed. preface by Madeleine Rebérioux (le Signe, 1981).

Labori, Marguerite-Fernand. *Labori. Ses notes. Sa vie* (Paris: Attinger, 1947).

Lazare, Bernard. *Une erreur judiciaire* (Paris: P.-V. Stock, 1897).

Leblois, Louis. *L'Affaire Dreyfus. L'iniquité. La réparation* (Paris: A. Quillet, 1929).

Péguy, Charles. *Notre Jeunesse* (Paris: Gallimard, 1913).

Scheurer-Kestner, Auguste and Leblois, Louis. *Ligue des droits de l'homme et du citoyen* (1898).

Schwarzkoppen, Count Maximilien von. *Les Carnets de Schwarzkoppen. La vérité sur Dreyfus,* translated from the German (Paris: Rieder, 1930).

Stock, P.-V. *Mémorandum d'un éditeur: l'Affaire Dreyfus anecdotique* (Paris: Stock, 1938).

Vaughan, Ernest. *Souvenirs sans regrets* (Paris: 1902).

Zola, Émile. *L'Affaire Dreyfus. La vérité en marche* reed. preface by Collette Becker (Paris: Garnier-Flammarion, 1969).

General Works on The Affair

Baumont, Maurice. *Aux sources de l'Affaire Dreyfus* (Paris: Productions de Paris, 1959).

———. *Au cœur de l'Affaire Dreyfus,* reed. (Paris: Librairie Del Duca, 1976).

Chapman, Guy. *The Dreyfus Case* (London: Rupert Hart-Davis, 1955).

———. *The Dreyfus Case: a Reassesment* (Wesport, Ct.: Greenwood Press, 1979).

Charensol, Georges. *L'Affaire Dreyfus et la IIIᵉ République* (Paris: 1930).

Charpentier, Armand. *Historique de l'Affaire Dreyfus* (Paris: Fasquelle, 1933).

———. *Les côtés mystérieux de l'Affaire Dreyfus* (Paris: Rieder, 1930).

Cherasse, Jean-A. *Dreyfus ou l'intolérable vérité* (Paris: Pygmalion, 1975).

Dardenne-Cavaignac, Henriette. *Lumières sur l'Affaire Dreyfus* (Paris: Nouvelles Éditions latines, 1964).

Derfler, Leslie. *The Dreyfus Affaire* recueil articles (Boston: 1963).

Dutrait-Crozon, Henri. *Précis de l'Affaire Dreyfus* (Paris: Librairie d'Action française, 1924).

Erhardt, André. *A travers l'Affaire*: "Henry et Val-Carlos" (Paris: Klincksieck, 1977).

——. *A travers l'Affaire Dreyfus (cont'd): "le silence de Val-Carlos"* (Strasbourg: librarie Becker, 1979).

Figueras, André. *Ce canaille de D…reyfus* (Paris: Publications A. Figueras, 1982).

Foucault, André. *Un nouvel aspect de l'Affaire Dreyfus* (Paris: les Œuvres libres, 1938).

France, Jean. *Autour de l'Affaire Dreyfus. Souvenirs de la Sûreté générale* (Paris: Rieder, 1936).

Garros, Louis. *Alfred Dreyfus: l'Affaire* (Paris: Mame, 1970).

Gauthier, Robert. *Dreyfusards!* (Paris: Gallimard-Julliard, 1965).

Georges, Roux. *L'Affaire Dreyfus* (Paris: Librairie Perrin, 1970).

Giscard d'Estaing, Henri. *D'Esterhazy à Dreyfus* (Paris: Plon, 1950).

Guillemin, Henri. *L'Énigme Esterhazy* (Paris: Gallimard, 1962).

Halasz, Nicholas. *Captain Dreyfus: History of a Mass Hysteria* (New York: Simon and Schuster, 1955).

Hoffman, Robert L. *More than a Trial: the Struggle over Captain Dreyfus* (New York: The Free Press, 1980).

Johnson, Douglas. *France and the Dreyfus Affair* (London: Blandford Press, 1966).

Kayser, Jacques. *L'Affaire Dreyfus* (Paris: Gallimard, 1946).

Kedward, Roderick H. *The Dreyfus Affair* (New York: Harper and Row, 1965).

Lewis, David L. *Prisoners of Honor: the Dreyfus Affair* (New York: Morrow, 1973).

Lombarès, Michel de. *L'Affaire Dreyfus. La clef du mystère* (Paris: Robert Laffont, 1972).

Maur, Joe. *Le Juif sur l'île du Diable ou Critique de la raison impure* (Berne: Steiger, 1898).

Mazel, Henri. *Histoire et psychologie de l'Affaire Dreyfus* (Paris: Robert Laffont, 1972).

Miquel, Pierre. *L'Affaire Dreyfus* (Paris: PUF, coll. Que sais-je, 1973).

Id. *Une énigme? L'Affaire Dreyfus* (Paris: Dossier Clio, PUF, 1972).

Paléologue, Maurice. *Journal de l'Affaire Dreyfus 1894–1899—L'Affaire Dreyfus et le Quai d'Orsay* (Paris: Plon, 1955).

Paraf, Pierre. *La France de l'Affaire Dreyfus* (Paris: Droit et Liberté, 1978).

Peter, Jean-Pierre, "Dimensions de l'Affaire Dreyfus," *Annales ESC*, XVI, no. 6, November–December 1961.

——. "L'Affaire Dreyfus" *(Encyclopædia Universalis)*.

Reinach, Théodore. *Histoire sommaire de l'Affaire Dreyfus* (Paris: 1924).

Salmon, André, *L'Affaire Dreyfus* (Paris: Émile-Paul frères, 1934).

Schecter, Betty. *The Dreyfus Case: A National Scandal* (Boston: Houghton Mifflin, 1965).

Snyder, Louis L. *The Dreyfus Case: A Documentary History* (New Jersey, 1973)

Sorel, Georges. *La Révolution dreyfusienne* (Paris: M. Rivière, 1911).

Villemar, H. *Dreyfus intime* (Paris: Stock, 1898).

Weil, Bruno. *L'Affaire Dreyfus*, translated from the German (Paris: Gallimard, 1930).

Zevaès, Alexandre. *L'Affaire Dreyfus* (Paris: Sphinx, 1931).

The Affair in Politics

Ageron, Charles Robert. *France coloniale ou Parti colonial* (Paris: PUF, 1978).

Bredin, Jean-Denis. *Joseph Caillaux* (Paris: Hachette Littérature, 1980).

Chastenet, Jacques. *Histoire de la IIIe République*, vol. III (Paris: Hachette, 1955).

Dansette, Adrien. *Le Boulangisme 1886–1890* (Paris: Perrin, 1946).

Daudet, Léon. *Panorama de la IIIe République* (Paris: Gallimard, 1936).

Faure, Sébastien. *Les Anarchistes et l'Affaire Dreyfus* (Paris: le Libertaire, 1898).

Goguel, François. *La Politique des partis sous la IIIe République* (Paris: le Seuil, 1958).

Lagardelle, Hubert. "Le Socialisme et l'Affaire Dreyfus", *Mouvement socialiste*, February 15–March 15, 1899.

Levillain, Philippe. *Boulanger, fossoyeur de la monarchie* (Paris: Flammarion, 1982).

Mayeur, Jean-Marie. *Les Débuts de la IIIe République, 1871–1898* (Paris: Seuil, 1973).

Nordmann, Jean-Thomas. *La France radicale* (Paris: Gallimard-Julliard, 1977).

Pisani-Ferry, Fresnette. *Le Général Boulanger* (Paris: Flammarion, 1969).

Rebérioux, Madeleine. *La République radicale?* (Paris: le Seuil, 1975).

Rioux, Jean-Pierre. *Nationalisme et Conservatisme: la Ligue de la patrie française 1899–1914* (Paris: Beauchesne, 1977).

Sorlin, Pierre. *Waldeck-Rousseau* (Paris: A. Colin, 1966).

Sternhell, Zeev. *La Droite révolutionnaire en France, 1885–1914* (Paris: Seuil, 1978).

———. *Ni droite, ni gauche, l'idéologie fasciste en France* (Paris: le Seuil, 1983).

———. *Maurice Barrès et le Nationalisme français* (Paris: A. Colin et Fondation nationale des sciences politiques, 1972).

Weber, Eugen. *L'Action française* (Paris: Stock, 1972).

Willard, Claude and Botticielli, Émile. *Le Parti ouvrier français, l'Affaire Dreyfus et l'entente sociale: les guesdistes* (Paris: Éditions sociales, 1981).

Intellectuals and Ideologies

Baal, Gérard. "Un salon dreyfusard; des lendemains de l'Affaire à la Grande Guerre: la marquise Aconati-Visconti et ses amis," *Revue d'histoire moderne et contemporaine*, July–September 1981.

Barrès, Maurice. *Scènes et Doctrines du nationalisme* (Paris: Félix Guven, 1902).

———. *Mes cahiers* (Paris: Plon, 1939).

Blum, Antoinette. "Romain Rolland face à l'Affaire Dreyfus," *Relations internationales*, no. 14, Summer 1978.

Cahm, Éric. "Les étudiants de Paris en janvier 1898," *Bulletin de la Société d'études jaurésiennes*, October–December 1978.

Capteran, abbé Louis. *L'Anticléricalisme et l'Affaire Dreyfus* (Toulouse: Imprimerie régionale, 1944).

Capitan-Peter, Colette. *Charles Maurras et l'idéologie d'Action française* (Paris: Seuil, 1972).

Charle, Christophe. "Champ littéraire et champ du pouvoir; les écrivains et l'Affaire Dreyfus," *Annales ESC*, no. 2, March–April 1977.

Dansette, Adrien. *Histoire religieuse de la République* (Paris: Flammarion, 1965).

Debray, Régis. *Le pouvoir intellectuel en France* (Paris: Ramsay, 1980).

Girardet, Raoul. *Le Nationalisme français* (Paris: A. Colin, 1966).

Jackson, A. B., *La Revue blanche, 1899–1903* (Paris: Minard, 1960).

Lacouture, Jean. *Léon Blum* (Paris: Seuil, 1977).

Larkin, Maurice. *Church and State after the Dreyfus Affair* (London: Macmillan, 1974).

Launay, Michel. "Jaurès, la Sorbonne et l'Affaire Dreyfus," *Bulletin de la Société d'études jaurésiennes,* VII, no. 26, 1967.

Leroy, Géraldi. *Péguy* (Paris: Presses de la Fondation nationale des sciences politiques, 1981).

Lévy, Louis. *Jaurès: Anthologie,* preface by Madeleine Rebérioux (Paris: Calmann-Lévy, 1982).

Maurras, Charles. *Au signe de Flore* (Paris: Grasset, 1933).

Mayeur, Jean-Marie. "Les catholiques dreyfusards," *Revue historique,* no. 530, April–June 1979.

Mitterand, Henri. *Zola journaliste* (Paris: A. Colin, 1962).

Nora, Pierre. "Ernest Lavisse: son rôle dans la formation du sentiment national," *Revue Historique,* CCXXVIII, no. 128, July–September 1962.

Rabaut, Jean. *Jean Jaurès,* preface by M. Rocard (Paris: Librairie Perrin, 1981).

Rebérioux, Madeleine. "Histoire, historiens, dreyfusisme," *Revue historique,* no. 518, April–June 1976.

———. "Zola, Jaurès et France: trois intellectuels devant l'Affaire, *Cahiers, naturalistes,* no. 54, 1980.

Revue française de sciences politiques, "Le intellectuels dans la société française contemporaine," Special issue of *RFSP,* vol. IX, no. 14, December 1959.

Smith, Robert J. "L'atmosphère politique à l'École normale supérieure à la fin du XIXᵉ siècle," *Revue d'histoire moderne et contemporaine,* XX, 1973.

Sorel, Georges. *Réflexions sur la violence,* reed. (Genève: Slatkine, 1981).

Sternhell, Zeev. *Maurice Barrès et la nationalisme français* (Paris: Presses de la Fondation nationale des sciences politiques, 1972).

Wilson, Nelly. *Bernard Lazare, Antisemitism and the Problem of Jewish Identity in the Late 19th Century* (New York: Cambridge University Press, 1978).

The Army at the Time of the Affair

Arbieux, Capitain d'. *L'Officier contemporain. La démocratisation de l'Armée* (Paris: Grasset, 1911).

Becker, Jean-Jacques. *Le carnet B. Les pouvoirs publics et l'antimilitarisme avant la guerre de 1914* (Paris: Klincksieck, 1973).

Bedarida, François. "L'Armée et la République," *Revue historique,* July–September 1964.

Chalmin, Pierre. *L'Officier français de 1815 à 1870* (Paris: M. Rivière, 1957).

Déroulède, Paul. *De l'éducation militaire* (Paris: undated).

Gaulle, Charles de. *La France et son armée* (Paris: Plon, 1971).

Girardet, Raoul. *La Société militaire dans la France contemporaine 1815–1939* (Paris: Plon, 1953).

Gohier, Urbain. *L'Armée contre la Nation* (Paris: Revue blanche, 1898).

Jung, Général. *La République et l'Armée* (Paris: Fayard, 1892).

La Gorce, Paul-Marie de. *La France et son armée* (Paris: Fayard, 1963).

Lasalle, Colonel G. *Manuel de l'organisation militaire* (Paris: 1892).

Mitchell, Allan. "The Xenophobie Style: French counter espionage and the emergence of the Dreyfus Affair," *Journal of Modern History,* University of Chicago, vol. 52, no. 3, 1980. *Revue d'Histoire moderne et contemporaine* XXIX, July–September, 1982.

Ralston, David B. *The Army of the Republic—The Place of the Military in the Political Evolution of France, 1871–1914* (Cambridge: Cambridge University Press, 1967.)

Serman, William. *Les Officiers français dans la Nation* (Paris: Aubier, 1982).

Literature and The Affair

Anglès, Auguste. *André Gide et le premier groupe de la NRF* (Paris: Gallimard, 1978).

Barrès, Maurice. *La Roman de l'énergie nationale. Les déracinés* (Paris: Gallimard, 1898).

Benda, Julien. *La Jeunesse d'un clerc* (Paris: Gallimard, 1937).

Bloy, Léon. *Le Salut par les Juifs* (Paris: Demay, 1892).

Charles, Christophe. "La lutte des classes en littérature: *l'Étape* de Paul Bourget *et la Véité* d'Émile Zola." Proceedings of the Orleans colloquium on writers and the Dreyfus Affair, October 1981, forthcoming.

Delhorbe, Cécile. *Les Écrivains français et l'Affaire Dreyfus* (Paris: Attinger, 1932).

France, Anatole. *Histoire contemporaine—. L'anneau d'améthyste. Monsieur Bergeret à Paris* (Paris: Calmann-Lévy, 1966).

———. *L'Île des pingouins* (Paris: Calmann-Lévy, 1947).

Gerbod, Françoise. "La représentation de l'Affaire Dreyfus dans *Notre Jeunesse,*" Proceedings of the Orleans colloquium on writers and the Dreyfus Affair, October 1981, forthcoming.

Lunel, Armand. *Nicolo-Peccavi ou l'Affaire Dreyfus à Carpentras* (Paris: Gallimard, 1926).

Martin du Gard, Roger. *Jean Barois* (Paris: Gallimard, 1913).

Mauriac, François, "L'Affaire Dreyfus vue par un enfant," preface to *Cinq Années de ma vie* by Dreyfus (Paris: Fasquelle, 1962).

Morand, Paul. *1900* (Paris: Flammarion, 1958).

Péguy, Charles. *Notre Jeunesse* (Paris: Gallimard NRF, 1913, 1933).

Proust, Marcel. *Jean Santeuil* (Paris: Gallimard NRF, 1952).

Renan, Ernest. *La Réforme intellectuelle et morale* (Paris: M. Lévy, 1871).

The Role of the Press

Bellanger, Claude. *Histoire générale de la presse française*, vol. 3 (Paris: PUF, 1972).

Boussel, Patrice. *L'Affaire Dreyfus et la presse* (Paris: A. Colin. 1960).

Cazenave, Elizabeth. "L'Affaire Dreyfus et l'opinion bordelaise," *les Annales du Midi,* January–March 1972.

Delmaire, Danièle, "L'antisèmitisme du journal *la Croix du Nord* pendant l'Affaire Dreyfus (1898–1899)," in *De l'antijudaïsme antique à l'antisémitisme contemporain* (Lille: Presses Universitaires de Lille, 1979).

Jurt, Joseph. "L'Affaire Dreyfus: le rôle de l'opinion," *Bulletin de l'Amitié judéochrétienne*, no. 4, 1981.

Manevy, Maurice. *La Presse de la IIIe République* (Paris: Grasset, 1967).

Ponty, Janine. "La presse quotidienne et l'Affaire Dreyfus 1898–1899," *Revue d'Histoire moderne et contemporaine*, XXI, April–June 1974.

———. "*Le Petit Journal* et l'Affaire Dreyfus," *Revue d'histoire moderne et contemporaine*, XXIV, 1977.

Sorlin, Pierre. *La Croix et les Juifs* (Paris: Grasset, 1967).

Anti-Semitism

Andics, Helmut. *Histoire de l'antisémitisme* (Paris: Albin Michel, 1967).

Arendt, Hannah. *Sur l'antisémitisme* (Paris: Calmann-Lévy, 1973).

Aubery, Pierre. *Les Milieux juifs de la France contemporaine à travers leurs écrivains* (Paris: 1967).

Beau de Lomenie, E. *Drumont et la capitalisme national* (Paris: J. J. Pauvert, 1967).

Byrnes, Robert F. *Antisemitism in Modern France,* part I: "Prologue to Dreyfus" (New Brunswick, New Jersey: Rutgers University Press, 1950).

Crémieu-Foa, Ernest. *La Campagne antisémitique. Les duels. Les responsables* (Paris: Alcan-Lévy, 1892).

Desportes (abbé Henri). *Le Mystère du sang chez les Juifs de tous les temps* (Paris: Savive, 1889).

Duroselle, Jean-Baptiste. "L'antisemitisme en France de 1886 à 1914," *Cahiers Paul Claudel*, VII, la Figure d'Israël, NRF, 1968.

Drumont, Édouard. *La France juive. Essai d'histoire contemporaine* (Paris: Flammarion, 1886).

Eisenberg, Josy. *Une histoire de peuple juif* (Paris: Fayard, 1974).

Finkielkraut, Alain. *L'Avenir d'une négation* (Paris: Seuil, 1982).

Furet, François. "Les Juifs et la démocratie française," in *l'Atelier de l'Histoire* (Paris: Flammarion, 1982).

Girard, Patrick. *Les Juifs de France de 1789 à 1860, de l'émancipation à l'égalité* (Paris: Calmann-Lévy, 1976).

Gougenot des Mousseaux. *Le Juif, le Judaïsme et la Judaïsation des peuples chrétiens* (Paris: 1869).

Kriegel, Annie. *Les Juifs et le Monde moderne* (Paris: Seuil, 1977).

Lazare, Bernard. *L'Antisémitisme. Son histoire et ses causes,* reed. (Paris: éditions de la Différence, 1982).

Leroy-Beaulieu, Anatole. *L'Antisémitisme* (Paris: Calmann-Levy, 1897).

Marrus, Michaël R. *Les Juifs en France à l'époque de l'Affaire Dreyfus* (Paris: Calmann-Lévy, 1972).

Marx, Karl. *La Question juive* (1844).

Pascal, R. P. de. *La Juiverie* (Paris: Gantier, 1887).

Petit, Jacques. *Bernanos, Bloy, Claudel, Péguy: quatre écrivains catholiques face à Israël* (Paris: Calmann-Lévy, 1972).

Pierrard, Pierre. *Juifs et Catholiques français (1886–1945)* (Paris: Fayard, 1970).

Poliakov, Léon. *Histoire de l'antisémitisme* (Paris: Calmann-Lévy, 1973).

Rabi, Wladimir. *Anatomie du judaïsme français* (Paris: Éditions de Minuit, 1962).

Renan, Ernest. *Judaïsme et christianisme*, reed. (Paris: Copernic, 1977).

Sartre, Jean-Paul. *Réflexions sur la question juive* (Paris: P. Morihieu, 1946).

Sorlin, Pierre. *La Croix et les Juifs* (Paris: Grasset, 1967).

Toussenel, Alphonse. *Les Juifs, rois de l'époque* (Paris: 1845).

Trigano, Samuel. *La République et les Juifs* (Paris: les Presses d'aujourd'hui, 1982).

Verdès-Leroux, Jeannine. *Scandales financiers et antisémitisme catholoique* (Paris: le Centurion, 1969).

Wilson, Stephen. *Ideology and Experience: Antisemitism in France at the time of the Dreyfus Affair* (The Littman Library of Jewish Civilization, 1982).

———. "Le Monument Henry: l'antisémitisme à la fin du XIXe siècle," *Annales, ESC,* no. 2, March–April 1977.

———. "The Antisemitic Riots of 1898 in France," *Historical Journal,* XVI, 1973, no. 4.

———. "Antisemitism and Jewish Response in France during the Dreyfus Affair," *European Studies Review,* 6, 1976.

Winock, Michel. *Édouard Drumont et Cie. Antisémitisme et fascisme en France* (Paris: Seuil, 1982).

The Economic and Social Crisis

Bouvier, Jean. *Les Deux Scandales de Panama* (Paris: Julliard, coll. Archives, 1964).

———. *Les Rothschild* (Paris: A. Fayard, 1967).

———. "Le mouvement d'une civilisation nouvelle," in Georges Duby, *Histoire de la France* (Paris: Larousse, 1970).

Bouvier, Jean. *Le Mouvement du profit en France au XIXe siècle* (Paris: Mouton, 1965).

Cameron, Rondo. *La France et la développement économique de l'Europe au XIXe siècle* (Paris: Seuil, 1971).

Daumard, Adeline. "L'évolution des structures sociales en France à l'époque de l'industrialisation," *Revue historique,* April–June 1972.

Lévy-Leboyer, Maurice. "Histoire économique et sociale de la France depuis 1948" (cours de l'IEP de Paris, Paris, 1952).

———. "La croissance économique en France au XIXe siècle," *Annales ESC,* July–August 1968.

Lhomme, Jacques. *La Grande Bourgeoisie au pouvoir (1830–1880)* (Paris: PUF, 1960).

Palmade, Guy. *Le Capitalisme français au XIXe siècle* (Paris: A. Colin, 1961).

Pernoud, Régine. *Histoire de la bourgeoisie française,* vol. II: "Les temps modernes" (Paris: Seuil, 1981).

Prost, Antoine. *Histoire de l'enseignement en France 1800–1967* (Paris: A. Colin, 1968).

Rioux, Jean-Pierre. *La Révolution industrielle, 1790–1880* (Paris: Seuil, 1971).

Sorlin, Pierre. *La Société français, 1840–1914* vol. I (Paris: Arthaud, 1969).

Weber, Eugen. *Peasants into Frenchmen* (Stanford: Stanford University Press, 1976).

TABLE OF ILLUSTRATIONS

Archives Historiques de l'Armée, photo Julliard, p. 6
Bibl. Historique de la Ville de Paris, p. 13b
Bibl. Nat., photo Julliard, pp. 8, 17b, 26, 29b
Photo Bibl. Nat. Paris, pp. 10, 11, 14, 22, 25b, 27, 28
Bundesarchiv, Koblenz, p. 4
Cliche E.R.L., pp. 1, 2a, b, 7
Harlingue—Viollet, pp. 11b, d
Jean-Louis Lévy, pp. 9a, b, 15a, b, 18c, 19a, b, 20, 30b, 32b
Private collections, pp. 16a, c, 18a, c, 23a, b, d, 31a, b, 32a
Roger Viollet, pp. 13, 16b, 17a, 18b, 24
Photothèque Plon, pp. 12a, 17a, b, 21, 25a, 30a, c
Shark/Edimedia, pp. 8a, 29b
Coll. Tallandier, p. 12c
in Reinach *Histoire de l'Affaire Dreyfus*, pp. 3, 5

Cover: photothèque Plon.

INDEX